CONTENTS

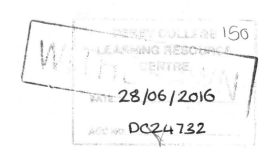

INTRODUCTION

Welcome to our book!

This book follows on from our AS and Year 1 textbook and provides you with clear and complete coverage of the A-level applied psychology topics, as well as helping you to revise the research methods and psychological themes. The chapters devoted to the compulsory topic of Issues in Mental Health (Chapter 1) and the four chapters for the options (Chapters 2–5) all follow the same pattern. They provide you with details of the background, key research and application for each of the topics within all of the options.

Remember, you will study Mental Health plus only **two** of the optional areas of applied psychology, as indicated in the table below.

Topic	Background	Key research	Application (with examples)
SECTION A – Issues in Mental Health (Chapter 1) (compulsory)			
The historical context of mental health	Historical views, defining abnormality and categorising mental disorders	Rosenhan (1973) page 13	Characteristics of an affective disorder, a psychotic disorder and an anxiety disorder
The medical model	Biochemical, genetic and brain abnormality explanations of mental illness	Gottesman *et al.* (2010) page 28	Biological treatment of one specific disorder (*antidepressant drugs* and *electroconvulsive therapy*)
Alternatives to the medical model	Behaviourist and cognitive explanations, and one explanation from humanistic, psychodynamic or cognitive neuroscience	Szasz (2011) page 46	Non-biological treatment of one specific disorder (*cognitive behavioural* and *humanistic therapies for depression*)
SECTION B – two options from below			
Option 1: Child Psychology (Chapter 2)			
Intelligence (Biological)	Defining intelligence and biological influences on intelligence	Van Leeuwen *et al.* (2008) page 62	At least one method of assessing intelligence (*Raven's progressive matrices*)
Pre-adult brain development (Biological)	Brain development risk-taking behaviour	Barkley-Levenson and Galván (2014) page 73	At least one strategy to reduce risk-taking behaviour (*graduated driver licensing*)
Perceptual development (Cognitive)	Studying perceptual development in babies and animals.	Gibson and Walk (1960) page 83	At least one play strategy to develop perception in young children (*sensory integrative therapy*)
Cognitive development and education (Cognitive)	Cognitive development and the education of children	Wood *et al.* (1976) page 94	At least one strategy to improve revision or learning (*mnemonics*)
Development of attachment (Social)	Attachment in babies and failure to attach	Ainsworth and Bell (1970) page 104	At least one strategy to develop an attachment friendly environment (*attachment* and *family centred care*)
Impact of advertising on children (Social)	Television advertising, stereotyping and children	Johnson and Young (2002) page 113	At least one strategy to reduce the impact of advertising which is aimed at children (*developing media literacy*)

OCR A L
PSYCHOLOGY
YEAR 2

Matt Jarvis • Julia Russell
Lizzie Gauntlett • Fiona Lintern

OXFORD

OXFORD
UNIVERSITY PRESS

Great Clarendon Street, Oxford OX2 6DP

Oxford University Press is a department of the University of Oxford.

It furthers the University's objective of excellence in research, scholarship, and education by publishing worldwide in Oxford New York Auckland Cape Town Dar es Salaam Hong Kong Karachi Kuala Lumpur Madrid Melbourne Mexico City Nairobi New Delhi Shanghai Taipei Toronto

With offices in

Argentina Austria Brazil Chile Czech Republic France Greece Guatemala Hungary Italy Japan South Korea Poland Portugal Singapore Switzerland Thailand Turkey Ukraine Vietnam

Oxford is a registered trade mark of Oxford University Press in the UK and in certain other countries

© Oxford University Press 2016

The moral rights of the authors have been asserted

Database right Oxford University Press (maker)

First published 2016

British Library Cataloguing in Publication Data

Data available

978 019 8332763

10 9 8 7 6 5 4 3 2 1

MIX
Paper from responsible sources
FSC® C007785

Printed and bound by Bell & Bain Ltd, Glasgow

Paper used in the production of this book is a natural, recyclable product made from wood grown in sustainable forests. The manufacturing process conforms to the environmental regulations of the country of origin.

Author dedications
To Louis and Nathaniel, with love. LG
To Dad, with love. JR

Acknowledgements
The authors would like to thank Patricia Briggs for her unending patience, hard work and good humour.

The publishers would like to thank the following for permission to reproduce photographs:

Cover: Tischenko Irina/Shutterstock; **p7**: Anita Ponne/Shutterstock; **p8**: NATIONAL MUSEUM, DENMARK/MUNOZ-YAGUE/ SCIENCE PHOTO LIBRARY; **p10**: Time Life Pictures/ Mansell/The LIFE Picture Collection/Getty Images; **p13**: © Simon Cook/Alamy; **p14**: (t) © CinemaPhoto/Corbis, (b) Duane Howell/The Denver Post via Getty Images; **p17**: (t) Boris Mrdja/Shutterstock, (b) imging/Shutterstock; **p21**: Alan Poulson Photography/ Shutterstock; **p26**: SvetlanaFedoseyeva/Shutterstock; **p28**: tobkatrina/Shutterstock; **p31**: (t) CORDELIA MOLLOY/SCIENCE PHOTO LIBRARY, (b) WILL & DENI MCINTYRE/SCIENCE PHOTO LIBRARY; **p35**: 'Little Albert', Watson, J. B. and Rayner, R. (1920) 'Conditioned emotional reaction', Journal of Experimental Psychology 3, 1-14, Archives of the History of American Psychology, The Drs. Nicholas and Dorothy Cummings Center for the History of Psychology, The University of Akron; **p37**: Dragon Images/Shutterstock; **p43**: MAURO FERMARIELLO/SCIENCE PHOTO LIBRARY; **p47**: Barbara Alper/Getty Images; **p58**: altanaka/ Shutterstock; **p59**: DenisNata/Shutterstock; **p60**: viki2win/Shutterstock; **p62**: Jeremy/ Shutterstock; **p63**: Felix Mizioznikov/Shutterstock; **p68**: Jason Winter/Shutterstock; **p69**: Monika Wisniewska/Shutterstock; **p71**: Igor Morski; **p72**: Lisa F. Young/Shutterstock; **p73**: Evan Lorne/Shutterstock; **p76**: Yellowj/Shutterstock; **p80**: GEOFF TOMPKINSON/ SCIENCE PHOTO LIBRARY; **p84**: Gibson, E.J. & Walk, R.D. (1960) The Visual Cliff. Scientific American, 202, (4), 64-71, Archives of the History of Psychology, The Drs. Nicholas and Dorothy Cummings Center for the History of Psychology, The University of Akron; **p86**: (tt) Oksana Kuzmina/Shutterstock, (tb) Tsekhmister/Shutterstock, (mt) Miniature world/Shutterstock, (mb) Pakhnyushchy/Shutterstock, (bt) Tsekhmister/ Shutterstock, (bb) Rich Carey/Shutterstock; **p88**: g215/Shutterstock; **p90**: W.E. Hill (1915); **p95**: Ekaterina_Minaeva/Shutterstock; **p98**: bogdan ionescu/Shutterstock; **p100**: oliveromg/Shutterstock; **p101**: Thomas D. McAvoy/The LIFE Collection/Getty Images; **p102**: (t) Andrey_Kuzmin/Shutterstock, (m) szefei/Shutterstock, (b) wonry/Shutterstock; **p103**: Zdorov Kirill Vladimirovich/Shutterstock; **p108**: Portra Images/Getty Images; **p109**: Liudmila P. Sundikova/Shutterstock; **p111**: Monkey Business Images/Shutterstock; **p113**: Aleksandra Zaitseva/Shutterstock; **p115**: Angela Waye/Shutterstock; **p116**: Ollyy/ Shutterstock; **p124**: VADYM SHPONTAK/Shutterstock; **p125**: Mary Evans Picture Library; **p128**: © Angela Hampton Picture Library/Alamy; **p137**: (t) Forensic Science International, 156 (1) pp.74-8 'Contextual information renders experts vulnerable to making erroneous identifications' I. Dror, D. Charlton, A. Peron. With permission of Elsevier, **p140**: Ton Keone/Visuals Unlimited, Inc./SCIENCE PHOTO LIBRARY; **p141**: Reprinted from Forensic Science International, 181, Lisa J. Hall, Emma Player, Will the introduction of an emotional context affect fingerprint analysis and decision-making?, 2008, with permission

from Elsevier; **p144**: Rich Legg/Getty Images; **p145**: Created using FACES software, with kind permission from www.facesid.com; **p151**: © Mark Harvey/Alamy; **p154**: © FREDRIK VON ERICHSEN/epa/Corbis; **p156**: Tinseltown/Shutterstock; **p162**: © Jason Smalley Photography/Alamy; **p164**: Kuzma/Shutterstock; **p165**: Susan Watts/NY Daily News via Getty Images; **p167**: © Sean De Burca/Corbis; **p168**: © Kumar Sriskandan/Alamy; **p169**: pixinoo/Shutterstock; **p174**: © Roger Bamber/Alamy; **p175**: East News/REX Shutterstock; **p179**: Philip G. Zimbardo, Inc.; **p181**: © ACE STOCK LIMITED/Alamy; **p183**: © Marmaduke St. John/Alamy; **p191**: Photick/Shutterstock; **p192**: Linda Bucklin/Shutterstock; **p193**: (t) De Visu/Shutterstock, (b) Earl D. Walker/Shutterstock; **p194**: Gena Melendrez/ Shutterstock; **p200**: © picturesbyrob/Alamy; **p201**: © Patrick Durand/Sygma/Corbis; **p202**: (t) Markus Gann/Shutterstock, (b) Mikhail Starodubov/Shutterstock; **p207**: foto Arts/ Shutterstock; **p209**: © Image Source Plus/Alamy; **p221**: Lichtmeister/Shutterstock; **p224**: (t) © Rob Walls/Alamy, (b) BSIP/UIG Via Getty Images; **p226**: Reprinted with permission. © (2015). SAGE Publications. All rights reserved. from (2014) Evaluation of a configural vital sign display for intensive care unit nurses; **p229**: With permission from Dazkir, S., & Read, M. Furniture forms and their influence on our emotional responses toward interior environments. Environment and Behavior, 44 (5), 722-732., Elsevier, 2011; **p231**: Iakov Kalinin/Shutterstock; **p233**: (l) Kevin Eaves/Shutterstock, (r) © Pete Hill/Alamy; **p234**: (t) science photo/Shutterstock, (b) Mark Bernard/Shutterstock; **p236**: (t) With permission from Lindal, P., and Hartig, T., Architectural variation, building height, and the restorative quality of urban residential streetscapes, Journal of Environmental Psychology, 33, 26-36, Elsevier, 2013, (b) Zeynep Demir/Shutterstock; **p237**: (l) Matthew Dixon/Shutterstock, (r) With permission from Kahn, P. H., Jr., Friedman, B., Gill, B., Severson, R.L., Freier, N.G., Feldman, E.N., A plasma display window? The shifting baseline problem in a technologically-mediated natural world. Journal of Environmental Psychology, 28, 192-199, Elsevier, 2008; **p241**: © Gruffydd Thomas/Alamy; **p246**: © moodboard/Alamy; **p247**: Photofusion/Universal Images Group via Getty Images; **p249**: © Tribune Content Agency LLC/Alamy; **p257**: mrcmos/Shutterstock; **p258**: Juergen Faelchle/Shutterstock; **p259**: Kappri/Shutterstock; **p262**: Monika Wisniewska/Shutterstock; **p263**: Ljupco Smokovski/ Shutterstock; **p265**: gpointstudio/Shutterstock; **p266**: AlexanderNovikov/iStockphoto; **p267**: (t) Lana K/Shutterstock, (b) sfam_photo/Shutterstock; **p269**: Monkey Business Images/Shutterstock; **p272**: (t) viafilms/Getty Images, (b) © WENN Ltd/Alamy; **p274**: Ilya Andriyanov/Shutterstock; **p275**: Fotokostic/Shutterstock; **p276**: Nicholas Piccillo/ Shutterstock; **p277**: (t) concept w/Shutterstock, (b) Stefan Holm/Shutterstock; **p279**: Volt Collection/Shutterstock; **p281**: © Juice Images/Alamy; **p282**: © Blend Images/Alamy; **p283**: Stephane Boussoutroux/123RF.com; **p284**: Andrii Kaderov/123RF.com; **p286**: dotshock/123RF.com; **p287**: Jose Luis Pelaez Inc/Getty Images; **p289**: © Tammy Abrego/ Alamy; **p291**: © Juice Images/Alamy; **p292**: mooinblack/Shutterstock; **p293**: sainthorant daniel/Shutterstock; **p294**: Eugene Onischenko/Shutterstock; **p295**: fstockfoto/ Shutterstock; **p296**: Sergey Toronto/Shutterstock; **p298**: © Cultura Creative (RF)/Alamy; **p299**: You can more/Shutterstock; **p337**: Julia Russell

Artwork by Paul Moran and Oxford University Press.

Index by Indexing Specialists.

The authors and publishers are grateful to the following for permission to reprint copyright material:

American Association for the Advancement of Science for table from Rosenhan, D.L. (1973) On being sane in insane places. *Science*, 179 (4070), 255.

Cambridge University Press for figure from Carroll, J.B. (1993), *Human cognitive abilities: A survey of factor-analytic studies.* Cambridge University Press, New York, NY.

Elsevier for tables from Hall, L.J. & Player, E. (2008) Will the introduction of an emotional context affect fingerprint analysis and decision-making? Forensic Science International, 181, 36-39; and for table from Wells, M.M. (2000) Office clutter or meaningful personal displays: The role of office personalization in employee and organisational well-being. *Journal of Environmental Psychology*, 20 (3), 239-255.

The Home Office Police Department Police Research Group for table from Chenery, S., Holt, J. and Pease, K. (1997) Biting Back II: Reducing Repeat Victimisation in Huddersfield. *Crime Detection and Prevention*, London, England, Series Paper 82.

National Audit Office for figure from C&AG's Report, Ministry of Justice and National Offender Management Service: Managing the prison estate, Session 2013-14, HC 735, 12 December 2013, Figure 3, p.14.

Schizophrenia International Research Society for figure from Simon, J.J., Billler, A., Walther, A., Roesch-Ely, D., Stippich, C., Weisbrod, M. & Kaiser, S. (2010) Neural correlates of reward processing in schizophrenia. *Schizophrenia Research*, 118, 154-161.

The Southern Medical Association for table from Freedman, A.M., Warren, M.M., Cunningham, L.W. & Blackwell, S.J. (1988) Cosmetic surgery and criminal rehabilitation. *Southern Medical Journal*, 81 (9), 1113-1116.

Springer Science+Business Media for extract from Gans, J, Cole, M.A., Greenberg, B. (2015) Sustained Benefit of mindfulness-based tinnitus stress reduction (MBTSR) in adults with chronic tinnitus: a pilot study. *Mindfulness*, University of California, San Francisco.

John Wiley and Sons for extracts from Lord, K.R. (1994) Motivating recycling behaviour: A quasi-experimental investigation of message and source strategies. *Psychology & Marketing*, 11 (4), 341-358.

Every effort has been made to contact copyright holders of material reproduced in this book. If notified, the publishers will be pleased to rectify any errors or omissions at the earliest opportunity.

Option 2: Criminal Psychology (Chapter 3)			
What makes a criminal? (Biological)	Physiological and non-physiological explanations of criminal behaviour	Raine *et al.* (1997) page 129	At least one strategy for preventing criminal behaviour (*plastic surgery for prisoners*)
The collection and processing of forensic evidence (Biological)	Motivating factors and bias in the collection and processing of forensic evidence.	Hall and Player (2008) page 137	At least one strategy for reducing the bias in the collection and processing of forensic evidence (*independent analysis of the latent mark and comparison print, the filler-control method* and *working in isolation*)
Collection of evidence (Cognitive)	Collecting and using evidence from witnesses and suspects	Memon and Higham (1999) page 147	At least one strategy for police interviews (*the PEACE model* and *Forensic Hypnosis*)
Psychology and the courtroom (Cognitive)	The persuasion of juries by witnesses and defendant characteristics	Dixon *et al.* (2002) page 156	At least one strategy to influence jury decision making (*inadmissible evidence, the CSI effect* and *the use of fMRI scans*)
Crime prevention (Social)	Influences on crime: neighbourhoods and zero tolerance policies	Wilson and Kelling (1982) page 165	At least one strategy for crime prevention (*situational crime prevention*)
Effect of imprisonment (Social)	Responding to criminal behaviour: punishment and reform	Haney *et al.* (1973) page 176	At least one strategy for reducing reoffending (*anger management*)
Option 3: Environmental Psychology (Chapter 4)			
Stressors in the environment (Biological)	Environmental stressors and biological responses	Black and Black (2007) page 194	At least one strategy for managing environmental stress (*cognitive-behaviour therapy*)
Biological rhythms (Biological)	The effects of disrupting biological rhythms	Czeisler *et al.* (1982) page 204	At least one strategy for reducing effects of jetlag or shift work (*schedule changes, power naps during shift breaks, controlled exposure to light and dark,* and *drugs*)
Recycling and conservation behaviours (Cognitive)	Factors influencing conservation behaviours and recycling	Lord (1994) page 211	At least one technique used to increase recycling or other conservation behaviour (*normative messages*)
Ergonomics – human factors (Cognitive)	Observing workers: cognitive overload in the workplace	Drews and Doig (2014) page 224	At least one workplace design based on ergonomic research (*the size of the space and the size of the furniture,* and *Feng Shui*)
Psychological effects of the built environment (Social)	The built environment, urban renewal and wellbeing	Ulrich (1984) page 233	At least one example of environmental design used to improve health/wellbeing (*restorative environments*)
Territory and personal space (Social)	Territory and personal space in the workplace	Wells (2000) page 242	At least one office design strategy based on research into territory or personal space (*open-plan offices, hot-desking,* and *working at a treadmill*)

Option 4: Sport and Exercise Psychology (Chapter 5)			
Arousal and anxiety (Biological)	Optimising arousal: controlling and measuring anxiety	Fazey and Hardy (1988) page 259	At least one technique for managing arousal and anxiety in sport (*cognitive-behavioural therapy*)
Exercise and mental health (Biological)	Benefits of exercise to mental health	Lewis *et al.* (2014) page 267	At least one exercise strategy to improve mental health (*dance, cardio-vascular exercise, green exercise*)
Motivation (Cognitive)	Self-efficacy and confidence: imagery and sports orientation	Munroe-Chandler *et al.* (2008) page 274	At least one strategy for motivating athletes (*intrinsic and extrinsic motivation, manipulating self-efficacy* and *using imagery to develop confidence*)
Personality (Cognitive)	Personality: its measurement and relationship to sport	Kroll and Crenshaw (1970) page 281	At least one strategy for using knowledge of personality to improve sports performance (*identifying and preparing potential elite athletes, matching athlete and sport,* and *modifying personality to fit with the demands of sport*)
Performing with others (Social)	Teams, coaching and leadership	Smith *et al.* (1979) page 288	At least one strategy for improving team performance (*team building and coach development*)
Audience effects (Social)	Audience effects: facilitating and inhibiting performance and the home advantage	Zajonc *et al.* (1969) page 294	At least one strategy for training for and playing spectator sports (*developing automatic processing through practice* and *increasing athlete resilience*)

Each topic includes an Evaluation section illustrating how the topic relates to the issues and debates, including: nature/nurture, freewill/determinism, reductionism/holism, psychology as a science, ethnocentrism, and usefulness of research, as well as ethical and methodological issues.

Each chapter ends with a set of Practice Questions, with sample answers and comments to help you to prepare for your examinations.

At the end of the book there are two further sections. Chapter 6 provides an A to Z of research methods terms. This will be useful to help you throughout the year in understanding the key studies and research used as evidence for the various theories and applications you will learn about. In addition, it will provide an easy-access revision aid for the research methods paper you will sit at the end of the year. To assist you further with this, there is a set of practice research methods questions with sample answers. Finally, Chapter 7 provides guidance to help you to manage your revision effectively, and includes a summary of all the key studies in an 'In Brief' section (pp.322–7). This will help to remind you of the essential elements of each study.

This book aims to help you to engage as deeply as possible with issues relevant to applied psychology so that you improve your understanding and your exam performance. There are boxes alongside the text throughout, including ones providing in-depth explanations of important points (Key Ideas), questions giving tips to prepare you for the exam (Question Spotlight) and taking it further (Stretch & Challenge), and ones to check your recall of mathematical and statistical issues (Maths Moments). In addition, there are opportunities to conduct practical activities (Do-It-Yourself and Activities) and to use the Internet to help you (Web Watch).

Good luck and enjoy!

C1
ISSUES IN
MENTAL HEALTH

Clinical psychology is the area of psychology concerned with understanding issues in mental health. Researchers in this area may study abnormal behaviour in individuals, how it is influenced by biological and environmental factors, and the ways in which mental disorders can be treated. In this chapter we will consider three broad topics:

1 **The historical context of mental health:** We will explore historical views of mental illness. Definitions of the term 'abnormality' will be considered, as will the categorisation of mental disorders. We will consider the contribution of Rosenhan's (1973) study on being sane in insane places. Finally we will explore the characteristics of one affective disorder (depression), one psychotic disorder (schizophrenia) and one anxiety disorder (specific phobias).

2 **The medical model:** We will consider in turn biochemical, genetic and brain abnormalities as explanations of mental illness. We will look at key research by Gottesman *et al.* (2010) regarding disorders in the offspring of psychiatrically ill parents, before considering the biological treatment of one specific disorder (depression).

3 **Alternatives to the medical model:** We will look at both the behavioural and cognitive explanations of mental illness. We will also discuss three other explanations of mental illness, of which you must learn one from the following: humanistic, psychodynamic and cognitive neuroscience. Szasz's (2011) key research on the 'myth' of mental illness will then be examined. Finally we will learn about a non-biological treatment (cognitive-behavioural therapy) of a specific disorder (depression).

HISTORICAL CONTEXT OF MENTAL HEALTH

BACKGROUND

Historical views of mental illness

Although the medical model is the now dominant explanation of mental illness (see Topic 2), this has not always been the case. Long before the advent of modern medicine, unusual patterns of thinking and behaviour were accounted for in many different ways: as an indication of witchcraft, arising from intense religious experiences, or the result of internal imbalances within the body.

Our recognition of mental disorder and treatment reaches back to prehistoric times, and can be seen in evidence such as trepanning of skulls (see Figure 1.1). One of the oldest medical documents in existence was composed around 1550BC in Egypt, and demonstrates an understanding of specific disorders such as depression (Smith, 1974). In Ancient Greece, Hippocrates is credited with developing one of the first systems of classifying mental illness, including mania, paranoia, epilepsy and hysteria. He proposed the theory that such disorders occurred as a result of an imbalance of different fluids, or 'humours', in the body (e.g. blood, phlegm, yellow bile).

Reliance on humours as an explanation of mental illness persisted well into the Middle Ages. Later, during the European Renaissance, there was a greater focus on observation and classification of illness by symptoms and causes. Gradually, the classification of mental disorders in Europe and the USA became dominated by biological typology and medical ideas regarding disease, in recognition of the changing cultural beliefs and knowledge about its origins.

The history of psychiatric treatment is simultaneously fascinating and terrifying. Until the nineteenth century, there was no public provision for those suffering mental illness, and most ended up in workhouses, prisons or private 'madhouses'. These were generally highly unsuitable settings as they were run for profit rather than for the therapeutic benefit of residents. The Madhouse Act of 1774 introduced licensing and inspections of madhouses, and towards the start of the nineteenth century, county asylums began to open. By mid-nineteenth century each region of the UK had a mandate to care for their mentally ill in lunatic asylums, and a period of mass construction ensued. One of the first mental health hospitals is the Bethlem Royal Hospital in London, whose extraordinary history is outlined in Figure 1.2.

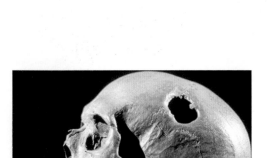

Figure 1.1: Trepanning is a surgical procedure involving the piercing of the skull to create a hole from which evil spirits were supposedly released. It was used for the treatment of seizures, migraines and mental disorders for thousands of years across many cultures

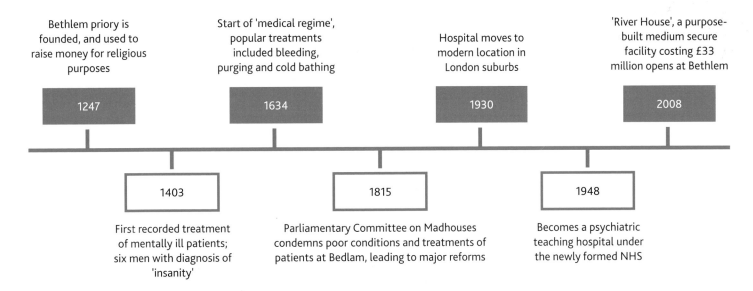

Figure 1.2: Historical overview of Bethlem Royal Hospital
Source: South London and Maudsley NHS Trust website, 2014

The legal and social changes of this period were associated with changing views of mental illness. Concepts of 'madness' and 'lunacy' had long been rich sources of entertainment in literature, theatre and art (Foucault, 1961). The practice of publicly viewing inmates at madhouses and asylums continued until as late as 1815. However, the mentally ill were increasingly viewed as treatable and requiring compassion. In the UK, a religious group known as the Quakers led early humanitarian reform of asylums. Residents were encouraged to rest, engage in physical work, such as gardening, and talk with others.

Improvements for patients were slow, however, and the rapid expansion of institutionalised care meant overcrowding and poor living conditions persisted well into the twentieth century. Modern psychiatric treatments were offered, including insulin treatment for schizophrenic patients, as well as electroconvulsive therapy (ECT) and lobotomies. All of these have been discontinued, except for ECT, which is still used, albeit rarely, to help relieve symptoms of severe mood disorders. One of the most significant advances in mental health treatment was the introduction of medication for the asylum patients, such as chlorpromazine, the first anti-psychotic drug. There was also a growing recognition and development of various forms of 'talking' therapies which could benefit patients.

By the 1960s the Victorian-era asylum system had lost the support of the incumbent Conservative government. It felt that ordinary hospitals could offer some care to those with mental health issues, and widespread availability of medication meant increasing numbers could self-manage their illness. Plans were made to reduce funding for maintaining the large, specialist institutions in favour of a 'care in the community' model. Over the subsequent 25 years, asylums closed down as community mental health services in the UK came to offer the majority of provision.

This coincided with important changes in how mental illness was viewed. Changes in vocabulary, such as in the use of the terms 'mental health' and 'service user', reduced the stigma associated with the terms 'mental illness' and 'patient'. The anti-psychiatry movement, which we will explore in Topic 3, challenges the conventional constructs of power in the way we talk about mental health.

So do we now agree where the line is between normal human behaviour and 'abnormality'?

ACTIVITY ✳

The language of mental health has undergone huge transformation over time. There are many powerful words used to describe those with mental health issues. Consider the list of words below. What are the origins of the words? What can they tell us about different historical views of mental illness?

Word	Origin and significance
Lunatic	
Crazy	
Insanity	
Madness	
Bedlam	

Defining abnormality

As we will see in the key research, there are problems defining which human behaviours can be regarded as abnormal. It is one of the most controversial areas in psychology, mainly because diagnosing an individual as 'abnormal' or 'mentally ill' has serious implications for their subsequent treatment.

Abnormality is the term used by psychologists to describe a range of thinking and behaviours. There are many ways of defining abnormality. One of these definitions is known as *statistical infrequency*. In this conceptualisation, behaviour that is rarely seen in the general population might be considered abnormal. It is based on the idea that in measurable characteristics, such as anxiety or intelligence, most people's scores will group around a central average, and the number of people attaining scores much lower or much higher than the average will be fewer. In other words, looking at an overview of a measurable trait such as IQ will produce a normal distribution of scores.

Figure 1.3: Mechanical restraints for mentally ill residents were commonplace prior to the reform of the asylums in the early 1800s

Figure 1.4: Normal distribution of IQ scores across the general population

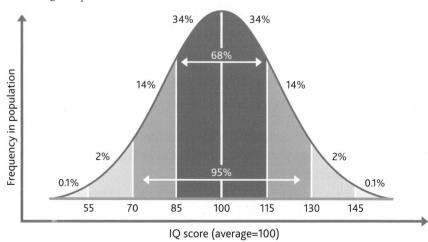

Although this method works well for reliable measurements of particular qualities, it is not a sufficient measure for diagnosing abnormality. To take the example of IQ, it is not helpful to those individuals with the highest or lowest scores to be labelled 'abnormal', as they may well be perfectly happy and function well in society.

An alternative definition of abnormality is known as *deviation from social norms*. This denotes behaviour that can be seen as a departure from what one society or culture defines as acceptable. This involves a judgment based on the context in which the behaviour occurs. While there are behaviours that might be universally considered morally unacceptable, much of what we consider socially acceptable has a strong cultural and historical context. That is to say that over time, or within different groups, there are huge discrepancies between what each would consider normal.

A third and final definition of abnormality relates to *maladaptiveness*. This refers to when a person's way of thinking, emotional responses or actual behaviour is dangerous or prevents them from functioning well. This might be because they are deliberately self-harming, or less directly their behaviour might be impeding the success of their relationships or ability to hold down a job. For example, someone with obsessive-compulsive disorder might be consistently late for work because of lengthy and elaborate cleaning routines. This definition is broader than the other two in that it allows for individual differences; in some cases a person's behaviour might appear abnormal but does not cause them any great difficulty or risk. Individuals may be described as eccentric or outspoken in such cases, but don't warrant a psychiatric diagnosis.

All three definitions – statistical infrequency, deviation from social norms, and maladaptiveness – play some role in the diagnosis of mental disorders, though none is sufficient on its own. Typically a person who is a risk to themselves or others (maladaptiveness) and scores abnormally highly on a depression checklist (statistically infrequency) may receive a diagnosis. Conformity to or deviation from social norms has also influenced classification of abnormality across different contexts, as we will explore next.

STRETCH & CHALLENGE

There have been a number of socially constructed 'mental illnesses' over the course of history. Research the following terms and discover the specific social context in which they existed. You may be surprised at how recently some social attitudes have changed:

- Hysteria
- Homosexuality
- Nymphomania

ACTIVITY ✳

When considering the accuracy of how we diagnose mental illness, it is useful to consider what is meant by 'abnormality'. Read the following examples and answer the questions below:

A   A maths teacher by day, who is also a cage-fighter and a transvestite dancer

B   An unmarried teenager who falls pregnant from a one-night stand

C   A 50-year-old man who in his leisure time wears a nappy, acts like an infant and drinks milk from a baby's bottle

D   A young man who hears the voice of god, and then wanders the desert for 40 years

E   A woman who takes 1–2 hours to leave her flat each day because she has to wash her hands 16 times, and check three times that each window in the house is locked and that switches are turned off.

1   Which of these cases would you consider abnormal, and why?

2   To what extent are our ideas about what counts as 'abnormal' fixed and unchanging within different contexts?

Categorising mental disorders

Attempts to formally classify abnormality have been made by psychiatrists – doctors with medical training who consider mental disorders as equivalent to other forms of illness. The medical model of mental illness tries to determine the appropriate treatment for an individual by establishing categories of symptoms that form an identifiable disorder. Psychiatrists use the Diagnostic and Statistical Manual of Mental Disorders (**DSM**) to classify abnormal behaviour and diagnose patients. It was originally published in 1952 by the American Psychiatric Association, and since that time has undergone periodic reviews. It is the handbook that mental health professionals in the USA, UK and much of the world regard as the authority on mental disorder diagnosis.

Currently in its 5th edition, the manual contains descriptions, symptoms and other criteria to allow reliable diagnoses of 157 disorders. The process of completing the latest edition involved around 160 international researchers and clinicians with expertise in neuroscience, biology, genetics, statistics, epidemiology, social and behavioural sciences, and public health (APA, 2014). Existing collective knowledge and new research determine how disorders are removed or changed from one edition to the next. A selection of DSM-5® chapter categories are given in Table 1.1.

TABLE 1.1: CATEGORISING MENTAL DISORDERS

Major categories of disorders	Disorder example, with selected diagnostic criteria
Neurodevelopmental disorders	**Severe intellectual disability (intellectual development disorder)** IQ score below 70 Individual requires support for all activities of daily living
Obsessive-compulsive and related disorders	**Trichotilliomania (hair-pulling disorder)** Recurrent pulling of hair, resulting in hair loss Hair-pulling causes distress or impairment in social functioning/work context
Trauma- and stressor-related disorders	**Post-traumatic stress disorder** Exposure to actual or threatened death, serious injury or sexual violence Involuntary recurrence of memories of event Hypervigilance (extreme alertness) Sleep disturbance
Somatic symptom disorders	**Conversion disorder (functional neurological symptom disorder)** One or more symptoms of altered voluntary motor or sensory function that cannot be explained by medical issues, e.g. seizures, slurred speech or paralysis
Feeding and eating disorders	**Pica** Persistent eating of non-food substances over a period of at least one month Eating behaviour is not part of a culturally or socially accepted practice
Disruptive, impulse control and conduct disorders	**Pyromania** Deliberate fire setting on multiple occasions Fascination with fire, or pleasure at setting/witnessing fires
Substance use and addictive disorders	**Gambling disorder** Persistent and recurrent problematic gambling leading to distress or impairment of function May need to gamble with increasing amounts to achieve excitement Lying to conceal involvement with gambling Lost or endangered a relationship, job or other opportunity as a result of gambling behaviour

Some changes reflect changes to social attitudes and conventions, such as the replacement of the diagnosis 'mental retardation' with 'intellectual disability (intellectual development disorder)', along with greater emphasis on adaptiveness over IQ score in diagnosis. 'Autism spectrum disorder' is a new name encompassing four previously separate disorders (autistic disorder, Asperger's disorder, childhood disintegrative disorder and pervasive developmental disorder). This is in recognition of the consensus from mental health professionals that these are actually a single condition with different levels of symptom severity in two core domains.

DSM-5® contains several new depressive disorders, including disruptive mood dysregulation disorder and premenstrual dysphoric disorder. It also includes a new chapter on obsessive-compulsive and related disorders (now recognised as distinct but aligned with anxiety disorders). Among new inclusions is 'hoarding disorder', a persistent difficulty in parting with possessions, even those of little value, which leads to such accumulation of belongings that it becomes difficult to maintain a safe environment.

KEY IDEAS

DSM – the Diagnostic and Statistical Manual of Mental Disorders is published by the American Psychiatric Association and provides standard criteria for the classification of mental disorders. It is regularly revised, and the version currently in use is DSM-5®.

Reliability refers to how consistent a test or tool is. In this case, a diagnostic test is considered reliable if it can produce similar results when used again in similar circumstances.

Validity is the extent to which a test measures what it is intended to measure. In this case, the extent to which the diagnostic criteria can be used to accurately diagnose someone experiencing a mental illness.

Figure 1.5: Extreme hoarding may cause distress to the hoarder and/or those around them

Rosenhan and others have criticised the medical model of mental illness as part of what is known as the 'anti-psychiatry movement'. While they accept that mental suffering and deviant behaviour *do* exist, they question whether the most useful way of understanding such behaviour is through a rigid system of classification. One of the most serious criticisms levelled at psychiatry is that it actually increases the suffering of those who receive a mental health diagnosis. This is because it removes control from the patient, who can then be manipulated for political or social purposes. A second major issue that concerned Rosenhan was the **reliability** and **validity** of diagnosis: to what extent can the sane be consistently and accurately distinguished from the insane?

Figure 1.6: Actor Jack Nicholson in the 1975 film version of Ken Kesey's *One Flew Over The Cuckoo's Nest*, which brought the anti-psychiatry movement to the attention of the masses

QUESTION SPOTLIGHT!

As you will see, Rosenhan's research is composed of two separate but related studies. Ensure you can clearly describe the aims, methods and results from each study.

Figure 1.7: Psychologist Dr David L. Rosenhan of Stanford University

KEY RESEARCH

Rosenhan, D.L. (1973) On being sane in insane places. *Science*, Vol. 179 (4070), 250–258.

Aim

The aim of the study was to investigate whether the sane can be reliably and accurately distinguished from the insane. In Study 1, this involved finding out whether normal, sane individuals would be admitted to psychiatric hospitals, to see if and how they would be discovered. In Study 2, this involved examining whether genuine patients would be misidentified as 'sane' by various hospital staff.

STUDY 1

Method

Sample

Eight pseudopatients were adults over the age of 20 and included Rosenhan himself. They had a variety of professions: one was a psychology graduate student in his twenties, while other participants were psychologists, a pediatrician, a psychiatrist, a painter and a housewife. Three pseudopatients were female, the remaining five were male. They all used false names, and those with careers in mental health claimed to have an alternative occupation to avoid attracting any special attention from staff. Rosenhan was the first pseudopatient and his involvement was known only to the hospital administrator and chief psychologist.

The settings were also varied. To make the findings generalisable, pseudopatients sought admission to a variety of hospitals. Twelve hospitals were chosen, across five different states in the USA. They ranged from old and shabby, to modern and new. The sample included public, private and university-funded hospitals. Staff-to-patient ratios also varied greatly.

Design and procedure

After calling the hospital for an appointment, the pseudopatient arrived at the admissions office of the hospital and asserted that they had been hearing voices, which were unclear but were saying 'empty', 'hollow', and 'thud'. These words were chosen by Rosenhan as they were thought to imply a crisis about one's existence, but, at the time the study was conducted, there was no literature linking this to a known mental health disorder. Pseudopatients all reported that the voices were unfamiliar and were of the same sex. All other details of the pseudopatient's life, relationships and experiences were given truthfully to the doctoral staff, with the exception of their name, participation in the current study, and occupation.

Pseudopatients entered the study understanding that they had to be released from the institution by their own means, by convincing staff they were sane.

On the ward, the pseudopatients behaved 'normally' and attempted to engage others in conversation. They indicated to staff that they were no longer experiencing any symptoms. Pseudopatients obeyed the rules and routines of the ward, and pretended to take medication they had been prescribed without fuss. Although pseudopatients found the experience as a whole distressing and unpleasant, nursing staff recorded in their notes that they were friendly and cooperative.

This main study can be considered to be a field experiment. The independent variable was the 12 different hospitals. The dependent variable was the admission of participants to hospital, the diagnoses they received, and the recordings of their experiences on the ward. The study was also a participant observation: researchers acted as genuine patients while keeping a written record of their personal experience in each institution.

In four hospitals, the pseudopatients also observed staff responses to a specific request. They approached a member of staff and asked: 'when am I likely to be discharged?' Responses to this question were recorded and compared to a control condition at Stanford University that involved asking university staff a similarly simple question.

Results

Pseudopatients were successfully admitted at all 12 hospitals. Despite ceasing to show any symptoms of insanity once admitted, pseudopatients were not detected by staff in the hospitals. Failure to recognise sanity therefore was not related to the quality of the hospital. All except one received diagnoses of schizophrenia, and were discharged with a diagnosis of 'schizophrenia in remission'. In this way, patients discharged carry a **label** of mental illness beyond the hospital.

The length of stay in hospital ranged from 7 to 52 days, the average stay lasting 19 days. During the first three trials, 35 out of a total of 118 genuine patients voiced suspicions about the sanity of the pseudopatients. They made accusations such as 'You're not crazy ... you're checking up on the hospital', while none of the hospital staff raised such concerns. Rosenhan found a strong tendency towards type 1 errors in diagnosis, which is when a healthy person is diagnosed as ill.

Rosenhan found that, once admitted with a diagnosis of mental illness, subsequent behaviour by pseudopatients was interpreted in light of their diagnosis. He calls this the 'stickiness of psychodiagnostic labels'. Examples of 'pathological behaviour' from the observers' experiences included:

- When pacing in the hospital corridors from boredom, pseudopatients were asked by the nurse if they were nervous.
- When recording behaviour in notes on the ward, pseudopatients were described by the nurse as 'engaging in writing behaviour'.
- When waiting outside the cafeteria entrance before lunch, pseudopatients were described as demonstrating the 'oral-acquisitive' nature of their conditions.

Experience of hospitalisation was overwhelmingly negative and unpleasant. Hospital staff avoided interaction with patients. On average, attendants spent only 11.3% of their time seeking staff-interaction. In the case of both the medical centre and hospitals, individuals experienced most depersonalisation (see page 16) from psychiatrists and more cooperation from lower ranking, less powerful staff and interns.

KEY IDEAS

The term 'labelling' has a special meaning in this study. It is used to mean a tag that is attached to a person that refers to their mental illness. However, it is not just a description; it carries with it a negative social and personal meaning.

TABLE 1.2: SELF-INITIATED CONTACT BY PSEUDOPATIENTS IN HOSPITALS COMPARED TO OTHER GROUPS

Contact	Psychiatric hospitals		University campus (non-medical)	University medical centre		
	(1) Psychiatrists	(2) Nurses and attendants	(3) Faculty	(4) 'Looking for a psychiatrist'	(5) 'Looking for an internist'	(6) No additional comment
Responses (%)						
Moves on, head averted	71	88	0	0	0	0
Makes eye contact	23	10	0	11	0	0
Pauses and chats	2	2	0	11	0	10
Stops and talks	4	0.5	100	78	100	90
Mean number of questions answered (out of 6)	*	*	6	3.8	4.8	4.5
Respondents (no.)	13	47	14	18	15	10
Attempts (no.)	185	1283	14	18	15	10

Source: Rosenhan (1973), p.255

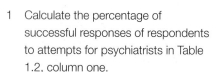

MATHS MOMENT

1   Calculate the percentage of successful responses of respondents to attempts for psychiatrists in Table 1.2, column one.
2   Calculate this for column 2 and compare to your answer for question 1. How does this finding support Rosenhan's arguments about powerlessness and depersonalisation?

KEY IDEAS

Powerlessness is a key idea used in this piece of research. It refers to the loss of authority or control an individual has to make their own legal or personal decisions. As well as a lack of control, the pseudopatients also experienced a loss of their sense of personhood: they ceased to be treated as individuals by staff. This can be described as **depersonalisation**.

Powerlessness was evident in each institution. In addition to the restricted contact with staff, personal privacy was inadequate. For example, patients' rooms could be entered and examined by any member of staff without warning or justification. There was a lack of confidentiality in terms of patients' case notes, which were read openly by casual members of staff who had no therapeutic input with the patient. Patients' personal hygiene and waste evacuation were monitored, and toilet cubicles had no doors. Even the initial physical examinations were conducted in a semi-public room.

The **depersonalisation** of patients was also a key finding. There were instances where ward staff attendants engaged in physical abuse of patients in the presence of other patients. This behaviour ceased in the presence of staff because they could be considered credible witnesses. In one instance a nurse undid part of her uniform to adjust her bra in full view of male patients on the ward. A total of 2100 pills were administered to pseudopatients (although only two were swallowed). Many other patients also disposed of their medication, but this was not challenged by staff as long as patients remained cooperative.

Rosenhan argues that depersonalisation has several causes. First, the staff's attitudes towards the mentally ill affected their treatment of the patients. They may have distrusted and feared patients, while also wanting to help them. Rosenhan suggests that this combination of opposing feelings could have led them to avoid interaction with patients.

Second, the formal hierarchical structure of the hospitals could also have contributed to the depersonalisation experienced by patients. Those with the highest status within the hospital were those who had least contact with the patients. Average daily contact time with doctoral staff per patient was just 6.8 minutes. As doctoral staff serve as role models to the rest of the nurses and support staff, this could also have been a contributing factor. There might be other practical considerations that contribute to the experience of powerlessness and depersonalisation, including financial pressures, staff shortages, and over-reliance on medication to treat patients.

As seen in this study, Rosenhan is highly critical of diagnostic labels. He describes the labelling process as 'counter-therapeutic', suggesting that it actually does the patient more harm than good. He is also critical of the type of environment that perpetuates labelling: he describes psychiatric hospitals as special environments, 'in which the meaning of behaviour can be easily misunderstood' (Rosenhan, 1973).

Instead of focusing on labelling an individual as 'insane', Rosenhan supports alternative models of treatment including the services of community mental health centres and behavioural therapy programmes. These options could potentially reduce the stigma associated with being institutionalised, as well as offering more individualised treatment with an element of control for the individual.

Rosenhan also asserts that raising hospital staff's awareness of the issues faced by psychiatric patients could change the experience of hospitalisation. If frontline mental health staff had an experience similar to his own and that of his other pseudopatients, he believes it might increase their sensitivity to the position of hospitalised patients.

STUDY 2

Method
Sample
Participants were psychiatric staff at one research and teaching hospital who had been briefed on the findings of the main study. Judgements were made on 193 patients who were admitted for psychiatric treatment.

Design and procedure
Staff were informed that at some point during a three-month period, one or more pseudopatients would attempt to gain admission into the hospital. Each staff member was asked to rate each patient – either at admission or on the ward – according to the likelihood that the patient was an imposter. A 10-point scale was used, with '1' reflecting the strongest belief that the patient was a pseudopatient, and '10' the strongest belief that that patient was genuine.

Results
All staff that had close contact with or responsibility for the patient made judgements on the 10-point scale. This included attendants, nurses, psychiatrists, physicians, and psychologists. It was found that 41 of the patients admitted during the three-month period were rated with high confidence to be pseudopatients by at least one member of the staff. Of these, 23 were suspected by at least one psychiatrist, and 19 were suspected by a psychiatrist and at least one other staff member.

No pseudopatients actually presented themselves to the hospital for admission during the period of this study. This secondary study lends evidence to Rosenhan's argument about the lack of reliability in diagnosis. In this instance, psychiatric staff committed a type 2 error by identifying mentally ill patients as healthy.

Figure 1.8: Powerlessness and depersonalisation – patients experienced a continual lack of privacy: patients' rooms were entered without permission, and toilet cubicles were not fitted with doors

WEB WATCH @

BBC Radio 4 revisits Rosenhan's pseudo-patient study, gaining access to his unpublished personal papers to discover how it changed our understanding of the human mind, and its impact 40 years on.

http://www.bbc.co.uk/iplayer/console/b00lny48

Figure 1.9: Pseudopatients accepted their prescribed medication without protest, and disposed of it later. It was found that many genuine patients did the same.

QUESTION SPOTLIGHT!

Make sure you understand what is meant by both a type 1 and type 2 error. Can you explain the difference between the two in relation to Rosenhan's study?

STRETCH & CHALLENGE

Rosenhan's full study makes for an interesting read. You can access it here:

http://www.psychblog.co.uk/as-study-full-text-references-spec-2008-282.html

Conclusions

Rosenhan's research challenges the idea that psychiatric professionals can effectively distinguish between individuals who are sane and those who are insane. He found that:

1 Psychiatrists are unable to reliably identify sane pseudopatients (type 1 error: false positive).

2 Psychiatrists also fail to reliably detect insanity (type 2 error: false negative).

3 Within the 'insane' environment of the psychiatric hospital, an individual's behaviour is perceived in a distorted manner, which can maintain a diagnostic label.

APPLICATION: CHARACTERISTICS OF MENTAL DISORDERS

In this topic we have considered what is meant by abnormality, and looked at attempts to categorise mental illness. We will now turn to specific examples of three different types of disorder: affective, psychotic and anxiety disorders.

Affective disorder: depression

Affective disorders include a broad group of illnesses affecting mood which can range from mild to severe. Typically individuals may experience marked feelings of sadness, emptiness, or irritability; in other cases mania, euphoria or rage are also prevalent. What sets these disorders apart from the ordinary 'highs and lows' of life are their damaging impact on the individual's capacity to function.

Previously referred to as the 'common cold' of mental illness, because of its high prevalence, depression is one example of an affective disorder. Recent national statistics show rates of depression or depression and anxiety occur in around one fifth of the population (BPS, 2013). There are several different types of depression classified in the DSM-5®; here we will specifically consider major depressive disorder.

The experience of a person in a major depressive episode is one of sadness and hopelessness. They may deny their feelings or express themselves as feeling 'blah'. In some cases their mood may be more accurately noticed by those around them: it can be seen in their facial expression or demeanour, through atypical angry or tearful outbursts, or in social withdrawal. Individuals suffering the disorder may lose appetite, or eat excessively. They may also have difficulty sleeping or sleep to excess. Psychomotor agitation can occur – this is an inability to relax or keep still, and may also include pacing or handwringing. Similarly, delay to psychomotor responses can be noticed, such as excessive pauses before speaking, or slowed body movements. In more severe cases, suicidal ideation (fantasies of taking one's own life) may be frequent. This can range from passive thoughts ('I don't want to wake up in the morning') to more specific plans of suicide.

> **Box 1.1: Symptoms of major depressive disorder**
>
> Main symptoms (present in past two weeks):
>
> - Depressed mood for most or all of the day, nearly every day
>   and/or
> - Loss of interest or pleasure in all or most activities
>
> Other possible symptoms include:
>
> - Significant weight/appetite loss or gain
> - Frequent insomnia or hypersomnia (excessive sleeping)
> - Inability to relax or sit still, or excessive lethargy
> - Daily fatigue or loss of energy
> - Excessive feelings of worthlessness or guilt
> - Loss of concentration or ability to think
> - Recurrent thoughts of death, suicidal ideation, suicide attempt or plan

Symptoms of a major depressive disorder (detailed in Box 1.1) must be present every day or nearly every day to be considered as part of a diagnosis, over the course of at least two consecutive weeks. Fatigue and sleep disturbance are among the most commonly reported symptoms, however depressed mood or the loss of interest in pleasurable activities are the only two essential criteria. Instances of major depressive episodes tend to begin at puberty and peak in the 18-to 29-year-old age range, with females experiencing between 1.5 to 3 times higher rates than males. In children and adolescents, mood may appear irritable rather than sad.

Major depressive episodes can reoccur (e.g. with an interval of at least two months), and vary in severity from mild to moderate and severe. The course of the illness is also highly variable: some individuals only ever experience one episode, or go for long durations in remission (period of recovery without symptoms). The risk of recurrence diminishes over time spent in remission. The diagnosis of a major depressive episode may change, for example if an individual subsequently experiences a manic episode, or lives with the symptoms for longer than two years (or one year for children or adolescents). In these cases, a diagnosis of another affective disorder becomes more appropriate, such as bipolar disorder or persistent depressive disorder (dysthymia).

Psychotic disorder: schizophrenia

Schizophrenia is a long-term mental health condition that affects people's thoughts, emotions and behaviour. It is often described as a 'psychotic disorder'. This refers to the experience of the disorder as a loss of contact with reality; those with the diagnosis come to perceive things around them very differently from others.

Symptoms of schizophrenia are sometimes described as either positive or negative. 'Positive' symptoms refer to the addition of new behaviours, such as the onset of hallucinations or delusions. 'Negative' symptoms, on the other hand, include a removal or loss of normal function, such as a lack of outward emotion or a reduction in speech. Hallucinations may take many forms, and involve hearing, seeing and even feeling things that don't exist. Delusions, by contrast,

WEB WATCH @

It is difficult for someone who does not have schizophrenia to imagine what it feels like to experience hallucinations, paranoia and delusions. You can read the stories of those with an inside perspective on the illness here:

http://www.nhs.uk/Conditions/
Schizophrenia/Pages/Stuarts-story.aspx

refer to beliefs people may have that are not based on reality. A common example of this might be the paranoid belief that family, friends or healthcare professionals are 'out to get' the person who is ill, when they are actually trying to help.

Often the symptoms of schizophrenia are not immediately recognisable. Changes may begin slowly, in the form of social withdrawal or in the appearance of apathy, which may be mistaken for a normal 'phase' of adolescent behaviour. These periods can then become acute, meaning the person experiences severe positive symptoms which may lead to diagnosis and psychiatric interventions.

As you can see from the summary in Box 1.2, symptoms of schizophrenia may overlap with those of other disorders. Importantly, a diagnosis should only be given if symptoms are not better explained by underlying medical issues or substance use. They must also have a negative effect on the normal functioning of a person. For instance, someone who claims to hear voices but who exhibits no other symptoms and shows a good level of functioning in society would not fit the criteria.

Box 1.2: Symptoms of schizophrenia

Main symptoms (present during period of one month):

- Delusions
- Hallucinations
- Disorganised speech

Other symptoms include:

- Highly disorganised or catatonic behaviour
- Negative symptoms (e.g. reduced expression of emotion)

Around 1 in 100 people will be diagnosed with schizophrenia during their lifetime, making it a fairly common serious mental health disorder. Males are typically diagnosed in their late teens, with the average age of diagnosis for women being several years later (around age 25). Men are more likely to experience hospitalisation as a result of their illness. As a long-term condition, those with the diagnosis will never be 'cured' and are likely to require ongoing treatment to help manage their symptoms. However, the majority of those diagnosed with schizophrenia live normal lives. Contrary to media stereotypes, very few people with the diagnosis ever engage in violent behaviour towards others. Aggressive behaviour is not a symptom of schizophrenia, and those with the diagnosis are more likely to be a danger to themselves, or at risk of harm from others.

Anxiety disorder: specific phobias

Anxiety disorders are those that involve feelings and behaviours characterised by excessive and persistent fear or anxiety. Fear is an emotional response to a real (or perceived) threat, whereas anxiety is the expectation of that threat.

Many of us may relate to being afraid of or disliking certain animals, such as spiders or snakes. However, in a minority of people these negative feelings towards specific animals, objects or situations are much more extreme and have a serious impact on their lives. Specific phobias are one type of anxiety disorder, affecting around 6% of people in the UK. Among the more common phobic stimuli are animals (insects or dogs), the natural environment (heights or water), situations (travelling in a lift or aeroplane) and injury (blood or injections). However, there are a huge variety of phobias; some more unusual ones include pteronophobia (fear of feathers or being tickled by feathers), spectrophobia (fear of mirrors or looking at your own reflection) and zemmiphobia (fear of mole rats). The key symptoms of specific phobias are outlined in Box 1.3.

> **Box 1.3: Symptoms of specific phobia**
> - Phobic stimulus provokes immediate fear and anxiety
> - Phobic stimulus is deliberately avoided or endured with strong anxiety or fear
> - Fear and anxiety caused by stimulus is disproportionate to the actual danger it poses
> - Phobic distress is persistent, lasts 6 months or more
> - Phobia causes significant distress and impairment in areas of functioning such as social life or work

A 'phobia' is an intense, severe and irrational fear that produces a physiological response, such as sweating, shaking and increased respiratory rate. While transient fear of some objects is fairly normal, a phobia will be intense and severe, and even the anticipation of the phobic stimulus can induce anxiety. Typically, someone who has a specific phobia will actively avoid encountering it, they will minimise contact in any way possible. For example, someone who has a fear of dogs might walk a long route home from work to avoid seeing a neighbour's pet, or they might never visit local parks. Their phobia is likely to have a significant impact on their lives and prevent normal functioning. Someone with a fear of water might never learn to swim, avoid travelling anywhere by boat, and avoid any occupation that could involve working on or near water.

Individuals who have specific phobias often realise that their reaction to the phobic stimuli is disproportionate. It is likely that people experience multiple phobias: 75% of people with a specific phobia fear more than one object (APA, 2013). The disorder is also more commonly diagnosed in certain groups than others: adolescents and females are particularly likely to have a specific phobia. There are also gender differences between types of phobic stimuli: animal and natural phobias are more common in females than males, whereas blood and injury type phobias are experienced roughly equally by both genders.

Figure 1.10: No laughing matter: pteronophobia is 'feather fear' or the fear of being tickled by feathers

DO IT YOURSELF

Design a questionnaire to investigate gender differences in phobias. Include a list of common phobias. You may wish to consider using a Likert scale to measure individuals' responses. Summarise your findings in a bar chart. Do they support the idea that there are gender differences for specific phobias?

EVALUATION

Methodological and ethical issues

The key research raises important questions about the reliability of diagnostic processes and about how to treat patients. Rosenhan highlights problems with using classification systems such as DSM-5® through his fundamental challenge to the assumptions of psychiatry. Arguing that the criteria for disorders are too vague and arbitrary has paved the way for research into how subjective bias can undermine and distort diagnosis. In the UK, Kirkbride *et al.* (2012) found that diagnostic rates of schizophrenia were disproportionately high in black males as compared to white males. This shows how Rosenhan's findings can be applied to revealing racial bias in the diagnosis of mental illness.

While research such as Rosenhan's could be considered to be high in ecological validity, the researchers' experiences cannot be entirely valid, as they were not experiencing genuine symptoms of insanity. Using participant observers compromises the validity of the research, as observers could lose their objectivity. For example, they might have over-empathised with other patients and distorted their reports of staff behaviour.

There are important ethical considerations around the use of terms such as 'insanity' and 'madness'. Historically these terms have been used to describe people who suffer mental health problems, and they have highly negative implications. As we saw from Rosenhan's research, labelling those who suffer from disorders can be 'sticky', affecting them not only during periods of treatment but also in periods of good mental health, leading to discrimination. As well as recognising the importance of language, we must consider the appalling treatment of people with mental illness, even in recent history. Many treatments involved pain and permanent damage to the bodies and minds of individuals, some of whom would have been kept in institutions in terrible conditions against their will. Today there are still serious ethical implications around mental health treatment, in balancing the cost and effectiveness of talking therapies, and in trialling new drugs.

There are also specific ethical issues around researching mental health issues. The British Psychological Society (BPS) guidelines on conducting research with participants specify that those with mental health issues require additional consideration due to their vulnerability. Even in Rosenhan's research, hospital staff were unaware that they were participants in a study, which raises a number of ethical issues. Staff in Study 1 did not give their informed consent to take part in this study. They were deceived by pseudopatients who sought admission to the hospital, and misled into administering medication and treatment to them as though they were genuine patients. The nature of the environment was potentially harmful for the pseudopatients, who had to seek discharge from the hospitals by their own efforts. Pseudopatients witnessed physical and verbal abuse, which was not only highly distressing, but from which they had no immediate means of escape.

QUESTION SPOTLIGHT!

What ethical implications do you see when labelling mental illness, and how are these exemplified in Rosenhan's findings?

Debates

Usefulness of research

Rosenhan's findings question the validity and reliability of psychiatric diagnosis, as well as raising concerns about the treatment received by patients in mental health institutions. This has clear implications for the profession in terms of reviewing diagnostic processes and bringing to the forefront issues concerning patient experience. Therefore it makes sense that Rosenhan's explanations for these experiences, and his suggestions for how to improve conditions, focus on educating staff and changing the fundamental methods of practice involved in the diagnosis and treatment of the 'insane'.

Nature vs nurture

Historically, mental illness has been attributed to a range of causes both internal and external to the individual. The belief that certain disorders were caused by possession by evil spirits could also be considered 'supernatural' rather than a result of nature or nurture. As we considered, there are several ways of defining abnormality. Those that involve cultural perspectives – i.e. deviation from social norms and maladaptiveness definitions – argue for a strong role for the environment determining what is abnormal. For example, in some cultures eating insects might be seen as abnormal behaviour and a symptom of mental illness, whereas it might be normal practice in another culture.

The key research by Rosenhan explores this idea further, examining the way in which the environment, or the way in which we are nurtured, affects our mental health and the treatment we receive from others. He found that once labelled mentally ill, it was difficult to have one's behaviour perceived as anything other than abnormal. This was seen in the interpretation of writing as obsessive, and in the way in which patients were largely ignored when speaking to hospital staff.

Freewill vs determinism

Rosenhan's key research is important to the debate about the influence of freewill versus determinism. In the design of Study 1, pseudopatients had to find a way to be discharged from the hospital. Even though they had voluntarily presented themselves for admission, some of them remained in hospital for as long as 52 days. Their freedom to leave the institution was determined by psychiatric staff, which remains the experience of some mental health service users today, for example those who are sectioned under the Mental Health Act.

Rosenhan recognised determinism in the treatment of psychiatric patients in more subtle ways. He considered that once a patient had been given a diagnosis of a mental disorder, they were forever labelled with the diagnosis, which could have repercussions for their lives while in remission. This is reflected in the DSM-5®, which asks clinicians to specify that a patient is 'in remission'. In some ways, even though someone may recover from a period of illness and never experience symptoms again, they have a sticky label of 'mentally ill', the stigma of which can affect how others treat them.

Reductionism and holism

Considerations about reductionism are highly relevant to evaluating definitions of abnormality. Using statistical infrequency to determine abnormality is truly one-dimensional; the single factor that determines normal from abnormal is the frequency with which a particular symptom or trait is experienced in the general population. Deviation from social norms also offers a relatively limited picture of abnormality, relying on the specific values of the culture one is part of. Judging abnormality as behaviour or thinking that is maladaptive is more holistic; it considers different aspects of functioning and what is relevant to the individual's social, cognitive and emotional needs in context. For example, to define someone's behaviour as maladaptive could affect their employment prospects, social functioning, or whether they are endangering themselves or others.

The DSM system of classification for mental health disorders intends to offer a range of criteria to enable clinicians to make diagnoses. Some criteria are necessary for a diagnosis; some are additional or optional. The system is explicitly designed to include a broad spectrum of symptoms, patient's background, and cultural context. For example, we considered specific phobias as an example of an anxiety disorder. As well

as the diagnostic criteria, the age and cultural background of the individual are considered in order to determine how irrational a certain fear is – a holistic process of diagnosis. For example, an infant who becomes hysterical and anxious at being left by his or her mother might be more normal than a 45-year-old who exhibits similar behaviour at maternal separation. However, some would argue that simply trying to capture the nature of mental illness through a list of criteria is reductionist and cannot offer a complete picture of each disorder.

Individual vs situational explanations

Mental health is often discussed as an area of individual difference in psychology. As we have seen from the different definitions of abnormality, the terms 'infrequency' and 'deviation from norms' reflect the idea that there are individual explanations for the atypical experience of mental illness. History has viewed the mentally ill as unusual cases afflicted by disorder, which has resulted in stigma and isolation in institutions such as madhouses. Systems of classification such as the DSM are used to diagnose individuals; the assumption is that those individuals display objectively recognisable symptoms such as those we have considered in depression, schizophrenia and specific phobias.

The study by Rosenhan (1973), however, shows how situational factors can cause us to misinterpret 'abnormal' behaviour in individuals. In his study, the behaviour of the pseudopatients was wrongly thought by staff to be a result of mental illness, when it was actually a product of the hospital environment. Importantly, Rosenhan maintains that there is a situational explanation for the powerlessness and depersonalisation experienced by psychiatric patients. Failures of the institutions studied were just that: institutional. The negative behaviour of staff towards patients as a whole reflected the culture and expectations of dealing with the insane in psychiatric hospitals.

Psychology as a science

Throughout history, views on mental illness in Europe and the USA have shifted from religious or spiritual explanations towards scientific explanations. Instead of blaming psychotic disorders on demonic possession, people now search for biological explanations for mental illness, such as hormone or neurotransmitter issues or genetic causes. This involves the uses of objective measurement such as DNA or blood testing, and brain-scanning techniques. It is also reflected in the treatments offered to those with mental health issues, as in the use of biological treatments such as chemotherapy.

Definitions of abnormality range from highly scientific to fairly subjective. Measurement of statistical infrequency to determine abnormality can involve the use of validated scales such as IQ, whereas determining maladaptiveness relies on a subjective interpretation of how well someone functions within their environment. Attempts to classify disorders and offer diagnostic criteria follow the scientific traditions of medicine and biology, providing reliable and valid tools for mental health diagnosis. However, diagnosis relies on self-report or observation by others – measures that are difficult to quantify. The DSM-5® cannot be considered wholly reliable and valid, and certainly has many detractors.

STRETCH & CHALLENGE ◎

You can discover more about the evolution of the DSM from its very first edition to its present form here: http://psychcentral.com/blog/archives/2011/07/02/how-the-dsm-developed-what-you-might-not-know/ Considering the many changes to classification that have occurred, what do you see as the advantages and disadvantages of applying objective criteria to diagnosing mental disorder?

THE MEDICAL MODEL

BACKGROUND

As we have seen, by the twentieth century mental illness was widely seen as the province of the medical profession, and there was a corresponding emphasis on biological explanations and treatments. The very language of psychopathology is grounded in the medical model, the most obvious example being that mental health conditions are often called mental 'illnesses'. By the 1950s drugs existed to treat depression and schizophrenia. Purely biomedical explanations and treatments have always been controversial and this controversy continues today. However, advances in neuroscience have allowed us a much better idea of what variations in brain functioning correspond to the experience of mental illness, and this, combined with an increasing influence on the part of pharmaceutical companies, means that mainstream psychiatry is currently more biomedical in outlook than ever before.

The biomedical model (or 'disease' model) of psychopathology views psychological disorders as being the result of biological malfunction or disruption, for example to brain chemistry or electrical activity in a brain region. The underlying causes of symptoms are viewed as biological in origin, for example faulty genes or brain damage. The medical model also assumes that mental disorder can be understood as illness in the same way that physical conditions can. It can thus be classified, diagnosed and treated by medical personnel in the same way as physical disease. Biomedical approaches to treatment are based on the idea that we can correct or at least reduce the effects of these malfunctions or disruption. Medical treatments are biologically based, including drugs, surgery and the application of electric shocks, magnetic fields and bright light.

The biochemical explanation of mental illnesses

For us to think, feel, or make a decision or act on it, our brain cells must transmit information in the form of electrical impulses around the brain. Where each brain cell ends there is a gap, or synapse, leading to the adjacent brain cell. For information to pass from one cell to the next, chemicals called neurotransmitters must pass across the synapse. Different neurotransmitters are important in different parts of the brain and are believed to be important in regulating different mental processes. One class of explanation for mental illness involves the possibility that symptoms are the result of abnormal neurotransmitter levels or action.

The monoamine hypothesis of depression

A group of neurotransmitters called the monoamines appear to be involved in depression. These include serotonin, noradrenaline and dopamine. Depression involves lowered mood and disruption to activity levels, leaving patients either more or less active than they would be under normal circumstances. It is believed that dopamine plays an important role in regulating our mood, while noradrenaline is particularly implicated in activity levels. Serotonin may be important in controlling the activity of noradrenaline and dopamine.

WEB WATCH @

For a look at the range of diagnosable mental illnesses, check out the World Health Organisation's classification here:

http://apps.who.int/classifications/icd10/browse/2015/en#/V

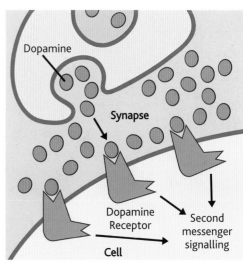

Figure 1.11: The action of dopamine at a synapse. This action appears to be disrupted in schizophrenia

KEY IDEAS

Schizophrenia is a serious mental illness diagnosed in around 1% of the population. It is more commonly diagnosed in men and typically begins in the sufferer's teens or twenties. There are two classes of symptom in schizophrenia. Positive symptoms are those that are in addition to normal experiences, and include hallucinations – most commonly voices – and delusions – powerful irrational beliefs, often of persecution or being a famous person. Negative symptoms involve the loss of a normal experience, and include apathy, reduction in speech and incoherent thinking. Schizophrenia is widely regarded as a biological condition, and the standard treatment is by antipsychotic drugs.

Figure 1.12: If one of these identical twins develops depression there is a moderately increased risk that the other will also do so

One version of the monoamine hypothesis of depression says that reductions in serotonin levels, which typically follow stressful events, lead to a failure to regulate normal dopamine and noradrenaline function. This in turn disrupts mood and activity levels. A different version of the monoamine hypothesis says that the disruption to monoamine levels is the result of abnormally high levels of an enzyme that breaks down the monoamines, reducing their action and disrupting the passage of information around the brain.

The dopamine hypothesis of schizophrenia

Dopamine (or DA) is widely believed to be important in the functioning of several brain systems that may be implicated in the symptoms of **schizophrenia**. Early versions of the dopamine hypothesis identified a possible role for high levels of dopamine in certain lower parts of the brain, which could account for some symptoms of schizophrenia. For example, an excess of dopamine in those centres of the brain responsible for speech production may cause hallucinations of voices.

More recently, a new take on the dopamine hypothesis has focused instead on reduced dopamine levels or activity in the brain's cortex (Goldman-Rakic *et al.*, 2004). Thus low levels or activity of dopamine in the pre-frontal cortex, which is responsible for thinking and decision-making, may explain other symptoms of schizophrenia, including apathy and incoherent thought or speech.

It is of course possible that both these hypotheses are correct, and that disruption to the dopamine systems in different parts of the brain are responsible for different symptoms of schizophrenia.

Genetic explanations for mental illness

As humans we randomly inherit half our genetic material from our mother and half from our father. The total genetic make-up of an individual is known as the 'genotype'. **Genes** are sections of DNA that contain the instructions for producing physical structures, including the brain, and organic chemicals, such as neurotransmitters and the enzymes that break them down. It is probable that genes exert an influence on individual psychological characteristics, including mental illness, by influencing the nature of physical structures of chemical levels in the central nervous system.

It is unlikely that any mental illness is purely the result of genetic factors. However, it does appear that some people are more vulnerable than others to developing mental health problems as the result of their genetic make-up. The extent of genetic vulnerability varies widely between different mental illnesses. Depression – at least in its more minor and common forms – appears to be only moderately affected by genes. However vulnerability to schizophrenia appears to be much more heavily influenced by genetic variations.

Genetic vulnerability to depression

There is no suggestion that most types of depression are only or primarily the result of genetic vulnerability. The strongest predictor of depression is experience of stressful life events. However, we do not all respond to stress in the same way – some of us are more resilient than others. It may be that our genes have important effects on how resilient or vulnerable we are to the impact of life-stress.

Rather than just look at whether there appears to be a genetic influence on conditions such as depression, modern research is homing in on the influence of particular genes and how those genes may interact with the environment, together influencing symptoms. Researchers have been particularly interested in the serotonin transporter gene, which is responsible for producing serotonin in the brain. This gene comes in three forms, varying in the length of its two strands; long-long, long-short and short-short. It is believed that the short form leads to inefficient serotonin production. This may mean that people with the short-short form of the gene are less resilient than others to the effects of stress and are more vulnerable to responding to stress with depression.

Genetic vulnerability to schizophrenia

Schizophrenia runs in families. However, this does not mean that schizophrenia is genetic in origin, because family members tend to share aspects of their environment as well as many of their genes. A better reason for thinking that schizophrenia is genetically influenced comes from looking at the way risk of schizophrenia co-varies with our genetic similarity to a family member with the condition. For example, we share 100% of our genes with an identical twin, 50% with a sibling or parent, and so on. There is a strong relationship between this genetic similarity and the shared risk of developing schizophrenia. This is shown in Figure 1.13, which presents the findings of Gottesman's (1991) large-scale family study.

KEY IDEAS

Genes are sections of DNA. Each gene carries the necessary information for the production of a physical structure or chemical. There is no clear beginning and end to a gene – we simply note that variations in particular sections of DNA are associated with particular characteristics, and label these sections genes. In psychology it is important to understand that genes do not code for psychological characteristics. They simply code for production of something physical. However, it is likely that variations in physical structures, and in levels of certain chemicals, can affect certain psychological characteristics, including mental illness.

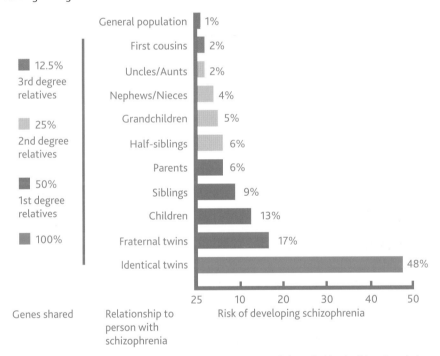

Figure 1.13: The relationship between genetic similarity and shared risk of schizophrenia in family members

It used to be believed that there was a single 'schizogene' that made some people particularly vulnerable to schizophrenia (Meehl, 1962). It now appears however that a number of genetic variations each make us slightly more vulnerable. Schizophrenia can therefore be described as **polygenic**. It also appears that schizophrenia is **aetiologically heterogeneous**, i.e. different combinations of factors can lead to similar symptoms. The fact that schizophrenia appears to be both polygenic and heterogeneous in its origins has made it very hard to pin down what genes might be involved in it, and how they might lead to symptoms.

KEY IDEAS

How genes work in combination
A characteristic is said to be **polygenic** if it is influenced by a number of different factors, including multiple genes. Schizophrenia is an example of such a characteristic, being influenced by over 100 genes and also by environmental factors. The aetiology of a characteristic is its origins. Characteristics that result from a single cause or a single combination of causes are said to be aetiologically homogeneous (i.e. its origins are the same). Something is said to be **aetiologically heterogeneous** if it can result from more than one cause or combination of causes. It seems likely that schizophrenia is aetiologically heterogeneous.

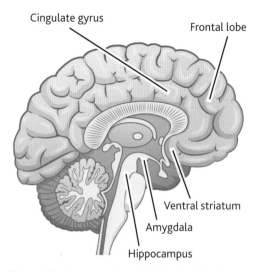

Figure 1.14: A cross section of the brain, showing some key areas believed to be involved in mental illness

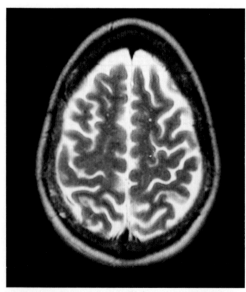

Figure 1.15: There are two distinct halves to the brain. There is evidence that the left brain in particular does not work normally in schizophrenia

In the most comprehensive published study so far, Ripke *et al.* (2014) combined all previous data from studies linking variations across the whole human genome to schizophrenia. The genetic make-up of 37,000 patients with schizophrenia was compared to that of 113,000 controls, and 108 separate genetic variations were found to be associated with increased risk of schizophrenia. Genes associated with increased vulnerability to developing schizophrenia included those coding for the functioning of a number of neurotransmitters, including dopamine. This is significant as it shows how genetic vulnerability and the dopamine hypothesis can be understood together.

Brain abnormality

The human brain is an incredibly complex system. We have already discussed how its delicate chemistry can be disrupted, with depression being associated with low monoamine levels and schizophrenia being linked to unusually high and low levels of dopamine in different parts of the brain. Other aspects of brain structure and function are also associated with mental illness. For example, certain structures in the brain may develop with a different size or shape, and levels of electrical activity can be higher or lower in particular brain regions. There is evidence showing that our central nervous systems do not function normally when we suffer from certain conditions. Particular areas of the brain also appear to malfunction during mental disorder, although it is unclear whether this is simply due to the abnormal neurotransmitter levels or to a separate phenomenon.

Brain abnormality in depression

There is some evidence for brain abnormality in depression. Some studies have suggested a role for the frontal lobes, the region at the front of the brain cortex that is particularly involved in thinking. Coffey *et al.* (1993) compared the size of the frontal lobes in depressed patients and non-depressed controls using MRI-scanning technology, and found that the mean frontal-lobe volume in the depressed patients was significantly smaller. A PET-scan study by Milo *et al.* (2001) has also shown that the frontal lobes in depressed patients do not draw on blood flow in the brain as they do normally (this is called 'hypoperfusion'). Interestingly, Milo *et al.* found that blood flow to the frontal lobes improved immediately following ECT (see page 31), suggesting that this may be how ECT works.

Brain abnormality in schizophrenia

There is evidence to suggest that in schizophrenia the left hemisphere of the brain does not function normally. Purdon *et al.* (2001) compared the force applied with the right and left hand in 21 patients with schizophrenia and in a control group. Ten of the treatment group were then given anti-psychotic medication and tested again. The untreated group were significantly weaker in the right hand, though not the left. This effect disappeared after treatment. This suggests that schizophrenia involves a problem with the left-brain, and that anti-psychotic drugs help correct this.

There is also evidence to suggest that the negative symptoms of schizophrenia, such as loss of motivation (or 'avolition'), are associated with brain abnormalities. Motivation – in particular, the anticipation of reward – is believed to involve a brain region called the ventral striatum. Juckel *et al.* (2006) have measured activity levels in the ventral striatum in schizophrenia and found lower levels of activity than those observed in controls. They also found a negative correlation between activity levels in the ventral striatum and the severity of overall negative symptoms. This suggests that at least this symptom of schizophrenia is connected to abnormal function of the ventral striatum.

Hallucinations are also associated with abnormal brain function. Allen *et al.* (2007) scanned the brains of patients experiencing auditory hallucinations, and compared them to controls, while they identified segments of pre-recorded speech as either their own or from other people. Lower activation levels in two brain regions – the superior temporal gyrus and anterior cingulate gyrus – were found in the hallucination group, who also made more errors than the control groups. It can be concluded from this that abnormal function in these areas is associated with hallucinations in schizophrenia.

MATHS MOMENT 🖩

The following graph (adapted from Simon *et al.*, 2010) shows a correlation between apathy and levels of electrical activity in the brain's reward system in schizophrenia

1. Correlations can be positive or negative, and weak or strong. What sort of correlation is shown in this graph?
2. What statistical test would you use to test the significance of these results? Explain the reasons for your choice.

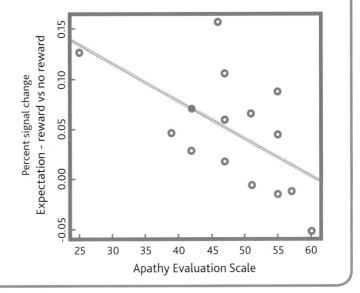

Figure 1.16: Correlation between apathy and levels of electrical activity in the brain's reward system in schizophrenia

KEY RESEARCH

Gottesman, I.I., Laursen, T.M., Bertelson, A. & Mortenson, P.B. (2010) Severe mental disorders in offspring with two psychiatrically ill parents. *Archives of General Psychiatry* 67, 252–257.

Aim

The aim of this study was to examine how vulnerable the children of two parents with mental illness are to developing a mental illness themselves. Specifically, the researchers were interested in vulnerability to any mental disorder of children of parents suffering from schizophrenia or bipolar disorder.

Method
Sample

Participants were drawn from a population of approximately 2.7 million Danish people born before 1997 who had an identifiable mother and father. The data was sampled in 2007, so the minimum age for participants was 10 years. From this population a sample was selected of 196 couples, both of whom had a diagnosis of schizophrenia, and their 270 children; and 83 couples, both of whom had a diagnosis of bipolar disorder, and their 146 children. This sample represented the target group of families where both parents had a severe mental illness. For comparison, samples where only one parent had a diagnosis of either schizophrenia (8006 couples with 13,878 children) or bipolar disorder (11,995 couples with 23,152 children) were also drawn. Rates of mental disorder were also recorded from the remainder of the population where neither parent had either schizophrenia or bipolar disorder.

Design and procedure

This type of study is called a cohort study because it involves looking at a cohort of a population, i.e. the population born between between two dates. In this case the study is a natural experiment because it involves comparing two or more naturally occurring groups. The independent variable (IV) is parental schizophrenia or bipolar disorder. The dependent variable (DV) is a diagnosis of any mental illness.

The IV was operationalised as parents receiving a diagnosis of schizophrenia, bipolar disorder, or a related psychotic condition in accordance with the World Health Organisation's system for classification and diagnosis of mental illness: the International Classification of Disease (ICD). The DV was operationalised as offspring receiving a diagnosis of any mental illness according to the ICD. This was represented by the cumulative risk of developing mental illness from 10 to 52 years of age – shown in Figure 1.13.

Results

For both schizophrenia and bipolar disorder the risk of mental illness was much greater for offspring of two parents with a diagnosis: 27.3% of offspring with both parents having a diagnosis of schizophrenia had developed schizophrenia by age 52, rising to 39.2% for schizophrenia and related conditions, and 67.5% developed a mental illness of some sort. For offspring with one parent diagnosed with schizophrenia the risk was 7% of a diagnosis of schizophrenia and 11.9% for any diagnosis. For those with neither parent having any diagnosis, the risk was 1.12% for schizophrenia and 14.1% for any mental illness.

Figures were similar for bipolar disorder, with 24.95% of offspring of two bipolar parents developing the disorder by age 52, 36% developing either bipolar disorder or depression, and 44.2% a mental illness of some sort. Of those with one bipolar parent 4.4% developed bipolar disorder themselves, and 9.2% a mental illness.

Conclusion

Having both parents with a serious mental illness is associated with a significantly increased risk of developing not only that disorder but mental illness in general. Having one parent with a serious mental illness carries a lower risk. This provides useful information for genetic counselling, which involves advising people of their own risks of developing an illness or of passing on genetic vulnerability to their children.

APPLICATION: BIOLOGICAL TREATMENTS

Depression can be treated biologically using drugs and/or electroconvulsive therapy (ECT).

Antidepressant drugs

Traditionally, most people approaching their GP with symptoms of depression have been prescribed antidepressant drugs. There are a number of different antidepressant drugs and these work in slightly different ways. Generally, though, antidepressants work by raising the levels of monoamine neurotransmitters in the brain.

Monoamine oxidase inhibitors (MAOIs) prevent the breakdown of serotonin, noradrenaline and dopamine, so that levels of all three monoamines build up. Tricyclics prevent serotonin and noradrenaline being reabsorbed after they have crossed a synapse, again increasing their levels. Although these now old-fashioned antidepressants are effective in reducing symptoms, because they interfere with a number of neurotransmitters they can have serious side effects. Tricyclics, for example, can cause drowsiness, dry mouth and constipation.

Newer antidepressants tend to work on one monoamine only. Selective serotonin reuptake inhibitors (SSRIs), such as Prozac and Seroxat, stop serotonin being reabsorbed and broken down after it has crossed a synapse, and noradrenaline reuptake inhibitors (NRIs) do the same with noradrenaline. It is important to have a number of anti-depressants available because individual patients vary quite a lot in how they respond to each drug, both in terms of effects on their symptoms and side effects. Different people present with different symptoms, and this can influence the choice of drug. NRIs, for example, may be particularly useful for motivating patients whose depression has left them very inactive.

Different types of antidepressant are prescribed in different circumstances. Gender is an issue here; women suffer more side effects than men from tricyclic antidepressants so the latter are perhaps more appropriate for men. Women generally tolerate MAOIs well, but these are highly toxic drugs so they are perhaps not appropriate when the patient is considered to be at high risk of suicide (National Institute for Clinical Excellence, 2004).

Electroconvulsive therapy (ECT)

ECT is an alternative medical procedure for treating depression. The procedure involves administering an electric shock for a fraction of a second to the head, inducing a seizure similar to that experienced in epilepsy. This seizure generally lasts between 15 and 60 seconds. In most cases the shock is bilateral (i.e. it is given to both sides of the head). This is generally considered to be more effective than unilateral ECT (given to one side of the head only), although it is also more likely to lead to side effects. A typical course of treatment might run for two to three weeks, with the ECT being repeated between 6 and 12 times in all.

ECT is a controversial treatment. In its early use the shock was relatively large and given without anaesthetic or muscle relaxants. The resulting fits sometimes resulted in broken bones and occasionally burns to the brain. Modern ECT involves small shocks given for short periods (typically 800 milliamps for a fraction of a second), given under anaesthetic and using drugs such as succinylcholine to paralyse muscles and so prevent broken bones.

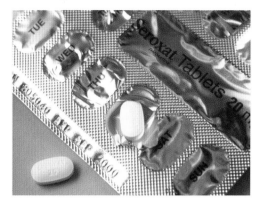

Figure 1.17: Antidepressant drugs are reasonably effective but many psychologists feel they are overused

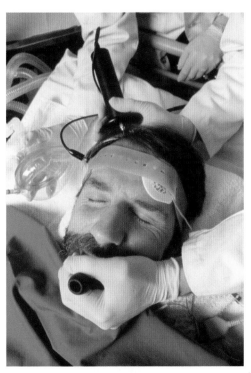

Figure 1.18: A patient being prepared for electroconvulsive therapy

EVALUATION

Ethical issues

There are some serious ethical issues associated with the biomedical approach, in particular with treatments. It is widely believed, for example, that antipsychotic drugs have sometimes been used in hospitals as a 'chemical cosh', to make patients calmer and easier for staff to work with, rather than for any benefit to the patients. Although short-term use of antipsychotics to calm agitated patients is recommended by the National Institute for Health and Care Excellence (NICE), this practice is seen by some as a human rights abuse (Moncrieff, 2013).

There are also ethical issues around the side effects of medical treatments. Antipsychotics have side effects, ranging from the mild to the fatal. Older antipsychotics such as Chlorpromazine are associated with side effects including dizziness, agitation, sleepiness, weight gain and itchy skin. Long-term use can result in central nervous system damage that manifests as involuntary facial movements, such as grimacing, blinking or lip smacking. This is called **tardive dyskinesia**. Occasionally antipsychotics produce a powerful reaction called neuroleptic malignant syndrome – this can be fatal.

 KEY IDEAS

The side effects of antipsychotics can be serious. **Tardive dyskinesia** is believed to be the result of the brain becoming too sensitive to the effects of dopamine. Dopamine is important in muscle movement, and this 'supersensitivity' to it causes ordinary levels of dopamine to trigger involuntary movements, most seriously to the face, where inability to control expression leads to serious difficulties in social interaction. Tardive dyskinesia has become less common as smaller doses of antipsychotics have become the norm. It is also less of a problem for newer antipsychotic drugs. However, the condition is incurable and hard to treat, so it is regarded as a serious problem.

Debates

Usefulness of research

Research into biomedical aspects of mental illness is useful in that it has given rise to a range of treatments, including drugs and ECT, and in the sense that we have a fairly good idea how effective treatments are likely to be. For example Arroll *et al.* (2005) reviewed studies that investigated the effectiveness of antidepressants prescribed by GPs. Ten studies were found that compared tricyclics with placebos, three comparing SSRIs with placebos, and two comparing both with placebos. Overall, 56 to 60% of patients treated with antidepressants improved, as opposed to 42 to 47% of people given the placebo. SSRIs took longer to work but had fewer side effects. This study suggests that both tricyclics and SSRIs are moderately effective when prescribed by GPs.

Similarly, there is a large body of evidence to support the idea that antipsychotics are moderately effective in tackling schizophrenia. Thornley *et al.* (2003) reviewed studies comparing the effects of a standard antipsychotic called Chlorpromazine to control conditions in which patients received a placebo (so that their experiences was identical except for the presence of Chlorpromazine in their medication). Data from trials with a total of over 1100 participants showed that Chlorpromazine was associated with better overall functioning and lesser symptoms than in placebo conditions.

Nature vs nurture

The biomedical approach to mental illness leans more to the nature side of the nature–nurture debate than do alternative psychological approaches to explaining and treating mental illness. There is an emphasis on genetic vulnerability to mental illness. Other biological factors – such as abnormal brain structure and function, and abnormal biochemistry – are often explained within the biomedical approach as the result of genetic factors. However, the biomedical approach does not ignore environmental factors, it simply looks at aspects of the biological environment. Thus a range of environmental factors – including oxygen starvation during birth, prenatal exposure to the flu virus, and childhood head injuries – have been explored in relation to mental illness within the biomedical approach. This balance of nature and nurture is a strength of the approach.

Most of the time when we talk about 'nurture' we are referring to aspects of the psychological environment, such as love, care, etc. However, there is also a biological environment, and this is important in understanding some mental illness, in particular schizophrenia. Be clear when answering a question involving the nature–nurture debate that nature = genetic influence, and nurture = all aspects of environmental influence, both biological and psychological. Although in everyday speech we might use 'nature' and 'biology' interchangeably, the nature–nurture debate is not about biological vs psychological influences.

Freewill vs determinism

The biomedical approach to mental illness is fairly deterministic. Symptoms are seen as determined by brain or biochemical abnormality, which are in turn determined by genetic vulnerability or some aspect of the biological environment. There is little room in this approach for free will. This is seen as a weakness by psychologists from some approaches, in particular the humanistic approach (see page 31), where particular value is placed on the human capacity for free will.

Reductionism and holism

The biomedical approach can be seen as reductionist. Specifically it is guilty of biological reductionism. This means that the mind is reduced to the brain, and the many aspects of human experience are reduced to a set of biological events. We often think of this as a weakness, and in some ways it is. We are more than simply the sum of our brain cells and chemicals, and when we take a biomedical approach we miss out on this complexity. However, it is not possible to study the whole of human nature at the same time, so this kind of reductionism is necessary for the scientific process. The reductionism of the biomedical approach is therefore both a strength and a weakness.

Individual vs situational explanations

The biomedical approach emphasises the role of genetics, brain chemistry and abnormal brain structure and function in individual differences between people, including mental illness. However, sociologists and social psychologists point out that actually many aspects of our functioning, including mental health and illness, are influenced not just by our individual differences but also by the situations in which we find ourselves. Mental illness is associated with a range of situational variables, such as stress, urban living and poverty, and these factors are not adequately taken into account when we adopt a purely biomedical approach. This is a weakness of the approach.

Psychology as a science

The biomedical approach grew out of the science of biology, and has continued to be conducted in a scientific manner. The approach is firmly based on research, and biomedical explanations for mental illness are supported by research. Cutting-edge scientific techniques are used to study biomedical explanations – for example, the scanning techniques used to study brain abnormality, and the genome-wide sequencing used to find associations between genes and mental illness. Biomedical treatments are also tested by scientific research and supported as reasonably effective. This emphasis on scientific techniques is a strength of the approach.

We started this topic by saying that the biomedical model is controversial, and we have touched on some issues. For a comprehensive review of criticisms of the biomedical model read the following article from the Community Mental Health Journal:

http://psychrights.org/research/Digest/Pending/biomedicalization.pdf

You may wish to divide into two groups and debate the pros and cons of this approach to mental illness. Alternatively, draw up a list of arguments for and against.

ALTERNATIVES TO THE MEDICAL MODEL

BACKGROUND

You may notice that in this section we will take a different approach to this topic. This is because, as well as two compulsory explanations for mental illness:

- behavioural
- cognitive

you also need to learn one other explanation from the following options:

- humanistic
- psychodynamic
- cognitive neuroscience.

We have also included a choice of treatments as the applications that follow the background explanations. You will notice there are additional sections on evaluation to support these options.

THE BEHAVIOURIST EXPLANATION OF MENTAL ILLNESS

In the previous section we considered the medical model, but processes of learning can also be used to explain the origin of mental disorder. In other words, abnormal behaviour is assumed to be learned in the same way as any other types of behaviour are learned. This can occur through different types of learning, known as classical and operant conditioning.

Classical conditioning

Classical conditioning happens when an emotional response, such as fear or anxiety, becomes associated with a particular neutral stimulus. It was famously demonstrated by Pavlov (1903), who taught dogs to salivate when they heard noises that they had come to associate with the presentation of food (see Web watch). If a person is regularly exposed to a particular stimulus together with an unpleasant experience, then the stimulus will come to elicit a fearful or disgusted response. In cases where the experience is extremely unpleasant or distressing, just one coupling with the stimulus may be sufficient to create a lasting association.

One example of this is the case study of Little Albert by Watson & Rayner (1920) who demonstrated that phobias can be learned through classical conditioning (see Activity). Little Albert was a healthy, normal 11-month-old infant who, in a series of trials, was exposed to a sudden loud noise that would cause him to burst into tears. The experimenters presented a white rat to Little Albert and then struck a hammer against a metal bar to induce fear. This

WEB WATCH @

Remind yourself about the basic principles of classical conditioning by playing the Pavlov Dog Game:

http://www.nobelprize.org/educational/medicine/pavlov/pavlov.html

procedure was repeated. Eventually Little Albert only had to see the rat and he demonstrated a fearful response: crying and crawling away.

Although the phobia was deliberately induced, the process could be applied in real-life situations. For example, people may develop hydrophobia (fear of water or drowning) as a result of falling into water (neutral stimulus) at a young age, not being able to swim and being submerged (unconditioned response of fear/panic), and developing a powerful lifelong aversion to water (conditioned response).

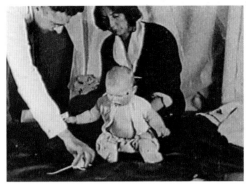

Figure 1.19: Watson & Rayner (1920) demonstrated that phobias can be acquired through classical conditioning

ACTIVITY

You can watch video footage in many places online of Watson & Rayner's study of Little Albert (1920). Complete the exercise below to show how the infant developed a phobia of white, furry objects:

Before conditioning	Unconditioned Stimulus (UCS)	>	Unconditioned Response (UCR)
	-------------------		-------------------
During conditioning	Neutral Stimulus (NS) + Unconditioned Stimulus (UCS)	>	Unconditioned Response (UCR)
	--------------- + ---------------		-------------------
After conditioning	Conditoned Stimulus (CS)	>	Conditioned Response (CR)
	-------------------		-------------------

Operant conditioning

Another behaviourist explanation for mental disorder is operant conditioning. Operant conditioning explains how the consequences of different behaviours (also known as reinforcers) shape subsequent behaviour. Humans learn by consequence: when behaviour is reinforced, be it through food, money or other reward, that behaviour becomes more likely to be repeated (Skinner, 1938). Conversely, behaviour that is not reinforced but instead is punished is less likely to be repeated (although punishment is generally thought to be much less effective than reinforcement).

This process is easily observed through the example of addictive behaviour, e.g. addiction to alcohol, drugs or gambling. If someone tries gambling and has some success, their behaviour is reinforced. We all enjoy winning! What starts as a voluntary behaviour can become 'addictive'; the player experiences a compulsive need to keep playing. One reason gambling is particularly addictive is that it creates an intermittent **schedule of reinforcement**. This actually has a stronger behavioural effect than continuous positive rewards, because the gambler often loses, but still 'hangs in there' hoping their luck will change.

THE COGNITIVE EXPLANATION OF MENTAL ILLNESS

The cognitive account of mental health is more concerned with the processes of thinking, attention and perception that underlie abnormal behaviour. Cognitive psychologists found that the behaviourists' approach ignored the ability of

KEY IDEAS

A **schedule of reinforcement** is the set of rules for giving rewards for behaviour. A continuous schedule of reinforcement would mean that each time the correct behaviour is displayed, the individual is reinforced (e.g. receiving praise for every correct answer given in class). Variable schedules of reinforcement do not reinforce every desired behaviour, but instead may do so in different ratios (e.g. every third correct behaviour) or at different intervals (e.g. every 3 minutes). Variable schedules, especially variable ratio schedules such as those used by slot machines in pubs and casinos, tend to produce behavioural change quickly.

people to reflect on and consciously control their own behaviour. The cognitive explanation addresses symptoms and causes of mental disorder through examining irrational or maladaptive beliefs.

Essentially the cognitive explanation relies on the idea that the cognitions of a person with a mental illness are somehow faulty; it is the way in which they perceive and think about situations that causes the difficulty, rather than the situation itself. A person who tends to think negatively will make associated thinking errors or biases that warp their emotions and behaviour.

Cognitive distortion is another term for irrational thinking. An individual forms an inaccurate perception of reality that may be highly negative or disturbed – the opposite of wearing 'rose-tinted glasses'. There is nothing deliberate or controlled about cognitive distortion; it occurs automatically (Beck, 1976). The cognitive theory of emotional disorders was outlined by Beck and later by his student, Burns (1989). They recognised that while adverse events happen in everybody's lives, in some individuals, specific distortions of thought can lead to negative emotional and behavioural outcomes such as anxiety and depression. Examples of some of the main cognitive distortions appear in Table 1.3.

TABLE 1.3: COMMON COGNITIVE DISTORTIONS		
Cognitive distortion	**Description**	**Expressed as thought**
Over-generalisation	Viewing one unfortunate event as part of a neverending defeat or struggle	'Everything always goes wrong for me'
Filtering	Giving greater consideration and focus to negative aspects, while ignoring or downplaying positive ones	'It doesn't matter that I passed the test because I got that one silly question wrong and let myself down'
Catastrophisation	Making a mountain out of a molehill; feeling that a situation/outcome is or will be far worse than it actually is or turns out to be	'I got the customer's order wrong; I'm bound to get fired now. I'll never get a job again'
Dichotomous reasoning	All-or-nothing thinking; the world is viewed as black and white	'He's perfect, nothing ever goes wrong in his life – he's so good at everything!'

Source: adapted from Burns (1989)

But where do these maladaptive thinking patterns originate from? Beck suggested that they form in childhood, as we acquire information about particular aspects of the world. This process is known as 'schema development'; different disorders are characterised by different schemas. For example, depression involves a triad of negative schemas (see Figure 1.20). In this disorder, early experience forms dysfunctional beliefs, which may then be triggered by adverse life incidents (e.g. death of a loved one, illness, or loss of a job or relationship), and which activate the underlying assumptions. From then on, incoming information is processed with a negative bias, resulting in all the emotional, cognitive and behavioural symptoms of depression.

Beck's theory about the influence of schemas on subsequent processing has also been applied to anxiety disorders. It is important to note that although difficult early experiences and dysfunctional beliefs may lead to the development of the negative cognitive triad, this does not mean the person will develop a mental disorder – for this, a trauma or serious life incident is also required. Beck and other cognitive theorists believed that the nature of schema formation and information processing could be changed through therapeutic techniques, some of which form the main, non-medication treatment options for anxiety and depression.

ACTIVITY ✳

Refer to Beck's Cognitive Triad shown in Figure 1.20. Construct the thoughts that might accompany each of the three aspects to illustrate the cognitive distortion of someone with depression.

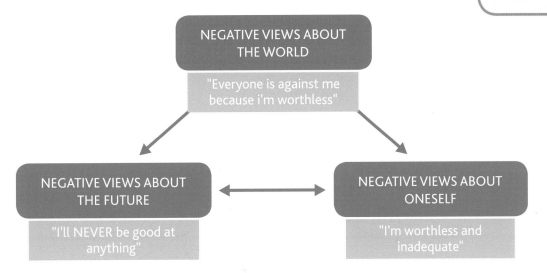

Figure 1.20: Beck's Negative Cognitive Triad (1967)

COGNITIVE-BEHAVIOURAL THERAPY FOR DEPRESSION

Cognitive-behavioural therapy (CBT) is now the most commonly used form of psychological therapy, both generally and in particular for depression. It usually takes place once a week or fortnight for between 5 and 20 sessions. CBT involves helping patients to identify irrational and unhelpful thoughts and trying to change them. This involves showing patients the links between their thinking, behaviour and emotions, for example, through drawing diagrams. The rationale for CBT is that our thoughts affect our feelings and behaviour, so by changing our thoughts we can make ourselves feel better. Some forms of CBT also focus on directly encouraging changes to behaviour.

According to the British Association for Behavioural and Cognitive Psychotherapies (BABCP), the aims of CBT in treating depression are as follows:

1   To re-establish previous levels of activity
2   To re-establish a social life
3   To challenge patterns of negative thinking
4   To learn to spot the early signs of recurring depression

Figure 1.21: In CBT therapists may use diagrams to show patients the links between their thinking, behaviour and emotions

KEY IDEAS

Much of what takes place in **cognitive-behavioural therapy (CBT)** is very cognitive: argument and reality testing work by changing cognitions. However, CBT does build in behavioural techniques where appropriate. A major sign of depression is a person's withdrawal from the kinds of activities that they previously enjoyed. This can be treated by behaviour activation. This involves encouraging and perhaps rewarding the patient for re-engaging with fun activities such as socialising.

Therapy is collaborative; the therapist and patient will agree on what the patient wants to change. The therapist may then ask the patient to express their negative beliefs, for example in relation to their social life. A depressed patient might believe that there is no point in going out as they won't enjoy it. The therapist might respond to this by vigorous argument to convince the patient that they will in fact enjoy going out.

The cognitive-behavioural therapist might also combine behaviour activation, in which patients are encouraged to take part in activities they normally enjoy but they have ceased to engage in since becoming depressed, with reality testing, in which the patient is encouraged to record in a diary that they enjoyed the activity. This evidence can be used to challenge the patient next time they say that there is no point in doing something because they wouldn't enjoy it.

EVALUATION

Debates

Usefulness of research

CBT is widely considered to be extremely useful. It is recommended as the first-line treatment of depression. Butler *et al.* (2006) reviewed studies of CBT and found 16 published meta-analyses, each of which included the results of several smaller studies. Based on this very large body of evidence they concluded that CBT was very effective for treating **depression**. The Royal College of Psychiatrists and the National Institute for Health and Care Excellence (NICE) recommend CBT as the most effective psychological treatment for moderate and severe depression.

Nature vs nurture

The cognitive approach has elements of both nature and nurture. The types of faulty cognitions that may cause depression, for example, are part of underlying cognitive structures (nature) that are influenced by learning and experience (nurture). By contrast, the behaviourist explanation relies entirely on nurture, proposing that maladaptive behaviours such as gambling or irrational fear are a product of external environmental stimuli. Elements from both approaches influence CBT as a treatment for mental illness, which in turn draws on innate cognitive processes and environmental stimuli, through behavioural activation.

Freewill vs determinism

The behaviourist explanation of mental illness can be considered fairly deterministic. This is because maladaptive behaviours are seen as a product of interaction with the environment, and there is little to suggest that we can change or influence them. On the other hand, the cognitive approach suggests that the way in which we think about negative events can change our patterns of behaviour. This can be seen in action during CBT sessions, where clients are encouraged to confront cognitive distortions in order to improve their emotional health.

Psychology as science

Behaviourists look to take a highly scientific approach to their work. In offering an explanation of mental health, they seek a causal link between a known event in a person's life which has resulted in a particular outcome. For example, a frightening experience of near-drowning could cause a subsequent phobia of water. Cognitive explanations are harder to demonstrate empirically, because they rely on clients' self-report of distorted cognitions and maladaptive behaviours. CBT is an approach that combines these cognitive and behaviourist principles. It can be considered scientific in part because it is evidence-based; there is considerable evidence to support its effectiveness.

THE HUMANISTIC EXPLANATION OF MENTAL ILLNESS

Humanistic psychology deliberately aims to understand human nature using simple principles and a minimum of theory. Humanistic psychologists reject both psychiatric diagnosis and complex theories such as those favoured by psychodynamic and cognitive therapists, relying instead on a number of basic assumptions about human nature. These include the ideas that people are basically good and have a tendency to grow as individuals and fulfil their potential. Psychological problems result when external forces prevent us achieving this growth.

Within this philosophy, classification and diagnosis of mental disorder are seen as unhelpful; a person's symptoms can be better understood as their individual response to the blockage of their growth.

Carl Rogers' theory

In the field of mental health Carl Rogers has been the most influential of the humanistic psychologists. He proposed that understanding healthy psychological development depends on two ideas: the actualising tendency and the self-concept.

The actualising tendency

Rogers (1959) believed that humans are primarily motivated by the need to actualise, i.e. to fulfil their potential and achieve the best level of 'human-beingness' they can. The relationship between the environment and the ability to actualise can be understood using the analogy of a flower, which will grow to its full potential only if the conditions are right. Just as a flower is constrained by the availability of environmental variables such as light, water and nutrients, so people flourish and reach their potential only if their environment is good enough. An unconscious process of valuing guides us towards choosing behaviours that will help us fulfil our potential. This valuing process can, however, be prevented from operating by the use of strict social rules and by a poor self-concept. Rogers believed that people are inherently good and creative. They can however become destructive when their valuing process is interfered with.

The self-concept

Rogers noticed that in therapy patients would often make reference to themselves, saying things like 'I'm not being my real self' or 'I wonder who I really am'. Rogers began to place great importance on this emphasis on the self and how people thought of themselves. Rogers (1961) proposed that a particularly critical aspect of the self-concept is our self-esteem. Self-esteem means essentially how much we like ourselves. Rogers believed that we hold in our mind an image of our self as we currently are and an image of our ideal self, or how we would like to be. If these two self-images are congruent (the same), we will experience a good level of self-esteem.

The development of congruence and the resulting healthy self-esteem depends on our receiving **unconditional positive regard** from others in the form of acceptance, love and affection. Without unconditional positive regard

 **KEY IDEAS**

Rogers believed that people need **unconditional positive regard** in order to develop good self-esteem. Unconditional positive regard means being loved and valued, irrespective of our behaviour. Parents should try to give children unconditional positive regard even when they have to regulate their behaviour. The same principle applies in therapy: a therapist may be horrified at a client's behaviour but they still value them as a person.

WEB WATCH @

You can watch a short clip of Carl Rogers outlining some of his ideas here: https://www.youtube.com/watch?v=o0neRQzudzw

we cannot self-actualise. Some children lack unconditional positive regard from their families in childhood. Harsh, inattentive parenting, or parenting that involves conditional love, i.e. love that is available only if the child conforms to certain conditions, is likely to lead to low self-esteem in adulthood, and such individuals are thus vulnerable to mental disorder, especially depression.

APPLICATION: HUMANISTIC THERAPY FOR DEPRESSION

Person-centred counselling is used to treat depression, and the process is very much the same as for treating any symptom. Remember that the humanistic approach generally rejects the idea of classifying and diagnosing mental illness. Humanistic counsellors refer to those in therapy as 'clients' as opposed to 'patients'. This reflects the fact that they see the therapist and client as equal partners rather than as an expert treating a patient. Humanistic counsellors do encourage clients to focus on and explore feelings, but, unlike psychodynamic therapists, they are completely non-directive, refraining from asking clients to focus on or explain things they have said. Rogerians do not offer interpretations but merely encourage the client to keep on talking in the belief that they will eventually find their own answers. One reason why Rogers rejected interpretation was that he believed that, although symptoms do arise from past experience, it is more useful for the client to focus on the present and the future than on the past.

The core conditions for personal growth

Rogers worked towards personal fulfilment in his clients. Rather than just liberating them from the effects of their past experience, as psychodynamic therapists do, Rogerians try to help their clients to achieve personal growth and eventually to self-actualise. Rogers (1961) suggested three core-conditions, which facilitate clients in their personal growth.

1. **Empathy** – the ability to understand what the client is feeling. An important part of the task of the person-centred counsellor is to follow precisely what the client is feeling and to communicate to them that the therapist understands what they are feeling.
2. **Congruence** – also called genuineness. This means that, unlike the psychodynamic therapist who generally maintains a 'blank screen' and reveals little of their own personality in therapy, the Rogerian is keen to allow the client to experience them as they really are.
3. **Unconditional positive regard**: Rogers believed that for people to grow and fulfil their potential it is important that they are valued as themselves. The person-centred counsellor is thus careful to always maintain a positive attitude to the client, even if they are disgusted by their actions.

As Mearns & Thorne (1988) point out, we cannot understand person-centred counselling by its techniques alone. As humanistic psychology is primarily a philosophical system the person-centred counsellor is distinguished by their positive and optimistic view of human nature. The philosophy that people are essentially good, and that ultimately the individual knows what is right for them, are the essential ingredients of successful person-centred work.

EVALUATION

Debates

Usefulness of research

The humanistic approach has practical applications in therapy and education. Rogers' idea that unconditional positive regard is of psychological benefit is the basis of a humanistic therapy, called person-centred or Rogerian counselling. However, it is also widely considered to be a necessary – though not sufficient – element of all psychological therapies. The emphasis on individual free will is also important in education, where it is important not to see students' potential as determined by their prior experiences. Person-centred counselling is undoubtedly useful for many clients. Greenberg *et al.* (1994) reviewed the results of 37 outcome studies looking at the effectiveness of person-centred therapy in a variety of situations and conditions. They concluded that person-centred counselling is as effective as other approaches to therapy, and more successful than no treatment at all.

Nature vs nurture

The humanistic approach has elements of nature and nurture. Rogers talked about the human need to receive unconditional positive regard in order to achieve good self-esteem. This is an innate need – an example of nature. However, the provision of unconditional positive regard is nurture, this nurture leading to a congruence between the self and the ideal self. The fact that the humanistic approach takes account of both nature and nurture is a strength of the approach.

Freewill vs determinism

Of all the approaches to psychology, the humanistic approach is the least deterministic and the one with the greatest emphasis on free will. To humanistic psychologists such as Rogers, although we are influenced by our early experiences, for example unconditional positive regard, we have the ability to make decisions about how we would like to be and make decisions to achieve that state. The humanistic attitude towards people is very positive, and this positivity has applications in therapy and education, where people can be encouraged to become who they would like to be.

Reductionism and holism/psychology as science

Most approaches to psychology are reductionist, i.e. they reduce the complexity of human nature to something simpler in order to make it easier to understand and to study. Thus behaviourists reduce people to a series of learnt behaviours and cognitive psychologists reduce people to information-processing systems. Humanistic psychology does not do this, but instead looks at the whole person. It is the most holistic and least reductionist of the psychological approaches. This is a strength in the sense that it is a realistic rather than an oversimplified view of the person. On the other hand it is very hard to study people scientifically without being reductionist, and this means that the humanistic approach has produced very little scientific research. The humanistic approach can be said to be unscientific, and this is a weakness.

THE PSYCHODYNAMIC EXPLANATION OF MENTAL ILLNESSES

This is one of the older approaches to treatment of mental illness, dating back to the work of Sigmund Freud in the late nineteenth and early twentieth centuries. This is a very theoretical approach to mental illness, emphasising the influence of the unconscious mind (i.e. aspects of the mind of which we are not consciously aware) on symptoms and the influence of early trauma and the quality of early relationships on later mental health. Whereas the behavioural and cognitive approaches are based on scientific research the psychodynamic approach is clinically derived, i.e. it is based on what patients have said to therapists.

Freud's hydraulic model

Freud got the idea of the **hydraulic model** from literature, where phrases such as 'to cry oneself out' and 'to blow off steam' were commonly used to describe emotional responses. These phrases suggest that the mind is a system

KEY IDEAS

Freud's **hydraulic model** sees emotion – what Freud called psychic energy – as having the same properties as physical energy, i.e. it can be stored, transformed or discharged, but not destroyed. Negative emotions resulting from early trauma or from resentment at poor quality early relationships are repressed. However, this can lead to symptoms. An aim of psychodynamic therapies is to discharge pent-up emotion in a process called catharsis. This relieves symptoms.

in which psychic (mental) energy behaves in much the same way as physical energy. Freud believed that, like other forms of energy, psychic energy could be discharged or transformed but not destroyed. Trauma and the inability to express instincts resulted in a build up of psychic energy that led to the symptoms of mental disorder. One of the aims of psychodynamic therapy is catharsis, the release of accumulated psychic energy.

Freud's ideas about sexual trauma and fantasy

Freud's view of psychosexuality is the most socially sensitive and controversial aspect of his theory. In his early work Freud proposed seduction theory, in which he emphasised the role of childhood sexual abuse in causing psychological problems. He famously put it thus: 'whatever case and whatever symptom we take as our starting point, in the end we infallibly come to the realm of sexual experience' (Freud, 1896:p193). The term 'sexual experience' is quite broad and describes a range of sexual traumas. An example is in the case of Anna O, whose deafness in early adulthood was linked to her childhood experience of eavesdropping on her parents having sex (Breuer & Freud, 1896). However Freud identified sexual abuse as a major cause of psychopathology.

In his later work Freud shifted his emphasis from real sexual abuse to sexual fantasy. In the light of our current knowledge about childhood sexual abuse this is widely considered to be a serious mistake. In the case of Dora (Freud, 1905), Freud suggested that Dora's symptom of psychological loss of voice was not the result of the trauma of being molested by a family friend but due to suppressing her desire for him.

Freudian theory of depression

Freud (1917) proposed that some cases of depression could be linked to experiences of loss of a parent, or rejection by a parent. Freud drew a parallel between the feelings we have as adults when in mourning for a lost loved-one and the experience of depression years after a childhood loss experience. An important part of adult mourning is anger, and Freud proposed that the same anger is important in children's responses to loss. The child's anger at being 'abandoned' through separation or rejection cannot be expressed because of love for the object of the anger, and instead is repressed, turning inwards and causing guilt and low self-esteem as the ego 'rages against itself' (1917:p257).

A psychodynamic explanation for schizophrenia

Schizophrenia is a complex and serious mental illness involving hallucinations – most commonly voices speaking critically to or about the patient, and delusions – irrational beliefs such as that the sufferer is being persecuted. Another psychodynamic approach came from Fromm-Reichmann (1948). Based on her patients' accounts of their childhoods, she proposed the existence of a **schizophrenogenic mother**. The term 'schizophrenogenic' refers to a factor that causes schizophrenia. Fromm-Reichmann proposed that where families were characterised by high emotional tension and secrecy, and where the mother was cold and domineering in her attitude, children were at high risk of developing schizophrenia. Fromm-Reichmann drew a link between the secrecy in the family and the development of delusions of persecution.

APPLICATION: PSYCHODYNAMIC THERAPIES FOR DEPRESSION

Psychodynamic therapies originated with the work of Freud. The original form, classical psychoanalysis, is very intensive, taking place four or five times per week and lasting for several years. Psychoanalytic psychotherapy is slightly less intensive and long term, typically one or three times per week for one to five years. Traditionally patients in psychoanalysis lie on a couch, and patient and analyst do not face each other. Nowadays, particularly in psychotherapy as opposed to psychoanalysis, patient and therapist are more likely to be facing each other, seated on comfortable chairs.

In psychoanalysis or psychoanalytic psychotherapy there is no attempt to teach the patient more constructive patterns of thinking or behaviour. Instead the emphasis is on exploring the patient's past and linking it to their current symptoms. Early experiences of loss or rejection are particularly important in depression, so these in particular may be explored. The patient may vividly recall these experiences (this is called abreaction) and 'discharge' the associated emotion (this is called catharsis). They may thus become very angry or upset. Often these negative emotions can become transferred on to the therapist, who can be treated as if they were the absent or rejecting parent. The therapist can feed this back to the patient, who can thus gain insight into the way they transfer their anger on to other people. From a psychodynamic perspective the relationship difficulties often associated with depression are often the result of transferring anger from early losses. In the more modern brief psychodynamic therapy (BDT), rather than waiting for negative emotions to be transferred on to the therapist, patients are educated about the links between their current functioning and their past experiences.

Figure 1.22: Traditionally patients in psychoanalysis lie on a couch

EVALUATION

Debates

Usefulness of research

In spite of the scientific limitations of Freudian theory, psychodynamic therapies have proved useful for many people. Psychodynamic therapies aim to discharge pent-up emotion (see the hydraulic model, page 41) and also to give patients insight into their condition and its possible origin, so that they can begin to exercise more free will and prevent their past experiences determining their symptoms. Because some psychodynamic therapies are long-term and expensive they are uncommonly used now in the UK National Health Service, however they are recommended by the National Institute for Clinical Excellence (NICE) (2004), for example for complex cases of depression. This practical application is a strength of the approach.

Nature vs nurture

The psychodynamic approach acknowledges the importance not only of nature in the form of instincts, but also of nurture in the form of parenting. Freud identified two basic instincts: eros, the life instinct, and thanatos, the death instinct. He also explored how these interact with parenting behaviour. So, for example, during the Oedipus Complex a child's life instinct is expressed towards their opposite-sex parent, while their death instinct is directed towards the same-sex parent. The fact that both nature and nurture are part of psychodynamic theory is a strength, however most modern psychologists disagree with Freud's idea of instincts and his emphasis on particular interactions with parents, such as the Oedipus Complex.

Freewill vs determinism

The psychodynamic approach is fairly deterministic because it emphasises the way our current feelings and motives are determined by our unconscious mind, which contains both instincts and mental representations of our early relationships. However, the approach also offers the possibility of free will because we can gain some insight into these unconscious influences through dreams, slips of the tongue and interpretations from a therapist. Once we are aware of these influences we can make conscious decisions to act in particular ways – this is free will. This recognition of both deterministic factors and the potential for free will is a strength of the approach.

Psychology as a science

The psychodynamic approach is widely seen by modern scientists as poor science. Freud's ideas were derived from self-analysis and interpretations of what his patients said to him in therapy. This contrasts with modern psychological theory which tends to be the product of systematic research on larger groups of participants. Another reason why Freudian theory is seen as poor science is the difficulty involved in testing his ideas in a scientific manner. By its very nature the unconscious mind is not observable and Freud's theory often fails to lead to predictions that can be tested through research. Freud's own evidence tended to be in the form of case studies, which are not repeatable and can be interpreted in different ways.

KEY IDEAS

Post-traumatic stress disorder (or **PTSD**) is an anxiety disorder caused by exposure to great stress. It is best-known in armed-services personnel who have been in combat, but also often follow incidents of violence or sexual assault. The major symptom distinguishing PTSD from other anxiety disorders is flashbacks, in which the sufferer re-experiences the event and its accompanying anxiety.

THE COGNITIVE-NEUROPSYCHOLOGICAL EXPLANATION OF MENTAL ILLNESS

The cognitive-neuropsychological approach is one of the newer psychological approaches to mental illness. It is based on our growing understanding of the relationship between cognitive function and brain function. Brain function has a direct effect on cognitive function and changes in brain state can manifest as changes in cognitive functions. In some mental illness, for example, **post-traumatic stress disorder (PTSD)** and schizophrenia, it is likely that cognitive symptoms are the direct result of an underlying abnormality in brain function.

A cognitive-neuropsychological model of post-traumatic stress

Scott & Stradling (2001) have developed a cognitive-neuropsychological model for PTSD by combining our understanding of the role of memory cues and the activity of an area of the brain called the amygdala. The main symptom that distinguishes PTSD from other anxiety disorders is the re-experiencing of the traumatic event, complete with the full range of sensory and emotional experiences present at the original event. This can be seen as a powerful cue-dependent memory, triggered by seemingly insignificant sights, sounds or smells related to the traumatic event.

Scott & Stradling (2001) have combined this cognitive understanding of PTSD with what we know of brain function in PTSD. Traumatic memories are particularly associated with activity in the amygdala. When cues such as a sound, sight or smell trigger the 'alarm' in the amygdala, the alarm is 'switched off' by the hippocampus, an area of the brain particularly associated with recent memories. However PTSD patients appear to have a smaller hippocampus than the norm, so the hippocampus fails to turn the alarm off. The amygdala therefore continues to sound the alarm, reproducing the original physical state that accompanied the trauma together with the sensory memories of the trauma. This explains the experience of flashbacks in PTSD.

A cognitive-neuropsychological model of schizophrenia

Schizophrenia is characterised by disruption to normal information processing. It appears that the negative symptoms of schizophrenia, such as reduced speech and difficulty in coherent thought are associated with reduced activity in an area of the brain called the ventral striatum. Hallucinations are associated with reduced activity in the temporal and cingulate gyri.

Frith (1992) identified two kinds of dysfunctional information processing caused by brain dysfunction that may underlie some symptoms of schizophrenia. Our metarepresentation is the cognitive function that allows us insight into our own actions and intentions. It is the same cognitive ability that allows us to makes sense of the actions of others. We would expect that a problem with the brain's metarepresentation system would impair our ability to recognise our own thoughts. This could explain experiences such as hallucinated voices and delusions, for example, the experience of feeling we have thoughts projected into our mind by other people.

Frith also proposed an important role for the brain's central control system. Central control is our cognitive ability to suppress automatic responses while we carry out deliberate behaviour. Sufferers with schizophrenia tend to suffer *derailment* of sequences of thoughts and words because each word triggers associations and the patient cannot suppress their automatic responses to these. This could be the result of failure of the brain's central control system.

MATHS MOMENT 🖩

Stirling *et al.* (2006) compared patients with a diagnosis of schizophrenia with a group of controls on a range of cognitive-neuropsychological tests including the Stroop Test, in which participants have to name the ink-colour of colour words, suppressing the automatic response of reading the colour-word (e.g. identifying 'red' when the word 'blue' is written in red ink). They obtained the following results:

	Times	
	Mean	**Standard deviation**
Schizophrenia	123.20	65.52
Controls	58.12	11.26

1. What do the means for the two conditions suggest about the effect of schizophrenia on cognitive tasks?
2. What do the standard deviations for each condition show?
3. Identify one strength and one weakness of the mean as a measure of central tendency.

EVALUATION

Debates

Usefulness of research

This approach is useful in being able to explain the usefulness of both biological and cognitive approaches to treating mental disorder. For example there is evidence to show that the most effective treatment for schizophrenia is a combination of antipsychotic drugs and cognitive-behavioural therapy. Only the cognitive-neuropsychological approach fully explains why this combination of altering brain functioning on a biological level and altering cognitions should be so effective. This practical application is a strength of the approach.

Nature vs nurture

The cognitive-neuropsychological approach takes account of both nature and nurture because it explains the brain abnormality that underlies abnormal cognition as the result of both genetic factors and experience. For example, abnormal cognition in schizophrenia may be influenced by disruption to the dopamine system and/or reduced activity in the ventral striatum. Neuropsychological research has linked these abnormalities to both genetic vulnerability and **traumatogenesis**, in which traumatic experience in early life affects the development of the brain. This ability to account for the role of both nature and nurture is a strength of the approach.

 KEY IDEAS

For decades psychologists have noticed that trauma in the first few years of life substantially increases the risk of developing a mental illness later. **Traumatogenesis** means trauma as the origin of something. Recently neuroscientists have begun to propose mechanisms by which traumatic experience might affect the developing brain, leaving the individual vulnerable to later mental illness. This is not currently fully understood.

Freewill vs determinism

The cognitive-neuropsychological approach is quite deterministic as it sees our cognitions and resulting behaviours as being determined by brain functioning. For example, in post-traumatic stress our experience of flashbacks is determined by an environmental cue triggering an alarm response in the amygdala. In schizophrenia our experience of hallucinations is determined by brain abnormality that is itself the product of genetic abnormality or traumatogenesis, in which normal brain development is disrupted by traumatic experience. However, the approach is not entirely deterministic – cognitive therapy for schizophrenia involves teaching patients to recognise that hallucinations and delusions are not real and to exert free will by ignoring them.

Reductionism and holism/psychology as science

Cognitive psychology is often said to be guilty of 'machine reductionism', reducing the complexity of the human mind to an information-processing system. Biological psychology is equally described as reducing humanity to a central nervous system. Cognitive neuropsychology can be seen as doubly reductionist! On the one hand, reductionism oversimplifies the human experience, and this is a weakness. On the other hand, without being reductionist it is very hard to study people scientifically. So in this way the reductionism of the cognitive-neuropsychological approach can be seen as both a strength and a weakness.

KEY RESEARCH

Szasz, T. (2011) The myth of mental illness: 50 years later. *The Psychiatrist,* 35, 179–182.

Aim

In this study, Szasz revisits his famous essay 'The Myth of Mental Illness', and his book of the same name (1960, 1961). He considers the current medicalisation of abnormal behaviour in the light of his earlier arguments.

Method

Szasz's paper is an essay on psychiatry and how it affects those who experience mental health issues. As such it is not a study and does not involve participants or a specific procedure.

Findings

Szasz, a trained psychiatrist, began writing his early work during the 1950s. At this time, the mental health profession was moving away from psychodynamic therapies and towards the medical model which, as we have seen, involved greater reliance on drug therapies and formal systems of diagnostics. He describes his original work, 'The Myth of Mental Illness', as rejecting the image of patients as passive victims of biological events, and also outlines his views of psychiatry as 'coercive' (i.e. exerting forceful pressure on patients) and a denial of human rights. It is clear that Szasz views psychiatric intervention as an important moral question that should concern all of society, not just the mentally ill or those that treat them.

He returns to this question 50 years later in this key research. Szasz outlines the changes that have taken place in US mental healthcare over the intervening period, including:

- changing attitudes towards 'incurable' patients who were previously confined to mental hospitals
- blurring of distinctions between private and state psychiatry, the overlap between medical hospitals and mental hospitals, and voluntary/ involuntary confinement
- new legal responsibility on mental health professionals to prevent patients causing harm to themselves or others.

Overall, Szasz describes the drive to **medicalise** and **politicise** the US mental health system, which has taken away credibility from alternatives to the medical model of mental health. It has been politicised in the sense that those who hold power (politicians) have openly declared that mental illness is just like any other physical illness. It is medicalised in the sense that it can be diagnosed (e.g. via diagnostic statistical manuals) and treated accordingly.

Szasz rejects the current medical paradigm, and argues that mental illness is a metaphor. He suggests that while some mental illnesses might be discovered to have a physical cause, this means they were never 'mental illnesses' but are, instead, undiagnosed physical illnesses. Szasz dismisses the idea that mental illness is a subtype of physical ailments. Instead he proposes that the term 'mental illness' actually refers to the judgement of some people about the disturbing or socially unacceptable behaviours of other people whom they label 'mentally ill'. He draws on the controversial insanity defence used by defendants in court; it seems as though we reject the idea that there are bad people in the world for the idea that bad behaviour is the product of mental disorder.

In other words, our underlying worldview is that people are inherently healthy/good until afflicted by mental illness, which makes them unhealthy/ bad. This has important implications for human freedom, as Szasz outlines. By adopting this pseudo-medical approach, psychiatry and society denies people both a responsibility for wrong-doing, and also their liberty from the oppression of the mental health system. The person as the potential sufferer loses their importance; it is the illness that is to be treated. Because of their duty to protect patients and those around them, the psychiatrist acts as a jailer, imprisoning the patient in the system and denying them their right to seek, accept and reject medical diagnosis and treatment.

Szasz argues that psychiatrists wield incredible power; they alone are qualified to categorise, label and treat the person whom society deems as disturbed. The way in which this is normalised in society means the mental health system is 'insulated' or protected from criticism as it is seen as morally

Figure 1.23: Thomas Szasz (1920–2012) was an academic, psychiatrist and outspoken sceptic of the mental healthcare system

 **KEY IDEAS**

Medicalisation refers to the categorisation or treatment of a behaviour or event as a medical problem. This term is often used when it is perceived as unjustified. For example, midwives may feel that pregnancy and labour are 'medicalised' – treated as an illness that requires medical intervention.

Politicisation means to make a phenomenon become political in nature. For example, wearing religious symbols in schools has become highly politicised in some countries: politicians debate and make laws about what might once have been considered a private matter for the individual.

QUESTION SPOTLIGHT!

Can you see the link between Szasz's argument and the debate over freewill and determinism in psychology?

STRETCH & CHALLENGE ◎

Explain why you think Szasz's ideas are still considered radical by many mainstream mental health professionals. Do you agree that the medical model of mental health is a form of social control?

and medically legitimate. Suddenly, having a mental illness becomes a synonym for becoming a patient.

Conclusion

Szasz concludes that:

1 The medicalisation and politicisation of psychiatry over the past 50 years has led to a dehumanised model of care.
2 Mental illness should be regarded as a metaphor; a fiction.
3 Szasz rejects the moral legitimacy of psychiatry as it violates human liberty.

EVALUATION

Ethical issues

Szasz's article does not collect data directly from participants, so in many senses it can be considered free of ethical issues. However, Szasz's work on beliefs about mental illness is socially sensitive and highly controversial. For those experiencing mental health difficulties, it could be very distressing to have their illness described as a 'myth', when they perceive their symptoms and diagnosis as real, and may have experience of effective treatment. It could also be argued that Szasz's theory overstates the case against the medical model of mental illness, and risks bringing the professions of psychiatry and psychology into disrepute.

Debates

Usefulness of research

Szasz's work had a huge impact on the world of psychiatry and psychology. It became well-known to both critics and supporters, and has been influential in movements to empower service users in mental health. By suggesting that mental illness is a myth, Szasz further divides devotees of the medical model and those anti-psychiatry advocates. These criticisms are important in psychiatry and psychology, because they make us question the effectiveness, appropriateness and morality of invasive treatments such as drug therapy, ECT and involuntary confinement of those with mental health issues.

Nature vs nurture / individual vs situational explanations

The theory that mental illness is a myth rejects the idea that mental health problems could have a hereditary or other biological cause. Szasz's argument suggests that what we call mental illness is purely a social construct and thus has an environmental explanation. In other words, mental illness is not an abnormality experienced by individuals as a result of their particular biological or emotional functioning; it is a product of psychiatrists' particular views on mental 'health'.

Freewill vs determinism

The cognitive-neuropsychological approach is quite deterministic as it sees our cognitions and resulting behaviours as being determined by brain functioning. For example, in post-traumatic stress our experience of flashbacks is determined by an environmental cue triggering an alarm response in the amygdala. In schizophrenia our experience of hallucinations is determined by brain abnormality that is itself the product of genetic abnormality or traumatogenesis, in which normal brain development is disrupted by traumatic experience. However, the approach is not entirely deterministic; cognitive therapy for schizophrenia involves teaching patients to recognise that hallucinations and delusions are not real, and to exert free will by ignoring them.

Reductionism and holism / psychology as science

Szasz can be thought of as offering a more holistic view of mental illness; that although symptoms may be real, the diagnoses they attract can be explained by a wider understanding of society and psychiatry's processes of labelling. The medical model of mental illness, as Szasz argues, is reductionist in that it offers only one (in his view, incorrect) interpretation of a variety of human behaviour. This is an oversimplification of human experience, because it seeks to make mental illness akin to physical illness. Thus, Szasz's argument can also be evaluated as 'unscientific' because he explicitly rejects science as an appropriate method for studying and treating mental illness.

PRACTICE QUESTIONS

Section A: Issues in mental health

1 **(a)** Outline **two** characteristics of an affective disorder. **[2]**
(b) Contrast **two** definitions of abnormality. **[3]**

2 Gottesman *et al.* (2010) investigated inheritance of mental illnesses. With reference to the key research, discuss the effect of inheritance when both parents have a mental illness. **[5]**

3 Suggest how non-biological treatment can be used to treat **one** specific disorder. **[5]**

4* Compare a biological explanation with **one** other explanation of mental illness. **[10]**

5* Discuss the nature/nurture debate with regard to the psychodynamic explanation of mental illness. **[10]**

---

1 (a) Outline two characteristics of an affective disorder. [2]

Liam's answer:

Phobias are where you are really, really scared of something, like water or heights, which are common. There are also lots of weird phobias like feathers, mole rats and mirrors. You can treat them with different therapies like cognitive behavioural therapy and PCT.

Rina's answer:

In depression, one symptom is sadness. This is more than just feeling a bit fed up, it has to last most of the day and most of the week for at least two weeks. Another symptom is often having sleep problems, which can be being too sleepy (called hypersomnia), or not being able to sleep (called insomnia).

We say: Liam knows some things about phobias but hasn't describe the symptoms, he has just named a selection of phobias and mentioned how they could be treated, neither of which were asked for. The only relevant part of the answer is the very first statement, which relates to the DSM diagnostic criterion of 'Marked fear or anxiety about a specific object or situation'. He could have gone on to say that his examples – such as feathers or mirrors – are out of proportion to the actual danger, or any other of the criteria.

We say: Rina has given a short, but concise answer that elaborates on two of the criteria from DSM-5® for a major depressive disorder ('depressed mood' and 'frequent insomnia/hypersomnia'). She has given details such as frequency ('often' in relation to sleep disturbances) and duration (two weeks).

---

1 (b) Contrast two definitions of abnormality. [3]

Liam's answer:

Abnormality is about being different, this can be based on numbers, like in the normal distribution, where being abnormal is being outside of two standard deviations from the norm, so you would be in the top or bottom 2.5%. Alternatively, it can be based on social norms, whether you do things that most people would think were unacceptable – like hearing voices and talking back to them. This explains differences between cultures, as different societies think different things are unacceptable.

We say: Liam's answer includes a description of two alternative definitions of abnormality, but he has not made any attempt to contrast them, so he hasn't answered the question. He could, for example, have drawn a contrast using the idea of culture, explaining how social norms can, but statistical norms cannot, account for the differences that he identifies as existing. He could have gone on to illustrate this using his example of hearing voices, which in some cultures is not seen as abnormal.

Rina's answer:

One way to define abnormality is statistical norms. This is based on abnormality being infrequent in the population, so if you are very unusual, like outside the 95% of the spread in a normal distribution, then you are abnormal. This is just based on maths and doesn't take into account how well someone functions, which is exactly what the maladaptiveness definition does do. This says that abnormal behaviour is doing things that are dangerous or that cause poor coping, such as failing in social relationships or jobs. This means someone who was really clever – so outside the statistical norm – but gets on fine in work and life would be abnormal according to stats but not maladaptive.

We say: Rina answers all aspects of this question, using her brief outlines of the two definitions to draw a contrast between them, which she then illustrates at the end with an example.

2 Gottesman *et al.* (2010) investigated inheritance of mental illnesses. With reference to the key research, discuss the effect of inheritance when both parents have a mental illness. **[5]**

Liam's answer:

In the Gottesman et al. key study, the risk of getting a mental illness like schizophrenia or bipolar disorder was tested. They did an experiment comparing the risk of diagnosis with schizophrenia, bipolar disorder, or any other mental illness. They used thousands of Danish people and their children so the findings would be generalisable, so we can draw conclusions about inheritance in general. The risk for bipolar was 4% and for schizophrenia it was a bit bigger, 7%, compared to virtually nothing for parents who weren't mentally ill. The odd thing is that for children with any mental illness, the highest risk was for children with parents who were not mentally ill, which was 14%, whereas it was only 9% for bipolar and 12% for schizophrenia. This means inheritance isn't all that important in general, though it might matter for specific disorders.

We say: Liam discusses both disorders but mistakenly considers the data for only one parent, except for the figure of 14% for 'any disorder' for parents without a diagnosis. This means that, although his description of the study is relevant to the question, the results are incomplete at best, and he isn't able to come to an appropriate conclusion.

Rina's answer:

Gottesman et al. studied the risk of becoming mentally ill (the DV) when one or both parents had a diagnosis of either schizophrenia (SZ) or bipolar disorder (BP) (the IV). The data looked like this:

	% offspring with a diagnosis				
	Parents not mentally ill	One parent with SZ	Both parents with SZ	One parent with BP	Both parents with BP
SZ	1	7	27	X	X
BP	X	X	X	4	25
any	14	12	68	9	44

This shows that inheritance is really important because, for both SZ and BP, the risk of offspring having the same disorder is higher with 2 parents affected than with 1, by about 4 times as much. For SZ it's also much more than the percentage of people with neither parent who are mentally ill. This means there must be some kind of genetic factor, though it could be the environment that the parent creates by being mentally ill, because there's also a higher risk of any other mental illness. This means that getting a genetic predisposition from both parents is much riskier than getting one from just one parent.

The results could also mean that inherited factors just make you vulnerable to mental illnesses generally, and what you end up with depends on other things – which could be more genes or could be the environment. Also, the fact that even with both parents with a mental illness the risk is nothing like 100% suggests that inheritance isn't everything. If you have two blue-eyed parents you always get a blue-eyed child, but it isn't like that with SZ or BP.

We say: This is a good answer from Rina, which gives a little information about Gottesman et al.'s method, and plenty of detail about the results. This is followed by a good discussion which applies the results to the question effectively. Note also that Rina has used abbreviations but has explained them – always remember to do this.

3 Suggest how non-biological treatment can be used to treat **one** specific disorder. [5]

Liam's answer:

Carl Rogers was a humanistic psychologist who said that we all move towards self-actualisation like a flower coming into bloom, but if we don't have enough water we end up with a mental illness. Our good environment means being valued so we get to continue to be good and creative but if the environment is too strict for us to flower we wilt just like a plant without water. He thought self-esteem was really important, so we need to like ourselves – if we think we are who we think we should be, then our image and our ideal match and we have good mental health. It's something called UPR that gives us high self esteem, that's when people accept us and love us just for who we are without having to prove it all the time. So parents who say 'I don't like you, you're a naughty boy' damage their children. They ought to say 'I like you I just don't like what you are doing right now'. So PCC is all about making sure people have the chance to feel accepted and to grow, by giving them lots of UPR, and letting them decide for themselves.

Rina's answer:

CBT is used for depression. The patient goes for therapy once a week, or so, for a series of sessions. The sessions help them to identify irrational and unhelpful thoughts and then to change them, making them more rational. This works because our thoughts affect our emotions and behaviour, so if we change our thinking we feel better. The therapist may also try to change behaviour directly.

The therapist uses several techniques. Cognitive ones include drawing diagrams for patients to show them the links between their thinking, behaviour and emotions, and arguing with them about their negative thinking, such as never enjoying going out. These aim to change their thinking. Encouraging them to actually go out and do stuff challenges their behaviour. This is called reality testing and they write down their experiences in a diary, which means they have a record of

We say: Much of what Liam is saying is a good explanation of the humanistic approach (although he gets muddled between people and plants at one point). However, this is not what the question is asking. Although he could have used the information about the humanistic approach to explain the therapy he mentions (PCC – person centred therapy, which he should have stated), he hasn't done so. For example, if he had discussed its use with depressed clients, he could have linked his description of giving people the chance to flourish to the first of the core conditions for personal growth, of empathy. He could then have used his comments about self-esteem to discuss the second core condition of congruence, and finally his illustration of unconditional positive regard (UPR) could have been contextualised within a counselling framework.

having had fun which the therapist can then use to challenge their beliefs again later. The therapist might also reward them for going out as this will help to re-establish previous levels of activity and a social life. These things tackle the behaviour aspect, hence cognitive-behavioural therapy – the depressed person's false cognitions are altered and their reduced behaviours are increased again, removing the symptoms and the cause.

We say: Rina needed to explain the abbreviation 'CBT' at the beginning of her essay, rather than leaving it until the end. In other respects, this is a good response, with a discussion of both how CBT is used in practice and how it works in theory.

4* Compare a biological explanation with **one** other explanation of mental illness. **[10]**

Liam's answer:

The biological approach says that mental illnesses are caused by biology – the brain, neurotransmitters and genes. Everything we feel and do happens by communication between brain cells, which is done by neurotransmitters going across synapses, which are gaps between neurons. Neurotransmitters are just chemicals but how much of each one we have, and how well they work, is important in mental illnesses.

Monoamines are neurotransmitters that control mood and they go wrong in depression. They include serotonin, noradrenaline and dopamine, but they have different roles in mental illness. Noradrenaline is linked to lowered activity levels, like not wanting to go out or do anything and dopamine is linked to mood, so perhaps feeling sad all the time. Serotonin seems to be more central, controlling both noradrenaline and dopamine so having a wider effect on all the symptoms of depression.

A theory called the monoamine hypothesis suggests low serotonin causes depression, especially after stress, like being bereaved. This then leaves people unable to keep their dopamine and noradrenaline under control and it's this that messes up their mood and activity. But it could be that having lots of the enzyme that breaks down monoamines means you don't have enough of any of them and this is the cause of all the symptoms.

Dopamine is important in schizophrenia, making people hear voices when there is too much in the speech areas of the brain. This is called hallucinations and is a positive symptom. But according

We say: It is unfortunate that Liam hasn't answered the question. He has written an excellent discussion of the biological approach, but has not considered it in relation to another approach to explaining mental illness (cognitive or any other). His essay does not, therefore, fulfil the requirements of the question.

to Goldman-Rakic et al. (2004) not enough dopamine in the pre-frontal cortex causes negative symptoms, making people apathetic and muddling their thinking and speech. It might even be that both ideas are right but happen in different parts of the brain so cause different symptoms. As schizophrenia can be treated with drugs, this suggests it is biological in origin, which is different from the cognitive explanation.

Rina's answer:

Neurotransmitters are our biological control system in the body and brain, making us feel, think and act. When they go wrong our mental health can suffer. In depression our feelings change and we become more sad, and mood is controlled by dopamine (DA). Drugs like MonoAmine Oxidase Inhibitors (MAOIs), which control dopamine, improve depression, showing that low dopamine is a possible cause. Our behaviour changes too, with people being unable to motivate themselves. Drugs that increase noradrenaline (NA) can help with this, suggesting a different neurotransmitter system is involved. MAOIs can help with this too as they increase NA as well as DA. Other drugs, like tricyclics and Prozac, affect another neurotransmitter serotonin, and are effective too.

The evidence about neurotransmitters and drugs shows that depression has biological causes, this is different from the cognitive idea. Whereas the biological ideas focused on our feelings and actions, i.e. emotions and behaviour, the cognitive approach considers mainly our thinking. Although, in CBT, thinking and behaviour is treated, so in this respect the two approaches are similar.

Cognitive psychology considers the symptoms in relation to their causes, so if faulty thinking can be changed, maladaptive behaviours will change. This is different from the biological approach, which aims to change faulty biology and solve the behavioural problems directly, without changing thinking first. This makes the two approaches different. In this way, biological explanations of mental

We say: This is an excellent essay from Rina. It describes a biological explanation quite briefly but then considers this is detail in relation to the cognitive explanation. She makes many different comparisons, identifying similarities as well as differences and discussing these in full. There is good analysis, with comparisons in relation to many of the debates.

An alternative way to make comparisons would have been in terms of methodology or ethics. The biological explanations tend to rely on evidence from laboratory experiments, often initially on animals, whereas cognitive explanations may use case-study based research. This also raises different ethical issues, which could have been discussed.

illness are more reductionist than the cognitive ones. This is also important because the cognitive approach says that the negative thinking is like a downward spiral, it leads to lack of behaviours (like socialising) which reinforce the negative thinking. The biological approach doesn't say that depressive behaviour makes neurotransmitter problems worse, so this is another difference.

Another difference is in what causes the problems in the beginning. Biological imbalances might be caused by genes, at least they seem to be for schizophrenia, so could be for depression too – so there is an underlying biological cause to the neurotransmitter problem. The underlying cause of the cognitive problems are from our childhood according to Beck (1967). He says that depressed people must acquire negative schemas early in life and that these dysfunctional beliefs are only set into action by bad things happening, like deaths or losing your job – i.e. by the environment, not by genes. This means that cognitive explanations include situational factors whereas biological ones are purely individual.

This leads to an important difference in therapy. Cognitive therapy aims to undo the faulty thinking and replace it with functional thinking, so the emotional and behavioural symptoms go away. In biological drug therapy, the aim is to correct the lack of neurotransmitters and this also results in the removal of emotional and behavioural symptoms. These are similar in the sense that they are both determinist as they say that changing these things – thinking or neurotransmitters – will reduce symptoms.

The cognitive approach talks about a range of cognitive distortions, like over-generalisations, filtering and catastrophisation, so it is suggesting there are lots of similar factors all contributing to the depressive symptoms. This is similar to the idea that there are three different neurotransmitters, which are all too low, and all contribute in a biological way to depression. However, the factors from biological explanations are all from the nature side of the nature/nurture debate, whereas the cognitive ones include aspects of nurture such as what happens in our childhood or negative life events in adulthood.

Lastly, it is not impossible that the changes caused by early childhood disrupt our biology, or that drug therapies work by changing thinking and breaking the cognitive downward spiral. These would mean that both theories were right and were not really alternatives but all part of a bigger picture.

5* Discuss the nature/nurture debate with regard to the psychodynamic explanation of mental illness. **[10]**

Liam's answer:

Nature is all about biology and the cause of mental illnesses that come from genes, neurotransmitters or brain abnormalities which are all things we are born with, although Freud didn't ever talk about any of these things. Nurture is the influence of the environment, like our experiences with other people or problems in our lives like losing a job or getting a divorce, so it is things like this that change in our lives. Freud talked a lot about these things, mainly our parents. Psychodynamic explanations of mental illness talk about our unconscious mind, and these are a bit of both because we are born with them, but they are filled with the things that happen to us. Our dreams and slips of the tongue tell us what is in our unconscious mind.

A psychodynamic explanation of schizophrenia proposed by Fromm-Reichmann (1948) suggested that the mother's behaviour during an individual's childhood, being highly emotional and cold was the cause. The nurture aspect of the parenting behaviour would affect the nature aspect of the unconscious mind.

Therapy based on psychodynamic explanations works, so this suggests that Freud was right and NICE (2004) recommends this, for example for complicated depression. This works by the nurture effect of being with the therapist, which corrects the nature part, the unconscious mind.

We say: Liam's essay starts well with a clear distinction between nature and nurture, and he gives examples that are relevant to the psychodynamic explanation, although this is not sufficiently detailed. His example of schizophrenogenic mothers is correct, and he links it to the nurture aspect of the debate, but without any previous detail about the unconscious mind he couldn't write any more. His last section, on therapies, is linked to both aspects of the debate but again lacks the necessary detail to enable him to make this analysis clear.

Rina's answer:

Freud said mental illnesses came from the unconscious mind, this is something we are born with so it is basically an aspect of nature. All instincts are present from birth, and he says we have a life instinct called Eros and a death instinct called Thanatos. The hydraulic model was Freud's idea of the cause of mental illnesses. Evidence from what people say about their problems, like 'crying oneself out', suggested that psychic energy in the mind was like physical energy, building up and needing to be released. He said it was traumatic experiences, and being unable to express the instincts that caused a back-log of psychic energy, that resulted in symptoms of mental illness. So, although the instincts themselves are nature, the traumatic experiences – such as having cruel parents – are aspects of nurture. Also, being unable to release the built-up energy, for example if you are a bereaved man but don't want to be seen crying, is another illustration of nurture.

Psychodynamic therapy aims to release built-up psychic energy. This is called catharsis. As the therapy works, this is another example of nurture – the experiences with the therapist change the status of the mental illness. One way this is done is by letting the psychic energy out by expressing the pent-up feelings at the therapist, as if they were the problem parent. This provides a solution for the problem with nature, with the trapped instincts, by using the nurture from the interaction with the therapist.

Freud explained how nature and nurture can interact in childhood. In the Oedipus Complex a child's Eros is directed at the opposite-sex parent, and their Thanatos at the same-sex parent. So the instinct itself is nature but the interaction between the child and each parent is nurture. This helps to explain why problems in childhood, especially with parents, are a risk in the development of mental illnesses because both nature and nurture could be influential. For example, Freud (1917) said depression was sometimes linked to losing a parent or being rejected by them. Although the event with the parent is nurture, the psychic energy, which is trapped in as anger against the parent and guilt about themselves, is a nature aspect. Together these cause the symptoms of mental illness.

We say: This is a good essay from Rina, who has answered the question well, relating each point she has made to the nature/nurture debate and presenting both sides of the argument. She has also included a discussion of the way in which the two interact.

Although it is obvious that Rina knows what nature and nurture mean, it would have been wise to have begun the essay by making this clear.

C2
CHILD
PSYCHOLOGY

Child psychology is the study of the development of thinking and behaviour that occurs in children and young people. Researchers in this area may study individual children's behaviour, environmental factors and the impact of both on their development. In this chapter we will consider six important topics:

1 **Intelligence**: We will consider what psychologists mean by the term intelligence. Biological factors such as heredity will be considered, as in van Leeuwen *et al.*'s twin-family study (2008). We will then consider the use of IQ tests as a method of assessing intelligence.

2 **Pre-adult brain development**: The study of pre-adult brain development has been shown to have an impact on risk-taking behaviour. We will consider evidence of this, including key research by Barkley-Levinson & Galván (2014) and explore how to reduce risk-taking behaviours in the real world through Graduated Driver Licensing.

3 **Perceptual development**: We will examine the processes of perceptual development and how this can be studied in both human infants and animals. We will then consider the contribution of Gibson & Walk's 'take over cliff' research

(1960), before looking at how strategies such as Sensory Integrative Play help develop perception in children.

4 **Cognitive development and education**: Different cognitive abilities emerge over time; we will look at how this idea has changed children's education. We will look at the role tutoring can play when problem-solving with children, in the study by Wood *et al.* (1976), and then consider mnemonics as a strategy for improving revision.

5 **Development of attachment:** We will look at attachment processes and the consequences of a failure to develop attachments. Then we will consider Ainsworth & Bell's classic research using the 'Strange Situation' (1970), before exploring how family-centred care can be used in hospitals to create an attachment friendly environment.

6 **Impact of advertising on children**: Many children are exposed to television advertising on a daily basis. We will look at the impact of this through key research by Johnson & Young (2002) on gender stereotyping. Finally we will explore the use of media literacy in reducing the negative impact of advertising aimed at children.

INTELLIGENCE

BACKGROUND

We have previously considered Gould's (1982) article on early efforts to quantify human intelligence (Jarvis *et al.*, 2015, p.178). But what does the term actually mean? Intelligence is commonly understood as the ability to acquire and use knowledge and skills. Yet it has multiple uses in English; we might describe a fellow student as highly intelligent because they scored top marks in a test, or read a book in which an author raises some intelligent points; we might even describe a film as intelligent. In other words, intelligence is difficult to define because it may describe a multitude of talents: creative skills, originality, logical reasoning, or the ability to make critical judgements.

What do psychologists mean by 'intelligence'?

It may not surprise you to learn then that psychologists also offer competing definitions. Early theorists recognised the circularity of such arguments, as intelligence comes to represent whatever particular intelligence tests were testing (Boring, 1923). For instance, most modern IQ tests include logical reasoning exercises. An individual who scores highly on this type of test is considered intelligent; but only if you define being intelligent as being highly skilled at solving analogies!

Factor models

In the early twentieth century, psychologist Charles Spearman (who gives his name to Spearman's rank correlation coefficient) studied relationships between cognitive factors in schoolchildren. He observed a consistent correlation in performance across a number of unrelated academic subjects. Because of this relationship, Spearman proposed that mental ability could be understood as a single general factor, commonly referred to as 'g'. He suggested that the 'g' factor was responsible for success across a range of different mental tasks for each individual, and was likely to account for around 50% of **variance** across mental tasks. To give an example, say you are a whizz at algebra, and your best friend struggles with the subject. According to Spearman, around half of the variance could be explained by the 'g' factor. The remainder would be attributed to other influences, such as your desire to get a top grade, or because you have a more supportive teacher.

The single-factor theory of intelligence idea was further developed by Carroll (1993) into a model known as the three-stratum model. This model consists of a three-level hierarchy of intelligence: stratum I included around 70 narrow abilities and stratum II gathered these into several broad ability factors, which were overarched by the single 'g' factor introduced by Spearman (see Figure 2.2, page 60). Since then several theories have attempted to include a broader range of ability types and to move away from the idea of a single 'g' factor.

 **KEY IDEAS**

Variance is a measure of dispersion in a data set. It measures the size of the difference between individual numbers in a set of numbers.

Figure 2.1: Book smart – is possessing knowledge about different subjects the same as being intelligent?

STRATUM III		General intelligence (g)					
STRATUM II	Fluid intelligence	Crystallised intelligence	Memory and learning	Visual perception	Auditory perception	Retrieval ability	Cognitive speediness	Processing speed
STRATUM I				Specific cognitive abilities			

Figure 2.2: Carroll's three-stratum model of intelligence (1993)

These theoretical constructions have real implications for methods of measurement. Many tests of intelligence yield an individual numerical score, which relies on the existence of the single 'g' factor. We will return to this debate in the application section of this topic, as theories of intelligence are closely tied to methods of assessment. First, we will consider the biological origins and development of intelligence.

Influence of biological factors

Sex differences – neural anatomy and hormones

The relationship between sex and intelligence has been investigated by many researchers. In one major review of a range of intelligence measures, Halpern (1997) found evidence to indicate particular differences in cognitive abilities between the two sexes. For instance, women obtain higher than average scores in tests that involve tasks requiring verbal fluency and areas of knowledge such as foreign language. By contrast, he established that men perform better in tasks that involve **mental rotation** and scientific reasoning.

Figure 2.3: Square pegs and round holes: biological factors could account for sex differences in spatial reasoning tasks

One biological explanation for these differences is the way in which male and female brains are organised. Using MRI scans, Haier *et al.* (2005, see Figure 2.4) found that men have comparatively more grey matter in their frontal and parietal lobes, which are typically associated with motor skills and higher-level reasoning. In comparison, women had more grey matter in different areas of their frontal lobe and Broca's area; regions important for tasks like speech and writing.

STRETCH & CHALLENGE ◎

One debate that concerns psychologists is whether intelligence is a single construct, or whether humans possess 'multiple intelligences'. The idea of multiple intelligences was most famously developed by Howard Gardner (1983). Find out about this theory and write a short summary of each of the eight intelligences he describes. What advantages does this theory have over the idea of a single unified construct of intelligence?

 **KEY IDEAS**

Mental rotation is the practice of turning an object in our imagination to view it from a different perspective. A task of mental rotation might require a person to consider two objects and rotate them in their consciousness, to determine whether they are the same object in different positions.

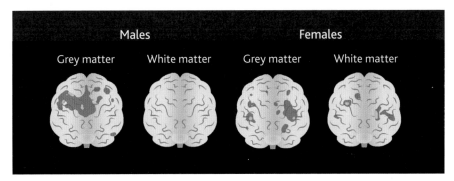

Figure 2.4: Illustration to show sex differences in grey matter distribution (adapted from Haier *et al.*, 2005)

Men and women have been found to achieve similar IQ results despite these differences in brain regions – which makes sense, as such tests involve a mixture of cognitive tasks (e.g. language-based *and* spatial ability measures). Neurological evidence currently suggests that there is no single underlying neuroanatomical structure for general intelligence, and that male and female brain designs may result in similar intellectual performance overall.

Another explanation for differences in intelligence between the genders could be differences in the amount of sensitivity to hormones. In a study of female-to-male transsexuals given testosterone prior to undergoing sex change, Van Goozen *et al.* (1995) found significant increases in visual-spatial ability combined with lowered scores on tasks involving verbal fluency. The effect was reversed for male-to-female patients who took cross-sex hormones, suggesting that hormones play some role in sex differences in particular cognitive abilities.

Genetic factors

Heredity is the phenomenon of children inheriting characteristics or traits from their parents. This occurs as particular genes and gene combinations are passed on from parents to offspring. Researchers are interested in understanding the 'heritability' of observable traits such as intelligence. This means they want to know the extent to which differences in genes and differences in environmental factors contribute to observed variations in intelligence within a population.

Studies that estimate the degree to which heredity influences cognitive ability often use **twin** or **adoption study methods**. Scarr & Weinberg (1978) compared the intellectual abilities of parents and their adopted and biological children. They found stronger correlations between biological relatives than between adopted relatives. This study suggests a greater role for genetic factors than shared environmental factors, and is further supported by evidence from twin studies. Plomin & Defries (1998) compared identical (monozygotic) and fraternal (dizygotic) twins on measures of spatial and verbal skill to find that similarity between identical twin scores was significantly greater than between fraternal twins, despite their shared environments. Other studies indicate that even when reared apart, identical twins shared higher concordance rates (i.e. they had more similar results) than fraternal twins who were reared together (Scarr, 1997).

Despite all this evidence, efforts to identify individual genes or gene combinations have so far only found genes with a minor influence on intelligence scores, and given results that have been hard for others to replicate. In a recent

KEY IDEAS

Twin studies involve the comparison of pairs of twin participants to analyse for similarities and differences, such as IQ scores or psychiatric illness. There are two types of twins: monozygotic (MZ) and dizygotic (DZ). Monozygotic (identical) twins originate from a single fertilised egg and share all of their nuclear DNA. Dizygotic (fraternal) twins, are 'non-identical' because they originate from two separate eggs. Although they gestate in utero simultaneously, they only share around 50% of their DNA, just like any other siblings with the same parents. Twin studies are useful for researchers trying to establish the influences of nature and nurture, because most differences between identical twins can be attributed to variations in their environment rather than genetics.

Adoption studies are another form of genetic study. They involve comparing particular traits or abilities in children who have been adopted to those of their biological and adoptive parents. In theory this allows a direct comparison of genetic and environmental influence, because adopted children share no genetic link with their adoptive families. So if heritability of a given behaviour is high, there should be a higher rate of concordance with biological than adoptive parents.

QUESTION SPOTLIGHT!

Can you see how studies of heritability of intelligence may relate to the nature-nurture debate?

 KEY IDEAS

Assortative mating is the name for non-random reproductive patterns that involve individuals with similar genes or observable characteristics mating with each other more often than we might expect if mating were purely random. There are many dimensions which are thought to influence assortative mating. Examples include shared religious beliefs and being of similar age or body size. Spouse and family studies show spouses resemble each other in IQ scores and similar measures such as educational achievement.

Figure 2.5: Assortative mating: are we more likely to chose partners with whom we share certain characteristics?

study by Desrivières *et al.* (2014), DNA analysis, MRI scans and intelligence testing of a large sample of teenagers identified the NPTN (neuroplastin) gene as important in explaining some variation. They found that, on average, individuals carrying a particular variant of the gene had a thinner layer of grey matter in the left cerebral hemisphere and performed less well on tests for intellectual ability. While this study has found some promising data, in reality our understanding of the heritability of intelligence is still in its infancy.

One issue with twin studies comparing MZ and DZ twins is that they often assume that parent phenotypes are uncorrelated. In other words, they do not consider that individuals might be more likely to have children with partners who have similar traits to themselves, i.e. **assortative mating**. These studies also may not measure interaction between genes and environment; failing to consider that certain environments might 'activate' a particular gene or *vice versa* (known as genotype-environment, GE interaction or epistasis). A third issue is that twin studies often ignore that parents may transmit not only their genes but also their environment to their offspring (known as genotype-environment correlation). An example of this might be healthy, fit adults who are active, play lots of sports and eat a healthy diet. Both adults and their offspring may be genetically predisposed towards such good health, but by sharing their lifestyle with their children, it makes it difficult to establish the contribution of nature or nurture. The issue with all these assumptions is that they may lead to 'estimation bias' where the influence of genetics on intelligence is either overestimated or underestimated.

ACTIVITY ✳

'Genotype' is the word used to describe an individual's internal, inherited information. It also refers to a specific gene responsible for particular observable traits such as eye colour. The expression of a genotype in this outward, visible form is known as a 'phenotype'. These terms can be tricky to remember, so try writing your own definitions of each.

KEY RESEARCH

van Leeuwen, M., van den Berg, S.M. & Boomsma, D. (2008) A twin-family study of general IQ. *Learning and Individual Differences*, 18, 76–88.

Aim

The researchers wanted to separate shared genetic from shared environmental effects on intelligence. They aimed to measure the relative influence of assortative mating, cultural transmission, and GE interaction and GE correlation. The researchers also wanted to investigate why spouses have similar intelligence scores to one another.

Method

Sample

Participants were drawn from the Netherlands Twin Registry, meaning they came from all over Holland. Two hundred and fourteen families of twins about to turn 9 years old, and who also had an extra sibling aged between 9 and 14 years, were invited by letter to participate (see Table 2.1). Of these, 112 families agreed to participate, 103 of which had full siblings willing to take part. The mean age of the twins was 9.1 years, with mean age of siblings at 11.9 years (range 9.9 years to 14.9 years). The mean age of biological mothers and fathers was 41.9 and 43.7 years old respectively. Only families with children without self-reported psychiatric problems, major medical issues, special educational needs or physical or sensory disabilities were included.

TABLE 2.1: NUMBER OF PARTICIPANTS ACCORDING TO SEX AND TWIN TYPE		
Twin type	**Monozygotic (identical)**	**Dizygotic (fraternal)**
Male	23	23
Female	25	21
Opposite sex	-	20

Design and procedure

This study used an extended twin design, which compared the intelligence test results of MZ and DZ twins, full biological siblings and biological parents. Including data from parents and siblings meant the effects of heredity and cultural transmission could be estimated at the same time.

Both parents and children gave consent to participate in the study and were compensated for their travel costs. Children were given a present for taking part. Families completed a questionnaire or DNA cheek swabs at home prior to the study for the purposes of confirming zygosity (whether children were identical twins or not).

Children completed a cognitive test known as Raven's Standard Progressive Matrices (SPM) in separate rooms. They were given verbal instructions and completed the test at their own pace. The test consists of 60 problems divided into five sets of 12 questions that become increasingly difficult as the set progresses. The test covers a range of cognitive abilities, from identifying missing puzzle pieces to completing analogies.

Figure 2.6: Two of a kind: identical (or MZ) twins are genetically identical, making them ideal participants for studies examining the relative influence of nature and nurture

WEB WATCH @

It may not be as easy as you might think to determine whether twins are identical or not. Same-sex DZ twins may also share a strong physical resemblance. Usually DNA testing is the only way to be certain, but questionnaires can also estimate zygosity. The Minnesota Twin Study website has one such example. Try answering the questions based on a pair of twins you know:

mctfr.psych.umn.edu/Zygosity Calculator.html

Adult participants completed a similar but more advanced test known as Raven's Advanced Progressive Matrices (APM). They were given written instructions and also worked at their own pace. Although the number and arrangements of questions and sets were slightly different, both types of test produced comparable results. Both tests are discussed in more detail in the Application section of this topic.

In their analysis of the data, the researchers used two different theoretical models to determine whether spousal resemblance could be better explained by phenotypic assortment or social homogamy.

Phenotypic assortment suggests that assortative mating occurs because individuals *choose* one another because they have similar intelligence levels. For instance someone might be more likely to begin and continue a relationship with someone they see as intellectually equal, or *vice versa* to end a relationship with someone they consider vastly more or less intelligent than them.

Social homogamy is the idea that because people with similar intelligence levels are clustered together in the same environment they are more likely to end up having children together. For example, individuals who meet each other at work and form relationships may have similar IQ scores and educational backgrounds they are not choosing each other on the basis of intelligence.

Results

The IQ measures derived from the cognitive tests were estimated using the Rasch Model (a way of estimating IQ based on the scores shown in Table 2.2). No statistically significant sex differences were observed across the whole participant group, or within individual groups (parents, siblings, twins). Furthermore, cultural transmission was not found to have any significant effect on the genetic variance of IQ. The absence of such common environmental effects shared by family members has been shown in other similar studies. This further diminishes the role for environmental factors in intelligence.

Spousal correlation for Rasch IQ estimates was moderately high (0.33), which confirms existing evidence that individuals are more likely to mate with partners of similar intellectual ability. The statistical modelling showed this is may be better explained by phenotypic assortment rather than social homogamy. In other words, it is more likely that individuals actually select mates with similar intelligence, rather than ending up selecting a mate with similar IQ because they are in the same social circle (social homogamy).

Environmental factors were found to be more important in children with a genetic disposition for low-IQ groups than those with a disposition towards high-IQ groups. This suggests a GE interaction wherein genetic and environmental factors affect one another to determine intelligence levels. This means that people with a certain genotype (i.e. lower IQ) are more sensitive to environmental influences than others.

TABLE 2.2: RAW IQ SCORES ON THE RAVEN'S PROGRESSIVE MATRICES (PRIOR TO RASCH MODEL ANALYSIS)

	Minimum	Maximum	Mean	Standard deviation
Fathers	4	36	27.0	6.5
Mothers	9	36	25.9	6.0
Male siblings	24	56	43.8	7.8
Female siblings	30	59	46.4	6.5
Male twins	13	50	36.7	8.6
Female twins	19	50	36.6	7.1

Note: Parental scores out of a maximum 36, offspring scores out of maximum 60.

Conclusion

The researchers concluded that:

1. The main influence on IQ level is genetic factors, however genes do interact with environmental factors to influence intelligence in significant ways.
2. Cultural transmission does not have a significant influence on variance in IQ.
3. Phenotypic assortment better explains spousal resemblance than social homogamy.

APPLICATION: ASSESSING INTELLIGENCE

As we have seen, a mixture of factors determines the intelligence of a given individual. Because the term is used differently by psychologists, intelligence is measured in different ways. You will already have considered the work of Gould (1982) as one example. He examined the mass mental testing of US army recruits by Robert Yerkes and others during World War One. In the next section we will consider a commonly used, modern IQ test and how effectively it assesses intelligence.

Raven's Progressive Matrices

Raven's Progressive Matrices (RPM) are one of the most popular non-verbal tests of intelligence in current use. Since the creation of the RPM, parallel versions of the test have been introduced as many of the items were becoming too widely known. The tests were developed by John C. Raven (1902–1970), an English psychologist and major contributor to the field of psychometrics – an area devoted to objectively measuring different psychological dimensions of individuals. He found that many existing tests were long and difficult to deliver, and so in 1936 he designed a test that was easier to administer and interpret. The name of the test comes from the way in which the test items are typically presented, in a grid or matrix of 6 × 6, 4 × 4, 3 × 3 or 2 × 2 (see Figure 2.7).

MATHS MOMENT 🖩

Calculate the range for each of the participant groups shown in Table 2.2.

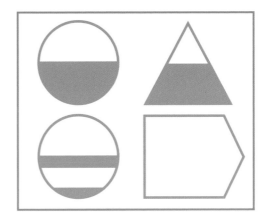

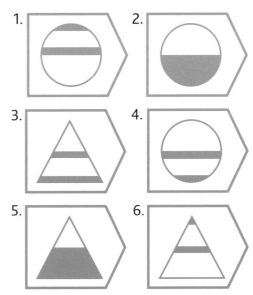

Figure 2.7: This is a made-up example of a 2 × 2 matrix problem, similar to the RPM items; participants chose the item from a selection to best complete the pattern

KEY IDEAS

Horn & Cattell noted the distinction between fluid and crystallised intelligence in the 1960s. They used the term 'crystallised' to refer to knowledge and skills that we accumulate over our lifespan – essentially knowledge that has solidified and strengthened. One example of this might be a test of vocabulary. '**Fluid intelligence**', however, refers to our ability to think and reason 'on the spot', often under the pressure of time when faced with new problems. This type of intelligence tends to peak and decline in humans as they get older.

WEB WATCH @

You can try out tests of mental rotation yourself here:

http://www.cambridgebrainsciences.com/browse/concentration/test/rotation-task

Try comparing male and female scores on the online test – do you notice any gender difference?

Raven wanted the tests to measure 'eductive reasoning'; the ability to infer or work out an answer based only on the information one has been given. The RPM is provides an incomplete, novel pictorial stimuli which participants have to make meaningful. So, for each test item participants have to select the missing aspect in a series of stimuli in order to complete a pattern. The RPM test is an example of what is known as a '**fluid intelligence**'.

The test itself now comes in three different versions, two of which were used in the key study by van Leeuwen *et al.* (2008). These are designed for participants of different abilities and are described in more detail in Table 2.3. The items on the test get progressively more challenging. This has important implications for scoring, because scoring a point on an easy item is quite different from getting a more difficult item correct. As such, models for interpreting results on the RPM do not simply produce total sum scores, but rely on calculations that take into account the difficulty of each item (e.g. the Rasch model used by van Leeuwen *et al.*, 2008).

TABLE 2.3: RAVEN'S PROGRESSIVE MATRICES		
Format	**Recommended group**	**Length and presentation**
Colour Progressive Matrices (CPM)	Children 4–7 years, the elderly and some groups with mental or physical difficulties	Typically 36 items (three sets of 12); mostly colour, may include some black and white items
Standard Progressive Matrices (SPM)	Children and young people 7–18 years*	60 items (five sets of 12) in black and white
Advanced Progressive Matrices (APM)	Adults aged 18+ years	48 items (set I includes 12 items, which may be used as practice to familiarise participants with the test; set II is 36 items)

*the APM is in some occupational assessments considered more appropriate for 'elite' adults; those who might be applying for higher managerial work roles, and the SPM considered suitable for those roles without such demands. However, in research such as van Leeuwen *et al.* (2008) there is the danger of the 'ceiling effect', where items on the SPM may be too easy for most adults. To avoid this, the APM is used to create a better spread of results.

Applications of the RPM

The test is particularly favoured in research with children, because items do not rely on language. Instructions can be given verbally instead, so young participants do not have to be able to read or write. For this reason the RPM may also be better suited to individuals with language or perceptual difficulties, hence the development of the coloured format.

Although they were originally designed for research purposes, the RPM are now used widely in clinical, educational and occupational applications. Many entrants into the military across the globe have routinely undertaken versions of the RPM, because of its relative cultural neutrality. This has allowed comparisons to be made about cognitive ability in these populations over time and between countries. Research into developmental disorders such as autistic spectrum disorders (ASD) prefer to use the RPM because they are non-verbal; communication impairment experienced by individuals with ASD therefore has less impact on the measure. Finally, the nature of the test items means that all versions of the test are comparable, meaning that test scores from the SPM undertaken by children can meaningfully be compared to those of adults who have completed the APM (van Leeuwen *et al.*, 2008).

RPM and the Flynn effect

The 'Flynn effect' is a frequently observed trend in IQ scores, and refers to the work of James R. Flynn who conducted longitudinal and cross-cultural research on various IQ testing programmes. He compared data from 14 nations which revealed overall gains in IQ scores ranging from 5 to 25 points in just one generation (Flynn, 1987). One way to explain this intergenerational gain is as a result of improved access to education and literacy rates across the later half of the twentieth Century. However, Flynn found that some of the largest gains occurred on culturally-reduced tests and tests of fluid intelligence, such as the RPM. The data set he analysed from the Netherlands can be seen in Table 2.4, with scores adjusted to allow for comparison from the start of the study period.

TABLE 2.4: IQ GAINS ON THE RPM FROM MALES AGED 18 YEARS IN THE NETHERLANDS

Year	Mean IQ score
1952	100.00
1962	106.20
1972	112.43
1981/2	121.10

Flynn found that simple gains in literacy or learned content could not explain this phenomenon, and instead saw an increase in problem-solving abilities as the cause. He concluded that IQ tests such as the RPM do not offer a direct measure of the single 'g' factor of general intelligence. Flynn suggests that IQ tests may measure an ability somehow related to intelligence (e.g. the ability to notice patterns). This could explain why, even though the tests do give an indication of intelligence, they do not produce stable results across generations.

The following example should illustrate Flynn's point. Placing greater emphasis in schools on teaching patterns and mental rotation of shapes could develop this specific skill in all children. The most intelligent children would be more likely to develop skill in mental rotation at a more advanced level, because it is linked to intelligence. Hence, the scores on tests involving this mental rotation would improve over time as a result of the educational focus, whilst still giving some indication of who the brightest children are. As Flynn noted, the problem with IQ tests is not that they fail to directly measure intelligence itself, but that they correlate too weakly with intelligence to offer a convincing measure of IQ.

MATHS MOMENT

1 Using the data in Table 2.4, round the mean IQ scores to the nearest whole number.
2 Plot a line graph to illustrate the data given in the table above.

QUESTION SPOTLIGHT!

It is important to understand the problems Raven faced when trying to assess intelligence. Can you explain one issue psychologists might encounter when designing ways to test intelligence?

EVALUATION

Methodological and ethical issues

The study of intelligence is controversial because it raises many socially sensitive issues. For example, when considering factors that influence the development of intelligence we looked at sex differences.. Suggesting that men and women are naturally more gifted at different kinds of cognitive activities can be prescriptive and limit equality of opportunity. Twin-study research, which supports the role of genetic factors in intelligence, is similarly deterministic, whereas findings from cross-cultural research, which identifies differences between nations, can be highly politically sensitive.

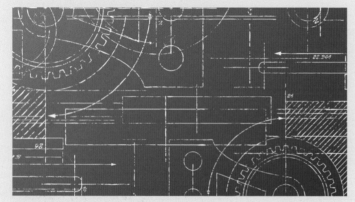

Figure 2.8: Genetic determinism: Are our genes blueprints for our futures?

The van Leeuwen *et al.* study (2008) considers the importance of these issues, and considers the contribution of genetics and environment in its discussion and interpretation of findings. The researchers also addressed specific ethical guidelines in order to protect its participants, such as the informed consent that was obtained from parents and children.

ACTIVITY ✳

You will have considered the issue of ethnocentrism in IQ testing within Gould's report on mass mental testing in US army recruits. Draw up a chart to compare and contrast the two tests. Make sure to compare the RPM to Yerkes' test in terms of cultural bias.

The van Leeuwen *et al.* (2008) study uses a complex twin-family design, theoretical modelling and statistical analysis to effectively measure the relative contribution of genetics and environment to the heritability of IQ. The researchers used a fairly large sample of families; however, by mere fact that the participants are all twins or twin relatives, the sample cannot be said to represent the general population.

The researchers adopted widely used standardised measurement tools and models (the RPM and Rasch model) that have been shown to have high levels of validity and reliability. However, questions remain about the validity of IQ tests such as the RPM owing to intergenerational increases in scores (the Flynn effect). Objective, value-free DNA tests were used for gene analysis alongside self-report measures, removing the possibility of researcher bias. Participants took the cognitive tests individually, having been issued with identical instructions. This allowed researchers to minimise the impact of extraneous variables, such as noticing other participants finishing their tests first.

Debates

Usefulness of research

Twin studies such as the key study of van Leeuwen *et al.* (2008) are useful as they offer one of the only ways to measure the relative contributions of environment and genetics to the heritability of IQ. One limitation of these studies, however, is that the sample population may be unrepresentative. Although the sample size is often large in such pieces of research, particularly in adoption studies, ethnic minorities and low-income families are often under-represented, which may distort results.

IQ tests and different models of intelligence are concepts that remain relevant in the fields of education and mental health, as well as in occupational psychology. Tests such as RPM have been adapted for use in determining an applicant's suitability for vocational roles, while cognitive tests are embedded in school entrance exams across the world to judge academic ability. The RPM and other IQ tests are used in clinical practice, for example in assessing and developing individualised support for patients with brain damage.

Nature vs nurture

This debate is essential to understanding factors influencing intelligence. As we have seen, a range of innate, biological factors such as hormones, brain anatomy and function and genetics are all implicated in the development of intelligence. However, while this may hold true for research that relies on traditional single-factor theories of intelligence, other conceptions of intelligence might indicate a stronger role for environmental influence.

Current research, such as van Leeuwen *et al.* (2008), continues to support existing evidence of the heritability of intelligence. Through the use of twin, adoption and family studies, it is clear that genetic factors do account for a large proportion of variance in IQ scores. What is less clear, and difficult to test experimentally, is the influence of environment on IQ and the interaction or correlation that exists between certain biological and cultural factors. For instance, van Leeuwen *et al.* (2008) concluded that while genetic factors are the main influence, environmental factors play a significant albeit smaller role.

Assessment of intelligence also has great relevance to the nature–nurture debate. Throughout this course you will have looked at several types of IQ test, and considered how an individual's background can influence their ability to score well on such tests. Yerkes' early mental tests with the US Army contained frequent, culturally specific references that would advantage native English speakers. Raven's Progressive Matrices are an example of a culturally reduced test, which seeks to avoid such bias. However, as Flynn (1987) points out, there is scope for intelligence scores to improve over time owing to environmental influence, even on tests of fluid intelligence. It is therefore questionable whether IQ tests can ever truly provide assessment of 'native' intelligence, or whether they will in some way be tainted by environmental influence.

Free will vs determinism

With so much evidence implicating biological factors such as heritability, it does appear that a significant proportion of variance in IQ can be said to be naturally determined. However, this may be an overly simplistic view, because it suggests that all natural influences are outside of our control, and that all environmental influences are a product of our own free choosing. While it is true that we cannot change our genetic make-up, the implications of this for observable intelligence are great.

In the study by van Leeuwen *et al.* (2008), for example, the researchers found that spousal resemblance was a likely product of phenotypic assortment. In other words, partners chose one another because they have similar IQs, implying the involvement of free will in how we select mates. Genetic transmission is not a product of purely random mating patterns. On the other hand, you do not get to choose your family! So, viewed from the alternative perspective, offspring have little or no control over their genetic make-up or environmental factors such as parental support for schooling.

Free will may also play a role in assessment of intelligence. However, this may well depend on the method of assessment used. Intelligence tests that measure fluid intelligence, such

as RPM, are assessing one's ability to think on the spot and reason about new situations. It might be difficult, therefore, for individuals to prepare for such tests, and as a result the outcome is likely to be determined by their innate cognitive abilities. On tests that rely on linguistic ability or cumulative knowledge (i.e. crystallised intelligence), individuals have more control over the outcome, by freely choosing to prepare thoroughly and revise in order to improve their performance.

Reductionism and holism

As we have seen from examining different theories of intelligence, some rely on more or less reductionist explanations. Gardener's theory of multiple intelligences embraces a more holistic view of intelligence as a number of different qualities within an individual. Conversely, the majority of mainstream intelligence research relies on the elusive 'g' factor, an overarching concept providing a single notion of intelligence. Attempts to define factor theories of intelligence have resulted in competing hierarchical models involving numerous broad and narrow traits that inevitably capture a more holistic view of intelligence (e.g. Carroll, 1993).

By definition, reductionist approaches seek to cut down explanations to the smallest of units. Looking at genetic explanations for intelligence in single genes is a mission being currently undertaken in research by Desrivières *et al.* (2014) and others. Yet it seems unlikely that genetics will ever offer a complete explanation of variance in IQ. This is made clear in the key research by van Leeuwen *et al.* (2008), who found an interaction between genetics and environment that requires further consideration.

Figure 2.9: Twin study researchers confirm zygosity through DNA testing

When measuring intelligence, assessments such as the RPM focus on a narrow range of eductive abilities – for example, mental rotation. Other types of IQ test are composed of different sections that measure a more comprehensive range of cognitive abilities. In current clinical work, 'cross-battery assessment' is frequently used. This involves using a combination of IQ tests or elements from different tests to produce a more holistic measure of intelligence than using a single assessment tool.

Individual and situational explanations

Theories of intelligence tend to suppose that intelligence is a stable personality trait that remains fairly consistent over the lifespan. In other words, someone who is an intelligent child is likely to become an intelligent adult. This may be the case whether intelligence is defined as a single factor or as multiple qualities; across different situations an individual's performance remains consistent.

Research generally confirms that intelligence is best explained by personality variables and not by situation, with longitudinal studies demonstrating clear correlation between IQ scores of the same individuals at different ages. In fact, for all the controversy over the existence of personality traits, most psychologists agree that to some extent intelligence exemplifies the one aspect of behaviour that remains consistent across a range of different situations. For example, the strong IQ concordance between MZ twins in the van Leeuwen *et al.* study (2008) points to a highly individualist explanation for intelligence.

There are of course some exceptions to this, in cases where variables such as illness, stress, and conditions such as dementia may influence one's cognitive abilities. A person of above-average intelligence might perform poorly on an IQ test administered as part of a job interview, in which case a situational explanation (for example, the influence of stress) might more appropriately explain their low score. Also, methods of assessing intelligence that rely on cultural knowledge or a high level of literacy, unlike the RPM, may better reflect the experience of a person's education than their intelligence. In this way, situational explanations can account for differences between ethnic groups on IQ tests.

Psychology as a science

Psychometric testing is the main method used to assess intelligence. It relies on models that typically consider intelligence as a single factor composed of broad and specific cognitive abilities. Psychologists have sought to use psychometric testing in the form of IQ tests to objectively measure these theoretical constructs, and by design they are standardised and repeatable. They produce quantitative data allowing statistical analysis. However, as we have seen, the methods used to test intelligence measure what they define as intelligence – there is no one agreed definition. Critics argue that this renders the process of measurement unscientific and somewhat self-defeating.

Nonetheless, measures such as the RPM and other IQ tests, such as the Stanford-Binet test, seek to collect empirical data, via standardised procedures. Efforts to remove confounding variables such as cultural knowledge have also increased validity. Research on factors that influence intelligence can also be considered scientific as they use objective, valid measurements such as DNA testing to isolate genes, and to confirm relatedness and zygosity within twin studies.

PRE-ADULT BRAIN DEVELOPMENT

BACKGROUND

The human brain grows at an amazing rate in the journey from conception to adulthood. Much of this development occurs in the first three months of life, during which time a newborn's brain grows at an average rate of 1% per day! It was once believed that virtually all important brain changes had occurred by the time a child reached the age of three. However, thanks to modern neuroimaging techniques, we now know that significant changes to the brain continue right through childhood, **adolescence** and into adulthood. Techniques including magnetic resonance imaging (MRI) scanning have allowed researchers to track changes to the organisation, grey-matter content and function of the brain across the lifespan.

Early brain development

At the time of birth, much of the spinal cord and brain stem are well developed, however, upper regions such as the limbic system and cerebral cortex, are still fairly immature. Interestingly, all the neurons in the cortex are produced while the baby is *in utero*, but they remain poorly connected until after birth. A huge number of synaptic connections are made during the first few years in the cerebral cortex, signalling the development of conscious actions, memories, thoughts and emotions.

This special period of synaptic production or 'exuberance' goes into overdrive during early childhood. It starts earliest in the visual cortex and eventually in the frontal and temporal lobes, the brain areas responsible for higher cognitive and emotional functioning.

Adolescent brain development

A dramatic change in synaptic production occurs in adolescence. Grey matter (which contains synaptic connections) reaches peak volume and begins to decrease in density across several cortical regions. It continues to do so through to early adulthood (early to mid-twenties), in a process called 'synaptic pruning'. Connections that are not used enough are eliminated; the environment is important in determining which connections are needed and which can be pruned away. In effect, this allows the brain to become more efficient in its use of energy, removing weaker, less essential synaptic connections in favour of strengthening those that are required. The prefrontal cortex is one of the last areas of the brain to undergo this key process of maturation, and studies suggest it may last into the early twenties (Huttenlocher, 1979). It continues to develop throughout adolescence, as adolescents gradually get better at abstract reasoning and anticipating outcomes.

 **KEY IDEAS**

Adolescence refers to the period of life that starts with the onset of puberty, and ends when the individual reaches adulthood. It involves both physiological and psychological development. Adolescence is defined by some as the teenage years, though the precise beginning and end of this period tends to vary widely between cultures. However, it is characterised by universally recognised types of behaviours, such as peer influence and increased risk-taking.

Figure 2.10: Less is more: The process of synaptic pruning refines and strengthens essential neural processing

Impact on risk-taking

The way in which adolescents' brains are developing along with hormonal changes in puberty can have a significant impact on their decision-making and behaviour. This process is combined with major environmental changes: moving schools and sitting exams; increased responsibility, such as part-time jobs or caring for younger siblings; greater independence in socialising and leisure activities. In many ways, adolescents are expected to behave in a grown-up way and make responsible adult choices, yet their brains are still functioning quite differently from those of their elders.

Adolescents are more prone to risk-taking and impulsivity than other age groups. Examples of this include more frequent drug use, injuries/accidents and unprotected sexual activity (Arnett, 1992). One reason for this is to do with the order in which various regions of the brain mature. The limbic system, which is involved in the processing of social and emotional information, develops earlier than the prefrontal cortex. For a period it dominates the executive controls of the prefrontal cortex, making risky decisions more common and more likely to occur under higher levels of social influence (Steinberg, 2008). For example, this means that adolescents might make poorer, riskier decisions about getting into fights than adults would.

Another process that emerges with the onset of adolescence involves the ventral striatum (VS) (Casey *et al.*, 2008). This area of the brain is often referred to as the 'reward centre', because it is highly sensitive to rewards. Early maturation of the VS encourages adolescents to engage in more adult activities that reap rewards (e.g. drinking, driving and sex) and to seek independence from their families. Adolescents' neurological function makes them sensation-seeking and drawn to novel behaviours. Because the prefrontal cortex is not fully mature, adolescents do not manage the risk involved in these activities in the same way as adults can.

Figure 2.11: Sex, drugs, rock 'n' roll and … the limbic system? Adolescent rebellion is the behavioural expression of neurological changes essential to healthy development

These differences do not mean that adolescent brains are 'immature' in the sense that they are defective in comparison to those of adults, rather that they are not fully developed. Neuroscientists suggest that these differences are probably highly adaptive, making adolescence a time of heightened risk and opportunity. Young people may have a greater tolerance for uncertainty than adults, which allows them to become more innovative and thus independent, developing new strengths and establishing social groups.

KEY RESEARCH

Barkley-Levenson, E. & Galván, A. (2014) Neural representation of expected value in the adolescent brain. *Proceedings of the National Academy of Sciences of the United States of America,* 111, 1646–1651.

Aim

In this study the experimenters investigated whether adolescents attach more value to rewards than adults do. They aimed to identify neural development of **expected value** (**EV**) in the brains of adolescents.

Figure 2.12: Expected value in action: many judge the low cost of a lottery ticket to be a worthwhile risk for winning the jackpot, despite the low probability of winning

Method

Sample

Nineteen adult participants between the ages of 25 and 30 (mean age 27.9 years; eight males and eleven females) and twenty-two adolescent participants aged 13–17 (mean age 15.6 years; equal mix of genders) took part in this study. They were all healthy right-handed individuals recruited from poster and Internet advertisements.

Design and procedure

This was a quasi-experiment carried out under laboratory conditions. The independent variable was the age of the participant (adult or adolescent), and the dependent variables were the differences in neural activation and behavioural responses to a gambling task. All participants gave their informed consent; the parental consent of those participants under age 18 was also obtained. They were acclimatised to the fMRI through a mock scan, and the experimenters collected information on participants' source and amount of income per month. This was to investigate whether differences between the two groups was due to the novelty of the reward rather than developmental differences (i.e. adolescents might have less experience of spending money, and value it more highly than adults).

Each participant was given US $20 to use as 'playing' money during the fMRI task. They were also informed that there was an opportunity to win up to $20 more in addition to their playing money, but that there was a possibility that they would lose it during the gambling. They had to decide for each trial whether they would be willing to gamble for their money. They were told one of the trials they accepted would be selected and played at the end of the scan for

QUESTION SPOTLIGHT!

Consider the impact of neurological changes on risk-taking. Can you see how the debate over free will and determinism links to the behaviour of adolescents?

💡 KEY IDEAS

Expected value (EV) is the sum of all of the possible outcomes of a particular choice multiplied by their probabilities. A person uses this to judge whether the risks involved in a certain course of action are worth taking in order to gain a reward.

QUESTION SPOTLIGHT!

If more of the adolescent participants were recruited through the internet and more of the adults through posters, how might this bias the sample?

real money, and the outcome would be added or subtracted from their overall payment of $20. This was done in order to encourage participants to risk-take as they would normally. In actuality, all participants were assigned a payment of between $5 and $10, to ensure no participants had to return money.

Participants were trained on how to use the computerised gambling programme prior to testing. In the task, participants were presented with a series of gambles across 144 trials. On screen they saw a 'spinner' with a 50% probability of gaining the amount shown on one side, and a 50% probability of losing the amount shown on the other side (*see* Figure 2.13). The amounts were given in whole dollars, ranging from losses of –$5 to –$20, and gains from +$5 to +$20.

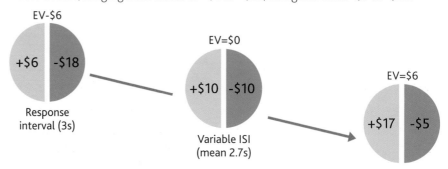

Figure 2.13: Example of three trials from the gambling task. Ps responded to each within 3s, with a brief interval between trials (ISI, or interstimulus interval). The EV of each trial is shown at the top to illustrate risk (not shown to Ps).

The experimenters collected both neural and behavioural data. Neural activation in response to the gambling task was observed and recorded using an MRI scanner at the same university research centre. Experimenters were particularly interested in activity in the ventral striatum (VS) – an area of the forebrain associated with valuation and reward. Behavioural responses of acceptance and rejection to each trial were recorded when the participants pressed computer keys.

Results
Neural activation
The fMRI data showed more activation of the VS in adolescents as EV increased. So, in cases where the expected value of the gamble was greater, this area of adolescents' brains became much more active than it did in adults. This was the case even when groups of participants were matched on income and overall acceptability of gambles, suggesting that adolescents do not have a special preference for money that might explain the difference.

Furthermore, even when similar gambling behaviour was being exhibited by both groups, VS activation was still much greater in the adolescent sample. This could be explained by the theory that adolescents are less skilled than adults at calculating the EV of gambles than adults; however the behavioural data did not suggest that adolescents were any less adept at discriminating advantageous from disadvantageous gambles.

Behavioural differences
In trials where no risk was involved (e.g. gain-only or loss-only), both groups made similar judgements. However, for both groups, an increased EV also increased the likelihood of accepting a gamble, although a higher EV had a greater influence on the response of adolescents than on adults (see Figure 2.14).

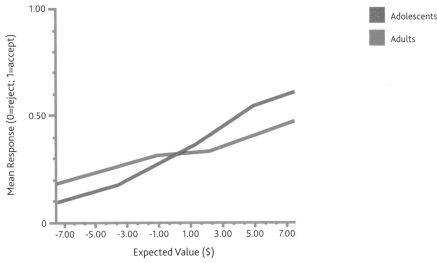

Figure 2.14: Graph comparing behavioural responses and expected value (EV) of both groups

MATHS MOMENT 🖩

1   The experimenters calculated the
     mean response for the gamble task.
     Why was this the most appropriate
     measure of average?
2   Outline one finding from the graph
     shown in Figure 2.14.

This 'hyperactive' reward sensitivity was therefore found to precede more advantageous risk-taking behaviour in adolescents. This suggests that adolescents were focused more on the higher amount they could win, and less concerned with the relatively smaller amount they stood to lose. Like adults, adolescents virtually never accepted gambles with a negative EV (i.e. more to lose, less to win). This suggests that adolescents were equally capable of avoiding disadvantageous choices as adults, and actually made better choices on advantageous gambles.

One explanation offered by the experimenters for these age differences is that they offer adolescents an evolutionary advantage. Being more willing to accept the risk of advantageous gambles may help them develop increased independence, so becoming self-reliant and more willing to explore and to find potential mates.

Conclusion

The researchers concluded that:

1   Adolescents place greater value on rewards than do adults.
2   Neural representations of value in adolescents are linked to increased risk-taking behaviour.

APPLICATION: REDUCING RISK-TAKING BEHAVIOURS USING KNOWLEDGE OF BRAIN DEVELOPMENT

Existing strategies to reduce risk-taking

The key research by Barkley-Levenson & Galván (2014) confirms that adolescents and adults are both able to reason about risk in similar ways. There is nothing defective *per se* with adolescents' ability to reason about outcomes, but rather that they chose to take more risks when the chance of reward is greater. As discussed at the start of this topic, this has an impact on the behaviour of adolescents, making them more vulnerable to harm from unintentional injury, for example.

For many years, heightened risk-taking behaviours were thought to be a product of the information that adolescents use when making decisions.

Figure 2.15: Need for speed: young drivers account for a huge number of road casualties each year

Interventions to reduce risk-taking were designed to alter knowledge, attitudes or beliefs. These included educating adolescents about the risks of substance use, reckless driving or unprotected sex. While these programmes improved young people's knowledge about such activities, it was not effective in changing their actual behaviour (Steinberg, 2008). This may be because adolescents lack the cognitive control to resist sensation-seeking, no matter how much information they are given about high-risk activities.

Changing context – graduated driver licensing schemes

The impact of risk-taking behaviour on the well-being of adolescents remains a serious cause for concern. A good proportion of adolescent deaths and injuries may be preventable, such as those involving car or motorcycle accidents, physical assaults, or drug or alcohol abuse. Drivers aged 16–19 in the UK are more than twice as likely to die in a crash as drivers aged 40–49, with one in four 18–24 year olds (23%) being involved in a crash within two years of passing their driving test (UK Department for Transport, 2014).

However, some strategies have been able to reduce these issues by giving greater consideration to the context in which risk-taking behaviours take place. Since we know that adolescent brains are more sensitive to social and emotional information, interventions that restrict the influence of these factors on decision-making may be more effective than education programmes.

One such intervention is the implementation of graduated driver licensing schemes (GDL). You might notice that much adolescent risk-taking – such as alcohol consumption or dangerous driving – often occurs in groups (Steinberg, 2008). Having peers present can make the rewarding aspects of risky situations even more appealing, increasing activation of the VS brain region. Limiting opportunities for risk-taking, or changing the socio-emotional context of such behaviour, can help reduce negative outcomes.

GDL schemes are in place in different countries across the world (the UK currently isn't one of them). They vary in how they are implemented, but essentially feature one or more probationary periods for new drivers, once they have qualified for their driving licence. In a GDL, probationary periods contain a number of restrictions designed to improve road safety: limits on the number and age of passengers, and restrictions on other risk factors such as alcohol consumption or night-time driving.

For example, in some GDL schemes in the United States, newly qualified drivers and young drivers have a night-time curfew prohibiting driving between 10pm and 5am, and often are banned from carrying passengers under the age of 30 (except in the presence of an older adult). Some GDL schemes also carry heavier penalties for mobile-phone use while driving, or impose lower alcohol limits until the end of probation. Table 2.5 compares different regulations for drivers across several schemes.

TABLE 2.5: COMPARISON OF GRADUATED DRIVER LICENSING SCHEMES

Country/region	Minimum age to pass test	Probationary period (after passing test)	Restrictions for probationary period
California, USA	16 years old	12 months	• No passengers under age 20 for duration of provisional period • Night-time driving restriction between 10pm and 5am
New South Wales, Australia	17 years old	3 years (includes two probation stages)	• Max. speed 90 kmph (approx. 56 mph) • Zero blood alcohol permitted • Night-time driving restriction limits one passenger under age 21 between 11pm and 5am • Immediate suspension for speeding offence
Hong Kong, China	18 years old	12 month period	• Max speed 70kmph (approx. 44mph) • May not drive in offside lane of three-lane carriageway • Motorcyclists may not carry passengers

Source: US Governor's Highway Safety Association webpage (www.ghsa.org), New South Wales Government Roads and Maritime Services webpage (www.rms.nsw.gov.au) and Hong Kong Government webpage (www.gov.hk), 2015

The UK Department for Transport recently published a review of research into the effectiveness of GDL schemes for drivers aged 17–19 years. The authors found that:

- GDL is consistently found to be effective at reducing collisions in countries where it has been implemented
- There are real potential public health benefits of a GDL system for new drivers
- The effectiveness of individual GDL schemes depends upon the number of restrictions implemented and how strictly they are enforced by authorities.

The report also estimates that implementing a GDL in the UK could save on average 4,471 casualties and £224 million annually (Kinnear *et al.*, 2013).

ACTIVITY ✳

What difficulties can you foresee with implementing a GDL scheme in the UK? Write a letter to the government outlining the neuropsychological evidence for why such a scheme might be effective.

DO IT YOURSELF 🔍

Test the difference in driving skills when driving alone or driving in the company of others. Use a driving simulation online, such as an interactive hazard perception test to design a simple experiment. One example is at:

http://www.billplant.co.uk/hazard/hazard.php

Was driving better or worse in the presence of others? What are some flaws with your study's design?

EVALUATION

Methodological and ethical issues

There are several difficulties with investigating brain development and risk-taking behaviours. One of these is the method used to examine brain activity and function. Researchers have to carefully select participants for research who are healthy individuals (free from mental or physical illness for example) and control for factors such as age, gender and handedness. If longitudinal studies are employed to observe development, there is a risk that participants may drop out of the study.

The study of Barkley-Levenson & Galván (2014) was ethically fairly sound. It did, however, involve fMRI scanning, which can cause participants discomfort and even feelings of claustrophobia. For studies involving adolescent participants, such as the key research, additional parental consent must be obtained. Furthermore, there could be an ethical objection to the risk-taking task in that it might actually increase the future likelihood of the participants' engaging in gambling, particularly as they were rewarded with real money.

QUESTION SPOTLIGHT!

Why did the researchers control for handedness? What impact might it have had on the study if both left- and right-handed people took part?

Another issue to consider is how psychologists measure risk-taking behaviour. There are different ways of doing this, many of which rely on self-report, which may incur social desirability bias. Adolescents may want to over- or under-report risk-taking, depending on the context in which they are asked. For example, teenagers interviewed about illegal drug-taking in a classroom at their school by an adult researcher may be reluctant to disclose information.

There were methodological limitations to the research by Barkley-Levenson & Galván (2014). They used a small sample size, which would be difficult to generalise from. They also lacked a pre-adolescent (8–12 years) participant group. Without this group it is not possible to say whether the observed difference is unique to adolescents or part of an ongoing developmental course. Although the researchers devised an objective measure of risk-taking through the computerised task, it lacks ecological validity and would be difficult to replicate in the real world.

STRETCH & CHALLENGE

Before the advent of modern brain-scanning techniques, psychologists often relied on case studies of individuals who had suffered brain damage in order to learn more about brain function and development. What ethical and methodological issues can you see with using case studies of brain-damaged patients?

Debates

Usefulness of research

Research into neurological change is useful in helping us to understand typical patterns of development and to identify relevant behavioural correlates. In the case of adolescents, hypersensitivity to reward can express itself in sensation-seeking behaviour. Combined with the relative dominance of the limbic system over the prefrontal cortex in this age group, this gives us a good explanation for increased risk-taking in this group.

The key research we have looked at refines this picture. It can explain why attempts to educate young people are less successful at promoting behavioural change than those such as GDL, which target social and emotional contexts. As discussed earlier, GDL as a strategy for reducing risk-taking in young drivers has been associated with significant reductions in road traffic accidents for this group.

Nature vs Nurture

The debate over the roles of nature and nurture in brain development has evolved hugely in recent years. It is now recognised that while some patterns of neurological changes are an innate process, stimulation from the environment plays a huge role in shaping development. One example of this is in synaptic pruning, which seems to be a universal, age-related process (nature), but one that is influenced by environment. The 'use it or lose it' principle means that the skills required for functioning in specific environments strengthen neural connections, while those that are not required are eliminated, specifically adapting to the individual's environment.

The key research by Barkley-Levenson & Galván (2014) revealed a difference in neural activation and gambling behaviour between adolescents and adults. They found that adolescents were highly sensitive to rewards when compared to adults. This suggests that changes in sensitivity to reward are likely to be part of a natural process of neural development.

However, the study did not explore reasons behind the onset of neurological change; nurture factors might still partly explain this.

Risk-taking behaviour and how it is reduced can be influenced by environmental factors. We have considered how being in a social group increases the reward factor in decisions to take risks. Strategies to improve the driving of adolescents include schemes such as graduated licensing. Placing restrictions on novice drivers controls the social and emotional context in which driving takes place (nurture). GDL also reduces the opportunity for taking risky decisions during the adolescent period, until the brain has had time to mature more fully (nature).

Free will vs determinism

Exploring the role of determinism in brain development and risk-taking behaviour is challenging. One reason for this is that it is easy to mistakenly assume that determinism refers only to biological changes in the brain, when in fact there are other forms of determinism that may stem from environmental factors. As we have seen in the nature vs nurture debate above, both have a role in shaping neurological development. However, risk-taking involves reasoning and decision-making by the adolescent, and for this reason there is a strong role for individual free will.

The key research focuses on gambling as a form of risk-taking. Both adults and adolescents employ reasoning when considering the expected value of a gamble. While adults have a more mature prefrontal cortex than adolescents have, behavioural choices are not fixed or determined. Indeed, other factors, such as personality type and family background, might play a role in adolescents' risk-taking tendencies.

Similarly, in GDLs and other schemes that are designed to reduce risky behaviour, there is a strong role for free will. While the social and emotional context in which the behaviour takes place can be manipulated, ultimately no such strategy can determine the course of an individual's behaviour. For example while risk-taking such as forms of drug and alcohol abuse is a real public health issue, it is often a minority of adolescent offenders who engage in such activities (Steinberg, 2008).

QUESTION SPOTLIGHT!

Having peers around makes the potential gains of risky situations more rewarding, because the setting influences the functioning of the ventral striatum.

Can you apply this idea to two different debates?

The study of brain development and its influence on risk-taking behaviour incorporates factors that involve both nature and nurture. Particular pieces of research into risk-taking can, in some cases, be considered reductionist. In the key research by Barkley-Levenson & Galván (2014), the experimenters identify differences in activation of the VS region, which they attribute to heightened sensitivity to reward in adolescents. While the authors acknowledge that there are other neural regions and environmental factors implicated in reward and risk, they are not explored in the study.

GDL could be considered a holistic strategy to reduce risk-taking behaviour in adolescents. It involves changing the context that places limitations on behaviour, extending the opportunity to gain driving experience under various conditions. It also delays full driving privileges until a later stage of neural development, which allows for further physical maturation.

Psychology as a science

Research into brain development and risk-taking tends to rely on laboratory-based procedures and uses objective, scientific measurements via brain-scanning techniques and computer simulations. This means that researchers such as Barkley-Levenson & Galván (2014) were able to control the environment and ensure that differences in gambling behaviours and neural activation were linked to age and nothing else. The scans or simulations also produce empirical data, through standardised, highly replicable procedures, such as the gambling task.

QUESTION SPOTLIGHT!

Adults are generally likely to have had more experience of gambling than adolescents. To what extent might this difference matter, and how could it have been controlled for in the study?

As with many applications, it is difficult to consider the implementation of GDL schemes in a scientific way. While it is partly based on current understanding of neurological development, the strategy takes place within real-world contexts that are extremely varied. It would be difficult to 'prove' that the implementation of GDL could effect changes in adolescents' levels of risk-taking, although current data on road-casualty reduction suggests that they are very effective (Kinnear *et al.*, 2013).

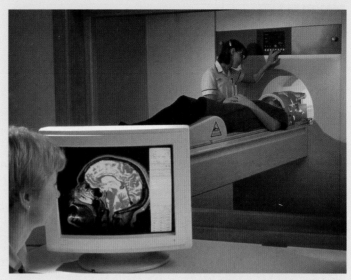

Figure 2.16: MRI scans can provide useful information about brain activity, but may cause discomfort to participants

PERCEPTUAL DEVELOPMENT

BACKGROUND

What do we mean by 'perception'?

Our perceptual systems are constantly at work, keeping us informed of what is happening in our environment and helping us to respond accordingly. We rely on these systems for our survival and quality of life; to cross roads safely, play a game of football or sing in a choir. It is through the process of sensation that we experience the world; being exposed to stimuli such as light, sound, smell, taste and touch through corresponding sensory organs. A closely related term is perception: the process by which our minds organise, process and make sense of sensory data. In this topic we will consider the how perceptual development has been studied in human and animals.

Development of perception in children

In humans, most perceptual capacities emerge in the first year of life. The development of perception is directed by an interaction between an infant's sensory experiences and its biological programming. The rate at which perception develops is truly extraordinary and of real interest to psychologists wanting to understand the interplay between brain development, perceptual processing and healthy functioning. In humans, sensory input comes from our senses: vision, hearing, taste, touch and smell. Our auditory, olfaction and tactile systems are already fairly well developed at the time of birth. The visual system is somewhat organised but still relatively immature and continues to develop over the first few weeks and months.

Visual perception

In many ways, vision must be considered our most important sense, as it often provides us with the most detailed information about what is happening in our environment. Below we will consider the early development of vision and its effect on infant perception. A number of *sensory abilities* develop over the first year of life, including:

- *Acuity* – One major difference between adult and newborn vision is the difference in optical acuity. 'Acuity' is the sharpness of our vision; the ability to detect fine detail. It is determined by how quickly eye muscles are able to contract and relax to allow the eye to focus. It also requires maturation of the fovea and retina (see Figure 2.17) in order to transmit a clear image. Newborn acuity is poor compared to that of adults; an infant can see at 6 metres what adults can normally see at 100–125 metres.
- *Binocular vision* – The ability to perceive depth is again determined in part by the strength of eye-muscle control. Humans have two eyes (binocular vision) which create a single 3-D image containing information

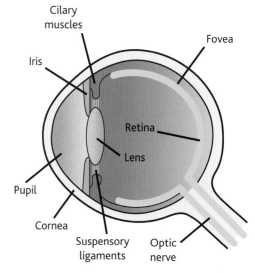

Figure 2.17: Cross-section showing the basic structures of the eye

Figure 2.18: Turn that frown upside down! Young infants show preference for coherent, typical faces over scrambled or blank faces (Goren, 1975)

WEB WATCH @

You can learn more about monocular cues such as size constancy at:

http://psylux.psych.tu-dresden.de/
i1/kaw/diverses%20Material/www.
illusionworks.com/html/size_constancy.
html

from both visual fields. This 'stereopsis' requires that both eyes are aligned and coordinated in their movements. A newborn's eyes do not move as well together as those of an adult because of poor muscle definition, so the result is immature depth perception.

- *Colour* – Sensitivity to colour develops as the cones of the eyes mature, though there is debate about the precise ages at which infants can differentiate colours, and how this ability is affected by factors such as brightness. Cones are cells that can be found at the retina and are responsible for colour vision, particularly in bright light. Very young babies have been found to prefer bold colours or high contrast, such as strong black-and-white graphics. This is not to suggest that newborns cannot perceive colour at all, as was once thought. Rather it means that their ability to perceive and prefer coloured stimuli, including highly saturated images (images of intense colour), emerges later.

We have already stated that perception is far more than just sensation; the development of the capacities outlined above have a significant impact on how visual information is made meaningful by the infant. Two key *perceptual abilities* are outlined below:

- *Facial recognition* – As their visual capabilities develop and they gain experience of their environment, infants change in their ability to recognise faces. Early research suggests an innate capacity for facial recognition (Fantz, 1963). However, it is difficult to distinguish whether it is a preference for visual complexity rather than for faces, e.g. babies may be more interested in a face than a blank circle because it has more lines and detail. Later research has confirmed findings on facial preferences, as infants show a preference for typical faces over scrambled faces (Goren, 1975).
- *Depth perception* – This is the visual ability to perceive the world in 3-D. Depth perception relies on a number of depth cues, including binocular cues as discussed earlier. Monocular cues (cues that can be provided by one eye only) include motion parallax, and size and shape constancy. These are discussed in greater detail in the key study. While research shows motion and size/shape discrimination is possible in newborns and very young babies, the point at which they use this information to inform depth judgments may not emerge until they are around 3 months old.

Studying perception in infants

Determining the nature and extent of infant perception is a truly challenging task for two reasons. First, it involves working with newborns and young babies, who would probably prefer to eat, sleep or cry than to take part in psychological research! As well as the formidable characteristics of the participant group, there is the additional challenge of trying to directly access and measure someone else's perceptions; a feat that is difficult to achieve with adults who can communicate and respond to instructions easily.

Consequently, psychologists have developed novel ways to investigate the development of perception in infants. Two main ways to study infant perception are habituation and preferential looking. Habituation is based on the idea that infants will get used to (and bored of) looking at familiar stimuli, but will show interest in novel stimuli. This allows researchers to investigate whether infants can discriminate between two different stimuli. For example, a red object is shown repeatedly to an infant until their heart rate or visual fixation drops to a stable level (habituation). A green object is then introduced to the visual field and any difference in response would indicate the infant can discriminate red from green. Preferential looking refers to the tendency of babies to prefer to look at new things. Two objects can be presented at once, and the researcher can record which, if either, the infant attends to more. This allows researchers to identify what stimuli babies prefer, e.g. in tests of facial recognition.

Studying perception in animals

Owing to the practical and ethical difficulties of conducting research using human infants, a number of studies into perception have involved animals, including the key research by Gibson & Walk (1960). One method used by psychologists is known as 'selective rearing', which involves raising an animal from birth under controlled conditions to observe the outcome.

An example of this is the work of Blakemore & Cooper (1970), who raised kittens from birth to five months of age in an environment containing either only vertical or only horizontal stripes. When exposed to a normal environment, which included both vertical and horizontal movement, kittens were 'blind' to the stimuli of which they lacked experience. Similar studies have used selective rearing techniques to investigate the effect of environment on the development of colour vision and depth perception (Sugita, 2004; Gibson & Walk, 1960).

Modern thinking on the processes of perceptual development is that it is very closely linked to motor development. Gibson, whose most famous work we will consider next, argued that without perception any action we take in our environment is essentially unguided and without purpose. As action requires both motion and perception, the two seem to be inextricably linked.

KEY RESEARCH

Gibson, E.J. & Walk, R.D. (1960) The visual cliff. *Scientific American*, 202 (4), 64–71.

Aim

The researchers investigated how humans and other animals perceive height distance, which is a specific form of distance perception. They were particularly interested in considering the stage at which human infants and other young animals develop the ability to perceive height distance.

Method
Sample

Participants were 36 infants ranging in age from 6 months to 14 months. The researchers also tested unspecified numbers of young animals from a range of different species including cats, rats, goats, sheep, turtles and chickens.

Design and procedure

The study was a laboratory experiment that used a novel set-up known as the 'visual cliff'. This set-up was specifically designed to test height distance perception, while also avoiding the danger associated with an actual fall. It

DO IT YOURSELF 🔍

Have a go at creating your own version of the visual cliff. You might want to use materials such as cardboard boxes, cellophane and patterned fabric.

Figure 2.19: On the edge: most infants avoided crossing over to the cliff edge, even when tempted to do so by their mothers

KEY IDEAS

Motion parallax is a visual depth cue that results from motion. As we move, objects that are closer move farther across our field of vision than do objects that are in the distance. This can make objects in the distance appear to move more slowly. For example, when you are riding on a bus, the markings at the edge of the road will whizz by quickly, while trees or buildings in the distance will move very slowly by comparison.

Relative size – the more distant an object is, the smaller the image of that object will be on the retina. For example, the squares on the patterned background to the shallow side of the cliff were the same size as those on the cliff side. However, they appear smaller to the eye because of relative size.

consisted of a board laid across a large sheet of heavy glass which was supported about one foot above the floor. On one side of the board a sheet of patterned material was placed directly underneath the glass; this became the 'shallow side'. On the other side a sheet of the same material was laid on the floor; this side therefore became the 'cliff side'. Although the cliff side was solid to the touch, visually the patterned material was clearly some distance lower. This created an illusion of depth.

Human trials

Each child was placed in the centre of the board as they were individually tested. The mother of each child was present, in order to motivate the babies to move while on the apparatus. The mother called the baby towards her, first from the cliff side and then from the shallow side. The behaviour of the child was observed and recorded.

Animal trials

The researchers also observed and recorded the behaviour of different animal subjects on the visual cliff, including a number of kittens that had been reared in total darkness for 27 days. Some of the animals came from the Cornell Behaviour Farm where Gibson worked.

Control trials

The researchers also performed a number of alterations to the set-up to check for any hidden bias, including changes to lighting, the pattern of the material used and the height distance for each side. They assessed the impact of each change one at a time, observing any differences in the behaviour of rats.

Separation of visual cues

Finally, in order to investigate the impact of different visual cues, the researchers introduced a variation that included two different materials being placed below each side (see Figure 2.20). The two cues involved in perceiving depth are: a) difference in object size (**relative size**), and b) **motion parallax**. To equalise and remove the cue from motion parallax, they placed patterns at the same level. Having a smaller pattern on one side meant that there was still a difference in spacing, so object size was the only cue at play. To eradicate the difference in object size cue and to test the motion parallax cue, the researchers used a larger pattern on the low side of the cliff to create a constant density to the pattern.

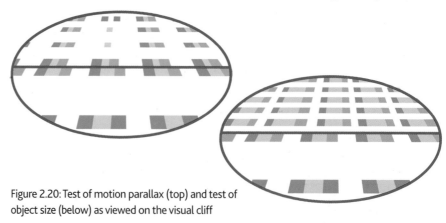

Figure 2.20: Test of motion parallax (top) and test of object size (below) as viewed on the visual cliff

Results

Human trials

All of the 27 infants who moved off the board crawled out on the shallow side at least once. Only three babies crept onto the deep side of the cliff. Many of the infants crawled away from the mother when she called to them from the cliff side edge. Other babies also cried when their mothers stood at the cliff side because they perceived their mothers to be unsafe to reach.

The babies appeared to be dependent on their vision to determine movement. They were observed looking down through the glass on the cliff side before backing away. Others would pat the glass with their hands, and despite being able to feel it, would still refuse to cross.

Gibson & Walk found that the babies' depth perception had matured more quickly than had their ability to physically move. Many supported themselves on the glass over the cliff as they manoeuvred awkwardly on the board, or backed out onto the glass as they moved towards the shallow side. So, despite perceiving the cliff's presence, it is likely that several would have fallen off if the glass had not been present.

Animal trials

The researchers found similar results when other species were placed on the visual cliff, although there were notable differences in the age at which depth perception and mobility developed. Table 2.6 offers a full comparison of the behaviour of different species used in this study. These findings suggest that in the animal species studied, depth perception emerges once an animal becomes mobile. This may serve an adaptive purpose, helping the newly mobile animal to survive by avoiding falls.

The kittens reared in darkness were equally likely to move towards the cliff side as the shallow side, and did not freeze or circle when placed on the cliff side. After one week under normal light conditions they behaved identically to kittens reared under normal conditions: they preferred the shallow side and froze or circled when placed on the cliff side. This suggests that light is necessary for visual maturation in these animals, and perhaps others.

Control trials

The results of the variations to the set-up found no hidden bias. When researchers replaced the patterned material with a plain gray surface on both sides, rats exhibited no preference for either side. When both patterned sides were raised to directly below the glass, the rats showed no preference for either side; when both sides were lowered evenly by 10 inches, the rats remained on the board. Finally, the researchers also manipulated the lighting angle to ensure there was no reflection on the glass imparting a different visual cue; in this trial the rats still had a strong preference for the shallow side.

Separation of visual cues

With only motion parallax to guide them, day-old chicks and rats reared in both normal and dark conditions showed a strong preference for the shallow side. However, neither of these animals showed as strong a preference for the shallow side as normal rats when guided only by object size. This finding suggests that motion parallax may be an innate visual cue, but that object size develops as a result of maturation.

MATHS MOMENT 🖩

Create a basic results table that shows the movements of the 36 human participants.

Calculate the percentage of babies who crawled to the shallow side, those who crawled off the edge, and those who remained stationary.

TABLE 2.6: COMPARATIVE BEHAVIOUR OF HUMANS AND DIFFERENT ANIMALS ON THE 'VISUAL CLIFF' APPARATUS

Type of animal	Age at testing	Behaviour on cliff	Natural behaviour and habitat
Human infants	6–14 months	Majority move towards shallow edge, exhibiting desire to reach mother but reluctance to move towards cliff side	Begin moving independently, usually by crawling or shuffling, at between 6 and 10 months
Chicks	24 hours	Always move towards the shallow side	Begin fending for themselves just a few hours after birth, e.g. scratching in the dirt for food, unlike many other bird species
Lambs and kids	As soon as they can stand/one day old	Never step onto the cliff side; become immobile (freeze or go limp) when pushed off onto cliff side	Can usually stand and walk within 24 hours
Rats	N/A	Move freely over both the shallow side and the cliff side, provided their whiskers are in contact with the glass	Usually begin walking around 3–4 weeks of age; nocturnal, so less reliant on vision; use touch cues from whiskers to perceive their environment
Kittens	4 weeks	Almost always choose the shallow side, freezing or circling when placed on the cliff side	Usually begin walking around 3–4 weeks of age; use tactual cues from whiskers, but also rely on vision to hunt
Aquatic turtles	N/A	While most move to the shallow side, 24% crawl towards the cliff side	Live in water; less likely to experience danger from falling

Conclusion

Gibson & Walk concluded that:

1   both nature and nurture influence the development of depth perception
2   binocular cues such as motion parallax are innate, while monocular cues such as size constancy are learned
3   humans and other animals have developed some depth perception by the time of the onset of mobility, which is specifically suited to the habitat and behaviour of their species.

APPLICATION: DEVELOPING PERCEPTION IN YOUNG CHILDREN THROUGH PLAY STRATEGIES

Sensory and perceptual difficulties

In this topic we have considered the normal or typical development of perception. The development of perception in humans and animals is affected by exposure to different types and levels of stimulation, and the individual's capacity to process and make sense of sensory information. In some cases abnormal perception can be explained by sensory deprivation, such as the dark-reared kittens who lacked normal depth perception (Gibson & Walk, 1960).

However, some people with developmental disorders, such as attention deficit hyperactive disorder (ADHD) or autistic spectrum disorders (ASD), may struggle to receive, process and make sense of the information provided by the senses. These individual differences are often most pronounced in very young children who may not meet the normal developmental milestones for sensation and perception that we learned about at the start of this topic.

Not all children with autism or other developmental disorders have sensory processing difficulties. However, some people with autism, for example, are hyper-sensitive (over-sensitive) to stimuli such as bright lights, but hypo-sensitive (under-sensitive) to other stimuli such as heat or pressure. Psychologists and therapists working with these children design interventions at early ages, to help facilitate their perceptual development through play.

Sensory integrative therapy as play

Psychologists often describe the development of perception according to the function of and changes to individual senses. However, perception occurs in a multisensory environment. Sensory integrative therapy (SI therapy) is one strategy designed to help people cope with sensory and perceptual difficulties. This strategy emerged from the work of A. Jean Ayres (1920–1988), an educational psychologist and occupational therapist who studied children with learning disabilities. She rejected the ideas that sensory systems develop independently or that they process sensory inputs in isolation (Ayres, 1961). Her theory of sensory integration outlined how our senses are neurologically organised for use and allow us to move, learn and function well in our environment. When sensory integration is impeded, developmental delay, and emotional and behavioural problems can often result. Ayres was also an advocate of evidence-based practice, and recommended a **therapeutic intervention** that incorporated sensation to develop multisensory perception.

 **KEY IDEAS**

A '**psychological intervention**' or '**therapeutic intervention**' is any kind of activity designed to support change in an individual – for example, therapy, treatment or access to a service that will improve someone's quality of life. Interventions for those with ASD might be designed to reduce core impairments of social interaction or communication, or associated difficulties such as self-injurious behaviour.

Figure 2.21: SI therapy involves a programme of multisensory play activities

Ayres proposed that interventions such as SI therapy could develop improved learning, visual and auditory perception, and advanced motor skills by facilitating synthesis of sensory perception. The role of the SI therapist is to conduct an initial assessment of the child's sensory issues, using a number of standardised tests of sensory integration. The nature of sensory impairment in young children with ASD or ADHD means that they will have highly individual sensitivities and needs. The therapist then develops a personalised treatment programme that uses appropriate techniques and tools to meet those needs.

The SI programme will involve a combination of different elements. In young children, these techniques are designed to be fun and engaging. Although they involve using tools and methods to improve developmental outcomes (and therefore sound like hard work!) the child's experience is intended to be fun, relaxing and enjoyable. The key to SI therapy is 'intrinsic motivation' – that is, the children should love the activities and they are their own reward. Examples of play activities and how they involve the different senses include:

• using brushes on the skin (touch and hand-eye coordination)
• sitting or rolling on a bouncy ball (vision and balance)
• being squeezed between exercise pads or wearing a weighted vest (pressure and movement)
• dancing to different types of music (sound and movement).

Some of these techniques might be uncomfortable for a person with typical sensory and perceptual abilities, and may even sound claustrophobic! The intervention depends very much on the experience and skill level of the therapist, who matches the techniques to the needs of each child. It also relies on feedback from the child engaged in the play activities, which can sometimes be difficult to obtain if the child is very young or has communication difficulties. The effectiveness of SI therapy is also measured through behavioural outcomes such as improved tolerance for stimulation, attention-building, improvements in perceptual abilities or general functioning.

Effectiveness of SI therapy

There is some evidence of the effectiveness of SI therapy, though research in the area is limited. In a small-scale study, Fertel-Daly *et al.* (2001) found use of a weighted vest for children with developmental disorders resulted in increased attention to tasks and a decrease in self-injury behaviours. Fazlioğlu & Baran *et al.* (2008) found that SI therapy programmes positively affected children with ASD, as compared to a control group who did not participate.

Although SI therapy is very popular and used across many settings with young children, it remains controversial. One reason for this is that there are insufficient numbers of well-designed studies to allow a clear assessment of whether or not it works. A recent meta-analysis of 25 studies involving SI therapy found that only a few studies had clear positive results, and most used small, non-randomised samples (Lang *et al.*, 2012). However, this research itself has been criticised for including studies involving forms of sensory stimulation that do not meet the criteria for SI therapy in its true form.

Different sorts of multisensory interventions have proved so popular that they are commonly used in less formal ways, often by unqualified practitioners outside of an intervention context. Tools and techniques are therefore used without adequate consideration of the objectives of therapy and ignore the specific needs of the child. In addition, they may not encourage active engagement in play and may not be reviewed regularly as part of ongoing research, contrary to what Ayres and other SI therapy creators advised.

EVALUATION

Methodological and ethical issues

The protection of participants from harm is essential in modern psychological research. As such it is now quite challenging to gain consent for studies of newborns. Methods can be intrusive and invade the privacy of parents and infants. For example, Gibson & Walk (1960) created conditions that induced distress in babies who felt they could not safely reach their mothers.

There are also ethical issues around the use of animals for investigations into perception. Gibson & Walk (1960) and others have used different species for sensory deprivation or selective rearing experiments. This could potentially cause suffering to the animals or long-term harm if the effects of deprivation were irreversible.

It could be argued that experimenting with animals is the only way to obtain the knowledge, as it would be too unethical or impractical to carry out such tests on humans. However, as Gibson & Walk found, there are considerable differences in perceptual development between animals and humans, which may make the methods more difficult to justify.

Furthermore, examining the perceptual process involves inferring how meaning is made from raw stimulation of the senses. As such it requires researchers to make certain assumptions about what participants are thinking, or about reasons underlying their behaviour. This is more challenging in the study of infant and animal perception because of the absence of communication. However, researchers in this field have developed elegant and unique solutions designed to improve control and reliability.

Additionally, in the Gibson & Walk study, there is the risk of exposing the participants to non-verbal cues that can influence the infant's behaviour. For example, the tone of voice or facial expression of the mother as she beckoned her child to crawl over the cliff side might have varied from those put forward when beckoning them to shallow side. These subtle cues could create extraneous variables that could bias the findings.

Debates

Usefulness of research

Research from infant and animal studies has been useful in creating timelines for visual perception in order to track 'normal' development in newborns and infants. Findings from these studies help parents and professionals to identify abnormalities that may arise and interfere with perceptual development. This may be especially important either to help treat conditions with corrective aids such as glasses or hearing devices, or to develop compensatory strategies such as learning sign language or Braille.

Further research into the effectiveness of applications such as SI therapy is needed. Current evidence using pilot studies or small-scale reviews suggest that it can be effective in improving motor function and moderating sensory difficulties, however the evidence overall is mixed.

ACTIVITY ✳

Do you agree with using animals in psychology research? Hold a class debate over using animals in research to help investigate perceptual development. Consider issues such as ethics and the usefulness of research.

Nature vs nurture

Human infants are born fairly well equipped in terms of their functioning sensory system, which suggests a strong role for nature. Perception involves using these systems to make sense of information and act accordingly using environmental information. Most psychologists avoid adopting an extreme nature or nurture position on perception and agree that both are influential and affect one another. Animal studies involving selective rearing, such as Sugita (2004), have shown that although the sensory capability may be present, without the right environmental stimulation, abilities such as depth perception and colour perception cannot develop.

The study by Gibson & Walk (1960) has been interpreted by some as evidence that depth perception is innate. Because the participants were young it might be presumed that any depth discrimination must have been inborn. However, as we now know, visual perception changes rapidly after birth, so the development of a crawling 6 to 14 month old would certainly be influenced by their environmental experience. Even research with newborns may not fully control for the influence of environment, as babies in the womb have been shown to be capable of sensing some light and sound.

In practical terms, this debate is highly relevant to those implementing strategies to help the development of perception in young children. As we have seen, some individuals may experience a lack of sensory integration or specific sensory aversions. Strategies that involve play activities, such as SI therapy, intend to nurture improvements in these children's perception.

Free will vs determinism

It would be contentious to describe perception as a direct, objective account of our environment; although some theorists have suggested this. Our abilities to perceive the external world depend on many factors – on the stimuli we sense, but also on our existing knowledge and expectations. Some psychologists argue that these factors emerge from our culture and life experience, shaping and determining how we perceive the world.

One example of this is can be illustrated through optical illusions (Figure 2.22). In some cases, we may not be able to avoid perceiving an object in a certain way, or be able to stop our brain making us believe something exists that isn't really there. Our perceptual processes work to make sense of the world, to make images, sounds and textures meaningful, and they can't easily be switched off!

Reductionism and holism

As we have seen, most theories of perception attend to the multiple influences of nature and nurture. This avoids giving a reductionist explanation of how perceptual processes emerge. Many theorists and researchers in this area look to neuroanatomy, cognitive processes and environmental exposure. Even early researchers such as Gibson & Walk (1960) and Ayres (1961) were explicit in basing their understanding of perception on what was known about neurobiology at the time, and expected a fuller account to emerge with new discoveries about the brain.

SI therapy could be considered a holistic strategy, as it involves an assessment of the functioning of the whole person. The therapist considers the child's abilities and difficulties, and what they can, need and want to do in their environment in order to function well. The tools and techniques that are used in the intervention are chosen specifically for the individual and intend to improve overall function, rather than develop one aspect of perception.

Psychology as a science

Research into the development of perception in infants and animal studies tends to rely on laboratory-based procedures, and to use objective, scientific measurements of heart-rate, gross movement and eye-tracking. This meant that researchers such as Fantz (1963) were able to control the environment, testing variables such as typical or scrambled faces in different manipulations. This allowed him to confirm or disprove different hypotheses about infant perception.

Gibson & Walk's research was scientific in that in allowed a high degree of control over the variables. They explored and ruled out potential bias from issues such as light reflection to improve validity. Additionally, the set-up of the visual-cliff apparatus was precise, which meant it was reliable; other researchers can repeat their experiment and expect to obtain similar results. The animal participants were carefully controlled too, which meant variations in results between, for example, light- and dark-reared kittens were due to their environmental condition and nothing else.

Figure 2.22: What do you see? Ambiguous pictures are optical illusions that can be viewed in multiple meaningful ways

TOPIC 4
COGNITIVE DEVELOPMENT AND EDUCATION

BACKGROUND

The study of cognitive development

One of the most important aspects of child psychology is the study of how children come to think and perceive information in the same way as adults. For a long time it had been assumed that children simply knew *less* than adults. For example, Bandura (1977) argues this in his theory of social learning, which is based on the idea that knowledge and skills increase over time through a process of observation and imitation. Development is therefore seen as quantitative, as what is known by the child is simply added to as they grow older.

Swiss psychologist Jean Piaget (1896–1980) was one of the first to study cognitive development in a systematic, structured way. He developed a theory of cognitive development which proposed that children are born with basic mental structures upon which all other knowledge and skills were built. Piaget used a range of different methods to explore how children's thinking evolved and became more sophisticated over time, and developed a universal stage theory of cognitive development (see Figure 2.23). This approach considers that children's thinking undergoes a qualitative change, emphasising that children do not think about the world in the same way as adults do.

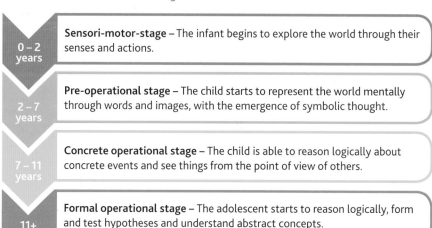

0–2 years	**Sensori-motor-stage** – The infant begins to explore the world through their senses and actions.
2–7 years	**Pre-operational stage** – The child starts to represent the world mentally through words and images, with the emergence of symbolic thought.
7–11 years	**Concrete operational stage** – The child is able to reason logically about concrete events and see things from the point of view of others.
11+ years	**Formal operational stage** – The adolescent starts to reason logically, form and test hypotheses and understand abstract concepts.

Figure 2.23: Piaget's stages of cognitive development

Piaget describes children's learning about the world as being based upon the creation and development of schemata. A 'schema' is a mental unit of knowledge about a particular aspect of the world, such as objects, events or sequences. For example, a young child may have acquired some knowledge and experience of dogs as a specific animal, which becomes grouped together in the child's

KEY IDEAS

Assimilation is the process by which new information and experience are incorporated into existing schema. For example, when a child sees a picture of a penguin for the first time they may call it a duck.

By contrast, **accommodation** happens when individuals encounter information that requires a reconstruction of existing mental structures, for instance when a child learns something that violates their pre-existing understanding. For example, when a child begins to notice differences in body size, colouring, habitat and behaviour between penguins and ducks, they have 'accommodated' the new animal and can refer to the two birds individually.

mind. If a child has a pet dog at home, they may come to believe that all dogs are friendly, have white fur and are called Max. However, our schemas become increasingly refined and detailed over the course of time, as a result of greater experience and cognitive maturity. Piaget calls the two processes contributing to the development of schemata **assimilation** and **accommodation**. Thus, an older child will have modified their schema of dogs in recognition of the fact that not all dogs are friendly, or white, or called Max.

Impact of cognitive development on education

Piaget's work has had radical implications for the field of education. Understanding that children develop cognitive abilities in a particular sequence means acknowledging that certain aspects of the world can only be understood at certain ages; that there are limits to what sort of problems a very young child can solve. This concept of 'readiness' has provided a useful framework for the school curriculum as it means the teaching of concepts can be organised around the developmental sequence. As an example, early science education should focus on teaching basic concepts such as features of the natural world, then move towards simple practical experimentation, and finally, with older children, towards abstract concepts such as the motion of waves or testing of hypotheses. Complete the activity in this section to see how Piaget's theory can be applied in educational settings (see *Activity*).

ACTIVITY ✳

Check your understanding of how Piaget's theory of cognitive development could be applied in education by completing the following exercise.

Identify which teacher is teaching which age group. How do you know?

A   Mr Lowry is teaching a class about fractions by using a pie he has cut into six pieces.

B   Miss Kahlo is teaching a class about a psychology study and has asked them to write their own hypotheses for a piece of research.

C   Mrs Murphy is encouraging her group to learn about texture through playing with materials such as dry cereal and cotton wool.

Although Piaget himself did not directly relate his theories to education, later researchers have drawn these links. Neo-Piagetian theorists such as Demetriou (1988) also place emphasis on the development of other cognitive abilities such as working memory, concentration span and information processing. As these abilities develop with age, teachers can approach more challenging concepts and advanced skills. Failure by teachers to recognise cognitive change or limitations can lead to frustrating classroom experiences where learners lack challenges or face tasks that are too far beyond their abilities.

Piaget has also influenced educational policy. One example of this was through the UK Government review of primary education, which led to the publication of the Plowden Report in 1967. The report emphasised individual learning, learning through play and discovery, and greater flexibility in the curriculum. The concept of discovery learning involves allowing children to actively learn through doing and exploring, rather than passively receiving tuition (Bruner, 1961). Benefits may include increased creativity, independence and ownership of learning. However, some critics of discovery learning suggest there is a lack of consistent evidence supporting its effectiveness in the classroom. There is some concern that, particularly for novice learners, pure discovery learning is unsuitable because learners may encounter problems in understanding that they cannot overcome independently.

The role of the other

So far we have examined theories of cognitive development that put the individual at the heart of the learning process. But what does this mean for the role of teachers and other learners? Lev Vygotsky was a contemporary of Piaget, but assumed a different stance to Piaget's universal stage theory of cognitive development. He argued for the centrality of language and social interaction in children's learning and development. Vygotsky suggests that infants are born with the basic cognitive abilities of memory, attention, sensation and perception, but require sociocultural interaction to develop higher mental abilities.

One of his key theoretical concepts is the *zone of proximal development* (ZPD). Vygotsky defines this as 'the distance between the actual developmental level as determined by independent problem solving and the level of potential development as determined through problem solving under adult guidance, or in collaboration with more capable peers' (Vygotsky, 1980, p.86). Thus he suggests that working with peers and adults are effective ways of developing more sophisticated and advanced skills.

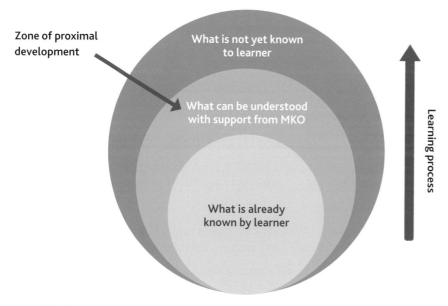

Figure 2.24: The zone of proximal development (ZPD)

Vygotsky advocated that teachers use paired or group activities to enable children to benefit from **more knowledgeable others (MKO)**, and develop the skills to achieve the task themselves. What we call 'collaborative learning' is based on Vygotsky's core belief that learning is a social process. Working with peers on paired or group activities allows us to question, evaluate and generate new ideas; the process or outcome becomes greater than the mere sum of its

KEY IDEAS

The **more knowledgeable other (MKO)** is a concept used to describe an individual who works alongside the learner to demonstrate ideas, strategies or behaviours that the learner can observe and internalise. MKOs include parents, teachers or tutors and older siblings, but also same-age peers or even technology, such as online tutors.

KEY IDEAS

Tutoring is a specific, small-scale educational interaction. One person assumes the role of expert or adult, who then teaches a particular skill or aspect of knowledge to a second person who is less adult or less expert.

parts. Collaboration can be as simple as a five minute discussion of a story in pairs, or as complex as a lengthy project where students work in a team to design, conduct and analyse a piece of research. There is a large body of fairly consistent evidence supporting the effectiveness of group work in educational settings. For example, Anderson *et al.* (1998) found that after engaging in group discussion of text, students showed substantial improvements in critical thinking and reasoning. The success of cooperative learning strategies are so great that they are now employed across the world in every subject area throughout preschool to university and even in adult training courses (Johnson & Johnson, 2009).

The ZPD is closely related to the concept of 'scaffolding', later introduced by Wood *et al.* (1976) in the key research for this topic. Scaffolding describes a method of instruction wherein the MKO (e.g. a tutor) will support the learner by structuring a task to make it achievable, given the learner's current ability. In contrast to Piaget and neo-Piagetian thinkers, Vygotsky believed the curriculum should lead the learner, not the other way around. The support provided by the MKO should be tailored to the individual learner, and as the learner becomes more skilled, the MKO will gradually reduce the level and type of support offered. We will now consider the study by Wood, Bruner & Ross (1976), which elaborates on the use of scaffolding with young children.

ACTIVITY ✳

It's important to understand how the role of the MKO can change over time, depending on learner need. Imagine that you have to teach someone to evaluate a piece of psychological research who has never done it before. Write out the steps you might use to scaffold their learning as you gradually reduce the amount of support offered.

KEY RESEARCH

Wood, D., Bruner, J.S. & Ross, G. (1976) The role of tutoring in problem-solving. *Journal of Child Psychology and Psychiatry*, 17 (2), 89–100.

Aim

This study intended to explore the process of tutoring. Researchers were interested in describing the instructional relationships between adult tutors and children in the context of skill acquisition and problem solving.

Method
Sample

The volunteer sample consisted of 30 children from the same region in the USA, from middle- or lower-middle-class families. The group included an even number of boys and girls, and included equal numbers of 3, 4 and 5 year olds.

Design and procedure

The participants were accompanied by their parents and tutored in individual sessions lasting between 20 minutes and one hour. A tutor was given the task of teaching children aged 3, 4 or 5 years to build a three-dimensional structure requiring a degree of skill that was beyond them. The tutor was required to instruct verbally but to let the children be as independent as possible in carrying out the task.

For the task, the children sat before 21 blocks of various shapes and sizes spread out in a jumble (p.92). Initially they were invited to play with the blocks for 5 minutes in order to get used to them. Then the tutor would usually take two of the smallest blocks and demonstrate how they could be connected, or if the child connected a pair themselves during free play, tell the child to 'make some more like that'. The tutor then recognised and responded to one of three responses of the child:

1   The child ignored her and continued to play with connecting blocks.
2   The child took the blocks they had just connected and manipulated them.
3   The child took new blocks and attempted to make something similar to what had already been made.

Assembly operations were divided into two categories: 'assisted', in which the tutor either presented or indicated the correct materials for assembly, and 'unassisted', where the child selected the materials. The experimenters noted when the constructed object did not meet required constraints (and were mismatched), whether the child rejected them or laid them down as assembled. If the child took them apart this was also noted. Interventions of the tutor were noted in one of three categories: 'direct assistance', a 'verbal error prompt' (e.g. 'does this [the mismatched construct] look like this [the matched construct]?') and thirdly, a straightforward prompt for the child to attempt more constructs (e.g. 'can you make more like this?').

Results

The median total number of 'acts' (putting blocks together, or taking a previously built construct apart) for each of the three age groups can be seen in Table 2.7.

Figure 2.25: Young children used inter-connecting blocks of different shapes and sizes under the guidance of a tutor to make constructs

MATHS MOMENT

1   Table 2.7 shows the median number of acts produced in each age group. Explain why this is the most appropriate measure of average.
2   The difference in the median number of acts between children aged 4 and 5 is described in the study as not significant. What does the term 'significance' mean in terms of statistical testing?

TABLE 2.7: NUMBER OF 'ACTS' AND PERCENTAGE OF UNASSISTED CONSTRUCTS BY AGE GROUP		
Participant age	**Median number of acts**	**% of acts that were unassisted constructs**
3	39	10
4	41	50
5	32	75

The older children selected two matching blocks without the need for previous trial and error more often than the younger ones did. The 3-year-old children took apart almost as many correct constructs as they put together. However, two-thirds of the time they also reconstructed without instruction to do so. This group was as likely as the 4-year-olds to reassemble correct constructs and not incorrect ones, showing that they were as able to recognise correct outcomes.

ACTIVITY ✳

Match up each of Wood *et al.*'s findings to aspects of Piaget's theory of cognitive development:

Finding	Theory link
• Older children showed less 'trial and error' than younger children	• Sensori-motor stage: Children in this stage explore the world through their senses and physical movement
• Younger children took apart around as many blocks as they put together	• Discovery learning: Children learn best through actively doing
• All children were physically engaged with matching the blocks, rather than simply following tutor instruction	• Pre-operational stage: Children in this stage form mental representations of the world around them

The greatest difference is seen in the interactions between tutor and different age groups. Three year olds paid little attention to verbal instruction. On average (median) the 3-year-olds rejected tutor instruction on 11 occasions compared to virtually none by the other children, who accepted assistance. Tutor interventions reduced by half between the 3- and 4-year-olds, and another half between 4- and 5-year-olds.

The differing roles of the tutor included:

- 3-year-olds – attracting them to the task through demonstration and providing tempting material
- 4-year-olds – a verbal prodder and corrector (reminding them of task requirements and correcting efforts as they seek to carry on)
- 5-year-olds – a confirmer and checker of constructions (as the children more firmly have in their minds the nature of the task)

Wood *et al.* also suggest that the tutor needs to consider the theory of how the task can be completed *and* the abilities of the child in order to give appropriate feedback.

The experimenters outline the following process of 'scaffolding' in relation to a theory of instruction:

1 *Recruitment* – get the learner interested in the task and its requirements.
2 *Reduction in degrees of freedom* – simplify the task, reducing the number of steps needed for completion.
3 *Direction maintenance* – keep the learner on task in spite the distractions; incentivise.
4 *Marking critical features* – mark out relevant features of the task, help identify the difference between what the learner has already achieved and the correct outcome; i.e. scaffolding.
5 *Frustration control* – employ strategies to make problem solving less stressful.
6 *Demonstration* – model the correct outcome or 'idealise' the act to be performed.

Conclusions

Wood *et al.* drew three main conclusions from this study:

1   Increasing age meant a greater likelihood of task success, and an improvement in the achievement of the more complex aspects of the task.
2   Although younger children might not be able to complete tasks as well as older children, they are often equally able to recognise when a task has been correctly achieved.
3   The level and type of support needed by children differed across age groups in line with the tutor's changing support with increased ability, as an example of scaffolding.

APPLICATION: IMPROVING LEARNING AND REVISION

Our knowledge of how the mind processes information can be applied in education to improve revision and learning through cognitive strategies. Cognitive strategies include any mental techniques for enhancing processes such as memory, concentration or problem-solving. Strategies are different from skills, because they require us to make conscious decisions and choices about the most appropriate and effective ways of achieving a particular goal. One example of such a strategy is known as 'mnemonics'.

What is a mnemonic?

A mnemonic is the term given to a technique for aiding the memory, typically when the information we need to recall is large in amount or quite unfamiliar. Mnemonics often rely on familiar information that we can easily recall to make memorising the new concepts much easier. Different **levels of processing** are involved in each mnemonic strategy, which means recall may be better using some types than others. Mnemonics can be thought of as cognitive 'shortcuts'; here we will consider visual and auditory mnemonics (involving structural and phonemic processing) and contrast them with non-mnemonic methods (involving semantic processing).

Structural processing – visual mnemonics

Mnemonics that rely on structural processing are usually quick and easy to learn, although they usually represent quite superficial learning. One of the oldest mnemonic devices dating back to Ancient Greece is known as the 'method of loci'. It involves visualising a place that you are familiar with, e.g. your home, workplace or a journey you take regularly. Each object or feature in this space then acts as pieces of the information you need to memorise. It may help to go in order to ensure all aspects of the information are recalled each time. By identifying a list of concepts you need to memorise and associating each with the location, you should be able to recall the linked information more easily.

Acronyms are probably the most well known mnemonics. An acronym takes the first letter of each word contained in a phrase or set of information to form a new word. For example, the word 'scuba' is actually an acronym for 'Self-Contained Underwater Breathing Apparatus'. Alternatively, when a string of words needs to be remembered, particularly in order, a common technique is to replace the words with ones that can be used in a simple, coherent sentence.

 **KEY IDEAS**

Levels of processing is a concept developed by Craik & Lockhart (1972). Processing takes place on a continuum of shallow to deep, where memory recall acts as a product of the depth of processing. In other words, if little effort is required to 'learn' the information, it may be too superficial to be recalled at a later time. On the other hand, meaningful learning (which usually requires lots of effort!) is more deeply encoded and can be better recalled in detail.

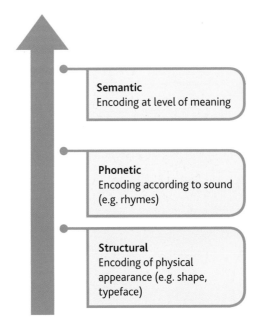

Semantic
Encoding at level of meaning

Phonetic
Encoding according to sound (e.g. rhymes)

Structural
Encoding of physical appearance (e.g. shape, typeface)

Figure 2.26: Levels of processing (Craik & Lockhart, 1972)

Figure 2.27: The order of the colours of the rainbow can be more easily remembered through the use of a mnemonic device

A well-known example of this might be the colours of the rainbow in sequential order (red, orange, yellow, green, blue, indigo, violet) are more easily remembered through the phrase 'Richard of York gave battle in vain'.

Phonemic processing – auditory mnemonics

Rhymes are also good mnemonic devices and may be even easier to recall than acronyms because of they involve deeper encoding. A rhyme is a simple poem that contains similar sounds at the end of each line. For example we use rhymes as children learning correct spelling such as:

> 'I before E,
>
> except after C'

Whilst devising and rehearsing rhymes do involve deeper forms of processing than structural strategies, they are still thought to be less effective at producing good recall than semantic processing.

Are mnemonics effective?

There is some evidence supporting the effectiveness of mnemonic devices as cognitive strategies for improving revision. Some mnemonics help us to condense information into 'chunks'. The capacity of our working memory capacity is quite limited, with most adults typically able to retain approximately seven items in their short term memory (Miller, 1956). Mnemonic devices such as acronyms, for example, maximise the short-term memory capacity by condensing a number of terms, items or concepts into a single word.

However, as we have discussed, most mnemonics rely primarily on shallow forms of processing. By contrast, 'semantic processing' involves more elaborate rehearsal of information, leading to deeper encoding and better recall. Semantic processing can involves techniques such as writing practice essays, explaining topics out loud to another person or creating detailed mind maps. In other words, lots more effort! However, understanding that processing occurs on a continuum means that we can create 'elaborate' mnemonics to deepen learning and improve recall.

One example of this is through linking the new information to existing knowledge already stored in our long-term memory. The method of loci technique can help create meaningful associations that might also improve recall. In a study of university students, Roediger (1980) found that participants instructed to use the method of loci technique performed better on a recall task than the control group, or those who were instructed to use simpler visualisation techniques based on structural processing.

Nonetheless, the use of mnemonic devices may be quite limited, depending on the type of information one is trying to learn or revise. It might be easier for us to create rhymes to remember elements of the periodic table in chemistry than to recall textual analysis of a Shakespearean play for instance. Similarly, some techniques require imagination in order to make meaningful associations or create rhymes or poems, which can be a challenge! Like all cognitive strategies, the effectiveness of these techniques relies on how skilled the individual is at choosing a suitable mnemonic for the information they are trying to learn.

EVALUATION

Methodological and ethical issues

There are many practical issues when conducting research with young children, particularly when attempting to study mental processes. As we learned at the start of this topic, children reason in quite different ways from adults, which can make briefing them about the aims of a task or collecting data difficult. Piaget developed a specific method for researching cognitive tasks, known as the 'clinical interview'; this relied on basing questions on the previous responses of the children. In other research, such as Wood *et al.* (1976), the tutor was also flexible and responsive to the child participant's behaviour. These approaches, though necessary for capturing the thinking and learning process, lower the reliability of the research and create data that can be difficult to compare.

As with much cognitive psychology, there are additional challenges around gaining insight into unseen mental processes. Researchers such as Roediger (1980) assessed the effectiveness of mnemonic techniques through comparing a specified strategy such as method of loci with a control group who were not given a specific method of memorisation. How can we be certain of which method participants in either condition used, given that it is an invisible process? This raises issues around the validity of the conclusions we can draw about the effectiveness of cognitive strategies.

As discussed at the start of this chapter, addressing ethical issues is especially important when conducting research with children and young people. However, as with many early psychological studies with children, researchers such as Piaget, Vygotsky and Wood *et al.* were less concerned with explicitly stating how consent was obtained or what measures were in place to protect participants' well-being. However, we might infer from the nature of the tasks described in the research that it is unlikely that any children experienced any significant physical or emotional distress.

STRETCH & CHALLENGE

You could be asked to consider in what ways theory or research into cognitive development and education is socially sensitive. Ensure you can explain what is meant by this term. Why do you think a concept such as Piaget's stage theory could be considered socially sensitive?

QUESTION SPOTLIGHT!

Piaget's theory of cognitive development is based on his clinical interviews with his own children, and other samples of Swiss children. He was cautious not to suggest that his findings could be applied to all children.

Can you think of why this might be, and what issues might be posed by using this restricted sample?

ACTIVITY

Locate the British Psychological Society's 'Code of Human Research Ethics' here:

www.bps.org.uk/sites/default/files/documents/code_of_ human_research_ethics.pdf

Search the document for guidelines about working with children. How would researchers interested in cognitive development go about obtaining children's consent to participate in an ethical manner?

Debates

Nature vs nurture

This debate is highly relevant to the study of cognitive development, because it is primarily concerned with questions about whether children's mental processes are determined by their innate qualities or by external environmental influences. One argument for suggesting that such development is innate comes from Piaget's cognitive stage theory. He argues that the ages at which children achieve certain cognitive abilities are fixed and universal. Piaget's process of discovery learning, however, relies on suitable conditions in the environment; an important aspect of nurture. By contrast, Vygotsky argues for the importance of sociocultural factors and the influence of language. These nurturing influences offer children 'tools' that are specific to the environments in which they are raised. He does not deny that some mental processes are innate, but suggests that without the guidance of MKOs children cannot develop higher cognitive abilities.

Evidence from studies such as Wood *et al.* (1976) suggests that collaborative learning processes such as scaffolding rely on both nature and nurture. Tutors in the study interacted in a range of ways, depending on the age and ability of the child. The results of the study show children's construction abilities improved with age, which suggested an innate element to cognitive development.

Free will vs determinism

In this topic, this debate is linked to the nature vs nurture debate, as Piagetians would argue that children are pre-determined to develop new cognitive abilities at fixed ages, along the lines of the theory of universal stages. However, the opportunities discovery learning presents allow freedom for all kinds of learning to occur. Those child psychologists who recognise the significance of sociocultural influences could also be considered deterministic, as the cognitive development of individual children depends on the learning of language and appropriate instruction by the MKO.

It is important to emphasise that children are not simply products being constructed in a factory of education; there are many other variables that can influence their cognitive development. As the study by Wood *et al.* (1976) shows, the interactions between tutors and children are individualised and moderated by other factors within the child's control. These might include their choice of behaviour on the day, for example, how cooperative they were being, how shy they were feeling, or even how polite they were to the tutor.

QUESTION SPOTLIGHT!

1   How might cognitive strategies such as use of mnemonics be influenced by our natural preferences?
2   To what extent do you think a student has control over his or her exam result? (Consider how revision strategies outlined in this chapter could influence this.)

Psychology as a science

Methods used to assess cognitive development in children such as observation and clinical interviews may be considered somewhat unscientific because they are open to biased interpretation. For example, Piaget conducted his observations alone, so the data may reflect a subjective interpretation. Other researchers, such as Wood *et al.* (1976), use multiple observers and coders to classify data, which reduces the risk of bias and make the method more scientific.

However, in some ways Wood *et al.*'s study can be described as unscientific. It does not seek to establish cause and effect but instead describes the nature of the interaction between child and tutor. The researchers do collect some quantitative data, however, which allows them to reasonably assert a relationship between age and cognitive ability. The main findings of the study, however, are qualitative and reflect the observers' interpretations of a unique social interaction.

Figure 2.28 The nature of one-to-one methods of instruction such as tutoring means each interaction is unique

Usefulness of research

It is difficult to overstate the impact that theories of cognitive development have had on the evolution of the education system. Although Piaget did not explicitly make recommendations for methods of formal education, his theories have nevertheless influenced teaching practices worldwide, encouraging teachers to engage children actively in their own learning. By introducing the idea that children think differently to adults he created a focus on the process of thinking, not just on the outcome. These theories also influenced the Plowden Report (1967) which overhauled the existing English primary education system and had the express intention of placing the child at the centre of the educational process.

'Scaffolding', as introduced by Wood *et al.* (1967), has also been influential in education. It is still widely used in many forms that you would recognise: 'contingent scaffolding' takes place when a teacher sets an activity, then travels around the room to different students asking questions, providing encouragement or corrections – all tailored to the individual's level of need. More recently, scaffolding can be seen as influential in the realm of online or virtual learning environments (VLEs), where interactive learning is supported via blogs, wikis, instant messaging and live chats.

DEVELOPMENT OF ATTACHMENT

BACKGROUND

This topic will lead us to consider what psychologists mean by the term 'attachment'; how it develops in humans and how early attachment experiences can affect us in later life. Attachment refers to the enduring emotional bond that exists between two people. Psychologists studying attachment note that attachments have the following essential qualities:

- proximity-seeking (wanting to be close to the other person)
- separation anxiety or protest (displeasure or distress at leaving this person)
- happiness at reunion (experiencing pleasure at being close to the other person again).

While we form numerous attachments throughout our lives, our first is generally considered to be the most important. Child psychologists have sought to understand the nature of infants' relationships to their attachment figure, to identify different styles of attachment, and to consider the purpose and consequences of attachment. You will notice that in earlier research the attachment figure studied is usually the mother, as she was almost always the primary carer.

Attachment in humans

John Bowlby (1907–1990) was an English psychoanalyst whose ideas about infant attachment are still widely accepted today. Like many psychoanalysts he was concerned with how early experience shapes our mental health. He was also influenced by ethology, which is the scientific study of animal behaviour. Bowlby looked to apply some of its principles to human behaviour, including the concept of 'imprinting'. Imprinting occurs during a **critical period**, and is when the animal 'imprints' or learns to recognise the characteristics of its parent. This was famously observed by Lorenz (1935) (see Figure 2.29) in geese, who imprint the first suitable stimulus they see shortly after hatching, whether or not it has feathers!

As attachment behaviours such as imprinting can be observed in other species, Bowlby (1957) came to believe that they serve an evolutionary purpose. In prehistoric times, the world would have been much more dangerous for human infants, who are heavily reliant on their caregivers for their basic needs. Those babies who formed attachments with carers and maintained proximity lowered the risk of being eaten by predators and encountering other dangers. This is an example of adaptive behaviour, whereby humans and other animals become more suited to survival in their environments.

Bowlby proposed that human infants possess adaptive mechanisms for eliciting parental responses. What good is it to be well-bonded to a carer if they

 **KEY IDEAS**

The **critical period** is the term used in developmental psychology and biology referring to an important stage in the life of a human or animal that is important for its later function. During this time it may, for example, acquire language or form an emotional bond. If this process does not occur within the critical period, it may later be difficult or even impossible for the change to occur. The idea of a critical period has been revised in child psychology and is now often referred to as the 'sensitive' period. This reflects the evidence that even when the window for change is missed, under the right circumstances children can still develop the missing capacities and skills later in their lives.

Figure 2.29: Feathered friends: Konrad Lorenz demonstrated that imprinting can occur between geese and humans within the 'critical period'

are not responsive to your needs? He suggested that there are several innate behaviours that are key to shaping and controlling parenting responses. These are known as 'social releasers', and each is an example of adaptive function (see Table 2.8).

TABLE 2.8: EXAMPLES OF SOCIAL RELEASERS

Infant behaviour	Description	Parenting response
Smiling 	At five weeks babies begin smiling at visual stimuli; quickly this is refined to smiling more often at recognisable, familiar faces	Elicits attention, smiling and interaction; strengthens the attachment bond
Crying 	Infant cries are distressing and difficult to ignore; babies cry when they are hungry, cold, frightened or in pain and require adult intervention	Parent learns through negative reinforcement to pick up the child to alleviate crying; elicits response to meet specific need or to encourage proximity
Sucking 	Required in order to obtain milk, however non-nutritive sucking (such as sucking a dummy) is common and has been shown to pacify or alleviate a baby's distress	Baby is offered breast milk, bottle or object to suck, requiring proximity from caregiver

Individual differences in attachment

Mary Ainsworth worked alongside Bowlby in London at the Tavistock Clinic, investigating the effects of maternal deprivation on infants. Later, she and her colleagues developed a method for assessing the nature and quality of attachment between infants aged 12–24 months and their caregivers. They developed a procedure known as the 'Strange Situation' – an important tool used across the world to investigate how attachments vary between different individuals. This is outlined in greater detail in the key research section for this topic (see page 104). By using the Strange Situation procedure, Ainsworth and others developed a system for classifying different attachment types, as outlined in Table 2.9.

TABLE 2.9: AINSWORTH *ET AL.* (1978) ATTACHMENT TYPES		
Attachment type	**Name**	**Behaviour in the Strange Situation test**
Type A	Insecure-anxious/avoidant	• baby avoids proximity to mother at reunion • baby not distressed by mother's absence
Type B	Secure	• baby actively seeks and maintains maternal proximity • baby may show distress at mother's absence
Type C	Insecure-ambivalent/resistant	• baby simultaneously seeks and resists maternal contact
Type D*	Insecure-disorganised	• no one clear pattern of behaviour • inconsistent/bizarre responses to maternal separation and reunion

*introduced by Main & Soloman (1990)

Figure 2.30: Unbearable? Crying is one of the most powerful weapons a baby has to attract adult attention because it is so loud and distressing

Ainsworth argued that infants with mothers who showed high levels of responsiveness and who were sensitive and accessible to their infants in the first year of life were likely to develop Type B secure attachments. Conversely, infants who had experienced abuse or whose mothers had experienced mental health problems might develop insecure, confused attachments, such as Type D. We will now consider how individual attachments develop and what they mean for a child's development.

Difficulty forming attachments

One of Bowlby's main contributions to this field of study was his concept of an internal working model for attachment (Bowlby, 1969). Internal working models are essentially organised representations of experience that provide a framework for understanding the self and guiding new behaviour (Collins *et al.*, 1996). Bowlby describes the model as a 'working' one because it is dynamic and subject to change.

He suggested that children form a mental representation of their first attachment relationship, which then forms a model for later relationships, including attachments to their own children. According to the theory, children who form kind, loving bonds with their primary attachment figure will internalise the relationship as a model for future attachments. Likewise, Bowlby claims that children who have been abused or neglected will be more likely to go on to reproduce those patterns of behaviour.

The idea of an internal working model of attachment is an aspect of Bowlby's work that is hotly contested. There is good evidence to suggest that attachment types may be transmitted across generations, however it is too simplistic to suggest that a good upbringing will result in being a great parent, or that suffering abuse as a child will perpetuate a cycle of abuse. One reason for this is that the attachment style that a child has with one parent is not a reliable indicator of the attachment style he or she has with the other parent (Fox *et al.*, 1991). Furthermore, Bretherton *et al.* (1989) suggest it may be likely that individuals can maintain several internal working models that may help them to make sense of their different social roles (son or daughter, friend, sibling, spouse or parent).

STRETCH & CHALLENGE

You can read more about Bowlby's research into the effects of maternal deprivation by searching online or in books concerned with child psychology. Look out for his 1944 work on early maternal deprivation and psychopathy, known as the '44 Juvenile Thieves' study.

But what happens if children fail to form an attachment at all during their early years? This was one of Bowlby's first concerns, which he addressed in developing his maternal deprivation hypothesis (1951). He noted two potential outcomes arising from a failure to form a close bond with a primary carer within the first 18 months to 2 years (see Key Idea on the critical or sensitive period, page 101):

- Affectionless psychopathy: the inability to feel empathy, guilt or affection towards others. This has a profound affect on the ability to develop and maintain relationships with others. Bowlby also found evidence to suggest that affectionless psychopathy is associated with criminality (see Stretch & Challenge).
- Developmental retardation: Bowlby linked the critical period for the development of attachment with a period of cognitive development. Without the presence of an attachment figure, intellect could be 'retarded', i.e. delayed.

Later in his work, Bowlby acknowledged that he may have overstated the consequences of maternal deprivation. Current research suggests that children are more resilient to adverse early experiences than was previously realised. Rutter (1981) makes the important distinction between deprivation (separation from attachment figure after attachment has been formed) and privation (total lack of attachment bond). Evidence from case studies such as 'Genie' (Curtiss, 1977) and others indicates that extreme emotional and cognitive impairment is associated with privation rather than deprivation.

Furthermore, in instances where children have failed to form attachments within the critical or sensitive period, they can still achieve normal developmental outcomes. Rutter (1981) studied children from Romanian orphanages who were subsequently adopted by families. He found that the majority of adoptees formed attachments to their new caregivers and had no lasting developmental problems.

We will now look more closely at Ainsworth & Bell's (1970) investigation into quantifying mother–infant interactions, and the implication of this for promoting attachment-friendly environments.

KEY RESEARCH

Ainsworth, M.D.S. & Bell, S. (1970) Attachment, Exploration and Separation: Illustrated by the Behavior of One-year-olds in a Strange Situation. *Child Development*, 41 (1), 49–67.

Aim

To investigate the interaction between infant attachment behaviour, response to unfamiliar situations, and separation from and reunion with the maternal attachment figure.

Method

Sample

The participants in this study were 56 one-year-old babies and their mothers from white, middle-class family backgrounds. Families were contacted for participation via their paediatricians from private practices. Of this sample, 23 had been observed longitudinally from birth onwards and were observed in the Strange Situation at 51 weeks old. The 33 remaining babies were observed when 49 weeks old.

Design and procedure

The study was a controlled observation. It used a standard procedure which the researchers called the Strange Situation. This involved eight separate episodes, followed in the same order by all participants.

It was designed to encourage explorations of the new environment, while remaining not so strange as to frighten the babies. For example, the stranger used in the study was required to approach gradually, avoiding abrupt or alarming behaviour – this sort of approach would normally scare an adult! In addition, episodes were ordered so that the least 'disturbing' would occur first. Ainsworth & Bell wanted to avoid heightened attachment behaviour, and observe more typical reactions.

The observation took place in a room which was arranged to contain 2.75m × 2.75m cleared floor space, divided into 16 squares to allow for accurate recording of location and movement. One end of the room contained a child's chair surrounded by toys. At the other end was a chair for the child's mother and near the door (arranged to form a triangle) was a chair for the stranger.

The baby was placed at equal distance between the chairs at the base of the triangle and allowed to move about freely. The mother and stranger were instructed beforehand as to their roles.

Eight episodes of the Strange Situation:

1. Mother (M) carried the baby (B) into the room.
2. M put B down in the specified place, and then sat quietly in her chair, participating only if B sought her attention. (Three minutes.)
3. A stranger (S) entered, sat quietly for one minute, conversed with M for one minute, and then gradually approached B, showing him a toy. At the end of the third minute M left the room unobtrusively.
4. If B was happily engaged in play, S was non-participant. If he was inactive, she tried to interest him in the toys. If he was distressed, she tried to distract him or to comfort him. If he could not be comforted, the episode was cut short; otherwise it lasted three minutes.
5. M entered, paused in the doorway to give B an opportunity to spontaneously move towards her. S then left unobtrusively. After B was again settled in play M left again, after pausing to say 'bye-bye'.
6. The baby was left alone for three minutes, unless he was so distressed that the episode had to be cut short.
7. S entered and behaved as in episode 4 for three minutes, unless distress required the episode to be cut short.
8. M returned, S left, and after the reunion had been observed, the procedure ended.

QUESTION SPOTLIGHT!

This study uses an opportunity sampling technique. Looking at the sort of participants who took part, could you explain how it might be biased?

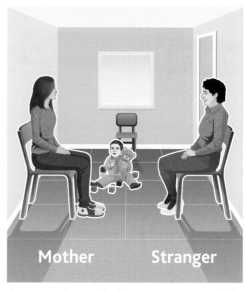

Figure 2.31: The standard room arrangement of the Strange Situation

DO IT YOURSELF

It can be tricky to remember each of the eight episodes of the Strange Situation when you are reading about it for the first time. Work in a small group to act out the procedure outlined above, taking on the roles of mother, baby, observer and stranger. It might help to nominate one group member to coordinate and time the rest of the group.

WEB WATCH @

You can watch a video showing the Strange Situation procedure here:

https://www.youtube.com/watch?v=s608077NtNI

STRETCH & CHALLENGE

One way which researchers in this study collected data was via time sampling. What are the advantages and disadvantages of this method? They also used an intensity scale to rate the infant's behaviours. Why do you think they wanted to transform the qualitative observations into a numerical score?

In an adjoining room, two observers described the behaviour as they observed it, speaking into a tape recorder. This recorder also picked up a timer click at 15 second intervals. The recordings were then transcribed and coded. In four cases, an additional coding was made which showed a very high rate of reliability. Two quantitative measurements were taken from the narratives:

1   A frequency measure of three types of exploration: locomotor (bodily movement), manipulatory (touching and moving things with hands), and visual (looking and examining), as well as crying. For each 15-second interval in which the behaviour occurred, a score of 1 was given.

2   The infant's behaviour towards their mother or the stranger, coded on 7-point scales of intensity for:
    −   *proximity- and contact-seeking behaviours*: e.g. approaching and clambering up, reaching or leaning
    −   *contact-maintaining behaviours*: e.g. clinging, holding on, resisting release or protesting once contact is lost
    −   *proximity- and interaction-avoiding behaviours*: e.g. ignoring the adult by looking, turning or moving away
    −   *contact- and interaction-resisting behaviour*: e.g. angry, ambivalent attempts to push away the adult seeking to make contact, squirming to get down once picked up, throwing or pushing away toys when offered
    −   *search behaviour*: e.g. following the mother to the door, trying to open or banging on the door, remaining looking towards the door.

The first four interactions were scored with the mother during episodes 2, 3, 5 and 8, and with the stranger during episodes 3, 4 and 7. The fifth, 'search behaviour' was scored for separation episodes 4, 6 and 7. Intensity ratings considered the frequency, strength and duration of each behaviour. Across 14 randomly selected cases the two scorers again showed very high levels of inter-rater reliability.

Results

Exploratory behaviour

Overall, the amount of exploratory behaviour decreased when the stranger entered the room in episode 3, and remained low during episode 4 after the mother left. During episode 5 visual and manipulatory play increased as the mother attempted to interest the baby in play. When this was attempted by the stranger in episodes 4 and 7 there was no such increase.

Crying

There was no significant increase in crying during episode 3, which suggested that babies did not find the stranger alarming in the presence of their mother. During episode 4 the mother left and crying increased and then declined again on her return at episode 5. There was an increase at episode 6 when the baby was left alone. The stranger returned at episode 7 and there was no significant decrease, which suggested that crying was caused by the mother leaving, rather than the baby being alone.

Search behaviour during separation

Search behaviour peaked during episode 6 when the baby was left alone: 37% of babies cried minimally during episode 6 but searched strongly; 20% cried to a much greater extent but searched only a little; 32% cried and searched.

Proximity-seeking and contact-maintaining behaviours

Contact-maintaining behaviour increased during episodes 5 and 8, which were the times at which the mother returned to the room. Overall, proximity-seeking and contact-maintaining behaviours were less frequent and less strong towards the stranger. A few babies sought contact with the stranger, though much less than they did with their mother. In cases where the stranger picked up a baby to offer comfort, some babies did cling and resisted being put down.

Contact-resisting and proximity-avoiding behaviours

Contacting-resisting behaviours were observed in around one-third of babies in relation to the mother during her first return, and in around half at her second return. Nearly all babies who scored highly in contact-resisting behaviour also scored highly in contact-maintaining behaviour. This behaviour represents ambivalence towards the mother: wanting to be held but at the same time becoming irritated and resisting contact.

There was little proximity-avoiding behaviour during the first episodes, as mothers were instructed not to seek interaction. However, it occurred in approximately 50% of babies during each of the reunion episodes. During episode 3 approximately one-third of babies avoided the stranger, which declined at episode 4 and again during episode 7. Around 50% of babies did not avoid either the mother or the stranger.

Conclusion

In this study, Ainsworth & Bell showed that in unfamiliar situations, avoidance or approach behaviour is influenced by proximity of the mother. They concluded that:

1 in threatening situations, attachment behaviour increases.
2 the attachment figure is used as a secure base for exploration by the infant.
3 there are observable differences in attachment styles; attachment can look different between different pairs.

APPLICATION: DEVELOPING AN ATTACHMENT-FRIENDLY ENVIRONMENT

Maternal deprivation

Earlier we considered some of the theoretical concepts that John Bowlby introduced to the study of infant attachment. In 1951, he submitted a report to the World Health Organisation (WHO) as part of an international programme concerned with the welfare of homeless children. The WHO report contained data that Bowlby had collected on the effect of maternal deprivation on homeless and disturbed children from across Europe and the USA. His research found negative outcomes for children across a range of contexts associated with infant–mother separations.

Bowlby was well aware of the importance of proximity and stability in forming secure attachments. Children were often being removed from family homes and sent to live with foster families or in group homes, because they were born to unmarried mothers, or lived in impoverished and overcrowded homes. He argued that in most cases (with the exception of abuse and neglect), offering aid in the

Figure 2.32: Hospital visits for parents and relatives of sick children used to be heavily restricted

WEB WATCH @

Joyce Robertson was a writer and researcher who worked alongside her husband James to study the effects of separation on young children, particularly in hospitals. You can read more about the life, work and films of James Robertson and his wife Joyce Robertson on this website:

www.robertsonfilms.info

form of financial assistance and support from social services to these families was far preferable to separation.

Children's experiences of hospitalisation

As well as obvious implications for social work and adoption policy, the WHO report and related research also changed hospital practices across the world. During the 1950s, children's experiences of hospitals were far different from what we expect today. Visits from parents were actively discouraged, and minimal visiting hours were enforced – in some cases limited to just one hour a week.

Bowlby collaborated with a social worker named James Robertson to study the effects of hospitalisation and parental separation on young children and babies. They found that the hospitalised children suffered emotional damage from their experiences. Their findings were supported in a documentary film created by Robertson entitled '*A Two-Year-Old Goes to Hospital*' (Robertson, 1952), which illuminates the suffering of a young girl's experiences in hospital.

Subsequently, the British government commissioned the Platt Report (Platt, 1959) into the welfare of children in hospital. The resulting recommendations were that visiting be unrestricted, that mothers should be permitted to stay in hospital with their child, and that medical and nursing staff be trained to better understand the emotional needs of children.

Attachment and Family-Centred Care

Modern hospital policies have changed dramatically since the work by Bowlby (1951) and Robertson (1952). This is partly in recognition of the fact that a patient's well-being involves more than just physical aspects; the child still has emotional and social needs that are best met by their primary carers. Visits to hospital can last hours, days or even months for some sick children, and provoke deep feelings of fear and vulnerability.

In order to create more attachment-friendly environments, many institutions – particularly maternity units and children's hospitals – have adopted models of Family-Centred Care (FCC). There are many ways in which this model has been implemented, but broadly speaking, different types of FCC encourage the same values:

- to share information about a patient with the patient and their families openly
- to respect and honour individual differences and choices
- to work in partnership with patients and families to make joint decisions and negotiate care
- to care 'in context' – medical care and decisions should reflect the child within the context of his or her family, education, interests and community.

Source: Kuo *et al.* (2012)

Family-centred services support the implementation of open visitation policies. Parents of children staying in hospital often have permission to be with them 24 hours a day. For example, in specialist institutions such as Great Ormond Street Hospital for Children, in London, parental accommodation is provided on the ward or nearby for at least one parent. This allows for the child to stay physically close to their attachment figures. According to Bowlby (1969), for primary caregivers to be readily accessible is essential for maintaining attachment with very young children during the critical or sensitive period. Siblings, other relatives and friends are also permitted to visit patients, which is important for maintaining other attachment relationships. Wards may offer different visiting periods to allow for visits outside of school or traditional working hours to accommodate other family members.

Another way in which hospitals may create attachment-friendly environments is through engaging parents with their children's care. Examples of this might include personal care tasks, such as bathing and dressing, or reading and singing to them to provide entertainment or comfort. Many wards have policies in place to ensure medical staff encourage and facilitate this type of engagement. This means that parents can continue to respond to their children's needs within the hospital environment, allowing them to keep some sense of routine and family life. A recent systematic review of hospitals implementing these policies found overall positive outcomes in measurements of health status and satisfaction with care, as well as family functioning (Kuhlthau *et al.*, 2011).

EVALUATION

Methodological and ethical issues

So far in this section we have considered the difficulty of measuring the concept of attachment. Much depends on what we determine normal attachment behaviour to look like; Ainsworth's attachment styles suggest that Type B 'secure' attachments are ideal and prevalent. In cross-cultural research, however, this is not always the case. A cross-cultural meta-analysis by Van Izjendoorn *et al.* (1988) found that while secure attachments were the most common type across a number of nations, there were variations in patterns of insecure attachments. Many of these differences can be explained in terms of variations in child-rearing practices. The classification system devised by Ainsworth *et al.* may be seen as somewhat ethnocentric, as it does not account for these cultural differences.

Furthermore, the Strange Situation is a controlled observation, which means it may lack ecological validity. Some would contest this and argue that brief infant–mother separations and reunions frequently occur in real-life. However, studying attachment behaviours in the real world is also inherently problematic. For example, measuring outcomes for young patients treated in wards with open visitation policies is often achieved through self-report measures rather than direct observation, and with a focus on short-term rather than long-term outcomes.

The concept of 'sensitive mothering' put forward by Bowlby and Ainsworth is a controversial idea, as is the notion of the critical or sensitive period. Mothers in particular may experience a great deal of pressure to remain consistently accessible and highly responsive to their children's needs, particularly in the first few years. This has implications for women who remain at home during this time, or who return to work either full- or part-time. Mothers may face depression or feelings of a loss of identity when needing to provide full-time care for a young child, or guilt and anxiety at leaving the child in order to return to work.

Figure 2.33: Balancing work and family life is a challenge for many parents

There are further ethical implications for research in the area of maternal deprivation. Many studies, such as Curtiss (1977) and Bowlby (1944), use case studies of those who have failed to form attachments. In this area, it is one of the only methods available to investigate the effect of privation or deprivation in humans. However, some case studies can be viewed as exploitative and not serving the young participants' best interests, or in the case of Genie, failing to protect her right to privacy.

ACTIVITY ✳

Short video clips are available online that show the case study of Genie (Curtiss, 1977). There may be other examples of children affected by extreme privation that you know about. How do you feel about the life stories of these children being publicly available – have they been treated ethically by researchers?

The Strange Situation procedure used by Ainsworth & Bell (1970) includes episodes of separation and reunion designed to induce anxiety and distress. Although the stages are brief and are curtailed in cases of extreme upset, the procedure could be considered unethical. Furthermore, infants of the age used in the study have no real understanding of the purpose of the test, and if or when they would be reunited with their mothers.

One final ethical consideration for this topic is around the effectiveness of care and visitation policies for hospitalised children outlined earlier. While parents and children tend to be more positive about their experiences, there is a lack of rigorous evidence supporting the overall effectiveness of FCC in contrast with more traditional models (Shields *et al.*, 2012).

Debates

Nature vs nurture

Bowlby and other proponents of the evolutionary view of attachment view it as an innate process that ensures the survival of the infant, through mechanisms such as social releasers, imprinting and proximity-seeking behaviour. Indeed, infants will form attachments even when their caregiver is negligent or abusive. The quality of the attachment and subsequent internal working model are developed through the sensitivity and responsiveness of the caregiver. So, while there is a strong, natural predisposition to form an attachment, the quality of the relationship and developmental outcomes for each child is dependant on the nurturing they receive.

Ainsworth and others support this view, assigning labels to the different types of attachment created by varying levels of maternal sensitivity. However, one criticism of this view is that it ignores another innate quality in infants; their temperaments. Babies are often described as having 'easy' temperaments (they are cheerful, with predictable moods and routines) or 'difficult' temperaments (they are irritable

or unpredictable). Psychologists believe that temperament may have a strong biological basis, and, along with nurturing, is likely to impact attachment measures such as the Strange Situation.

Free will vs determinism

The biological need to attach, as understood by Bowlby and others, is a necessary and inevitable process for human beings. The evidence suggests that the security of the infant's first attachment has a significant influence on their internal working model, subsequent relationships and other cognitive and social outcomes. However, other factors, such as the sensitivity and accessibility of the caregiver, can have a major role in the development of individual attachments, as shown by Ainsworth *et al.* (1978). There is some flexibility in the formation of attachment, for example as demonstrated by Rutter's (1981) work on adoption. It would be wrong, therefore, to say that attachment type is biologically or environmentally determined.

One example of this might be the way in which parents and relatives choose to and are able to involve themselves in children's care while in hospital. Changes in institutional policies over time have meant that relationships can be better facilitated and the child's attachment needs prioritised. Open visitation policies allow parents to maintain proximity to their children, to strengthen close, nurturing relationships, and to minimise the emotional trauma involved in prolonged periods of hospitalisation.

Reductionism and holism

As we have seen, Bowlby's notions of the internal working model and his maternal deprivation hypothesis have both been hugely influential in attachment theory. However, they both place great emphasis on the primacy of the mother–infant relationships, at the cost of ignoring other important attachment figures, such as fathers, siblings and other carers. To reduce the idea of the internal working model of attachment to a blueprint of the mother–infant attachment is somewhat reductionist.

The strategy outlined in this topic for creating attachment-friendly environments looked at the example of separation during hospitalisation. Traditionally, a sick child would have been treated in hospital by medical professionals with a clear, singular focus on eradicating the physical illness or injury. Using modern, family-centred policies, such as involving family members in both decision-making and practical aspects of care, is intended to treat the child in a more holistic manner. It takes into account their needs as a whole person: physiological (i.e. treating their illness) as well as emotional and social (i.e. maintaining family connections).

Psychology as a science

By definition, attachment is a bond that exists between two people. As such, it is quite a difficult thing to quantify and measure. For example, Bowlby's idea of an internal working model is highly conceptual, which makes it problematic for researchers to study scientifically. Much of Bowlby's empirical work, such as the 44 Thieves study (1944), involves retrospective consideration of maternal deprivation and uses restrictive samples of vulnerable young people, which again makes it difficult to draw conclusive causal links.

However, much work in attachment theory has used observational techniques, that is, the watching and recording of infant-mother behaviour, such as in the Strange Situation. Ainsworth & Bell (1970) devised the procedure and ways to code observed behaviour in a reliable manner. The procedure itself is highly controlled, using a prescribed set-up, with standardised actions and timings, and has been replicated in numerous studies worldwide.

Usefulness of research

While there have been many revisions to attachment theory since its conception, much of the work of Bowlby, Ainsworth and others remains highly influential across many areas of social policy (see Application, page 107). As mentioned earlier, Ainsworth & Bell's Strange Situation test is still used in current attachment research. It has also been modified for use in studies concerned with infant-father attachments (Grossmann *et al.*, 1981) and sibling attachments (Stewart, 1983), further enhancing our understanding of the different kinds of infant relationships.

Figure 2.34: Sibling relationships can also influence our attitudes and behaviour

Research into specific strategies to facilitate attachment, such as FCC in hospitals, is still relatively limited. It has been questioned as a model of care because it can be difficult to implement effectively. One reason for this is that it encourages high levels of parental involvement, which hospital staff may feel interferes with their ability to treat patients. Also, families may feel they are expected to offer input on their child's care that is beyond their capabilities, which may be stress-provoking. More research is required in this area to determine the effectiveness of these policies, including their long-term effects on facilitating attachment.

THE IMPACT OF ADVERTISING ON CHILDREN

BACKGROUND

Children and television

It is well known that many children and adolescents (and adults for that matter!) spend considerable amounts of time exposed to sources of media. Having access to countless media outlets increases children's exposure to both positive television content (e.g. educational programmes) and negative content (e.g. inappropriately sexualised content or violence). For almost as long as television has existed, people have been concerned about its influence on children. These concerns are worthy of investigation, in the context of the accelerated commercialisation of television in the UK over recent years. There are now vast numbers of for-profit channels, including many specifically targeted towards young children that are supported by advertisers' fees.

Children as consumers?

In this context, young people now make up a recognised consumer market. In countries such as the UK, where parents may have a fair amount of disposable income, children are a target audience for products such as toys, holidays, food and beverages all designed to meet their needs and appeal to their wants. For example, Pine & Nash (2002) found that children who watch more commercial television than non-commercial television tend to request far greater numbers of toys from Father Christmas. With advertising becoming an increasingly dominant feature of children's daily environments, psychologists are interested to know whether advertisements directed towards children offer models of how to speak and behave.

Research has consistently shown a correlation between children's viewing and their learned behaviours and attitudes. In 1963, Bandura *et al.* replicated their earlier study on the transmission of aggression, this time using video-recorded aggressive models. Children who observed video-recorded behaviour displayed similar levels of aggression to those who observed a real-life model, and in both conditions children displayed considerably more instances of aggressive behaviour than the control group. This suggests that televised role models may have similar levels of influence on children's subsequent behaviour.

Stereotyping in television advertising

Some theorists argue that advertising engages viewers or consumers in a much larger cultural process than we may at first be aware of. They suggest that advertisers need to create a market for products such as children's toys, and to do this, advertisers use messages that draw on and perpetuate existing dominant ideas about gender, ethnicity and class (Bem, 1993). Often, these may involve the use of **stereotypes**.

KEY IDEAS

The term **stereotype** refers to a fixed impression or belief that one has about an individual, based solely on their membership of a particular group. Stereotypes can be positive or negative (e.g. 'all women are caring' or 'all men lack empathy'), and may be based in truth or may be wholly inaccurate. Stereotyping is the process by which people use stereotypes to make sense of their world, which can lead to prejudice (positive or negative feelings towards others based on their group membership) and/or discrimination (positive or negative treatment of others based on their group membership).

There is a lot of evidence to suggest that cultural stories about gender are shared and exaggerated through the advertising of children's toys. For example, Smith (1994) analysed TV adverts during children's programmes, and concluded that adverts featuring only one gender were gender-role stereotypical. Typical portrayals of girls might include nurturing, passive behaviours, while boys are shown as action-oriented and powerful. Limiting gender roles within advertising limits children's ideas about how they play and what they play with, and may ultimately limit the types of roles they will try out as adults (Smith, 1994). Psychologists are therefore interested in the types of behaviour encouraged by TV models and whether children are vulnerable to accepting the sorts of messages portrayed in advertising.

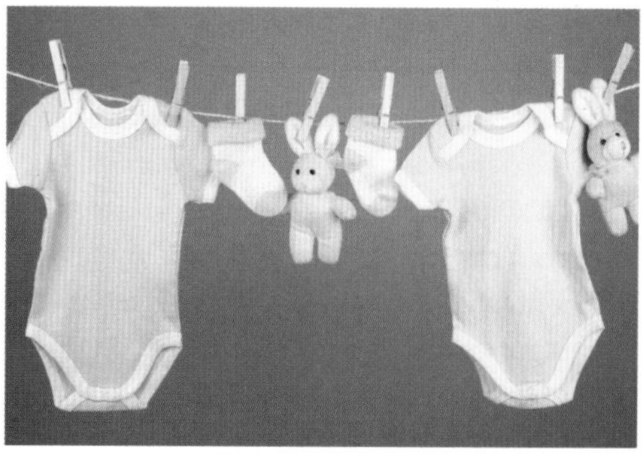

Figure 2.35: Pretty in pink? Advertisers create bigger markets for girls and boys by drawing on cultural ideas about gender identity

KEY RESEARCH

Johnson, F.L. & Young, K. (2002) Gendered voices in children's advertising. *Critical Studies in Media Communication*, 19 (4), 461–480.

Aim

The aim of the research was to determine whether advertisers scripted television adverts differently for females and males of school age, linking toys to gender stereotypical roles.

Method

Sample

Samples of children's television cartoon programmes on commercial (for profit) networks, regional independent New England stations, and the television channel 'Nickelodeon' in the autumn of 1996 and 1997 were video-recorded for this study. The sample was repeated again in the autumn of 1999.

Fifteen half-hour programmes were recorded in 1996 and 1997, and 24 half-hour programmes in 1999. The total number of adverts included between the beginning and end of programmes was 478. This included 149 in 1996, 133 in 1997 and 196 in 1999. The range of adverts per programme was 8.2 to 8.9. Adverts were classified in one of five product categories (see Table 2.10).

TABLE 2.10: SAMPLE OF ADVERTS DISPLAYED BY CATEGORY		
Category	**Example**	**Number of adverts**
1. Food and drink	e.g. breakfast cereal	216
2. Toys	e.g. dolls	188
3. Educational/public service	e.g. anti-drug campaign	21
4. Recreation	e.g. theme parks	19
5. Video/film promotion	e.g. film trailer	20
6. Other/miscellaneous*	e.g. credit cards	14
Total		478

* this category was added for the 1999 sample only

KEY IDEAS

A **content analysis** is a method of research that can involve examining the content of all kinds of material, from interview transcripts to video to newspaper articles. The researcher first identifies and creates categories suitable for their aim, then each time an example from the category appears in the material it is counted to produce quantitative data. **Discourse analysis** is slightly different in that it critically analyses the use of vocabulary, tone and other features of speech to interpret meaning.

DO IT YOURSELF

Have a go at a content analysis similar to that of Johnson & Young (2002). Identify several children's TV programmes at different times of day and record them. Using the girl-oriented, boy-oriented and girl/boy-oriented categories, code the gender of the voice-over used in each advertisement. Enter your results in a table and summarise your findings. Do they support or contradict the key research?

MATHS MOMENT

1   How have the numbers of boy-oriented toy adverts changed over time? Support your answer with data from the Table 2.11.

2   Draw a bar chart to illustrate the data contained in the combined column of Table 2.11.

Design and procedure

This study was a **content and discourse analysis**. Researchers found that a large percentage of adverts in their sample was made up of toys, and as these were most open to gender elaboration, they were analysed further. This analysis further categorised the toys by gender target audience into the following groups:

1   Adverts targeted to boys in which boys were depicted
2   Adverts targeted to girls in which girls were depicted
3   Adverts targeted to both boys and girls either because both genders were featured or because there was no gender-specific content.

Researchers identified gender in advert voice-overs, as well as the presence of gender exaggeration in voices. For example, this could be female voices that were high pitched and excited, or male voices that were deep and powerful-sounding. They analysed speaking lines of males and females, and the use of the word 'power' in male-oriented adverts. They also considered the following verb elements in these five categories:

1   *Action verb elements* – verbs that relate to physical movement (e.g. crawl, fly, jump, race)
2   *Competition/destruction verb elements* – action verbs directly related to competition or destruction (e.g. crush, fire on, knock out, pounce, slam, stomp)
3   *Power/control verb elements* – verbs referring to target consumers or speakers in the advertisement as possessing power over someone or something (e.g. control, defeat, rule, take)
4   *Limited-activity verb elements* – verbs not involving explicit action (e.g. beware, get, go, know, look, talk, wait, watch)
5   *Feeling and nurturing verb elements* – a type of limited activity linked to emotions and caring (e.g. cuddle, loves, taking care of, tuck you in).

Results

In total, 188 toy adverts were recorded. When combined, adverts for boy-oriented toys outnumbered those oriented towards girls, with relatively few gender non-specific adverts (see Table 2.11).

TABLE 2.11: GENDER ORIENTATION OF TOY ADVERTS				
Gender orientation	**1996**	**1997**	**1999**	**Combined**
Boy oriented	47.6% (30)	42.1% (24)	70.6% (48)	54.8% (102)
Girl oriented	30.2% (19)	49.1% (28)	23.5% (16)	33.0% (63)
Boy and girl oriented	22.2% (14)	8.8% (5)	5.9% (4)	12.2% (23)
Total	n = 63	n = 57	n = 68	n = 188

The naming of many toys reinforced opposing or polarised gender stereotypes. For example, the researchers identify 'Big Time Action Heroes' and 'Tonka Mega Crew' which stress size as an important feature for boy-oriented toys, in comparison to 'Juice 'n' Cookies Baby Alive' and 'Bedtime Bottle Baby' which portray parenting as a female-oriented quality.

Types of toy were also categorised and measured. Boy-oriented adverts were dominated by action figures and, by 1999, the emergence of hand-held electronic games and computer-related toys. Girl-oriented adverts included 'posable figures', such as Barbie dolls, and animal figures. Posable figures were depicted in scenes of limited activity, compared to the action figures of boy-oriented adverts. Researchers suggest this reinforces stereotypical ideas regarding the play activity of boys and girls.

Adult actors provided the voice-over for the majority of adverts, with all boy-oriented and boy/girl-oriented adverts voiced by a male. The majority of girl-oriented adverts were voiced by a female (89%). Further voice analysis showed that gender exaggeration was present in 80% and 87% of voice-overs for boy-oriented and girl-oriented adverts, respectively. This exaggeration was not generally present in the toys aimed at both boys and girls.

Feeling and nurturing verb elements were absent from boy-oriented toy adverts, though were present in 66 girl-oriented adverts. By comparison, the use of *competition/destruction* verb elements in boy-oriented adverts was over 12 times greater than in girl-oriented adverts. Verb elements of *limited activity* were more present in girl-oriented adverts despite occurring often in boy-oriented adverts. *Agency and control* verb elements were more prevalent for boy-oriented toys than for girl-oriented toys. Least variation was found in frequency of use of *action* verb elements between boy-oriented and girl-oriented adverts. Differences were however found in the images associated with each action verb (e.g. 'throw' or 'take off' for boys; 'skip' or 'twirl' for girls.)

Some advertisements contained more than one voice, meaning the actors or voiceover would speak in turn during a conversation. There was a difference in the way speaking turns were used in adverts. Over half of the girl-oriented adverts contained speaking turns, compared with less than a quarter of the boy-oriented adverts. The researchers suggest that this presents the young audience with verbal models which reinforce stereotypes in which females engage in talk, while males prefer action to words.

In addition, adverts in which girls and boys were together, the scripting displayed polarised views of gender behaviour. For example, girls responded with affirmation to lines said by boys, showing boys as having positions of power within the group. The word 'power' or 'powerful' was found in one fifth of boy-oriented adverts, but was used only once in a girl-oriented advert, when it was part of the name of a toy manufacturer.

Conclusion

The researchers concluded that:

1   Gender stereotypes underlie television adverts as they portray males and females through traditional gender stereotypical discourse.
2   Reasons for gender-stereotypical portrayal might include reliance on historically successful marketing strategies and/or profitability in creating gender-specific consumer-behaviour (i.e. creating markets for both male and female products).

APPLICATION: STRATEGIES TO REDUCE THE IMPACT OF ADVERTISING AIMED AT CHILDREN

As we have seen, television advertising targeted at children can reinforce stereotypes such as traditional gender roles and encourage gender-stereotypical play. It has also

QUESTION SPOTLIGHT!

Can you see how children's inability to understand the purpose of advertising could relate to the debate about free will and determinism?

Figure 2.36: Don't believe everything you see on TV: children and young people may become more media literate through learning about persuasive advertising techniques

STRETCH & CHALLENGE ◎

This section outlines one example of a media literacy programme. Can you find other examples of such programmes? Consider how they are similar to or different from Media Smart, and whether they may be more or less effective.

Figure 2.37: One Media Smart resource aims to educate children about how advertising can influence young people's perceptions of body image

WEB WATCH @

You can check out the MediaSmart website for the UK here: www.mediasmart.org.uk

The site is divided into three areas: for parents, children and teachers. You can trial sample activities and the aims of the programme, as well as read further information on the effectiveness of media literacy programmes.

been heavily criticised by organisations such as the Food Standards Agency (FSA) for encouraging unhealthy eating habits and obesity in young people. For example, the FSA has found that promotion of food to children is dominated by television advertising of pre-sugared cereals, soft drinks, confectionery, savoury snacks and fast-food outlets (Carvel, 2003). As a result of an increasing awareness about this, some governments (e.g. Sweden) have legislated against all advertising aimed at children below a certain age. Others have imposed legal restrictions on the nature, timing and content of advertising aimed at children and rely on self-regulatory bodies, such as the National Advertising Standards Agency in the UK. We will consider one way to reduce the impact of advertising, the development of 'media literacy'.

Why 'media literacy'?

One reason these safeguards are deemed necessary is because research shows that young children perceive TV adverts in different ways from older children and adults. Pine & Nash (2002) reviewed studies of the effects of adverts on young children and found that many children below 7 to 9 years of age lack an understanding of persuasive intent, meaning they do not know when they are being manipulated or lied to by adults. Furthermore, they are unaware of the purpose of adverts, i.e. that they are intended to sell a product. It may even be the case that this awareness does not develop until as late as 12 or 13 years of age (Linn, De Benedictis & Delucchi, 1982).

New educational strategies designed to increase media literacy in children have now emerged in order to address some of these issues. Becoming media literate essentially means developing a critical awareness of mass media and advertising, including the ability to analyse and evaluate different media sources. In this way, children can be taught to better understand when they are being manipulated or having information presented to them in a misleading way. The intention of media literacy is that young people might become more sceptical about the messages presented to them by media sources, and can make healthier choices as a result.

'Media Smart' and 'Be AdWise'

There are several media literacy programmes in use in the UK, of which Media Smart is one example. Media Smart is a non-profit programme designed for children aged 6 to 11 years. The programme is funded by advertising businesses in the UK, and is also supported by both the UK government and the EU. The materials are written and reviewed by a group of experts who are academics and education specialists in media literacy, and the programme has been rolled out to several other European countries.

It has a particular focus on advertising literacy, and provides free educational materials to primary schools. 'Be AdWise' is a set of resources produced by Media Smart that aim to teach young people to think critically about advertising within the context of their daily lives, using real-life examples and brands. Resources are designed to teach children how advertising works and about the persuasive methods that they might see used, ranging from celebrity endorsements to the use of mood music.

EVALUATION

Methodological and ethical issues

One key issue around investigating the influence of media and advertising on children is that it is difficult to approach the area without any preconceived ideas. That is to say, many researchers may already have formed beliefs about the positive and negative effects of different forms of media and advertising. When conducting qualitative research such as discourse analysis, it can be challenging to put aside these personal beliefs and to interpret material objectively.

Johnson & Young (2002) attempt to establish validity and reliability through using a systematic coding method. However, while we might not dispute whether a voice is male or female, it could be argued that defining 'gender exaggeration' in a voice-over is a matter of interpretation. Furthermore, the idea of a 'stereotype' itself is somewhat difficult to define, and can change across time and between cultures. This adds another layer of complexity for researchers trying to find ways to investigate the presence of stereotypes in advertising.

The researchers use content and discourse analysis. One advantage to this method is that it minimises ethical concerns, as the data that is collected does not directly involve human participants. Thus, there is no risk to others. The nature of the material being analysed is unlikely to be offensive, is publicly available, and does not require formalities such as briefing or gaining consent.

However, other research in this area works more directly with children and teachers, such as studies evaluating the effectiveness of media literacy programmes (e.g. Buckingham *et al.*, 2007). In such cases, the informed consent of the schools and participants needs to be obtained. There are further issues of protection in some research into media and advertising, particularly in cases where research may involve examining the impact on young people's body-image perceptions or risk-taking behaviours (e.g. alcohol consumption).

Debates

Nature vs nurture

This debate links to the study of the impact of advertising because of the high levels of exposure many children have to a range of media sources. In the study of Johnson & Young (2002), the discourse in advertisements reflects specific cultural gender stereotypes about masculine and feminine play, which, for example, define female roles as nurturing and male roles as dominant or aggressive. Furthermore, the use of media literacy programmes for children could be considered a specific environmental influence that moderates the impact of advertising messages.

However, as we learned from Bandura *et al.*'s (1961) research on the transmission of aggression, boys were found to be more likely to imitate physical aggression than girls (Jarvis *et al.*, 2015, p.82). This theory might offer an alternative explanation for innate toy preferences, and subsequent marketing strategies.

Free will vs determinism

The idea of determinism is highly relevant to this topic, as the idea that media can influence young people's perceptions and choices implies a certain lack of free will. The evidence suggests that young children lack the capacity to decipher the true intentions of advertisements and how they may be targeted as an audience. Johnson & Young's (2002) study highlights how pervasive stereotyping is in televised toy advertising, giving consistent, highly gendered messages to children.

Current research does, however, indicate that media-literacy education can positively influence children's ability to analyse, critique, and even produce their own media messages (Worth & Roberts, 2004). This may be because the methods of such programmes are based on developing critical thinking in the form of 'media scepticism', which challenges children to deconstruct messages in advertising and actively filter information. For example, Kupersmidt *et al.* (2010) surveyed school children who had recently completed a media-literacy programme aimed at discouraging tobacco and alcohol use. They found that an increase in critical thinking about media advertising and media-message deconstruction skills reduced adolescents' intention to use substances in the future. This suggests that, with increased media literacy, individuals are better able to exercise free will and be sceptical about advertising messages.

Reductionism and holism

This area mainly concerns social psychologists and media theorists who appreciate that media is a powerful influence on children's behaviour, but not the only influence. For example, strategies to control the impact of advertising on children and research evaluating these strategies consider a range of factors that could influence their success. In the study by Kupersmidt *et al.* (2010), researchers focused on the impact of the media-literacy programme on attitudes towards alcohol. However, they also measured and reported on the impact of other factors, such as parental involvement and peer behaviour, which also influenced the adolescents.

The study by Johnson & Young (2002) did have a clear focus on gender. However, the researchers noted that certain ethnicities may also be portrayed in stereotypical ways. For example, races other than Caucasians were under-represented, and the only advert in which an African-American male took a prominent role had him speaking in a 'rap' style, whereas Asian children had virtually no speaking parts at all. While it would be unreasonable to expect one study to consider all of these factors, there is research into advertising that explores forms of stereotyping other than gender. For example, another content analysis of a large number of television advertisements conducted by Coltrane & Messineo (2000) considered the portrayal of racial stereotypes in addition to gender. They found that African American males were shown as aggressive, whilst images of white women were often highly sexualised.

Individual and situational explanations

The background information contained in this topic outlines situational explanations for why children might be influenced by advertising and the stereotypical messages it may contain. Research has shown that the greater the level of exposure to media advertising, the greater its influence, as we learned from Pine & Nash's (2002) study on children's Christmas present requests.

On the other hand, when considering how media-literacy programmes can be used to lessen the effects of such advertising, it is important to consider individual differences. Although media literacy programmes in general have been shown to be effective, they seem to work best when they developing critical-thinking skills in individuals. Better critical-thinking skills have been found to correlate with higher levels of media scepticism (Kupersmidt et al., 2010), indicating that they may be more effective for some people than others.

Psychology as a science

Much research into the effects of media and media advertising on children takes place in real-world settings, which means it is ecologically valid. However, experimenters often lack control over variables such as family setting, or may rely on self-report measures to determine how much television is watched. These methods, while practical, lack scientific rigour and may be open to response bias. For instance, in order to appear more socially acceptable, parents may under-report how many hours of TV they let their children watch.

Methods such as the content and discourse analysis used by Johnson & Young (2002) do not rely on direct observation or experimentation. As such they cannot be described as scientific because they involve elements of interpretation (e.g. gender exaggeration in voices). However, the researchers clearly outline a systematic process of categorisation and coding that could be easily replicated.

Usefulness of research

The key research of Johnson & Young (2002) is useful in that it highlights the overt gender stereotyping that occurs in children's advertising. Other studies into the impact of advertising on children's behaviour have also raised awareness of regulating media sources in order to reduce problems prevalent in the UK, such as childhood obesity.

Determining how effective media-literacy programmes are remains a source of some debate. Much depends on exactly what outcome such programmes are aiming for – whether they are aiming to protect children, to enact behavioural change, or simply to provide them with the skills required for living in a world dominated by technology.

Media Smart commissioned an independent evaluation of the effectiveness of its resources (Buckingham et al., 2007). Data was collected from online surveys and telephone interviews with teachers, as well as from classroom observations. The findings showed that the majority of teachers liked the Media Smart materials and found them to be effective at teaching children about advertising literacy. Most teachers found the materials engaged children and were successful in teaching the language of advertising. However, the report also found that some teachers lacked confidence or expertise when delivering the materials, and that the activities might be more effective if embedded within other National Curriculum subjects.

ACTIVITY ✲

Design a leaflet for parents that provides them with information about encouraging media literacy in their children. You may wish to read more about media-literacy programmes such as Media Smart and Be Adwise. Include sections to help them explain:

- who makes advertisements
- why advertisements are made
- how advertisers use different text, colour and sound.

PRACTICE QUESTIONS

Remember that in any exam paper you will only get a set of questions on one of the six sub-topics.

TOPIC 1: INTELLIGENCE

(a)* Explain how the research by Van Leeuwen *et al.* (2008) could be used to understand similarities and differences in the intelligence of twins. **[10]**

(b)* Assess the role of biological factors in intelligence. **[15]**

(c)* Thelma is worried about her son. He seems very bright in some ways; he is generally making excellent progress at school. However, in three subjects his report was terrible and Thelma is wondering whether an intelligence test would help her to understand why.

Discuss how an intelligence test might be conducted and what the results might, or might not, tell Thelma about her son. **[10]**

TOPIC 2: PRE-ADULT BRAIN DEVELOPMENT

(a)* Use the study by Barkley-Leveson and Galván (2014) to explain how neuroscience can help us to understand differences between adolescent and adult brains. **[10]**

(b)* Assess the reliability of research into brain development and risk-taking. **[15]**

(c)* Dr Shah's research team studies risky behaviour in adolescents. She has a young research student called Dan who is designing a new project. He has to choose a topic other than gambling.

Choose any risk-taking behaviour other than gambling and discuss how Dan might plan and conduct a new piece of research and what he might find. **[10]**

TOPIC 3: PERCEPTUAL DEVELOPMENT

(a)* Using the research by Gibson & Walk (1960), explain how experimental studies can be used to understand perceptual development. **[10]**

(b)* Assess the role of science in psychology, using Gibson & Walk's study of perceptual development as an example. **[15]**

(c)* Sally is a nurse at a post-natal clinic specialising in sensory awareness. She advises parents on ways to help their newborn babies to develop well.

Discuss how Sally's knowledge of studies of perceptual development in children and animals will influence the suggestions she makes to the parents she meets. **[10]**

TOPIC 4: COGNITIVE DEVELOPMENT AND EDUCATION

(a)* Explain how the research by Wood *et al.* (1976) could be used to improve children's learning in an educational setting. **[10]**

(b)* Assess the usefulness of research into cognitive development in children in the context of education. **[15]**

(c)* Leroy is a new teacher at Park School and has a lunchtime craft group with students aged between 6 and 10 years old. He is aware that the older and younger children might have different needs when learning crafts such as sewing and woodwork.

Discuss how Leroy's understanding of the cognitive development of children will impact on the way he treats the children in his group. **[10]**

TOPIC 5: DEVELOPMENT OF ATTACHMENT

(a)* Explain how the research by Ainsworth & Bell (1970) could be used to identify children with attachment problems. **[10]**

(b)* Assess ethical problems with the use of children in Ainsworth & Bell's study of the development of attachment. **[15]**

(c)* Kate works with infants at a nursery, some of whom find adjusting to the nursery very difficult. Her boss has asked her to provide a leaflet for parents about possible changes the nursery could make to become a more attachment-friendly environment.

Discuss a strategy that Kate could suggest that could help to develop an attachment-friendly environment either for use in the child's home or in the nursery. **[10]**

TOPIC 6: THE IMPACT OF ADVERTISING ON CHILDREN

(a)* Explain how the research by Johnson & Young (2002) helps us to understand the influence of advertising on children. **[10]**

(b)* Assess problems of sampling bias in the study of the influence of television advertising on children. **[15]**

(c)* Carly runs a preschool nursery and although some parents are happy that the children are allowed to watch appropriate television shows during the day, others have raised concerns about whether the children should be allowed to watch the advertisements between programmes.

Discuss the evidence that television advertising may influence the children at the nursery. **[10]**

TOPIC 2: PRE-ADULT BRAIN DEVELOPMENT

(a)* Use the study by Barkley-Leveson and Galván (2014) to explain how neuroscience can help us to understand differences between adolescent and adult brains. **[10]**

Liam's answer:

In an experiment, Barkley-Leveson and Galván tested gambling. It was an ethical study because all the participants were over 18, except the adults who were 13–17, so this wasn't very ethical because it was encouraging them into bad habits. Though they did make sure that the ones who weren't very good at gambling didn't lose out because they all got some winnings, which was quite ethical though maybe it was even worse and it would have been more ethical if they'd all lost to put them off gambling. They found that the adolescents were more likely to gamble than the adults, because young people are more likely to take risks.

We say: Although Liam clearly has some knowledge of the correct study, he isn't answering the question. There is no mention of the neuroscience aspect of the procedure and the results, although hinting at the right general idea of risk-taking, do not indicate what was really found in the study. He needed to spend less time talking about ethics, and more time looking at the use of brain-scanning and what this showed.

Rina's answer:

Barkley-Leveson and Galván (B-L & G) compared adults and adolescents, looking at brain activity when they gambled. The bigger the risk, the more activation, but this pattern was stronger in the younger participants, showing that they took even more risks. These results show that neuroscience matters because the pattern was true even when social factors were taken into account, such as income, because this is an obvious difference between older and younger people, and how much they thought gambling was okay. Neuroscience was also more important than their actual behaviour. Even when they were doing the same sorts of things, like only winning or only losing, the expectation of winning still made the adolescents' brains light up more than the adults' brains. The bit that lit up was the ventral striatum, which makes judgments about how valuable something is. This is important because the results also showed that both groups could avoid losing gambles well, but the adolescents took bigger risks when there was less certainty of winning, but because they made good choices, they won more. B-L & G thought this was because the brain is a biological structure so is affected by evolution. Adolescents

We say: This is a very good answer by Rina. It offers both good knowledge of the procedures in the study and links this effectively to an understanding of neuroscience. The link to evolution at the end is an effective conclusion.

taking bigger but good risks would have been rewarded by their ventral striatum so take even more risks. They would have become more independent and had sex earlier, so would have passed on more of their good genes – early in evolution but maybe not now.

TOPIC 3: PERCEPTUAL DEVELOPMENT

(b)* Assess the role of science in psychology, using Gibson & Walk's study of perceptual development as an example. **[15]**

Liam's answer:

Science is all about experiments and controls. Psychologists use experiments – that's what makes psychology a science. In an experiment there is an IV and a DV. The IV is the independent variable. This is the thing that the experimenter controls to make two conditions in an experiment. Like in Gibson and Walk's study there were the children and the animals. The DV is the thing the experimenter measures, like in Gibson & Walk's study they measured whether the animal or baby fell off the cliff.

Controls matter in experiments. That's another thing that makes psychology a science. Controls are where the experimenter keeps everything the same. In Gibson & Walk's study they didn't really have good controls because they used different species of animals, like turtles, as well as babies. Also, the different sides of the cliff were different heights, they should have kept them the same.

We say: Liam has raised some relevant points about what makes psychology scientific. These points do relate to Gibson & Walk's study of perceptual development, but they are mainly generic points and where Liam has tried to link them to the study, he has made some mistakes, such as with the IV and the controls. Liam has misreported the species used and, although there were comparisons between species on the basis of their life histories, the key IVs were grey versus patterned cloth, the pattern density of the squares, and light or dark rearing. He could also have mentioned controls such as having non-reflective glass on both sides of the cliff. There were also things that Gibson & Walk did not control, although not those noted by Liam, which are incorrect. For example, the young rats tested had had some opportunity to learn, unlike the day-old chicks.

Rina's answer:

Perceptual development is investigated scientifically, mainly using a deductive approach, for example Gibson & Walk had the theoretical basis of evolution to predict differences in development of depth perception in different species and the concept of motion parallax to predict what animals would do. This meant they could write testable hypotheses like 'young animals will choose the deep side more than old ones' or 'dark reared cats will choose the deep side more than light-reared ones', which is another feature of a deductive approach to science. Hypotheses have to be falsifiable, which they are because the younger animals, or the dark reared ones, could have been better.

In science, hypotheses are tested by manipulation of variables in controlled situations, which Gibson & Walk did. They standardised the procedure and used quantitative methods – counting the number of deep-/shallow-side crossings. This is an objective measure, which is often difficult with observations but you would be unlikely to judge animals crossing to the 'deep' or 'shallow' side differently than someone else. The standardisation is important because it makes the procedure replicable, and because Gibson & Walk got similar results with different species, such as chicks and rats, this suggests their results were reliable. So, as this area has theories, objective testing and replicability, it is scientific.

We say: Rina's essay started off well, with good analysis of the deductive method using appropriate examples. In the second paragraph, the points about controls and standardisation are relevant but are not illustrated with examples from the study. The final discussion of quantifiable measures and objectivity is better as it is substantiated with evidence, adds balance to the essay and ends in a conclusion based on the previous argument. However, the argument is entirely one-sided. It would have been even better to have seen some evidence that Rina understood that there are limitations to the scientific approach in this area, such as having to use limited numbers of animals or the difficulty of different species opening their eyes or becoming mobile at different times after birth.

TOPIC 4: COGNITIVE DEVELOPMENT AND EDUCATION

(c)* Leroy is a new teacher at Park School and has a lunchtime craft group with students aged between 6 and 10 years old. He is aware that the older and younger children might have different needs when learning crafts such as sewing and woodwork.

Discuss how Leroy's understanding of the cognitive development of children will impact on the way he treats the children in his group. **[10]**

Liam's answer:

Leroy could work with the children making wooden things. This would help their cognitive development as it would be active learning. Piaget says this is important. It helps children to discover things so they can fill up their schema. They might have schema for solid things and be able to expand the schema to include wood, this would be assimilation. They might have to make another schema for soft things, and could accommodate wool into it in the sewing club. It would be a bad idea for Leroy to let them use sharp needles as they might hurt themselves and this is against the ethical guideline of protecting participants from harm. The older children would be safer as they have more schema for different

We say: Liam's answer does contain some relevant material. He has identified the importance of active or discovery learning and correctly attributed this is Piaget. He goes on to explain how this contributes to the development of schema and successfully illustrates assimilation and accommodation, differentiating between the two. He also recognises that the understanding of older children would be more sophisticated and that this would determine what Leroy could do. However, the focus of Liam's essay is on the children's learning, rather than the way Leroy should decide how he helps them. Liam could have continued his final paragraph to include the different ways Leroy could work with the older and younger children, using Piaget's or Vygotsky's ideas. Finally, there is some irrelevant material in Liam's essay, for example his comments on the children hurting themselves – they are not participants in an experiment but children at Leroy's school.

things so would probably already know about dangerous things like needles, and saws and drills for woodwork, so they would be able to do different things from the little ones.

Rina's answer:

Following Piaget's ideas, Leroy would have to treat the younger and older children differently. The ones aged 6 and 7 would still be in the pre-operational stage so would only be beginning to use symbolic thought. That means they might find it hard to follow instructions, even easy ones with pictures, as the instructions would be representing what they had to do. They would be better off being shown directly how to do things like sewing a shape. The older ones would be in the concrete-operations stage so would be able to think logically if the thing they were working on was in front of them, so they could work out how to do something practical quite well. They might not be able to follow written instructions without pictures though, because this would need abstract thought which they wouldn't have yet (because it's formal ops).

Leroy could also simply let the children try and get it wrong sometimes. This would be discovery learning, which Piaget also said was important. However, he would need to look at each individual child because although they all go through the stages in the same order they do it at different times so he can't assume that all the 7 year olds would think the same way.

If Leroy believed Vygotsky he would try to scaffold the children. As he has different aged children he could get the older ones to be MKOs for the younger ones. He or the 10 year olds could help the younger ones through their Z.PD, maybe showing them how to do sanding in woodwork or how to thread a needle in sewing.

We say: Rina's answer covers many relevant ideas. The descriptions of the stages are relevant and correct, although she could have said more about the pre-operational children's needs and about discovery learning. In the final paragraph, Rina could have expanded on what the zone of proximal development (ZPD) is and how more knowledgeable others (MKOs) help. Importantly, Rina should have explained the two acronyms to ensure that the examiner knew she understood.

C3

CRIMINAL

PSYCHOLOGY

Criminal psychology includes a consideration both of psychological explanations for criminal behaviour and of the contributions psychology can make to the success of detecting and sentencing suspects and treating or punishing convicted criminals. Research in this area therefore studies a range of ways in which psychology can improve the processes involved in the judicial system and reduce the risk of criminal behaviour. In this chapter we will consider six important topics:

1 **What makes a criminal?:** We will consider the causes of criminality, looking at physiological factors such as brain areas associated with criminal behaviour, which will be explored through Raine et al.'s (1997) brain-scanning study, and also non-physiological explanations. We will then examine facial surgery as a strategy for preventing criminal behaviour.

2 **The collection and processing of forensic evidence:** We will look at motivating factors and biases in the collection of forensic evidence, including key research by Player & Hall (2008), and explore strategies for reducing bias in this context.

3 **Collection of evidence:** We will explore a variety of ways in which evidence can be collected from suspects and from witnesses before examining the review of the cognitive interview process conducted by Memon & Higham (1999). We will also look at other strategies for police interviews.

4 **Psychology and the courtroom:** We will begin by looking at a range of witness and defendant characteristics that may have an effect on the decisions made by juries. The key research, conducted by Dixon et al. (2002), examines the effect of accent and we will also consider other factors that may impact on jury decisions.

5 **Crime prevention:** We will explore how changes at the neighbourhood level and zero-tolerance policies can impact on criminality. This will be considered through the specific example of the work by Wilson & Kelling (1982): 'Broken Windows'. We will conclude with a discussion of situational crime prevention.

6 **Effect of imprisonment:** We will start by discussing punishment, imprisonment and reform, and then explore the study by Haney et al. (1973) on a prison simulation. We will then look at the use of anger management as a strategy to reduce reoffending.

WHAT MAKES A CRIMINAL?

BACKGROUND

Some criminals are 'specialists' in one particular activity, such as arson or fraud. Others are 'generalists', engaging in a range of crimes such as violent behaviour, theft or illicit drug use. The question arises: What causes such behaviours? Specifically, 'Are criminals born or made?' – that is, does their behaviour come from some innate physiological predisposition, or are there non-physiological factors, such as life experiences, that mould behaviour down a path to criminality?

Physiological explanations of criminal behaviour

If criminal behaviour has a physiological cause, this suggests that it is controlled genetically and is therefore the product of evolution. Early observations of prisoners originally published by Lombroso in his book Criminal Man (1876) suggested they had similar features, such as prominent jaws and brow ridges and large ears (see Figure 3.1). From the perspective of **natural selection**, Lombroso, saw such characteristics as primitive in terms of evolution. If such an explanation were correct, it would be physiological in nature, although Lombroso himself also acknowledged the role of other factors such as social ones. He even went so far as to describe prisons as 'criminal universities', as they provided an environment in which criminal behaviour could develop.

QUESTION SPOTLIGHT!

Lombroso's ideas seem very 'unscientific', but it would be perfectly possible to test them in a scientific way. Consider what makes a topic within psychology 'scientific' and how you could test Lombroso's theory objectively.

Overall, Lombroso's ideas are quite holistic. Why?

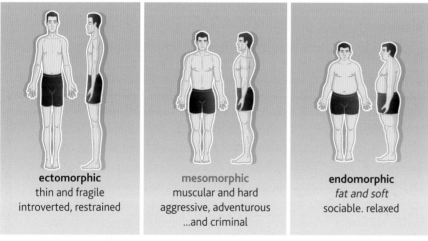

ectomorphic
thin and fragile
introverted, restrained

mesomorphic
muscular and hard
aggressive, adventurous
...and criminal

endomorphic
fat and soft
sociable. relaxed

Figure 3.2: The criminal body type

Sheldon (1942) identified three body types: ectomorphs, mesomorphs and endomorphs (see Figure 3.2). He proposed that the mesomorphs were more likely to be criminals. Although Sheldon found a difference in body types between students and delinquents, there has been little subsequent evidence to support the theory. Even if there were a link between big, muscular bodies and criminality, this might not be causal; several other explanations could account for this pattern. Bigger, muscular children and adults might discover, for example,

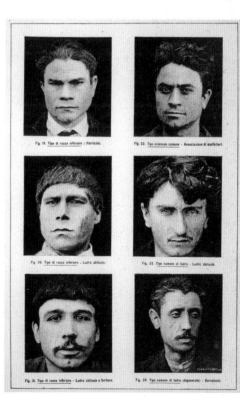

Figures 3.1: Images of criminal types assessed by Lombroso

KEY IDEAS

Charles Darwin proposed the theory of evolution by **natural selection**. This idea suggests that over very long periods of time, organisms change because random mutations occur, some of which are beneficial. Individuals whose differences are advantageous characteristics are more likely to survive and reproduce (survival of the fittest). The new characteristics therefore become more common in the population.

that they can achieve things more easily by force than by hard work. This is an example of operant conditioning (see page 128). Alternatively, their appearance may prejudice those around them, causing other people, including those in the criminal justice service, to respond to them as 'criminal types', thus encouraging such behaviour, or being more inclined to give them custodial sentences. This is an example of a self-fulfilling prophecy (see page 128). Finally, the mesomorph body type may be more common in those from poor backgrounds, as a result of a poor diet and more manual labour. If poor backgrounds are also associated with higher rates of criminality, a link between body type and criminality may exist, but not for the reasons suggested by Sheldon.

Modern physiological explanations for criminality focus on genes. This does not mean there is a (single) 'gene for crime', rather that there may be *many* hereditary factors contributing to the *risk* of criminal behaviour. As men are more likely to exhibit criminal behaviour than women, one early genetic approach considered the difference between genetically normal men (those with XY sex chromosomes) and those with the genetic abnormality XYY. Jacobs *et al.* (1965) found that XYY men were more aggressive than XY men and, although they represent only 0.001% of the population, they made up 1.5% of prisoners. While this difference is large, the pattern is probably better explained by differences in intelligence. XYY men are less intelligent than average, so may be more easily swayed towards crime, especially as they may find earning a living more difficult.

Nevertheless, there are other links between criminality and genetic patterns. The simplest of these is that criminality runs in families. For example, Osborn & West (1979) found that only 13% of the sons of non-criminal fathers had convictions, whereas 40% of sons of criminal fathers had convictions. Of course, such effects may not be purely genetic, but evidence suggests that genes are partly responsible. This can be explored using studies of twins and of adopted children.

Twin studies

Monozygotic or 'identical' twins (MZs), share 100% of their genes, whereas dizygotic or 'non-identical' twins (DZs) share only 50% of their genes on average (see page 61). Any characteristic that is (at least in part) genetically controlled should show greater resemblance in monozygotic than dizygotic twins.

Lyons *et al.* (1995) studied records of misbehaviour and juvenile crime in thousands of twins. The MZs were not a lot more similar than DZs, suggesting that the environment is important in determining early criminal behaviour. However, records of criminal and aggressive behaviour in *adult* twins showed that the MZs were indeed more similar. This suggests that genetic factors become more important in adulthood. This pattern can be understood in terms of how much effect the environment can have. For children, external influences on behaviour are controlled – such as not watching violent television or being made to play with 'sensible' friends – so twins, whether they are MZs or DZs, would all be quite similar. As adults, however, individuals can make choices, and it appears that when DZs have this freedom, their behaviour becomes more different, suggesting a genetic effect.

Adoption studies

In twin studies, it is difficult to separate genetic effects from those of the twins' similar environments. In adoption studies, the two factors can be explored independently. Similarities between biological parents and their children suggest that genes are important, whereas similarities between adoptive parents and their children suggest that the environment is important.

The findings of two studies looking at the similarity between sons and their biological and adoptive parents in terms of criminal records are summarised in Table 3.1. Although the overall rates are different between the two studies, they show the same patterns:

- Having biological parents with a criminal record increases the chance of sons also having a criminal record, suggesting that genes influence criminality.
- Having adoptive parents with a criminal record increases the chance of sons also having a criminal record, suggesting that the environment influences criminality.
- Having biological and adoptive parents with a criminal record increases the chance of sons also having a criminal record even more, suggesting that the influences of genes and the environment on criminality add together.

TABLE 3.1: ADOPTION STUDIES OF CRIMINALITY			
Biological parents have criminal record	**Adoptive parents have criminal record**	**% of sons with criminal record** (Mednick *et al.*, 1987)	**% of sons with criminal record** (Bohman, 1995)
No	No	13.5	2.9
Yes	No	20.0	12.1
No	Yes	14.7	6.7
Yes	Yes	24.5	40

Non-physiological explanations of criminal behaviour

At AS level, you learned about Bandura *et al.*'s (1961) study and the theory of social learning. This idea can be used to explain the acquisition of criminality. As shown in Table 3.1, unrelated parents affect their children's behaviour, and one way this could happen is if they act as models, so children acquire criminal behaviour by observing and imitating parental crime.

Bandura (1977) suggested that learning occurs when the observer pays attention to the model, when they are able to remember and reproduce what they have observed, and when they are motivated to do so. Motivation may be created by the model, explaining why there are differences in the effectiveness of models. High-status and powerful models (such as parents, but also older peers or celebrities) are more effective, as are same-sex models and those who are likeable. Another motivating factor is *vicarious reinforcement*. This is when the observer sees the model receiving positive reinforcement for their actions, which makes imitation *by the learner* more likely. For example, if one child observes a peer bullying others for their pocket money the learner is watching not only a behaviour they could imitate (the bullying) but the rewards gained by the model (the stolen money). As this rewards the model, they become a more effective model for the learning of criminal behaviour.

MATHS MOMENT

Compare the findings of Mednick *et al.* and Bohman shown in Table 3.1 by estimating ratios or by drawing a pie chart. Comment on how similar or different the two sets of results are in relative rather than absolute terms.

QUESTION SPOTLIGHT!

Using the theory of social learning, explain why evil cartoon characters are potentially dangerous role models for children.

KEY IDEAS

Rewards and punishments change behaviour: this is **operant conditioning**. Nice consequences, or **positive reinforcement**, increase the frequency of the behaviour they follow, where as unpleasant consequences, or **punishment,** reduce the frequency of the behaviour.

Figure 3.3: Is our expectation of criminal behaviour a cause of criminality?

In general, observers with high self-efficacy, i.e. those who believe they can imitate the behaviour they are witnessing, are more likely to learn. However, in criminality, low self-esteem may also be important. Trzesniewski *et al.* (2006) found that adolescents with low self-esteem were more likely to engage in criminal activity as adults than those with higher self esteem, even when other factors, such as socio-economic status, were controlled for. In addition to the effects of social learning, **operant conditioning** will occur if the observer receives direct positive reinforcement for the criminal behaviour they have learned. For example, if a child uses violence and is rewarded, perhaps gaining sweets by threatening others, their behaviour is being positively reinforced so will increase in frequency. Although this is separate from the effects of social learning, it adds to the likelihood of imitation. A child could also gain positive reinforcement for imitated violence through the feeling of power over others or increased status. For example, imitating the violent actions of a popular TV villain could increase a child's popularity. These consequences are reinforcers, so would increase the frequency of the child's behaviours. Such effects were demonstrated experimentally by Bandura (1965), who showed that a child was more likely to copy an aggressive adult model if the child was reinforced – and less likely to if he or she was punished.

Bandura *et al.*'s studies were based on an artificial experimental setting. An alternative to this is to gather correlational data. Eron *et al.* (1972) measured the level of violence in TV programmes watched by 7–8 year olds and measured the children's aggressiveness, and found a positive correlation. By their teens, there was an even stronger positive correlation between the violence viewed and aggressiveness in boys (though not girls). Importantly, the more violence the boys had watched as children, the more likely they were to be violent criminals as adults (Eron & Huesmann, 1986).

People can affect our behaviour directly, by being models, or by reinforcing us. An alternative way we can be influenced by others is through their expectations. The self-fulfilling prophecy (SFP) suggests that the stereotyped beliefs somebody holds can affect the behaviour of another person. This is because beliefs affect behaviour. The holder of the false beliefs may respond in ways that elicit the expected behaviour from the other individual. This would confirm their expectations and reinforce their stereotype. With regard to criminality, the SFP suggests that this can happen if an observer expects others to engage in criminal behaviour. This expectation causes the observer to behave in ways that elicit criminal behaviour because their stereotyped beliefs change the way they interact socially. As a consequence, the anticipated criminal actions are demonstrated, confirming the initial beliefs. For example, a new girl at school is believed by other students to be a thief. As a result, they treat her with contempt and blame her for missing items. She can see that she is being treated differently from the other students, so feels she may as well do what they have accused her of. The students' initial response to her becomes the trigger for her subsequent real thefts.

In a naturalistic study, Jahoda (1954) looked at aggression in the children of the Ashanti people. A male child is traditionally given a 'soul name' determined by the day they were born, which is believed to affect his character. 'Monday' boys are thought to be calm, and 'Wednesday' boys aggressive. Jahoda found that 22% of violent offences were committed by boys with 'Wednesday' names, but only 7% by 'Monday' boys. This suggests that the cultural expectations about the boys' natures and the explicit labels – their names – resulted in the boys being treated differently. As a result, the boys acted in line with the expected differences.

Ageton & Elliott (1974) suggested that treatment of youth offenders by the police and courts could lead to further deviance. In a longitudinal study of delinquent boys, they found that those who were not caught had higher self-esteem and less of a delinquent view of themselves. SFP can explain this, as only the boys who were caught would have been exposed to negative responses from others (e.g. their families, the police or the courts), and these responses would have led to the boys exhibiting behaviours to fit their 'criminal' label. Alternatively, it may be that those who were not caught had higher self-esteem precisely because they had evaded arrest.

The self-fulfilling prophecy can also explain recidivism (repeat offending). Once an individual has the label of 'criminal', this is hard to shift. As people reinforce the label by their responses, it becomes part of the individual's self-concept, producing further deviant behaviour. We should therefore be cautious of labelling people as 'problems' as this may worsen their behaviour.

KEY RESEARCH

Raine, A., Buchsbaum, M. & LaCasse, L. (1997) Brain abnormalities in murderers indicated by positron emission tomography. *Biological Psychiatry*, 42 (6), 495–508.

Aim

To study brain activity in murderers and non-murderers using **positron emission tomography** (**PET**) to find out whether there were differences in areas thought to be involved in violent behaviour.

Method
Sample

The experimental group ('murderers') consisted of 39 men and 2 women (with a mean age of 34.3 years). Each had been charged with murder or manslaughter and pleaded 'not guilty by reasons of insanity' but had been convicted. The control group ('non-murderers') was matched for sex and age and, for six participants, a diagnosis of schizophrenia. Their mean age did not differ significantly from that of the experimental group. No participants took any medication for at least two weeks prior to testing.

Design and procedure

The participants were brain scanned during a **continuous performance task** (**CPT**). This was chosen because it increases activity in brain areas of interest in normal participants.

The participants were allowed to practise the CPT. Then, 30 seconds before being injected with a fluorodeoxyglucose tracer for the PET scan, the participants began their full CPT session. This ensured that the novelty of the task would not

KEY IDEAS

A **continuous performance task** (**CPT**) is a visual vigilance task. The participant watches brief stimuli (e.g. numbers or letters) that appear one after the other, pressing a button each time a specified stimulus appears. This controls for variations in sensory stimulation in the room, which could cause differences in brain activation that could obscure differences between the groups of participants.

Positron emission tomography (**PET**) is a brain-scanning technique in which the participant is injected with a radioactive tracer that is used in energy production (respiration) by the brain. The molecules of the tracer (e.g. glucose) travel through the blood and their breakdown is detected by a scanner. The brain scans indicate the level of activity in areas of the brain using different colours.

The following text is a description of the CPT used in Raine *et al*.'s study, taken from Buchsbaum *et al*. (1990): 'Single digits (0–9) were presented for 40 minutes at a rate of one every two seconds. Subjects were told to press a button using their right hand each time that they detected the digit 0 and that it was equally important to respond to zeros and not respond to non-zeros. Targets were presented irregularly with a probability of occurrence of 0.25. Stimuli were presented silently by rear projection on a 24cm × 24cm screen…'.

Produce and try out a test that replicates the task required of participants, using PowerPoint, for example.

STRETCH & CHALLENGE

The CPT was tested for split-half reliability. This produced an *r* value of 0.843, which was significant at *p*≤0.001. Describe how this reliability test could have been done and explain what the findings mean.

KEY IDEAS

The **limbic system** is a collection of structures lying beside the thalamus on both sides of the brain, which includes the amygdala, hippocampus and hypothalamus. It plays a role in many functions, including: emotion, processing of social information, motivation, learning and memory.

appear as an 'event' on the brain scan. The CPT continued for 32 minutes. After this, PET images of 10 horizontal 'slices' through the brain were taken at 10mm intervals. Two techniques were used to identify brain regions:

- *Cortical peel technique*: used for lateral areas (on the sides/surface of the brain) including the superior frontal, middle frontal and inferior frontal gyri, and areas of the temporal, parietal and occipital lobes.
- *Box technique*: used for medial areas (inside the brain) including the superior frontal gyrus, anterior medial frontal gyrus, medial frontal gyrus and orbital gyrus.

The scans were analysed for activity levels in many different brain areas — see Table 3.2 for some of these.

Results

In analysing the results, all tests were two-tailed. Means and standard deviations were calculated for the two levels of the independent variable (IV) for the activity of each brain area (some of these results are presented in Table 3.2 and Figure 3.5). The murderers had significantly less activity in the lateral, medial and parietal prefrontal cortical areas of the brain compared to controls, and also in the corpus callosum. They had abnormally asymmetrical activation in areas of the **limbic system**, including the amygdala (less activation on the left but more on the right), and lower activation on the right in the temporal lobe/hippocampus and in the thalamus.

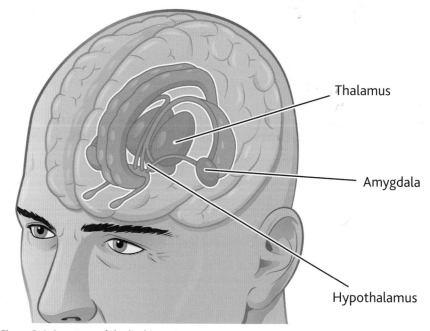

Figure 3.4: Structure of the limbic system

TABLE 3.2: GROUP MEANS FOR MURDERERS AND CONTROLS FOR ACTIVITY IN DIFFERENT BRAIN AREAS

	Left hemisphere		Right hemisphere	
	Control	**Murderer**	**Control**	**Murderer**
Lateral prefrontal cortex	1.12	1.09	1.14	1.11
Medial prefrontal cortex	1.25	1.2	1.22	1.17
Parietal cortex	1.15	1.1	1.17	1.13
Corpus callosum	0.68	0.56	0.67	0.56
Amygdala	0.97	0.94	0.83	0.88
Temporal lobe and hippocampus	0.95	0.91	0.93	0.96
Thalamus	1.09	1.09	1.09	1.15

Note: the values in red are significantly lower for the murderers; the values in green are significantly higher for the murderers.

Conclusion

The areas identified as having abnormal activity are associated with aggressive behaviour (amygdala, hippocampus, thalamus), a lack of fear (amygdala), impulsiveness, i.e. lowered self-control (prefrontal cortex), and problems with controlling and expressing emotions (amygdala, hippocampus, prefrontal cortex). All of these could lead to an increased risk of committing acts of extreme violence. They are also linked to problems with learning conditioned emotional responses and failure to learn from experiences, which could account for the type of violent offences committed (linked to the hippocampus, amygdala and thalamus). Finally, effects on areas associated with learning could lower IQ, which links to lower chances of employment and a higher risk of criminality (prefrontal and parietal cortex). As a consequence, one factor increasing the risk of committing a serious crime such as murder appears to be abnormal brain activity.

APPLICATION: A BIOLOGICAL STRATEGY FOR PREVENTING CRIMINAL BEHAVIOUR

Plastic surgery for prisoners

Even if the ideas of Lombroso and Sheldon have no scientific backing, it remains the case that we associate physical abnormalities with misbehaviour and criminality. These links arise early in childhood, for example with exposure to 'handsome princes' and 'ugly villains'. Such portrayal is not limited to male characters – think of the ugly sisters in *Cinderella*. This is an interesting example. The sisters were ugly before they were wicked. Could this be an example of a self-fulfilling prophecy? If we view people's characteristics in a stereotyped way, does our reaction risk causing them to take a potentially criminal pathway in life? If so, then one way to improve the chances of someone with a physical deformity avoiding a career in crime, or to reduce recidivism, is to improve their appearance. Not only might this prevent the consequences of negative responses from others, but it might also boost their self-esteem. How could this be done? Through reconstructive surgery to correct facial defects, making the individual's appearance better.

MATHS MOMENT

Explain why the measure of central tendency used in Table 3.2 was the mean rather than the mode.

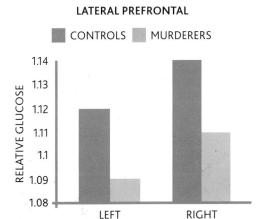

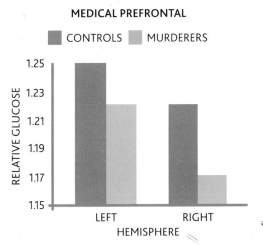

Figure 3.5: The level of brain activity indicated by the rate of use of glucose in murderers compared to controls

WEB WATCH @

Read this news article:

http://articles.chicagotribune.com/1986-01-31/features/8601080691_1_texas-prisoners-plastic-surgery-inmates

This is based on the situation described in an article (Spira *et al.*, 1966), which can be read in full for free here:

http://www.jprasurg.com/article/S0007-1226(66)80080-2/pdf

QUESTION SPOTLIGHT!

Explain why it was important for Lewinson to record the recidivism rate for inmates in general as well as those who had received facial surgery.

Plastic surgery therefore has potential as a biological strategy to prevent criminal behaviour. As early as the 1950s, the success of plastic surgery with criminal offenders was being reported in police literature (e.g. Bankoff, 1952). Lewinson (1965) went further, conducting 450 facial reconstruction operations in a prison population, including both men and women, and observing consequent behaviour both in prison and after release. In this systematic study, conducted over a period of 10 years, Lewinson took four factors into account when selecting prisoners for surgery: their age (although younger inmates potentially had more to gain, by age 40 they had often a strong desire to change); the number of offences (early offenders, with fewer than five offences, usually first-, second- or third-time offenders); the type of offence (drug addicts were usually but not always rejected, and sex offenders were not considered); and reasons for seeking surgery (embarrassment about a congenital defect, the desire for improved function, to correct defects to be able to perform prison duties better or to be eligible for a better job in the prison, or to be more presentable on release). There was always a long waiting list and prisoners noted that it was the only time anyone had shown any interest or care with respect to their deformity. The operations conducted were predominantly for congenital defects or previously broken noses, but also for deformed ears, receding chins and removal of facial scars.

Lewinson observed that the most obvious and immediate change was psychological – an increase in cooperation with authority and participation in prison activities. Following surgery, the inmates were also more likely to want to learn a trade. The effect was therefore to raise morale and reduce hostility. The recipients were grateful to the surgeon and nursing staff, and generated an interest in the operations among other inmates. Importantly, the recidivism rate for the 450 inmate patients was 42%, considerably less than the 75% rate for the general inmate population.

One problem, although rare, was that some patients, benefiting perhaps from their improved appearance, shifted from crimes such as breaking and entering and theft to more subtle, anti-social crimes such as those of confidence tricksters.

Successes were reported by Kurtzberg *et al.* (1968) in their comparison of recidivism in prison inmates receiving correction of facial disfigurements compared to a non-surgical control group and by Freedman *et al.* (1988), who compared recidivism rates following cosmetic surgery for inmates in general and those convicted of violent crimes in particular (see Table 3.3).

TABLE 3.3: RECIDIVISM RATES OVER A THREE-YEAR PERIOD	% of prisoners reoffending		
	Number of years post-release		
	1	2	3
Baseline prison population	14	32	36
Cosmetic procedure group	8	17	25
Cosmetic procedure group incarcerated for violent crimes	3.3	7.7	15

Source: Freedman *et al.* (1988)

Such successes suggest that the operations were, either directly or indirectly, responsible for the difference in recidivism. By bringing the prisoners into close contact with people who care about them as individuals (especially when their services are given for free, as in the case of the surgeon in Lewinson's study), giving them time and individual attention, and making them feel that they are worthy of this effort, will all enhance self-esteem. This is so regardless of the outcome of the surgery. In addition, the expectation of an improved appearance, whether or not this is a reality, can enhance self-perception. Since self-esteem is independently related to the risk of criminality, this is one possible causal influence. Furthermore, the individual's altered self-perception, both within the prison and on release, means that the responses they will elicit from others will be different from those they had before. The difference in their interactions with others breaks the cycle of the self-fulfilling prophecy and gives them a 'new start', in which other people treat them as non-criminals, thus eliciting non-criminal behaviour.

Experimental evidence from Stroomer *et al.* (1998) suggests that improved appearance may not be the causal factor, but rather that, post-operatively, patients tend to have different expressions, hairstyles or make-up. Their study compared independent judgments of 'liking' of facial photographs – pre-operative versus digitised post-operative ones that were identical to the pre-operative ones except for the correction of the deformity. The results showed that only two of the 15 patients (12.5%) were identified as having a more likeable appearance after surgery. On the one hand this evidence suggests that the operations themselves made only subtle differences to physical appearance, but on the other hand, it confirms that the procedure initiates a positive cycle that changes the individual's self-perception which in turn impacts on their social interactions.

EVALUATION

Methodological and ethical issues

In methodological terms, the research by Raine *et al.* used brain scanning, which is often thought of as a valid and reliable measure: we assume brain activity cannot be affected by demand characteristics, for example, raising validity and since the measures are technological they should be reliable. However, the precision of the location of scans in different participants is hard to maintain, so comparisons may be less valid than they appear, and scans still need to be interpreted, leading to the potential for lowered reliability. The generalisibility of the results is also limited as the range of criminals used was so small – those committing other crimes may have different patterns of abnormal brain activity. In fact, two controls groups are necessary – one for equally violent but non-criminal behaviour and another for equally criminal but non-violent behaviour. In addition, Raine *et al* observe that psychiatric controls other than for schizophrenia may have been appropriate to ensure that comparisons were valid. Nevertheless, the study offered a large sample considering the constraints on recruitment and the extensive matching and restriction on drug use controlled for several potential confounding variables.

Studying explanations of crime inevitably leads to research with inmates. This raises clear ethical issues – to what extent can they give informed consent? Prisoners should have the same right to withdraw as any other participants, but to what extent does a prisoner feel they can exercise this right? They may be more vulnerable to persuasion to participate simply because they are bored.

Debates

Biological explanations of crime suggest a hereditary disposition towards criminality, supporting the role of **nature** but the evidence does not indicate that this is an exclusive effect. Instead, the findings show that while genes may increase or decrease the risk of this outcome, the **nurture** perspective is important too. The social environment provides models who may or may not demonstrate crimes and, where this behaviour is seen – either in life or in the media – it may or may not lead to rewards or punishments, for the model or for the learner. Such consequences will contribute to the likelihood of acquiring criminal behaviour. Indeed, Raine *et al.* observe that even their findings showing brain activity differences do not mean that violence is determined purely by nature.

We assume that people have a choice about whether they engage in criminal behaviour or not, i.e. that we have **freewill**. The effect of facial surgery on inmates is an interesting example of the extent to which this may not be so. An individual who had been punished for a crime by imprisonment should, according to operant conditioning, be less likely to reoffend but in reality many released prisoners do. Changing the way they think about themselves and respond to others alters that risk suggesting that their behaviour is **determined** by both their self perceptions and the perceptions of others. Nevertheless, even when related factors are identified, such as brain activity in the case of Raine *et al*'s study, these factors alone do not preclude the potential for each individual to make a choice about their behaviour. Factors exist which may increase the risk of criminal behaviour but this does not remove the ultimate responsibility

for that action from any individual criminal. Clearly such findings are **socially sensitive** as they have direct implications for the punishment or treatment of criminals.

STRETCH & CHALLENGE

To what extent is it important in terms of justice that psychology makes a clear distinction between factors which cause criminality and factors which are related to criminality?

To assume that criminality was caused by any one factor, such as genes, learning or the self-fulfilling prophecy, would be **reductionist**. Instead, a more **holistic** view should be taken, considering the interaction of a range of factors on the individual, such as was demonstrated in the adoption studies on page 127.

Criminal behaviour is, by its very nature, hard to study because it is illegal and therefore hidden. Any study of criminals is by definition typically a study of those who failed to avoid getting caught. This makes criminality hard to study **scientifically**: the tendency of criminals to lie, the biased samples and the difficulties of observing actual criminal behaviour first hand mean that its objectivity is restricted.

Nevertheless, the study of the causes of criminality can provide **useful** guidance for society. Firstly in terms of reducing risks: knowing that children may learn behaviours from criminal models has led to restrictions on children's late-night TV viewing and their access to films through certification. Secondly, our understanding offers guidance for rehabilitation, for instance indicating the importance of self-esteem in prisoners and, as a more radical step, the use of surgery.

COLLECTION AND PROCESSING OF FORENSIC EVIDENCE

BACKGROUND

Crime scenes, fingerprints and psychology

You might think aspects of forensics like finger-printing would be outside the realm of psychology. However, mistakes are made with fingerprint analysis and if these are the product of human error, such problems would enter the psychological domain. In forensic analysis, there are two obvious competing motives. Analysts are motivated to catch criminals by identifying suspects but are also motivated to catch the right criminals, i.e. to avoid making mistakes.

Motivating factors and bias in the collection and processing of forensic evidence

Psychology offers an insight into the motivating factors and biases that can affect this decision-making. Charlton *et al.* (2010) interviewed 13 fingerprint analysts and produced an in-depth description of their main motives. They summarised these as: rewards (job satisfaction linked to skills); hope and satisfaction related to catching criminals and solving crimes; factors linked to case importance (e.g. serious or long-running cases); feelings associated with searching for and finding matches; and the need for closure on cases and fear about making mistakes.

In the analysis of crime-scene evidence, the ridge details of **fingerprints** are analysed and compared by expert analysts. Their job is to decide whether the ridge details on a suspect's finger(s) match those on **fingermarks** collected from the crime scene. Such marks are often poor quality, incomplete, smudged, distorted or obscured. Two fingerprint experts therefore complete the identification processes in order to verify the judgments made and reduce the likelihood of misidentifications.

Problems with fingerprint analysis

Studies have demonstrated a lack of consistency in fingerprint analysis. For example, Dror *et al.* (2011) found that individual fingerprint examiners differed both from one another (inter-observer consistency) and from themselves over time (intra-observer consistency). One reason for this is the range of cognitive factors that can bias decisions. Comparing fingerprints is an information-processing task and involves processes such as attention and visual searching, which you considered in the core studies by Moray and Simon & Chabris. You may recall how pertinent information could sometimes draw a person's attention, and irrelevant information could distract them. The same ideas might be important in fingerprint analysis when analysts compare the fingermark from the crime scene (the **latent mark**) to the comparison print (from a suspect). This is because it is a visual search task looking for, and comparing, specific ridge details from many categories (see examples in Figure 3.7).

WEB WATCH @

There are may fingerprint analysis activities online that illustrate the essence of the matching process with varying degrees of entertainment and accuracy. Try the following:

http://www.wonderville.ca/asset/fingerprint-activity (an animation that allows you to check a latent mark against several sets of prints)

http://www.newscientist.com/gallery/mg20527522600-guess-the-fingerprints (a matching exercise between pairs of latent marks and suspect prints).

KEY IDEAS

Fingerprints are the fine patterns you can see on the pads of your fingers and thumbs. Each one is (probably) unique. Compare the patterns on each of your fingers, or compare your hand to someone else's – you will see some differences. Our fingers can leave a trace of this pattern on surfaces we touch: this is called a '**fingermark**' or '**latent mark**'. The term 'latent mark' is more general, it can apply to the patterns of ridges left, for example, by palms or the soles of a person's feet. On some surfaces, these marks can be clear enough to be used by forensic analysts to determine whether they match the prints of a known suspect. These known (or 'comparison') fingerprints are taken in controlled conditions so they are of high quality.

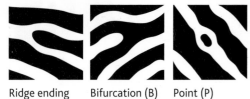

Ridge ending (A)   Bifurcation (B)   Point (P)

Figure 3.7: Three examples of ridge details (minutiae) in fingerprints

Source: adapted from Schiffer & Champod (2007), p.118.

a)   b)   c)   d)

Figure 3.6: Compared to a latent print (c) fingerprints can be unambiguous non-matches (a), or can be very similar (b) and (d). Fingerprints (b) and (d) are from identical twins, one twin being the source of the latent print.

Evidence such as Dror *et al.* (2005) shows that only decisions about ambiguous prints, such as (b) and (d), are affected by biases caused by factors such as emotional context.

As fingermark clarity decreases, interpretation becomes more difficult and subjective, and therefore more open to bias. One motivating factor for this bias is the circumstances of the case and the pressure that the fingerprint expert feels they are under. Decision-making is affected by emotional context, so much of what we call 'rational' thinking is partly emotionally governed judgments (Simón, 1998). Considerable evidence exists to show that context directly affects visual perception (see Figure 3.8 for an example). In an experimental study with non-experts, Dror *et al.* (2005) showed that, when decisions are made about fingermarks, a high-emotion context increases the likelihood of a 'match' decision being made with an ambiguous pair. University student participants were given pairs of fingerprint images and had to decide whether they matched. Although context made no difference to judgments about unambiguously similar or different pairs, a context based on a crime involving personal harm (rather than a minor crime such as theft) made the participants more like to say that ambiguous pairs matched. The emotional context was based on the nature of the crime, such as an attempted murder, and on photographs (for example, a neutral photograph of a lamp, or a graphic one of a large knife wound on a dead person's face). These created a bias in the participants' decision-making: the more emotive the context the more motivated the analysts were to find a match.

It might seem impossible for a fingerprint analyst to 'see' ridgemarks that are not there – but do you see a diamond in Figure 3.8 and does the shading in region A differ from that in region B? The subjective contours of this illusion show how the perceptual system can distort data so that we see things that are not actually there.

It is interesting to note that even a little experience may help. Schiffer & Champod (2007) investigated the effects of both case context and pre-exposure to the latent mark and found that neither affected the accuracy of analysis by forensic science students. However, errors are sometimes made even in high-profile cases – by highly experienced and practised analysts – hence the need to search for causes of misidentifications and ways to reduce such problems. For example, in a report from the US Department of Justice, the problem of 'circular reasoning' is identified. In one case, examiners looking at a suspect's prints found 10 points of unusual similarity between the suspects fingerprint and the fingermark from the crime scene. This, it is suggested, caused them to 'find' further (non-existent) points of similarity (see also Figure 3.9). This suggests that the motivating factor of the need to solve the crime may influence decision-making.

STRETCH & CHALLENGE ◎

Use the ideas from Moray and Simon & Chabris to explain how pertinent or irrelevant information might disrupt attention and visual searching in the context of fingerprint analysis. You might also have noticed a similarity between the lines in Figure 3.7 and the lines on the walls of the kittens' environment in Blakemore & Cooper's study. In fact, fingerprint analysts develop feature detectors for ridge patterns rather in the way that the kittens developed (or did not develop) detectors for horizontal or vertical lines (see the Web Watch below for more information).

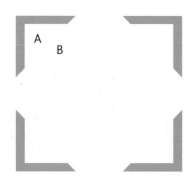

Figure 3.8: What shapes do you see?

KEY RESEARCH

Hall, L.J. & Player, E. (2008) Will the introduction of an emotional context affect fingerprint analysis and decision-making? *Forensic Science International,* 181 (1), 36–9.

Aim

In the UK, the Metropolitan Police Fingerprint Bureau gives fingerprint experts assigned to a case a copy of the crime scene examination report which provides details of the nature of the crime (although the report has no photographs). This means that the examiner making decisions about the match of prints is exposed to potentially high-emotion background material. This study aimed to investigate whether:

- the fingerprint experts were emotionally affected by the case details in the report, and
- emotional context would bias the judgments of expert analysts (as was the case with the students in Dror *et al.*'s study).

Method

Sample

The sample consisted of 70 fingerprint experts working for the Metropolitan Police Fingerprint Bureau whose experience ranged from less than 3 months to over 30 years (mean 11 years). Most dealt with crimes ranging from burglaries to terrorism although 12 were managers (not active practitioners but remaining on the UK Register). All were volunteers who responded to a request (which did not provide details) to take part in an experiment. The data collected were recorded anonymously using a unique reference number for each expert.

Design and procedure

To be certain that the experts' decisions in the experiment were correct, a fingermark from a known source was made. This was scanned and superimposed onto an image of a £50 note on a card so that the background image, and contrast control, obscured most of the ridge detail (see Figure 3.10). The latent mark was thus only just identifiable. A separate sample of experts of varying experience confirmed the mark was of poor quality and an ambiguous match to a set of 10 prints from the donor. Although the experts are not normally given fingermarks on card, this can happen, and the colour, size and detail of the image were typical of the quality and clarity regularly seen.

Each participant was given an envelope with a test mark card (with a sheet saying it was from the right forefinger), the 10-print fingerprint and the scene examiner's report. It was thus a typical case report except for the advice about it being from the right forefinger, which was included for speed. This process replicated the verification stage of the identification process.

They each also had a fingerprint magnifying glass and a Russell Comparator (an optical magnifier) to compare images. The participants were randomly assigned to groups of eight and asked to treat the experiment and the task like an ordinary case and a normal day, moving around and talking to each other (but not about the experiment or the fingermarks). There was no time limit.

WEB WATCH

You can read more about the relationship between fingerprint analysis and psychology here:

https://www.ncjrs.gov/pdffiles1/nij/225335.pdf

Figure 3.9: This latent mark was misidentified as belonging to a terrorist involved in train bombings in Madrid, Spain, in 2004. The highly emotional context may have been responsible for creating a motivational context, which led to the misidentification of Brandon Mayfield – whose prints were already in a database – as the bomber.
Source: FSI, 156 (1), p.75 (2005)

QUESTION SPOTLIGHT!

Consider the information about Hall & Player's sample. Comment on the extent to which their procedure was ethical.

Figure 3.10: A fingermark similar to the one used in the study.

KEY IDEAS

Stages of fingerprint analysis – The examination of a latent print follows a four-stage process, the ACE-V, which stands for Analysis, Comparison, Evaluation, and Verification. In this process, an initial examiner conducts the first three of these and annotates documents about the fingerprint analysis, directing the verifier to ridge details used in their conclusions. The verifier may then agree or disagree. In some instances, the verifier is blind to the initial examination and examines the latent mark independently.

The research method was an experiment, so the participants were assigned to one of two levels of the independent variable of emotional context: low-emotion context or high-emotion context. It was therefore an independent measures design, with half of the participants in each condition. The difference was in the nature of their examination report. For the low-emotion condition, the context referred to a forgery (a 'victimless' crime which carries a minor sentence), which said: *'Suspect entered premises and tried to pay for goods with a forged £50 note. The forgery was spotted by cashier. Suspect then decamped.'* For the high-emotion group the report referred to a murder (i.e. a crime with a clear victim and a severe sentence). The report was the same except the last sentence which read: *'Suspect then fired two shots at victim before decamping.'* The two dependent variables were whether the analysts reported feeling affected by the context-creating scenarios and whether this affected their final decision about the fingermark.

After their analysis, the experts were asked to make a judgment about the print as they would normally (see also Table 3.4), i.e. to say whether:
- the mark was an *identification* (a match),
- the mark was not an identification [an *exclusion*] (not a match),
- the mark was *insufficient* – not enough detail to undertake a comparison, or
- there was insufficient detail to establish identity; some detail in agreement but not enough to **individualise** [*inconclusive*].

TABLE 3.4: THE POSSIBLE ERRORS FINGERPRINT ANALYSTS CAN MAKE

		Appropriate outcome as determined by experts			
		Identification	**Exclusion**	**Inconclusive**	**Insufficient**
Examiner's decision	*Identification*	CORRECT	False positive	False positive	False positive
	Exclusion	False negative	CORRECT	False negative	False negative
	Insufficient	Missed an identification	Missed an exclusion	CORRECT	Missed an insufficient
	Inconclusive	Missed an identification	Missed an exclusion	Missed an inconclusive	CORRECT

Source: US Department of Commerce (2012).

They were asked to elaborate on the findings, providing observations and opinions. Finally, via a feedback sheet, they were asked whether they had referred to the crime scene report prior to their assessment of the marks. If they had done so they were then asked whether they felt the information had affected their analysis.

Results

Only 57 of the 70 participants read the crime scene examination report before examining the prints. With regard to the first aim, 52% of the 30 who had read the high-emotion context scenario felt affected by the information in the report, significantly more than the 6% who had read and felt affected by the low-emotion context scenario. This indicates that there is a relationship between the type of context and the perceived effect on the experts.

Figure 3.11: What is the middle character?

Depending on whether you read across (so the context is one of letters) or down (so the context is one of numbers), your perception will change. This illustrates how the interpretation of a visual image – just like a fingermark – depends on the visual or mental context in which it is viewed.

For the second aim, to find out whether this effect altered the experts' decisions, the difference in decisions between the two groups was compared. The final decisions made by the experts (Table 3.5) are very similar for the two emotional contexts and no significant difference was found.

TABLE 3.5: THE EXPERTS' FINAL OPINIONS OF FINGERMARK COMPARISON WITH DELIBERATELY OBSCURED TRUE MATCH

	Number of experts giving final opinion as:				
	Identification	Insufficient not suitable for comparison	Some detail in agreement but not sufficient to identify	No identification	Total number of experts
High-emotion context	6	15	13	1	35
Low-emotion context	7	12	16	0	35

Source: Hall & Player (2008) p.38.

The participants were asked if they would be prepared to present the mark in court, i.e. about their confidence in the difference between the set of clear prints and the ambiguous fingermark. This explored whether they were more motivated or obliged to try to explain an identification in the high-emotion context. Figure 3.12 shows that more were sufficiently confident in the low-emotion context (20%) than in the high-emotion context (17%), although this relationship was not significant.

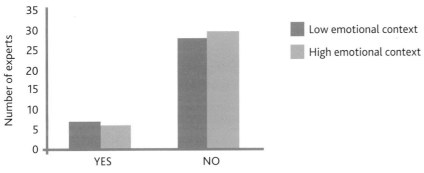

Figure 3.12: The number of experts willing to present the fingerprint evidence in court
Source: Hall & Player (2008) p.38, Figure 2.

Conclusion

Emotional context does affect experts' feelings but it does not influence the final outcome of their analysis (because no difference was observed between the high- and low-emotion contexts). In comparison to the findings of Dror *et al.* (2005), this shows that experienced fingerprint experts are better at doing analyses in a detached manner than non-experts.

KEY IDEAS

Individualisation is being able to isolate a particular suspect by determining that the latent print could have only come from that person. Historically, this was assumed to be a universal or absolute judgment because every finger was believed to have a unique pattern of ridges and other features that was fixed over the lifespan. Nowadays it is considered to be a judgment made with high confidence that the two prints are sufficiently similar to have come from the same source.

MATHS MOMENT

Note that the percentages of participants who felt affected by the crime-scene examination report are only those who *reported* to the experimenters that they felt affected – others may have felt affected but *not* reported this. Would the absence of any such participants from the totals have increased or decreased the percentages described as affected?

The statistical test used in this analysis was a Chi-square test. The results of this test were: $\chi^2 = 17.920$, df = 1, $p < 0.0001$. Of these three numbers, which is which of the:

- figure calculated using the formula 'number of rows $-1 \times$ number of columns -1',
- observed value,
- the significance level?

Consider these four factors separately and together:

- The participants were aware that they were participating in an experiment.
- The participants were encouraged to treat the experiment as a 'normal day's work'.
- The participants were prevented from talking to each other about the study.
- The one ambiguous mark was the only piece of forensic evidence in the case.

To what extent did these factors affect the ecological validity of the study?

APPLICATION: STRATEGIES FOR REDUCING BIAS IN THE COLLECTION AND PROCESSING OF FORENSIC EVIDENCE

ACTIVITY

Using instructions online, take fingerprints of members of your class and put them on good-quality white card. Allow each person to make one extra print of one digit, putting this print on other materials, such as rough card, coloured card, crumpled paper, smooth fabric, etc. This will 'degrade' the print, simulating the loss of clarity in a real latent print. See if you can match each single 'latent print' to its owner. Use the diagrams in Figures 3.7, 3.14 and 3.14b (or use ones online).

Fingerprints are traditionally taken with ink, as described here:

http://www.ehow.co.uk/how_6319152_fingerprints-ink.html

and here:

http://www.wikihow.com/Take-Fingerprints

or can be done very successfully with pencil and paper, as described here: http://www.instructables.com/id/Get-your-fingerprint/

Figure 3.13: What motivates a fingerprint analyst to make a match?

The evidence from the key research above suggests that the fingerprint experts, unlike non-experts, were not biased in their interpretation of forensic evidence (and nor, according to Schiffer & Champod (2007), were student fingermark analysts). However, other evidence is contradictory and there may be a variety of possible causes of error. Hampikian *et al.* (2011) reported that there have been many DNA exonerations and concluded that forensic science is far from flawless. In fact, only 2% of the 149 cases examined were ones in which the original (wrongful) convictions were based on fingerprint evidence (mistaken eyewitness identification was, for example, a far greater problem). Nevertheless, that any mistakes are made at all suggests that the process could benefit from improvements. Fingerprint analysts are only human, and are subject to the same biases and emotional and motivational influences that affect other aspects of our decision-making. For forensic analysts, however, the consequences of errors can have grave effects on others. Charlton *et al.* (2010) interviewed 13 experienced fingerprint examiners, who indicated that they derived satisfaction from catching criminals, especially in high-profile, serious, or long-running cases. They identified positive emotional effects associated with matching fingerprints and a need for cognitive closure, that is, to reach a definitive conclusion. However, these factors, which would tend towards making a (potentially erroneous) match, were tempered by a fear of making errors. In this section we will consider several ideas as strategies for reducing error in the collection and processing of forensic evidence.

a.

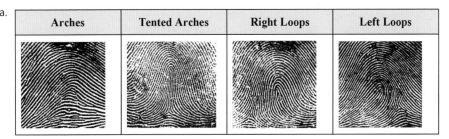

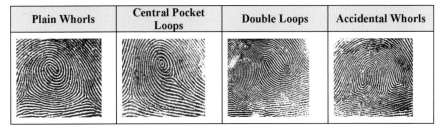

b.

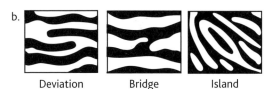

Figure 3.14: (a) Fingerprint types (b) Three further types of minutiae

Source: Expert Working Group on Human Factors in Latent Print Analysis (2012), (a) p.56, Figure 3.1; (b) pp.58–9.

Combating expectation: independent analysis of the latent mark and comparison print

As we discussed on page 135, Dror *et al.* (2011) found that fingerprint examiners differed in terms of inter- and intra-observer consistency. One important recommendation from this study was that the initial analysis of the latent mark should be done in isolation from the comparison print. This was because their study showed that if the experts had viewed a comparison print before analysing the latent print they identified fewer key elements of the print (minutiae) than if they had not. Dror *et al.* suggest that this is because the latent mark sets up cognitive expectations that affect the attention-guided visual search, i.e. knowledge of what might be there biases what is actually found. This is important as analysts need to be objective in their examination, although Dror *et al.* also observe that the comparison print may instead serve to optimise the visual search, so the best compromise would be to examine the latent mark in isolation and subsequently review this analysis after seeing the comparison print.

Kassin *et al.* (2013) support this strategy, observing that examiners should work in a linear rather than a circular way – progressing *from* the crime scene evidence *to* comparison with a target, rather than exploring these either together or alternately. They suggest that this will eliminate the possibility of the target (the comparison print) influencing how the information from the source (the latent print) is processed and the significance that is given to it. Once the analysis of the comparison print is complete, viewing the latent mark can usefully guide the examiner to reconsider particular areas of the print for minutiae, but this should be limited, for example, to those features that were inconclusive in the initial analysis.

Combating circular reasoning and bias: the filler-control method

Dror *et al.* (2013) identified several related problems: contextual bias, having a target suspect, and circular reasoning. Analysing prints in the absence of case information such as confessions and eyewitness identification helps to avoid bias to an extent, although it does not avoid the assumption that any individual identified as a suspect is likely to be the perpetrator. To overcome these issues,

QUESTION SPOTLIGHT!

You will be familiar with the effects of expectation in everyday life. Imagine you have lost a textbook. You are sure the cover has a blue pattern. Which books, that are not in fact the one you are looking for, are you most likely to spot in your search? What would happen if, in fact, the book were orange? Relate these two examples to the situation experienced by a fingerprint analyst who has a latent mark (which is not, in fact, from the perpetrator) and a closely matching comparison print.

STRETCH & CHALLENGE

Use your understanding of the role of filler questions in questionnaires to explain how the filler-control method should work in a forensic context.

KEY IDEAS

Forensic confirmation bias is the tendency for an individual's pre-existing beliefs, expectations, motives, and situational context to affect they way in which they collect, perceive and interpret evidence in a criminal case.

Dror *et al.* suggest that the examiner should be given not just one sample print for comparison but six, consisting of the comparison print (from the suspect) plus five plausible alternatives or 'fillers'. The task would not then simply be deciding whether the comparison print is a match for the latent print but would instead be to determine which print, if any, matched the evidence from the crime scene or victim. This filler control method is like the 'line-up' used for visual identification of a suspect by eyewitnesses, which has been shown to be the most effective procedure (Wells *et al.*, 1998). Miller (1987) demonstrated that a similar 'line up' procedure for analysing forensic hair samples was also less likely to produce false-positives (misidentifications) than the standard process. So, in the filler-control method, the examiner is working 'blind' to the information about which print belongs to the suspect. This avoids the bias inherent in decision-making that asks 'Is this similar enough?' as it instead asks the question 'Which is the most similar?'. While it still does not offer a complete solution, by removing the knowledge that a particular print is potentially that of the perpetrator, the examiner can be more objective.

Combating context effects: working in isolation from other evidence and other conclusions

In line with the evidence from Dror *et al.* (2005) described on page 136, Kassin *et al.* (2013) suggest that the *examiner* should be unaware of crime-scene information, including whether the suspect has confessed, and should avoid contact with the victims and their families. Furthermore, they propose that the *verifier* should be blind both to this information and to the initial conclusions of the examiner, indeed preferably they should even be unaware of who this examiner was. Awareness of such information could lead to a forensic confirmation bias, i.e., in this instance, to finding evidence of a match between prints.

One final suggestion from Kassin *et al.* is that forensic science education should include some basic psychology – most notably, experimental methods and, as has been addressed in this topic, aspects of perception, judgment, decision-making and social influence that impinge on the effectiveness of the role of forensic analysts.

EVALUATION

Methodological and ethical issues

Much research in this area uses as participants fingerprint analysts in their daily work or data from actual cases (such data following DNA exoneration). Such studies have high ecological validity in the sense that they are based on real-life instances of forensics at work. However, even in the case of the key study by Hall & Player, there are some ways in which the procedure was clearly artificial, not least in that the participants knew they were in an experiment and knew the cases were not real. In other studies, the participants may not be forensic experts, taking the generalisibility one step further from the reality of an analyst faced with the emotional and motivational impact of decision-making that potentially determines freedom or incarceration, rightly or wrongly.

Even when studies are based on experts in the workplace, there is a balance to be met between strong ecological validity, such as participants following their normal daily routine, and controls, such as ensuring that they do not talk about the case. In reality, such conversations may help (or hinder) decision-making and such influences are excluded in experimental situations. This makes them more controlled but less realistic.

Hall & Player's key study, although conducted in the workplace, may not have been entirely realistic for the participants. Apart form knowing that they were in an experiment, there were several ways in which the situation was unlike a real case. They were given not only the full set of 10 fingerprints, but also a test-mark card illustrating the same finger as the latent mark (in order to speed up the process of analysis and to mimic the verification process). In addition to the whole fingermark set also being on card, there were differences in the presentation of the case details too. As the mark was presented on a £50 note, the case report implied a high probability that it belonged to person who presented the note to the cashier (although, in fact, few participants commented on this possibility). In addition, it was the only piece of evidence being presented in the case, which could have raised the apparent level of responsibility on the analyst. However, this was a constant between both groups so should not have affected the overall results. Finally, the participants knew they were not dealing with a 'live' mark – i.e. they were aware it was not from a current investigation – which could have affected their motivation. However, to have placed it covertly into their normal workload would have required significant and potentially unjustifiable deception.

In the broadest sense, psychology has a responsibility to improve quality of life. In this respect, it is essential that psychological knowledge is used to benefit society, in this case to ensure the fair and just treatment of suspects. In the specific case of studies on fingerprint analysts, qualitative research has revealed that they feel pressure both to convict criminals and to avoid making mistakes. When under the scrutiny of experimenters, these conflicting motives may be stressful. In the Hall & Player study, there were many steps to ensure the ethical acceptability of the study. The participants were volunteers so were willing to participate and, while not fully informed, they were already fingerprint experts so understood what would happen in the course of the study. Similarly, as they were already working in forensics, the high-emotion context information would not have been shocking, so the potential for harm in that respect was minimal. Finally, by using reference numbers not names to identify participants, confidentiality was assured. This was especially important as any mismatches of prints could reflect badly on an individual's competence in their job.

Debates

Usefulness of research

Clearly research such as this has direct implications for the judicial system and, interestingly, these may be more extensive than is apparent at first glance. While this study is based, necessarily, on a restricted sample of expert analysts and focuses on a narrow task – of comparing finger marks – the conclusions about problems and possible solutions may have wider implications. It is not only in the domain of fingerprints that forensic experts' decision-making is based on visual analysis of degraded or limited evidence under emotional pressure. The same may apply to decisions about matches for forensic samples such as hair, or even DNA. The issues of confirmation biases and of emotional context, and the corresponding recommendations for improved procedures, may therefore generalise to other practices.

Freewill vs determinism

The consideration of ways to improve the accuracy of fingerprint analysis shows that, in spite of the analysts' strong desire to make correct decisions, they are prey to many potential influences. This illustrates the extent to which we do not have free will. While reporting that they are emotionally affected by contextual information, some evidence suggests that analysts do manage to remain impartial. Other evidence suggests that when viewing stimuli such as latent marks, cognitive processes are in part determined by unconscious effects such as expectations and biases, which can detrimentally affect decision-making about matches between prints.

Reductionism and holism

Decision-making, as this topic shows, is the product of a complex interaction of factors. Not only are biological considerations important, such as the specialisation of the perceptual system to certain types of stimuli, but higher cognitive, emotional and social ones too. The diversity of factors considered in this approach to an aspect of forensic psychology is therefore relatively holistic.

Psychology as a science

Ways to improve analytical processes in forensics rely on some of the same strategies that are used to maintain objectivity in psychological experiments. Analysts, like experimenters, benefit from being blind to key information that could influence the way they collect and interpret data. Another way to avoid bias is to hide the 'real' information among other irrelevant but plausible items, as is done with filler questions designed to hide the key items in questionnaires. In forensics, the (potentially) 'real' prints can be presented within the context of similar 'filler' prints.

COLLECTION OF EVIDENCE

BACKGROUND

Collection and use of evidence from witnesses and suspects

There are several ways in which the police can collect information, including the use of identity parades and identikits. Perhaps the most important technique that the police use is to interview both witnesses and suspects. This section will look briefly at the use of line-ups and identikits before focusing on the techniques of police interviewing.

Identity parades

Identity parades (or line-ups) are used when the police have a suspect and need a witness (or a victim) to confirm that this is the person they are looking for. An identity parade is traditionally a line-up of around six individuals, including the suspect and a number of 'foils'. The witness is ideally on the other side of a one-way glass screen, so they can not be seen, and has to identity the perpetrator from the line-up.

Line-ups suffer from a number of weaknesses, including the fact that witnesses feel under pressure to choose someone. This is because they make the reasonable assumption that the suspect is one member of the line-up. This bias can be easily reduced by telling witnesses that the person may or may not be in the line-up, or, even more effectively, showing the witness the people in the line-up one at a time (without telling them how many there are in total) and asking them to make a decision on each one individually.

One of the most prominent researchers in this area is Gary Wells, an American psychologist from Iowa State University. He has conducted research into a range of factors that affect line-ups, including some in which he manipulated the confidence of the eye witness by giving them false feedback about the accuracy of their decision. In this study, participants watched a poor-quality video from a shop camera showing a man entering a store. They were then told that this man had murdered the shop's security guard and they were asked to pick him out from a photo line-up. The person was not in the line-up, so whatever choice was made, the participant would be incorrect. One group of participants were told that they had chosen the correct person, one group were told that they had chosen the incorrect person and a third, control group, were given no feedback on their choice. They were then asked a number of questions including:

- *'How certain were you that the person you identified from the photos was the gunman that you saw in the video?'* and
- *'On the basis of your memory of the gunman, how willing would you be to testify in court that the person you identified was the person in the video?'*

Figure 3.15: Identifying a suspect in a line-up

The results showed that the people who received the confirming feedback ('*you chose the correct person*') were more certain of their accuracy, and said that they would be more willing to testify. These are worrying results as they suggest that reactions from the police to correct line-up identifications could have significant effects on witness testimony later in court. As with the other methods of collecting evidence, every effort needs to be made to reduce any possibility of leading questions or other form of bias. In the case of line-ups, one suggestion is that police adopt a **double-blind** procedure, where the officer running the line-up is not aware which is the suspect and which are the foils, so that they are unable to unconsciously pass on any clues to the witness.

Identikits

These are techniques for producing an accurate image of someone to fit a witness's description. These images would have been originally produced by police artists who would spend hours with a witness in order to produce a hand-drawn likeness. During the 1970s this moved on to what we know as photo-fit, which builds up a picture of a face by selecting features (eyes, nose, mouth, etc.) from a large bank of photographic images. This system was obviously able to be used much more widely as there was no need for artistic skills, although they often produced very odd-looking faces. More recently, a number of 'facial composite' systems have been introduced (including FACES, E-FIT and SketchCop). Although most police departments now use computer-based systems such as these it is interesting to note that the FBI still uses police artists to create their likenesses.

KEY IDEAS

Double-blind is a research methods term meaning that neither the participants nor the experimenter know what is expected. If the experimenter is 'blind' to the experiment, then they cannot influence the outcome, either consciously or unconsciously.

WEB WATCH @

For more of Gary Wells' research into line-ups, as well as other topics related to eyewitness memory, visit his website:

https://public.psych.iastate.edu/glwells/

Figure 3.16: An image produced using FACES software

ACTIVITY ✳

Creating a recognisable image is harder than you might realise. If you try to describe the face of someone you know well – what shape is their face? what shape is their nose? – you will quickly realise that facial recognition is based on the whole face, rather than an awareness of each individual feature. Now try this task.

This website – hosted by the Open University – allows you to create your own images: http://www.open.edu/openlearn/body-mind/photofit-me

See if you can produce a photo-fit of the same person that other people can recognise. Would they recognise themselves? Why not ask someone who knows you well to try to create a photo-fit of you?

Interviews

The standard interview (SI)

Police have traditionally received very little training in interviewing techniques and have been free to 'ask whatever questions they feel are relevant, frequently interrupt, ask short-answer questions, and follow inappropriate sequences of questioning' (Brewer, 2000, p.49). This is termed the standard interview in many texts, although it is important to understand that this term does not refer to a specific technique. This issue will be discussed later in this chapter. After careful analysis of the 'standard interview', Fisher *et al.* (1989) identified a range of problems. These included numerous interruptions and an over-reliance on short-answer questions at the expense of long-answer questions designed to elicit more detail and to improve recollection. Pedzek *et al.* (2007) also provides evidence that pushing the witness to answer questions is likely to result in false information being provided. Fisher's work culminated in the development of the cognitive interview, which starts with the assumption that there is always more information in the witness's memory than they have initially recalled.

The cognitive interview (CI)

The cognitive interview is a specific interviewing technique that has been developed using knowledge of cognitive processing. It has four stages, which are followed in order:

1 *Context reinstatement*. This is based on research that has shown that recall is improved when we recall in the same (or similar) context to the one in which the material was learnt. Police interviewers should encourage the witness to reinstate the context in their mind. This might mean recalling environmental factors such as the placement of furniture, the temperature, or any particular sounds or smells, as well as recalling how they were feeling or what they were thinking at the time. Police interviewers may encourage the witness to close their eyes and imagine themselves back in the situation.

2 *In-depth reporting*. The second stage is to ask the witness to tell the story of what happened, in their own words, and in as much detail as possible. There should be no interruptions, and witnesses should be encouraged to report everything that they can recall, even if it seems irrelevant. The interviewer's job in this stage is to encourage and support rather than ask questions.

3 *Narrative re-ordering*. The third stage is to ask the witness to recall the story again but from a different perspective or from a different starting point. For example, they may be asked to start at the end and tell the story backwards, or to start in the middle. Reporting a story backwards means that later elements provide cues to earlier ones, rather than the other way around.

4 *Reporting from different perspectives*. Finally, the witness is asked to tell the story again, but this time from the perspective of another witness. It is acknowledged that some of this may be speculation but, as with the other stages, this may produce cues that generate new memories.

There have been many studies into the effectiveness of the cognitive interview. One of the earliest ones was conducted by Fisher *et al.* (1989), who compared the performance of experienced detectives, before and after training, in cognitive interviewing techniques, and compared their post-training performance with that of a control group. This was a field experiment with repeated measures.

The sample for this study was 16 experienced detectives from Florida. Seven completed the cognitive interviewing course and the rest acted as the control group.

Each detective recorded five to seven interviews over a period of four months and in total 88 interviews were recorded, mainly with victims of commercial robbery or handbag snatching. After this had been completed, seven of the detectives underwent four training sessions of one hour each, and then a further 47 interviews were recorded. Interviews were transcribed and scored by independent judges and the numbers of relevant, factual and objective statements were recorded.

The results showed that 47% more information was recorded in the post-training interviews, and six of the seven detectives in this group did better post-

ACTIVITY ✳

Conducting a cognitive interview

Context reinstatement. Imagine that you are interviewing someone who witnessed a theft from a large supermarket. Suggest questions that could be used to help the witness reinstate the context of witnessing the theft.

Reporting from a different perspective

Think about the last time you went out with a group of friends. Tell the story of where you went and what happened from your perspective. Now tell the story again from the point of view of one of your friends.

training, with only one doing worse (and the researchers note that this detective was not using the strategies that had been suggested during the training). When the trained group were compared to the control group, 63% more information had been recorded in the interviews conducted by the trained detectives. This study clearly shows that the cognitive interview technique is effective and further suggests that the training is relatively easy to provide.

The enhanced cognitive interview (ECI)

The enhanced cognitive interview (ECI) contains the same four techniques as the CI, but adds social aspects to the setting and procedure which appear to improve communication. This includes ensuring that distractions are kept to a minimum, allowing pauses, and being as sensitive as possible to the needs of the interviewee. The interviewee is also encouraged to strengthen the context reinstatement by the use of focused memory techniques such as imagery.

KEY RESEARCH

Memon, A. and Higham, P.A. (1999) A review of the cognitive interview. *Psychology, Crime and Law*, 5 (1–2), 177–196.

This is a **review** rather than a report of a single piece of research. The authors have structured their review around four key themes, which are:

1 The effectiveness of the various components of the cognitive interview
2 The relationship between the cognitive interview and other interviewing methods such as the standard interview and the structured interview
3 Different measures of memory performance and the effect this has on research findings
4 Interviewer variables and the effect of training quality on interview performance.

The effectiveness of the various components of the cognitive interview

We have already looked at the components of the cognitive interview. In their review, the authors attempt to identify exactly which component of the cognitive interview is the effective component. One way to do this is to isolate each of the components of the CI and test their effectiveness individually. Surprisingly, there do not seem to have been many pieces of research that have set out to do this. However, they do report one of Memon's own studies (Memon *et al.*, 1996), in which college students were interviewed using one of three cognitive techniques: context reinstatement, changing order (or narrative re-ordering) and changing perspective. A control group were simply asked to 'try harder'.

In this study no significant differences were found across the four groups. However, a later study by Milne (1997) compared the full CI procedure with each of the individual components (context reinstatement, changing order and changing perspective). Although she found no differences across the different component groups, she did find that the full CI procedure produced more recall than all of the single component groups, with the exception of the cognitive reinstatement group.

 **KEY IDEAS**

A **review** article is an article that brings together a number of pieces of research conducted by other authors, rather than reporting original research by the author. They are extremely useful in that they may identify themes or conclusions that have been identified by a careful examination of a wide range of research, or they may explicitly assess a number of pieces of research against objective criteria. There are journals that specialise in publishing review articles.

QUESTION SPOTLIGHT!

Identify as many differences between the cognitive interview and a standard police interview as you can.

This leads the authors of the review to conclude that context reinstatement is the most effective component of the cognitive interview. They claim that the instruction to change perspective or to recall in reverse order have not been shown to be effective by themselves. However, they do admit that it is possible that it is the combination of techniques that is effective rather than any single component. To test this idea would require the testing of every possible combination of techniques to discover which one, or which combination, was the most effective.

The relationship between the cognitive interview and other interviewing methods such as the standard interview and the structured interview

In early research studies into the effectiveness of the CI, the CI was most commonly compared with the standard interview. However, as we have already seen, the standard interview is not a standardised set of procedures and is associated with a number of inappropriate interview techniques, such as firing lots of questions at the interviewee very fast, using too many short-answer or leading questions, and constantly interrupting. Clearly the CI offers many advantages over the standard interview, but it is almost impossible to compare the two as they differ in so many ways. For example, the reviewers suggest that the increased effectiveness of the CI may be due to the fact that interviewers have had some training in interview techniques (perhaps to avoid the negative aspects of the standard interview described above) and not because they are using specific CI techniques. Trained interviewers may also be motivated in comparison with those who have had no training. It is also impossible to control for individual differences in the styles of interviewers using the standard interview as there would be so many.

They conclude that this was a useful comparison for researchers to begin with, when the key question was whether the CI was better than the procedures used by the majority of police. However, the research has now moved on to attempting to determine the effectiveness of individual components of the CI rather than simply measuring its effectiveness as a whole. They therefore recommend that researchers do not use the standard interview as a comparison group in future research. Instead, they suggest comparisons with the structured interview, which encourages interviewers to build rapport, to allow time for narrative descriptions and to avoid interrupting or rushing witnesses. However the SI and the CI are different in that the specific cognitive procedures (e.g. context reinstatement) are found only in the CI. Research has found that the CI produces more information than the SI, although there is no difference in accuracy rates. Because the sole difference between the two is the use of the cognitive procedures, this will offer researchers a better comparison group for establishing the effectiveness of these techniques.

Different measures of memory performance and the effect this has on research findings

The authors begin this section with the observation that researchers examining the effectiveness of the CI might usefully examine the measures of memory that they are using. They claim that the majority of studies measure performance in terms of a percentage of correct statements or an absolute number of correct and incorrect statements. This causes problems as it neglects to consider the amount and nature of unreported information. We also know from laboratory research that the CI results in people reporting more information than they might in an SI. Measures of memory need to be able to take account of the fact that the CI may be changing an interviewee's understanding of what it is that the interviewer wants.

ACTIVITY ✳

Design a study to test memory for an event. You could begin by showing a group of participants a video. Ask them to recall as much as they can. Now you need to make some decisions about how you are going to code their answers

- Are you going to count how many things they remembered? Is 'a man with red hair and a beard' one item or two, or possibly even three?
- Is remembering a number plate more difficult (and therefore worth more points?) than remembering the make or colour of the car?
- Are you going to count inaccurate items separately, or are you going to calculate the proportion of correct information from all the information that was recalled?
- Would counting how many words someone used to recall a memory be a useful measure?

Hopefully this will illustrate to you how many possible ways there are to measure memory and the effect that the choice might have on the results and conclusions from your study.

You could try out two different techniques. Once you have shown participants a video and asked them to recall everything they can, code their answers using two different techniques and display the results in a graph or table. Which technique do you think was more appropriate?

Interviewer variables and the effect of training quality on interview performance

Another problem affecting research into the CI surrounds the amount of training that the interviewers are given. This would appear to vary from study to study. In some studies, it was reported that interviewers were given a written list of instructions to follow, but no formal training, while in other studies the CIs were conducted by interviewers simply reading the questions without any instructions.

Research has shown that cognitive interviewers report that conducting a CI is significantly more 'demanding and exhausting' than conducting an SI. This would suggest that the CI places greater cognitive demand on interviewers and may well produce more errors. This is why Memon & Higham claim that the quality and quantity of training is an important issue, and support this argument with another of Memon's own studies in which she demonstrated that four hours training in CI procedures produced no significant increases in the amount of information recalled when compared to an SI (Memon *et al.*, 1994).

It is also possible that individual differences such as attitudes, motivation and prior experience of the interviewers also need to be taken into account. The study by Memon *et al.* (1994) also revealed that many police officers showed considerable resistance to their training, failed to follow instructions, and

QUESTION SPOTLIGHT!

Suggest what individual characteristics might make someone a good interviewer and what individual characteristics might make someone a poor interviewer.

used poor questioning techniques in both the CI and the SI. This may also be dependent on who is providing the training – the response to training provided by senior officers may be very different from the response to training provided by a researcher from the local university. They also suggest that another useful approach to the study of the effectiveness of CI might be to develop some way of establishing a baseline score for individual interviewer performance, which could be compared to their scores after training.

Finally, they make recommendations for training. As well as suggesting a minimum of two days training, they also suggest that individual differences be considered here, so that officers who have both the potential and the motivation to make good interviewers might be guided toward the role of investigative detective, while others might be guided towards other aspects of police work. However, they do acknowledge that this assumes that poor interviewers will not benefit from good training, as well as assuming that those who are already good interviewers will become even better interviewers through this use of training.

Conclusions

The authors conclude that there is still the need for good research into the CI. In particular, researchers need to establish appropriate comparison groups and suitable measures of memory. Even if comparisons are restricted to other techniques with clear protocols, such as the SI, individual differences still remain a significant challenge for researchers.

APPLICATION: STRATEGIES FOR POLICE INTERVIEWS

We have considered the cognitive interview (CI) in some detail already in this chapter. This, along with the enhanced cognitive interview (ECI), are well established strategies for police interviews. In this section we will examine the PEACE model of interviewing, as well as the use of forensic hypnosis.

The PEACE model of interviewing

Training police officers in interview skills now follows the PEACE model, which consists of five key elements:

P   Preparation and planning
E   Engage and explain
A   Account, clarification, challenge
C   Closure
E   Evaluation

P is for preparation and planning

Interviewers are encouraged to plan their interviews carefully. This may include plotting a timeline of what is already known, collating all the information that is known about the interviewee and setting out objectives for the interview. They might produce a list of 'facts' that need to be verified and they will also have to acknowledge any practical issues in relation to the interview. For example, where will the witness be interviewed, is the witness under 16, is the witness considered vulnerable, or are there any language barriers that need to be considered. Plans for interviews should be written down.

E is for engage and explain

Interviewers need to engage with the witness, they need to form a rapport with them rather than simply sitting down and firing questions at them. They should explain the purpose of the interview to the interviewee and ensure that the interviewee understands.

A is for account, clarification, challenge

Interviewers should allow the witness to first give their account of the event with no interruptions. They should use open questions rather than closed questions, summarise information that has been given to them, ask the interviewee for clarification or further details, and keep summarising, repeating and questioning until everything is clear. If the interviewee is not being honest or is keeping something back, this will be the point at which this becomes evident. By challenging the statements made by the witness, the interviewer can identify inconsistencies or deceptions. Note that this is very similar the structured interview (SI) already mentioned.

C is for closure

Interviewers should close down the interview appropriately. This will reinforce the rapport that was established earlier and ensure that witnesses will be more likely to speak to them again in the future. The interviewer should make sure that they have told the interviewee that they can contact officers again if they need to and should make sure that they have all the necessary contact details.

E is for evaluation

This is where the interviewer needs to evaluate the interview that they have just conducted. They need to establish whether everything that was required has been covered or if there were any inconsistencies that were not followed up. This is an extremely important part of the process.

Forensic hypnosis

Forensic **hypnosis** can help in the investigative process. It is based on the assumption that witnesses may be able to retrieve information under hypnosis that was not available to them otherwise. Unfortunately, the research that has been conducted into forensic hypnosis has tended to support critics who argue that it places witnesses in a suggestible state where they can be easily misled by an interviewer. Forensic hypnosis is used more often in the US than in the UK. Dwyer (2001) cites a case reported by Kalat (1993) in which police hypnotised a young boy whose mother had disappeared. Under hypnosis the son reported that he had seen his father murder his mother and chop up her body. Although there was no other evidence, the father was sentenced to life imprisonment for her murder. Some months later the woman turned up unharmed. Brewer (2000) cites a case reported by Orne (1979) of a witness who described in detail an event that it later turned out he could not possibly have witnessed as he had been out of the country at the relevant time.

Laboratory research has also supported the claim that witnesses are more suggestible under hypnosis. Sanders & Simmons (1983) showed participants a video of a pickpocket, followed by an interview and an identity parade. One group of participants were hypnotised and their results were compared to a group that were not hypnotised. The hypnotised group were less accurate in identifying the suspect, less accurate in answering questions, and more likely to be misled

Figure 3.17: Police conducting an interview with a witness

 **KEY IDEAS**

Hypnosis is an artificially induced trance that resembles sleep, and is characterised by heightened susceptibility to suggestions. It has many applications, including helping people to give up smoking, to manage pain, and as an aid to psychotherapy. It is the suggestible state that allows it to be a useful psychotherapeutic tool, but which also makes it a highly unreliable technique within a forensic context

WEB WATCH @

Can a polygraph detect when someone is lying? Read some of the research here:

http://www.apa.org/research/action/polygraph.aspx

by factors such as a foil in the identity parade wearing the same jacket as the perpetrator.

Finally, Gibson (1982) identifies a number of problems with the use of forensic hypnosis including increased errors, alteration of true memories, the ease with which false information can be suggested and the ease with which people can lie.

EVALUATION

Methodological and ethical issues

The key study by Memon & Higham is a review article, which means that the researchers are not reporting on research that they have conducted themselves, but rather are attempting to bring together a body of research on a specific topic. This can be a very useful process as it can identify a number of important themes, and establish conclusions that are consistent over a number of pieces of research. Memon & Higham have organised their review under four separate headings, each of which makes a valuable contribution to our understanding of the effectiveness of the cognitive interview. It is possible that other researchers might select different articles (a different sample) to include in a review, and might also identify different themes and conclusions. It is not possible to assess the reliability and validity of a review in the same way that this can be done for a piece of experimental research. One of the strongest themes emerging from this review is the suggestions that are made in terms of how research into this area should be conducted.

Within the review and within this topic as a whole, we have considered a number of studies of the cognitive interview, as well as the use of line-ups and forensic hypnosis. These are often laboratory studies rather than studies of real-life criminal investigations. In laboratory studies it is obviously possible to control extraneous variables, which would not be possible in real-life experiments, but these studies may lack ecological validity. It may be that memory for 'faked' events in laboratory situations is affected in different ways than the memory might be for a real-life (and possibly highly emotive) event. Such laboratory research needs to be considered in conjunction with studies that have been carried out in real-life

situations. We have briefly mentioned the use of case study evidence as well as studies that can be best described as field experiments where the performance of interviewers with and without training, or before and after training, has been compared. These have more ecological validity, although they present serious problems in terms of identifying the effect of individual variables such as level of training, motivation and other individual characteristics. Memon & Higham's research is important in bringing research together so that these methodological issues can be addressed.

The studies discussed here raise little in the way of ethical issues. The review by Memon & Higham does not raise any ethical issues at all, as the authors did not collect any data directly. However, it is possible to consider ethical issues raised by research within the general topic area. If people are shown faked events, either staged or on video, for the purpose of research into line-ups or identikits for example, then researchers need to ensure that these events will not cause distress. It is possible that events in participants' own lives mean that they could be extremely distressed by events that may appear relatively harmless to others. More importantly, the research conducted in this area is likely to have significant effects on the way police investigators do their jobs. Researchers should be mindful of this responsibility and ensure that they conduct high-quality research and do not allow flawed or poorly controlled research to influence policy decisions.

Debates

Usefulness of research

Following on from the discussions above, it is clear that both conducting research into this area and reviewing research in this area can have useful applications. Police interviewing has changed significantly since the introduction of the cognitive interview, with both improved recall and reduced errors. Similarly, the bias originally inherent in police line-ups has been dramatically reduced as a result of the work of researchers such as Gary Wells. It is also highly useful to be sceptical of strategies such as forensic hypnosis, which do not have the weight of research evidence to back them up.

Psychology as a science

Science applies scientific principles of control and manipulation of variables in order to establish cause-and-effect relationships. The review by Memon & Higham illustrates the importance, as well as the difficulty, of applying these principles to the examination of the effective components of the cognitive interview. They demonstrate that much of the early research did not apply these principles appropriately, as it was not possible to identify precisely which component was the effective one and neither were these studies utilising appropriate control groups. This reinforces the fact that research that is not properly 'scientific' will fail to convince an academic audience.

More interestingly, both the revised approach to line-ups and the cognitive interview can be seen to apply the principles of scientific research directly to their own procedures. For example, Wells suggests applying the principles of double-blind research to the way line-ups are conducted in order to avoid the possibility of demand characteristics being transmitted to the witnesses. The cognitive interview focuses on the reduction of bias and the repetitive nature of some of the components could be understood to be a type of internal check on the reliability of the information that is being provided.

PSYCHOLOGY AND THE COURTROOM

BACKGROUND

How juries can be persuaded by the characteristics of witnesses and defendants

Juries are made up of ordinary men and women and it is therefore reasonable to suggest that their final decisions may be affected by the same processes that affect our everyday decisions about the people we meet. Our impressions of other people are largely formed through stereotyping – that is the process of using one piece of information about someone to make assumptions about other characteristics that they might have. Juries may therefore be affected by the appearance, attractiveness, dress, age, race and accent of the witness and the defendant.

How does attractiveness influence juries?

A study by Stewart (1985) investigated the impact of appearance on jury decisions. The hypothesis for this study was that there would be a negative correlation between the attractiveness of the defendant and the severity of the punishment. In other words, the prediction is that as the attractiveness of the defendant increases, the severity of the punishment decreases.

This study was unusual in that Stewart observed real trials. He was not able to observe any of the conversations that the jury had while in the jury room but he sat in the public gallery and watched the trials. Altogether he observed 60 trials in Pennsylvania, USA. The defendants were mostly male (56 male and only 4 female), and a range of ages; 27 were black, 3 were Hispanic and 30 were white. There was a team of eight observers (who were all white) and each was given a standard rating form. Each trial was observed by at least two observers.

Observers rated the defendants on a range of scales. These included their physical attractiveness, neatness, cleanliness and quality of dress. These four items were combined to produce a score for attractiveness. Several other ratings were also carried out and this included posture.

Stewart checked the data and found no correlation between race and attractiveness, and a high level of agreement between raters (0.78). However, the attractiveness scores were negatively correlated with punitiveness – that is, the less attractive the defendants were judged to be, the more severe the punishment. The additional item, posture, also showed this negative correlation on its own.

In an **experimental study**, Sigall & Ostrove (1975) asked 120 participants to suggest a sentence for burglary or fraud, either with or without seeing a photograph of the defendant. The photographs showed either a physically attractive or a physically unattractive person. The results showed that

Figure 3.18: What assumptions might you make about this person? How do you think a jury might respond to this person if they were a witness? What if they were the defendant?

💡 KEY IDEAS

It is not permitted to investigate or observe the decision-making process of real juries. Therefore most research has been conducted by creating simulations. This means that research is created with mock juries in a range of experimental conditions, some of which attempt to recreate the entire courtroom experience. Despite attempts to simulate the processes of a real courtroom, **experimental studies** are always going to lack ecological validity and this needs to be kept in mind throughout this chapter.

participants suggested significantly longer sentences for burglary when the photo was of a physically unattractive defendant, but the reverse effects when the crime was fraud. In this condition, the photo of the attractive defendant produced the longer sentence.

How does race influence juries?

There are many studies with mock juries that have indicated that there are racial biases in jury decisions. Pfeifer & Ogloff (1991) showed that white university students rated black defendants as more likely to be guilty than white defendants, and this effect was even stronger when the victim was described as white. In real trials, there is also evidence that black defendants are more likely than white defendants to receive prison sentences when found guilty of similar crimes. Furthermore, in America, offenders found guilty of murdering a white victim are much more likely to receive the death penalty than offenders found guilty of murdering a black victim.

The O.J. Simpson trial was regarded as a race-related trial by many (Brewer, 2000). O.J. Simpson is a black American former professional football star and actor who was tried on two counts of murder after the deaths of his ex-wife, Nicole Brown Simpson, and waiter Ronald Lyle Goldman, in 1994. The case was one of the most publicised criminal trials in American history. Simpson was finally acquitted after a trial that lasted more than eight months.

Researchers identified a difference in the way that black Americans and white Americans responded to the trial, which was televised. White Americans tended to see Simpson as guilty owing to the weight of evidence against him, whereas black Americans were more likely to interpret the presented evidence in terms of police misconduct.

How does the way language is used affect juries?

Another factor that has been shown to influence the impression of witnesses is the language that they use. Lakoff (1975) studied the effect of using frequent 'hedges' while talking, such as saying 'I think' or 'perhaps', or rising in intonation at the end of a sentence, which makes it sound as though you are asking a question. Both male and female witnesses who used this type of language or speech pattern were perceived as less intelligent, less competent, less likeable and less believable than those who did not.

How does accent affect juries?

The Birmingham accent (or 'Brummie' accent) has attracted a great deal of attention from researchers into accents and is consistently evaluated more negatively than rural regional accents or so-called **received pronunciation** (**RP**). Mahoney & Dixon's study conducted in 1997 showed that defendants with Brummie accents were perceived as more guilty than defendants with non-Brummie accents, and that a 'black Brummie' accent was perceived as the most guilty, especially for blue-collar crimes such as theft. It is a later study conducted by Dixon that we will examine as the key study for this section.

Another study that has investigated the effect of accent was conducted by Seggie (1983). Seggie's research was conducted in Australia and investigated the effects on rater's perceptions of guilt of three accents: British RP, broad Australian and Asian. Participants listened to tape recordings of the 'accused'

💡 KEY IDEAS

Received pronunciation (RP) is the term used for the accent often described as 'typically British'. Speakers of RP will avoid non-standard grammatical constructions and localised vocabulary that are typical of regional accents. RP is not specific to a region of the UK and does not contain any clues about the speaker's geographic background, although it does reveal a lot about their social and/or educational background. It is the accent on which pronunciations in dictionaries are based and it is used in research often as the accent to which other accents are compared. It has possibly been studied more than any other accent, even though estimates suggest that only between 2% and 3% of the UK population speak it. It is largely unheard in Scotland, Northern Ireland or Wales, and should perhaps be described as an English rather than a British accent.

Figure 3.19: Ozzy Osbourne has a Brummie accent

KEY IDEAS

'Blue-collar crime' and 'white-collar crime' are terms that were originally used to refer to the class of the person committing the crime. Blue-collar crimes were typically those crimes committed by someone from the working class and white-collar crimes were typically those crimes committed by people from the middle or upper classes. Now the terms have slightly different meanings. Blue-collar crime now refers to acts that are considered to be the result of emotional outbursts, most notably anger and passion, and include crimes that cause injury to people or property, such as burglary, theft, sex crimes, assault and drug crimes. White-collar crime now refers to crimes that are committed in a business setting and are generally non-violent. They have been referred to as 'paper crimes' and include fraud, forgery and embezzlement.

pleading his innocence and were then asked to assess his guilt. Not only did Seggie find that accent influenced the responses given by the rater but he also found that this depended on the type of crime (**blue-collar** crime versus **white-collar crime**). More guilt was attributed to the broad Australian accent when the suspect was accused of assault, and more guilt was attributed to the British RP accent when the suspect was accused of theft.

KEY RESEARCH

Dixon, J.A., Mahoney, B., Cocks, R. (2002). Accents of Guilt Effects of Regional Accent, Race, and Crime Type on Attributions of Guilt. *Journal of Language and Social Psychology*, 21 (2), 162–168.

Aim
This research set out to test the hypothesis that a Brummie-accented suspect would produce stronger attributions of guilt than a standard-accented suspect. The study also tested whether the race of the suspect and the type of crime would influence this effect.

Method
The study investigated three independent variables, as shown in Figure 3.20. This is described as a 2 × 2 × 2 factorial design.

Black		White		Black		White	
Blue collar (armed robbery)	White collar (cheque fraud)	Blue collar (armed robbery)	White collar (cheque fraud)	Blue collar (armed robbery)	White collar (cheque fraud)	Blue collar (armed robbery)	White collar (cheque fraud)
Brummie accent				Standard accent			

Figure 3.20: Conditions of the experiment

The study took place in the Department of Psychology at University College, Worcester. The sample consisted of 119 white undergraduate psychology students (24 male and 95 female) with a mean age of 25.2 years. They participated as part of their course. The authors also note that as the research was concerned with the reactions of individuals who did not speak with a Brummie accent, participants who grew up in Birmingham were eliminated from the study.

As you can see from the table above, three variables produces eight conditions. Participants were randomly assigned to these conditions and were then asked to listen to the appropriate recorded conversation. This was based on the transcript of a real interview, which took place in a British police station in 1995 and involved a middle-aged male police inspector interviewing a young male suspect who pleaded his innocence. This scenario was recreated using actors hired for the study.

A standard-accented student in his mid-40s played the role of inspector, and the role of the suspect was played by a student in his early 20s who spoke with a standard accent. He was a natural code-switcher (in other words, he could switch between different accents) who had grown up near Birmingham and had also lived in various parts of England.

To manipulate accent types, two versions of the police interview were created: the first in which the suspect spoke with a standard accent and the second in which he spoke with a Brummie accent. The authors refer to these as 'guises' and they conducted a pre-test of the validity of these guises. More than 95% of people in the pre-test were able to identify the regional identify of the Brummie speaker. The Brummie accent was rated higher than the standard accent for strength of accent, and no differences were found between the two in terms of loudness or pitch, although the Brummie accent was rated as higher in terms of speech rate.

The other variables were manipulated by giving the participants different information. Crime type was manipulated by having the suspect accused of different criminal acts. In the blue-collar condition the suspect was accused of armed robbery, and in the white-collar condition he was accused of fraud (specifically, trying to use a stolen cheque).

The race of the suspect was manipulated by varying the racial cues provided to participants within the taped interview. At one point during the interview, the police inspector provided a physical description of the person who committed the crime and this varied across the experimental conditions.

QUESTION SPOTLIGHT!

Why was it a good idea to eliminate those potential participants who spoke with a Birmingham accent?

QUESTION SPOTLIGHT!

Why it is important that the two accents did not differ in terms of loudness or pitch? What would the problem have been if there had been a difference in one or both of these?

Box 3.1: Excerpt from the transcript of the taped exchange between suspect (S) and police officer (PO)

PO: *Okay, would you like to just briefly tell me what your understanding is of the arrest?*

S: *Well, eh, I was told last night that I was arrested on suspicion of armed robbery [cheque fraud]?*

PO: *Okay. Are you involved in that robbery [fraud]?*

S: *No, I'm not.*

PO: *In any way, are you involved in that robbery [fraud]?*

S: *Not in any way whatsoever. It's absolutely not true, not true at all. I speak only for myself and I am not involved in any armed robbery [cheque fraud], in any way whatsoever.*

PO: *Well the person that carried out this crime is described as male, White [Black] put at 5'9" tall…*

Note. The type of crime and race of the suspect variables were manipulated by varying the transcript as indicated in this extract.

STRETCH & CHALLENGE

Do you think these two crimes are equivalent? If yes, how could you double-check this? If no, how could this potential confounding variable be dealt with?

Once they had listened to one recording, the participant completed two sets of rating scales:

1. Rating the suspect's guilt on a 7-point scale from innocent to guilty, and
2. Using the Speech Evaluation Instrument (SEI), which is a measure of language attitudes developed by Zahn & Hopper (1985). This measures language attitudes on three dimensions: superiority, attractiveness and dynamism.

Statistical analysis revealed significance differences on only one factor: superiority. This showed that the Brummie suspect was rated lower on superiority than the standard-accent suspect, and this confirms findings of other research that show that non-standard speakers score lower on competence-related ratings than standard speakers.

ACTIVITY

You could test the effect of ruling information inadmissible using a very simple experiment. Give a group of participants a list of words to remember. They could be all similar words, for example, all food items or all animals. As part of your instructions, tell them not to remember one word ('gorgonzola', perhaps, or 'elephant'). It is guaranteed that they will all remember the word that they were specifically instructed to forget!

QUESTION SPOTLIGHT!

Why was it a good idea to select participants from those who were currently serving on jury service? What difference do you think it would have made if Broeder had selected students as his participants?

Results

A three-way Analysis of Variance (ANOVA) was performed on the guilt ratings. The Brummie suspect was rated as more guilty than the RP suspect (significant at $p<0.05$), as had been hypothesised. In addition, the analysis also revealed that the Brummie accent/black suspect/blue-collar condition had the highest guilt ratings. The authors also report that the suspect's levels of superiority and attractiveness significantly predicted guilt, but that levels of dynamism did not predict guilt. This suggests a number of possible further studies. Perhaps non-standard speakers are perceived as more guilty because their speech (and hence their testimony) is less assured or less confident and so we associate this more with characteristics such as 'shifty' and 'untrustworthy'.

APPLICATIONS: INFLUENCING JURY DECISION-MAKING

The influence of inadmissible evidence

If you have ever watched a courtroom drama, the chances are that you will have seen the judge rule something as 'inadmissible'. This means that, for various reasons, the person should not have said what they did and the jury are instructed to disregard what they have heard.

But surely barristers know what they can and can't say in court? Is it possible that they say inadmissible things as a deliberate strategy? A study by Broeder (1959) suggests that they might.

Broeder conducted his study to examine the effect of information being ruled inadmissible by a judge. Is it possible that being told to disregard information makes it even more important?

Broeder's study was a laboratory experiment and, although forming a mock jury, the participants that Broeder selected were actually members of the public who were serving on jury service at the time they participated. The experiment was conducted at the University of Chicago Law School.

Groups of participants were allowed to listen to tapes of evidence from a trial and were asked to deliberate as if they were actually the jury for this case. In one part of the research, 30 experimental juries listened to a case of a woman who was injured by a car driven by a careless male driver.

Broeder found that when the driver said that he had liability insurance, the jurors awarded the victim an average of $4000 more than when he said he had no insurance ($37,000 compared to $33,000). This suggests that juries will make larger awards to victims if an insurance company has to pay.

It is the next finding that it more interesting. If the driver said he was insured and the judge ruled that information inadmissible (told the jury to disregard it) then the average award to the victim increased to $46,000. In other words, when the juries learned that the driver was insured, they increased the damage payment by $4000. When participants in another condition were told that they must disregard this information, they used it even more, increasing the damage payment by another $13,000. This research is supported by many other studies that have demonstrated that banned information acquires even greater importance.

The CSI effect

The CSI effect refers to the impact of the television show *CSI* (and similar shows) on the way in which jury members perceive evidence. Schweitzer & Saks (2007) refer to the way in which the show portrays forensic science as 'high tech magic', and claim that this has produced unrealistic expectations in viewers. Perhaps they have unrealistic expectations about evidence, and therefore they expect too much of the prosecution (and may acquit if the evidence does not match their expectation) or they have an exaggerated faith in evidence, thus making it harder for the defence to convince. This tendency is apparently particularly strong when it comes to DNA evidence, although research with potential jurors has demonstrated that they often do not understand what this evidence is, and, more worryingly, the less they understand, the more likely they are to regard this evidence as infallible.

However, a study by Kim *et al.* (2009) did not support the notion that exposure to *CSI* (or similar programmes) impacted at all on the way jurors made decisions about evidence.

The impact of fMRI scans as evidence

A company called No Lie MRI is attempting to get its tests allowed in American courts as evidence. Although the debate about whether this should be allowed or not is a fascinating one, here we will be considering the way in which such evidence might influence juror decisions. In a study by Weisberg (2008), 330 students at Colorado State University were asked to read a short account of a criminal trial, in which the defendant was accused of killing his estranged wife and her lover. The account contained summaries of the testimonies given, the cross-questioning, and the evidence submitted. In one version, fMRI evidence was cited (referring to increased activation of frontal brain areas when the defendant denied killing his wife) and other versions contained reference to polygraph readings, thermal imaging technology, or no lie detection technology at all.

Participants who read the version containing the fMRI evidence were far more likely to say that they considered the defendant guilty. The fMRI evidence was also more likely to be mentioned by participants when asked what had contributed to their evidence. However, it is important to note that if the participants were given a different version again, in which an expert witness warned of the limitations of the fMRI evidence, the proportion of people seeing the defendant as guilty dropped back in line with the other non-fMRI conditions.

This strongly suggests that MRI evidence could be far more influential than other types of evidence, and the decision whether to begin allowing this in court is a complex one.

WEB WATCH @

You can read more about 'No Lie MRI' on their website:

www.noliemri.com

WEB WATCH @

This is a fascinating read on the impact of neuroscience on the courtroom

http://www.nytimes.com/2007/03/11/magazine/11Neurolaw.t.html?_r=1&

EVALUATION

Methodological and ethical issues

Almost all jury research suffers from the problem of ecological validity. Given that is not permitted to observe or investigate the decision-making processes of real jurors, most researchers opt for simulations, with a greater or lesser amount of realism. Reading an account of a crime would be low in realism, while taking part in a fully simulated trial would be much higher in realism, although much more complicated and expensive to conduct. The key research by Dixon discussed here obviously has little ecological validity as participants simply listened to a very short extract of a (faked) police interview and then made their decisions. However, the advantages of the methodology chosen by Dixon is that the researchers were able to control many possible confounding variables, ensuring that the accent, for example, could be isolated as an independent variable and its effect studied. It simply would not be possible to do this in the real world as this would require two trials that were identical in every single detail apart from the accent of the defendant, and this is an impossibility. Another strength of Dixon's study is that he allowed participants to deliberate in groups as if they were making a decision in a jury, which contrasts strongly with much mock jury research, which simply asks people to read an account of a trial and then make a judgment.

An alternative method for studying jury decisions is to observe real trials, which would obviously have much higher ecological validity. Observers are allowed only in the public gallery of a court, and are not privy to any information other than that which is available to anyone watching the trial. However, as we saw in the study by Stewart, observations of many trials does allow researchers to draw broad conclusions about the effect of factors such as attractiveness and race.

One final possibility for jury research is to consider the use of a 'shadow jury' – a group of participants who sit through the trial (in the public gallery) as if they were members of the jury and then make a decision in the same way that the jury does. This has some real advantages in terms of ecological validity, although participants will be aware that their decision has no real consequence for the defendant and this might be a crucial difference. If the shadow jury comes to a different verdict than the real jury, what conclusions could be drawn from this?

Sampling also needs to be considered. The study by Dixon used psychology students as participants and this was most probably done as a form of opportunity sample within a research methods class. This is common practice for obvious reasons but it does mean that the final sample may not be strongly representative of a wider population. The sample did exclude those from Birmingham, as this would no doubt have skewed the data, but even so this is not a sample that would allow for wider generalisations. In contrast to this, the study by Broeder used real jurors. Although they only listened to tape recordings of evidence, which would have had low ecological validity, the fact that they were serving on real juries at the time would have made the whole experience more realistic to them and this may well mean that we would be safer making generalisations from this study. Finally, the observational study conducted by Stewart observed 60 trials. This is a relatively small number to generalise from, especially when you consider that although the sample did include defendants from a range of racial backgrounds, there were only four female defendants and the trials were all observed in one area of the US only.

In terms of ethical considerations, all psychological research should protect people from harm or distress. It is possible that participants in any mock jury research might be distressed by the information that they are presented with, although this is unlikely in the study by Dixon as no particularly graphic details were included in the recording. Participants may have felt some pressure to participate given that this was part of a taught course and no information is given about their right to withdraw. The issue of consent and observation might also be considered in relation to the observation conducted by Stewart. It could be argued that a courtroom is a public place and that it is therefore appropriate for defendants to be observed in this way, but you might also argue that such observations invade a person's privacy and should not be conducted.

We might also consider the socially sensitive nature of this kind of research. How might people from Birmingham feel on reading the results of the study by Dixon? How would you feel if you read that people of your race are likely to be given harsher sentences than people of other races? Would people be pleased that the bias has been recognised (and as such can be addressed in courtroom instructions to jurors), or might they be upset by the negative stereotypes that appear to exist around their accent?

ACTIVITY

Explore the theory of the self-fulfilling prophecy. Explain how this could be relevant in understanding how people might react to findings such as these.

There is a bigger problem here. Not all studies have shown a relationship between defendant characteristics and the decisions made by juries. Bull & McAlpine (1998) suggest that it is highly likely that studies that find no effect of appearance (or accent or race or any other characteristic) are not accepted for publication. This means that the research that is published may itself not be representative of all the research that has been conducted.

Debates

Usefulness of research

Clearly the results from research in this area can be useful in a number of ways. First, it would suggest that if you are a defendant, you should make every effort to appear neat, clean and well dressed. Attempting to speak clearly and avoiding strong colloquialisms or hesitations is also likely to help. This same advice could be given to witnesses who will have their evidence taken more seriously if the jurors form positive impressions of them. Is it possible that the results of studies such as this could be used to inform jurors of the pitfalls of being swayed by appearance or accent? Perhaps trials should be conducted in very different ways so that the jury cannot actually see the defendant. Perhaps their testimony could be presented in some way so that their voice was not heard directly and therefore the characteristics of

their speech could not affect the impressions formed. These are highly speculative ideas but ones that could at least lead to some fascinating research. The study by Broeder, as we have already seen, suggests that lawyers could turn the rules about the inadmissibility of evidence to their advantage and just occasionally state something that they know (or hope) will be ruled inadmissible so as to lend it greater weight when jurors are making their final decision.

Ethnocentrism

Ethnocentrism refers to a bias in interpretation. It can be defined as the tendency to use our own ethnic or cultural groups' norms and values to define what is the norm for everyone. It is not ethnocentric to select a sample of participants from one particular culture but it would be ethnocentric to make the assumption that findings from one cultural group might easily be applied to any other cultural group. Much psychological research into factors affecting jurors' decisions has been conducted in the US and the UK. It would be ethnocentric to publish this research as though it could be applied to people in general, rather than people from a specific sub-cultural group. In effect, what this is doing is ignoring the fact that culture might be a very important variable in explaining all sorts of behaviours. This is not to accuse any of the research described in this topic as being ethnocentric, but simply to highlight the importance of cultural factors in understanding behaviours.

It is also possible to refer to an ethnocentric bias being displayed by the participants in these studies. Assuming that people who are more likely to have certain characteristics because of their race or their accent may also be considered ethnocentric.

CRIME PREVENTION

BACKGROUND

The cost of crime to the community is high. It can be counted in loss of earnings to individuals and businesses, in covering the costs of criminal damage, as well as the considerable impact crime has on the lives of people living in the community. Psychologists studying ways of preventing crime can help to find ways to reduce its negative impact. In this section we will consider how the features of neighbourhoods and zero-tolerance policing can help prevent crime.

Features of neighbourhoods

Have you ever wondered why some neighbourhoods experience more crime and antisocial behaviour than others? While there are many explanations of why crime occurs, one important factor is the environmental features of neighbourhoods. In the1970s, Oscar Newman began to consider why many modern housing developments built since the Second World War were 'failing'. High-rise flats had become increasingly popular, in part because of the maximised use of space. However, their residents were experiencing rising crime rates and poor quality of life.

Figure 3.21: The lack of defensible space in high-rises is linked to high rates of crime and vandalism

ACTIVITY

There are several examples of high-rise estates and housing projects that are considered poor examples of environmental design for crime prevention. Select one of the following (or find your own):

Pruitt-Igoe project, St Louis, USA

Red Road Flats, Glasgow, UK

Aylesbury Estate, London, UK

For what purpose were these projects undertaken? What has been the impact of their design on the lives of residents? Can you think of any other reasons why they might be considered 'failures'?

Newman (1972) introduced the concept of 'defensible space'. Space is considered defensible if it can be clearly perceived as belonging to a particular person or small group of people. One of the issues with blocks of flat is that their design means there are numerous spaces that do not 'belong' to anyone: stairwells, landings, lifts, parking areas and shared gardens. This type of territory is considered to be of 'secondary' significance, as residents feel a diminished sense of responsibility for these areas.

As well as the lack of defensible space offered by this type of accommodation, the neighbourhoods themselves often consisted of a number of high-rise buildings. Residents would struggle to distinguish who lived in their buildings or neighbourhood, which could make identifying potential criminals more difficult. Newman argued that these factors lead to a reduced sense of community, with criminal activity less easily detected or challenged. On the other hand, Newman argued, well-designed housing developments could have a positive impact on crime rates and quality of life.

Newman & Franck (1982) investigated the relationship between features of neighbourhoods and their impact on crime by looking at real housing developments in the USA. A survey of residents found a positive correlation between building size and fear of, or actual experience of, criminal activity. In order to prevent crime, residents need to see and be seen in their neighbourhoods, as well as to feel safe to report or challenge crime. These findings are supported in England – Bramley & Power (2009) found that people living in higher-density areas are more likely to consider crime to be a problem in their area than respondents in lower-density areas.

TABLE 3.6: FEATURES OF NEIGHBOURHOODS THAT DETER CRIME	
Crime prevention principles	**Feature of neighbourhood**
Improve control of access to properties	Use one single, clear point of entry for buildings to clearly mark public and private space. This limits options for criminals to enter or escape through multiple, covert points of entry.
Increase opportunities for surveillance	Well-designed street lighting which illuminates the face, but minimises glare and shadows.
Create and maintain a sense of ownership	Plant trees and place benches in communal outdoor spaces to increase useage and increase opportunity for meeting neighbours whilst observing strangers.

Source: Adapted from Crowe (2000)

Newman's ideas about the impact of physical design on crime, fear of crime and quality of life continue to be influential. Current initiatives in many countries use principles of environmental design to deter crime in neighbourhoods. Some examples of the features used in urban planning today are outlined in Table 3.6. Later in this chapter we will look at a strategy for using environmental and situational factors to prevent crime, but first we will consider another important aspect of crime prevention: how police work to actively stop crime form happening in communities.

Zero-tolerance policies

The term 'zero tolerance' is a type of policing that involves dealing with ALL kinds of crime, rather than just serious offences. It is based on three core principles:

1   Address all types of criminal acts, in order to prevent escalation to more serious crime; 'nip things in the bud'.
2   Police officers should be confident to tackle even the lowest level crimes and antisocial behaviour that come within the remit of the law.
3   Low-level crime can be tackled with low-intensity, humane methods by officers to create an environment that is then inhospitable to more serious crime.

Dennis (1997) describes this as 'confident policing'. There are several well-known examples of zero-tolerance policies, two of which we will consider here.

By the early 1990s, New York City had long held the dubious honour of being considered one of the crime capitals in the world. As a large and complex city,

Figure 3.22: Under zero-tolerance policies, low-level crime such as vandalism is targeted by police

it has a correspondingly large and heavily bureaucratic police force. In 1994, Bratton attributed the city's poor record on crime to a number of factors. These included an overwhelmed emergency dispatch system (911 calls), intense pressure on officers to investigate and solve crimes quickly, and a preference for motorised policing over foot patrols.

When Bratton took his position as Police Commissioner in 1994, he tasked the force with reducing 'crime, disorder and fear'. Supported by the then newly elected Mayor Rudolph Giuliani, who had campaigned on such a platform, this initiative re-framed the objective of policing away from detecting crime and criminals and led to a new focus on reducing crime that negatively affected quality of life. It placed dual emphasis on tackling serious crime and on police officers addressing low-level crimes such as vandalism, loitering and vagrancy. Bratton's directive was based on the theory of 'broken windows' outlined in the key research for this topic (Wilson & Kelling, 1982). Around 7000 new police officers were recruited, many to engage with members of the community during foot patrols. These approaches were linked to a huge fall in serious crime rates; hotspots for crime were identified and criminal acts were prevented rather than reacted to. Bratton reported an overall drop in crime rate of 37% in three years, and an impressive 50% drop in the homicide rate.

At around the same time, Hartlepool, a far smaller town in the UK, had also introduced zero-tolerance policies on crime. The town did not suffer the same rates of high-profile violent crime as New York City, but had nonetheless undergone a steady decline in terms of crime, with overall crime rates having doubled in the 12 years prior to 1994, and burglary figures having tripled. This meant that the county council was wasting resources on dealing with the consequences of crime, such as cleaning up graffiti and mending public property.

Ray Mallon took up an appointment with the town's police division in 1994 to implement new strategies to tackle the crime rate. He used the idea of zero tolerance and related tactics to reduce crime and regain control of the streets on behalf of and with the consent of citizens. While officers were to show compassion for those with mental-health issues, and tolerate harmless high spirits, they were trained to pay attention to and not ignore anti-social behaviour in order to prevent problems from escalating. This would break deterioration of safety and dereliction of neighbourhoods, while restoring the community's confidence in the ability of the police to protect and maintain order. Low-level offenders were to be known to police officers, who would address their nuisance behaviour face-to-face and be seen to be 'keeping an eye on things' (Dennis & Mallon, 1997).

The strategy was two-pronged: addressing crime in juveniles early, in order to cut short future criminal paths, while also tackling minor offences, could in some cases lead to the detection of other offences and suspects. Zero tolerance proved successful in reducing the overall crime rate in Hartlepool by 27% in two years, with even greater reductions in offences such as car theft, which fell by 56% (Dennis & Mallon, 1997).

Zero-tolerance policies have attracted major criticism, however. It has been pointed out that crime rates have fallen since the early 1990s all over both the UK and USA, without the use of the tactics employed in New York and Hartlepool. Also, the huge increase of police officers in New York means that the drop in crime could have occurred no matter which policing strategies were used. In both cases, the police forces in question enjoyed the full backing of politicians, and were under immense pressure to make zero tolerance work to bring down crime.

Pollard (1998) cautions that when zero tolerance involves heavy-handed aggression, it may well create short-term improvement, but can risk alienating local communities in the long term. In recent incidents in the USA, routine police stops of citizens have escalated into brutal encounters that have highlighted tensions between police and community members (see Stretch & Challenge). The causes of crime are numerous and complex, and keeping neighbourhoods orderly and dissuading individuals from committing crime requires a coordination and cooperation by other public services such as local schools, waste management services, community mental-health teams and social services (Pollard, 1998). In the next section we will consider an article that was instrumental in changing attitudes about the role of policing in preventing crime.

KEY RESEARCH

Figure 3.23: Bill Bratton is the current NYC Police Commissioner and acts as an advisor to the London Metropolitan Police

Wilson, J.Q. & Kelling, G.L. (1982) The police and neighbourhood safety: Broken windows. *Atlantic Monthly*, 127, 29–38.

Aim
The aim of the article was to challenge existing beliefs about the fear of crime and the role of the police. The authors explored links between disorder and incivility to subsequent occurrences of serious crime in communities.

Method
Sample
This article is a discussion piece that proposes a theory of neighbourhood safety and crime and therefore does not use a particular sample. However, the authors do make reference to the Newark Foot Patrol Experiment. Newark is a city in New Jersey, USA, which took part in a statewide initiative started in the mid-1970s called the 'Safe and Clean Neighbourhoods Program'. The programme was designed to improve the quality of community life.

Design and procedure
As mentioned, the article does not outline an experimental piece of research but instead proposes a theory of crime. However, the authors consider Newark as a case study; a focus on one particular situation that is considered in depth. One of the researchers also engages in what could be considered naturalistic participant observation of police officers. Kelling accompanied different officers on foot patrol over many hours, observing their interactions with members of the community throughout neighbourhoods in Newark.

Findings and implications
Results of the Newark Foot Patrol Experiment
The authors report that existing attitudes towards foot patrol were negative: police chiefs felt it reduced the mobility and manageability of its officers, while the officers themselves viewed it as a kind of punishment. This was because it was considered hard work, and might reduce the chance of catching

STRETCH & CHALLENGE

In August 2014, an unarmed black teenager by the name of Michael Brown was shot by a police officer in Ferguson, Missouri. It sparked some of the worse riots the USA has experienced in many years. Consider how policies such as zero tolerance could lead to increased tensions between police and members of the community.

serious criminals. When the State of New Jersey implemented the foot-patrol experiment, police went along with it because it was funded, despite seeing it as a ploy to gain public support. To some extent, the authors report, these concerns were founded, because a 5-year evaluation of the programme by the Police Foundation found the increase in foot patrols had not reduced crime rates.

However, the evaluation did find that residents reported feeling as though crime had been reduced, and were taking fewer behavioural precautions to this effect (e.g. staying home with doors locked). The report also found the foot-patrol officers had higher morale and job satisfaction, as well as improved relations with the community. The authors suggest that rather than catching criminals who had perpetrated serious crimes, such as physical assault or armed robbery, the officers were actually preventing crime through maintaining public order.

The idea of 'order maintenance' is outlined in examples from the article. The foot patrol officers got to know the community, understanding who was a 'regular' or a 'stranger'. Although not all 'regulars' were 'decent' working people, those who were drunks and derelicts got to 'know their place'. This meant establishing informal rules to keep order – for example, drunks could sit on steps but not lie down, begging was forbidden, drinking was to be kept off the main streets. Officers established these rules alongside the residents, and both worked to maintain them. Residents felt more confident to report disorder because they felt something would be done about it; breaking these 'rules' lead to arrests being made. Officers also viewed it as their job to keep an eye on the strangers, while members of the community felt relieved and reassured when the police helped maintain order. Wilson & Kelling suggest that the use of police vehicles was a physical and mental barrier to engaging with members of the community and having their presence felt.

ACTIVITY ✳

Test out the broken windows theory for yourself—without breaking any windows! Design an observation to see how quickly an area or item can be neglected by the users of the environment. For example, place a full bin in a corridor and scatter a few pieces of litter nearby. After a time, has more litter been left on the floor, or do passerbys take it away with them? How could you change people's behaviour to keep the corridor tidy?

The broken windows metaphor

The authors argue that disorder and crime are inextricably linked. They draw on the well-established observation that when one window in a building is smashed and left unrepaired, psychologists and police tend to expect that the rest of the windows will soon be broken. Wilson & Kelling suggest that this is true in any neighbourhood, because a broken window left unrepaired suggests that no one cares about the property. They refer to an early experiment by Zimbardo (1969), who arranged to have a car without licence plates abandoned with its hood up in a rough inner-city neighbourhood, and a comparable vehicle on a street in a more up-market area. In the first instance, the car was quickly stripped and destroyed. In the second instance, the car remained untouched for over a week, until Zimbardo partially damaged it. Within hours of this damage, the car had also been badly vandalised. Wilson & Kelling note that both black and white citizens joined in the destruction, regardless of whether or not they appeared 'well-to-do'. They conclude from this that untended behaviour inevitably leads to the breakdown of community control, and that small instances of 'no one caring' can breed more serious crime.

The theory of broken windows has an effect on residents' attitudes. They become 'atomised', isolated from neighbours and less concerned with or involved in what happens in their community. For the elderly, this can have a disproportionately negative effect, as they are most vulnerable, and least likely to be able to move out of a neighbourhood that has fallen into decay. Out of fear they may stay home behind locked doors to minimise the risk of becoming a victim. The authors suggest that disorderliness in the community leads to increased fear of crime, isolation from others and lack of faith in police to act in the interest of the community.

Implications for the role of police

Wilson & Kelling point to a pattern of policing that has led to urban decay. Prior to the Second World War, they constructed the role of police as watchmen – keepers of public order and civility. The move from keepers of order to crime-fighting involved solving crimes, gathering evidence and making more arrests. The authors suggest that this changed the focus of police work away from community relations. So, applying the broken windows metaphor to crime, tackling low-level anti-social behaviour such as drunken disorderliness is not a priority for officers. Civilians do not feel as though police will be interested in helping, potential criminals perceive a lack of police or community interest in preventing crime, and so inevitably criminal activity escalates. The authors suggest that foot patrol officers have a key role in building community relations and collaborating with residents in preventing crime, in ways that are difficult for an officer inside a police patrol car.

Wilson & Kelling express concern over the legality of keeping order as opposed to fighting crime. Some methods used by officers on foot patrol involve informal rules, and the use of personal judgment to determine what is and is not permissible behaviour in public. Letting a homeless person off a charge of vagrancy might seem to make sense in an individual case, if that person isn't hurting anyone else. However, they argue that, applied universally, this would involve letting hundreds of vagrants off, which could 'destroy an entire community'. They point out that behaviour that is tolerable for one person may prove intolerable to another. For example, an elderly person might feel more fearful of walking past young teenagers loitering on a corner. The implication for policing is that officers must take into account the relationship between one broken window (a minor infraction of the law) and a thousand broken windows (a crime-ridden neighbourhood with low quality of life for residents). Thus they caution against decriminalising low-level criminal behaviour.

In order to prevent bigotry and discrimination, the authors propose appropriate selection, training and supervision of officers to help fairly maintain public order. They also see a role for organised citizen patrols; residents who volunteer to patrol streets and challenge disorder, though they note that there is little information on the effect these groups have on crime. They outline the

Figure 3.24: Who cares? Zimbardo found that the neglected appearance may encourage further criminal acts

QUESTION SPOTLIGHT!

Can you explain how Bratton's policy of zero-tolerance policing was influenced by this key research by Wilson & Kelling?

Figure 3.25: 'Ello, 'ello, 'ello … foot patrol officers may be instrumental in building good community relations

 **KEY IDEAS**

Rational choice theory as applied to crime suggests that individuals think about their decisions before they commit crime. In the majority of cases, people commit crimes for their own benefit, but they must perceive the benefits of committing crime as greater than the benefits of not committing crime. In other words, offenders are motivated by (a) a minimal likelihood of getting caught, and (b) anticipating a good outcome for themselves.

WEB WATCH @

Beat the burglar! Scroll your mouse over the interactive house featured on this website. Can you identify what situational crime-prevention strategies are being used in each case?

www.dorset.police.uk/default.aspx?page=5999

community-police relations within a large public housing project that had gradually improved over a number of years. Where once there were bad relations, an alliance had been formed – police had kicked out gang members and informal social control had been re-established – yet the legality and fairness of order maintenance was questionable. The authors suggest that the rights and needs of the community took precedence over any one individual's rights in this instance.

Wilson & Kelling conclude their article by reporting on the falling numbers of police recruits across the USA, and advise that police should identify those neighbourhoods at 'tipping point', i.e. still reclaimable by the community. Police resources could also be stretched through using off-duty police officers to engage in patrol work in housing projects and on public transportation. While acknowledging the tension between preventing broken windows and the demand for concentrating police resources on high crime areas, the authors maintain that police must keep order as well as fight crime.

Conclusion

In this article, the authors conclude that:

1   The relationship between low-level and serious crime can be understood using the broken windows metaphor.
2   Public order should be created and maintained collaboratively by police and the community.

APPLICATION: CRIME PREVENTION

Situational crime prevention

Continuing with the theme of community responsibility and neighbourhood crime, we will now consider ways in which crime can be prevented. 'Situational crime prevention' is a radical move away from traditional approaches that primarily target offenders. Crime is reduced by looking closely at the different aspects of the environment, in an attempt to minimise opportunity for crime or to make criminal acts appear too risky. Much of this work draws on Newman's original concept of defensible space, as well as **rational choice theory**. In this section we will consider three core principles underpinning situational crime prevention, before considering two case studies that have used these techniques to prevent crime.

Target hardening

Target hardening is an environmental intervention designed to alter the cost benefit of committing a crime. It makes the target of crime 'harder' i.e. more difficult and less attractive to potential offenders. Examples of this include bike locks, dye tagging and car-immobilisation systems that render the target difficult to use, move or sell. In some cases targets can be removed altogether, for example removing cash targets by paying wages using electronic payment or using debit cards. However, as you might imagine, while some targets might be hardened, criminals might subsequently change targets, for example by using identity fraud to commit theft. This is also known as 'displacement' of crime, and is one of the key criticisms of situational crime prevention.

Creating defensible space

Using situational crime prevention as a strategy is clearly linked to a theory we looked at earlier, Newman's idea of 'defensible space' (see page 162). The key ideas that foster ownership and responsibility over neighbourhoods have been of interest to investigators. For example, one way in which crime can be deterred is through controlled access (Newman, 1972; Crowe, 1991). Poyner and Webb (1987) found a significant reduction in vandalism and theft on a British housing estate following the introduction of measures such as entry phones, fences and electronic access to buildings. Put simply, if the risk of being observed or challenged when spraying graffiti, drinking in a communal stairwell or committing a burglary is too high, an offender may refrain from the activity.

Increasing risk of detection

The idea of increasing the risk of getting caught relates to Crowe's (1991) recommendations for maintaining defensible spaces in communities. You may be familiar with Neighbourhood Watch programmes, which bring ordinary members of the community together to increase surveillance, reporting and deterrence of local crime. A volunteer resident co-coordinator liaises between the police and community, they receive information and equipment to help prevent crime and encourage vigilance, such as luminous marker kits (for marking personal property such as bicycles), window stickers and signs to publicise the scheme, and personal safety alarms, all of which they can make available to members. Other situational methods of increasing the risk of detection include the use of CCTV in public spaces, adequate street lighting, and electronic tagging of items in shops.

Situational crime prevention: case studies
Alley-gating in Liverpool

Alleyways are often considered hotspots for crime – poor lighting, restricted opportunities for surveillance and lack of perceived ownership make them an environmental feature conducive to crime. They are common in certain neighbourhoods, particularly in industrial cities, such as Liverpool, where rows of terraced houses backing on to narrow alleys are very common. 'Alley-gates' are durable, lockable gates that restrict access to alleyways to local residents only, and prevent unauthorised entry. This case study used alley-gates as a device to reduce opportunities for potential offenders in cases of domestic burglary from 2000 onwards.

The process of introducing alley-gates was problematic – installation required resident permission, negotiation of public rights of way, bespoke manufacture of gates, and distribution of keys to all residents. In total, over 3,000 gates were installed, with each gate protecting approximately 1134 houses. Bowers *et al.* (2004) used a quasi-experimental design to compare the effect of alley-gating on burglary rates in Liverpool with adjacent areas over the same time period. Their comparison showed that burglary rates in the test area were reduced up to 37% compared to the control, with analysis suggesting around 875 burglaries had been prevented. However, there was some incidence of displacement, with small rises in burglaries committed in adjacent neighbourhoods.

Figure 3.26: Smile, you're on camera! CCTV is used to increase the risk of detection for offenders

Biting back in Huddersfield

'Biting Back' was a program introduced as part of the Police Operations Against Crime initiative between October 1994 and March 1996 in the Huddersfield area of England. It was specifically designed to help develop an understanding and prevention of repeat victimisation from domestic burglary and theft from cars. Previous research has shown that one of the biggest predictors of future victimisation is having previously been a victim of crime (Chenery, 1997). Huddersfield police identified repeat victims and offered rising levels of response and support according to the victims' experience. These measures included target hardening and increasing the risk of detection for offenders (see Table 3.7).

TABLE 3.7: SUPPORT OFFERED TO REPEAT VICTIMS IN THE BITING BACK PROGRAMME	
Level of response (number of incidents)	**Examples of support offered**
Bronze (first victimisation)	Personalised letter to the victim; crime prevention advice leaflet; discount vouchers for security equipment
Silver (second victimisation)	Visit from Crime Prevention Officer; police watch visits
Gold (third victimisation)	Increased police watches; temporary installation of alarms and covert cameras

Source: Chenery et al. (1997)

As well as the tiered response element, a network of coordinators, Crime Prevention Officers (CPOs), data analysts and victim liaison officers worked alongside community partners such as the local authority, the University of Huddersfield and local media to deliver information about crime prevention and victim support.

Evaluation of the project highlighted several important achievements including:

- A reduction in crime – domestic burglary fell by 30% and theft from motor vehicles fell by 20%
- Reduced levels of repeat domestic burglary
- No evidence to suggest that domestic burglary was displaced rather than prevented
- An increase in arrests from temporary alarms, from 4% of installations to 14%, and
- Improved quality of service to victims.

Source: Anderson (1997); Chenery (1997)

In conclusion, both these case studies show evidence for the effectiveness of situational crime prevention. Each does this by minimising the opportunity for crime to occur and reducing the attractiveness of committing an offence. However, critics argue that it fails to deal with the other underlying causes of crime: the motives and behaviour of offenders. While the strategy focuses on building community cohesion, perception of safety, and quality of life, some people might feel programmes involve an overreliance on the work of members of the community.

DO IT YOURSELF

As you can see from the examples given in this section, different situational crime prevention techniques may be more effective than others. Design and test a questionnaire to investigate people's attitudes towards specific measures to 'target harden' and increase risk of detection. Consider who your sample will be and why this might be important.

EVALUATION

Methodological and ethical issues

There are some methodological issues around zero-tolerance policing and the Newark Foot Patrol Experiment outlined in the key research. Despite reported success in terms of cutting crime rates and/or reducing the fear of crime, there is controversy about the measuring of results. In the key research, Kelling acts as participant observer alongside the officer. In doing so, the officer may be perceived to have 'back-up' and appear to be more effective. The researcher may have an idea of what they hope to find and create reporter bias, for instance.

As we have seen, Pollard (1997) also queries the long-term outlook for assertive approaches to tackling disorder. As much of the research on the effectiveness of crime prevention strategies and zero tolerance take place shortly after the intervention, it can be difficult to assess its long-term effects. Other critics point to extraneous variables occurring in communities that could account for reductions in crime rates A famous example of this is the simultaneous decline in the use of crack cocaine, which some believe can better explain the sudden drop in the New York murder rate (Bowling, 1999).

There are practical issues involved in situational crime prevention and designing neighbourhoods so that they abide by the principles of defensible space. One of these is the costs involved in installing and maintaining equipment to deter crime, such as the alley-gates in the Liverpool project, or high-tech video recording equipment. Likewise, the cost of employing more police officers to spend time patrolling neighbourhoods on foot is high. However, there is an argument that these measures pay for themselves if they are effective at reducing crime rates overall.

One of the main criticisms of zero tolerance is made on ethical grounds. Effectively, such policies prevent police from using their discretion (as Wilson & Kelling advised against in their broken windows metaphor). On the surface this might seem to encourage a more fair and ethical approach to tackling crime, because it reduces subjectivity in the decisions of individual officers. However, it also means personal histories and mitigating circumstances are often disregarded. One implication of this is that some groups in society, e.g. those with mental-health issues, alcohol or drug dependency, or learning difficulties may become more vulnerable under zero-tolerance initiatives. Some critics also caution that the alienation of police from the community can also lead to a brutal and militaristic treatment of suspects.

Some techniques used in situational crime-prevention strategies may also be considered unethical. One of the core principles is increased surveillance and increasing the risk of detection for offenders. In practice this has involved an explosion in the use of CCTV and other forms of tracking and monitoring. Because such techniques do not discriminate between criminals and law-abiding citizens, this means that all of us of who venture into public spaces, use credit cards, visit websites, and so on, have our image or data recorded. Some people argue that this has lead to a 'Big Brother' culture, where it has become commonplace to invade individuals' privacy.

Debates

Usefulness of research

Research into the effectiveness of situational crime prevention is useful in psychology in that it complements alternative strategies, such as working with individual offenders. Many safety measures outlined as forms of situational crime prevention are in use in our everyday lives. For example, locking our doors, avoiding poorly lit roads and alleyways, and installing alarms are behaviours and safeguards that we all may benefit from. Situational crime prevention involves considering the particular risks involved in each instance as well as the type of offenders we are trying to deter. This strategy plays a key part in UK crime policy, so it has wider applications in improving conditions in society. Evidence of this can be seen in the alley-gating and Biting Back case studies, which demonstrate the effectiveness of target hardening and increased surveillance in some contexts.

Since the major successes of initiatives in places such as Huddersfield and New York City, zero-tolerance initiatives remain popular, yet controversial. Inspired by Wilson & Kelling's broken windows theory and work of the Newark Foot Patrol Experiment, there are fears that they encourage overly aggressive police tactics that may alienate communities. Additionally, we have considered how drops in crime rates in cities such as New York City may be difficult to verify owing to naturally occurring extraneous variables, such as trends in illegal drug use. So while zero-tolerance practices may be effective, the research supporting this in practice is difficult to interpret accurately.

Freewill vs determinism

Wilson & Kelling's theory of broken windows could be considered deterministic because they suggest that even single instances of anti-social behaviour will inevitably breed increasingly more serious problems for communities. They argue against the exercise of freewill and discretion by police officers in offering leniency in some cases. This is because, just as in zero tolerance policing, ignoring low-level crime is thought to be a 'slippery slope'.

Individual and situational explanations

This is one of the most important debates when evaluating theories and strategies to prevent crime. Almost everything we have considered in this section relies on a situational explanation for why crime occurs and how it can be prevented. For example, we considered the use of defensible space and zero-tolerance policing in crime prevention. Defensible space explicitly relies on features of the environment that may make crime more or less likely, such as the design of building exits or the effects of high-density living. Similarly, the theories of broken windows and zero-tolerance policing consider the community as a whole, rather than focusing on individual differences, which may make some people more likely to commit offences than others. Perhaps most clearly, situational crime prevention involves implementing measures to protect targets of crime and reduce the opportunity for offences to occur rather than dealing with individuals who perpetrate offences.

ACTIVITY ✳

Zero-tolerance policies have been implemented outside of community policing. Research their use in the context of prisons or school, for example. How transferable is the concept to these environments?

TOPIC 6
EFFECTS OF IMPRISONMENT

BACKGROUND

Responses to criminal behaviour

Punishment and reform are two kinds of responses to criminal behaviour which we will explore in this section. In many cases they may be linked. For example, imposing a prison sentence on a burglar serves as a form of punishment for breaking the law, but it may also have the intention of reforming the individual to reduce the likelihood of reoffending. Punishments for offenders come in various forms, ranging from fines and community service to imprisonment, probation, or even capital punishment (the death penalty). Reform on the other hand involves changing or improving the behaviour of offenders; there are many techniques for changing those factors that contribute to reoffending, such as anger-management programmes (see Application section, page 180).

It is important to bear in mind that responses to criminal behaviour serve distinct purposes, and that the question of how criminals should be treated is a controversial one. For example, if the purpose of punishment is mainly punitive, society seeks retribution for the crime as the offender faces a particular consequence for their actions. Another purpose might be to deter the individual or other would-be offenders from committing such a crime. Alternatively, restrictive punishments, such as prison, parole or electronic tagging, limit the ability of offenders to reoffend, which serves to protect the community. The idea that criminals can be reformed and afforded another chance to live freely in the community is the main concern of psychologists working to treat offenders.

Forms of punishment

The idea of punishment as a way of shaping human behaviour is a type of operant conditioning that comes from the work of B.F. Skinner (1938). In the behaviourist tradition, punishment is a form of response-stimulus conditioning where undesirable (in this case, criminal) behaviour is reduced through the application of an unpleasant stimulus (e.g. a fine or imprisonment). As this definition relies on the unpleasant stimulus causing a reduction in unwanted behaviour, it is essential to explore whether 'punishment' for crimes actually leads to a reduction in reoffending.

Probably the first sort of punishment for criminal behaviour you might think of is imprisonment. You can see the increasing prison population figures in Figure 3.27. In UK institutions, prisoners' lives are tightly controlled. Offenders spend around 25 hours a week engaged in 'purposeful activity', i.e. work, education and training, programmes addressing their offending, and drug or alcohol treatment where required. Inmates have basic food and clothing provided, with privileges such as television in cells being earned through

ACTIVITY ✳

Consider the following. To what extent does each method punish prisoners, prevent reoffending, or promote reform?

- Writing a letter of apology to victims
- Death penalty
- Monitoring by parole officers
- Engaging in psychological therapies
- Speeding fine

good behaviour and paid for by the individual inmate. There is considerable demand for space in UK prisons, with around a quarter of institutions reporting overcrowding in cells (Prison Reform Trust, 2012).

MATHS MOMENT

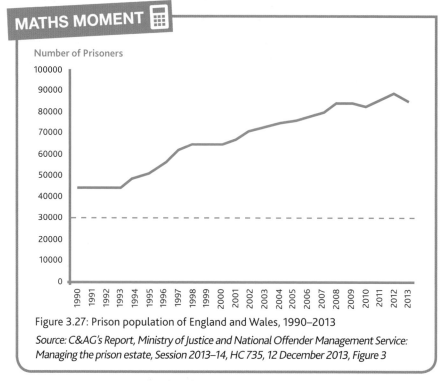

Figure 3.27: Prison population of England and Wales, 1990–2013

Source: C&AG's Report, Ministry of Justice and National Offender Management Service: Managing the prison estate, Session 2013–14, HC 735, 12 December 2013, Figure 3

Encouraging reform

But what relationship does this increasing number of offenders behind bars have with rates of reoffending? In the UK, prison has a poor record for reducing reoffending, with 47% of adults being reconvicted within one year of being released. These rates are currently even higher for children and young adults, suggesting that imprisonment does not necessarily have the deterrent effect we might expect. However, reoffending rates in the UK are considerably lower than in some other countries, such as the USA, perhaps owing to the greater emphasis and resources placed on education and employment training for UK offenders.

What about other forms of punishment? In recent years, a move towards non-custodial sentencing has been pursued for a variety of non-violent crimes. A major UK longitudinal study, '***Surveying Prisoner Crime Reduction'***, found that probation supervision was more effective than a custodial sentence of less than a year in reducing one-year reoffending rates (Prison Reform Trust, 2012). Similarly, community orders are a popular method of punishing low-level crime. These can involve sentencing offenders to undertake compulsory unpaid work, such as removing graffiti or cleaning up derelict areas (e.g. between 40 and 300 hours). While there is dispute over whether community orders can eliminate reoffending, rates of re-offence for offenders sentenced to community orders tend to be lower than reconviction rates for offenders with prison sentences.

Limitations of punishment and reform

There are serious challenges to accurately assessing rates of reoffending and understanding 'what works'. Statistics can be difficult to interpret in meaningful ways, because of the many factors involved in criminal punishment. These

Figure 3.28: Giving back to the community: offenders sentenced to community orders may be required to perform unpaid work to benefit the local area, such as litter-picking or graffiti removal

may include the individual's circumstances before imprisonment, the nature of their crime; the conditions of the prison where they were confined and the interventions they participated in during imprisonment. It is also difficult to control for the support offenders receive both immediately and in the long-term following release, which might influence their likelihood of committing future crime. Perhaps most significant is that reoffending as measured through conviction rates and/or offender self-report significantly under-estimates the actual rate of reoffences, with crime-rate statistics indicating much higher rates of offending (Prison Reform Trust, 2012).

Imprisonment as a form of punishment may lead to high rates of reoffending, in part because of the profound effect it has on most aspects of the individual's lives. Imprisonment involves isolation from family, friends and community; relationships have to be rebuilt when the offender leaves prison. Having a criminal record and large gaps in work history can also make finding suitable employment and housing especially difficult. The conditions within different institutions and the personal experience of imprisonment can also have a significant impact on an offender's sense of identity and connection to the outside world.

ACTIVITY ✳

For current information on UK prisons, and to see what life is like inside the prison system, download an app from the Prison Reform Trust. It is also available at the following link:
www.prisonreformtrust.org.uk/Publications/Prisonthefactsapp

Reoffending rates may be notably higher for some groups of offenders than others. One such example is people diagnosed as 'psychopaths'. As we considered previously for AS/Year 1, psychopaths are characterised by a lack of empathy for others, combined with a high drive to satisfy aggressive self-interest. As they find anti-social behaviour gratifying and rarely exhibit genuine remorse for criminal behaviour, they are highly resistant to therapeutic treatment. In some cases, it is believed that treatment programmes such as social-skills training or anger management actually make these offenders more skilled at manipulating others and securing early release/parole (Porter *et al.*, 2009).

The experience of imprisonment

So far we have considered that an individual's experience in prison involves a complex interaction of factors. Personality variables, the extent of prison crowding, and peer-group affiliation can all influence an individual's experience. However, in the research we will consider for this topic, situational factors are considered of primary importance. A study was undertaken by Philip Zimbardo and his assistants on behalf on the US Navy in order to establish the causes of conflict between guards and prisoners in naval prisons (Haney *et al.*, 1973). Previously, a dispositional explanation of conflict had been accepted – that the 'guard mentality' attracted individuals who were insensitive and cruel, whereas prisoners were aggressive people characterised by a lack of respect for law and order.

Zimbardo rejected this hypothesis and wanted to investigate how poor conditions in prisons could be explained by the social roles prisoners and

QUESTION SPOTLIGHT!

Can you explain why it might be difficult to make a fair comparison between the success rates of offenders who have prison sentences and those who have community orders?

Figure 3.29: Philip Zimbardo was the senior researcher in the Haney *et al.* study, which is why it is often informally referred to as 'Zimbardo's study'

Why do you think the researchers carried out their investigation as a naturalistic observation (i.e. in a real prison)? How does this link to the debate over situational vs dispositional explanations of behaviour?

guards were expected to play in their environments. He believed that by increasing our understanding of the social processes underlying the experience of imprisonment, training could be developed to improve the violent and harsh conditions of prison life that existed at the time.

KEY RESEARCH

Haney, C., Banks, W.C. & Zimbardo, P.G. (1973) Study of prisoners and guards in a simulated prison. *Naval Research Reviews*, 9, 1–17.

Aim
The aim was to investigate the effect of being assigned to different roles (either a prison guard or prisoner). This was done in order to critically evaluate whether the resulting attitudes and behaviour could be better explained by situational or dispositional factors.

Method
Sample
The 24 participants were male volunteers who had responded to a newspaper advertisement to participate in a psychological study of 'prison life'. Three of these men never participated in the study. They acted as standbys in case a prisoner or guard dropped out, but were never required. They were offered payment of $15 per day. The participants were selected from 75 respondents who had all completed a questionnaire about their physical and mental health, family background, attitudes towards psychopathology and any previous involvement in crime. Those selected were judged to be the most mature, physically and mentally stable, and least antisocial. The participants were predominantly white middle-class college students who were not known to one another prior to the experiment.

Design and procedure
This experiment used a specifically designed simulated environment: a mock prison. The independent variable was the role randomly assigned to participants; either guard or prisoner. Of the 21 participants, 11 took on the role of guard, 10 became prisoners. The dependent variable was the behaviour of the participants during the experiment, which was collected through video and audio recordings, as well as direct observation. The researchers also gathered data through post-experiment interviews and questionnaires.

The prison environment was created in the basement of a campus building at Stanford University. It consisted of three small cells measuring 1.8m × 2.75m. Each cell housed three prisoners, who were each assigned a cot and bedding. In a nearby area, several rooms formed the guards' quarters, which included interview rooms, space for relaxation, and bedrooms for the warden and superintendent. A small room was also allocated for use as a 'prison yard'. Finally, a small, unlit room across from the prisoners' cells was designated for 'solitary confinement'.

All participants consented to play their assigned role for 24 hours a day for a maximum of two weeks. They were guaranteed to have their basic living needs such as meals and medical provision met, although they were warned that some of their basic rights (e.g. privacy) would be denied if they were assigned the role of the prisoner. Participants were randomly assigned roles as guard or prisoner and asked to be home ready to start the experiment on a given Sunday evening. They received no further instruction as to how to behave in their roles.

Participants who were allocated the role of guard attended a briefing meeting the day before the prisoners arrived. They were met by the prison's superintendent, Philip Zimbardo, the warden (a research assistant) and the other researchers. Participants were informed that the investigators were aiming to simulate a prison environment. While the men believed the researchers were observing the prisoners' behaviour, they were actually equally interested in recording and analysing the behaviours of the guards.

The guards were instructed to 'maintain the reasonable degree of order within the prison necessary for effective functioning', but forbidden from using physical aggression. Their induction included a review of their administrative duties, instructions on how to manage the prisoners' routines (mealtimes, recreation and work) and how to complete 'critical incident reports', in case of any unusual occurrences. The guards were also involved in finalising arrangements of the bedding and furniture in the prison, as well as devising the rules of the prison, along with the warden. The guards then worked three at a time on eight-hour shifts, in between which they were allowed to return home.

The 'prisoners' had a very different induction to the experiment. Local police assisted in 'arresting' participants at their homes without warning, 'charging' each on suspicion of robbery. Each man was read his rights, handcuffed and searched before being driven to a police station in a marked car. The police officers behaved professionally and the participants were not told that the study had begun; their arrest was in some cases witnessed by neighbours and family. Fingerprints and mugshots were taken at the station in accordance with genuine procedures. The participants were detained in a real cell, before being blindfolded and transported to the simulated prison.

Once at the prison, prisoners were stripped naked and sprayed with a delousing agent (this was actually a deodorant spray). They were then ordered to stand naked and alone in the 'yard' before being issued with their uniform, led to their cell and instructed to remain silent. The warden read the rules of the prison, which the prisoners had to memorise and follow. In an effort to depersonalise the prisoners, they were to be referred to by a number rather than their actual name throughout their confinement.

The prisoners were permitted three toilet visits and allowed three plain meals each day, as well as a two-hour period for reading or writing. Prisoners had to be counted three times a day, in order to check they were present, and test they had memorised their number and the prison rules. Additionally, they were given compulsory work assignments and allowed limited privileges such as visiting hours, exercise periods and the chance to watch films.

Both the prisoners and guards wore uniforms. The guards wore military style plain khaki shirt and trousers, with reflective sunglasses, a night stick and whistle. This outfit prevented eye contact with prisoners, and conveyed a sense of control and dominance. By contrast the prisoners wore a loose fitting smock bearing their prisoner number on the front and back. They were not given underwear, and were made to wear rubber sandals and a hat made from a stocking (similar to a hair net), and a chain and lock was placed around their ankles. They were permitted no

WEB WATCH

You can visit the official Stanford Prison Experiment website here to learn more:

www.prisonexp.org

QUESTION SPOTLIGHT!

Why do you think Haney *et al.* went to such lengths to make the experiment so realistic? Is this a strength or a weakness? Explain your ideas.

personal belongings, but were issued with basic personal hygiene items (e.g. soap and toothbrush). The ill-fitting, generic attire stripped the prisoners of their normal appearance and diminished their masculinity. Although the uniforms each group wore were very different, they were both designed to increase the participants' group identity while reducing their individuality.

Results

It was found that the behaviour of the participants was strongly affected by the role they had been assigned in the experiment. Both groups demonstrated a negative tendency in their speech and behaviour, which was interpreted to mean that individuals were 'internalising' the environment and their roles. The experimenters identified a number of processes that contributed to the changes observed in participant behaviour (see Table 3.8).

Reality of the simulation

Participants found the situation believable; it stopped being just an experiment to them and took on a special meaning. Throughout the observations, it was noticed that around 90% of conversations between prisoners were about their situation in the prison, as opposed to talking about their personal backgrounds or other topics. The same was true for discussions among the guards, even though they spent two-thirds of their time outside of the setting. Although the experimenters recognised that there were limitations to the realism of the mock prison, such findings suggested a preoccupation with the simulation that went beyond superficial role play.

Pathology of prisoners and guards

Even though there was no 'script' for how the two groups should behave towards one another, they took it upon themselves to engage in hostile, rude and even dehumanising encounters. The majority of interactions were initiated by guards as commands or verbal affronts which were impersonal and contained few references to personal identity. Prisoners were generally passive in their responses, and while physical violence was expressly forbidden, they still experienced less direct forms of aggression at the hands of the guards.

Some of the guards were openly hostile and cruel. For example, one guard detained a prisoner in solitary confinement longer than was specified in the rules, and also attempted to conceal this from the experimenters who he perceived as too lenient. However, others adopted a 'tough but fair attitude' and played by their own self-imposed rules. The most hostile guards assumed leadership roles, creating an aggressive culture among the group. Basic rights such as eating and sleeping times were quickly reframed as privileges, and privileges such as movie rights were soon cancelled; the prisoners were rendered powerless. Guard behaviour intensified in hostility on a daily basis, despite corresponding intensification in prisoner distress. Throughout the study, the guards had been consistently punctual in arriving for their shifts. Only one individual expressed any sympathy for the prisoners, and this was not openly admitted. This was interpreted by the researchers as evidence that the guards had come to enjoy their positions of power and control. Zimbardo refers to this as the **pathology of power**.

The prisoners, on the other hand, came to experience what Zimbardo called **pathological prisoner syndrome**. They moved from disbelief at the prison conditions to rebellion against the rules, then eventually towards more collective action, such as forming a prisoner grievance committee. When all these efforts failed, prisoners began to act more out of individual self-interest and cohesion was lost. The prisoners varied in the ways in which they coped with the prison conditions. Contrasting coping strategies included being 'good', siding with guards and being obedient, or becoming 'sick', showing signs of extreme emotional distress. When questioned on day four, 3 out of 5 prisoners said they would forfeit the money incentive they had been offered if they could be released, yet no attempts to escape were made.

As a result, the study was concluded earlier than the planned for 14 days. After just six days, the behaviour of the participants had become so concerning that it was called to a halt by the researchers. In fact, five prisoners had been released earlier than this because they were showing signs of emotional trauma (shown by episodes of crying, anger and anxiety). Interestingly, while calling a halt to the experiment was a welcome relief to the prisoners, the guards seemed genuinely disappointed to be finishing early.

KEY IDEAS

Pathology in this study refers to thinking and behaviour that deviates from healthy psychological functioning. The term **pathology of power** refers to how guards enjoyed their dominance over prisoners. Zimbardo describes **pathological prisoner syndrome** as an equally self-perpetuating process which left the participants in a state of passive dependency.

STRETCH & CHALLENGE

Consider the police procedures that are used during arrests. How do you think these procedures make people feel confused, fearful and dehumanised?

TABLE 3.8: PROCESSES INVOLVED IN CREATING PRISONER AND GUARD PATHOLOGY		
Process	**Description**	**Evidence**
Loss of identity	The uniqueness of each individual was reduced through use of a uniform, and through the use of prisoner ID numbers rather than names. Prisoners were de-individuated to the guards and observers, as well as to themselves.	When introduced to a priest who visited the prison, some prisoners introduced themselves by their numbers rather than using their own names.
Arbitrary control	Guards exercised power over prisoners in random and capricious ways. Their decisions about punishments and rewards were unpredictable and unfair, which lead to submissive behaviour and an attitude of learned helplessness from the prisoners.	A prisoner who smiled at a joke might be punished, whereas not smiling at a joke at another time might also be punished.
Dependency and emasculation	The result of arbitrary use of control created a network of dependency for even the most basic needs. The style of the prisoners' uniform and lack of underwear made them move in feminine ways and provoked insults.	Going to the toilet involved prisoners having to publicly request permission (which was not always granted), then being escorted blindfolded and handcuffed to the facilities by guards.

Conclusion

Overall Haney *et al.* (1973) conclude that:

1. The behaviour of the participants is best explained by situational, not dispositional factors.
2. Some residual differences exist between how people individually manage their social roles.
3. The findings of the study should be used to inform guard training programmes.

Figure 3.30: Guards and prisoners in the Stanford Prison Experiment

Source: Haney et al. (1973)

KEY IDEAS

Cognitive-behavioural therapy (CBT) is a form of therapy that originated through the work of Albert Ellis. It focuses on resolving problems through encouraging clients to challenged distorted thoughts in order to change dysfunctional feelings and behaviour. (See also pages 37–38.)

APPLICATION: REDUCING REOFFENDING

The process of identifying, implementing and evaluating treatments for offenders is complex. The interventions used to reduce reoffending should be based on the psychological and practical needs of offenders (Thomas-Peter, 2006). Often, the more complex needs an offender has, the more likely they are to offend again. For example, someone who has experienced abuse as a child, and abuses illegal substances, may require multiple interventions in order to change their behaviour. In this section we will consider one way of improving the emotional well-being of offenders as a way of reducing reoffending.

Anger management

The rationale for treating anger is the assumption that anger is the cause of violent crime. While we all understand what it is like to feel angry, in some cases these feelings can lead to destructive and violent behaviour. Novaco (1975) suggests that some violent offences occur when offenders express their anger in antisocial ways towards inappropriate targets. If offenders can learn to control or manage their anger, this should lead to a decrease in violent behaviour, both in prison settings and when the offender returns to the community.

Anger-management programmes are based on a **cognitive-behavioural** model of treatment which can be carried out in group or individual therapy settings. They are used with a range of client groups, but here we will refer to their application to offenders. The aim is to teach offenders to recognise feelings of anger, control their angry behaviour, and resolve conflict in positive ways (Novaco, 1975). These three stages form the basis of most anger-management programmes.

Stage 1: Cognitive preparation. The offender must learn to identify situations that serve as triggers that lead to angry outbursts. Common examples of these might be feeling ignored or humiliated. They are also taught to be mindful of internal cues that they are starting to feel angry. These could be physical signs such as increases in rate of breathing, heart rate or muscle tensing. It could also include noticing irrational thoughts that accompany the situation such as a disproportionate sense of injustice.

Stage 2: Skills acquisition. Offenders learn different relaxation techniques to use when they have identified anger-provoking situations. These can include regulating breathing, slowly counting to ten, or, where possible, removing themselves from the situation. Sometimes, social-skills training in negotiating and assertiveness is used to help offenders learn how to resolve conflicts without resorting to violence.

Stage 3: Application practice. The skills and awareness learned in previous stages is applied in practice. This is often done through role play, which allows offenders to practice in a controlled, non-threatening environment, such as during therapy sessions. The end result of the programme is to practise the learned techniques until they become natural and automatic responses that replace violent responses.

Figure 3.31: Can learning to control anger reduce offending?

In the UK, the main anger-management course used in prison settings is Controlling Anger and Learning to Manage it (CALM). The programme consists of 24 two-hour sessions that aim to reduce the frequency, intensity and duration of anger. As the majority of violent offences are committed by male offenders, CALM is specifically targeted to benefit men. There are six stages of CALM, which are similar to those outlined above. CALM teaches offenders to focus on thinking patterns that lead to criminal behaviour and learn how to solve their problems without getting angry. It also aims to improve offenders' communication skills and help them to develop strategies to prevent relapses of anger.

Does it work?

Across different client groups, it has been shown that successful anger management interventions can reduce instances of violence as well as decreased self-reported feelings of anger (DiGiuseppe & Tafrate, 2003). More specifically, research by Feindler *et al.* (1994) found that anger-management training led to improvements in self-control, improved problem-solving ability and a reduction in offending in young men.

However, others suggest it may have limited effectiveness, as some violent offences are not motivated by anger, but in order to achieve specific goals (Howitt, 2009). For example, at AS-level/Year 1 we considered research into psychopathic offenders, who are unlikely to benefit from anger management. A study by Rice (1997) found that psychopaths given anger-management or social-skills training showed increased rates of reoffending, possibly because the skills and confidence they gained from the programme made them more effective at manipulating others.

Additionally, there is evidence to suggest that the effectiveness of programmes is limited when the individual's level of motivation to participate is low; for instance when participation is compulsory. This applies to the offender population, where participation may be court-ordered, or seen as helpful for gaining parole rather than as a benefit in itself. Studies such as Heseltine (2010) have found a positive correlation between offender readiness to participate and successful programme outcomes.

One major study has evaluated the effectiveness of CALM. Ireland (2000) conducted a natural experiment that compared 50 prisoners who had completed CALM to a control group of 37 men. The study used self-report methods to assess the effectiveness of anger management, as well as the observations of prison officers.

STRETCH & CHALLENGE ◉

Anger management is just a type of programme designed to reduce reoffending. Find out more about alternative interventions, such as drug-abuse counselling or psychodynamic therapy. What do you see as the similarities and differences between different approaches?

Participants in the CALM programme rated themselves as less angry, as did the prison officers. 92% of CALM offenders showed improvement on at least one 'angry behaviour' measure, which suggested the programme has short-term effectiveness. However, 8% deteriorated, which supports the idea that some groups of offenders are unlikely to benefit from such a programme.

EVALUATION

Methodological and ethical issues

There are some methodological difficulties with studying punishment and reform as a response to criminal behaviour. We have examined some issues with collecting quantitative data and the effectiveness of various forms of punishment on reoffending rates. These include problems with comparing data from different sources, as well as the validity of self-report data or imprisonment rates as a reflection of actual reoffending. It is also difficult to collect qualitative data on the experiences of offenders, as they may be reluctant to be interviewed or observed. For example, it would be challenging to conduct a naturalistic observation in prison, as behaviour will be confounded by personality variables and the histories of prisoners and guards.

A main strength of the key study by Haney *et al.* (1973) was how the researchers were able to balance control of such variables with some ecological validity. The guards and prisoners were randomly allocated and were selected using carefully implemented criteria to reduce confounding variables. Zimbardo was able to make the experience as true to life as possible, for example by having the prisoners arrested at their homes. This contributed overall to the validity of the findings, because participants became immersed in their social roles and engaged in naturalistic interactions that could be generalised beyond the mock prison setting. However, the sample of the study was limited to white, college-educated males, which makes it unrepresentative. The realism of the environment was somewhat limited as participants were aware that they were taking part in a study, and there was an absence of the worst aspects of prison life, such as the threat of real violence and discrimination.

There are also major ethical concerns around methods of punishment and reform as responses to criminal behaviour. There is little doubt that punishment such as imprisonment is a challenging personal experience that has a largely negative impact on the life of the individual offender. It can also have an effect on the mental health of offenders. There are measures in place to reduce the incidence of self-harm, suicide and assaults in prisons, which reflect concern over the increase of these behaviours during imprisonment. There is also debate about discrimination experienced by different groups of offenders – those with pre-existing mental-health conditions, those with learning difficulties, and those from Black and ethnic-minority backgrounds are often over-represented in prison populations.

STRETCH & CHALLENGE ◉

What do the BPS guidelines for conducting research with human participants say about working with prisoners? Why do you think these measures are in place?

The Stanford Prison Experiment has attracted much criticism over the years around the ethical issues it created. It breaches many principles that guide research within psychology. For instance, the study deceived the participants, who were 'arrested' at the start of the experiment. There was overwhelming evidence of psychological harm and distress being experienced in the study, yet it took several days before it was abandoned. However, it could be (and has been) argued that conducting the study in this way was one of the only practical ways to learn more about conflict in prisons, in order to serve the purpose of reducing the problem in real life. Zimbardo felt that the benefits to our understanding outweighed the distress caused by the study.

Debates

Usefulness of research

Research into various methods of punishment and reform play a key role in establishing what works in reducing reoffending. For example, studies that explore what makes anger management effective (e.g. 'readiness' to participate) can make treatment more targeted and cost-effective in reducing instances of violent crime. Reducing reoffending is an important societal goal because of the high impact of crime on victims, families and the wider community, as well as the cost of offender rehabilitation.

Figure 3.32: Readiness to participate in therapy is essential for effective treatment

The usefulness of the research by Haney *et al.* (1973) is somewhat impacted by the ethical limitations of the study. Infamous studies of this type have given psychology a bad name; some might consider that the damaging impact on the reputation of the discipline outweighs its value as a piece of research. Nevertheless, the study has been extremely influential in bringing situational explanations greater acceptance in mainstream psychology. It has also inspired further study into the relationships of power and tyranny in prison settings. One example of this is the BBC Prison Study (see *Activity*), which revisited similar issues to the Stanford experiment and challenged some of the original findings (Reicher & Haslam, 2006).

Reductionism and holism

The argument that the behaviour of inmates in prisons can only be explained by situational variables is perhaps given too much weight by Haney *et al.* (1973). Not all the participants behaved in the same way; some prisoners were more resilient than others to the humiliating conditions in which they found themselves, and some guards were less cruel than others in their exercise of power. It is likely that our personalities are important to how we react as individuals in different situations. The way in which we adopt social roles is not simply reduced to a situational explanation of behaviour.

Individual and situational explanations

The issue of individual and situational explanations for behaviour is key to understanding the effects of imprisonment. As a response to criminal behaviour, methods of punishment and reform involve both. When issuing sentences, the individual's personal circumstances may well play a role in the type of punishment they receive. Likewise, programmes to treat and reform prisoners, such as anger management, are chosen to meet the needs and motivation of different categories of offenders. However, forms of punishment such as community orders, or treatment programmes such as anger management may not be effective for certain individuals, such as those diagnosed as psychopathic.

Applied to the key research by Haney *et al.* (1973), Zimbardo has been criticised for over-emphasising the situational explanation. An alternative explanation for the findings is that the behaviour of both groups originated from stereotypical ideas about social roles that they then play-acted. Either way, there is still evidence that individual differences influenced the thinking and behaviour of both guards and prisoners. Furthermore, Zimbardo acted as superintendent in the prison; he acted as leader to the guards and gave them instructions on how to behave. It could be that his personality was an important factor in influencing the subsequent actions of the guards.

ACTIVITY ✳

Visit the BBC Prison Study website to get an overview of the project. Briefly compare this research to that of Haney *et al*. (1973). How does this help us to understand the differences between the findings of the two studies?

PRACTICE QUESTIONS

Remember that in any exam paper you will get a set of questions on only one of the six sub-topics.

TOPIC 1: WHAT MAKES A CRIMINAL?

(a)* Explain how the research by Raine *et al.* (1997) could be used to understand physiological explanations of criminal behaviour. **[10]**

(b)* Assess the individual/situational debate with regard to explanations of criminal behaviour. **[15]**

(c)* Scarlett is worried about her son Josh and his friends. They are often involved in fights at school and she thinks Josh might have started stealing. Josh's dad was always aggressive and is in prison for theft. Scarlett is wondering what might be causing Josh's behaviour.

Discuss how a criminal psychologist might apply their knowledge of two different explanations of criminal behaviour to help Scarlett to understand possible causes of Josh's behaviour. **[10]**

TOPIC 2: THE COLLECTION AND PROCESSING OF FORENSIC EVIDENCE

(a)* Using the research by Hall & Player (2008), explain how motivating factors and bias could affect the collection and processing of forensic evidence. **[10]**

(b)* Assess the methodological issues involved when researching the ways in which motivating factors and bias could affect the collection and processing of forensic evidence. **[15]**

(c)* A series of high-profile armed robberies have been committed in a town called Lymdon recently. Forensic experts have been processing the evidence. There are several possible suspects, including one with a previous conviction for possession of weapons.

Discuss how motivating factors and bias could affect the collection and processing of forensic evidence in this case. **[10]**

TOPIC 3: COLLECTION OF EVIDENCE

(a)* Explain how the research by Memon & Highman (1999) could be used to improve the way evidence is collected though police interviews. **[10]**

(b)* Assess the extent to which research into the collection of evidence from suspects and witnesses raises and/or solves moral issues for society. **[15]**

(c)* Daryl is a detective who believes he could improve the success of interviews with suspects. He has suggested asking witnesses to sleep at the police station and playing them sounds known to have been audible at the time of the incident, such as dogs barking, traffic noise or music.

The witness would then be woken up and re-interviewed.

Discuss how a psychologist could investigate whether Daryl's new interview technique could improve the collection of evidence. **[10]**

TOPIC 4: PSYCHOLOGY AND THE COURTROOM

(a)* Using the research by Dixon *et al.* (2002), explain how juries can be persuaded by the characteristics of witnesses and defendants. **[10]**

(b)* Assess the validity of research into how juries can be persuaded by the characteristics of witnesses and defendants. **[15]**

(c)* Darcy has been looking at the local news and has seen two pictures of people accused of theft. They have lots of piercings. She wonders if, like accents, piercings might affect the decision-making of the jury.

Discuss how a psychologist could investigate whether Darcy is right in believing that seeing a suspect with lots of piercings might affect the decision reached by a jury. **[10]**

TOPIC 5: CRIME PREVENTION

(a)* Using the research by Wilson & Kelling (1982), explain how the features of neighbourhoods and zero-tolerance policing can help prevent crime. **[10]**

(b)* Assess the ethical issues in crime prevention with regard to features of neighbourhoods and zero-tolerance policing. **[15]**

(c)* Shona has been thinking about crime in her village. Petty things such as graffiti and stealing garden gnomes are beginning to happen. She is wondering what might have led to it and what the community might do to stop it.

Discuss how a psychologist could design a practical strategy to tackle the problems that Shona has seen. **[10]**

TOPIC 6: EFFECTS OF IMPRISONMENT

(a)* Explain how the research by Haney *et al.* (1973) could be used to understand the effects of imprisonment. **[10]**

(b)* Assess the role of social factors in understanding the effects of imprisonment. **[15]**

(c)* Tim is only 20 years old and may go to prison for a crime he committed while drunk. His parents feel it was totally out of character and that being in prison will do him more harm than good. They are asking various people Tim knew to present arguments on his behalf.

Discuss how a psychologist might apply their knowledge of punishment and reform to argue against Tim being imprisoned. **[10]**

TOPIC 1: WHAT MAKES A CRIMINAL?

(b)* Assess the individual/situational debate with regard to explanations of criminal behaviour. **[15]**

Liam's answer:

The individual approach to explaining criminality suggests that the cause is something to do with the person, this might be something they are born with, like their personality, or it might be to do with their experiences, like the way they were brought up. In a way this is partly situational, because it is the environment that is involved in their development here, like the association between poorer educational opportunities and higher crime, but this is really to do with the effect it has on each person, so is still an individual explanation. In the situational approach, experiences matter immediately, like directly triggering a criminal act. For example, Wilson & Kelling showed that broken windows set up a culture of criminality, this is a situational effect.

The findings of the Zimbardo study showed that people thought there were individual causes of behaviour, like the prisoners believing the guards were nasty because they were bigger, but in fact this wasn't the case. The evil behaviour of the guards was caused by the situation.

We say: In some ways, Liam has written a good answer here. He has explained the two aspects of the debate clearly and has illustrated each one with an example. He has used two studies to illustrate the situational argument and, although neither are from the directly relevant section of the specification, they do provide useful evidence. Note that although it is common to refer to 'Zimbardo' in relation to the prison simulation, the study is really Haney *et al*. The main problem, however, is that by using evidence from other areas of the specification, Liam has said too little about 'explanations', which was the focus of the question. Nevertheless, the discussion about the extent to which the environment is responsible for individual explanations as well as situational ones is well argued.

Rina's answer:

Natural selection picks individuals with successful characteristics and sometimes criminality is advantageous, e.g. when stealing or fighting gets you better resources. Darwin's theory would therefore say that individuals would evolve with the capacity for crime because it helps them to survive. So theories such as Sheldon's body types could be explained by bigger, stronger individuals being better at fighting – an explanation on the individual side.

Genetic explanations suggest individual factors too, like Lyons et al.'s study of twins, which showed that genetically identical MZ.s were more likely to share criminality in adulthood than less similar DZ.s. An individual factor that might matter is self-esteem. A study looked at adult

We say: Rina's answer starts of well, clearly establishing the two opposing arguments. For each one she has provided explanations and some discussion, including evidence – although she didn't attempt to spell Trzesniewski et al. (2006), the reference for the self-esteem study! Towards the end of the essay Rina seems rushed. She would have been better off covering fewer explanations and expanding her discussion. For example, more details about how role models can explain criminality and more discussion of the evidence would have been better than her brief comments in the final paragraph. In her haste, Rina hasn't drawn a conclusion at the end of the essay, which is a pity because the arguments she presented were good and this could make a big difference to the mark.

criminals and found they were likely to have had low self-esteem as adolescents. It's likely to have been this individual factor, as the pattern was the same across social classes so it wasn't just a situational difference because of what social class they were in.

Alternatively, Sheldon's criminal types could also come from the situation, as bigger people could be positively reinforced when they did do something illegal and this might be more likely (maybe) to happen to them than to skinny wimps. Though this doesn't really work for some crimes, when being little might be an advantage – maybe shop-lifting or getting through open windows to commit burglaries.

Another big situational factor is role models. Research by Eron looked at boys who watched violent TV but then when they were older the ones who watched the most had worse criminal records. Even this could be other things though. Maybe they watched a lot of bad TV because they weren't well parented. Or it could be operant conditioning. The self-fulfilling prophecy is another situational explanation, supported by Jahoda (1954).

TOPIC 2: THE COLLECTION AND PROCESSING OF FORENSIC EVIDENCE

(c)* A series of high-profile armed robberies have been committed in a town called Lymdon recently. Forensic experts have been processing the evidence. There are several possible suspects, including one with a previous conviction for possession of weapons.

Discuss how motivating factors and bias could affect the collection and processing of forensic evidence in this case. **[10]**

Liam's answer:

The lines on fingerprints are called ridge marks. Fingerprint analysis is about counting these and looking for patterns like points, bridges and islands. These help to tell prints apart and to say if they are the same because no two fingerprints are ever exactly the same, not even identical twins, or at least that was supposed to be the idea, but now it's more like in a stats test whether there's much of a chance that they could be the same person's.

Being a fingerprint analyst is a bit like being one of Blakemore & Cooper's cats – you begin to see the lines you've seen the most really well. So fingerprint experts get really good at seeing ridge patterns. But they also see things that aren't there, like the B13 illusion – it depends on how you look at it. It's the same with fingerprints, if you believe it's 12 … 14 you see 13, so if you believe it's the suspect's print, you'll see the bridges and islands they've got. These problems with perception mean that experts might be motivated to say two fingerprints are the same. Even if they've never been to Lymdon if people are getting hurt it matters so they want to catch somebody.

> **We say:** Much of Liam's essay is irrelevant. There is too much detail about how fingerprint analysts examine prints, and not enough about the biases they are affected by. Towards the end of the essay, where Liam begins to answer the question, he muddles up bias, which he has explained quite well, with motivation, which he hasn't mentioned at all until the very last sentence.

Rina's answer:

Evidence, such as fingerprints and even DNA samples, has to be interpreted, so although it is a physical piece of evidence, like a gun or shoe, judgments have to be made about whether the evidence does or doesn't match up to a suspect. It's this matching that involves the psychological problems of motivation and bias. In the Lymdon case, experts such as fingerprint analysts might have heard about it as it is described as high profile, and the fact that they are dangerous crimes would matter too, since this makes analysts more likely to want to get a conviction. This work involves looking at two samples, like two fingerprints or two DNA records to see if they are the same, matching up the suspect with the perpetrator. These visual judgments are affected by perceptual biases, like the tendency to 'fill in the gaps' in a visual illusion, because our perceptual system looks for contours, and this can lead to mistakes. These mistakes are more likely to happen when we think we are going to see them. So another thing that makes us likely to see something is expecting it, similar to Moray's study where we sometimes hear our own name. In fingerprinting,

> **We say:** Rina's essay is quite good, tackling both biases and motivation and using a range of information to explain her answer, including studies and concepts such as expectation and contours in illusions. However, some ideas are not explained in sufficient detail. For example, the study by Schiffer & Champod could have been used to explain the effect of seeing the suspect's print before the latent mark, rather than just saying 'it's obvious'.

if you see the suspect's print before you look at the one you
are analysing of course you are going to see similarities, it's
obvious.

　Biased decision making is even worse when we are
motivated to find a match. Lots of evidence from fingerprint
studies show that mistakes are more likely when working
in high-emotion contexts. Dror et al. (2005) showed that
with information about a gory crime, fingerprint analysts
matched ambiguous prints that didn't really match. Though
Hall & Player (2008) only found that they felt affected –
they actually weren't less accurate with information about
the crime. Maybe this was because Hall and player didn't use
gory pictures.

TOPIC 4: PSYCHOLOGY AND THE COURTROOM

(a)* Using the research by Dixon *et al.* (2002), explain how juries can be persuaded by the characteristics of witnesses and defendants. **[10]**

Liam's answer:

Dixon's first study found more people with London accents were
found guilty than ones with non-London accents. This was even
worse if they 'sounded black' and worse still if the crime was
something like theft, done by workers in blue overalls. All this
means having a bad accent makes you more likely to get found
guilty if you have done the sort of crime linked to your social
group.

　Then in 2002 Dixon did the study again with Birmingham
accents. This time he found having an accent, being black, and
doing a blue collar crime all led to guilty verdicts. This is bad if
you are an innocent, black boy from Birmingham accused of
armed robbery. Amazingly, the study was done with a student
who could do a perfect normal accent and a Brummie accent
because he had grown up in Birmingham. This means the whole
study was really well controlled as everything else about him
was kept the same. Dixon said that this might be because posh
accents are more confident so are believed more. Courts ought to
try to stop the jury taking notice of this.

We say: Liam was having a bad day when he wrote this essay. He describes Mahoney & Dixon's study but is muddled because he says the defendants had London accents instead of Birmingham accents. He then gets confused about 'blue-collar workers' – ones in manual jobs. 'Blue collar' used to refer to crimes committed by working-class people but now tends to mean, as Liam says, crimes such as theft. The paragraph's saving grace is that Liam observes that the link between accent and perceptions of guilt isn't straightforward – it depends on the crime. In the second paragraph, Liam focuses on the correct study and all of his description is accurate, although some of it is more detailed than it is relevant or useful here. He ends the essay with a brief attempt at a summary.

Rina's answer:

In the courtroom, ordinary people make decisions about guilt or innocence but stereotypes can bias their decisions. We might not even be aware of them, but guilty people may go free or innocent people may get convicted. Psychology tries to sort this out. Stewart showed that in real cases, attractive defendants were acquitted more. Generally, though, you can't go in to real courts to see the jury so research is done on mock juries, as with Pfeifer & Ogloff (1991), who found that white students judged a black defendant as guilty more than they did a white one. Both studies suggest that how a defendant looks affects how fair juries are. This means juries should be careful about judging people based on their appearance, whether it is attractiveness or race, but, in reality, it's impossible to stop people noticing these things unless you hide the defendant, and even then there might media information about the suspect or there might be other clues, such as in their voice.

   The voice does matter. Lakoff (1975) found that witnesses who sounded unsure, e.g. saying 'perhaps', or ending sentences like questions, were thought of as less clever and not so believable. Seggie (1983) found speech mattered for defendants too. People who were accentless were less likely to be thought of as guilty of assault than ones with Australian or Asian accents. Interestingly, this posh accent meant they were more likely to be thought of as guilty of theft. This shows that the effect of accents is complex as the type of crime was linked to particular social groups, meaning that in different situations juries might be biased in favour of or against different groups, so guiding juries to avoid it would be hard.

   Research by Dixon et al. looked at the differences between people who were black or white, accused of robbery or fraud, with Brummie or standard accents. Participants listened to basically the same interview but in different accents and with different information about the crime, then rated the suspects' guilt. They found that the Brummie accent led to higher guilty ratings. Even though the study used

We say: Rina's essay here is quite well balanced, with discussion of three different factors – attractiveness, race and accent – and a critical consideration of the key research, although the latter is quite brief. The ideas from the studies have been applied to the way in which juries can be persuaded, and the critical evaluation at the end of the discussion of Dixon *et al.* offers both appropriate evaluation of the study and reapplies that criticism to the question.

university students not real jurors, it shows how easily
a defendant's or a witness's characteristics might sway
people's judgments, especially as it was even the same person
doing the voices. It's possible, though, that juries wouldn't be
persuaded so easily. In a real situation there is much more
evidence so the accent would be less important to the decision
and the importance of accents might be less than other things
like gender or age.

C4

ENVIRONMENTAL PSYCHOLOGY

Environmental psychology is the study of the relationship between people and the natural and built environment. This includes the influences of the environment on human experiences, behaviour and well-being (Steg *et al.*, 2013), as well as factors influencing environmental behaviours. In this chapter we will look at six topics:

1 **Stressors in the environment:** We will look at environmental stressors, particularly noise and its effect our health, and examine a field study by Black & Black (2007) exploring the links between aircraft noise and stress and hypertension in residents nearby. Finally, we will examine strategies for dealing with stressors.

2 **Biological rhythms:** We will look at circadian rhythms and the impact of disrupting these through shift work or jet lag. A study by Czeisler *et al.* (1982) demonstrated how knowledge of circadian rhythms can be applied to help reduce the negative effects of shift work. We will also look at various strategies for reducing the effects of shift work and jet lag.

3 **Recycling and other conservation behaviours:** We will examine conservation behaviours and the factors that influence our tendencies to conserve or recycle. A study by Lord (1994) explores the effectiveness of different types of message and message sources for increasing recycling behaviour. We will also examine techniques used to increase recycling or other conservation behaviours.

4 **Ergonomics:** Here we consider cognitive overload and the impact of observation in the workplace. Drews & Doig (2014) address cognitive overload in intensive care nurses and develop a new configural display to reduce cognitive load and facilitate faster decision-making. We also consider a range of other factors involved in ergonomic workplace design.

5 **Psychological effects of built environment:** We will consider the impact of the built environment and urban renewal on our well-being, specifically how a view of the natural environment may speed up recovery after an operation (Ulrich, 1984). We will also look at how environmental design can be used to improve health and well-being.

6 **Territory and personal space:** Here we explore issues of territory and personal space in the workplace. Wells (2000) explores the role of office personalisation in employee and organisational well-being, and we consider strategies for office design based on research in this area.

STRESSORS IN THE ENVIRONMENT

BACKGROUND

What is stress?

Stress has been defined as the 'response we get when the demands of our environment are greater than the capacity we have to deal with them' (Oliver, 2002).

In order to understand stress we need to understand two concepts: the stressor and the stress response. The stressor is any stimulus that requires an adjustment or an adaptation in order to be able to deal with it. Such a stimulus can obviously be either external (for example, noise, overcrowding or temperature) or internal (for example, worry or anxiety), but in this chapter we are considering the impact of environmental stressors. The response to stress is a biological or a physiological one and is sometimes described as the 'fight or flight' response – a term first used by Cannon in 1932.

Biological responses to stress

The fight or flight response involves the activation of the sympathetic-adrenal medullary (SAM) system which regulates adrenaline release. This causes a rapid increase in blood pressure, blood coagulation and heart rate. It also causes blood

ACTIVITY ✳

Researchers in this area have identified that major life events are one source of stress, but so are 'daily hassles' such as oversleeping or not being able to get a seat on the bus. The kinds of things that will stress a student in the UK are likely to be very different from those of someone working in a high-powered job in New York or someone struggling to feed her children in a remote part of East Africa, Make a list of everything that has stressed you in the last week. Try to put them in order, from the least stressful to the most stressful.

Ask other people in your class to do the same thing and see if you can develop a list of what stresses this group of people the most. Produce an advice leaflet or a poster suggesting how people could cope with this sort of stress.

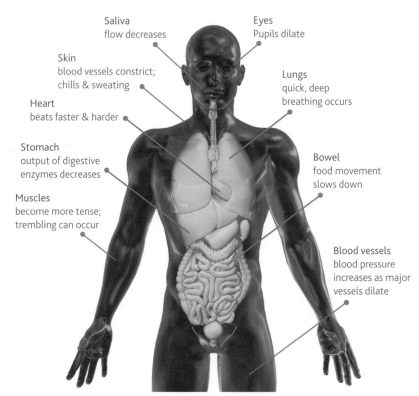

Figure 4.1: The fight or flight response

sugar levels to rise rapidly (to provide energy) and digestive processes to slow down. Once the emergency has passed, the system returns to its normal state of equilibrium, which is called homeostasis (*homeo* = similar + *stasis* = standing still). Cannon's work had focused on the body's response to acute threat, by which he meant short-lived emergencies. In the 1950s Selye began to consider the adaptation of the body to chronic stress, or longer-lasting stressful situations. Selye proposed a three-stage response to stress which he termed the General Adaptation Syndrome or GAS.

TABLE 4.1: THE STAGES OF THE GENERAL ADAPTATION SYNDROME (GAS)	
Stage 1: alarm	A threat or stressor means that the body prepares itself for fight or flight, as described above
Stage 2: resistance	If the situation continues, the body tries to adapt to or cope with the long-terms demands of the stressful situation
Stage 3: exhaustion	Ultimately the bodily resources will become depleted; this is where damage to the body starts to occur

The two models of stress described here are primarily physiological models. In contrast, psychological models of stress focus on the influence of psychological factors on stress responses. One of the best known models is the transactional model proposed by Lazarus (1966). In this model, stress is not simply a physiological response to an external event, but is affected by 'cognitive appraisal', i.e. the way that we think about the stressor (for example, the level of control that people perceive they have), and by the different coping strategies that we have available to us.

What are environmental stressors?

There are many kinds of environmental stressor: for example, noise, crowding, poor housing quality, poor neighbourhood quality, traffic congestion. Take a few moments to consider the environment you are in at this moment. What are you aware of? Is anything irritating or annoying you? Can you do anything about it?

Noise

Noise is any sound, especially one that is loud, unpleasant or that causes disturbance. It can be defined simply as unwanted sound. The intensity of noise is measured in decibels, although other measurements may also be important when investigating the effects of noise. These might include the pitch (or frequency) of the noise, whether the noise is continuous or intermittent, or how long it goes on for. Other factors such as the level of predictability of the noise and the amount of perceived control we have over the noise are also key factors to consider.

TABLE 4.2: EXAMPLES OF NOISE AND THEIR DECIBEL LEVELS	
dB	**Examples**
150	Jet take-off at 25 m. This would cause ruptured ear drums
130	Machine-gun fire at close range. 32 times as loud as 70dB
110	Rock concert. This is the human pain threshold; 110dB is 16 times as loud as 70dB

Figure 4.2: Where you would prefer to be?

Figure 4.3: This would be around 100 decibels. How do you think you would feel if you were exposed to noise like this over an extended period of time? How would you feel if you could hear this noise from inside your house?

WEB WATCH @

This website will give you an idea about how loud 70 decibels is:

http://www.dangerousdecibels.org/ education/information-center/decibel-exposure-time-guidelines/

QUESTION SPOTLIGHT! ☆

Why do you think that being able to control noise is important?

We all know that intense, unpredictable and uncontrollable noise can irritate and annoy us. However, chronic noise can produce more serious stress symptoms and can affect performance, social behaviour and health. Studies (**natural experiments**) have shown that children attending school near an airport had higher noradrenaline levels and higher resting blood pressure than children living in quieter areas (Evans, Bullinger & Hygge, 1998). We also know that people who work in very noisy environments suffer from high blood pressure (Tomei *et al.*, 2010).

Noise can also have significant effects on motivation. A study conducted by Glass and Singer (1972) showed that when participants were exposed to loud noise in a laboratory they showed less ability to persist at a task *when the noise was removed*. This lack of motivation can therefore be seen as an after-effect caused by the cognitive load of working while exposed to loud noise. The effects were significantly reduced when participants were able to control the noise.

Another fascinating **natural experiment** on the effects of noise comes from Bronzaft (1981) who looked at the effect on reading ability in children attending a school close to a railway line. Those children who had their lessons in classrooms on the noisy side of a school (next to the train tracks) were found to have significantly lower reading abilities than those children whose classrooms were on the other (quieter) side of the school. Interestingly, Bronzaft also discovered that after major noise-reduction work had been carried out at the school, classroom location no longer had any effect on reading ability.

DO IT YOURSELF 🔍

Design a piece of research to investigate whether children growing up near a busy road suffer any negative effects in terms of their cognitive skills, compared to children growing up in quieter locations. What problems might you encounter in attempting to control for extraneous variables?

KEY RESEARCH

Black, D.A. & Black, J.A. (2007) Aircraft noise exposure and resident's stress and hypertension: A public health perspective for airport environmental management. *Journal of Air Transport Management.* 13 (5), 264–276.

Aim

The aim of this study was to explore the impact of aircraft noise on the health of a community of people living in the areas surrounding Sydney Airport in Australia.

Specifically, the researchers wanted to find out if the 'health related quality of life' was worse in a community exposed to aircraft noise than in a community not exposed to this noise. They also wanted to explore whether long-term exposure to aircraft noise was associated with elevated blood pressure.

Initially the researchers carried out a **pilot study** with 100 people, which allowed them to check the reliability of the noise stress scales and the noise sensitivity scales that were going to be used in the main study. They found that several items on each scale could be removed as they were duplicating the results of other items.

Population and sample

The study was conducted in the area surrounding Sydney Airport. The locations chosen were exposed to 50 or more occurences of aircraft noise exceeding 70 decibels. This level was chosen as it is the level at which noise interferes with normal conversation, listening to the radio or watching the television.

Control areas for comparison were selected in locations not exposed to aircraft noise and matched in socio-economic status to the exposed areas.

A total sample size of 1500 people was chosen. The researchers calculated that they needed to start with a sample this size for two reasons: first, the pilot study had indicated that the likely response rate would be around 50%, so this initial number would leave a good sample size of respondents even with a large dropout, and secondly, large samples are required to allow for meaningful comparisons to be made on health scores.

Method

Noise measurement

Noise stations were set up outside randomly selected households. Households that were close to other significant sources of noise – such as railway lines, industrial areas and major highways – were excluded. Data was collected from 26 noise stations surrounding Sydney airport and 3 stations in the control area, between 7am and 6pm on various days between October 2003 and November 2004. There is a nightime curfew at Sydney airport from 11pm to 6am, and an ethics committee restricted noise measurements late in the evening or at night due to safety concerns for the researchers.

Health measurement

Questionnaires were sent to survey participants with a covering letter explaining that the research was on environmental noise rather than on airport noise. This was in an attempt to reduce the likelihood of an increased response rate of those residents who are especially annoyed by aircraft noise, as this would have created a bias.

The researchers measured subjective health outcomes using items from validated, internationally recognised surveys (e.g. SF-36, designed by Ware & Sherbourne, 1992). The questionnaire measured seven major characteristics for each participant, which were as follows:

1 Health-related quality of life
2 Hypertension
3 Noise stress
4 Noise sensitivity
5 Noise annoyance
6 Demographic characteristics
7 Confounding factors

For each health measure, a summary score in the range of 0 to 100 was obtained, with a higher score indicating a more positive health status.

KEY IDEAS

Clearly most research in environmental psychology is conducted through the use of **natural experiments**. Remember that a natural experiment is one where the independent variable is manipulated already within the natural environment rather than being manipulated by a researcher in an often unnatural or controlled setting. This gives natural experiments relatively high levels of ecological validity and relatively low levels of control. Laboratory experiments, in contrast, tend to have relatively low levels of ecological validity and relatively high levels of control.

A **pilot study** is a study conducted with a small number of participants to try out the procedures of a study and to check for any problems.

QUESTION SPOTLIGHT!

Why is it important to match the locations for socio-economic status? How might this have been done?

STRETCH & CHALLENGE

The researchers claimed to be concerned with the effects of environmental noise generally rather than airport noise specifically. Is this kind of cover story a type of deception? Are there any ethical issues with this?

STRETCH & CHALLENGE ◎

There are many potential confounding variables here. Suggest as many effects as possible for each one of these variables. Consider how these potential confounding variables could have been controlled.

Results

In all, 796 responses were received, with 704 of these filled in completely. This gives a total response rate of just under 50%. Not surprisingly, the response rate from the noise-exposure area was slightly higher than that from the control area, probably as the topic of the questionnaire had greater relevance for this group.

Demographics

There were some significant differences between the two groups. The age range in the total sample was from 15 to 87, although the control group had an average age four years higher than that of the noise-exposure group. There were also significantly more female participants in the control group. However, participants in the noise-exposure group had higher educational qualifications and better employment statuses than the control group. The groups were similar in terms of household income and consumption of alcohol and salty foods. There were more smokers in the noise-exposure group, but this group took more exercise than the control group, which had higher levels of obesity. Finally, only 3% of the control group had insulated their homes from noise, whereas 37% of the noise-exposure group had had some type of noise insulation installed.

Health measures

Subjects in the noise-exposure group had significantly higher levels of reported noise stress and aircraft noise annoyance. They also had significantly lower scores on the mental health measures. People in the aircraft noise-exposure group had lower scores on health measures than those people in the control groups. The significant differences were as follows:

1 *Relationship between health quality of life factors and aircraft noise*
   Further analysis revealed that the mean scores for physical functioning, general health, vitality and mental health were significantly lower in the noise-exposure group than in the control group.

2 *Prevalence of hypertension and aircraft noise*
   The authors conclude that long-term aircraft noise exposure was significantly associated with chronic noise stress, and that chronic noise stress was significantly associated with a prevalence of hypertension (high blood pressure).

Conclusions

There is clear evidence here for the negative health effects of exposure to aircraft noise, but what solutions, if any, can the researchers suggest?

In other parts of the world (Hong Kong and Jakarta for example), the negative health impact of aircraft noise has been largely eliminated by relocating the airports away from populated areas. For Sydney airport, such a move would be almost impossible. There are some noise-management strategies that might be considered, such as operating parallel runway operations, and simultaneous approaches and take-offs, unless wind speeds and directions necessitate the use of other runways. The researchers also suggest that it might be possible to extend curfew hours, set an hourly cap on take-offs and landings, or offer an improved building insulation scheme.

These are all practical noise-management possibilities, but researchers approaching the issue from a more psychological perspective might consider ways to reduce the stress experienced by individuals living in the affected areas.

Black & Black argue that to their knowledge, no study has attempted to alleviate noise stress other than through the use of drugs. However, the literature on stress in general offers suggestions for stress management that include behaviour modification techniques (such as those used by Kahn *et al.* (1988) in an attempt to alleviate stress associated with environmental noise in an intensive care unit setting in Rhode Island) and cognitive behaviour therapy (CBT), as well as more recent developments in mindfulness.

APPLICATION: MANAGING ENVIRONMENTAL STRESS

Clearly, there are many practical strategies that aim to reduce the effects of environmental stressors such as noise. There may be changes that can be made to buildings such as double glazing, soundproofing and increased insulation as ways of reducing noise, changes to building regulations and changes to the operating hours of airports or other heavy industry.

In this section we will concentrate on psychological strategies that may help people cope with environmental stressors such as noise.

Mindfulness

Mindfulness is described as a mental state achieved by focusing awareness on the present while calmly acknowledging feelings and body sensations. It is a type of meditation based on principles of Buddhism and is gaining increasing recognition within Western psychology and psychiatry as a technique for reducing the symptoms of a range of conditions, including anxiety, obsessive compulsive disorder and depression.

In one recent study (Gans *et al.*, 2015), mindfulness was used to treat **tinnitus** (a ringing in the ears). It is estimated that roughly 10% of the UK population suffer from this condition and the numbers are particularly high among veterans returning from military service. Typically, studies have used white noise to distract sufferers from the ringing or buzzing noises, i.e. noise that contains many frequencies with equal intensities. (You will have heard white noise when tuning a radio. It is the 'static' that can be heard in the unused frequencies.) However, in this study Gans *et al.* found that practicing mindfulness helped patients find some relief from the stress caused by tinnitus.

Although their study was only a very small one (with just seven participants), Gans *et al.* report that self-reported scores in the tinnitus handicap inventory – which included social and occupational functioning, sleep habits, depression, and anxiety – had decreased immediately after the study and continued to decrease 12 months later.

'We found that perceptions of chronic tinnitus changed, with participants noting that they felt an increased tolerance, acceptance and courage to live with it, even after 12 months of completing the program,' said Gans. 'People commented that tinnitus no longer seemed like a dreadful curse; it was just another sensation that could be annoying but was not insurmountable.' (Gans et al., 2015)

Although tinnitus is not an environmental stressor, this study suggests that mindfulness could be useful in reducing the effects of noise such as that experienced living near to an airport.

WEB WATCH @

This website contains a lot of useful information and some videos on the use of mindfulness: http://www.mindfulnet.org/page2.htm

 KEY IDEAS

Tinnitus is generally defined as an auditory perception of sound that is not produced externally. Tinnitus may have many causes, including aging, hearing loss, prolonged exposure to loud noise, head injury, or the use of some prescription drugs and over-the-counter medications. Tinnitus is not an environmental stressor, in the sense that the noise is not from an external source, but it is reasonable to suggest that a technique that relieves the stress associated with tinnitus might also be applied to those who suffer from the stress caused by environmental noise (or other stressors).

KEY IDEAS

Imaginal exposure therapy asks the client to imagine the feared or stressful stimuli (in this case, the noise) rather than putting the person in the actual situation. In this way they can describe their feelings and develop coping strategies in a safe context and can stop if their stress levels get too high.

Cognitive behaviour therapy (CBT)

Leventhall *et al.* (2008) report successful outcomes from using CBT to increase coping strategies for sufferers of low-frequency noise. A small group of nine participants were evaluated before and after a series of interventions. Participants were assessed on the extent to which they reacted to low-frequency noise, its impact on their quality of life, the effectiveness of their coping strategies, and their personality type.

It was hypothesised that the stress experienced as a reaction to the noise could be treated with a combination of the following therapeutic strategies:

1   Reassurance, explanation and support
2   Relaxation therapy
3   General stress management advice and coping skills
4   **Imaginal exposure therapy**. This was based on the idea that, as there were some overlaps between the reaction to the noise and phobias, that a form of imaginal exposure therapy might be used to desensitise the participant to the sound.

Six group sessions of two hours each were held that included general discussions, the teaching of coping skills, relaxation therapy and self-hypnosis. Participants were also given handouts explaining the techniques and a CD of common relaxation exercises for stress, and were assigned homework to practise the relaxation twice daily.

At the end of the six sessions, participants were assessed on all the same measures that had been taken prior to the intervention.

The first key finding is that the participants' scored reactions to the noise were reduced in comparison to their pre-intervention scores. For example, scores on sleep disturbance dropped from 83% to 72%, and scores on problems relaxing dropped from 78% to 62%. In terms of quality of life, physical well-being scores were improved and participants reported lower anxiety levels. Supporting this improvement were increased scores on coping with the noise.

Although this is a very small scale study which only involved a short term intervention, there is evidence here to conclude that relaxation and other psychotherapeutic techniques can be effective in reducing the stress caused by environmental noise.

WEB WATCH @

Psychologists investigate a mystery 'hum'!

http://www.bbc.co.uk/news/magazine-13752688

ACTIVITY ✳

You are an environmental psychologist who is researching the effects of noise. You have been contacted by a group of people who are concerned about the possible expansion of Heathrow Airport and the effect that this might have on residents in nearby areas. Using your knowledge of this subject, provide the group with a summary of evidence that they can use to support their argument against the expansion of the airport.

STRETCH & CHALLENGE ◎

You could also advise the group of possible coping strategies for those people who are already affected by the airport noise.

EVALUATION

Methodological and ethical issues

The study by Black & Black could be considered to be a quasi-experiment (or natural experiment) as the independent variable of noise exposure occurred naturally rather than being manipulated by the experimenter. This will inevitably mean that the study has lower levels of control than if it had been based in a laboratory environment, but will also mean that the study has higher levels of ecological validity. Black & Black were studying the effects of noise exposure in an area surrounding Sydney Airport and so identified a control group for comparison. They matched this control group on socio-economic factors. Although they do not go into great detail about this matching in their article, this will mean that the area surrounding the airport is being compared to an area with similar housing and where people have similar incomes. This matching will allow for comparisons to be drawn more effectively. Overall the researchers sampled 1500 people and received 704 responses, with slightly more responses coming from the noise-exposure group than from the control group. This is a fairly typical response rate for a questionnaire (in fact possibly slightly higher than you might normally expect), and the fact that more people from the noise-exposure group returned their questionnaires can be explained in terms of the increased salience of the topic to them. It is always interesting to consider whether the people who did return the questionnaires are likely to be any different from the people who did not, but in relation to this study, we are unable to answer this question. This may also prove to be something of a weakness. If you are asked about something that is a major source of stress to you, it may be likely that you would exaggerate the symptoms you were experiencing in order to make the problem seem worse, possibly in the hope that something might be done about the noise. Questionnaires in general may have both strengths and weaknesses. Strengths include that they are relatively quick to complete and their anonymity may encourage people to complete them honestly, but they can also suffer from a range of weaknesses, including leading questions, bias, and demand characteristics.

The sample size used in the study by Black & Black was large, but the sample used in the two studies looking at coping with environmental stressors were both very small. It is always possible that individual differences had significant effects on results when sample sizes are very small, as they are in the studies by Gans *et al.* and by Leventhall *et al.* In both these studies, too, it is important to consider the possibility that there are alternative explanations for the results. Perhaps the group discussions about how people felt about the low-frequency noise was a significant factor in reducing stress for Leventhall *et al.*'s participants, or perhaps simply the fact that someone was taking their concerns seriously was enough to reduce participants' stress and anxiety in both of these studies, regardless of the specific interventions.

There are few ethical issues raised by the Black & Black study, as people were not being exposed to noise for the purposes of the experiment. Had this been the case, then clearly this would have raised issues relating to the protection of the participant. The participants were not harmed in any way by taking part in this study and consent was gained through the return of the questionnaire (which was anonymous, and it is highly unlikely that anyone would have objected to the minor deception involved). It is perhaps possible that participants found some of the questions quite personal and maybe slightly upsetting to think about, although they could simply have chosen not to complete such questions (note that this would have produced a further bias in the sample). Interestingly, the authors report that the university ethics committee restricted the noise measurements that could be taken late in the evening and through the night out of concern for the safety of the researchers, although they clearly recognised that the research created no ethical issues for those taking part.

Debates

Usefulness of research

This research has identified significant effects of living near an airport and it is obviously useful to have done this. The researchers discuss the impact of their research in terms of public policy (for example, restricting further developments, and increasing the noise insulation scheme), and if their results benefitted people in these practical ways then the research was indeed useful. Along with other studies detailing the negative relationships between noise and illness, or between noise and quality of life, this evidence could certainly be used to attempt to prevent the expansion of airports or the building of new airports (or other noisy industry) close to large residential areas. Interestingly, however, there are few specific applications for helping people deal with noise, and those that have been discussed are applications of more general therapeutic approaches, such as cognitive behaviour therapy, which have their own strengths and weaknesses.

STRETCH & CHALLENGE ◎

Research cognitive behaviour therapy and its strengths and weaknesses. A recent meta-analysis published by Johnsen & Friborg (2015) suggests that CBT may not be as effective as once thought. You can read a summary of this paper here: http://digest.bps.org.uk/search?q=+CBT

Reductionism and holism

It could be argued that this research is relatively holistic in that it considers both biological and social factors relating to the effect of noise exposure. The range of questions asked in the questionnaire means that a variety of variables are being considered. Solutions discussed by the authors are also relatively holistic: while responding to the effects of noise exposure by offering drug treatments could be considered a reductionist approach, the variety of suggestions, ranging from changing public policy through to cognitive strategies such as the ones discussed earlier, do offer a more holistic understanding of the problem and possible solutions.

Figure 4.4: Residential housing close to Sydney Airport

BIOLOGICAL RHYTHMS

BACKGROUND

What are biological rhythms?

Biological rhythms are common in the natural world. These are the rhythms that govern much of our physiological functioning. The most important biological rhythm that will be considered in this section is the **circadian** rhythm (from *circa* = about and *die* = day), referring to a rhythm that repeats approximately every 24 hours. Green (1994) estimates that there are around 100 different circadian rhythms in mammals, which include sleeping, waking, body temperature, urine flow, digestion, blood pressure, hormone release, and many other aspects of normal bodily function. In this section, we will examine the disruption to the circadian rhythms caused by shift work and jet lag.

The key question in relation to circadian rhythms is whether they are endogenous (meaning that they occur naturally) or exogenous (meaning that they are dependent on external cues such as a change in light). There is a great deal of evidence for humans and other mammals possessing internal/endogenous timing mechanisms (sometimes referred to as pacemakers). A famous study was conducted in 1972, when Michel Siffre spent two months living in isolation in a cave, with no access to any exogenous cues. Researchers monitoring his sleep-wake cycle discovered that, although it was erratic to begin with, it soon settled down into a roughly 24-hour cycle.

So, what role do exogenous/external factors play in our biological rhythms? It would seem as though they are equally important as the internal factors. While our endogenous pacemakers can time our biological activities, these activities are also controlled by external events such as changes in light and darkness. External events that help to set the timing of biological activities are called zeitgebers (from the German word for 'time-giver'). The body uses cues both from its own internal processes and from the environment (for example, the time on the clock, social activities, the light-dark cycle, and meal times) to keep these various rhythms in check. For example, body temperature is highest during the afternoon and early evening and lowest in the very early morning (typically just before sunrise). We tend to fall asleep (and stay asleep) as our body temperature falls, and find it harder to sleep as our body temperature rises again. If a person works shifts, the low body temperature in the early hours of the morning produces feelings of fatigue and disorientation as well as making it much more difficult to sleep during the day.

The disruption of bodily rhythms

Our bodies can adjust relatively easily to small changes in the external world, such as the changes of the seasons, or the losing or gaining of an hour when the clocks change in spring and autumn. However, when zeitgebers change dramatically, such as when we work at night or fly half way around the world,

Figure 4.5: Michel Siffre in isolation in the cave

our internal clocks are not able to adjust fast enough and, for a while, our physiological processes – such as hunger and the sleep-wake cycle – become desynchronised from the outside world.

The most extreme example of this is the experience of jet lag. If you fly to the USA, you might leave the UK at 9 o'clock in the morning and spend 6 hours on the aeroplane, but because of the 5-hour time difference you will arrive at 10 o'clock in the morning – just one hour later than when you left. It is hardly surprising that later in the day your body will still respond as if it is time for bed, although it is only mid-afternoon in the USA. This desynchronisation of internal and external factors is what produces the feelings of tiredness and disorientation that we describe as jet lag. Studies by Czeisler *et al.* (1982) and others have demonstrated that the most effective way to overcome the feelings of jet lag is to respond to the zeitgeibers, rather than to the messages that your body is sending you. So, if you travel from the UK to the USA, you need to try to stay awake as long as possible to ensure that your sleep-wake cycle adjusts to the external zeitgebers as soon as possible.

Jet-lag symptoms are notably much more severe when travelling from West to East than when travelling from East to West. An East-to-West journey means that our internal body clock is **phase advanced** and the re-synchronisation of our internal and external body clocks is far easier than when our internal body clock is **phase delayed** and ends up hours behind external clock time. So you are more likely to experience severe jet lag when travelling from the USA to the UK than when travelling from the UK to the USA.

Figure 4.7: Phase advance and phase delay

Figure 4.6: We can adjust easily to small changes in the external world, but it is harder to adjust to bigger changes

Shift work, which produces a similar de-synchronisation of body rhythms and zeitgebers to jet lag, is a system of employment where individuals work irregular hours, sometimes during the day, sometimes through the night. It is common in a range of occupations, including nursing, the police force and other emergency services; the leisure industry; mining, and other industrial work where production never stops; customs and immigration; and transportation services. A shift worker's working pattern may change regularly (perhaps weekly), meaning that they will spend most of their time in a state of physiological discomfort as they try to adjust to rapidly changing zeitgebers. Shift work is the focus of the study that will be examined here.

ACTIVITY

Research the effects of jet lag in a little more detail. Have you been on a long-haul flight? If you have, try to remember any symptoms that you may have experienced. Do you know someone who regularly flies to the USA and back for work? If you do, ask them to describe any symptoms that they might have experienced.

Produce a short advice leaflet that explains why jet lag occurs and what can be done to reduce its effects.

What problems can shift work cause?

A shift worker has to function (for at least some of the time) on a schedule that is not 'natural'. Constantly changing schedules can have many different effects. Upsetting the body's natural circadian rhythm can cause sleep deprivation or other sleep problems, and disorders of the gastrointestinal and cardiovascular systems. It can also exacerbate existing medical problems, and increase our susceptibility to minor illnesses such as colds (Harrington, 2001; HSE, 2006). Individuals who work shifts are also more likely to have a poor diet and to consume an excess of caffeine. Perhaps most significantly, shift work can cause severe disruption to relationships and family life.

Recent research by the International Agency for Research on Cancer (IARC) concluded that there was sufficient evidence to consider shift work as carcinogenic (that is, causing cancer). This was based on what they referred to as 'limited evidence' of carcinogenicity in humans and sufficient evidence of carcinogenicity in experimental animals. This included one study demonstrating that incidence of breast cancer was higher in women who worked night shifts on a long-term basis, than in women who did not work at night. These results were consistent with animal studies that showed that constant light, dim light at night, or simulated chronic jet lag can all increase tumour development. Although the exact causes of this association are not fully known, it is suggested that these findings are linked to the disrupted circadian rhythms caused by exposure to light at night, which alters sleep activity, suppresses the production of melatonin and may cause irregularity in the genes involved in tumour development.

Rotating shift work has been implicated in 'human error' connected with general issues of health and safety as well as with more serious accidents, for example at nuclear power plants or in air crashes. Fatigue and shift-working arrangements were cited as major contributory factors in incidents such as the Bhopal gas tragedy, the Clapham Junction rail disaster, and the catastrophic nuclear accident at Chernobyl (HSE, 2012). Fatigue is also a recognised contributing factor in patient-safety incidents such as drug errors (Health Service Journal, 2005).

KEY IDEAS

Make sure that you understand the difference between **phase advance** (getting earlier) and **phase delay** (getting later). These concepts will be crucial in understanding the key study that follows.

In terms of shiftwork, phase advance means a backward shift, so that workers work nights, then afternoons and then mornings. This causes the sleep-wake cycle to advance, effectively shortening the typical 24-hour cycle. In contrast, phase delay would mean a forward shift, so that workers work nights, then mornings and then afternoons. This delays (or lengthens) the sleep-wake cyle.

QUESTION SPOTLIGHT!

Experimental studies in this area have largely been conducted with animals, as experimental studies of this type with humans would be considered unethical. Consider whether we should conduct this type of research on animals. How could the link between shift work and illness be investigated in humans?

QUESTION SPOTLIGHT!

What are the differences between natural experiments and field experiments? Identify at least one strength and one weakness of each.

KEY RESEARCH

Czeisler, C.A., Moore-Ede, M.C. & Coleman, R.M. (1982) Rotating shift work schedules that disrupt sleep are improved by applying circadian principles. *Science*, 217 (4558), 460–463.

Aim

This research examines the experiences of individuals working on rotating shift patterns (where shifts change on a regular basis). The researchers predict that rotating shift workers are most often dissatisfied with the aspects of the working schedule that violate their circadian rhythm. They suggest that when schedules are redesigned to take into account what is known about circadian rhythms there will be an increase in satisfaction with their shift schedule, improvements in health and productivity, and reductions in staff turnover. This study tests this in a real work environment.

Method

This study has two parts. The first part compares workers on existing shift patterns (rotating versus non-rotating shift workers) and so can be seen as a **natural experiment**, as the variables were not manipulated for the purpose of the experiment. The second part is better described as a **field experiment**, as the researchers then manipulated the shift-work patterns so that the workers on phase-advancing schedules were divided into two groups: the first group continued to change shifts every week, and the second group rotated shifts by phase delay every 21 days.

Sample

A group of 85 male rotating shift workers aged between 19 and 68 (with a mean age of 31.4) were compared with a control group of 68 male non-rotating shift workers aged 19 to 56 (with a mean age of 27.3). All workers were employed in comparable jobs at the Great Salt Lake Minerals and Chemicals Corporation in Utah, USA. For the 10 years before this study was conducted, workers on shifts had had their shifts rotated so that each worker worked an 8 hour shift for 7 days before being moved to the preceding shift. This means that the shift order was midnight to 8am for seven days, then 4pm to midnight for seven days, and then 8am to 4pm for seven days. (Remember that this is referred to as a phase-advance shift pattern and that a phase-delay shift pattern would mean that the shifts were getting later with each shift change.)

Procedure: Stage 1

Each worker completed the job description and health indices of Smith, Kendall & Hulin (1969) and a sleep-wake and schedule preference questionnaire. The response rate was 84 per cent.

Results: Stage 1

Key findings included:

- The workers on rotating shifts reported significantly more sleep problems than the non-rotating workers, and 29% of the shift workers reported falling asleep at work at least once in the previous three months.

- Workers on rotating shifts also commonly reported that the schedules changed too often, and a huge majority (81%) reported that it took 2 to 4 days for their sleep patterns to adjust after each change in schedule, with 26% claiming that their sleep never adjusted fully before the next change in shifts.

Procedure: Stage 2 – intervention

The researchers then designed a new shift system that would incorporate what was known about circadian timing systems. In order to design their new shift system, they focused on two key issues. The first of these was the **direction of the rotation** and the second was the **interval between the changes in shifts**. Remember that phase delay (shifts getting later) is known to be easier to adjust to, and the first part of this study provides evidence that the time interval between shift changes was not long enough for people to feel that they had 'caught up'.

Thirty-three workers continued to change shifts every week, and 52 others rotated shifts by phase delay every 21 days. Before this new shift pattern was implemented, all workers and managers attended a presentation given by the researchers which covered the basic properties of the circadian sleep-wake cycle, and which also gave suggestions for adjusting their sleep time to their schedule.

Workers completed questionnaires evaluating the shift patterns three months after the introduction of the new schedules.

Results: Stage 2

Key findings included:

- Workers preferred delay rotating schedules over advanced rotating schedules.
- Among those in the 21-day phase-delay group, there was a significant reduction in the complaint that schedules changed too often.
- Rotators on the 21-day phase delay had increased scores on both the schedule satisfaction index and the health index.

Personnel turnover and plant productivity were analysed nine months after the introduction of the new schedules, and this demonstrated that:

- Staff turnover in the rotating-shift group was reduced to the same level as that of non-rotating shift workers.
- The production of potash harvesting increased significantly after the introduction of the new schedules.

Conclusions

This study demonstrates that workers clearly preferred the phase delay direction of rotation, and that the change to this shift schedule also produced improvements in health, an increase in productivity, and a decrease in staff turnover. This study was published in 1982 and represented a major contribution to the developing understanding of the effects of shift work. Czeisler *et al.* note in their conclusion that concern over the possible health risks of shift work is growing and that it is hoped that designing shift schedules around circadian principles will help to minimise the effects of temporal disruption.

APPLICATIONS: REDUCING THE EFFECTS OF JET LAG/SHIFT WORK

There have been several strategies suggested for dealings with problems caused by shift work. These include:

- Schedule changes
- Behavioural interventions
- Controlled exposure to light and dark
- The use of drugs to promote sleep, wakefulness or adaptation.

Schedule changes

The first suggested strategy is simply to staff straight shifts, meaning that people consistently work the same hours with no shift rotation at all. However, it is often quite difficult to staff the night shifts as they are understandably less popular and those workers on continuous night shifts will still have problems when trying to adjust to daytime activities on days off and holidays.

Another strategy is to rotate rapidly from one shift to the next. This is common in many occupations in this country, where people might work two day shifts, followed by two night shifts, followed by four days off (often working 12-hour rather than 8-hour shifts). Rapid rotation produces several beneficial effects, including improvements in total sleep length and leisure-time activities, improved sleep quality and sleep duration, improvements in blood pressure and reduced use of stimulants. Changing from 8-hour to 12-hour shifts also produced several beneficial effects including increased sleep quantity and quality, and improved physical fitness.

A final set of strategies for dealing with the problems of shift work include measuring the ability of individuals to cope with working and/or sleeping on abnormal schedules and selecting those with the greatest tolerance, or giving people a level of control over their shift patterns. Research into 'self-scheduling', where people are able to sign up for their preferred shifts, demonstrated improvements in work-life balance and in performance and motivation. Stress levels, absenteeism and staff turnover were all reduced, and there were either minimal or no effects on direct organisational costs. However, this type of system will not be suitable for all workplaces.

The findings reported above reflect a wide range of possible shift changes although it is important to remember that these types of study are typically conducted in a single organisation with a small sample of shift workers and with self-reported rather than objectively measured health outcomes. However, it can be concluded that forward-rotating shifts (i.e. phase-advancing shifts) quickly rotating shifts, and flexible working conditions all produce the most positive health effects.

Behavioural interventions

There appear to be relatively few studies in this area, although those that have been conducted tend to focus on encouraging shift workers to increase their physical activity and make positive lifestyle changes, such as improving their diet. These changes are then shown to improve such factors as increased aerobic capacity or improved blood pressure, all of which will help mitigate against the increased risk of illness. One interesting development is the relatively new research area of power naps.

QUESTION SPOTLIGHT!

We have just seen that allowing people some control over their shift patterns was beneficial. In the previous topic we saw that having some control over the source of a noise made the effects less stressful. Why do you think control is such an important concept to consider in environmental psychology?

Body temperature is at its lowest between 3am and 6am (this is called the circadian nadir). Night workers often associate this time with feeling cold, shaky and nauseous, as well as feeling sleepy or drowsy. This is a normal reaction, as the body is naturally biologically programmed to be least active at this time. This means it can be difficult to stay awake especially if the work demands are relatively low, as they might be if you were a security guard in an empty building or on duty in a residential home and everyone is asleep. Eating or drinking something warm can help, although remember that shift work can be associated with poor diets and an overconsumption of caffeine. Could it help to take a nap?

In 2006, the Royal College of Physicians recommended that junior doctors working the night shift should take a short restorative nap, or power nap, of between 20 and 45 minutes each night to reduce the risk of fatigue. They argued that a nap during the night is essential for maintaining vigilance and alertness. Further studies have also recommended power napping as having a positive effect on concentration levels and the speed of reflexes, and we saw earlier that disruption to circadian rhythms has been implicated in accidents caused by human error. A qualitative study of critical-care nurses in Canada found that 10 out of 13 nurses who regularly napped during breaks reported several benefits, including improved energy, mood, decision-making and vigilance. Researchers in this study also identified organisational and environmental barriers to napping during breaks, including the perceptions of managers and colleagues and a lack of appropriate facilities (Fallis *et al.*, 2011). So, it is important that employers are encouraged to consider the evidence base supporting the benefits of power napping and consider how this could be put into practice.

Controlled exposure to light and dark

It is generally agreed that exposure to light during the night is the key variable that links shift work to a range of negative health outcomes. If people are then exposed to light for the rest of the 24-hour period it easy to see how circadian rhythms would be affected. In order to reduce these effects, bright-light treatment (using a light box) is used to suppress melatonin release and increase body temperature and cortisol production in workers during the night shift Light-blocking goggles or glasses in the morning after night work are used to have the opposite effects. Studies have found beneficial effects from bright-light treatment on body temperature, and cortisol and plasma melatonin concentration, as well as positive effects on sleep. This provides evidence for circadian adaptation, including melatonin release during daytime sleep, when both bright-light exposure and light-blocking goggles were used.

Drugs to promote sleep, wakefulness or adaptation

Melatonin is a hormone produced by the body as part of the circadian rhythm. When it is dark, higher levels of melatonin are released compared to the amount released during the daytime. Increased levels of melatonin cause sleepiness. Melatonin pills can be bought without prescription to help sleep during the day and to help align the circadian rhythm with working at night. Hypnotics are sleep-inducing drugs that have been used to lengthen daytime sleep following night shifts. Stimulants can also be used to increase alertness, although studies in this area show mixed results and long-term use of stimulants are highly addictive and can cause side effects, including feelings of hostility and paranoia, as well as increased body temperature and an irregular heartbeat.

Figure 4.8: Are power naps effective for shift workers?

ACTIVITY

You are a psychologist working for a large airline company and have been asked to look at working patterns within the air traffic control department, as high levels of staff absence have been reported. Air traffic controllers currently work 8-hour shifts on a phase-advance system. Using your knowledge of circadian rhythms, the effects of shift work and the possible strategies for reducing these effects:

1 Suggest why there might be high levels of staff absence in the air traffic control department.
2 Suggest possible strategies that could be implemented to try to reduce the levels of staff absence.

EVALUATION

Methodological and ethical issues

This study by Czeisler *et al.* is in two parts. The first part is a natural experiment, as no variables were manipulated, and the second part is a field experiment, where variables were manipulated within the natural environment.

A strength of the natural experiment is greater ecological validity, as the independent variable (rotating versus non-rotating shift workers) already existed and was not artificially manipulated or created for the purposes of the experiment. However, natural experiments also have weaknesses, and the fact that there is no control over the independent variable may mean that extraneous variables (particularly individual differences) are difficult to identify. The first part of the study raises few, if any ethical issues. It is not made explicitly clear whether the workers had the choice of participating or not but the completion of a questionnaire can be seen as giving consent.

The field experiment, when the researchers artificially manipulated the shift patterns, also has high ecological validity as it is being done within the participants' natural environment, although this does raise some ethical issues. The researchers were manipulating the shift patterns that some (but not all) of the participants worked. Is this ethical? What if the new shift pattern were to have negative effects on the workers? Could this be counted as distress and failing to protect the participants? In fact, the new shift patterns were successful and so this question does not apply, However the question that then applies is whether it is ethical to provide the new shift pattern to only some of the workers initially. Perhaps the workers that stayed on the old shift patterns while the study was taking place would have liked to have been in the experimental group.

The sample was relatively small but extremely narrow in its focus. All the participants worked in the same industry and all were male. This does reduce the generalisability of the results to an extent, although it also produces a highly homogenous group for study, reducing the possibility of participant variables, which could have been a major factor to consider had the participants come from a range of industries.

Data was collected through self-report questionnaires and in this study the response rate was 84%. This is very high for a questionnaire study, probably owing to the fact that the questionnaires were given out within a work environment rather than simply posted to people's home addresses. It is always possible that participants do not tell the 'whole truth'

in questionnaires and there may be some reason why they may want to exaggerate the negative effects of shift work (in the same way that the participants in the previous study may have wanted to exaggerate the extent to which the airport noise affected them), but the questions here were relatively straightforward and the data relating to staff turnover would have been objective and unbiased.

Debates

Usefulness of research

This was clearly a very useful study. As a result of this one study and its intervention, the shift patterns for workers in this workplace were changed. This is part of a larger body of research that supports the idea that phase delay has fewer negative effects on shift workers than phase advance. The applications discussed in this topic also provide a range of useful suggestions for those who work shifts, as well as for those who are responsible for staffing in organisations that require 24-hour cover. These applications also approach the problem from a variety of angles, including changing the shift patterns or changing shift workers' behaviour patterns, through to the use of light boxes or drugs.

Nature vs nurture

The topic of biological rhythms demonstrates the interaction between the biological and the environmental. Humans have 'natural' circadian rhythms (discussed in the introduction to this chapter), but we also know that these rhythms are influenced by external factors called zeitgebers, allowing us to adjust at least to minor changes in the external environment (such as the demands of our jobs). However, the fact that we have negative responses to working nights, or rapidly changing shifts, or travelling across the Atlantic, suggests that our innate biological rhythms are at least partially quite resistant to change. Many of the strategies for dealing with the effects of shift work are attempts to reduce the mismatch between internal factors (nature) and external factors (nurture).

The situational–individual debate clearly overlaps here. It is the interaction between the individual and the situation that produces the negative effects such as jet lag or sleeping problems. Possibly the most useful interventions are those that recognise that both nature and nurture, situation and individual need to be considered in producing the most effective results.

RECYCLING AND OTHER CONSERVATION BEHAVIOURS

BACKGROUND

What are conservation behaviours?

Environmental issues are gaining in importance all the time although it is important to realise that this is a relatively new development. Conservation behaviours are any behaviours that are environmentally friendly. Although the key study in this section will focus on recycling behaviours, conservation behaviours can range from simply making sure that you put the correct items into the recycling bin at home or in college, to trying not to waste water, through to more radical lifestyle changes, such as trying to produce zero waste.

> **ACTIVITY** ✳
>
> Try to work out how much rubbish you have produced in one week. Then consider what proportion of this has been recycled. Could you do better? How?

What factors influence your recycling or other conservation behaviours?

This is a huge area of research in contemporary environmental psychology and it is possible to look only briefly at a few key factors here. We will examine the importance of values and social norms in determining conservation behaviours.

Values

Schwartz (1992) describes certain values – such as freedom, equality, and also pro-environmental behaviours – as 'trans-situational' goals that serve as guiding principles in the life of an individual. Values include beliefs about the desirability or undesirability of certain states. It is important to remember that values are relatively abstract concepts, and knowing which values someone holds may or may not help us make predictions about their behaviour. Individuals may hold many values and some may be more important to them than others. However, in terms of research, Steg *et al.* (2014) argue that the study of values can be useful as they provide a relatively efficient way of describing and explaining behaviour. More importantly, some attempts to change behaviours have chosen to focus on changing values as a way of influencing specific behaviours.

> **WEB WATCH** @
>
> How environmentally friendly are you? Calculate your environmental footprint here:
>
> http://footprint.wwf.org.uk/

> **WEB WATCH** @
>
> Lauren Singer has been living a 'zero-waste' lifestyle for over two years. Nothing she has used has ended up in landfill. You can read a little more about this here, as well as watching the video 'Going off the Grid':
>
> http://www.upworthy.com/is-it-possible-to-live-without-producing-trash-she-proves-it-is

Figure 4.9: How much rubbish do you produce?

STRETCH & CHALLENGE

Research the study conducted by Tajfel (1970). You can find a very clear outline of his research here: http://www.holah.karoo.net/tajfelstudy.htm Tajfel was not studying environmental behaviours but prejudice and discrimination, but there are significant overlaps between the decomposed game technique and the methodology used by Tajfel. Think about what this tells us about values. In what ways can broadly defined values be used to predict different behaviours?

KEY IDEAS

You will be familiar with the concept of **altruism** from Levine *et al.*'s (2001) study of cross-cultural helping behaviour. Altruism can be defined as selflessness – behaviour that may be detrimental to one's own health or safety while favouring the survival of others Examples of altruism are all around us, from tiny acts of kindness such as holding the door open for someone or giving a small donation to charity, to the acts that make headlines such as when people risk their own lives to save another. There are differing explanations for altruism, with social psychologists explaining it as a form of pro-social behaviour governed by social norms, and neuropsychologists suggesting that altruistic acts activate reward centres in the brain, producing positive emotions.

Value theories
1 Social value orientations

This reflects the extent to which people care about their own and others' outcomes in a social dilemma. People may have a broadly cooperative value orientation, a broadly individualistic orientation or a broadly competitive orientation. A person's social value orientation (SVO) can be assessed using the decomposed game technique developed by Liebrand (1984), which is an activity where participants have to choose between options that offer points to themselves or to another person.

In the example below, if the participant chose Option A this would indicate a cooperative orientation as it would lead to the maximum joint gain. If they chose Option B this would indicate an individualistic orientation as it is the option that maximises their own personal gain. A competitive orientation would be indicated by the choice of Option C as it maximises one's personal gain relative to the other person.

Which one would you choose?

	Option A: Co-operator	Option B: Individualist	Option C: Competitor
Points to self	700	900	700
Points to other	700	300	0

Source: adapted from Steg *et al.* (2014)

2 Biospheric values

Recently, environmental psychologists have argued that it is important to distinguish between biospheric and altruistic values. **Altruistic** values reflect a concern with the welfare of other humans, whereas biospheric values reflect a concern for the environment and for nature for their own sake (rather than in terms of how they will benefit humans). Both altruistic and biospheric values are likely to be predictors of pro-environmental behaviours, as such behaviours will usually benefit both humans *and* the environment. However, in other cases these values may conflict, such as when deciding whether to vote for a 'green' or a 'socialist' political party, or choosing between a product that is organic and a product that is fair trade.

Social norms

Social norms are socially acceptable ways of behaving. Social psychologists have studied social norms for many years and there have been many pieces of research supporting the notion that our behaviour is at least partially determined by the behaviour of others. We will be examining the power of social norms in the Application section of this chapter (see page 216).

ACTIVITY

You will be familiar with the work of Stanley Milgram, but Solomon Asch conducted even earlier research into conformity. Find out what he did, and what conclusions can be drawn from this research.

Research has suggested that we tend to underestimate the influence of norms on environmental behaviour. Research carried out by Nolan *et al.* (2008) investigated the willingness of individuals to conserve energy. Nolan *et al.* found that participants' behaviour was more likely to change as a result of their being given normative information about the better conservation behaviours of other households in the neighbourhood, rather than if they were given information about conserving energy for reasons of environmental protection, social responsibility or saving money. However, when asked to rate the importance of the differing information in terms of its effect on their behaviour, the normative information was rated consistently lower than messages about environmental protection and saving money.

KEY RESEARCH

Lord, K.R. (1994) Motivating recycling behaviour: A quasi-experimental investigation of message and source strategies. *Psychology & Marketing*, 11 (4), 341–358.

Aim

This research investigates the effectiveness of a range of different types of messages designed to increase compliance with a recycling programme in the United Sates. The investigators manipulated several variables including message appeal (positive or negative) and message source (advertising, publicity and personal). This generated eight hypotheses, which are outlined in Box 4.1.

Note that testing these hypotheses will require a control group. The researchers are predicting that all the experimental groups taken as a whole (regardless of which type of message they receive) will show improved attitudes to recycling and increased recycling behaviours compared to those who receive no message at all.

Box 4.1: Hypotheses

Hypothesis 1:
Attitude towards recycling is improved for households receiving an advocacy message, relative to unexposed (control) households.

Hypothesis 2:
Delivery of an advocacy message yields an increase in observed recycling with households receiving no message (control) showing no significant change in curbside collection amounts.

Hypothesis 3:
Consumer beliefs about positively valenced benefits of recycling are more readily formed upon exposure to an advocacy message than are beliefs about negatively framed consequences of failure to recycle.

Hypothesis 4:
Positively framed messages result in a more favourable attitude towards recycling than negatively framed messages

Hypothesis 5:
Consumer belief in negatively framed arguments about the consequences of failure to recycle is greatest when those arguments are conveyed in the form

of a publicity-generated news story, and least when they appear as part of an advertising campaign.

Hypothesis 6:
Among consumers exposed to negatively framed messages, attitude towards recycling is most favourable when the message is conveyed in the form of a publicity-generated news story.

Hypothesis 7:
Messages conveyed via social influence (i.e. from a personal acquaintance) result in a more favourable attitude towards recycling in a positively framed than in a negatively framed condition.

Hypothesis 8:
An advocacy message from a personal acquaintance elicits a greater increase in recycling behaviour than a comparable message from an advertising or news (publicity) source, with strongest behavioural change arising in the personal influence/negatively framed message condition.

The first two hypotheses are simply predicting that those households receiving any type of message in relation to recycling will show improved attitudes to recycling and increased recycling behaviours. The other six hypotheses make more specific predictions about the effect of the type of message (positive or negative) and the source of the message.

Overall the researchers are predicting that positively framed messages will be more effective than negative messages but that of the negative messages, the news story will be the most effective . Interestingly, when the message comes from a personal acquaintance, the positive message will result in more positive attitudes to recycling but negative message from a personal acquaintance will result in the biggest change in behaviours.

Method

The authors refer to this a quasi-experimental field study but it may be more appropriate to consider it as a field experiment. The design is what is called a full factorial 3 × 2 design. This means that there were three message sources (advertisement, newspaper article and personal letter from an acquaintance) and two message framing conditions (positive and negative). This is shown in the figure below, which also shows that investigating the effects of these two variables requires six experimental conditions (and a control group).

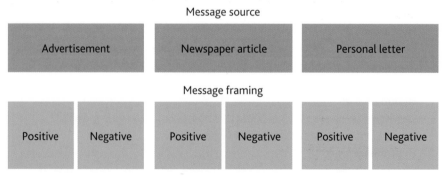

Figure 4.10: Conditions and variables of the study

The key theme in the material in all six experimental conditions was to attempt to increase participation in the community curbside recycling collection. If the message was a positively framed one, it focused on the environmental benefits of recycling, the savings to the community and the personal and social satisfactions arising from full participation in the recycling programmes. If the message was a negatively framed one, it focused on the physical, social and environmental risks and consequences of failing to recycle. If the material was an advertisement, it looked like an advertisement from a (fictional) company selling environmentally friendly products. In the newspaper article condition, the same material was described as having recently appeared in a local newspaper. Finally, in the personal letter condition, the information appeared as a letter signed by a student assistant of the researchers and sent to the participant from a personal acquaintance.

Box 4.2: Positively framed message

"In September 1990, the City of Buffalo began a curbside recycling program, and surrounding communities in the Buffalo metropolitan area have since followed suit. The first six months of the Buffalo program saw the recycling of more than 10 million pounds of what was formerly considered garbage. This, according to Buffalo Mayor James D. Griffin, equates to savings of 90,929 trees, 320,926 cubic feet of landfill space, and a 62 percent energy saving, or an estimated $92,678 saving in waste disposal costs.

The recycling trend is taking the nation by storm, as Americans in ever greater numbers enjoy the satisfaction of preserving our environment and reining in unnecessary government expenditure on excessive garbage disposal. Aside from being a responsible, cost-effective way to help solve some of our disposal problems, recycling helps preserve our natural resources, reduce pollution, and save energy. And as environmental consciousness takes on increasing significance within our culture, the practice of recycling is looked up to as one mark of a responsible, involved and caring member of the community.

We thus have an opportunity to preserve our quality of life and to earn the respect of our contemporaries and the appreciation of those who follow us. The City of Buffalo and surrounding towns each accept newspapers, magazines, corrugated cardboard, glass bottles and jars, metal cans, and plastic containers for weekly curbside pickup. Please join us in pledging full participation in our community's recycling program. Be a part of Buffalo's and America's bright future by recycling today."

Source: Lord (1994), pp.55–56

Box 4.3: Negatively framed message

"The refuse disposal problems which have plagued America's largest cities in recent years are now being felt in Erie County and other metropolitan areas of comparable size. Americans threw out 196 million tons of refuse in 1990, more than twice as much as in 1960. Communities like our own face the prospect of exceeding the capacity of landfills within half a decade at our current rates of disposal. This places at risk the beauty of our surroundings and the health of our families.

Without a marked reduction in the rate of refuse disposal, stiff measures may be required to preserve the quality of life in our neighbourhoods. Possible actions include severe limits on the amount of garbage a household can set out for curbside collection, steep fines for exceeding those limits or failing to separate recyclable items, a graduated fee schedule which increases with the amount of garbage set out by a household, and refuse sorting programs in which municipal sanitation departments bear the responsibilty of sorting household garbage into landfill, incineration and recyclable categories (supported by massive increases in local taxes).

Thankfully, responsible behaviour on our part may alleviate the problem and eliminate the need for the painfull solutions described above. The City of Buffalo and surrounding towns all have curbside recycling programs which accept newspapers, magazines, corrugated cardboard, glass bottles and jars, metal cans and plastic containers. Please join us in pledging full participation in our community's recycling program. Together we can thwart this menace to our community's future."

Source: Lord (1994), p.56

Sample

The sample comprised 140 households in a metropolitan community served by a recycling programme. **Quota sampling** was used in all but the personal letter condition to ensure that the households in each condition represented the diverse socioeconomic characteristics of the area.

Data collection

On recycling collection day in week 1, the student assistants discreetly observed and recorded the contents of the recycling bins of the test households (both experimental and control groups). The following day they left the stimulus message (whether advert, newspaper article or personal letter) at the front doors of the households in all six experimental conditions. They did not engage in any face-to-face communication.

On recycling collection day in week 2, the student assistants repeated their observation of the households' recycling bin. The following day they contacted and delivered a questionnaire to the adult member of the household who was most involved with the sorting and taking out the recycling. This person was given the questionnaire, assured that their responses would be kept anonymous, and asked to return the completed questionnaire in a sealed envelope. This stage included both experimental and control groups.

KEY IDEAS

Quota sampling could not be so strictly applied in the personal letter condition because the letters were sent to the personal acquaintances of the student assistants. However, the student assistants were asked to target certain characteristics in order to achieve a sample that matched the participants in the other groups as closely as possible.

The observation form

This recorded the number of items placed in the recycling bin in each of the categories of materials accepted for recycling. The article does not give us the full list, but examples include such items as newspapers/magazines, cardboard, glass bottles and jars.

The questionnaire

The questionnaire contained a variety of items required to allow the researchers to fully test their hypotheses.

Beliefs in the arguments raised by the messages was assessed by asking the participants to rate the truthfulness of a number of statements using a 7-point scale from *definitely false to definitely true*. This was also done in the control condition although obviously the control group participants had not seen these statements before and the experimental group participants would have seen only some of them before. The questionnaire also included four 7-point semantic differential items which measured attitude towards recycling (*good-bad, wise-foolish, harmful-beneficial, favourable-unfavourable*). All participants were asked for demographic data, such as age, gender, highest qualifications and annual income. Finally, the attitude towards the message they had been exposed to in the experimental group (but not the control group, for obvious reasons) was measured using eight semantic differential items (*good-bad, wise-foolish, harmful-beneficial, favourable-unfavourable, persuasive-unpersuasive, uninformative-informative, weak-strong and believable-unbelievable*).

Results

The change in recycling behaviour was measured using the differences in the total number of items put out for recycling in the week before the message was sent out and in the week following the message.

Hypothesis 1 predicted that those households that received a message would show more positive attitudes towards recycling than those households in the control group. Looking at the data as a whole, there is support for this hypothesis with the results showing a more favourable attitude towards recycling in the experimental groups than in the control groups.

However, when each specific condition is compared to the control group, some differences emerge. The personal-positive, advertising-positive and publicity-negative conditions all showed significantly more positive attitudes than the control group. The advert-negative and publicity-positive groups also showed more favourable attitudes, but these differences were not great enough to reach significance (i.e. the likelihood of a chance result was $p < 0.10$). In the personal-negative condition there were no differences in attitudes. The authors therefore claim partial support for Hypothesis 1.

Hypothesis 2 predicted that those households receiving a message would show increased participation in the recycling programme, compared to the control group. Combining all the experimental groups together showed that this was the case. There was a mean increase of 3.93 items put out for recycling compared to 0.22 for the control groups.

Hypothesis 3 predicted that positively framed messages would be more effective. This was also supported. Those exposed to positively framed messages reported higher levels of belief in the statements underpinning the message than

STRETCH & CHALLENGE

Identify potential limitations with this measure of the extent of change in the households' recycling behaviour. Suggest ways in which these limitations could be overcome.

WEB WATCH @

You can read a newspaper article about the findings of this study here:

http://www.buffalo.edu/news/releases/1994/11/3060.html

participants in the control condition and those participants in the negatively framed message conditions. There was little difference between the responses of those in the negatively framed message conditions and those in the control condition.

Hypothesis 4 was also supported, with respondents in the positively framed message conditions showing a more favourable attitude to recycling than the participants in the negatively framed conditions.

Hypothesis 5 was not supported. There is no evidence to support the idea that publicity-generated material (newspaper articles) would be more effective than advertisements.

Hypothesis 6 proposed that negatively framed messages would be most effective when conveyed in a publicity generated news item. This is partially supported, as publicity-generated news items were more effective than messages from a personal acquaintancem, but did not differ from messages presented as advertisements.

In the personal influence condition, attitudes towards recycling were higher in households receiving the positively framed message than among those in the negatively framed message condition. This confirms Hypothesis 7.

Finally, the greatest behavioural change came from a negatively framed message conveyed by a personal aquaintance, providing support for Hypothesis 8.

Conclusions

Overall the authors conclude that responses to appeals to increase recycling are complex, and have not fully been explained by this research. Certainly the positively framed messages appear to have the greatest effect on recycling behaviours and respondents are clearly more prepared to believe in positively framed messages than in negatively framed ones. However, the source of the message also has an effect, and this may be particularly significant in terms of negatively framed messages. If a negatively framed message comes from a personal acquaintance this seems to increase the power of the argument. Finally, the advantage shown by advertising over other source messages was unexpected, and the authors identify this as a potential angle for further research, along with exploring the effect of messages containing both positive and negative messages.

APPLICATION: INCREASING RECYCLING AND OTHER CONSERVATION BEHAVIOUR

There have been numerous attempts to change people's behaviour. In this section we will examine some of the strategies that have been used. In the first study we will examine the role of normative messages (linking to the role of social norms discussed in the introduction to this section) in changing people's behaviour. Secondly, we will consider the relationship between knowledge about environmental issues and related attitudes and behaviours, and finally we will examine the effect of messages that lead us to believe that science is developing solutions to environmental problems.

The first study we will examine was conducted by Cialdini *et al.* (2003), who worked with a large hotel to encourage guests to reuse towels rather than having them replaced each day. The researchers randomly assigned cards with one of five different messages to 260 guest rooms, each with one of the following messages:

- *Help the hotel save energy*
- *Help save the environment*
- *Partner with us to help save the environment*
- *Help save resources for future generations*
- *Join your fellow citizens in helping to save the environment*

QUESTION SPOTLIGHT!

Which of these messages do you think will be the most effective one and why?

The last message, which described a social norm (i.e. it suggests that this is what most people did) was the most successful one. Of the guests who had this card in their room, 41% recycled their towels. The next most successful messages were those urging environmental protection and the benefit to future generations, which led to about 31% reusing their towels. The least successful was the message emphasising the benefit to the hotel. Only 20% of guests with that card reused their towels.

Cialdini *et al.* found the results of this study to be consistent with the social psychological theory that when people are figuring out what to do in a new situation, they take their cue from what seems to be other people's normal behaviour – the social norm. Thus, using descriptive norm messages that say 'Everybody's doing it!' in order to promote conservation-minded actions may be most effective. The research also implies that the typical 'save the planet' awareness campaigns may not be that effective at encouraging specific behaviours, owing to their lack of specificity and their failure to give information about what 'everyone else' is doing.

ACTIVITY ✳

Design a poster for your school or college that contains a normative message about recycling. You could test the effectiveness of your poster by taking measurements of recycling behaviour for a week before you put the poster up, and then again for a week after the poster has been up.

There are several ways in which recycling behaviour could be measured.

You could observe people in your school or college canteen and record whether they use the recycling bins or not. You could observe the amount of litter left around the college. Or you could count the number of items placed in recycling bins. You could also ask people directly about their behaviour. All of these measures will have their own strengths and limitations.

The study by Cialdini *et al.* makes us aware that our intuition may not always be correct. You might have thought, quite reasonably, that a direct instruction to do or not to do something would be more effective that a normative message. A study conducted by Sunblad *et al.* (2007) also challenges our assumptions. In this research, researchers were trying to establish how knowledge about climate change was associated with how worried they were about climate change. To measure the levels of knowledge, researchers gave 44 statements about climate change to 621 participants ranging from 18 to 75 years old. These included statements from several areas: facts about the state of the climate, causes of climate change, and consequences of climate change for weather, sea, glaciers and human health. Participants simply had to rate the statements as true or false.

ACTIVITY ✳

Design an educational programme for school-age children that focuses on increasing knowledge about the health consequences of environmental change. Consider the ethical issues that your suggestions may raise.

Examples of statements describing the impact of climate change on human health:

- It is probable that mortality by lung oedema and heart problems during heat waves in Sweden will increase in the next 50 years. (True)
- It is probable that an increasing number of mosquitos and ticks within 50 years will cause more cases of human diseases in Sweden, due to climate change. (True)
- Climate change will increase the risk in Sweden for diseases transferred by water (e.g. diarrhoea) in the next 100 years. (True)
- Negative health impacts caused by climate change will globally affect humans in the countryside more than humans in the cities. (False)
- The health effect that might arise due to climate change in the next 50 years only concerns humans who live in tropical areas. (False)

The researchers found that it was the *level of knowledge about the human health consequences* rather than their knowledge about the state of the climate, climate change, or the other consequences of climate change that showed the strongest predictive power in terms of how worried they were about climate change. This strongly suggests that in order to change people's behaviour, future research should concentrate on the development of educational programmes that focus on increasing knowledge about the health consequences of environmental change.

A recent study by Meijers and Rutjens (2014) examined the effects of positive information about scientific progress in combatting climate change. In a series of studies, students were divided into two groups. Those in the first condition were given a positive article to read, which explained that medical advances and new technologies were being developed that would combat climate change. In the second condition, students read a negative message about the limited nature of technological solutions to environmental problems. Compared to those who read the negative article, those who read the positive article were less likely to display pro-environmental actions and intentions and were more likely to agree with statements such as 'waste sorting is unnecessary'.

This is fascinating and has powerful implications for the way we present information about the progress of science in combating climate change. These findings may be explained in terms of our willingness to believe that other forces are in control (for example: our parents, the government, God, and now science). This has echoes of bystander behaviour – if someone else is doing something we need neither to act nor to worry about acting or not acting.

Finally, did you calculate your environmental footprint earlier in this chapter? Did it make you think about anything in your life that you could change? The chances are that the changes you would need to make are so huge that you wouldn't really know where to start. You know that you need to change your behaviours but the reality is difficult. This is similar to knowing that you should go to the gym more often, or stop eating so many sweets, or give up smoking. This creates what Leon Festinger (1957) called *cognitive dissonance*: an uncomfortable feeling of tension when there is a mismatch between your behaviour and your attitudes (e.g. *I do care about the environment but I can't reduce my environmental footprint to the extent that I should,* or *I know I should give up smoking but it is too difficult).* The behaviour change is challenging and often an easier way to reduce the dissonance is to change our attitudes to bring them in line with our existing behaviour. In terms of smoking, this might be someone arguing that it helps them to relax or that their grandfather smoked all his life and lived to be 103. In terms of environmental behaviour we may argue that the changes that we can make individually would have no effect or that (see above) scientific progress will solve these problems so we don't have to worry.

Brook (2011) demonstrated this in a study that showed when people who were not concerned about environmental issues were given negative feedback about their environmental footprint, this actually made them even less sympathetic to environmental causes. This suggests that negative footprint feedback may even reduce environmentally sustainable behaviours, and Brook suggests that one strategy might be to provide practical information alongside the footprint feedback, outlining practical strategies for change.

One very encouraging piece of research into moral development suggests that the current focus on environmental issues is having an effect on the way children make judgements about harm against the environment. Hussar and Horvarth (2011) found evidence of biocentric reasoning (referring to the moral standing of nature itself) in children as young as 6 years old, whereas previous research conducted in the 1990s had showed biocentric reasoning not developing until adolescence. It will be fascinating to see how this change in reasoning impacts future generations.

EVALUATION

Methodological and ethical issues

This study is described by the authors as a quasi-experimental field study but it is probably more appropriate to think of it simply as a field experiment, with independent variables manipulated in the real world. The key strength of field experiments is their increased ecological validity but this will have to be considered against the reduced levels of control that are possible. However, in this study the researchers did use quota sampling to ensure first that all the households in the entire sample represented the area, and secondly that the groups were as similar as possible. This is clearly a strength of the way in which the research has been conducted, but it is not possible to control for all the possible differences that may exist among the different households. There are several other potential confounding variables that have not been considered. Simply taking one measure of recycling before the message was delivered and a second measure after the message was delivered leaves the results potentially lacking in validity. One

household may have had a party that week, and this – rather than the receipt of the message – might explain the increase in their recycling. Returning to collect data for a number of weeks might also have been more appropriate as perhaps people didn't read the message until part-way through the week (when they had already put a lot of recyclable rubbish into the non-recyclable rubbish bin), or perhaps these kinds of messages need time to affect behaviour. The researchers may have missed some significant behavioural changes by not conducting their study over a longer period of time. It is also possible that participants engaged in more recycling behaviours while away from their homes and the observation of the recycling bins would obviously not have been able to collect this data.

The researchers collected data in two main ways. First, they observed (and counted) the number of items placed in the recycling bin. This is a fairly straightforward measure, although it is difficult to imagine how a student researcher 'discreetly' observed and recorded this information. Minor errors in counting may well have occurred but the categories (glass, cardboard, newspapers, etc.) seem well defined, and it is unlikely that there would be major issues of inter-rater reliability here. The second form of data collection was through questionnaires which are often problematic, suffering from a range of problems including non-completion and social desirability bias. It is also not made clear in the study whether the researchers were able to ensure that the person completing the questionnaire was the person who had read the message, or indeed was the person responsible for recycling.

The sample for this study was relatively small, especially when you consider that there were six experimental groups and a control group. This is likely to reduce the generalisability of the findings.

The key research by Lord does not raise any significant ethical issues although it does raise the question of how people would feel if they knew someone was looking in their bins! In some countries, taking things out of bins is illegal, and although the vast majority of people would not mind this, they might be slightly anxious if they saw someone emptying out their recycling bin and counting its contents.

Some other research in this topic area may raise more significant ethical issues. Are people being deceived if they are part of a study to see which type of message in a hotel leads to most environmentally friendly behaviours? Would they mind if they knew? This may be a very minor example but the study by Sunblad *et al.* (2007) (discussed on page 217) exposed participants to a number of potentially distressing true *and false* statements about the consequences of climate change. This would require lengthy debriefing to ensure that people were not left believing false information. However, it is clearly important to conduct research into environmentally friendly behaviours, particularly when that research is able to identify strategies for improving people's behaviours, and so a cost-benefit analysis might conclude that mild levels of distress are acceptable.

Debates

Usefulness of research

All research into environmental behaviours will have useful applications as the research is refining our understanding of what motivates people to engage in such behaviours and what strategies are effective in attempting to change environmental behaviours. The key study by Lord demonstrates not only the effectiveness of communication from personal aquaintances but also the perhaps surprising finding that negatively framed messages from a personal source are the most effective of all.

Lord also finds that advertising as a source of the message was surprisingly effective and deserving of more research. The research studies considered in the applications section demonstrate the complex relationship between attitudes and behaviour and highlight the importance of social norms in environmental behaviours.

Individual and situational explanations

Once again, environmental psychology focuses on the situational (environmental) factors that determine people's behaviour. Here we have seen the powerful influence of messages from personal acqaintances and the power of social norms in determining people's behaviour. These are ideas that have existed in social psychology for a very long time, but are being newly applied to this topic area. What is still missing is a consideration of individual differences and the role of personality factors in determining such behaviours.

Ethnocentrism

Ethnocentrism is a complex idea. It is often misunderstood as a sampling problem and research is criticised for being ethnocentric because it looks only at one particular culture. This is not the meaning of ethnocentric. Ethnocentrism means making the assumption that findings from one cultural group can be easily applied to any other cultural group. Psychology has been dominated by white, middle-class male and northern European thinking for most of its history – in terms of both its researchers and participants. This has led to a situation where Western psychology has created a norm for human behaviour against which all other cultures are judged and often found wanting.

It is possible that most of the research into pro-environmental behaviours comes from this Western perspective, reflecting the current focus on the environment that exists in these cultures. It could be considered ethnocentric to assume that, for example, the finding that biocentric reasoning is developing earlier is true of all cultures. It is far more likely that other cultures may have developed biocentric reasoning much earlier than in the West and to a much higher level, and it is the West that is only now catching up.

ERGONOMICS – HUMAN FACTORS

BACKGROUND

In this chapter we will be examining the concept of cognitive load and the extent to which workplace design can reduce cognitive overload. In order to understand this concept we will first look at at the way information is stored in memory.

Models of memory

The multi-store model of memory

Atkinson and Shiffrin (1968) produced one of the earliest models of memory which simply proposed that memory is made up of a series of stores arranged in a linear fashion (see below). This model sees memory as information flowing through a system and has sometimes been described as an information processing model (using the analogy of a computer) with input, process and output.

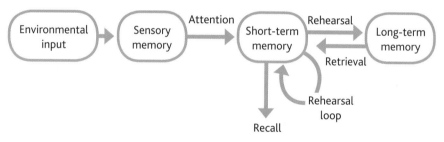

Figure 4.11: The multi-store model of memory

In very basic terms, this model proposes that information is initially detected by the sense organs and enters the sensory memory. If it is attended to it will move to short-term memory, and if not it will be lost. Information is transferred to long-term memory through rehearsal, which is one of the key concepts of this model. If rehearsal does not occur, then information is forgotten, lost from short-term memory through the processes of displacement or decay.

Atkinson's and Shiffrin's (1968) model was extremely successful, particularly in terms of generating huge amounts of research into memory. However, this research soon revealed that this original model was overly simplistic in its explanation of memory and information processing. Both short-term memory and long-term memory are now seen as more complex systems rather than simple unitary stores. The most important development in the context of this chapter is the replacement of the concept of short-term memory with the more complex model of working memory.

Figure 4.14: Cognitive overload

KEY IDEAS

Cognitive load refers to the amount of mental energy used to complete a task. Cognitive load is high when a task is complex and is increased even further when the individual has to mentally attend to more than one task (or source of information) at the same time. If the cognitive load is too great (sometimes referred to as **cognitive overload**) this can have the effect of reducing optimal performance, because one cannot completely concentrate on the target task.

QUESTION SPOTLIGHT!

How many different types of information do you think there are? Take a minute to think about all the information that is surrounding you at this moment.

Working memory

Working memory is short-term memory. However, rather than all information going into one single store, there are different systems for different types of information.

Figure 4.12: The working memory model
Source: Baddeley and Hitch (1974)

Working memory consists of a **central executive** which controls and coordinates the operation of two subsystems: the phonological loop and the **visuo-spatial sketch pad**. The central executive is the driving force and allocates data to each of the subsystems. It is also responsible for cognitive tasks such as mental arithmetic and problem solving.

The visuo-spatial sketch pad can be thought of as the inner eye. This component of working memory stores and processes information in spatial form and is also important in navigation.

The **phonological loop** consists of two parts, and can be thought of as the inner ear and the inner voice. The phonological loop deals with spoken and written material and consists of the **phonological store (or inner ear)** which is linked to the perception of speech and can hold information for one or two seconds. The second part, the **articulatory control process (or inner voice)** is linked to the production of speech and rehearses and stores verbal information from the phonological store.

All of these parts of working memory are seen as independent of each other and are assumed to have limited capacity (that is, there is a limit to the amount of material that they can deal with). This idea of a limited capacity links with the idea of cognitive load, which we will examine next.

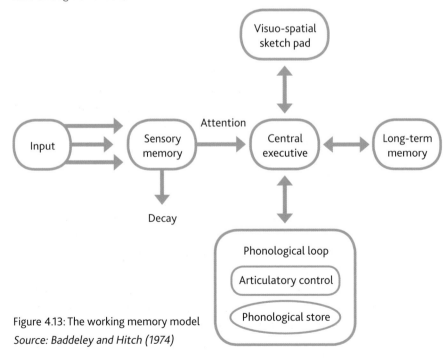

Figure 4.13: The working memory model
Source: Baddeley and Hitch (1974)

Cognitive load

Theories of cognitive load have been applied in several areas, including education and the workplace. In both of these the idea is that note should be taken of the 'cognitive architecture' of the learner or the worker. In other words, when designing educational strategies or workplace equipment we need to be mindful of the fact that, cognitively speaking, we have a limited working memory and a comparatively unlimited long-term memory. It is the limited working memory that carries the risk of cognitive overload, especially when performing a new or highly complex task. As we will see, this knowledge can be put to good use when designing visual display units to be used by staff in intensive care units, where key details need to processed at the highest possible speed. Cognitive overload can lead not only to stress and anxiety but also to indecisiveness and poor decisions.

Ergonomics

Ergonomics is the applied science of equipment design and is based on the study of people's efficiency or productivity in their work environment and how this is affected by the equipment they are using. This may include the ways in which workers use and interact with specialised equipment, as well as factors such as the impact that the design of simple workplace features – for example, desks and chairs – may have on worker fatigue. You may have seen office chairs that are advertised as 'ergonomically designed', which means that the designers have taken into account the physical characteristics and needs of the person, as well as the requirements of the role that the person must fulfil. This is often referred to as human factors engineering. We will be examining a study that used knowledge of cognitive load and our ability to process information in order to produce visual display units that should not only allow faster recognition of crucial information, but also, by preventing cognitive overload, reduce errors and omissions.

The impact of observation in the workplace

This relates to a number of key concepts from social psychology. Here, we need to examine some key concepts from the area of social psychology, including social facilitation, audience effects and co-action effects. Social facilitation is a broad term referring to any improvements in performance that are due to the presence of other people. Audience effects are exactly the effect of being watched while you do something, whereas co-action effects refer more specifically to working with other people.

WEB WATCH @

This site will give you more information about social facilitation. Make notes on how audiences can improve performance on a task and when they might have the opposite effect.

http://www.spring.org.uk/2009/06/
social-facilitation-how-and-when-
audiences-improve-performance.php

STRETCH & CHALLENGE

The idea of cognitive load has also been applied in criminal psychology where research has demonstrated that lying produces cognitive load that may be associated with observable behaviours. One of these studies was conducted by Mann, *et al.* (2002) and is called 'Suspects, lies and videotapes: an analysis of authentic high-stake liars'. There is plenty of information about this study online and you can read the original paper here:

http://ruby.fgcu.edu/courses/cpacini/
courses/common/highstake_liars.pdf

ACTIVITY ✳

Make a list of tasks or activities in which you think performance would be improved by the presence of either an audience or a co-worker, and a list of tasks and activities in which you think performance would be harmed by the presence of other people.

Keep this in mind as we examine the key study in which nursing staff are asked to make fast judgements in already stressful situations. How much extra stress might being observed create, and what might be the likely effects of this?

ACTIVITY ✳

Chunking refers to the grouping together of individual pieces of information to allow us to process them (and remember them) more easily. This might be as simple as trying to mentally 'chunk' a shopping list into 'fruit and vegetables', 'tinned food', etc., rather than trying to remember a whole list.

Look at the following two lists. It is probably harder to make sense of the first list than the second list:

List 1 PCDVDBBCHDMIITV

List 2 PC DVD BBC HDMI ITV

Ergonomics draws on such ideas in the design of equipment. For example, in terms of visual display units, colour could be used to group similar information together.

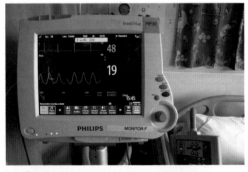

Figure 4.15: Patients may be monitored from their bedside or from a central monitoring station

KEY RESEARCH

Drews, F.A. & Doig, A. (2014) Evaluation of a configural vital sign display for intensive care unit nurses. *The Journal of Human Factors and Ergonomics Society*, 56 (3), 569–580.

Background

The intensive care unit (or ICU) is a specialised hospital environment designed for the continual monitoring of critically ill patients. Display units in intensive care units give staff information such as blood pressure, oxygen saturation, heart rates and respiratory rates. Traditional systems display this information numerically. Although graphical display systems (using images either as well as or instead of numbers) have been developed for specific roles such as anaesthesiologists working in an operating theatre, it is crucial to remember that this role may differ in significant ways from the role of an intensive care nurse on the ward. An anaesthesiologist will remain with one patient and be able to monitor their vital signs *constantly*. Nurses in intensive care units, on the other hand, may have more than one patient (often in different rooms) and are likely to be monitoring patients only *intermittently*. They may also be monitoring them in a number of ways – from their bedside as well as from remote monitoring displays sited centrally in a ward. This means it is crucial that the display units allow them to identify key information and respond to this as accurately and as quickly as possible.

Aims

This research has two aims: the first was to develop an ICU monitoring display that presents vital signs *trend information* and patient-specific physiological variability to support the detection and identification of acute physiological changes in patient state. In other words, rather than a numerical display of the vital signs as they are at a given moment (which would require the observer to process whether this is stable or whether this is signifying a change that requires action), the monitoring display being considered here would display the *trend* in the data and so would clearly show the nurse not only that a change had occurred but also the direction of that change.

Secondly, the research aims to test whether the improved ICU monitoring display decreases the mental demand associated with nurses' monitoring of patients. In other words does the newly designed display unit reduce the cognitive load on the staff?

The design requirements for the new units were initially established through interviews with nurses, literature reviews and interviews with data visualisation experts. It was crucial that the new display should include data representing changes in the patients' vital signs (trend data, numerical data and variability). The designers followed general design principles, such as the reduction of visual clutter, as well as using colour coding and geometric shapes to visually convey changes in vital signs.

The designers asked three experienced ICU nurses to review each successive prototype, which resulted in the final version of the configural vital signs (CVS) display.

The final version included two key elements designed to support effective data integration and rapid patient state identification. These were as follows:

1 The Current State Object (CSO), which provided information about the current state of the patient and also indications of the variability in the patients' [patients'] vital signs.
2 Shapes and colours were utilised to increase the speed at which this information could be processed. For example different measurements were presented in different colours and colour was also used to represent vital signs measurements. Blood oxygen saturation levels were represented as follows:

Methods

Sample
Forty-two registered nurses participated in the research. All had critical-care training and a minimum of one year's ICU experience.

Design
This was an independent measures design. Participants were randomly assigned to either the CVS display group or the control group. The CVS group were exposed to the newly designed CVS display and the control group were exposed only to a simplified version displaying just the numerical data section of the CVS (i.e. no trend data). Participants in the control group could access the trend information (without the visual momentum aspect of the CVS) by a single key press. This use of a one-touch procedure to access trend information is similar to that used with traditional ICU displays.

Four different patient scenarios were developed. Three scenarios tested whether the CVS display led to better decision-making than the traditional display. Note that in all these scenarios the information required to make a correct assessment was available on both displays. The fourth scenario was designed to represent a stable patient and was used to determine whether the CVS display allowed for faster recognition of a 'normal patient' (i.e. one without acute physiological changes). The scenarios were developed by an ICU doctor and an ICU nurse who had not been involved in the design of the CVS display.

Each participant had to respond to each of the four scenarios, with order of presentation randomised. The order for each participant in the CVS condition was matched with a participant in the control condition.

Procedure
The study took place in the Applied and Basic Cognition Laboratory of the Department of Psychology at the University of Utah. Participants were given a standardised 20-minute training which explained the functions of the display. Participants were told to verbally evaluate the patient's physiological status, interpret the data and recommend appropriate interventions as quickly and accurately as possible. Participants then received specific patient information (medical diagnosis, medical history and medication history). They were then presented with scenario-specific clinical information for four patients. (These scenarios reflected conditions of early sepsis, septic shock, pulmonary embolism and a stable state.) They were given 5 minutes (300 seconds) to complete each scenario. A paper patient record was also provided for clinical context (as this would be supplied for a 'real' patient in ICU).

Figure 4.16: Visual representation of blood oxygen saturation levels

QUESTION SPOTLIGHT!

Although this study took place in a hospital environment with real nurses, these were 'fake' patient scenarios and did not refer to real patients whose health depended on the decisions made by the nurses. Explain why this is an appropriate way to test new equipment.

After the scenarios were complete, participants were asked to complete 7-point Likert scale questions concerning the clinical desirability of the CVS display and the realism of the scenarios.

The most important data related to the speed of response and the accuracy of the data interpretation. Response time was measured from the start of the scenario to the time when the nurse verbalised his or her assessment. If no assessment was given within 300 seconds then 300 seconds was recorded as the response time. Accuracy was determined by whether the nurse correctly identified the patient state. Data was analysed (using an ANCOVA, or analysis of covariance) to compare responses between each display condition within each scenario, and to take into account further variables of nurses' years of experience and years of experience in the ICU. Independent t-tests were used to compare response times between each condition and Mann Whitney U tests used to compare accuracy between each condition. The percentage of nurses in the control display condition who accessed the trend data was also calculated.

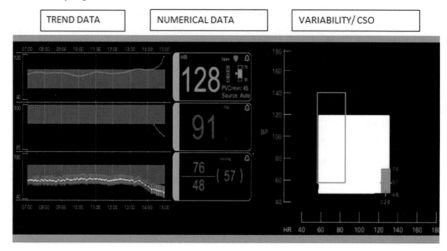

Figure 4.17: The configural vital signs (CVS) display
Source: Drews and Doig (2014), Figure 1, p.572

Results

Speed of response

The most important result is that the nurses were able to respond significantly faster to the CVS display than to the traditional display. The difference equates to a 30% improvement in response time using the CVS display.

Accuracy of response

Overall, the nurses in the CVS display condition were able to correctly identify the patient's condition more frequently than the nurses in the control condition. There were statistically significant differences in the septic shock condition and the pulmonary embolism condition. The stable condition narrowly missed significance, and no difference was found in the early sepsis condition.

Information access

In the control display condition only one nurse in each scenario accessed the trend data. This was a different nurse in each scenario.

Nurses rated the realism of the scenarios highly with a median rating of 6 (SD = 0.43) and the desirability of the CVS display also with a median of 6 (SD = 0.57).

STRETCH & CHALLENGE ◎

Why would an independent t-test be used to compare the response times between the two conditions and a Mann-Whitney U test be used to compare the accuracy between the two conditions?

Conclusions

The new CVS display produced faster response times. For two out of the three abnormal scenarios, nurses were, on average, 43% faster in interpreting the data. Accuracy also improved by a third or more when using the CVS displays in these two scenarios.

This strongly suggests that a display that integrates vital signs information and displays trending information can improve nurses' assessment of a patient in at least some clinical conditions.

However, there were no differences found in the early sepsis condition. This may be because nurses may rely on increases in temperature as a primary indicator for early sepsis and this was not included in the displays. Further studies are clearly needed to examine a much wider range of clinical events as well as larger numbers of vital signs.

It is important to consider the fact that nurses only infrequently accessed the additional information in the control condition. This may be because of the additional effort required and suggests strongly that display designs should avoid creating any impediments to the access and use of information. This does strongly support the authors' conclusions that incorporating trend data into a primary ICU display will facilitate more rapid trend detection.

Unfortunately, at least at the time of publication of the article, it would appear that the numerical display is still the one most typically used in intensive care units. This study, along with many other pieces of research with similar findings, have the potential to reduce the cognitive load associated with the role of intensive care nurse, and therefore to improve patient care.

> **MATHS MOMENT** 🖩
>
> The difference in response times between the two display conditions was significant as $p < .001$
>
> What does this mean?

APPLICATION: ERGONOMIC RESEARCH IN WORKPLACE DESIGN

There are many aspects of workplace design that could be considered in this section, for example the relative advantages and disadvantages of open-plan offices and hot-desking systems. However, this will be covered in the final environmental psychology topic (see page 240), and so in this section we will examine issues relating to the arrangement of furniture within rooms and to the use of colour.

The size of the space and the size of the furniture

Okken *et al.* (2013) have conducted a fascinating study examining whether people feel more comfortable talking about private matters in a larger room with a large desk, rather in than a small room with a small desk. This would have obvious implications for workplaces where professionals such as human resources staff, doctors or counsellors require clients to be relaxed and truthful.

Participants were asked to speak to a female researcher and were allocated to one of four conditions:

1. A small desk giving an interpersonal distance of 80cm in a small room (16 square metres)
2. A small desk giving an interpersonal distance of 80cm in a large room (19.8 square metres)

3   A large desk giving an interpersonal distance of 160cm in the same small room (16 square metres)

4   A large desk giving an interpersonal distance of 160cm in the same large room (19.8 square metres)

The participants were videoed being questioned about substance use, sexuality and emotions by the female researcher, who was unaware of the real purpose of the study.

Participants claimed that they felt more at ease and less inhibited in the larger room although this was only the case when the larger room also contained the larger desk. This could suggest that the intimacy of a smaller desk overpowers the disinhibiting effect of a larger room.

Participants were also videoed and their behaviours coded by coders who were unable to tell the room size and desk size (and were also unaware of the purpose of the study).

In the larger room, participants leant forward more and had a more open posture. They leant on the larger desk more than on the smaller desk, and made more eye contact with the interviewer than in the smaller room. Their answers also showed the effect of being in a larger, more spacious room. Participants used more words to describe their substance use, talked for longer and in more personal terms about sexuality, and gave more intimate answers to questions about emotions.

Okken and her colleagues suggest that these findings could be used to support the development of flexible office environments, including extendable desks and room dividers.

There is an interesting confounding variable in this study. Although the interviewer was unaware of the aim of the study, she took part in all four conditions and therefore was herself possibly influenced by the size of the desk and the size of the room. One of the effects of this might have been to produce significant demand characteristics.

Feng Shui

You have probably heard of Feng Shui – the Chinese art of arranging rooms and buildings in such a way as to have positive effects on those that use them. A study conducted in 2011 by Sibel Dazkir and Marilyn Read compared the effects of curvilinear (round) and rectilinear (straight-edged) furniture on people's emotions. This study used computer generated images of four rooms and 100 undergraduate participants completed an online survey that asked them to rate how each room made them feel in terms of happiness, hopefulness, sociability and how much time they would like to spend in them. Two of the rooms contained curvy, rounded furniture arranged in different ways, and the other two rooms contained straight-edged, angled furniture arranged in the same two formations as in the previous rooms. All the images of the rooms were presented in greyscale (without the use of colour) and included no patterned decor.

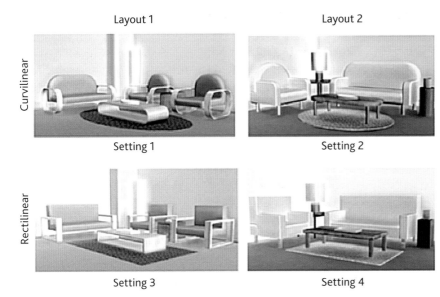

Figure 4.18: The images used in Dazkir and Read's study. Which one makes you feel most sociable?

Although the ratings were fairly negative for all the rooms, the rooms with the rounded furniture received higher pleasure and approach ratings than the rooms with the rectilinear furniture. Although these findings need to be replicated in real rooms (and with the additions of variables such as colour, pattern and texture) it does seem as though the curvilinear furniture is more appealing.

Interestingly, however, it is rectilinear furniture that is more commonly found in office communal areas. This is likely to be due to be cost, but it is also possible that the managers don't want people to feel sociable.

Colour

Finally, how does colour affect us? A study by Genschow *et al.* (2014) has monitored the levels of aggressive behaviour of male prisoners in Switzerland in detention cells which were painted either entirely pink (walls, ceiling and floor), or white with grey floors. Both sets of prisoners showed aggression at the end of three days, but there was, no difference found between the two groups.

There have been many studies into the effects of colour on cognition but these have not produced very reliable results. One study suggests that this is because different colours are effective for different types of cognitive tasks. In a series of computer-based tasks, where the background screen was either red or blue, Mehta & Zhu (2009) have shown that red is effective when tasks require careful attention to detail, whereas blue is more effective when tasks require creativity.

EVALUATION

Methodological and ethical issues

Although the study by Drews & Doig provides evidence that the configural vital signs (CVS) display was effective, it is not possible to draw clear conclusions about *why* performance was better in the CVS condition. There were differences both in terms of what information was presented on the primary display screen and also how this information was presented. This means that further studies will be required to evaluate the relative contributions of each of these factors. This study focused only on the development of an ICU vital signs display, and it is clear that additional work will be required to integrate other information, such as ECG and temperature.

The data was collected through a simulation, which had relatively low ecological validity. The nurses were experienced ICU nurses but would have been aware that this was not a real-life situation. This does not detract from the finding that nurses interpreted the data from the configural display faster than from a traditional monitoring display but it does mean that more realistic simulations are required as well as clinical evaluations. On the other hand, the fact that it was experienced ICU nurses who took part in the trials of this new display system is a definite strength of the study.

The study by Okken *et al.* had high levels of ecological validity as participants were unaware that they had been placed in different rooms and did not realise that the room was one of the variables being examined. However, there is a fascinating confounding variable in this study. The female interviewer conducted interviews in all four rooms, although she had not been made aware of the purpose of the study. She may have guessed the purpose of the study, in which case her behaviour may have changed depending on the room she was in, but more interestingly, she may not have guessed but may have also been affected by the room size and layout in the same way that the participants were. If participants leant forward more, had a more open posture and made more eye contact, then possibly so did the interviewer. This could have had a far greater effect on the participants' behaviour and responses than the room size and layout.

Dazkir & Read showed participants furniture styles and shapes via computer images, and Mehta & Zhu manipulated colour through the background on a computer screen. Both these studies can be said to lack ecological validity although it should always be remembered that studies such as these allow for high levels of control of variables and allow us to see the relationships between independent and dependent variables clearly. These relationships can then also be studied in more realistic environments once we have a better understanding of the effects of a range of possible variables that may interact.

There are few ethical issues raised by this key study, or indeed by any of the other research discussed here. The nurses knew that they were participating in a simulation and so were not deceived or distressed in any way. However, a more realistic simulation might involve the deception of participants, which would raise ethical issues, and certainly clinical trials of any new equipment need to be considered very carefully as patient safety must always be paramount.

Debates

Usefulness of research

This research was conducted as part of the process of developing an ICU vital signs display. More work is needed to incorporate other typical ICU information into the displays (such as ECG and temperature). However this research has the potential to be extremely valuable and will result in faster and more accurate responses from staff in ICU. Unfortunately, it is likely that such equipment will be expensive and this will delay its introduction into ICU departments.

Some of the other studies discussed here also offer useful suggestions for workplace design, from the size of the room required for different kinds of interactions through to the possible effects of different furniture and the use of colour. These might not be as significant as the development of visual display units that can speed up responses to the needs of critically ill patients, but very small changes can contribute to environments so as to reduce cognitive load and promote more effective cognitive processing.

Individual and situational explanations

Once again, a primary focus of environmental psychology is the interaction between the person and their environment. Throughout this section we have seen that psychology, particularly cognitive psychology, is able to provide us with an understanding of the 'cognitive architecture' required to complete a task, which can then be applied in practical ways to reduce cognitive load and improve functioning. It is important to remember, however, that in any examination of the ways in which individuals interact with their environments, there are going to be large numbers of variables that will all have to be considered both within the individual and within the situation. Isolating these variables in highly controlled laboratory tasks allows us to examine them separately, even though we know that they do not operate in isolation in the real world.

PSYCHOLOGICAL EFFECTS OF THE BUILT ENVIRONMENT

BACKGROUND

Both Western and non-Western cultures have long held the view that contact with nature can promote health and well-being. Steg *et al.* (2014) describe one of the earliest references to the health-giving properties of nature found on an ancient Sumerian clay tablet, which describes the paradise garden of Dilmun as a place where 'human beings are untouched by illness', and Hippocrates (460–370BC) stressed the importance of a scenic environment for health. In the early 18th century the then British Prime Minister William Pitt summed up the health functions of the capital city's many parks when he referred to them as the 'lungs of London' (cited in Steg *et al.*, p.48).

In fact Steg *et al.* argue that this notion is so 'intuitively valid' that is only very recently that people have felt the need to apply scientific research principles to this area. It is probable that the poor health and increased incidence of stress-related illness, particularly in the Western world, has been a significant factor in the development of this research. So, although the concept of the relationship between nature and health is an ancient one, the body of scientific research providing evidence of this is relatively recent, as researchers become increasingly interested in the impact that the built environment and urban renewal have on our well-being.

ACTIVITY ✳

Figure 4.19
What effect does nature have on us? Why are pictures of beautiful beaches and wide open spaces so attractive to us? Discuss these questions with a partner.

What is health?

In the Western world, health is often conceptualised as the 'absence of diseases', demonstrating the power of the biomedical model in these cultures. From this perspective, disease is seen as a purely biological process that is the result of exposure to a certain pathogen (a disease-causing agent, such as a bacteria or a virus). In striking contrast, the biopsychosocial approach sees health as a multidimensional concept involving biological, social and psychological components. This approach can also be seen to focus on promoting health rather than merely preventing illness. Any research or application of research looking at the relationship between nature and health can be placed within this approach.

Investigating the relationship between nature and health

Comparing life in urban areas with life in rural areas is methodologically very difficult. We can only compare existing populations and this means that there are numerous uncontrolled variables, such as lifestyle and employment opportunities, income and housing, to name but a few.

So even though cities are likely to produce higher levels of stressors than rural areas, we must be careful not to draw overly simplistic conclusions from this. However, we do know that stress related illnesses such as heart disease is more common in cities (Levine *et al.*, 1988) although we would need to consider the confounding variable of employment related stress here. Respiratory diseases are also higher in urban areas which may be explained in terms of pollution. Mental health problems are also thought to be more common in the city although this too may be due to other variables. Potentially those people in rural areas are able to access greater support networks.

The key research by Ulrich (1984) that we will examine in detail in this topic was published in the prestigious journal *Science* and, according to Steg *et al.* (2014), provided the first reliable empirical evidence that exposure to nature may have restorative effects.

How can we investigate restorative environments?

Much of the evidence of the restorative power of the natural environment unfortunately fails to include control groups. So, although researchers may show the positive health impacts of a range of nature-based therapy programmes, the lack of a control group not exposed to the same nature variable makes it difficult to determine exactly what is causing the improvement. Recently, researchers have applied a far more scientific approach to the study of restorative environments. This will often involve healthy volunteers receiving some sort of stress induction (for example, being asked to perform difficult or even impossible tasks, or watching a scary movie). They are then randomly assigned to groups that are exposed to either natural or built environments. Measurements of stress would be taken before the stress induction, after the stress induction and then after the exposure to the natural or built environment. A change from stage 2 (after the stress induction) to stage 3 (exposure to the natural or built environment) indicates the restorative power of the environment. Studies typically use affective measures (e.g. ratings of happiness/stress levels), cognitive measures (e.g. score on an attentional task) or physiological measures (such as heart rate or cortisol levels).

Such research has consistently confirmed that exposure to the natural environment is restorative.

Ulrich argues that people's initial response to any environment is one of generalised affect – we have either a generally positive reaction (we like it) or a generally negative reaction (we dislike it). He suggests that positive responses are triggered when certain environmental features are present, such as vegetation, depth and texture. Such immediate generally positive responses provide a break from stress and reduced levels of arousal. It is possible that such reactions have their roots in human evolutionary history, as lush vegetation and other natural features would offer many resources such as food, shelter and safety. Humans may have developed a biological preparedness to display positive affective responses in such conditions.

DO IT YOURSELF

Design a piece of research to investigate whether a walk on the beach will lower stress levels. State your hypotheses clearly, outline how you would operationalise your independent variable, and outline how you would measure your dependent variable.

Identify at least one potential confounding variable that you would have to take in consideration.

STRETCH & CHALLENGE ◎

We considered the fight or flight response to stressful environments on page 192. Stressful environments create high levels of physiological arousal, whereas the kinds of environments we are discussing in this topic seem to produce the opposite effects. Compare the likely physiological responses to each of these pictured environments.

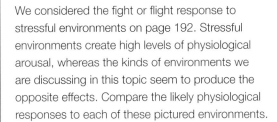

Figure 4.20

KEY RESEARCH

Ulrich, R.S. (1984) View through a window may influence recovery from surgery. *Science*, New Series, 224 (4647), 420–421.

Aim

The aim of this research was to compare the recovery of a group of patients who had undergone gall bladder surgery and who had either a view of trees or a view of a brick wall. Ulrich begins his paper by commenting that, for Americans and Europeans at least, there is a marked preference for natural scenes over urban ones. Previous studies had already shown that views of the natural environment, especially when they contain water, sustain interest and attention longer than urban views. Because Ulrich argues that such views elicit positive feelings and reduce fear in stressed participants, it is therefore reasonable to assume that such views might also have a positive influence in other situations. Here he is proposing that a view of the natural environment will have a positive effect on the recovery process.

Method

The study was conducted by analysing data on recovery rates from a surgical ward in a 200-bed hospital in Pennsylvania, USA. Being in hospital is a stressful situation and, if you are recovering from surgery, your view is likely to be limited to what can be seen outside the window. Ulrich was able to obtain and analyse data relating to all patients allocated to rooms on the second and third floors of

Figure 4.21: How would these views make you feel?

a three-storey wing of the hospital, between 1972 and 1981. On one side of the wing, windows looked out on a small stand of deciduous trees, and on the other side the windows looked out onto a brick wall.

Although Ulrich did not collect the data directly, he was able to compare the recovery rates of patients allocated to the rooms with a view of trees to the recovery rate of patients allocated to the rooms with a view of a brick wall. He was able to do this as the rooms on either side of the building had many identical features, which included:

- The same nurses allocated to rooms on both sides of the building
- The rooms were all the same size
- The rooms all contained two beds
- The furniture was arranged in the same way in each room
- Each room had an identically sized and positioned window
- The size and position of the window allowed an unobstructed view of the outside for each patient.

Ulrich argues that essentially, the rooms differed only in what could be seen out of the window.

Sample

The sample consisted of the records from patients who had undergone a cholecystectomy (a relatively common gall bladder surgery). Included in the study were the records from patients who had this operation between 1st May and 20th October in the years of the study. Records from those whose operations took place outside this time were excluded, as the trees had no foliage at these times of the year. Data from patients who were younger than 20 or older than 69 were also excluded, as was that from patients who developed serious post-operative complications, or who had a history of mental health problems.

The remaining patient data was then matched so that one member of each pair referred to a patient who had a view of the trees and the other to a patient who had a view of the brick wall. The patient data was also matched on the following characteristics:

- Same sex
- Same age (within five years)
- Being a smoker or a non-smoker
- Being within normal weight limits or outside normal weight limits
- General nature of previous hospitalisations
- Year of surgery (to control for any possible changes in procedure)
- Floor level
- Data from patients on the second floor was also matched on the basis of the colour of their room (rooms on that floor alternated between blue and green).

The final sample consisted of the data from 46 patients (23 pairs), with 15 pairs of data from female patients, and 8 data pairs from male patients. An attempt to further match the patient data on the basis of which surgeon had conducted the operation was only partially successful as there were so many surgeons. This matching was done for seven pairs. However, Ulrich stresses that for the remaining pairs, the distribution of the surgeons was similar. There was no instance when patients of the same doctor all had the same view.

Results

Data was collected from patient records by a nurse described as having 'extensive surgical experience'. The nurse did not know which scene was visible from a patient's window.

Five types of information were taken from each record, as follows:

1. Number of days of hospitalisation
2. Number and strength of analgesics taken each day
3. Number and strength of doses for anxiety (including barbiturates and tranquilisers)
4. Minor complications such as headaches and nausea that required medication
5. Nurse's notes relating to a patient's condition or course of recovery.

1 Number of days of hospitalisation

This was defined as being from the day of surgery to the day of release.

Ulrich found that patients with views of trees spent shorter periods of time (an average of 7.96 days) in hospital than those with views of the brick wall (an average of 8.7 days). This was analysed using a Wilcoxon Matched pairs signed rank analysis and was significant at $p<0.025$.

2 Amount of painkillers

The average number of doses per patient was calculated for:

- Period 1: the day of surgery and the first recovery day
- Period 2: days 2 to 5 after surgery
- Period 3: days 6 and 7 after surgery

Ulrich expected that for the first period, there would be no difference between the groups, suggesting that because they would have been in so much pain (and under the influence of such strong drugs) they would take no notice of the view out of the window. He also suggested that by days 6 and 7 there would be also be little difference (and to support this he reports that only 45% of the sample took any painkillers after the fifth day). In effect he is interested in the difference in painkiller use for days 2 to 5 after surgery.

He found no significant difference in painkiller usage between the tree-view group and the wall-view group for Periods 1 and 3, but, as expected, there were significant differences between the groups during Period 2 (days 2 to 5 after surgery). Patients in the tree-view group took milder painkillers, such as aspirin, and far fewer of the moderate or strong painkillers that were available, whereas patients in the wall-view group took far more moderate and strong painkillers. Overall, the difference in doses taken by the two groups was significant at $p<0.01$.

3 Anti-anxiety drugs

No significant difference between the groups was identified. However, wall-view patients had been given more doses of narcotic analgesics (painkillers that also make the patient sleepy) and this may have had the effect of reducing their need for anti-anxiety medication.

4 Minor complications requiring medication

There was a lower incidence of minor complications in the tree-view group, although this difference was not statistically significant. Once again, the relatively higher doses of medication given in the wall-view group may be responsible for this.

MATHS MOMENT

It is interesting that Ulrich made the decision to treat this data as ordinal rather than interval because the surgery was performed at different times of day and the times at which patients were discharged were also different. If he had calculated this as number of hours of hospitalisation, what sort of data would this have been?

5 Nurse's notes relating to a patient's condition or course of recovery

The nurse's notes consisted of comments about the patient's condition up to midnight of the seventh day after the day of surgery. These notes were coded as either positive or negative. For example:

Positive notes	Negative notes
In good spirits; Moving well	Upset and crying; Needs much encouragement

An average of 3.96 negative notes was identified for the patients with the view of the brick wall, compared to an average of 1.13 negative notes for patients with the tree view. This was statistically significant. Ulrich compared statistically the numbers of positive notes identified for each group and reports only that, although more positive comments were recorded for the tree-view patients, this was not a statistically significant difference.

Conclusion

The data from the tree-view group revealed shorter post-operative stays in hospital, took fewer moderate and strong analgesic doses, had fewer negative evaluations from nursing staff and had slightly lower scores for minor post-operative complications. In conclusion, the analysis of the patient data provides evidence that a view of trees has a positive effect on the post-operative recovery process.

APPLICATION: IMPROVING HEALTH AND WELL-BEING THROUGH ENVIRONMENTAL DESIGN

Do you live in a city or in the country? Can you see green fields and trees when you look out of the window? Do you think that the environment you live in has an effect on your health? The study we have just looked at provides strong evidence for the restorative power of the natural environment, but compared this to a view of a brick wall. What if the alternative view had been of a bustling city centre or a beautiful church? Could a view of the built environment ever have restorative powers? In this section, we will consider a number of pieces of research which have investigated the extent to which environmental design can be used to improve health and well-being.

A recent study conducted in Iceland has investigated some of these issues. Lindal & Hartig (2013) presented 236 participants with 145 computer-generated images of streets. The researchers varied the degree of variety and complexity in the building design, and also the building height, varying this from one to three stories.

Participants were asked to imagine that they were walking down the street, mentally exhausted after work. They were asked to rate each streetscape for the following: its restorative potential, how much they liked it, its 'fascination' (what there was to explore and discover), and its ability to give a break from routine.

Although it has to be acknowledged that this study suffers from many limitations (including the low ecological validity and the relatively small architectural variation), the results did suggest that participants found greater architectural variation and lower building height to be associated with the

Figure 4.22: Examples of the images created by Lindal and Hartig (2013)

Figure 4.23: Is this a restorative environment?

perception that the environment was restorative. The researchers suggest this indicates that greater variety and complexity allow the mind to constantly find new items of interest, and that the negative effects of high buildings may stem from an evolutionary preference for openness for easier identification of predators. The study does offer support for the notion that the built environment may also be restorative.

Nisbet & Zelenski (2011) argue that modern lifestyles 'disconnect people from nature' and, as we have already seen, this may have negative effects on well-being. They found that outdoor walks in natural environments made people happier than indoor walks but, more significantly, they found that people made what they called affective forecasting errors, that is they consistently underestimated the positive effects of nature. Clearly, underestimating the positive (and restorative) effects of the natural environment is likely to mean that people fail to maximise their time in the natural environment. This is also likely to reduce their sense of being related to nature, a construct that they describe as being strongly associated with attitudes and behaviours supportive of environmental sustainability. (See 209-220 for a discussion of recycling behaviours and attempts to improve recycling behaviours.)

But what if you don't live near any green space? Could you watch the same images on a screen and have the same effects? Kahn *et al.* (2008) investigated this question by comparing the restorative effects of a view from a real window to the benefits of viewing a huge plasma screen linked to a live, high-definition camera recording of exactly the same view that was visible through the window.

Figure 4.25: Is a view on a screen the same as a view from a window? Kahn *et al.* showed that it does not have the same effect.

Figure 4.24: Spending time in an environment like this is likely to have both a restorative effect, and encourage attitudes and behaviours supportive of environmental sustainability

They used 90 student participants split into groups. In one condition, the participants completed their tasks at a desk in front of a window with a view of a pleasant natural scene beyond. In the second condition, a window-sized plasma screen showing the same scene had been placed so that it totally filled the window opening. In a final condition, participants sat at the same desk in front of the window with the curtains closed.

The participants were given a number of time-constrained and stressful tasks to complete. Heart rate was monitored to measure stress recovery during the rest periods between tasks.

WEB WATCH @

Biophilia refers to the affinity human beings have with the natural world. Investigate biophilic design by visiting this website:

http://www.terrapinbrightgreen.com/reports/14-patterns/

There was no difference between the group with the plasma screen and the group with the curtains closed. However, both these groups differed significantly from the group sitting with a view through the window, who showed much faster stress recovery rates.

So unfortunately, you can't replace a walk in the country or in the park with watching scenes of the countryside on your television or computer screen!

EVALUATION

Methodological and ethical issues

The first methodological issue to consider in relation to Ulrich's study is whether his conclusion is a valid one. His analysis of the patient data does support the idea that a view of trees has a more positive effect on patients recovering from surgery than a view of a brick wall, but does this actually demonstrate that it is the view of nature that is the important factor in the improved recovery? It is possible that the view of trees was more colourful than the view of the brick wall, or that there was more movement or complexity in the scene. Perhaps a view of a busy street would have been equally (or even more) effective, as it would have provided a constantly changing view for the patients.

However, this does not detract from Ulrich's study, which has many strengths. The fact that the rooms were extremely similar and differed only in terms of the view through the window removes many of the confounding variables that could influence the results. The room size and furniture arrangement, as well as the size and placement of the window, were all the same, and Ulrich ensured that there could be no effect from different nurses being allocated to different rooms. the patient data was also matched on an impressive number of factors.

As patients were unaware of the study (having recovered and gone home long before Ulrich collected the data from their medical records) and the nurse collecting the data did not know which group each patient was in, there is no chance of demand characteristics influencing the outcome of this study. However, the majority of the data collected was quantitative (number of days in hospital, amount of medication, etc.), with nurses' providing the only qualitative comments. Perhaps if future research were to be carried out into this question, it would be possible to conduct brief interviews with patients in order to ask them whether they liked their rooms, or to collect self-report data relating to feelings of pain, anxiety and stress throughout the recovery period.

Ulrich used a relatively small sample for this study, which may reduce the reliability of his findings somewhat. However, the careful matching of the data and the similarity of the two conditions in all but the view from the window may counteract this. It may be possible to generalise Ulrich's findings beyond patients undergoing the operation that he selected, but this may not always be appropriate. While it is highly likely that similar results would be found with many other medical conditions, it is also likely that for seriously ill patients, the finding that a view from a window can reduce post-operative recovery time is unlikely to be supported. However, it might be found that a view from a window helps patients relax or reduces their anxiety even though this may have little effect on their long-term prognosis.

There are few ethical considerations here. The data collected by Ulrich can be considered to be secondary data, as it was not collected directly from the participants for the purpose of this research. Ulrich took already existing data from medical records which allowed him to test his hypothesis. The data was actually collected from the medical records by a nurse and so Ulrich presumably did not have access to any personal data, allowing his participants to maintain their anonymity and confidentiality. No one suffered any psychological or physical harm or distress as a result of this study. It may be possible to suggest that the patients whose medical records were accessed were not asked for their consent but, providing that patient confidentiality is maintained, it is crucial that medical information of this sort is available for research purposes so that important trends are identifiable and factors that contribute to both positive and negative outcomes for patients can be identified.

A broader ethical question in relation to this whole topic area would arise if a researcher attempted to replicate this study as an experiment, meaning that patients would be randomly assigned to a 'tree-view' or a 'wall-view' condition. This would raise ethical issues, as we would be deliberately depriving the 'wall-view' group of something that might aid their recovery. This is where experimental research is useful, such as that conducted by Kahn *et al.* comparing the effects of a real view from a window with a computer image of a view or an obscured view. Despite its obviously low ecological validity this tests the effect of a nature view without raising this kind of ethical issue.

Debates

Usefulness of research

Clearly, any research that has the potential to improve people's lives is useful research. Ulrich's research, along with the research discussed in the Application section on page 236, demonstrate that investigating the restorative power of the natural environment is valuable. Designs for new housing, hospitals, workplaces and even whole communities could benefit greatly from the conclusions being drawn from this research. Nisbet & Zelenski demonstrate that people consistently underestimate the positive effects of the natural environment, and Kahn *et al.* make it clear that images of the natural world are no substitute for experiencing the natural world. All of this knowedge is valuable. Lindal & Hartig have also shown us that, by ensuring that it offers variation and complexity, even the built environment can produce some restorative effects.

Psychology as a science

We began this chapter by saying that the relationship between the natural world and health and well-being was for many years considered to be so obvious as to not need researching. However, with the increasing concern about the nation's health, the cost of health care and concern about environmental issues in general, investigators have finally begun to apply the principles of good scientific research to this area. We may know something intuitively, but if we wish those making economic decisions to take this into account, we need to provide scientifically collected evidence to support our arguments. The more that studies like the ones described here are conducted, the more weight these 'intuitive' arguments will have.

Individual and situational explanations

These studies clearly examine the complex relationship between the individual and his or her situation (or environment). The research that has been conducted into the restorative powers of nature clearly demonstrates the influence of situational variables on our behaviour. However, the picture is likely to be somewhat more complex and perhaps future research will begin to examine how this undoubtedly crucial relationship is influenced by individual differences such as personality or by cognitive factors such as expectations.

TERRITORY AND PERSONAL SPACE

BACKGROUND

Personal space

Personal space is a concept that was first identified by Katz in 1937 and was defined by Sommer (1969) as 'an area with invisible boundaries, surrounding a person's body, into which intruders may not come'. Some descriptions use the concept of a bubble surrounding us which can expand or contract according to the situation.

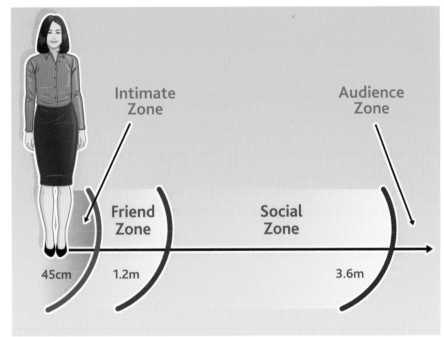

Figure 4.26: Zones of personal space

Source: Hall (1966)

Invasion of personal space

Maintaining our personal space allows us to avoid becoming stressed (remember the fight or flight response in previous sections) and perhaps threatened by people coming too close. One well-known study that investigated the effects of invasion of personal space was conducted by Felipe and Sommer (1966) in a large psychiatric hospital. Patients spent quite a long time outside, and the researchers arranged for a confederate to sit approximately 15 cm away from a patient who was sitting alone. If the patient moved, so did the confederate, keeping approximately 15 cm between them and the patient. They were compared to a control group of people whose space was not invaded in this way, and researchers timed how long it took patients to move out of the situation. Within 20 minutes, 65% of the invaded group had removed themselves from the situation compared to just over 30% of the control group. More interesting was the behaviour adopted by the invaded group in order to protect themselves from the space invasion. They turned away from the invader, folded their arms, and even began to talk to themselves, presumably to reduce the feelings of discomfort produced by the invasion. Felipe and Sommer also conducted a similar study in a university library where a confederate would sit either very close to or at varying distances from a target person. The closer they sat, the faster the target person would remove themselves from the situation. The researchers also reported the same defensive behaviours, such as turning away from the invader or building 'barriers' out of books.

Territory

The concept of territory was first used by Howard in 1948 and made popular in the work of Ardrey (1966). Territory refers to an area that is visibly bounded, in the sense of being marked ('staked-out') and relatively stationary. Territory is visible (in contrast to personal space) and is often home-based. Territorial behaviour (or territoriality) refers to the behaviours that a human or other animal display to claim and defend an area.

Altman (1975) has identified different types of territory, which he defines as primary, secondary and public.

Primary territories are relatively permanent areas, such as our homes or rooms within our homes. They have clear boundaries and are assumed to 'belong' to the individual so that it would be seen as socially inappropriate to enter without invitation or permission. You wouldn't walk into a stranger's garden or house without permission, and you may not feel comfortable entering someone else's room without their knowing that you are there.

Secondary territories are occupied on a more temporary basis and the occupant does not have complete control over them. A good example of a secondary territory would be a seat in a classroom. If you always sit in the same place for every psychology lesson you may feel a little upset to find someone sitting in 'your' seat.

Public territories are areas that are used by everyone. For example, desks and chairs in a library or seats in a common room would be considered public territories. You may use markers to claim your space, such as leaving your coat on a chair in the library or your towel on a sunbed – these markers are generally respected by others.

Territory and personal space in the office

Office work has changed dramatically in recent years. Advances in computer technology, especially with the use of the Internet, email and mobile phones, have made it much more possible for people to work from home. Also, socio-cultural changes, such as the rise of women in the workplace, have meant that more and more organisations are adopting flexible and family-friendly working practices.

Most office environments face the challenge of fitting a large number of people into a relatively small space, and open-plan offices obviously allow for more people than individual offices do. However, some workplaces are going further than this and moving to a situation where employees do not have their own permanent office space. Rather, the workplace offers a number of workspaces (desks or cubicles) that are not allocated permanently to anyone in particular. Workers are allocated (or simply find) a space for themselves each morning.

Figure 4.27: Why are we so unwilling to move markers placed on public territory?

QUESTION SPOTLIGHT!

Moleski & Lang (1986) suggest that the crucial factor in all of this is control. Personalisation allows people to feel in control. We have met this concept several times in environmental psychology. Try to explain the relationship between a feeling of control over your environment and a sense of well-being. Include as many examples as you can in your explanation.

Personalisation in the office

Personalisation is the deliberate decoration or modification of an environment by its occupants to reflect their identities (Sommer, 1974) and is a form of territorial behaviour. There is evidence to suggest that personalisation is associated with well-being as it may guard against negative physical, physiological and psychological consequences of inadequate privacy, such as stress, illness and anxiety. Inadequate privacy could be considered as another form of environmental stressor, with consequences similar to the effects of noise discussed earlier in this chapter.

If personalisation guards against negative effects, is it possible that it might do even more, and actually enhance our physical, physiological and psychological well-being? A study by Harris *et al.* (1978) suggests that personalisation allows employees to feel like individuals rather than just a 'cog in the machine'. Scheiberg (1990) demonstrated that personalisation produces positive emotional responses and allows employees to better deal with stress. Donald (1994) also argues that personalisation can potentially lead to greater job satisfaction and performance, and Cooper (1972) that it creates a greater sense of attachment to the workplace.

KEY RESEARCH

Wells, M.M. (2000) Office clutter or meaningful personal displays: The role of office personalization in employee and organisational well-being. *Journal of Environmental Psychology*, 20 (3), 239–255.

Aim

This study was conducted to determine whether office personalisation is associated with employee well-being and to consider the effect that gender has on this relationship. This led the researchers to propose four hypotheses.

1   *Men and women will personalise their office space differently.* This is a two-tailed (non-directional) hypothesis, although the authors do go on to say that they 'expect' women to personalise more than men, that men and women will use different items to personalise, and that personalisation will serve a different purpose for men and women.

2   *Personalisation will be positively associated with employee well-being.* Specifically, they propose that personalisation will be positively associated with satisfaction with the working environment, which will be positively associated with job satisfaction, which will be positively associated with employee well-being.

3   *Workspace personalisation will be more integral to the well-being of women than to that of men.* This is based on previous research that demonstrated that women personalise their homes more than men, and with more intimate items, suggesting that this is more important for their well-being.

4   *Companies that have more lenient personalisation policies will report higher levels of organisational well-being than companies having stricter personalisation policies.* The researchers suggest that organisational well-being can be seen through such factors as low turnover of staff, higher employee morale, and higher productivity.

QUESTION SPOTLIGHT!

What do you think? Is it important to personalise your space at home, college, school or work? Do you think that males and females personalise their space differently? If so, what reasons can you think of to explain this difference?

As well as setting out these four hypotheses, the authors also propose a model of office personalisation and employee well-being.

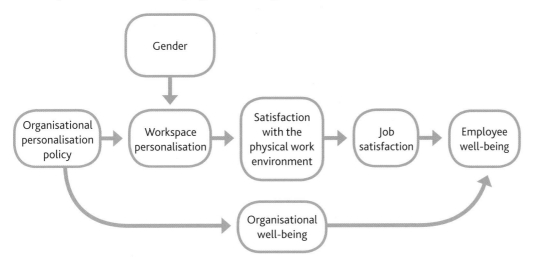

Figure 4.28: Wells' proposed model of the relationships between office personalisation, gender, employee well-being, and organisational well-being
Source: Wells (2000), p.243

First, and fairly obviously, this model is proposing that companies with more lenient personalisation policies will have substantially more personalisation than companies with stricter personalisation policies. Secondly, the model proposes that personalisation leads to greater satisfaction with the physical work environment, which will lead to greater job satisfaction. The model goes on to propose that greater job satisfaction will also enhance employee well-being. It also suggests that gender will influence personalisation, and that men and women will personalise for different reasons, to greater degrees, and with different types of personal items. Company policy is also seen as influential within this model – employees in companies with more lenient personalisation policies will report greater levels of organisational well-being. This will lead, in turn, to enhanced employee well-being.

Method
A survey of office workers was conducted at 20 companies in Orange County, California, during the winter and spring of 1997.

Sample
Twenty companies and their employees were recruited from 2000 companies who were participating in a larger project, the Small Business Workplace Wellness Project (SBWWP). For this study, only companies with more than 30 employees were eligible to be selected. This reduced the possible companies to 763, and a SBWWP contact person in each of these organisations was contacted to see if they were interested in taking part in a study of office environments and employee well-being. Only 20 companies were willing to participate and also met the criteria of having at least 15 workers in an office environment.

The final 20 companies included two manufacturing companies, two real-estate companies, three distributors, an air-conditioning company, a law firm, a relocation firm, a car dealership, a software developer, a home medical equipment company, a building materials distributor, a health-care office, an electronics repair company, a traffic-engineering firm, a vocational counselling office, a non-profit agency, and a hands-on learning science centre. The numbers of office-based workers ranged from 15 to 90. Participants were between the ages of 25 and 44, with slightly more males than females (there were 338 participants in the final sample; 187 male, 138 female and 13 who did not report their gender).

The response rate here is obviously very low and the researchers called around 100 of the companies that had not replied to see if they could obtain any further information about why they had not replied. The largest proportion (71%) stated that they did not have enough office workers to make them eligible, although 22% said they were too busy and 7% that 'they were not interested in research'. Although the researchers argue that the low response rate is not a major problem as this research is largely 'exploratory' and that the problems of getting organisations to participate is well documented, it is important to consider the extent to which the results from such a small number of agreeable companies can generalise to other workplaces.

The SBWWP contact at each organisation was given surveys for each of their office-based workers. In total, 661 surveys were given out. Each one was in a numbered, unsealed envelope and the office workers were asked to complete the survey and seal it inside the envelope and return to their SBWWP contact within 5 days. A total of 338 surveys were returned (an employee level response rate of 51%).

Procedure

All participants completed a survey, with some being selected as case studies, which involved a short interview and an observation of their workplace. The coordinator also completed a short organisational survey, which was broken into several sections. Details of all of the survey measures are summarised below.

In addition, a coordinator survey was completed by the coordinator in each organisation, which asked about the company's personalisation policy and organisational well-being. Of the 20 organisations, five agreed to participate as case studies. As well as completing the surveys, these organisations allowed the researcher to interview some employees and to observe and to photograph the workspaces. Fifteen women and eight men participated in this part of the study. Interviews lasted around 15 minutes and were structured interviews consisting of open-ended questions and were tape-recorded. Participants were asked about the items they were displaying and the importance of these items to them. They were also asked whether they thought being able to personalise their workplace affected their satisfaction with the work environment, their satisfaction with their job, and their overall well-being. They were also asked how they thought they would feel if their company were to prohibit personalisation.

After the interview, the researcher also observed the workplace of the case-study participants, and recorded the details on an observation checklist. This checklist consisted of: (1) a list of personalisation categories so that the number of items pertaining to each category could be counted; (2) space to list unusual items and themes; (3) a scale assessing aesthetic quality of the workspace (not including personalisation) and (4) the gender of the workspace occupant.

TABLE 4.3: SURVEY MEASURES USED BY WELLS *ET AL.* (2000)

	Measurement
Section 1: workplace personalisation	• The number of personal items displayed (excluding work-related items) • The types of personal items displayed • The degree to which the respondent would have liked to display personal items but did not due to workplace policies or norms • The extent of workplace rearrangement • Reasons for personalising/not personalising • The extent of personalisation of team spaces
Section 2: satisfaction with the physical work environment	This was assessed using Ferguson and Weisman's (1986) 'satisfaction with the work environment' scale, which consists of 9 items rated on a 5-point scale. Items include 'I like my workspace' and 'it is difficult to do my job in my workspace'.
Section 3: job satisfaction	This was assessed using Ferguson and Weisman's (1986) 'job satisfaction' scale. This has 5 items and is also rated on a 5-point scale. Items include 'In general, I like my job' and 'I am satisfied with the work I do'.
Section 4: well-being	This was assessed using a variety of measures, some designed by the researchers and some taken from already existing scales. Measures of global well-being included: • *How do you feel about your life as a whole?* (rated on a 7-point scale from delighted to terrible) • *How have you been feeling in general?* (rated on a 6-point scale from 'in excellent spirits' to 'in very low spirits') Measures of physical well-being included: • *How would you rate your health at the present time?* (rated on a 5-point scale from 'excellent' to 'poor') Psychological well-being included measures of the frequency with which respondents had experienced each of 20 symptoms, including poor appetite and crying spells (rated on a 4-point scale from 'rarely or none of the time' to 'most or all of the time'. This section also included the Global Stress Scale (Cohen *et al.*, 1983) which asks respondents to rate a number of stressful feelings or experiences (for example, nervous and stressed) on a 5-point scale from 'never' to 'very often'.
Section 5: employee perception of organisational well-being	Employee perceptions of the social climate (assessed with the Social Climate Scale; Stokols *et al.*, 1990), organisational climate (assessed with the Organisational Climate Scale; Taylor & Bowers, 1972), employee morale, productivity, performance and absenteeism.
Section 6: personality traits	Personality traits thought to be associated with office personalisation, such as need for affiliation, need for privacy and creativity. For example, the need for affiliation was assessed using the Sociability Scale (Cheek & Buss, 1981), which contains items such as 'I like to be with people' which are rated on 5-point scales from 'strongly disagree' to 'strongly agree'.
Section 7: demographic information	Demographic information such as gender, age, ethnicity, marital status, education, job title, length of time with the company and length of time in this workplace.

Results

Hypothesis 1: Men and women will personalise their workspaces differently

Table 4.4 summarise the reasons why respondents said they personalised their workspace.

TABLE 4.4: REASONS FOR PERSONALISING WORKSPACE

	Respondents said that they personalised their workspace ...
56%	to express their identity and individuality
30%	to improve the feel of the workplace
16%	to express their emotions
15%	to show that the workplace belonged to them
6%	to show their status within the organisation
5%	to control their interactions with co-workers
3%	because everyone else did

(Note: total = 131% as participants were able to give more than one response.)

Figure 4.29: A personalised office space

In terms of differences between men and women, the following significant results were achieved:

- More women than men personalised in order to express their identity and individuality, to express their emotions and to improve the feel of the workplace. However, more men than women personalised to show their status within the company.
- Women personalised to a greater extent than men. The average number of items (from the survey) was 7.68 for men and 11.12 for women. The observations supported this, with an average of 18.5 items for women and 8.3 for men,
- Men and women used different types of objects to personalise their workspaces. Women's spaces contained significantly more items relating to personal relationships, particularly friends and pets, and also more plants and more trinkets. Men's displays contained more sports-related items than women's. The observational data adds to this by revealing specific themes in the men's and women's displays. Women's family-related items consisted of photos of husbands, children and children's drawings. Another theme was animals, including pictures of pets and animal-themed posters, mugs, etc. Men displayed not only sports items but also items relating to their own achievements, such as diplomas, certificates and trophies.

The authors conclude that men and women differ significantly in their reasons for personalising, the extent of their personalisation, and the types of items displayed. Hypothesis 1 is therefore supported.

Hypothesis 2: Personalisation is positively associated with enhanced employee well-being

Three measures of personalisation were positively associated with satisfaction with the physical work environment. These were the number of personal items displayed, the association between how much the employee would like to personalise and how much he or she is allowed to personalise, and the extent to which the employee determined the arrangement of their workspace. Analyses also showed that satisfaction with the physical environment was associated with job satisfaction, which in turn was positively associated with employee well-being, including physical health and psychological well-being.

Hypothesis 3: Personalisation is more important to women's well-being than to that of men

There was no evidence from the survey data to suggest that personalisation is more important to women's well-being than to men's well-being. However, interview data suggested otherwise, with women being far more likely to comment positively on the effects of personalisation. When asked directly if personalisation affected their well-being, women said things such as: *'Yes, because they [these things] are a part of me, and it lets me express my identity',* and *'When I am away from my kids for so long during the week, just to look up to [pictures of] their faces once in a while makes it all worthwhile. It is a stress reliever.'*

Men seemed far less sure and gave answers such as: *'I've never thought about whether it makes me feel better or not. It is fun to come in and see all these things, though'* and *'Maybe, I guess, I don't really know how to answer that one.'*

Women were also far more likely to respond negatively when asked to imagine working for a company that restricted personalisation, with one woman stating that she wouldn't work for a company that would be strict, whereas men were less likely to care about this – although one man did suggest that '...*a company that wouldn't allow personalisation would probably have other strict rules that go with it, so it probably wouldn't be enjoyable.*'

So, although Hypothesis 3 was not supported (personalisation is not directly associated with women's well-being), the women interviewed thought that it was.

Hypothesis 4: Companies that have more lenient personalisation policies will report higher levels of organisational well-being than companies that have stricter personalisation policies.

This hypothesis was supported. Companies that allow more personalisation have a more positive organisational climate, a more positive social climate, higher levels of employee morale and reduced staff turnover. All these comparisons were statistically significant.

Conclusion

1   Men and women personalise their space differently: women personalise more than men, and tend to personalise with symbols of family, friends and pets as well as with trinkets and plants, whereas men tend to personalise with symbols of achievement and sporting items. Women tend to personalise to express their identities and emotions and to improve the feel of their workplace whereas men tend to personalise to show their status within the company.

2   Personalisation is positively associated with employee well-being. This is an indirect relationship that suggests that personalisation is associated with satisfaction with the physical work environment, which is positively associated with job satisfaction, which in turn is positively associated with employee well-being.

3   There is no difference in the importance of personalisation for men and women. The hypothesis that personalisation would be more important to the well-being of women than the well-being of men was not supported by the survey data, although it was supported by the interview data.

4   Companies with more lenient personalisation policies reported greater levels of employee morale, a more positive organisational climate, a more positive social climate, and a reduced staff turnover.

APPLICATION: EFFECTIVE OFFICE DESIGN

Are open-plan offices a good idea?

These days it is far more common for workers to be housed in large, open-plan offices than to be given their own private offices. There may be good economic reasons for this style, but is there any supporting evidence from psychological research? It might be reasonable to argue that workers can communicate with each other more effectively in an open-plan office, but they can also get distracted much more easily.

Kim & de Dear (2015) conducted a survey of over 42,000 office workers in 300 office buildings across America. They were asked to rate their satisfaction

STRETCH & CHALLENGE ◉

The authors suggest that women are more likely to try to make their workplace place look nice, perhaps in relation to their more traditional roles as homemakers. They also suggest that women may feel that the workplace is male and therefore need to personalise it. If men also feel that the workplace is 'theirs' (a more male space than a female space), this would also explain the fact that they don't need to personalise to the same extent. Evaluate this argument.

Figure 4.30: Would you like to work in this office?

WEB WATCH @

What is it like working in an open-plan office?

http://www.bbc.co.uk/programmes/b036wfzv

WEB WATCH @

Is hot-desking a good idea?

http://www.bbc.co.uk/guides/zgjmtfr

STRETCH & CHALLENGE

Do the same social norms apply in the virtual world as in the real world? Do we have a sense of personal space in a game such as 'Second Life'? This fascinating study by Yee *et al*. (2006) suggests that we do:

https://vhil.stanford.edu/pubs/2007/yee-nonverbal.pdf

WEB WATCH @

You can read more about Jane Carstairs' work here:

https://www.wlv.ac.uk/about-us/corporate-information/wlvdialogue/previous-issues/wlvdialogue---summer-2011/taking-the-hot-desk/

with several aspects of their office environment including temperature, lighting, privacy and ease of interaction, and their overall satisfaction with their personal workspace. Roughly two-thirds of the sample worked in open-plan offices (with or without partial partitions), a quarter had private offices, and a small number shared a single room with one other person.

Kim & de Dear found that workers in private offices were the most satisfied with their workspace. Those people that worked in open-plan offices were most dissatisfied with the privacy aspect of their working environment. This was particularly strongly felt in large open-plan offices with partitions. Although the partitions are designed to give a sense of privacy it is impossible to know who is listening to you or where other people are, and this makes people feel that noise is harder to predict and therefore it feels less controllable.

Hot-desking

Hot desking is the ultimate in non-territorial work space. Hot-desking means you do not have your own desk but work in a different place in the office each day. This may be at one of a few desks somewhere in a relatively small room, but in some organisations there could be hundreds of 'hot-desk' spaces. There may not even be enough space for everyone.

ACTIVITY ✳

What do you think the benefits to an organisation of a hot-desking policy might be? Although a classroom is not quite the same as an office, as students generally don't leave their things on (or in) a desk that belongs to them, it is usually the case that people have their usual seats.

For one week, in your classroom, allow no-one to sit in their usual seat but allocate the seats instead on a first-come, first-served basis. You could make this more interesting by creating some obviously desirable seating and some much less desirable seating. Ask people to report their feelings at the end of the week. You could also conduct an observation of student behaviour or record details such as whether people started arriving earlier to claim the best seats.

If your school or college has a common room, it might be interesting to replicate the study there.

Jane Carstairs, working at the University of Wolverhampton has been exploring the advantages and disadvantages of this kind of working environment for the employees. She argues: *'Having your own space allows people to gain control within that small environment and personalise it with pictures and little things that define their identity. The threats to that of the non-territorial office can result in a lack of motivation and even stress.'* She goes on to say that other studies have shown that people find working without personalisation quite stressful. This reinforces the point that we have been making throughout this chapter about the importance of perceived control and coping with stress.

Working at a treadmill!

We have looked at open-plan offices and at hot-desking, both of which are relatively common in workplaces across the world. We now come to a suggestion that is a little more unusual! Labonté-LeMoyne *et al.* (2015) report that working at a treadmill desk produces positive cognitive effects. This was a very small-scale study, where nine students were asked to spend 40 minutes reading text and emails on a computer while walking at 2.25km/h at a treadmill desk. There was a control group of another nine participants who read the same text and emails at a standard desk. When tested later, the treadmill group showed superior memory performance and reported that they had felt better able to concentrate during the reading task.

Tajadura-Jimenez *et al.* (2011) conducted a fascinating study that demonstrates that an iPod can be used to create a sense of personal space. They used the standard personal space experimental set-up, where participants were asked to walk towards an unfamiliar experimenter until they felt 'uncomfortable'. The experimental conditions were that this was done either in silence, while listening to music played in the room, or while listening to music played through headphones via an iPod. Music played through headphones via an iPod had the effect of shrinking the participants' sense of personal space so that they could be closer to the experimenter before they reported feeling uncomfortable.

Figure 4.31: Working at a treadmill desk

Methodological and ethical issues

The key study by Wells *et al.* used a survey method to collect data, along with some observation. They collected a huge amount of data using a variety of self-report measures. They do not say how long it might have taken individual participants to complete these surveys but it may have been a considerable amount of time. This might lead to some limitations. Self-reports can be unreliable anyway, with participants likely to be influenced by demand characteristics and social desirability bias. These factors may be even more important when a survey about your workplace is being completed. If you add to this the length of time that may have been required to complete the survey, it would be reasonable to suggest that some participants may have not completed them at all (the return rate was only 51%) and that, even if they were returned, they may have been rushed or completed with little thought.

There is an issue relating to the samples used in the study by Wells and in the studies reported in the applications section: a very small number of organisations agreed to take part in this study (less than 4% of the originally targeted companies), and only 51% of the employees in the companies taking part returned completed surveys. The companies

and the individuals who chose to participate may have been different from those who chose not to participate, and we have no way of knowing in what ways they may be different. It is always difficult to persuade organisations to take part in research because it is difficult to persuade businesses – especially small businesses – to take part in any research that might take their employees away from their work. The companies that did take part were small- to medium-sized companies (across a range of industries) and these might not be representative of larger companies. On the other hand, the study by Kim & de Dear (2015) surveyed 42,000 employees in 300 different organisations across America. It is likely that we would be safe in generalising the findings from this study to other organisations within the same country. The study by Labonté-LeMoyne *et al.*, looking at working at treadmills, used a tiny sample of just nine participants in both the experimental and control groups, and it would be unwise to generalise too far from these findings. However, this study may be seen as a starting point for more research into similar areas.

Some of the conclusions drawn by Wells *et al.* are the results of correlational analysis. For example, they conclude that personalisation is associated with higher well-being, but they have not demonstrated that this is a cause-and-effect relationship. Experimental research (manipulating the independent variable of personalisation) would be required for this.

In terms of ethical considerations, the study by Wells did not manipulate any variables experimentally but did ask participants for lots of information about their attitudes towards their work and their workplace. It is unlikely that any participants were distressed in any way by the questions they were asked, and they had the option to simply not complete the survey if they wished. No-one was forced to take part and no-one was deceived. The organisations received a report of the overall study's findings, a report of findings specific to their own organisation, and recommendations for simple changes to their work environment that might improve employee and organisational well-being. None of the studies mentioned in the Applications section raises ethical issues, although the study by Middlemist referred to in the introduction to this topic certainly did. He set up a periscope in a men's toilet in an American university to observe the effect of space invasion on the onset and duration of urination, finding (not surprisingly) that men took longer to begin urinating and continued for significantly shorter periods of time when a confederate of the experimenter was standing very close to them.

Debates

Usefulness of research

The research outlined here strongly suggests that there are significant benefits to allowing workers to personalise their workspaces. It would therefore seem reasonable to conclude that organisations should allow this. It may not be that simple, however. There may be good health and safety reasons why personal possessions should be kept to a minimum in some workplaces. Of course, organisations need to consider a wide range of factors when making these kinds of decisions, and economic considerations might prevail (see 'Generalisability'). However, wherever possible, office design should incorporate the knowledge that personalisation can be positive, and the provision of noticeboards, shelving, etc., for personal possessions might be incorporated helpfully and safely into the design.

Generalisability

It is difficult to apply results from one workplace to another workplace, because there are so many different factors to consider. Not everyone works in an office, and in other workplaces there may be other ways in which people personalise their spaces. People working in a shop, for example, may personalise their shared lunchroom. Perhaps simply being able to keep some of your own possessions in work, such as a mug or a change of clothes, is enough to increase well-being. Drivers often personalise their vehicles, perhaps for the same reason. In other workplaces it may simply not be possible. However, Wells *et al.* conclude that companies with a strict non-personalisation policy (such as those who have moved to a system of hot-desking) may nevertheless be more lenient and flexible in many other areas, such as offering flexible working hours, granting maternity and paternity leave, or allowing working from home. Such areas might outweigh any lack of personalisation when considering job satisfaction, and this would also mean we would need to consider the validity of measuring personalisation as a way of measuring job satisfaction.

Individual and situational explanations

Once again, we are considering directly the relationship between the individual and the situation, in this case the working environment. What the study by Wells *et al.* tells us is that the situation has a strong effect on the way people feel about their jobs, but that it affects men and women differently. Remember that men and women personalise their space differently: women personalise more than men, and women tend to personalise with symbols of family, friends and pets as well as with trinkets and plants, whereas men tend to personalise with symbols of achievement and sporting items. Women tend to personalise to express their identities and emotions and to improve the feel of their workplace, whereas men tend to personalise to show their status within the company. This does suggest that men and women interact with their environment in very different ways – ways that have only just begun to be investigated.

PRACTICE QUESTIONS

Remember that in any exam paper you will only get a set of questions on one of the six sub-topics.

TOPIC 1: STRESSORS IN THE ENVIRONMENT

(a)* Using the research by Black & Black (2007), explain the problems caused by environmental stressors and their impact on our biological responses. **[10]**

(b)* Assess the use of the biological approach in explaining the effect of environmental stressors on our biological responses. **[15]**

(c)* William lives in a big semi-detached house in a nice area but his neighbours bang on the wall at night and keep him awake. He feels trapped because he never gets out even though he knows he has time to.

Discuss how an environmental psychologist might apply their knowledge to help William to cope with or overcome the stress he is experiencing. **[10]**

TOPIC 2: BIOLOGICAL RHYTHMS

(a)* Explain how the research by Czeisler (1982) could be used to argue that there should be closer regulation of employers using shift work. **[10]**

(b)* Assess the nature–nurture debate with regard to biological rhythms. **[15]**

(c)* Sumiko is a psychologist who is starting work at a new airport. She is responsible for the health of the workers and hopes to create a happy, healthy working environment for its staff. Two key tasks are to organise the shift rota for ground staff and to improve conditions for air crew to reduce the effects of jet lag.

Discuss how Sumika could **either** design the shift work schedule for ground staff **or** the work schedule for air crew to minimise disruption to the workers' biological rhythms. **[10]**

TOPIC 3: RECYCLING AND OTHER CONSERVATION BEHAVIOURS

(a)* Using the research by Lord (1994), explain conservation behaviours and the tendency to conserve or recycle. **[10]**

(b)* Assess the ethical issues involved when researching recycling and other conservation behaviours. **[15]**

(c)* Imagine that your school or college has decided to 'Go Green' and wants to encourage recycling and conservation behaviours in students and staff, for example by recycling paper or conserving water.

Discuss how an environmental psychologist might apply their knowledge to develop a strategy for encouraging one type of recycling or conservation behaviour. **[10]**

TOPIC 4: ERGONOMICS – HUMAN FACTORS

(a)* Explain how the research by Drews & Doig (2014) could be used to demonstrate the importance of ergonomics (human factors) in the workplace**. [10]**

(b)* Assess the usefulness of research into ergonomics (human factors) in the workplace. **[15]**

(c)* Jared works on the interior design of cars. His current project is to devise a new layout for the controls in a lorry that will be driven on long-distance journeys. He has to consider the layout of the controls the driver can see and use, such as information about speed, navigation, temperature and fuel.

Discuss how an environmental psychologist might apply their knowledge of ergonomics (human factors) in the workplace to maximise ease of use and minimise the risk of cognitive overload as the driver deals with road and weather conditions, as well as other road users. **[10]**

TOPIC 5: PSYCHOLOGICAL EFFECTS OF THE BUILT ENVIRONMENT

(a)* Explain how the research by Ulrich (1984) could be used to improve the health and well-being of elderly residents in a nursing home. **[10]**

(b)* Assess the methodological issues involved when researching potential ways to improve health and well-being. **[15]**

(c)* Chris and Sam are planning to move house. They are looking for somewhere that will make them both happy, but they like different things. Chris likes city life and Sam prefers the countryside.

Discuss how an environmental psychologist might apply their knowledge of the effects of the built environment to make recommendations about what location they should chose. **[10]**

TOPIC 6: TERRITORY AND PERSONAL SPACE

(a)* Using the research by Wells (2000), explain the importance of territory and personal space in the workplace. **[10]**

(b)* Assess the individual and situational debate with regard to territory and personal space. **[15]**

(c)* Kate owns a company and is relocating to a new office building. She is planning large shared offices for each team. She is wondering whether it would be better to make each work area identical and fixed, or whether to allow the workers to personalise their space. She has decided to test which is better by allowing some teams more freedom than others.

Discuss how a psychologist could investigate which strategy is best. **[10]**

TOPIC 1: STRESSORS IN THE ENVIRONMENT

(b)* Assess the use of the biological approach in explaining the effect of environmental stressors on our biological responses. **[15]**

Liam's answer:

Stress is bad for you. The Systematic Adrenalin Model says that the hormone adrenalin is produced straight away when we get stressed. This makes us feel scared and has effects like speeding up the heart and breathing rate and opening our pupils. These are good responses if we need to run away or to fight. It means we can see better and have oxygen for our muscles. It's not so useful, though, if you are sitting in an exam room with a dry throat and shaky hands.

When we can't run away or fight the source of stress the body tries to adapt and we can cope for a while but eventually we burn out. So if you lived next to a runway the noise would be a stressor. You can't run away and you can't fight so your body goes into the SAM for no reason, and this exhausts it, so people who are stressed for a long time get sick. They end up with high blood pressure and they can't concentrate properly.

Rina's answer:

Stressors can be things in the environment and they are not biological, although there are also biological sources of stress. When an aspect of the environment is more than we think we can cope with, it becomes stressful. This is a cognitive evaluation rather than a biological one. What happens next, though, is biological – two of the fours Fs, fight or flight. A system called SAM controls this, sending out hormones that give us a rush. This is biological because it involves hormones. If the threat goes away, the SAM calms down.

If the stressor stays, the SAM isn't enough and we need the GAS to keep us on red alert. SAM is really the first stage of GAS, which Selye called the alarm stage. The next one is called the resistance stage and is biological because the body is coping with the problems caused by high blood sugar and heart rate from the alarm stage. For example Evans et al. (1998)

We say: Apart from getting the name of the SAM rather muddled (it should be the sympathetic-adrenal medullary system), Liam describes it well, including lots of appropriate biological detail. Unfortunately, Liam doesn't distinguish between the environmental factors, such as being in the exam room, and the biological responses that he describes. Although Liam doesn't refer to the General Adaptation Syndrome (GAS), he does describe the resistance and exhaustion stages, but again he makes no reference to biological or other explanations, which is a pity.

We say: Rina starts off well. She contrasts environmental and biological sources of stress, although the latter could have had an example or explanation, and then observes that because environmental stimuli only become stressful when they are threatening, this is a cognitive process. These are good comparisons to purely biological explanations. She then uses Cannon's idea of the SAM, without first explaining that is stands for the sympathetic-adrenal medullary system, and the explanation is far too simplistic. Her explanation of GAS is somewhat better and it was good to include some studies to support the ideas, although these could have been slightly more detailed.

The third paragraph again includes some appropriate analysis of the biological approach. It was good to include contrast to a non-biological explanation of stress.

found that children stressed by noise at school had higher blood pressure and this applied to adults at work according to Tomei et al. (2010) and at home according to Black & Black (2007) too.

   Bodies aren't very good at coping with long-term stress and eventually negative effects cause us to get sick, this is the exhaustion stage. These, like spending hours revising and sitting writing essays in exams, are environmental stressors that can put students into the exhaustion stage, but different students respond differently and this might be for social or cognitive reasons. For example, Lazarus says that it's the way that we interpret a stressor rather than what it is that counts. He called this cognitive appraisal. I might think examiners are out to trick me and get really stressed, whereas Liam might just think exam questions are what they are. My cognitive appraisal would result in me being more stressed than Liam.

TOPIC 2: BIOLOGICAL RHYTHMS

(c)* Sumiko is a psychologist who is starting work at a new airport. She is responsible for the health of the workers and hopes to create a happy, healthy working environment for its staff. Two key tasks are to organise the shift rota for ground staff and to improve conditions for air crew to reduce the effects of jet lag.

Discuss how Sumika could **either** design the shift work schedule for ground staff **or** the work schedule for air crew to minimise disruption to the workers' biological rhythms. **[10]**

Liam's answer:

Pilots get jet lag because they fly through time zones. This stops them sleeping well and can make them ill. It's better to change so time gets later, like in delay shifts, rather than trying to wake up when your body still thinks it should be asleep, which is what happens in advance shifts, so pilots should fly all the way around the world, only ever going from East to West. They could fly a plane from the UK to the US, then to China then Turkey then home. This way they would always be in phase delay and wouldn't get jet-lagged. It would extend their day each time they flew so their body clock would just run a bit slow rather than getting desynchronised.

We say: Liam's essay begins with a little description and sets the scene, but without answering the question. He then makes reference to delay and advance shifts, which is actually about shift work rather than jet lag, but the principle he is describing is correct. His idea for solving jet lag in pilots by flying all the way around the world is logically correct, but utterly impractical! He then goes on to make a reasonable point about exposure to zeitgebers but doesn't suggest when this exposure should be, or what the pilots should do when they are sleeping.

Czeisler says that pilots need zeitgebers to help them to adjust. These are factors from the outside in the environment that set the body clock. Sunlight is the most important one, so pilots should be allowed to get out and wander about at each destination, but also other things that happen regularly, like meal times, so they should go out and eat too.

Rina's answer:

Shift work in the airport is a problem because it causes sleep, gut and heart problems and makes workers likely to get sick, even get cancer. The IARC showed that constant dim light like you might get in an airport on night shift is linked to cancer. Sumika might also try to get the workers to eat better, not drink coffee and try to be nice to their families as all these things suffer when people work shifts. Ideally, each person in the airport should stick to the same shift all the time, different staff for day and night, then they wouldn't have to change at all, but people don't like doing nights.

Czeisler et al. (1982) tested rotating shift patterns by changing the cycle so factory workers changed shifts every week or every 21 days. Also, they all changed from phase advance to phase delay. The delay schedule was preferred and the people on the longer cycle were happier and healthier. The staff also left less and worked harder. This shows that schedules would be important for Sumika to sort out and people like it best if they can choose their own shift, but this isn't very practical as the airport needs staff round the clock, even if it does make people less stressed, and less likely to take time off or leave. So Sumika would have to plan shift times as phase delay with long periods such as 3 weeks.

Once they were on the shift cycle, Sumika should make sure the light is bright enough, so if ground crew are out in the dark they should have well-lit offices when they come indoors. This matters as if they see daylight when they are not at work, it would disrupt their circadian rhythms. Light boxes that give out really bright light would block melatonin

We say: The first part of Rina's introductory paragraph is correct and useful but is not, in itself, answering the question. The second part however, is relevant and correct and leads logically into her idea for shift patterns in the second paragraph. This, and the third paragraph, are well argued and use evidence effectively.

and cause cortisol release, so help to stabilise their cycles. This should counteract the risks of cancer reported by the IARC and reduce fatigue from sleep loss. This is important, as accidents in airports could be fatal, and incidents like the Clapham railway crash and Chernobyl were linked to fatigue and shifts according to the HSE (2012). The ground crew on the night shift might also use goggles to block out the light after work. Together these should improve sleep, helping to overcome the shift-work problems.

TOPIC 4: ERGONOMICS – HUMAN FACTORS

(a)* Explain how the research by Drews & Doig (2014) could be used to demonstrate the importance of ergonomics (human factors) in the workplace. **[10]**

Liam's answer:

Drews and Doig (2014) tested nurses with made-up information about patients with septic shock and pulmonary embolism to see if they could use new hospital monitors. The nurses had to decide if the patients were sick or not using either old black-and-white monitors or new colour ones. As there were lots of different colours (red, orange, pink, purple and blue just for breathing oxygen), this gives more different signals than just black and white, so makes the cognitive load for the nurses higher. Also, the new monitors were dynamic, with a real-time moving display for blood pressure and heart rate, but not temperature. So nurses on the new system had more information to process.

Nurses on the new system were faster, more accurate and accessed more information than the controls. They weren't any better at detecting early signs of septic shock because the new displays didn't include temperature, so they didn't have the right information.

So increasing cognitive load made the nurses more effective – for most things – in terms of speed and accuracy but that overloading them even more, with temperature information, would make them even better.

We say: Liam reports lots of accurate information about the study here and relates some of it effectively to the ideas of ergonimics. However, he has made two key mistakes. Firstly, the difference between the new and control displays wasn't simply about whether they were black-and-white or colour, but about the types of information they displayed and how simply it was presented. Secondly, Liam is muddled about cognitive load. High cognitive load is a bad thing, and the new design displays aimed to reduce (not increase) that load.

Rina's answer:

Ergonomics is about designing equipment and the immediate workplace environment so that people can do their jobs better, by feeling less tired or working faster. Drews & Doig (2014) tested the displays of information for nurses. Ergonomics is important here because nurses have a lot of data to take in simultaneously, i.e. high cognitive load, is because they monitor lots of patients at the same time, and they might even be in different rooms. They also have to keep track of information from different sources, e.g. talking to the patient, written reports and ward monitors, so need to recall information between each one or adjust to different outputs, adding stress to working memory. When they process this in their heads, they have to decide whether the patient's physiological state is getting better, worse or staying the same, so they have to think about a lot of information all at once, again increasing cognitive load. These tasks are even more difficult if they are in a group or overlooked by doctors or senior nurses, as they will feel pressured into making quick decisions under stress so might make mistakes.

The new monitoring system tested by Drews & Doig (2014) gave nurses information about trends such as blood pressure or heart-rate changes, so they didn't have to think about both past and present information to make a decision; they could see instantly if they were stable or not and whether any was good or bad. To make the new display easier to read they also designed it to be uncluttered and visually simple, with colour and shape codes to show changes in patient condition. For example, a bar that changed colour was used to show how much oxygen was in their blood. Two types of information were given separately: current state and past variation.

This system was ergonomically better because it took into account the things that nurses reported problems with. This clearly mattered as the nurses were 30% faster to spot important changes than on the old system and were also more accurate. This was probably because it reduced cognitive load as they could access information more easily. This shows that considering human factors, such as cognitive load, helps people to interact with systems more effectively.

We say: This is a very good essay from Rina, linking the study to the value of ergonomics very effectively. It would have been even better if a little more had been said about how the study was done, specifically that they investigated through interviews what nurses found difficult about the old system, and that there was a key difference between the conditions with regard to additional information, e.g. whether it was automatic (for the new display group) or had to be accessed by a key press. Rina could then also have given the relevant results and their implications for accurate and rapid detection of problems.

C5
SPORT AND EXERCISE PSYCHOLOGY

Sport and exercise psychology is a broad field ranging from the study of the psychological benefits of exercise to factors affecting sports performance. Some researchers in this area work in applied settings, for example with professional athletes. Others are more concerned with theoretical questions. In this chapter we will consider six important topics:

1 **Arousal and anxiety:** We will consider what psychologists mean by the terms 'arousal' and 'anxiety'. We then look in detail at the relation between arousal, anxiety and performance with particular regard to Fazey & Hardy's study of performance catastrophes. We then consider methods of anxiety reduction in sport.

2 **Exercise and mental health:** In this section we will consider the benefits of exercise for mood and mental health. In particular we look in detail at a study by Lewis et al., who researched the impact of dance on mood in patients suffering from Parkinson's Disease. We will then consider strategies for using exercise deliberately to improve mental health.

3 **Motivation:** We will consider the concepts of self-efficacy and sports confidence. We will then look in detail at the role of imagery in confidence, with particular regard to a study by Munroe-Chandler et al., and then consider methods of improving athlete motivation.

4 **Personality:** In this section we will look at the concept of personality and explore how it has been applied to understanding participation and success in sport. In particular, we examine Kroll & Crenshaw's study of the relationship between personality and choice of sport. In addition, we will apply an understanding of personality to improving sports performance.

5 **Performing with others:** This section is concerned with the psychology of teams, coaching and leadership. We will look particularly closely at a study by Smith et al. on the use of a cognitive-behavioural approach to enhancing the effectiveness of coaching, and will apply our understanding to improving team performance.

6 **Audience effects:** This section is concerned with the effect of audiences on performance, with particular regard to the study by Zajonc of performance in cockroaches (yes, really!). We then apply this understanding to the improvement of sporting performance in front of spectators.

AROUSAL AND ANXIETY

KEY IDEAS

Stress involves a mismatch between the demands of a situation and the ability of an individual to cope with these demands. Some psychologists emphasise the importance of the stressful situation and others the characteristics of the individual trying to deal with it. Competitive sport places considerable demands on athletes so the ability of the individual to cope with this is key to how well they perform. It is important to realise, however, that sometimes testing our ability to cope in a stressful situation can be a stimulating challenge and so a positive experience.

BACKGROUND

If you take part in sport yourself you will almost certainly have experienced good and bad performances. Some days you feel 'in the zone' and everything goes smoothly. On other occasions you just can't get going, or you might feel too 'up tight' and your nerves get the better of you. These performance variations are largely the result of differences in your levels of arousal and anxiety. At elite levels of sport there is often little difference in the skill, fitness or motivation of athletes. Perhaps the most important factor separating winners from losers at this level is the ability to cope with arousal and anxiety (Jones, 1991).

What do psychologists mean by 'arousal,' 'stress' and 'anxiety?'

Let's be clear about what we mean by 'arousal,' 'stress' and 'anxiety.' Arousal is our general level of physical and psychological activation. We are low in arousal when we are tired, bored or sleeping, and we are high in arousal when we are excited, anxious or angry. **Stress** can be defined as a mismatch between the demands of a situation and the ability of an individual to cope. A struggle to cope with the pressure of a situation can be seen positively as a challenge, or negatively as a crisis.

High and low levels of arousal and stress can be both positive and negative experiences. Anxiety however is always a negative emotional state in which we experience high arousal accompanied by worrying. There are various aspects to anxiety, and psychologists have made important distinctions between state and trait anxiety, and between cognitive and somatic anxiety.

A trait is a stable personality characteristic that remains fairly constant across a range of situations. An athlete high in trait anxiety is thus consistently anxious. State anxiety, on the other hand, refers to the anxiety experienced before and during competition. The concept of state anxiety is probably of more use in sport psychology, as it is the anxiety we experience while participating in sport that directly impacts on our performance and is open to reduction by psychological techniques.

The term 'somatic' comes from the Greek *soma*, meaning body. Somatic anxiety is thus bodily anxiety, or the physical sensation of anxiety. This involves increased heart and breathing rates, along with 'butterflies in the stomach' – the sensation of blood being diverted away from the digestive system. Cognitive anxiety, by contrast, refers to anxiety in the mind. This takes the form of anxious thoughts, for example of doubts about one's own ability, and of mental images, such as scenes of losing.

Figure 5.1: Athletes experience stress when the demands of a situation stretch their ability to cope

Arousal and performance

There are two traditional approaches used to explain the relationship between arousal and performance: drive theory and the inverted-U hypothesis. Hull (1943) proposed drive theory as a general explanation of human performance and motivation. According to drive theory, there are three major factors influencing performance: the complexity of the motor task, physiological arousal, and learned tendencies to respond to a task in a certain way. The higher the level of physiological arousal, the more likely we are to adopt our dominant response to a situation, i.e. the learned tendency to respond in a particular way. If the task is a simple one and our dominant response is the correct one, then higher arousal will be associated with better performance. This can be expressed as an equation:

performance = arousal × habit

Drive theory can also be shown graphically (see Figure 5.2).

Where the task is a complex one involving fine motor skills, or if the athlete has acquired bad habits and the dominant response for the situation is wrong, high levels of arousal will inhibit performance. Because arousal level is greater in competition than in practice, and increases according to the importance of the competition, drive theory predicts that the best performances of high-level athletes will take place in high-level competition. It also predicts, however, that, because novices are more likely to have bad habits, they would be more likely to make mistakes under pressure.

The inverted-U hypothesis originated from Yerkes & Dodson (1908). The principle is that for every motor task we can carry out there is an optimum level of physiological arousal. Performance is best at this level and drops off when arousal rises above or falls below it.

The optimum level of arousal for a task depends on the complexity of the motor skills used to perform that task. For a complex task involving fine motor skill, such as placing a dart in the bull's-eye, low levels of arousal are preferable. For gross tasks, such as weightlifting, the optimum arousal level is much higher.

Anxiety and performance

The emphasis in modern sport psychology is more on anxiety than arousal as a predictor of performance. We owe much of our modern understanding of this relationship to the work of Fazey & Hardy (1988).

KEY RESEARCH

Fazey, J. & Hardy, L. (1988) *The inverted-U hypothesis: A catastrophe for sport psychology.* British Association of Sports Sciences Monograph, No. 1, Leeds: The National Coaching Foundation.

Aim

This was a theoretical paper rather than an empirical study. The aim was to identify limitations with the inverted-U model of arousal and performance, making use of the distinction between somatic and cognitive anxiety, and to propose an alternative model, explaining the relationship between anxiety and performance.

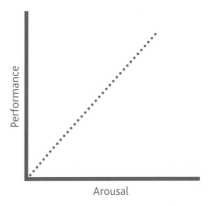

Figure 5.2: The relationship between performance and arousal for an expert performing a simple motor skill

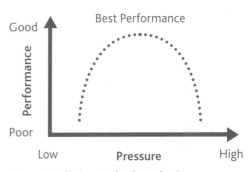

Figure 5.3: The inverted-U hypothesis

Figure 5.4: The optimum level of arousal for lifting weights is high

Method

The paper began with a review of problems with the inverted-U hypothesis of arousal and performance. Difficulties were examined under three headings:

- Difficulties with basic ideas
- Difficulties with evidence
- Difficulties with applications.

The authors then reviewed evidence concerning the relationship between stress and performance in other areas, for example in memory tasks, and the distinction between cognitive and somatic anxiety. They also looked at catastrophe models of behaviour, and considered whether Zeeman's model of stress and catastrophe could be applied to failure in sporting performance. Zeeman's model was demonstrated by a simple machine is shown in Figure 5.5.

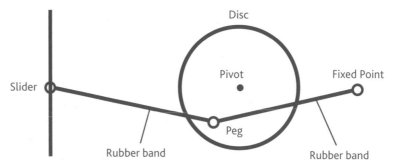

Figure 5.5: Zeeman's machine

When the disc is turned, the rubber bands are stretched until it passes a certain point where the tension is released and the disc jumps forward. Zeeman proposed that this is an analogy for the relationship between stress and performance. As stress increases so does performance until a point is reached where performance collapses. This is quite different to the smooth performance curve in the inverted-U hypothesis.

Based on Zeeman's model and the distinction between cognitive and somatic anxiety, Fazey & Hardy proposed a catastrophe model of the relationship between anxiety and performance.

Results

Three major problems were identified with existing literature concerning the inverted-U hypothesis:

- **Difficulties with basic ideas**. Most importantly many psychologists were using the terms 'arousal,' 'stress' and 'anxiety' interchangeably. In fact, while the inverted-U hypothesis described the relationship between performance and arousal, it did not adequately explain the more important relationship between *anxiety* and performance.
- **Difficulties with evidence**. There is a lack of consistent evidence for a particular relationship between stress and performance.
- **Difficulty in applying the model**. The inverted-U model predicts that when stress exceeds the optimum, performance will decline slightly, but that simply reducing stress slightly will bring back the optimum performance. In the authors' experience this is not the case and so the model has limited practical value.

Reviewing studies of the relationship between stress and performance suggested that in fact performance declines sharply once the optimum is exceeded. This is much more like the 'jump' shown when the disc in Zeeman's stress machine is turned.

Based on this evidence and the limitations of the inverted-U hypothesis, Fazey & Hardy proposed a catastrophe model to explain the relationship between anxiety and performance when athletes are performing under stress. Where physiological demand is high and cognitive demands are low, cognitive anxiety would be associated with good performance. However, where physiological demands are lower and cognitive demands are high, we would expect to see cognitive anxiety associated with poor performance. The authors illustrate this with a three-dimensional model, shown in Figure 5.6.

This is easier to understand in the form of a simplified two-dimensional diagram. In Figure 5.7 the green line represents performance in conditions of high physiological demand and low cognitive anxiety, the red line in conditions of high cognitive anxiety and low physiological demand.

Conclusion

By taking into account the difference between anxiety and arousal and between cognitive and somatic anxiety, and by using the analogy of Zeeman's catastrophe machine, the authors have produced a better model of the effect of anxiety and arousal on performance than the inverted-U hypothesis that most psychologists had previously used.

APPLICATION: MANAGING AROUSAL AND ANXIETY IN SPORT

Successful performance in sport depends largely on the ability of the individual to manage arousal and anxiety. Because anxiety has physiological and psychological dimensions its reduction can be approached on a physiological or psychological level. Biofeedback is an example of how arousal and the physiological aspects of anxiety can be tackled, while cognitive-behavioural therapy is an example of how the psychological aspects of anxiety may be addressed.

Biofeedback

Biofeedback is a strategy used to help people exert better control over their physiology. Arousal and anxiety involve physiological changes, such as increased heart rate and blood pressure. These are controlled by the autonomic nervous system, which works independently of our consciousness. Although we cannot directly perceive our heart rate and blood pressure, they have an effect on how we feel. So, for example, when we feel anxious, part of this unpleasant sensation will be the result of higher than usual heart rate and blood pressure.

The principle behind biofeedback is that the reason why we cannot normally control functions such as blood pressure and heart rate is because we cannot perceive them. Biofeedback aims to allow us to accurately judge our physiological state so that we can begin to learn to consciously control it. This involves using electronic instruments that measure autonomic functions

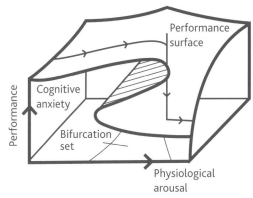

Figure 5.6: A 3-D image of Fazey & Hardy's model

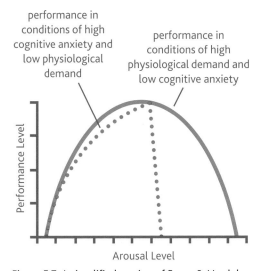

Figure 5.7: A simplified version of Fazey & Hardy's model

Figure 5.8: A GSR meter measures skin conductivity, a measure of anxiety

QUESTION SPOTLIGHT!

The specification asks for 'at least one technique to manage arousal and anxiety'. You should not therefore be asked specifically about biofeedback or CBT. Whether you learn one or both techniques, be sure you can write enough for an essay question.

and display them to us. Condron *et al.* (2008) identify the following as standard measures in modern clinical practice.

- EMG (electromyography): measures the electrical activity in muscle
- EEG (electroencephalography): measures brain waves
- GSR (galvanic skin response): measures sweatiness of skin
- HRV (heart rate variability): measures the variability in the time between heart beats, measured by an ECG (electrocardiogram) or heart monitor
- PST (peripheral skin temperature): measures skin temperature.

Each of these is a measure of physiological arousal, which in turn is a measure of anxiety and stress. Anxiety leads, for example, to increased sweating, reduced skin temperature, increased activity in muscles (twitchiness) and distinctive patterns in brain waves. Figure 5.8 shows the use of an GSR meter.

Electrodes are held in each hand. The more anxious the person becomes, the more they sweat and the more conductice their skin becomes. This means that more current passes between electrodes and the voltage displayed on the meter is higher. As the person successfully reduces their anxiety they can see the voltage decline on the meter. This helps gain conscious control over the anxiety levels. Anxiety is reduced by means of relaxation procedures. These include meditation and progressive muscle relaxation in which the patient focuses on relaxing groups of muscles in turn. It is possible to learn relaxation without biofeedback, but biofeedback helps by allowing the patient to see in real time when they are successfully reducing anxiety.

Biofeedback has been applied successfully to improving sports performance. De Witt (1980) described a case of a (American) football player who suffered from anxiety when having to catch a passed ball. He was asked to imagine various scenarios while he was connected to an EMG machine, which showed a pattern of muscle excitation suggesting anxiety. The football player was able to reduce his anxiety using relaxation techgniques, and helped by the fact that he could see his anxiety reducing on the EMG meter.

ACTIVITY

Using biodots

Ask your teacher if they or the science department have any biodots. These are a simple means of biofeedback. A biodot sits on your hand and changes colour according to your skin temperature, which is a crude measure of arousal. See if you can relax enough to change the dot colour.

Cognitive-behavioural therapy (CBT)

CBT has also been used to tackle anxiety in sport. Whereas biofeedback works on somatic anxiety, CBT works on cognitive anxiety. CBT involves identifying and modifying problematic thoughts that increase anxiety. For example, an athlete who believes they are likely to fail to perform well in a given situation, and that such failure would be a disaster, is actually more likely to mess up because these thoughts provoke so much anxiety. CBT would help this athlete by changing those thoughts.

The first stage of CBT is assessment. Puig & Pummell (2012) identify three aspects of assessment:

- Precipitating factors: what triggers anxiety, for example a particular sporting situation
- Predisposing factors: earlier experience where the tendency for anxiety was acquired, for example excessive pressure from parents
- Maintaining factors: any additional factors that lead to the anxiety being maintained, for example pressure from a coach or a sponsorship deal that depends on the athlete regularly winning

Dysfunctional automatic thoughts are then identified. These include 'I mustn't lose' and 'my opponents are probably better than me'. The therapist then puts together a hypothesis about how precipitating, predisposing and maintaining factors lead to the automatic thoughts, which in turn produce anxiety, including high physiological arousal. This is shared with the athlete.

Athlete and therapist then work together to test the validity of automatic thoughts. Some of these are probably irrational and can be challenged. For example, an athlete might say 'I know I'm going to lose.' A therapist would probably not say that this analysis was untrue, but they might ask the athlete to look closely at the evidence for the claim. Some automatic thoughts can be modified so as to be less threatening. An example is shown in Table 5.1 (from Puig & Pummell, 2012).

KEY IDEAS

CBT is the most popular form of psychological therapy practised by psychologists. The idea is to identify problem thoughts – these either come to the individual spontaneously or in response to particular circumstances – and to try to change them. This can involve arguing against the validity of the beliefs or testing them out. CBT sometimes involves directly changing behaviour as well as cognitions. This can, for example, involve desensitising people to situations that trigger anxiety or behavioural activation – getting people back into the habit of actively doing things rather than remaining passive.

TABLE 5.1: AN EXAMPLE OF MODIFYING AN AUTOMATIC THOUGHT USING CBT						
Situation	Mood	Automatic thoughts/ images	Evidence that supports hot thought	Evidence that does not support hot thought	Balanced thought	Mood
Before a match	Anxiety 80%	Everyone is better than me and I will lose this match.	I lost my previous match, the person I am playing won their previous four matches in a row.	I have only lost two of the last six matches, the other player has lost matches before too.	Although I may lose this match I may also win as I have done before. If I do lose there will be other opportunities.	Anxiety 50%

CBT can also involve working with deeper core beliefs. Negative core beliefs can be explored based on automatic thoughts. An example is shown below.

Therapist: 'what was going through your mind immediately before the match?'

Athlete: 'I was thinking that I was definitely going to lose.'

Therapist: 'And what would losing mean to you?'

Athlete: 'That people won't accept me as an athlete.'

Therapist: 'So what would that say about you?'

Athlete: 'That I'm a loser, a failure.'

The athlete's core belief here is that they are a failure. This kind of belief is common, but very dysfunctional. Core beliefs can be challenged by argument, or the therapist might set the athlete the task of asking 10 people whether they subscribed to the belief and collating the results.

Figure 5.9: Negative core beliefs are disabling but can be tackled by CBT

STRETCH & CHALLENGE ◎

Compare and contrast biofeedback and CBT. Draw up a table of similarities and differences. Which do you think would work better for you and why?

EVALUATION

Methodological issues

There are methodological issues in the study of sporting anxiety. As you can see in the previous section on usefulness of research, some of the research into interventions to tackle sporting anxiety has used very small samples. Studies such that of Lagos *et al.* and Turner & Barker successfully show that biofeedback and CBT can be effective in regulating sporting anxiety, larger samples are needed to establish how effective they are and what proportion of athletes benefit from them.

Another methodological issue concerns the validity of measures used to assess anxiety. Any study is only as valid as the measures used, and studies of sporting anxiety have tended to use a limited number of anxiety measures, based on self-report, i.e. questionnaires asking participants about their sport-related anxiety. All self-report measures are limited by their validity, which depends on a number of factors. There are concerns over the validity of sporting anxiety questionnaires, and this is a problem for this area of research.

Debates

Usefulness of research

We have seen in the application section that research into arousal and anxiety and their relationships to sporting performance have real-life applications. Fazey & Hardy's model predicts that regulating both physiological and cognitive anxiety can improve performance. Research into the use of biofeedback to control physiological arousal has supported its usefulness. For example in one recent study Lagos *et al.* (2008) describe the use of heart-rate variability biofeedback to help a golfer. After 10 sessions of biofeedback (no golfing instruction was given during this time) the golfer achieved his personal best, and his average score improved by 15 shots per 18-hole round.

There is also evidence to support the usefulness of CBT to regulate the cognitive aspects of sporting anxiety. Turner & Barker (2013) describe the use of REBT (a form of CBT emphasising vigorous argument with any beliefs that might impact on performance) with four elite youth cricketers. In all four cases competition anxiety was significantly reduced.

Nature vs nurture

Arousal and anxiety are influenced both by nature and nurture. It is possible to inherit a more reactive than usual nervous system (nature), and this will make us particularly likely to react to anxiety-provoking situations with high arousal. However, it is also true that experience (nurture) contributes to the experience of sporting anxiety. We have looked at an example of this in

the section on CBT. Predisposing factors for anxiety (Puig & Pummell, 2012) include experiences such as having parents that put us under great pressure to achieve and win. This kind of parenting is counterproductive because it can lead to high levels of cognitive anxiety that can trigger performance catastrophes.

Other early experiences that are likely to make us more anxious before sporting participation include those involving sporting humiliation. Losing is an inevitable part of sports training and need not cause a child great upset. However, humiliation is traumatic and likely to affect a developing athlete. Humiliation can result from being casually defeated and laughed at. There is an important role here for teachers and coaches to ensure that children who lose in competition or fail to grasp techniques do not experience humiliation.

Reductionism and holism

Some approaches to understanding the relationship between arousal and anxiety have been reductionist. Remember that reductionism is the tendency to reduce a complex aspect of human mind and behaviour to something simple like its biology. The inverted-U hypothesis is overly reductionist because it reduces the factors affecting performance to simply physiological arousal. It looks at the simple idea of arousal rather than the complex idea of anxiety. This is an example of biological reductionism. On the other hand, Fazey & Hardy's catastrophe theory is much more holistic because it considers both the role of physiological anxiety and cognitive anxiety.

Biofeedback is reductionist because it focuses simply on taking control of physiological arousal using a measure of arousal such as skin conductivity or muscle twitchiness. CBT on the other hand is more holistic because it looks at the ways in which cognitions can lead to increased physiological arousal.

Individual and situational explanations

The study of the relationship between performance and arousal and anxiety is firmly rooted in an individual differences approach. The emphasis is on the individual having a level of vulnerability influenced by genetic factors and acquiring anxiety responses through experience. For example, in Fazey & Hardy's model the emphasis is on individual levels of physiological arousal and of cognitive anxiety. However, situational factors also have a profound effect on sporting anxiety; team dynamics, leadership and spectator support all impact on anxiety and performance, and these are very much situational. We consider these factors later in the chapter.

TOPIC 2

EXERCISE AND MENTAL HEALTH

BACKGROUND

If you regularly take part in sport or other exercise you might notice that it has an effect on your mood. One reason for taking part in sport and exercise is because it appears to benefit our sense of well-being. Certainly if you are used to exercising and then don't for some reason you might feel irritable or down, and if we are feeling mildly depressed, anxious or irritable, some exercise might make us feel better. The benefits to physical health of regular physical exercise are well-known and straightforward to understand. The benefits to mental health are slightly less obvious and less well-established, but are nonetheless of great interest to psychologists.

What do psychologists mean by exercise and mental health?

Exercise

You will notice that this section of the specification is called 'sport and exercise psychology' rather than just 'sport psychology'. Sport and exercise psychology is a slightly broader field because it includes the study of non-competitive exercise as well as competitive sport. Exercise psychology has been recognised as a discipline in its own right since the 1980s (Moran, 2004). Exercise can be defined as physical activity undertaken in order to develop improved physical fitness. This is a broad concept. The kind of exercise a young able-bodied person might wish to undertake may be very different to the exercise suited to an older person or someone suffering from a physical disability. For some people, taking up exercise might mean taking a short walk each day. For others it might mean serious training of the kind associated with athletic training.

Exercise is usually of interest to psychologists for different reasons than is sport. Psychologists working in sport are primarily interested in understanding factors affecting performance and using this understanding to boost performance. Psychologists specialising in the field of exercise tend to be more concerned with understanding the benefits of exercise, motives for exercising, and ways to encourage people – not just athletes – to start and maintain regular exercise.

Mental health

Mental health and mental illness are examined in detail elsewhere in this book (see page 7). Briefly, mental health is often defined in terms of the absence of a mental illness. So if we are not suffering from severe enough symptoms of anxiety, depression, psychosis, etc., we can be seen as mentally healthy. However, many psychologists would see this as a very limited understanding of what it is to be mentally healthy. Jahoda (1958) suggested that, as well as lacking symptoms of

Figure 5.10: These two joggers are clearly happy

KEY IDEAS

Exercise is a sub-type of physical activity. Physical activity is a very broad category, including any movements of the body that require using energy. Exercise is purposeful physical activity aimed at improving the physical fitness of the exerciser.

KEY IDEAS

We all know what it is to have good and bad moods but to define **mood** any more scientifically than this is tricky. One way to think of moods comes from McNair *et al.* (1971). They identify six dimensions of mood: tension-anxiety, depression-dejection, anger-hostility, fatigue, inertia and confusion. These are measured by the Profile of Mood States (POMS), a popular test in sport psychology.

Figure 5.11: Aerobics improves mood in the short term

mental illness, to consider ourselves mentally healthy we should also be rational, have a realistic view of the world, be able to cope with stress, have good self-esteem, not depend on other people and successfully enjoy work, leisure and loving relationships. In short, we should be happy. Psychologists have studied the links between exercise and both mental illness and happiness.

Exercise and mood

It is well established that exercise has an acute (short-term) effect on mood. Hassmen & Blomstrand (2008) assessed mood before and after running a marathon in 106 male runners using the POMS. Although mood improved after the race, the authors noted that the improvement was less than typical of more moderate exercise. In another study Kennedy & Newton (1997) assessed mood with the POMS before and after aerobics classes of differing intensity. Mood improved irrespective of the intensity of the exercise.

Exercise and mental health

It seems then that exercise makes us feel better – at least in the short term. A related question concerns whether in the general population regular exercise is associated with lower levels of symptoms. A study from De Moor *et al.* (2006) addresses this question. For this study, 19,000 Dutch adults completed questionnaires about their mental health and exercise patterns. Exercisers were significantly lower in symptoms of anxiety and depression. However, they also differed in other characteristics, such as extroversion, so we cannot assume that the exercise was the cause of the better mental health.

Similar findings emerged in a study of 3400 Finns aged 25–64. A range of psychometric tests were administered in order to capture a holistic picture of mental health and well-being. Participants completed a standard test for depression, an anger scale, a cynicism and distrust scale, and a test of social integration. Participants who exercised twice or more a week scored significantly better on all these measures.

Explaining the benefits of exercise

Peluso & de Andrades (2005) have identified three possible psychological explanations to explain how exercise might prove beneficial to mental health.

- Distraction hypothesis is the idea that exercise shifts attention away from symptoms and their origins, allowing the patient relief from the cognitive aspects of mental illness and psychological distress.
- Self-efficacy hypothesis is the idea that exercise provides a challenge for the patient who can successfully take this on and therefore feel better about themselves.
- Social interaction hypothesis is the idea that the social interaction and likelihood of improved social support and developing positive new relationships through joint engagement with exercise improves coping ability.

They also suggest two possible physiological explanations for the link between exercise and mental health.

- Monoamine hypothesis is the idea that exercise boosts levels of the monoamine neurotransmitters – serotonin, noradrenaline and dopamine – that are known to be associated with depression and anxiety.

- Endorphin hypothesis is the idea that exercise triggers production of natural opiates – the brain's painkillers – called endorphins. The 'high' we get from these may override the negative feelings of depression and anxiety.

It is likely that all these mechanisms operate to some extent, but we have very little information about their relative importance.

KEY RESEARCH

Lewis, C., Annett, L.E. Davenport, S., Hall, A.A. & Lovatt, P. (2014) Mood changes following social dance sessions in people with Parkinson's Disease. *Journal of Health Psychology*, 19 (4).

Aim

Depression is a particular problem for patients with Parkinson's disease. Some, but not all, past studies have concluded that exercise is beneficial for mood in older people in general and for Parkinson's patients in particular. The aims of this study were to test whether dance would enhance mood in a group of older people, and to see whether this effect was different for those suffering from Parkinson's disease.

Method

Sample

A total of 37 people participated in the study; 19 were male and 18 female. They were aged between 50 and 80, the mean age being 65.5 years. Twenty-two participants had a diagnosis of Parkinson's disease. Physiotherapists rated this group as having mild to moderate Parkinson's. The participants were gathered through self-selecting sampling, either by responses to advertisements or through contacts in Parkinson's support groups.

Design and procedure

The study was experimental, using a mixed design. The two independent variables were Parkinson's status and short-long term exposure to dance. For the Parkinson's status IV, two groups were compared, those with a diagnosis of Parkinson's (experimental condition) and those without a diagnosis of Parkinson's (control group). This comparison was by independent measures. For the second IV, participants were assessed immediately after a dance class (short cycle) and after 12 weeks (long cycle). This part of the experimental design was repeated measures.

After completing a consent form, participants completed the Profile of Mood States in order to establish a baseline for their mood before the dance intervention. As well as the six subscales the POMS yielded a combined Total Mood Disturbance (TMD) score. Participants attended a 50-minute dance class run by a qualified instructor once a week for 10 weeks. Each dance class involved a 10-minute warm-up, 30 minutes of dance with a 5-minute break, and a 5-minute cool-down. The dance styles changed every two weeks and included Bollywood, Tango, Cheerleading, Old Time Music Hall, and Party dancing based on the Charleston and Saturday Night Fever. Participants completed a short form of the POMS called the BRUMS (Brunel University Mood Scale) after the first dance session, and the full POMS a few days after the tenth session.

Figure 5.12: A 'runner's high' results from the production of endorphins and improves mood

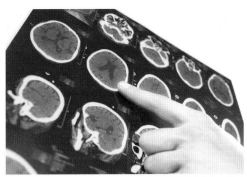

Figure 5.13: Parkinson's disease is caused by the loss of dopamine-producing cells in the *substantia negra* brain region

MATHS MOMENT 🖩

At the baseline, the Parkinson's group had a higher mean total mood disturbance than the control group (22.56 as opposed to 18.8), and a slightly larger standard deviation (33.3 as opposed to 29.59).

1. Define the mean and standard deviation.
2. Explain what these means and standard deviations tell us about the experimental and control groups in this study.

Results

Effect of 10 weeks of dance classes

Two participants, one from the experimental condition and one from the control group, dropped out. Five other participants failed to attend the final testing session owing to illness, holiday or other commitment. For the remaining participants in both groups TMD scores were significantly lower following the 10-week dance intervention. Changes in each POMS subscale were also analysed. Anger declined most significantly ($p<0.005$), with anxiety-tension also declining significantly ($p<0.038$). Vigour increased slightly but this did not quite reach significance. The effect of dance did not differ significantly between the experimental and control groups.

Effect of one dance class

All participants in both groups reported improvement in mood after a single dance class. TMD scores improved significantly from baseline ($p<0.033$). BRUMS subscales of tension-anxiety and vigour were significantly improved ($p<0.045$ for tension-anxiety and $p<0.016$ for vigour). Other improvements, e.g. in depression scores did not reach significance.

Conclusion

Dance improves mood in older people. A significant short-term improvement can be seen after a single session, and a larger improvement, maintained over a few days, results from a programme of sessions. The effect is significant on total mood disturbance and particularly significant for tension-anxiety (short and long cycle) and anger (long cycle).

APPLICATION: EXERCISE STRATEGIES TO IMPROVE MENTAL HEALTH

There are a number of ways in which exercise can be used to improve mood and mental health. Dance is one popular approach; aerobic exercise is another. In addition to these approaches there is increasing interest in so-called 'green exercise,' which involves interacting with the natural environment – for example gardening, walking or taking part in conservation work.

Dance

We have already seen in the key study in this chapter that weekly dance classes improve mood in older people, including those suffering from Parkinson's disease. Other studies have confirmed these benefits in younger people. In an Australian study McInman & Berger (1993) demonstrated that aerobic dance sessions improved mood in female students. As compared to controls, dancers improved very significantly in most dimensions of the POMS, with improvements reaching a significance of $p<0.001$ except for the vigour subscale.

However, not all studies have confirmed the benefits of dance for mental health. Other studies with older people have shown different findings. Alpert (2009) introduced 13 healthy women with a mean age of 68 to jazz dance, assessing their mood and balance before and after a course of sessions. Balance was improved, but not mood. Another study by Netz & Lidor (2003) found that swimming, yoga and Feldenkrais awareness through movement, but not dance, improved mood in 147 female Israeli teachers. These negative findings do not necessarily mean that dance is not beneficial for mood. It does seem, however, that there must be other variables – perhaps in the participants and perhaps in the nature of the dance classes – that moderate the impact of dance on mood.

Cardio-vascular exercise

We have already established that people who participate in regular exercise tend to have more positive moods (see page 266). However, this leaves us unclear as to whether exercise actually improves mood or whether some lurking variable, such as personality or physical health, affects both mood and the likelihood of exercise participation. Fortunately, experiments have established that mood can be improved by participating in vigorous aerobic exercise. Hansen, *et al.* (2001) carried out an experiment to test the effect of exercise on twenty-one 20–26-year-old students. They spent 10, 20 and 30 minutes on an exercise bicycle. Mood was assessed after each 10-minute session using a Profile of Mood States (POMS). Confusion, fatigue and negative emotion declined significantly after 10 minutes and again after 20 minutes. Extra exercise time beyond 20 minutes did not improve mood further.

Figure 5.14: Just 10 minutes on an exercise bike significantly improves mood

Other studies have focused on the effect of exercise on specific groups of participants. Arent, *et al.* (2000) meta-analysed the results of 32 studies looking at the effect of exercise on mood in older adults. It was concluded that regular exercise had a moderate but consistently positive effect on mood in older people. Other studies have examined the suggestion that exercise can relieve mood in people suffering from mood disorders. Bartholomew, *et al.* (2005) tested whether a single bout of moderately intensive exercise would improve mood in patients with a diagnosis of major depression. Forty participants were randomly assigned to either 30 minutes of quiet rest or 30 minutes of treadmill exercise, then both groups were assessed for mood using the POMS. Both conditions improved patients' mood but in different ways. Both groups reported a decline in anger, confusion, fatigue and tension. However, only the exercise group also reported improved well-being and energy.

Most research has involved aerobic exercise, which is oriented towards developing the health of the cardiovascular system. However, a smaller body of research has involved resistance exercise, which is oriented towards increasing muscular strength. A study by Katsura *et al.* (2010) reported that aquatic strength training in older Japanese adults was associated with improvement in POMS scores comparable to the effects of aerobic exercise. Currently there is only a small body of research into the benefits of resistance training for mood, so conclusions are uncertain.

Green exercise

Green exercise refers to the kind of exercise associated with enhanced awareness of the natural environment. It includes walking, dog-walking, gardening, horticulture and conservation work. A study reported by Peacock, Hine & Pretty (2007) looked at the effect of outdoor walking on mood. Before-and-after POMS scores were compared with a control group who walked indoors. Results were dramatic. Total mood disturbance improved massively in the outdoor walking group (*p*<0.01), but not at all in the indoor walking group. Results are shown in Figure 5.15.

Qualitative data also revealed something of why the outdoor walk might have been so effective. Comments included the following:

*   'It makes you feel good in the fresh air, looking at the water makes you feel relaxed. Joining in with other people. I like walking in the countryside.'
*   'Meeting others, visiting different places, fresh air, exercise and talking to others.'
*   'Getting close to God's beautiful creation.'
*   'Scenery.'

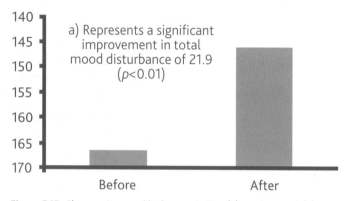

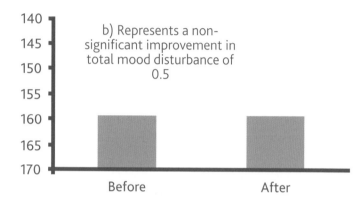

Figure 5.15: Changes in mood before and after (a) outdoor and (b) indoor walks

MATHS MOMENT 🖩

The study by Peacock *et al*. (2007) includes qualitative and quantitative data. Explain the difference between quantitative and qualitative data and suggest why using both kinds of data were helpful in this study.

EVALUATION

Methodological and ethical issues

There are some methodological strengths to the Lewis *et al.* study. A standard measure of mood was used. Several kinds of dance were incorporated into the programme so that if a particular dance style were ineffective this effect should be compensated for. Analysis compared both baseline and post-treatment scores and differences between the two groups – healthy controls and Parkinson's patients – so it was possible to tease out a range of possible effects.

There are, however, some methodological issues with the study that limit its usefulness. Because the study compared Parkinson's patients with healthy controls there could be no random allocation to conditions, so we don't know how closely the two groups were matched. The study is therefore a quasi-experiment rather than a true experiment and may be confounded by differences between the groups. The sample was also fairly small and this was made worse by the drop-out of some participants.

In terms of ethical issues, studies such as that conducted by Lewis *et al.* are important for understanding ways to alleviate suffering, so there is an argument that even if they put participants at risk they are still justifiable. However, if such studies are well enough designed they minimise risks in any case. To take the example of the Lewis *et al.* study, there are no issues of consent – participants gave full informed consent – and no deception was necessary. Several participants were allowed to not complete the study and no individual details published in the study made any individuals identifiable.

There is a risk that a participant might have suffered an injury during a dance lesson, but this risk was minimised by having classes run by an experienced instructor. Dance is also within the normal activities we might expect an older person to participate in, and participants were not exposed to additional risk beyond what we might reasonably expect them to experience in daily life.

Debates

Usefulness of research

One of the major strengths of this area of research is its enormous practical application. Currently mental illness accounts for millions of lost days to the economy and a huge cost to the National Health Service, not to mention the enormous personal suffering experienced by individuals. There is no suggestion that activities such as dance, aerobics or green exercise are a magic bullet that will cure most mental illness. However, it does appear that, especially in the cases of mild depression and anxiety, finding the right exercise for the individual may alleviate symptoms and improve quality of life for a lot of people. The National Institute for Clinical Excellence (2009) have recommended that exercise should be tried for moderate depression before formal treatment is considered.

Nature vs nurture

There are nature–nurture debates around both mental health and exercise participation. It seems that mental health is influenced both by multiple genetic variations and multiple developmental influences. Exercise is one of the environmental influences. This is important because, while we currently are not able to manipulate the genes that affect mental health, we can encourage people to participate in exercise and so improve their mental health. There is also something of a debate around exercise participation. People's natural activity levels are affected by their genetic make-up, but we can manipulate their environment by encouraging exercise participation.

Reductionism and holism

Mental health can be looked at in a reductionist or holistic way. Whenever we define mental health as the absence of symptoms this is reductionist because we are simplifying mental health. A more holistic approach to mental health is to look at the different dimensions of mood, as is done in research using the POMS. This includes measures of anxiety and depression but also of anger (a normal emotional experience), fatigue and vigour – physiological experiences of high and low energy levels. Much of the research into exercise and mental health, including the key study by Lewis *et al.* makes use of the POMS and so can be said to be quite holistic in approach.

Psychology as science

The study by Lewis *et al.* conforms to the standards of good science. The design was experimental. Independent variables were identified and manipulated. A standard measure of outcome (the POMS) was used, this having acceptable reliability and validity. The procedure would be straightforward to replicate.

MOTIVATION AND SPORT

BACKGROUND

In this section we are concerned with the importance of motivation for sporting performance. Picture yourself for a moment in the eighth round of a professional boxing bout. You are roughly level on points so it's all to fight for but you are exhausted and battered. If you give up, you could be in the pub in half an hour. This is an extreme example, but it is also more or the less the position many athletes find themselves in when in high-level competition. So why don't they give up? And what made them work hard enough to get to that position in the first place? Regardless of talent, athletes have to work extremely hard for their successes. On the other side of the coin, why do so many athletes reach the level they have aspired to for years then quickly fade away? This is the fascinating area of human motivation.

What do psychologists mean by motivation?

In the broadest sense, motivation is whatever makes us carry out behaviours – at least *goal-directed* behaviours, acts that are carried out deliberately for a purpose. Taylor & Wilson provide a sport-specific definition of motivation: 'the inclination to pursue and persist in activities related to one's sport' (2005: p.5). We are thus interested both in why athletes want to do sport in the first place, and in what makes them go to the considerable effort needed to continue and succeed in it.

When athletes are highly motivated 'they work hard in training and give 100% effort when competing' (Duda & Pensgard, 2002: p.49). They also tend to respond better to difficulties, which can include a losing streak, injury or loss of confidence. It is important for all those who employ, coach or teach athletes to understand the ways in which their own behaviour can affect the motivation of the athlete.

Intrinsic and extrinsic motivation

There is an important distinction between intrinsic and extrinsic motivation. This is absolutely central to understanding why people pursue sporting goals. Intrinsic motives are those that come from within the individual. We might, for example, relish the physical sensations experienced in sport, and derive personal satisfaction from improving our performance. Competition provides us with excitement, and training with friends can be a happy social experience. What these factors have in common is the pleasure associated with sport.

Extrinsic motives are the external rewards that we can gain from taking part and succeeding sport. These include the obvious rewards such as trophies and lucrative prizes and contracts, but also less obvious but nonetheless powerful rewards such as social status and attractiveness.

Figure 5.16: Boxing is exhausting and really hurts. Boxers must be extremely motivated to deliberately put themselves in this position

Figure 5.17: The rewards of extreme ironing are mostly intrinsic

ACTIVITY ✳

Which of these motivators would you class as intrinsic and which as extrinsic? Some may have elements of both so don't be afraid to debate them.

- The prospect of gaining the next belt in judo
- The chance of winning a place in the county rugby team
- The excitement of competing in extreme ironing at a famously challenging course
- The views you will see (weather permitting) if you climb Snowdon
- The experience of cycling with your new carbon-frame road bike
- The opportunity to tour with your college football team.

DO IT YOURSELF 🔍

As a group, record your own motives for participating in sport. What factors emerge as most important overall? To what extent are they intrinsic motives?

Research has strongly supported the importance of intrinsic motivation, both in the decision to participate in sport and in achieving a good performance. Studies to assess people's reasons for taking part in sport have tended to find that people report intrinsic rather than extrinsic motives. Ashford *et al.* (1993) interviewed 336 English adults (chosen on the basis of their use of a community sports centre) in order to ascertain why they participated in sports. Four intrinsic motivators emerged from their responses: physical well-being, psychological well-being, improvement of performance, and assertive achievement (defined as achieving personal and competitive goals).

Self-efficacy

Bandura (1982) introduced the concept of self-efficacy to sport psychology. Self-efficacy is often confused with self-esteem, but actually the two concepts are quite distinct. Whereas self-esteem is the emotional experience of how we feel about ourselves, self-efficacy refers to our beliefs about our abilities. As well as being a cognitive rather than emotional phenomenon, self-efficacy differs further from self-esteem in being situation-specific. Whereas our self-esteem is fairly constant and generalises across quite different situations, we can have different self-efficacy in different situations. If we have good sporting self-efficacy we believe we have a good level of skill in our sport and this generally has a positive impact on our motivation.

We get the information about our sporting abilities from several sources (Schunk, 1991). We draw on our past experiences of successful and unsuccessful performance. We can be persuaded by other people. We also look at the self-efficacy of our peers. If other people of similar ability believe they can do something, then it makes sense that we will also be able to. We also interpret our physiology. If for example we are in a relaxed state we might interpret this as meaning we can cope with the task at hand. On the other hand, if we are tense for whatever reason, we may interpret this as anxiety about being able to succeed, reducing our self-efficacy.

Figure 5.18: Experience of winning enhances self-confidence

KEY IDEAS

According to Paivio (1985) **imagery** serves cognitive and motivational functions, each of which can be divided into general and specific. Cognitive-general functions include planning routines or game plans. Cognitive-specific functions include rehearsing a move like a tennis serve or a free kick. Motivation-general functions include arousal regulation (calming down or psyching up before a match) and motivation-specific (imagining a goal like standing on a medal-winners' podium). Hall *et al.* (1998) extended the idea of motivation-general imagery to include motivation-general arousal (**MG-A**) imagery, which is about emotional regulation, and motivation-general mastery (**MG-M**) imagery, which is about mastery, self-confidence and mental toughness. The key study in this topic is concerned with MG-M imagery.

Sports confidence

This is a subtly different concept. Whereas self-efficacy refers to our beliefs in our abilities to carry out particular tasks or skills, sports confidence is about our beliefs around our ability to succeed in sport, i.e. to win. If we believe we are likely to win when entering a sporting situation then we can be said to be confident. This is different from having good self-efficacy, which would manifest as the belief that we are capable of the skills needed to perform well. Confidence is likely to be influenced by a range of factors:

- Prior achievement: past experience of sporting success suggests that we can be successful again.
- Self-regulation: confidence also requires that we can regulate our anxiety levels in the context of stressful situations.
- Climate: this refers to the general atmosphere in which we prepare for sporting events. A calm, supportive climate boosts confidence.

Confidence is believed to be one of the most consistent factors predicting success in competition.

Imagery and confidence

Bandura (1997) suggests that **imagery** is a way to enhance both self-confidence and self-efficacy. Imagery involves imagining scenes taking place. This can serve a range of functions, including enhancing motivation.

There is evidence to show that **MG-M** imagery is associated with higher levels of both self-efficacy and self-confidence. Mills, *et al.* (2001) found that athletes high in self-efficacy were more likely to use MG-M imagery than those low in self-efficacy. In another study, Callow, *et al.* (2001) showed that a 20-week programme of MG-M imagery enhanced the self-confidence of two of three elite adult male badminton players.

KEY RESEARCH

Munroe-Chandler, K., Hall, C. & Fishburne, G. (2008) Playing with confidence: The relationship between imagery use and self-confidence and self-efficacy in youth soccer players. *Journal of Sports Sciences,* 26 (14), 1539–1546.

Aim

Previous research into self-confidence and self-efficacy had focused very much on adult elite-level athletes. The aim of this study was to examine the relationships between imagery and self-confidence and self-efficacy in younger athletes competing at both recreational and competitive levels. More specifically, the relationships between MG-M imagery and self-confidence and self-efficacy were investigated in 11–14-year-old football (soccer) players who played at two levels, the Canadian House league (non-elite) and Travel League (elite). Two hypotheses were tested:

- MG-M imagery is a significant predictor of self-confidence and self-efficacy.
- The relationship between MG-M imagery and self-efficacy and self-confidence is stronger in elite than non-elite athletes.

Method

Sample

56 male and 69 female football players from South West Ontario, Canada, took part in the study. They were aged 11–14 years. 72 played at House (recreational, non-elite) level, and 50 played at Travel (elite) level. Three participants did not report their level, so their scores were removed from the analysis.

Design and procedure

The design included a quasi-experimental element in which imagery, self-confidence and self-efficacy were compared in the elite and non-elite footballers. There was also a correlational aspect to the design in which the relationships between imagery and self-confidence and self-efficacy were calculated using a Pearson's Product Moment Correlation. Imagery, self-confidence and self-efficacy were all assessed using standard measures.

Figure 5.19: Football was chosen for this study as it has clearly defined recreational and competitive levels

- Imagery was assessed using the Sport Imagery Questionnaire for Children. This consists of 21 statements scored from 1 (not at all) to 5 (very often). An example of a statement measuring MG-M imagery is: 'I see myself being mentally strong.'

- Self-confidence was assessed using the Competitive State Anxiety Inventory for Children (CSAI-2C). This is a 15-item questionnaire measuring confidence and anxiety.

- Self-efficacy was measured using the Self-efficacy Scale for Soccer (SEQ-S). This consists of five items assessing confidence in mental abilities each of which has a 100-point scale from 0 (no confidence) to 100 (complete confidence).

Player and parental consent were obtained, then players were asked to complete the questionnaires, along with some general information about age, gender, etc., before a mid-season training session. Participants took approximately 15 minutes to complete the questionnaire.

Results

As predicted, strong positive correlations were found between the use of MGM imagery and both self-confidence (0.64) and self-efficacy (0.66). These results were significant at the $p<0.01$ level. The use of all types of imagery was in fact correlated with confidence and self-efficacy but to a lesser extent than with MG-M imagery. There was also a strong correlation between self-confidence and self-efficacy. Table 5.2 shows the matrix of correlations.

TABLE 5.2: CORRELATIONS FOR IMAGERY, SELF-CONFIDENCE AND SELF-EFFICACY							
	CS	CG	MS	MG-A	MG-M	Confidence	Self-efficacy
CS	1.00						
CG	0.45**	1.00					
MS	0.46**	0.41**	1.00				
MG-A	0.43**	0.37**	0.50**	1.00			
MG-M	0.53**	0.52**	0.54**	0.58**	1.00		
Confidence	0.38**	0.42**	0.53**	0.52**	0.64**	1.00	
Self-efficacy	0.31**	0.41**	0.39**	0.43**	0.66**	0.64**	1.00

Note: **Correlation is significant at the 0.01 level (2-tailed).

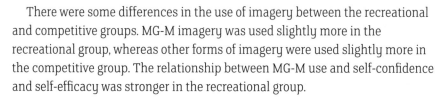
There were some differences in the use of imagery between the recreational and competitive groups. MG-M imagery was used slightly more in the recreational group, whereas other forms of imagery were used slightly more in the competitive group. The relationship between MG-M use and self-confidence and self-efficacy was stronger in the recreational group.

Conclusions

As predicted, MG-M imagery was a strong predictor of both self-confidence and self-efficacy, significantly stronger than other forms of imagery. However, counter to the second hypothesis the relationship between use of MG-M imagery and confidence and self-efficacy was stronger in the recreational group than in the competitive group. Overall differences in imagery and confidence/self-efficacy between the two groups were modest.

APPLICATION: MOTIVATING ATHLETES

Motivating athletes is one of the major tasks of the sport psychologist. This can be done in various ways.

Working with intrinsic and extrinsic motivation

Because intrinsic factors are so important in sporting participation, a key aim of research has been to improve our understanding of what influences intrinsic motivation. Amorose & Horn (2001) assessed 72 American college athletes aged 17–19 on their intrinsic motivation at the beginning and end of their first year of inter-college level participation. They were questioned about the time spent training, their coaching, and whether they had sports scholarships. Neither scholarship status nor time had any impact on the extent to which the participants maintained their initial levels of intrinsic motivation. However, the behaviour of coaches had a profound impact. Those whose coaches spent more time in instruction and less time in autocratic behaviour (i.e. throwing their weight about) tended to display significant increases in their intrinsic motivation during the year. There is clearly a practical application here: coaches can improve intrinsic motivation by focusing on developing technique.

Common sense suggests that if we throw some extrinsic motivation into the equation as well then we will increase the athlete's total motivation. This is known as the additive principle, shown in the equation below.

Intrinsic motivation + extrinsic motivation = maximum motivation

There are numerous extrinsic rewards available to top-class athletes. As well as the high salaries paid to some professionals, there may be prize money and sponsorship money. Athletes also have high social status and are likely to be considered a good sexual 'catch'. Until the 1970s it was standard wisdom to provide athletes with extrinsic rewards in order to make use of the additive principle. However, it seems that in this case common sense is wrong, and introducing large material rewards undermines rather than enhances intrinsic motivation. In one study, Sturman & Thibodeau (2001) tracked the performance of 33 American baseball professionals for two seasons before and two seasons after they signed lucrative new contracts. There was a sharp decline

Figure 5.20: Aggressive coaching can undermine intrinsic motivation

in performance as measured by batting average, number of home runs, etc., immediately following the new contract, and lasting for around one season. This suggests that the players' intrinsic motivation was undermined by their increase in salary. This leads us to a further practical application: keeping athletes focused on their intrinsic motives and not distracting them with a focus on extrinsic motivation.

Manipulating self-efficacy

There is no suggestion that self-efficacy is a complete explanation of sporting motivation, however it does appear to be one influence. Importantly, it is an influence that can be harnessed by coaches and teachers to improve motivation. Wells *et al.* (1993) demonstrated the power of manipulating self-efficacy. They randomly divided student participants into three groups and gave them weight-lifting tasks. In one condition the participants were given accurate feedback about how much they were lifting. In another condition they were misled into believing they were lifting heavier weights, and in the final condition they were misled into thinking they were lifting lighter weights. The three groups were then compared on how much they could lift, and the group who believed that they had lifted heavier weights than they really had were actually able to lift the most. This demonstrates both the power of self-efficacy and the ease with which a good coach can improve it, not necessarily by lying to athletes but by emphasising the positive aspects of their performance.

Using imagery to develop confidence

Recall the study by Callow *et al.* (2001). They tried out a 20-week training programme designed to use MG-M imagery on three adult badminton players. They assessed sporting self-confidence before and after the programme. Two of the three showed significantly improved confidence after the programme, while the third developed a more stable level of confidence. Callow & Waters (2005) demonstrated a similar impact on flat-race jockeys. Two of three jockeys showed significantly improved self-confidence following six sessions of imagery over three weeks. Jones *et al.* (2002) tested a similar programme with 33 female novice climbers and found that following four 1-hour imagery sessions they showed significant improvements in climbing self-efficacy as compared to a control group who undertook light exercise sessions instead.

Figure 5.21: False feedback has been shown to affect the self-efficacy of weight-lifters

Figure 5.22: Imagery training improved the self-confidence and self-efficacy of jockeys

EVALUATION

Methodological and ethical issues

The sample and sampling used in the Munroe-Chandler *et al.* study raise issues. The overall sample size was fairly small for a study of this kind – especially given that participants simply had to fill in questionnaires at their training grounds. The small sample size was compounded by the fact that there were four groups tasking part: recreational-male, recreational-female, competitive-male and competitive-female. The sampling method was by opportunity so participants may not have been representative of their population. It is also unclear whether there are cultural differences in the use of mental imagery, so it may be that the results gathered in Canada do not generalise internationally. That said, strengths of the study included that it was conducted on children and that it included both recreational and competitive athletes, extending the results from previous studies involving elite level athletes.

The study made use of user-friendly and standard measurement tools, the reliability of which had been previously tested. This is a strength of the methodology. However, the tools used have only moderately good reliability. The internal reliability for example of the imagery questionnaire is only 0.66–0.7. This is barely adequate for research purposes, and this is definitely a limitation of the study.

There is also a possible conceptual limitation in the distinction between self-efficacy and self-confidence. Although there is a clear theoretical difference between confidence in winning and confidence in technique it is not clear whether the questionnaires used to measure them adequately differentiated between them. The strong 0.64 correlation between self-efficacy and self-confidence suggests that they may not be distinct variables.

Ethics is a strength of the Munroe-Chandler *et al.* study. Participants agreed to take part and parental permission was obtained. There was little or no risk of harm or distress, and the study was conducted in 15 minutes or so before training, meaning that there was little chance for boredom and that participants' lives were not disrupted. Deceit and uninformed consent were not necessary for the study to work. This is a good example of a study where few ethical issues are raised and those that are are dealt with appropriately.

Debates

Usefulness of research

Usefulness is a strength of the Munroe-Chandler *et al.* study and others like it. Unlike some areas of sport psychology that are mostly of academic interest, there is a clear application for imagery research in working with athletes: imagery training improves performance, and studies such as this have shown that MG-M imagery is the most important type of imagery to use in training. The effectiveness of this type of training has been demonstrated with jockeys, badminton players and climbers (see page 277). Sport psychologists and coaches can directly apply results of these studies in their work to improve athletic performance.

Reductionism and holism

This approach to motivation can be described as reductionist. Human motivation is complex and involves a range of factors, from satisfaction of instinctive needs to learnt needs to achieve and to avoid failure. The mental images we form of motivational scenes can potentially tie into all these aspects of motivation, and this may be why it is a powerful technique to enhance sporting motivation. However, it would be a mistake to think that, just because we can enhance motivation using imagery, we can understand the complexities of human motives just with reference to imagery.

Psychology as science

Although we often think of reductionism as a weakness, it is necessary to carry out scientific research. By narrowing down the broad field of motivation to look in particular at the role of imagery, researchers such as Munroe-Chandler *et al.* have been able to carry out solid scientific research. Their study has good reliability and they used standard tools to measure well-established ideas: self-confidence, self-efficacy and imagery, testing hypotheses based on past research. This is good science.

PERSONALITY

BACKGROUND

Whether you take part in sport or not you may have a view about sport and personality. Think about people you know who participate in sport. Think as well about sporting personalities you will have seen on TV. Are they a particular type of person? How do they differ from other people you know who don't normally take part in sport? If you have ever met elite athletes, how about them? Is there a personality characteristic that marks them out as different to the run of the mill weekend amateur? And what about different types of sport? Forget physique for a moment – is a rugby player a different sort of person to a cyclist or golfer? If so why might that be? Psychologists have been fascinated with these questions and the idea of the sporting personality.

What do psychologists mean by personality?

According to the American Psychological Association, the word 'personality' refers to our 'individual differences in patterns of thinking, feeling and behaving'. In other words it is our personal characteristics – what make us distinctive from other people. There are many different ways to explain personality and its origins. Most sport psychologists have made use of **trait theories**. These identify key characteristics or *traits* of personality.

Trait theories of personality

Trait theories all aim to identify and describe the key traits that make us all different. The differences between different trait theories concern how many traits we have and what they are. The trait theories that have been most important in sport psychology are as follows

- Eysenck's three factor model. Hans Eysenck (1965) proposed that we can explain personality with just three traits; extroversion – liveliness and sociability, neuroticism – emotional instability and psychoticism – tough-mindedness.
- Cattell's 16PF (personality factors). Raymond Cattell (1956) took a different view and proposed 16 traits. These are shown in Table 5.3 on page 280.

Figure 5.23: What sort of personality might these rugby players have?

KEY IDEAS

Personality trait theories are different from other personality theories in that they are descriptive, i.e. their main aim is to describe the major aspects of personality. They are not usually causal theories, so they are not primarily about explaining where personality comes from. An exception comes from Hans Eysenck, who suggested that traits are primarily genetic in origin and are linked to activity in particular brain systems.

TABLE 5.3: CATTELL'S 16 TRAITS		
reserved	←→	outgoing
unintelligent	←→	intelligent
stable	←→	unstable
humble	←→	assertive
sober	←→	happy-go-lucky
expedient	←→	conscientious
shy	←→	adventurous
tough-minded	←→	tender-minded
trusting	←→	suspicious
practical	←→	imaginative
forthright	←→	shrewd
placid	←→	apprehensive
conservative	←→	experimenting
group-dependent	←→	self-sufficient
undisciplined	←→	controlled
relaxed	←→	tense

- Costa & McCrae's (1987) Five Factor Model. Based on the research conducted up to the 1980s, Costa & McCrae proposed that a 'Big Five' traits stood out as key to understanding human personality. These are extroversion and neuroticism, as in Eysenck's theory, but also openness to new experience, agreeableness (niceness), and conscientiousness.

Testing personality traits

Eysenck, Cattell and Costa & McCrae have all developed personality tests to assess people on their traits. These are self-rating inventories, i.e. banks of statements to which participants respond: yes/no in the Eysenck Personality Questionnaire; true/false in Cattell's 16PFl; and a 5-point strongly agree to strongly disagree for the Costa & McCrae 5-factor test, known as the NEO-PI. Each statement is related to one trait being measured. There are 240 questions in the NEO-PI, so if you are tempted to assess your own personality, make sure you set aside a reasonable length of time!

Sport and personality

Psychologists have studied the links between personality and sporting participation, sporting success and choice of sport.

Personality and sporting participation

Eysenck *et al.* (1982) suggested that people high in psychoticism and extroversion are more likely to take up a sport than others. This is because sport can provide both the social and physical stimulation craved by extroverts, and because those high in psychoticism are suited to the competitiveness and assertiveness/aggression involved in sport.

Some, though by no means all research has supported Eysenck's position. Francis *et al.* (1998) compared Irish female students who participated in university hockey clubs with a control group of female students with no formal involvement in sport. The hockey players scored significantly higher in

WEB WATCH @

There are many Internet sites where you can carry out personality tests. Usually these are not the same as the tests you read about in textbooks – the real NEO-PI and 16PF, for example, are heavily protected by copyright law.

This test uses items not from the NEO-PI but from another well-known test of the 'Big Five' personality traits:

http://personality-testing.info/tests/BIG5.php

Have a look at it if it interests you, but beware that you are not qualified to carry out psychometric tests on other people. Only look at your own scores if you are absolutely sure you won't be worried by the results. The main reason for looking at a test like this is not to assess your own personality but to think critically about the test. How valid do you think it is?

extroversion and psychoticism as measured by the EPQ. Although these results support Eysenck's view we need to remember that university hockey players cannot be taken as representative of athletes as a whole. Hockey is a team sport in which players typically build a close-knit team identity, and the high levels of extroversion found in hockey players may reflect team players rather than athletes *per se.*

Figure 5.24: Hockey players tend to be extrovert

Personality and sporting success

Tutko & Ogilvie (1966) proposed that athletic performance could be explained in terms of personality traits. They suggested 11 traits associated with performance: aggression, 'coachability', conscientiousness, determination, drive, emotional control, guilt-proneness, leadership, mental toughness, self-confidence and trust. These were measured by a self-rating inventory called the Athletic Motivation Inventory (AMI). It is generally agreed nowadays that the AMI had some serious flaws, both in the traits it identified (there is, for example, little evidence for leadership or coachability as stable traits) and in the items used to measure them. It is thus of little use in predicting performance.

Contemporary research using more widely accepted personality tests has provided some support for the idea that personality can impact on performance. Garland & Barry (1990) categorised 272 American university football players into different levels of skill and tested them with the 16PF. They found that four traits were significantly associated with skill; tough-mindedness, extroversion, group-dependence and emotional stability. Between them these traits accounted for 29% of the variance in skill level. However not all studies have found significant results and the link between personality traits and sporting success remains controversial.

Personality and choice of sport

Whereas results of studies into sporting participation and success have produced mixed results, there is stronger evidence linking personality to choice of sport. This makes sense when we stop and think about the different demands of different sports. For example, using Cattell's 16PF personality test, Schurr *et al.* (1977) found that team athletes were more anxious and extrovert than athletes favouring individual sports. The greater extroversion would be helpful working together in a team, whereas a solo athlete who has to manage anxiety on their own might be advantaged by low levels of neuroticism.

Differing levels of risk in different sports may also attract athletes with different personalities. Diehm & Armatas (2004) compared the traits of 44 golfers (a low-risk sport) and 41 surfers (high-risk) using Costa & McCrae's 5-factor personality test, the NEO-PI. Surfers were found to be significantly higher on the openness scale, meaning that they were more open to new experiences.

KEY RESEARCH

Kroll, W. & Crenshaw, W. (1970) Multivariate personality profile analysis of four athletic groups. *Contemporary Psychology of Sport,* 97–106.

Aim

The aim of this study was to compare the personalities of elite athletes participating in four different sports. Specifically the researchers aimed to

Figure 5.25: Karateka were the most serious and independent athletes

compare the 16 traits identified in Cattell's theory of personality in (American) football players, gymnasts, wrestlers and karateka (experts in karate).

Method

Sample

A total of 387 male athletes took part in the study. All competed at regional or national level so could be classified as 'elite' athletes. Football players (N=139) came from five university teams. The wrestlers (N=94) were selected from the Olympic team and the final stages of the Nationals. The 71 karateka came from five regional teams, and the 141 gymnasts from 14 college and university teams. Provided the athletes met the criterion of participating at regional or national level they were eligible for the study; the sampling method can thus be described as opportunity sampling.

Design and procedure

The design of the study was quasi-experimental. The independent variable was choice of sport; the four conditions were the main sports played by the participants. The dependent variables were the 16 personality traits measured by the 16PF.

All participants were administered form A of the 16PF, the self-rating inventory designed to measure Cattell's 16 personality traits. The 16PF comes in two versions, form A and form B. It is standard practice to use one or the other. The 16PF consists of approximately 200 statements each of which requires a true/false response.

Other tests were administered at the same time, including a 15-item lie scale taken from a mental health screening test called the Minnesota Multiphasic Personality Inventory. Lie-scales ask questions designed to tell if participants' responses to other questions are likely to be invalid because the person is either answering dishonestly or lacks self-awareness. An example of a lie-scale statement is 'I do not always tell the truth'. Participants who scored 7 or more out of 15 on the lie-scale had their 16PF data removed from the study.

Results

16PF scores were compared using both univariate and multivariate analyses. Univariate analysis involved comparing each possible pair of sports on each of the 16 personality traits. Multivariate analysis involved comparing all four groups of athletes on all 16 traits in a single equation. Multivariate analysis showed an overall significant difference in personality according to sport. Wrestlers and football players had very similar personality profiles, but these were quite distinct from the karateka and gymnasts, who were also quite distinct from each other. The biggest overall difference between groups was between footballers and gymnasts. The personality traits that varied most between groups were shy – venturesome and group dependent – self-sufficient.

Univariate analysis showed some interesting differences between particular characteristics of participants in different sports. For example, the major difference between footballers and karateka was in group dependence, the latter typically being much more self-sufficient. Gymnasts were significantly more shy than footballers or wrestlers, with karateka falling in between, with scores not significantly different to those in either group. Gymnasts were particularly intelligent and serious, karateka particularly conscientious and independent.

The extent to which personality predicted sporting choice was also tested. This is called maximum likelihood classification. Each participant was matched to a sport based on the closeness of their 16PF profile to that of the typical athlete in each group. Of the 387 participants, 196 were classified correctly (50.6%). As the most distinctive group, gymnasts were correctly matched to gymnastics 73.1% of the time. The other groups were matched correctly between 33.8% (karateka) and 39.5% (football players). We would expect that if chance alone was at work predictions would be accurate 25% of the time. A chi^2 test was carried out on this data, yielding a score of 93.72, significant at the 0.01 level.

Conclusions

There are significant differences in the personality profiles of athletes from different sports. The 16PF correctly predicted choice of sport around half the time. The most distinctive group were gymnasts, while the most similar profiles were found in footballers and wrestlers. The shy – venturesome and group-dependent – self-sufficient traits were the most important in distinguishing between athletes from different sports.

Figure 5.26: In the Kroll & Krenshaw study gymnasts were particularly shy, intelligent and serious

APPLICATION: USING KNOWLEDGE OF PERSONALITY TO IMPROVE SPORTS PERFORMANCE

Personality is unlikely to be the main factor affecting our success in our choice of sport. Our physique, role models and early experiences of spectating and trying different sports are probably more important. If we can predict someone's sporting success or choice of sport by knowing their profile of personality traits this may open up the possibility of identifying potentially successful athletes early and matching athletes to the 'right' sport for them – in the sense of the sport to which they are most psychologically suited. It may also be possible to modify aspects of an athlete's personality in order to help them adapt to their chosen sport. Both these strategies may have the potential to improve motivation and reduce anxiety.

Identifying and preparing potential elite athletes

In theory it may be possible to use personality tests to identify young athletes who, by virtue of their individual characteristics, may be particularly well suited to become elite athletes as adults. An early attempt to do this was by Tutko & Ogilvie (1969). They believed that those most likely to become elite athletes would score highly on particular traits. These were aggression, coachability, conscientiousness, determination, drive, emotional control, guilt-proneness, leadership, mental toughness, self-confidence and trust. They put together a self-rating inventory called the Athletic Motivation Inventory (AMI), which they claimed to measure these ten traits.

Later research did not support the ability of the AMI to predict athletic success, and some of these so-called 'traits' were badly thought-out. Most sport psychologists do not accept for example that 'coachability' is an aspect of personality. In a review Abbott & Collins (2004) conclude that in spite of decades of research no personality profile of the elite athlete has been found. As they say,

Figure 5.27: There is unfortunately no evidence that we can use personality measures to match children to their most appropriate sport

 **KEY IDEAS**

Team building is a process of increasing the cohesiveness of a team, i.e. to increase the emotional bonds between team members and between each member and the team as a whole. This is done in the belief that more cohesive teams perform better. Generally, evidence supports the idea that more cohesive teams do better so there is a sound basis for team building.

 STRETCH & CHALLENGE

Some (but not all) sport psychologists make a sharp distinction between academic and applied sport psychology. Generally, personality and sport is classified as academic sport psychology rather than applied. Having read this section, do you think personality research has a practical application in sport or is it just of academic interest?

Bjorn Borg and John McEnroe were well-matched tennis champions, but could not have been more different in personality.

There is thus no real application in using personality profiles to select future elite athletes. However, personality may influence sporting behaviour and therefore it can be an advantage to know an athlete's personality when starting work with them. For example Junge (2000) suggests that more venturesome athletes may not take adequate care when rehabilitating from injury and so may require particular care at that time.

Matching athlete and sport

Although there is clear evidence to show that there is a relationship between choice of sport and personality, this seems to take place naturally. There is no evidence to suggest that testing athletes' personality and nudging them towards particular sports helps them find the 'right' sport for them. Even if we could do this, personality is probably less important than physical factors anyway, so matching someone with their most psychologically appropriate sport would not necessarily mean they would perform best in that sport.

There is thus no real application in improving sporting performance by matching personality to sport. That said, there may be an application for personality testing in steering people who might have never considered taking part in sport towards a sport that they might enjoy. For example someone too shy and independent to get much out of team sports could be introduced to an individual sport like gymnastics, where they may enjoy participating and therefore perform better.

Modifying personality to fit with the demands of sport

By definition personality is *relatively* unchanging. However, where an athlete and their psychologist agree it would be beneficial, some aspects of personality can be tweaked in order to help an athlete achieve their best possible performances. For example, a footballer low in trust and group-dependence might not find it easy to work as part of a team. They might therefore require a personalised approach to coaching that is sensitive to this and pays particular attention to **team-building**. According to Bass & Avolio (1994) and Valle & Bloom (2008), this kind of personalisation is key to successful coaching.

Anxiety is also largely a product of personality, and techniques like CBT (see page 262) work to modify aspects of personality like trait anxiety. Studies showing that CBT improves performance through making athletes less anxiety-prone (e.g. Turner & Barker, 2013; see page 264) are essentially modifying a personality trait.

EVALUATION

Methodological and ethical issues

There are a number of methodological issues with the Kroll & Krenshaw study that limit its usefulness. The participants were chosen by opportunity sampling; this is unlikely to produce a representative group of each of the four groups.

This is particularly important in a study like this where the whole aim is to assess differences between the groups. This is made worse by the quasi-experimental design. In this study we cannot randomly allocate participants to conditions because the four groups *are* the conditions. It is therefore very important to match the groups as closely as possible, but that was not really possible in this study because of the sampling method. In particular the karateka were from local teams in a sport where there was not at the time a well-established hierarchy. It is possible therefore that the lack of elite status in the karateka in the study was a confounding variable, exaggerating their differences from the other athletes.

The study is also limited by the reliability and validity of the personality measure used. The 16PF has a test-retest reliability of between 0.56 and 0.79 over two months (Conn & Rieke, 1994). This is reasonable but not outstanding. There is also reasonable evidence for its predictive validity, i.e. personality profiles have been used successfully to predict academic achievement and health problems (Cattell & Meade, 2008). Although the reliability and validity of the 16PF are not too much of a weakness, there are now more reliable and valid personality tests available, and it would be interesting to know what sort of results we would find using them.

A strength of Kroll & Krenshaw's method was their use of a lie scale. This eliminated potential participants who were actually unsuitable for research involving self-rating inventories, either because of their dishonesty or lack of self-awareness. This in turn improved the validity of the procedure.

The Kroll & Krenshaw study is a good example of a psychological investigation that does not raise much in the way of serious ethical issues. Because there is no experimental procedure involved participants are not exposed to significant risk of harm or distress. No deceit or breach of privacy was necessary, and it would have been straightforward to pull out of the study if participants had wished to. Unfortunately you cannot carry out this kind of study yourselves as administering personality tests requires a certificate from the British Psychological Society. There are potential risks to participants' self-esteem whenever research involves psychometrics.

Debates

Usefulness of research

Research into personality and sport has produced some interesting findings but few of these have applications in the real world. Personality definitely falls under the heading of academic sport psychology rather than applied sport psychology. We cannot identify potential elite athletes using personality tests and, although personality is one factor in choice of sport, there is no evidence that we can use it to help athletes choose the sport in which they will perform best.

Although we can tweak aspects of personality like trait anxiety this does not really require an understanding of personality; it is more a case of working with an athlete to identify responses they would like to modify.

Nature vs nurture

Personality itself is an important topic within the nature-nurture debate. Some trait theorists, in particular Hans Eysenck, take a strong view that personality is primarily down to nature. Others however place more importance on the role of nurture, but it is widely accepted that both genes and environment are important in personality. Trait anxiety for example is likely to be influenced by both genetic and environmental factors. This is important as personality is associated with choice of sport; this means that both nature and nurture indirectly influence what sports we choose to participate through the intermediary factor of personality. In the context of sport the nature–nurture debate is also important because, if aspects of personality related to sport are at least partly a product of environment, then they are more likely to be open to modification by techniques like CBT.

Freedom vs determination

Personality and choice of sport, as studied by Kroll & Krenshaw, is an interesting issue in terms of the debate around freedom and determination. On a conscious level we have the experience of making choices to participate or not in sport and what sports to participate in. However, if these choices are influenced by our personality then perhaps they are less free than we think. Perhaps we are in fact largely determined. If our choices are subject to genetic influence this is called genetic determinism. If they are affected by our experiences this is called environmental determinism. Either way it seems likely that our sporting choices are not entirely free.

Individual vs situational explanations

Personality is all about individual differences. Personality theorists see individual differences as the key influence on behaviour as opposed to the situation. So from a personality perspective the reason Steve chose to take up karate while Dan opted to wrestle is because of differences in their personality. Actually, although personality may be important it is probably only part of the picture. Steve may have been influenced by the availability of a good local karate club, role models, or the experience of enjoying a good Chuck Norris film. These are situational factors. We simply don't know how important situational factors are in sporting success.

PERFORMING WITH OTHERS

BACKGROUND

Figure 5.28: How well a team works together profoundly affects performance

Even in solo sports we never really function in isolation. We have a coach, we have competitors, and we have a team, with whom we train and interact even if we don't perform in conjunction with them. In team sports this becomes even more complex and important as we interact with team members *during* competition as well as around it. Teams require leadership, and this comes from the captain and from the coach or coaches. Athletic performance can be profoundly affected by leadership and by how effectively a team works together. Some of the most brilliant athletes have had to leave teams and probably failed to reach their potential because they cannot work effectively with their team-mates, captains or coaches. David Beckham famously left Manchester United because of difficulties working with manager Alex Ferguson. More recently, Kevin Pieterson has been dropped from international cricket because of difficulties in getting on with other players.

What do psychologists mean by teams, coaching and leadership?

Teams and groups

A group can be defined as any 'two or more persons who interact with one another such that each person influences and is influenced by each other person' (Moorhead & Griffin, 1998: p.291). Obviously we tend to interact and be affected by those we spend time with, so we can be said to be in a group with anyone we spend time with. A team is something more specific; a number of people who work together, committed to a common goal. A team need not technically be a group, as such, because team members can be working for a common goal without ever coming into direct personal contact. For example, a national Olympic or Commonwealth squad are working for a common goal, but all individuals could fulfil their team roles without athletes from different sports ever meeting.

Leadership and coaching

Leadership can be defined as 'the use of non-coercive influence to direct and coordinate the activities of group members to meet a goal' (Moorhead & Griffin, 1998: p352). An effective leader organises team members and takes a key role in regulating the emotional and motivational climate in which the team operates. Leadership can be formal, such as that provided by team coach and captain. On occasion, other team members might also take on informal leadership roles in which they influence and inspire other team members.

Coaching is a special form of leadership. Coaching has been defined as 'an episodic process through which components of performance that require improvement are identified then developed (Knowles *et al.* 2006: p163). Leadership in the form of coaching is largely oriented towards improving athletic performance. This can be achieved through direct technique-oriented instruction or through enhancing motivation and team work. Over a million people in the UK coach athletes in a range of contexts.

Teams, leadership and performance

The major team variable affecting performance is its cohesiveness. 'Cohesion' literally means to stick together. Teams that stick together through success and failure because of their strong interpersonal bonds tend to achieve better results, even when they lack very high-achieving individuals. On the other hand, teams composed of brilliant individual performers often collectively underperform because the team has somehow failed to 'gel' together. This is an example of lack of cohesion, and illustrates that **team cohesiveness** is as important to a team's prospects as individual ability.

Many studies have shown a positive correlation between team cohesiveness and success. For example, Carron *et al.* (2002) assessed team cohesiveness in 18 basketball teams and nine football teams and found correlations ranging from 0.55–0.67 with successful performance. This is quite a strong relationship and suggests that cohesiveness is an important factor underlying team performance. However, correlation coefficients such as this show only a mathematical relationship between two variables; they don't show cause and effect. It may be that cohesive teams perform better or it may be that teams became more cohesive as a result of shared success.

In fact it appears that both these possibilities hold true. Slater & Sewell (1994) measured team cohesiveness and performance success in 60 university level hockey players three times; early, midway and at the end of the season. This allowed the researchers to see how cohesiveness early in the season related to later success and how early success related to later cohesiveness. They found that, although early success correlated positively with later cohesiveness, there was a stronger correlation between early cohesiveness and later success. This suggests that cohesiveness does in fact affect team success.

Leadership and performance

There are various styles of leadership. Lewin *et al.* (1939) identified three leadership styles. The authoritarian makes decisions without team input and expects unquestioning obedience from the team. At the other extreme, the laissez-faire leader leaves team members to get on without interference. They may help individuals, but tend not to direct the team as a whole. The democratic leader falls halfway between the authoritarian and laissez-faire styles. They make decisions but these take account of team members' views.

In sport, each leadership style can work but they are probably suited to different situations. Typically, democratic leadership is the most successful style (Jarvis, 2006), but it can run into problems when rapid decision-making is required under pressure. Authoritarian leadership allows direction of tired and disillusioned athletes who might give up if given a say, but most of the time it fails to allow team members to contribute their ideas. Laissez-faire leadership is usually the least effective style – it is really a lack of leadership!

KEY IDEAS

Team cohesiveness is the strength of the bonds between each individual team member and the team. This has two elements: the bond to each other individual in the team, and the bond to the team as a whole. It is believed that team cohesiveness is affected by a range of factors, including coaching, sharing of goals, communication and willingness of individuals to put the team first. Cohesiveness has a major effect on performance.

Figure 5.29: Cohesive basketball teams have been found to perform better

Coaching and performance

Jowett & Cockerill (2002) suggest that the key aspect of coaching is the quality of the coach–athlete relationship. This can be understood in terms of three key variables:

- Closeness: the emotional bond between coach and athlete
- Co-orientation: shared views, priorities and concerns
- Complementarity: co-operative behaviour between coach and athlete.

In a series of case studies and a larger study of 12 Olympic athletes Jowett and colleagues (Jowett & Cockerill, 2002) studied the closeness, co-orientation and complementarity of athlete–coach pairs and concluded that closeness was the most important variable. In all cases athletes placed the strongest emphasis on closeness. All the athletes reported that their motivation and confidence was linked to their experience of being cared for, liked, trusted and respected by their coaches.

Taking a different approach to understanding coaching, Chelladurai (1993) has pointed out that coaching activities involve decision-making, and suggests that we can understand the leadership displayed by coaches in terms of their decision-making style. Within this model decision-making is influenced by seven factors:

- Time pressure
- Importance of the decision
- Who has necessary information
- Problem complexity
- Group acceptance
- Coach's power
- Group integration.

Influenced by these factors, coaches select a decision-making style:

- Autocratic style: the coach makes the decision on their own
- Participative style: the coach involves the participation of athletes
- Delegative style: the coach delegates decision-making to athletes.

KEY RESEARCH

Smith. R.E., Smoll, F.L. & Curtis, B. (1979) Coach effectiveness training: a cognitive-behavioural approach to enhancing relationship skills in youth sports coaches. *Journal of Sport Psychology*, 1 (1), 59–75.

Aim

The aim of this study was to test the effectiveness of a training programme for baseball coaches working with children. Specifically, researchers compared trained coaches with untrained controls in terms of observed behaviours, athlete evaluations of self and coach and athletes' self-esteem.

Method
Sample

Taking part in the study were 34 male Little League baseball coaches from the Seattle area. Their mean age was 36.10 years and they had a mean of 8.37 years of experience. All coached 10–12–year-olds and 13–15–year-olds in three baseball leagues. 18 were randomly allocated to an experimental group and participated in the training programme. 16 were assigned to a control group and had no training. The uneven allocation to the two conditions was to allow for some coaches failing to attend the training. In reality all the coaches in the experimental group attended the training and three of the controls were lost due to teams merging or moving.

Design and procedure

The study was experimental, using an independent measures design. Because the participants were randomly allocated to conditions this was a true experiment rather than a quasi-experiment. The independent variable was the training programme; the two conditions were the experimental condition, in which participants undertook the training, and a control condition in which they did not. The dependent variables were measures of coaching quality. These included the following:

- Observed behaviours, including reactive and spontaneous behaviours recorded using a standard observation coding system called the CBAS. Reactive behaviours included reward, failure to reward, encouragement and punishment. Spontaneous behaviours included technical instruction, encouragement and organisation. Observers were 16 trained undergraduates.
- Player perceptions and attitudes were assessed by structured interview. 325 players were interviewed, 82% of the young people working with the coaches in the study. Interviews assessed player perceptions of coach behaviours.
- Attitudes to baseball were assessed by means of an 11-item questionnaire.
- Self-esteem was assessed by means of a standard questionnaire, the Coopersmith Self-Esteem Inventory. This has 14 statements rated on a 5-point scale from *not at all like* me to *very much like me.*

The aim of the coach training programme was to help coaches relate better to child-athletes, and to behave towards them in more positive ways, most importantly to offer more reinforcement and encouragement and less punishment.

Results

Data were available for most of the coaches for their previous season. No significant differences were observed. However following the training there were some differences between the two groups. Results are shown in Table 5.4 on p.290.

Figure 5.30: Little League baseball coaches were the subject of this study

TABLE 5.4: OBSERVED BEHAVIOURS IN THE TWO GROUPS

Behaviour category	Experimental		Control		F(1,29)
	M	SD	M	SD	
Reinforcement	25.99	8.13	20.51	5.24	4.51*
Neoreinforcement	3.28	1.82	2.77	1.31	0.74
Mistake-contingent encouragement	4.25	2.94	3.33	1.62	1.05
Mistake-contingent technical instruction	3.12	1.06	3.63	1.41	1.31
Punishment	1.48	1.40	1.67	1.43	0.14
Punitive technical instruction	0.62	0.83	1.04	0.82	1.87
Ignoring mistakes	1.70	1.06	1.73	0.85	0.01
Keeping control	1.18	0.81	1.46	0.36	0.51
General technical instruction	21.43	5.61	24.55	5.56	2.34
General encouragement	29.04	8.43	33.13	7.10	2.02
Organisation	4.80	1.73	4.67	1.86	0.04
General communication	3.11	1.54	2.30	0.96	2.83

$*p<0.05$

Coaches who had undergone the training programme were more likely to reinforce behaviour and to offer encouragement following mistakes. They were less likely to offer general instruction and general encouragement. On other measures there was little difference between the groups. The only behavioural difference that reached statistical significance was reinforcement. This was significant at the $p<0.05$ level.

Differences between players' ratings of coaches were greater than those in observed behaviours. Six behaviours were significantly different; trained coaches from the experimental group were described as more likely to reinforce, encourage after mistakes and offer general technical instruction. They were less likely to not reinforce good technique, punish and offer instruction of a punitive (i.e. punishing) nature. All these behaviours were targeted by the training intervention.

Player ratings of baseball and their coach also differed between the experimental and control groups. In particular players with coaches in the experimental group were significantly more likely to report liking their coach and wanting to play for them next year. Although self-esteem at the end of the season did not differ significantly between players working with coaches in the two groups, when changes in self-esteem from the previous year were looked at there was a marked improvement in the players with coaches in the experimental group ($p<0.05$) and a decline in self-esteem in those working with the control group.

Conclusions

Results show that the training programme for coaches had a significant impact on their behaviours towards their players and that these behavioural differences impacted on players' self-esteem and attitudes to the coach and other aspects of their sporting experience.

APPLICATION: IMPROVING TEAM PERFORMANCE

There are many strategies that can be tried in order to improve team performance. These include ways of working to improve team cohesiveness and to improve leadership and coaching.

MATHS MOMENT

Only one behavioural difference between the two groups achieved statistical significance.

1. The lack of other significant differences in the behavioural observations may be due to a Type 2 error. Explain what is meant by a Type 2 error.
2. In the player ratings of coach behaviours differences in general technical instruction reached a significance of $p<0.05$, differences in reinforcement reached $p<0.01$ and differences in punishment reached $p<0.001$. Explain what these three significance levels mean.

Team building

Making a collection of individuals function as an effective team is a key part of the coach's role. Strategies to develop team cohesion are known as *team building*.

Carron *et al.* (1997) offer a four-point model for team building. Their approach aims to increase team distinctiveness, for example by a uniform, to increase social cohesiveness, for example by holding team social events, to establish clear team goals, for example by having a team 'goal of the day' and to improve team communication, for example by having productive meetings. Their principles are summarised below:

- Every player should know the responsibilities of every other team member.
- Coaches should know personal information about each team member and use it to gain their trust and cooperation.
- Whole teams should have pride in sub-teams such as a rugby pack.
- Players should be actively involved in decision-making to give themselves a sense of ownership.
- Team members should know team goals and celebrate together when they are attained.
- Each team member should know their responsibilities and their individual importance to the team.
- Team members should be allowed to have disagreements.
- Teams should not have cliques within the team. This can be avoided by giving every member opportunities to perform and avoiding scapegoating.
- Training routines can be designed to show each team member how dependent they are on each other.
- There should be a focus on the positive, even when results are not good.

There is a clear rationale for team building in the sense that there is plenty of evidence to show that more cohesive teams tend to win more matches. However, does team building really increase cohesiveness? This has been tested in a number of experimental studies, but results have been inconsistent, and we cannot safely conclude that team building is effective. It is likely however that successful team building has a positive impact on teams, but that this is a skilled task, and some teams are harder to build than others. Also, team building can only improve cohesiveness where the team is lacking in cohesiveness in the first place. Thus studies on already-cohesive teams encounter a ceiling effect and have little impact. Some unsuccessful teams may have different problems, and team building is not a one-size-fits-all solution.

Coach development

We have already seen from the study by Smith, *et al.* that the practice of coaches can be improved by means of training programmes. Their approach was to improve the quality of interaction between coach and player by increasing levels of reinforcement and encouragement. This study demonstrated the effectiveness of the approach in the sense that trained coaches behaved in more motivational ways. However, the study did **not** demonstrate that teams with coaches who had undertaken the development programme were more successful in competition. This could of course simply have been a Type 2 error due to the small sample size.

KEY IDEAS

Team building

Team building is a process of increasing the cohesiveness of a team, i.e. to increase the emotional bonds between team members and between each member and the team as a whole. This is done in the belief that more cohesive teams perform better. Generally evidence supports the idea that more cohesive teams do better so there is a sound basis for team building.

Figure 5.31: Teams benefit from being allowed a say in decisions and to disagree

STRETCH & CHALLENGE

Imagine your school or college football team was underperforming. Looking at the individuals it appears that they should be doing well, however the results so far this season are very disappointing. Based on what you have read in this topic, how might you work with coaching and team cohesiveness to improve team performance?

It may be that the quality of coaching affects team success because it improves team cohesiveness. Ramzaninezhad & Keshtan (2009) studied this in 12 Turkish football teams. Coaching styles characterised by democratic leadership and high levels of social support was strongly associated with both team cohesiveness and success in competition. It appears then that coach development programmes improve the quality of coaching and that good coaching impacts positively on sporting success.

Figure 5.32: Coaching is important and can be improved by training

EVALUATION

Methodological and ethical issues

There are many methodological strengths to the Smith, Smoll & Curtis study. The design was experimental rather than quasi-experimental so coaches in the experimental and control groups were reasonably well matched, for example in match success. More importantly, where the children working with the coach-participants were found to be not well matched in self-esteem the authors dealt with this by analysing change in self-esteem across the two groups rather than just the scores at the end of the season.

There are however some methodological issues with the Smith, *et al.* study that limit its usefulness. For example the study is limited by the reliability and validity of the assessment tools used. The Coopersmith Self-Esteem Inventory was reported to have a test-retest reliability of 0.6 to 0.74. This is lower than ideal. Also the sample size was small and this may have led to Type 2 errors where no significant differences were reported, for example in observations of the two groups of coaches.

The Smith, *et al.* study is a good example of a psychological investigation that does not raise much in the way of serious ethical issues. Although there is an experimental procedure, there is little chance of harm or distress beyond what participants would have experienced anyway. Although child athletes in the control condition did not receive improved coaching they only received the same coaching as they would have done if they had not participated in the study. No deceit or breach of privacy was necessary. Children and their parents were assured that responses were confidential so there should have been no anxiety about coaches seeking revenge for bad reviews!

Debates
Usefulness of research

Sport is not only a multibillion pound industry, it is also an approach to improving the health of the nation and a talking point that unites diverse people as communities. It is therefore of great importance to society. Any strategies that lead to improvements in sporting performance are therefore important practical applications of psychology. Unlike some areas of research, studies of teams and leadership have clear practical applications. For example the quality of coaching can be improved by programmes like that used by Smith, *et al.* in their study.

Nature vs nurture

There is a nature–nurture debate around leadership i.e. are great leaders born or made? Certainly some of the most successful captains and coach-managers are highly charismatic personalities, and these personalities are undoubtedly influenced by genetic as well as environmental factors. We could never make another Jose Mourinho or Alex Ferguson! On the other hand, studies like that by Smith, *et al.* clearly show that it is possible to 'make' better coaches by developing their communication style to one that is more positive and supportive of athletes. Generally psychologists see leadership behaviour as open to change and therefore fall on the nurture side of the debate.

Individual vs situational explanations

Whenever we talk about the style of team work or coaching an athlete experiences we are speaking of situational factors. Social factors i.e. those involving interactions with other people are always situational. However, this emphasis on situational factors can lead us to forget about individual differences. Some athletes appear to be resistant to coaching or engaging in team work because of their personality (not mentioning a certain cricketer for fear of law suits), and this is clearly individual. Studies like that by Smith, *et al.* show that situational factors are important but neglect the role of individual differences in coachability and team-orientation.

Psychology as science

The study by Smith, *et al.* conforms to the standards of good science. It follows the classic scientific method; having observed that coaches with particular communication styles appeared to have better interactions with players, they tested experimentally whether developing the appropriate communication skills would lead to improvements in those interactions. Their procedure used standard experimental protocols like randomly allocating participants to experimental and control conditions.

TOPIC 6
AUDIENCE EFFECTS

BACKGROUND

If you have ever performed in competitive sports in front of people you will know that it feels very different to training on your own, even though you might be carrying out virtually identical actions. One reason for this is the effect of an audience. Being watched – whether by spectators or other athletes–can have a profound effect on our performance, making it better or worse depending on the circumstances. Imagine for a moment that you are performing in international competition in front of a television audience of millions. Now imagine you are performing for the benefit of the Olympic team selectors. These scenarios may have thrilled you with anticipation or filled you with dread! Either way you would feel and behave differently in those situations.

What do psychologists mean by audience effects

Audience effects are an example of social facilitation. **Social facilitation** is a general term covering the effects of *being in the presence of other people.* The simplest forms of social facilitation are co-action effects. These take place when other people are carrying out the same task alongside you. In sport this happens during competition or when training with teammates. As long ago as 1898 it was observed that cyclists training together rode faster than when on their own (Triplett, 1898). Triplett also found that children wound fishing reels faster in the presence of other children than when they were asked to perform the same action alone.

Audience effects occur in response to being watched. Depending on the circumstances being watched can have a positive or negative effect on sporting performance. A phenomenon widely believed to be linked to audiences is the home advantage effect (HAE). In most circumstances teams perform better playing at their home ground. This effect is greatest when the crowd is large (Nevill & McCann, 1998), so it is likely to be the result of being watched by a supportive audience.

Figure 5.33: Cyclists training together cycle faster

 **KEY IDEAS**

Social facilitation effects are simply the effects of the presence of others on performance. Co-action effects take place when we perform alongside others. Audience effects occur when we are being watched. Confusingly, social facilitation can include positive and negative effects of the presence of others, however we usually speak of facilitation in relation to improving performance, and inhibition in relation to worsening performance.

Figure 5.34: Only expert karateka can maintain the accuracy of kicks in the presence of this kind of audience

 **KEY IDEAS**

Extroversion is the extent to which a person is lively and sociable in their behaviour. All major systems for classifying personality traits include extraversion. See also page 279 for a full account of personality traits.

Effects of an audience

Most of the time having an audience facilitates better performance, although this may depend on the skill level and personality of the athletes concerned. A demonstration of audience effects comes from Michaels *et al.* (1982). They observed students playing pool in their Student Union and walked up to the tables and watched their game. This presence of an audience had the opposite effect on the below-average and above-average players. Those identified as below average in ability played worse in the presence of an audience, whilst those identified as above average played better. Similar results were reported by Bell & Yee (1989), who tested the accuracy of karate kicks in skilled and unskilled karateka in isolation and front of an audience. Accuracy declined for the unskilled group when the audience was present.

Individual differences in audience effects

There is strong evidence to suggest that audiences do not affect us all the same way. It seems that the effect of an audience on our athletic performance can be mediated by the personality of the athletes. Graydon & Murphy (1995) found that extroverts performed better in tennis serves than introverts when watched but worse alone. A review of factors affecting response to audiences by Uziel (2007) concluded that personality, in particular extroversion and self-esteem, is the most important factor affecting how we respond to the presence of an audience. Extroverts with high self-esteem respond best to audiences whereas introverts with low self-esteem respond worst.

Explaining audience effects

One explanation for audience effects comes from Zajonc (1965), who based his ideas on drive theory (see page 259). Zajonc proposed that the presence of others affects performance by raising arousal levels. Recall that, according to drive theory, heightened arousal produces improved performance when the task is simple and the athlete is an expert. However, higher arousal leads to worse performance when the task is complex or the performer is a novice. Zajonc suggested that because of this having an audience will lead to a better performance for experts but a worse performance for novices.

Cottrell (1968) suggested an alternative approach to explaining why audiences might lead to increased arousal. Evaluation-apprehension theory proposes that being watched by others leads to an increase in arousal because we believe we are being evaluated. If we believe that we are competent in the task being observed then we are likely to feel confident, and the effect on performance will be a positive one. If we know we are a novice however, then being watched is likely to cause us anxiety and mess up our performance.

Home advantage and disadvantage effects

'The home advantage is unquestionably a powerful influence on performance outcomes in many domains of sport. Athletes simply enjoy more success performing at home than on the road' (Wallace, *et al.* 2005: p.429). There are dramatic examples of the home advantage effect; between 1930 and 1994 no national football team, with the exception of Brazil, ever won the World Cup outside their own continent. Large, supportive audiences generally have a positive effect on performance. According to Pollard (1986), significant home advantage effects have been demonstrated in all major British sports, with 64% of points being scored by home football teams.

Both drive theory and evaluation apprehension theory can explain the home advantage effect. There are also many non-psychological 'common sense' factors that may give home teams an advantage over those playing away. These include familiarity with facilities, not having to travel and greater likelihood of favourable referee bias. There may also be an unconscious evolutionary effect at work; outside the sporting arena most disputes in humans and fights in animals are won by those on home territory (Fuxjager *et al.* 2009). It may be that an instinctive tendency to defend home territory mediates the physiological response to confrontation in the form of sport.

The home advantage effect is well known and fairly well understood. However there is also a home disadvantage effect. This is much less obvious and harder to explain, but it does appear that teams operating under very high pressure sometimes perform worse when at home. Jarvis (2006) gave the example of Sheffield Wednesday's 2001–2 season, in which, under pressure to avoid the relegation zone, they won many more games away than at home.

The home disadvantage effect takes place in conditions of high pressure. This gives us clues as to its causes. Wallace *et al.* (2005) suggest a cognitive explanation. Expert sports performance involves a high level of automatic information processing in which we can perform actions without conscious effort. This frees up our attention to focus on the game not ourselves. However, when players feel that they are being scrutinised under pressure they tend to focus attention on their performance rather than the game. This disrupts automatic processing of information and leaves us consciously performing skills in the same way as a novice would. This leads to the phenomenon of 'choking.'

Figure 5.35: Most of the time teams playing at home are advantaged

KEY RESEARCH

Zajonc, R.B., Heingartner, A. & Herman, E.M. (1969) Social enhancement and impairment of performance in the cockroach. *Journal of Personality & Social Psychology,* 13 (2), 83–92.

Aim
The aim of this study was to test the drive theory of social facilitation experimentally. More specifically the first experiment tested the hypothesis that the performance of cockroaches running a maze and a runway would be affected by the presence of other cockroaches, either as co-actors or an audience. The aim of the second experiment was to see whether the effects of the presence of other cockroaches would be maintained after they were removed.

EXPERIMENT 1

Method
Sample
Taking part in the experiment were 72 adult female cockroaches of the species *Blatta Orientalis.* For a week they had been kept in standard conditions of darkness at a temperature of 75°C and were fed a standard diet of apples.

Figure 5.36: Cockroaches dislike light so it is easy to motivate them to run a runway or maze in order to escape bright light

Design and procedure

The experiment used an independent measures design, with eight groups taking part in different conditions. Four groups of eight roaches were tested for co-action effects; alone-runway, co-action-runway, alone maze and co-action-maze. Four additional groups were tested for audience effects; runway-alone, runway-audience, maze-alone, maze-audience. Each cockroach performed ten times and their individual median time was recorded. The mean was then calculated for the roaches in each condition.

Cockroaches were placed in either a transparent runway (a straight passage) or a maze. A bright light was shone at one end, the start of the runway and to the side of the maze. Cockroaches dislike and avoid light so they were motivated to run to their goal, an area in darkness. In the co-action conditions two cockroaches were placed together at the start of the runway or maze. In the audience conditions they were alone in the passage but could see and smell (by means of air holes) other cockroaches outside it. The time taken for each cockroach to start running and to complete their run was measured.

Results

For the runway task, the simpler of the two, cockroaches started their run and completed it more quickly when in the presence of an audience or a fellow-cockroach. Average running times are shown in Table 5.5 below.

TABLE 5.5: RUNNING TIME AND STARTING LATENCY IN SECONDS FOR SUBJECTS TESTED ALONE, IN CO-ACTION, AND IN THE PRESENCE OF AN AUDIENCE

Treatment	Task							
	Runway				Maze			
	Alone		Social		Alone		Social	
Co-action								
Starting latency	8.25	(8)	6.88	(8)	10.56	(8)	11.19	(8)
Running time	40.58	(8)	32.96	(8)	110.45	(8)	129.46	(8)
Audience								
Starting latency	14.80	(10)	9.35	(10)	37.55	(10)	22.75	(10)
Running time	62.65	(10)	39.30	(10)	221.36	(10)	296.64	(10)
Both treatments								
Starting latency	11.89	(18)	8.25	(18)	25.56	(18)	17.61	(18)
Running time	52.84	(18)	36.48	(18)	172.06	(18)	222.34	(18)

For the more difficult maze task in which the cockroaches have to work out a route to their goal as well as run it, the effect was different. In the co-action condition cockroaches took longer to run the maze than when alone. However they ran the maze faster when in the presence of an audience than when alone.

Conclusion

Results were reasonably consistent with drive theory. Where the task was simple, i.e. the runway, participants performed better in the presence of others. When the task was more complicated they performed better without co-actors. The fact that this was reversed for the audience effects does not, however, fit neatly with drive theory.

MATHS MOMENT 🖩

Bar charts are particularly useful when comparing results from multiple conditions. Draw a bar chart of the results from experiment 1. Pay attention to the conventions of bar charts, so make sure you have a title, labelled axes and that bars do not touch.

EXPERIMENT 2

Aim
The first experiment established that the presence of other cockroaches affected performance. However, this left the question as to how the presence of cockroaches might have their effect. Experiment 2 tested the effect of visual and olfactory (smell) cues on performance.

Method
Sample
Taking part were 180 female *Blatta Orientalis* cockroaches. They were all kept in standard conditions of individual dark jars for four days before the experimental procedure.

Design and procedure
The design was independent measures, with participants allocated to one of six conditions. Three conditions involved the runway task and three the maze. In one runway and one maze condition participants performed alone. In one runway and one maze condition they performed with mirrored walls so simulate the visual stimulus of other roaches. In one runway and one maze condition they had the olfactory cues for the presence of other roaches provided by placing an egg carton impregnated with roach smell next to the runway or maze. As in the first experiment, time taken to start running and time taken to complete the task were recorded for each roach and averaged for each condition.

Results
In the runway condition both the visual and olfactory cues led to the cockroaches taking longer to run the runway than in the alone condition. In the maze condition the odour slowed them but the mirrors sped them up.

Conclusions
Results of Experiment 2 were ambiguous and did not easily fit with drive theory. One possible explanation is that mirrors and smells did not provide sufficient cues and that other cockroaches actually need to be present for real audience and co-action effects to occur. Another possibility is that the cues distracted the cockroaches and so worsened their performance.

APPLICATION: STRATEGIES FOR TRAINING FOR AND PLAYING SPECTATOR SPORTS

Performing in front of an audience requires both expertise and resilience. Expertise is important for the presence of other people to have a positive impact on performance. Resilience is important to avoid the phenomenon of choking, where under pressure tasks normally carried out automatically become conscious and so less efficient and vulnerable to distraction.

Develop automatic processing through practice
According to drive theory experts perform better in the presence of audience whilst novices perform worse. It follows then that we need our athletes to be experts rather than novices. A key feature of expert performance is **automatic**

 **KEY IDEAS**

Information can be processed in the mind consciously or automatically. When we consciously process information we think about it. This is useful when we are planning strategy, but in the thick of the action we cannot afford to think about every task as we perform it. This is where **automatic processing** comes in. When we have practised a skill enough it becomes automatic and we can carry it out without conscious thought.

Figure 5.37: Ball technique practice may be boring but makes technique expert enough to be performed under conditions of high arousal

Imagine your school or college football team was underperforming. Looking at the individuals it appears that they should be doing well, however the results so far this season are very disappointing. Based on what you have read in this topic what strategies might you suggest to improve team performance? Think for example about how you might develop expert performance and resilience.

processing for motor skills. Training that involves repetition of skills performance until they can be performed without conscious attention will thus equip athletes to perform in front of audiences.

Ericsson, *et al.* (1993) have suggested that around 10 years of deliberate practice can be necessary before skills can be performed expertly at an elite level. This highlights both the importance of intensive deliberate practice of technique in training. This is why so much sports training involves repetitively carrying out basic tasks pertinent to the sport. So for example footballers don't just play practice matches in training, they practice passing and tackling over and over again. Ericsson, *et al.* also highlight the importance of starting training young so that an athlete can achieve expert performance by the time they are at the optimum age for performance. It is hard to take up a sport as an adult and achieve elite performance – you are likely to get too old before you have mastered the techniques.

As spectators increase arousal levels in athletes and in turn make it hard to maintain automatic performance, so the heightened arousal resulting from spectators can also interfere with decision-making abilities. The answer once again seems to be intensive practice. In addition to making skills automatic, intensive deliberate practice can improve decision-making ability (Baker *et al.* 1993).

Increase athlete resilience

Spectators increase arousal and perhaps psychological aspects of anxiety as well. It follows that more psychologically resilient athletes will cope better with the presence of spectators. Sarkar & Fletcher (2014) have reviewed studies of resilience in athletes and identified five sets of factors underlying it:

* Positive outlook
* Confidence
* Focus
* Motivation
* Perceived social support

The strategies we looked at in topic 1 to help athletes cope with stress and anxiety are applicable here. Biofeedback can help by helping the individual athlete learn to regulate their own physiological arousal levels in the presence of spectators. This was demonstrated by Lagos (2008) in a case study of a golfer who was able to perform better when performing in front of a crowd (see page 262). CBT can also be helpful in making athletes more confident and focused so that they are not fazed by an audience, in particular this is likely to be helpful in tackling evaluation apprehension.

EVALUATION

Methodological and ethical issues
There are some methodological strengths to the Zajonc *et al.* study. The situation was tightly controlled so the results were unlikely to have been affected by situational extraneous variables. Internal reliability was very good as each cockroach had a very standardised experience. The choice of an independent measures design was justifiable as the participants' growing familiarity with the mazes might have

affected their performance if they had taken part in more than one condition. The use of time as the outcome measure is a strength as time can be objectively and accurately measured.

There are however some methodological issues with the Zajonc, *et al.* study that limit its usefulness. Although there is no issue with situational variables there is a problem with participant variables; cockroaches from different sources were used, and they were not randomly allocated to conditions. It is possible that the unexpected result in Experiment 1 where cockroaches ran the maze faster in the presence of an audience is the result of differences between the different batches of cockroaches used.

There is also a serious issue of extrapolating from data on cockroaches to humans. Whatever the reasons underlying the effects of audiences and co-actors for the cockroaches they may be quite different to those affecting humans. The human mind is vastly different to that of a cockroach and the type of cognitions that seem to affect humans in the presence of others – like evaluation apprehension – are probably not big issues for cockroaches.

As the study by Zajonc, Heingartner & Herman was carried out on cockroaches, this does not raise the same kind of issues as research using humans, so the things we usually think about when carrying out research – consent, deceit, harm, distress, debriefing, etc. – are not really applicable. That said, animal research does raise ethical issues of its own, and some psychologists reject the use of any animals for research on the grounds that they cannot give consent or demand withdrawal. However, in this study, cockroaches, which are believed to have limited awareness, were used. They were not harmed and the mild stress they experienced – a bright light – was something they would have experienced in their natural environment anyway. Therefore to most psychologists this study does not raise serious ethical issues.

Debates

Usefulness of research

Sporting performance can be powerfully affected by the presence of others, and sport is an important business in many ways. It follows therefore if we can do anything to understand this and accordingly help athletes this is an important practical application of psychology. Research in this area has applications for working with individual athletes; for example we can use biofeedback to learn to reduce the arousal response to the presence of others. We can use CBT to increase focus and confidence and thereby make athletes more resilient to evaluation apprehension. Research into the home advantage

and disadvantage effects can be applied to working with teams, in particular those under pressure.

Individual vs situational explanations

The presence of an audience and co-actors in sporting situations are situational factors. The research we have looked at in this topic, including the key study by Zajonc *et al.* clearly show that the presence of other people, whether as spectators or co-performing athletes, can have a profound effect on sporting performance. However, we have also seen that the effect of other people on performance is mediated by personality (see page 294). Athletes high in extroversion and self-esteem respond better to the presence of others and resilient athletes respond better to a range of stressful situations, including spectators. These are very much individual factors. We should therefore take account of both situation and individual differences when discussing audience effects and related phenomena.

Psychology as science

The study by Zajonc, *et al.* conforms to the standards of classical science. It was carried out under very tightly controlled laboratory conditions. Non-human participants were used, allowing much tighter control of variables than would be possible with humans – for example the cockroaches were kept in precisely the same conditions for days before the experimental procedure and fed a standard diet – all to eliminate possible confounding variables. Objective measures of behaviour in the form of time taken to run the runway or maze were taken. Time can be accurately measured, so there are no issues of reliability or validity of measurement tools.

Figure 5.38: Time is an objective measure of outcome that can be accurately measured, meaning that there are no issues of reliability or validity

PRACTICE QUESTIONS

Remember that in any exam paper you will get a set of questions on only one of the six sub-topics.

TOPIC 1: AROUSAL AND ANXIETY

(a)* Using the research by Fazey & Hardy (1988), explain the role of arousal and anxiety in sport. **[10]**

(b)* Assess the nature/nurture debate with regard to arousal and anxiety in sport. **[15]**

(c)* Lotty is an outstanding gymnast during training but often fails to perform as well as she should in competition.

Discuss how a sports psychologist might apply their knowledge of techniques to manage arousal and anxiety to help Lotty to perform the best she can. **[10]**

TOPIC 2: EXERCISE AND MENTAL HEALTH

(a)* Explain how the research by Lewis *et al.* (2014) could be used to improve mood in depressed Parkinson's patients. **[10]**

(b)* Assess the reductionism/holism debate with regard to exercise and mental health. **[15]**

(c)* Damian has been to see the mental health service at his workplace because his colleagues have been concerned about his mental health. The mental health nurse he saw suggested that he tries getting more exercise before any other treatment is considered. She is discussing with him the strategies he might consider for taking exercise.

Discuss one or more strategies that Damian might employ to improve his mental health through exercise. **[10]**

TOPIC 3: MOTIVATION

(a)* Using the research by Munroe-Chandler *et al.* (2008), explain self-efficacy and sports confidence in relation to imagery. **[10]**

(b)* Assess the ethical issues involved when researching self-efficacy and confidence in sport psychology. **[15]**

(c)* George is a good rugby player and could earn a lot of money if he were more motivated. His coach is looking for ways to motivate George.

Discuss how a sports psychologist could design a strategy to maximise George's motivation. **[10]**

TOPIC 4: PERSONALITY

(a)* Using the research by Kroll & Crenshaw (1970), explain the concept of personality, how it can be measured and its relationship to sport. **[10]**

(b)* Assess methodological issues involved when researching the role of personality in sport. **[15]**

(c)* Mrs Barker is Head of Physical Education at a school that wants to improve the competitive success of its pupils. She thinks it would be a good idea to select the pupils for different sports on the basis of their personality but a colleague suggests that the pupils should be allowed to choose and will change to suit their chosen sport.

Discuss how a knowledge of the role of personality in sports psychology could help Mrs Barker to design an effective strategy to improve her pupils' performance. **[10]**

TOPIC 5: PERFORMING WITH OTHERS

(a)* Using the research by Smith *et al.* (1979), explain how coach effectiveness training could be used to improve sports performance with others. **[10]**

(b)* Assess the debate about whether psychology is a science with regard to research on teams, coaching and leadership in sport. **[15]**

(c)* Mr Cook is a school Physical Education teacher. He wants to improve the performance of the school's football team.

Discuss how a knowledge of sport psychology could help Mr Cook to design an effective strategy to improve the football team's performance. **[10]**

TOPIC 6: AUDIENCE EFFECTS

(a)* Using the research by Zajonc *et al.* (1969), explain how the presence of others could affect sports performance. **[10]**

(b)* Assess the individual and situational explanations debate with regard to audience effects in sport. **[15]**

(c)* Daryl runs several clubs after college hours in different sports, including field and track athletics, football and netball. He wants to help to prepare his students for future competition with specific training for playing spectator sports.

Discuss how a sports psychologist could use their understanding of audience effects to help Daryl to design a suitable training programme. **[10]**

TOPIC 2: EXERCISE AND MENTAL HEALTH

(a)* Explain how the research by Lewis *et al.* (2014) could be used to improve mood in depressed Parkinson's patients. **[10]**

Liam's answer:

Lewis et al. (2014) compared 18 depressed people and 10 non-depressed people. This was the IV and it was an independent measures experiment. It was also a field experiment because the people were at a dance class. They also did a repeated measures experiment with different people, comparing them before and after classes and from class 2 to class 12. They used POMS and TMD to get a score of their mood. The classes changed every fortnight but had always had a warm-up, which is important for everyone, especially old people, half an hour of dancing – old dances like music hall and the Charleston, and more modern styles like Disco and cheerleading – then a break and a cool-down.

They found that the old people were in a better mood after each class and they improved over the 10 weeks, especially getting less tense and anxious and both after a class compared to the start of a class and both less tense and anxious and less angry by the end of the course compared to the start. So dance reduces depression.

Rina's answer:

Although Lewis et al.'s research didn't consider why exercise might help the Parkinson's patients, there are lots of reasons why it might help with their depression: it might take their mind off it by giving them something else to think about, it could make them feel more competent as they are achieving something, or, if they do their exercise in a social setting, such as through joining a class, they'd get social contact. All these are psychological reasons but there are also biological ones. Maybe exercise boosts neurotransmitters such as dopamine or endorphins, both of which are linked to depression.

The experiment used a self-selected sample of 22 Parkinson's patients and 15 controls. They were roughly equal genders

We say: Liam has really only described the study, rather than using the study to answer the question. Most of his description is accurate – in some ways clearer than Rina's, for example the before/after comparisons are well explained – and some of it is relevant. However, he goes into unnecessary detail in places as he isn't using the information very well. There are also some errors, such as suggesting that the two parts of the experiment used different participants (when in fact both comparisons were on the same participants, called a mixed design) and his conclusion, about depression, was not in fact supported directly.

We say: Rina's coverage of the study is really too brief, it is quite limited and lacks detail. Also, the number of participants Rina quotes are the number that started the dance classes, although only 28 in total finished and contributed to the final results analysis (so the numbers Liam is using are more appropriate). However, Rina does use the information from the study very effectively to answer the question. She links the ideas about what might cause depression to the findings of the study, so there is good application.

and an age range of 50–80. They also did the depression test in two conditions of exercise: after class and at the end of the 12-week course.

Dancing reduced mood disturbance for both Parkinson's and control participants over the whole course. This suggests that there might be some long-term psychological change, such as from socialisation or in having a sense of purpose. There was also a reduction in mood disturbance in the short term, suggesting an immediate physiological effect, such as boosting neurotransmitters. However, there was not a significant reduction in depression itself. So dance classes do improve mood in older people both over an individual session and over the whole course.

TOPIC 4: PERSONALITY

(c)* Mrs Barker is Head of Physical Education at a school that wants to improve the competitive success of its pupils. She thinks it would be a good idea to select the pupils for different sports on the basis of their personality but a colleague suggests that the pupils should be allowed to choose and will change to suit their chosen sport.

Discuss how a knowledge of the role of personality in sports psychology could help Mrs Barker to design an effective strategy to improve her pupils' performance. **[10]**

Liam's answer:

Mrs Barker should choose all the strong children to be footballers and wrestlers and all the little ones to be gymnasts. You need to be fit and big or heavy to be a good footballer or wrestler and the opposite to be a good gymnast, so the people she would choose for each sport would be different.

She could also do personality tests like the 16PF (A or B) which measures Cattell's 16 personality factors using 200 statements. She would have to check if the children were lying about their personality, so she could use a lie scale off the MMPI. This includes the statement 'I do not always tell the truth', which is a bit of an obvious way to detect whether children are lying. If the children score 7/15 or more on the lie scale they shouldn't be allowed to do sport at all as they wouldn't work well in a team because they might cheat or lie.

We say: At the start of his essay, Liam is talking about physical factors not personality, so this is irrelevant. His reference to using the 16PF is relevant but he needed to explain how Mrs Barker might use it. Also, Liam has misunderstood the lie scale. In the study by Kroll & Crenshaw, data from participants who scored 7/15 or more on the lie scale was excluded because the assessment of their personality might not have been valid. It was not used to reflect their ability to participate in team sports.

Rina's answer:

Kroll & Crenshaw (1970) showed that wrestlers, gymnasts and karate experts all had different personalities. This supports Mrs Barker's idea that she might segregate the pupils and direct them into different sports. The most serious and independent ones should go into karate, and the shy, intelligent, serious ones should try gymnastics. Less shy ones could try wrestling or football. You can see that there are some overlaps, though, like footballers and wrestlers both being adventurous and the serious ones could be put into karate or gymnastics. This means that Mrs Barker would have to do quite extensive analysis on each pupil to get the choice right and, even then, her colleague might be right as the similarities between sporting types might mean someone ends up in the wrong sport.

   Evidence from Tutko & Ogilvie (1969) initially showed that elite athletes differed in characteristics such as coachability, aggression, drive, emotional control, leadership, self-confidence and trust, which could be measured on the Athletic Motivation Inventory. However, this personality test has been criticised; for example, 'coachability' probably isn't a personality trait. Abbott & Collins (2004) point out that the tennis players Bjorn Borg and John McEnroe were about the same in terms of ability but had very different personalities.

   Instead, Mrs Barker could follow her colleague's advice and help the pupils to adjust to the personality needs of the sport they choose. A pupil who chooses football but isn't very trusting wouldn't work well in a team, so Mrs Barker could help him develop team-work through team-building exercises. For example, Ramzaninezhad & Keshtan (2009) found that Turkish football teams whose training encouraged team cohesiveness were more successful.

We say: This essay from Rina uses a diverse range of evidence: the key study as well as other evidence (including some that is relevant from another topic). She has presented a well-reasoned argument, considering ideas that both support Mrs Barker's plan and contradict it, and these are well organised. The use of named examples of sports and the associated personality traits helps to make the content of the essay relevant to the question.

TOPIC 5: PERFORMING WITH OTHERS

(b)* Assess the debate about whether psychology is a science with regard to research on teams, coaching and leadership in sport. [15]

Liam's answer:

Smith *et al.*'s study was scientific because it was a lab experiment. Lab experiments have an IV and a DV and use controls. They are good because you can be sure that the IV causes the changes in the DV, which means it is scientific. You can be sure of this because no other things that could change the DV are possible because all the extraneous variables are controlled in the laboratory environment. They used an independent measures design, which is scientific because you can be certain that there can't have been any risk of order effects like fatigue or practice effects, because the participants only did one of the conditions. This also means that they were less likely to respond to demand characteristics as they only encountered one type of coach so wouldn't have worked out the aim of the study like they would if they'd have seen both types of coach. It was also scientific because they collected quantitative data and analysed it using statistics.

In some ways psychology is not scientific, as it's difficult to replicate studies on people because they might feel different or behave differently just because of their mood or what time of day it is and not because of the IV. This would cause changes in the DV that you might think were caused by the IV, which would be a type one error.

Rina's answer:

To be a science, psychology needs to find cause-and-effect links between variables. To do this psychologists needs to conduct controlled studies to be sure the effects really are caused by the factors that they think are responsible – that is, the findings need to be valid. Also, they need to be reliable; they need to measure in a consistent way and get the same results.

We say: This essay by Liam contains lots of relevant, accurate material but it is not a very effective evaluation because he rarely links his ideas about science to examples from psychological research on performing with others. He only uses a single example, Smith *et al.*, but where he does give details they are relevant, such as his analysis of why the study is scientific because the risk of demand characteristics influencing the participants was low due to the experimental design chosen. If Liam had illustrated in this way each of the points he made, it would have been a much better essay. He could also be a little less definite, for example, 'you can be more sure that the IV causes the changes in the DV' and 'experiments aim to control extraneous variables'.

We say: Rina's essay covers a range of issues related to the scientific status of psychology (causal relationships, controls, validity and reliability), and illustrates them effectively with examples from studies from the topic, being quite specific about how they contribute to each issue. She also considers studies that are less scientific and explains why this is so, making the discussion well substantiated. However, Rina could have added a conclusion to her essay to complete it.

Smith et al.'s study shows that some sports psychology research is scientific. They used an experiment to show that the coach's communication style caused differences in interactions with players. They had controls such as randomly allocating participants to conditions so that the better players didn't all opt for one type of coaching strategy. Also, the children were compared between the groups to make sure they were similar. They were well matched for match success but weren't well matched for self-esteem, so Smith et al. tested changes in self-esteem rather than trying to compare the groups directly. All these things helped to improve validity. They also had a reliable way to measure the effects, they had a standard observation system and the observers were trained to ensure that they were consistent. The self-esteem questionnaire was also standardised and all of these helped to make sure that the results could be replicated.

Some sports psychology studies are less scientific, like Jowett & Cockerill's case study of athlete-coach pairs. They concluded that pair closeness was the most important variable but couldn't draw cause-and-effect conclusions as they hadn't manipulated closeness. To be scientific they would need to artificially change closeness of pairs and see if this affected performance.

Correlations are somewhere in between. Carron et al. (2002) found basketball and football teams had better team cohesiveness if they had better success. This isn't scientific because you can't tell whether cohesion affects performance or whether doing well makes the team closer. The cause-and-effect relationship isn't clear. In a way, though, Slater & Sewell's (1994) results do show this. They found that cohesiveness and performance success both got better over the course of a season.

RESEARCH METHODS A–Z

+   This is a 'plus' sign, which means 'add together'. Remember to add together numbers inside brackets first.

<   This means 'less than'. Remember that the 'small' end of the arrowhead is first, so it's less.

<<   This double arrowhead means 'much less than'.

>   This means 'greater than'. Remember that the 'big' end of the arrowhead is first, so it's greater.

>>   This double arrowhead means 'much greater than'.

~   This 'tilda' sign can mean many different things in the context of statistics. It is most likely to be used to mean either 'roughly equivalent to' or 'the same order of magnitude as'. Note that this is different from the 'bar' sign that is used over the letter x when referring to the mean.

≈   This sign means 'approximately equal to'.

≤   This combination of a 'less than' arrowhead and an equals sign means 'less than or equal to'. You are most likely to see this sign in the context of the significance level for a statistical test, e.g. '$p \leq 0.05$'.

≥   This combination of a 'greater than' arrowhead and an equals sign means 'greater than or equal to'.

A

Abstract – A summary at the beginning of a journal article, which usually includes brief details of the aim, method, results and conclusion.

Aim (research aim) – The purpose of an investigation, generally expressed in terms of what the study intends to demonstrate.

Alternative hypothesis – A testable statement predicting that there will be a difference or relationship between variables in an investigation.

Appendix (plural appendices) – Additional sections at the end of a journal article that can include samples of anonymous raw data and details of procedures or analysis.

Average – see **measure of central tendency**

B

Bar chart – A graph used to display nominal data and total or average scores. There are gaps between each bar that is plotted on the graph because the columns are not related in a linear way.

Behavioural categories – The independently and operationally defined units of events used in a structured observation to break a continuous stream of activity into discrete recordable events. They must be observable actions rather than inferred states.

Bias – An error in data (or data collection) that causes a systematic under- or over-estimation of a variable. This potentially leads to a difference between conditions that is not due to the IV but is caused by a flaw in the procedure. See also **sampling bias**.

Binomial sign test – A non-parametric statistical test used with nominal data from an experiment with a repeated measures (or matched participants) design, so is therefore looking for a difference in the DV between levels of the IV.

Blind – When a researcher does not know which level of the IV a participant they are testing belongs to. This arrangement, called a 'single blind procedure', helps to avoid experimenter bias. See also **double blind**.

BPS – see **British Psychological Society**

British Psychological Society (BPS) – This is a UK organisation that issues guidelines to help psychologists in research and practice to work ethically.

C

Case study – A detailed investigation of one instance, usually a single person (but could be a single family or institution), using techniques such as interviewing, observation and conducting tests, which is often done on rare instances that could not be created artificially but can provide useful information.

Causal relationship (cause-and-effect relationship) – A relationship between two variables such that a change in one is responsible for a change in the other, as in an experiment, in which the IV causes changes in the DV.

Ceiling effect – A problematic pattern of results in which the measure of a variable causes scores to cluster at the top of the range.

Central tendency – see **measure of central tendency**

Checklist – A list or table of behavioural categories used in an observational study to tally each event as it occurs.

Chi-square test – A non-parametric statistical test that is used with nominal data from an experiment with an independent measures design, so is therefore looking for a difference in the DV between levels of the IV.

Clinical case study – see **case study**

Closed questions – Test, interview or questionnaire items that offer a small number of explicitly stated alternative responses and no opportunity to expand on answers. They generate quantitative data.

Code of ethics – see **ethical standards**

Coding frame – A system for differentiating behaviours to be recorded in an observation, which uses abbreviations to represent different behavioural categories and their dimensions (such as severity). It may also include the operational definitions of the behavioural categories.

Competence – An ethical principle from the 2014 BPS Code of Human Research Ethics, which states that psychologists should maintain high standards, including advancing their knowledge, skills, training, education and experience.

Concurrent validity – A way to judge validity that compares measures of the same phenomenon in different ways at the same time to show that they produce similar results in the same circumstances. It is a type of **criterion validity**.

Confidentiality – An ethical standard relating to the principle of respect, which indicates that individuals' results and personal information should be kept safely and not released to anyone outside the study.

Confounding variable – A factor in an experiment that confuses (i.e. confounds) the results because it masks the effect of the IV on the DV as its influence is systematic. This can arise either because the additional variable acts in the same way as the IV, making the IV appear to be important when it is not, or because it works in the opposite way from the IV, making the IV appear to be unimportant when it is. One way to overcome such problems is through **random allocation**.

Consent – see **informed consent**

Construct validity – A way to judge **validity** by showing that the phenomenon being measured really exists, i.e. is based on an underlying construct, for example by justifying it in relation to a model or theory.

Content analysis – A technique for investigating information in material such as magazines, television programmes and transcripts of interviews. Content such as specific words, ideas or feelings can be divided into categories or coding units. These are counted to produce quantitative data. If they are described in detailed themes to produce qualitative data, this is called thematic analysis.

Control – A way to keep a potential extraneous variable constant so that it does not affect the DV in addition to or instead of the IV to ensure that a cause-and-effect relationship can be established.

Controlled observation – A research method in which behaviours are recorded in situations in which there has been some manipulation (e.g. of the social or physical environment) by the researchers. Such observations may be conducted in either the participants' normal environment or in an artificial situation such as a laboratory.

Correlation – A relationship between two measured variables indicating that a change in one variable is related to a change in the other (although these changes cannot be assumed to be causal).

Correlation coefficient – A measure of the strength of a correlation, usually expressed as an 'r' value between 0 and 1. A high value, e.g. $r=0.8$, means that there is a strong correlation, a negative value indicates a negative correlation, and $r=0$ means there is no correlation. This is often used to indicate reliability, so a higher value suggests better reliability.

Correlational analysis – A technique used to look for a relationship between two measured variables.

Counterbalancing – A procedure used to overcome order effects in a repeated measures design. Each possible order of levels of the IV is performed by a different sub-group of participants. This can be described as an ABBA design, as half the participants do condition A then B, and half do B then A.

Covert observation (non-disclosed observation) – A procedure in which participants are unaware that they are being watched, e.g. if the role of the observer is not known to participants., or if they are hidden. The observer may be participant or non-participant.

Credibility – Believability; the extent to which findings or explanations are plausible and trustworthy.

Criterion validity – A way to judge **validity** that compares two or more measures of the same phenomenon. In predictive validity this compares the same measure at different times to investigate whether the results on the first occasion will indicate the likely results on a future occasion. **Concurrent validity** is also a type of criterion validity.

Critical value – A value from a table for the appropriate statistical test to which an **observed value** is compared. This indicates whether the pattern in the results is significant. Three pieces of information are needed to find a critical value: the significance level (p), whether the hypothesis is **one-** or **two-tailed** and either N (the number of participants) or df (**degrees of freedom**, when using Chi-square).

Cross-cultural study – An investigation comparing variables such as mental health or attachment in people from two or more cultures.

Cross-sectional study – A way to investigate developmental changes by comparing separate groups of participants of different ages. Cross-sectional designs are quicker than **longitudinal** ones, but validity may be affected by the extraneous variable of individual differences between the participants in each age group.

D

d – This stands for 'deviation' or difference and is sometimes used in place of the difference between each score in the data set and the mean ($x-\overline{x}$) in the formulae for variance and standard deviation.

Debrief – An ethical standard relating to the principle of **responsibility**, which indicates that a full explanation of aims and potential consequences of a study be given to participants after participation to ensure that they leave in at least as positive a condition as they arrived.

Deception – An ethical standard relating to the principle of **integrity** (and of respect), which indicates that participants should not be deliberately misinformed (lied to) about the aim or procedure of the study. If this is unavoidable, steps should be taken beforehand to ensure they are unlikely to be distressed, and afterwards to ensure they are not.

Decimal form – Representing portions of numbers with values less than 1 using only 1/10ths, 1/100ths, etc. Each digit past the decimal point is one tenth of the size of the one before.

Deduction – A scientific method that develops hypotheses from theories, then tests these hypotheses by 'observation', i.e. empirically.

Degrees of freedom – In the Chi-square test this is used instead of **N** (the number of participants). It is the number of categories of data minus one and is calculated using the formula: (number of rows in the table $-$ 1) $\times$ (number of columns in the table $-$ 1).

Demand characteristics – Features of an experimental setting (the 'characteristics') that indicate to participants the aims of the study (hence the 'demands') and so can influence their behaviour.

Dependent variable (DV) – The factor in an experiment that is measured by the researcher. Changes in this factor are predicted to be caused by (i.e. dependent upon) changes in the independent variable.

Descriptive statistics – Ways to simplify or illustrate the data collected in a study to make it easier to understand, interpret or compare. These include **measures of central tendency**, **spread** and graphical representations.

Design – see **experimental design**

df – see **degrees of freedom**

Directional (one-tailed) hypothesis – A statement relating to the aim of an investigation which predicts how one variable will be related to another, e.g. in an experiment whether a change in the IV will produce an increase or a decrease in the DV or in a correlation whether an increase in one variable will be linked to an increase or a decrease in another variable. In statistical testing this is referred to as a one-tailed hypothesis.

Discussion – The section of a journal article that draws conclusions from the results of the investigation in the context of the research reported in the introduction. It may also raise any problems with the study and make suggestions for further research.

Dispersion – see **measures of dispersion**

Double blind – An experimental procedure that protects against both **demand characteristics** and **researcher bias**. It ensures that neither the researcher working with the participants nor the participants themselves are aware of which condition an individual is in.

DV – see **dependent variable**

E

Ecological validity – The extent to which findings derived from one situation generalise to other situations. This is affected by whether the situation (e.g. a laboratory) is a fair representation of the real world and whether the task is relevant (see **mundane realism**).

Errors (type 1 and 2) – see **type 1 errors**; **type 2 errors**

Estimation – A rough approximation based on some data or information that avoids a full calculation but provides a guide to the probable numerical answer.

Ethical standards – The specific guidelines suggested by the **BPS** in relation to the four ethical principles. They include consent, debriefing, protection of participants, deception, confidentiality and right to withdraw.

Ethnocentrism – Seeing the world from the point of view of one's own cultural group. Individual researchers have their own ethnic and national group and tend to conduct their research with participants from the same group so their findings and conclusions may be generalisible only to that specific group. Many classic studies in psychology were conducted in American universities using samples of undergraduate students who were, in the main, white and middle-class, so they may not be truly representative.

Event sampling – An observational data-recording method in which categories of behaviours, i.e. 'events', are recorded simultaneously and continuously (e.g. using tallies on a checklist).

Experiment – A research method in which the effect of two of more conditions of the IV on a DV is measured, and other variables are controlled, in order to investigate a cause-and-effect relationship.

Experimental conditions – The situations or tasks compared in an experiment characterising the levels of the IV. These may be compared to a baseline of a **control condition**.

Experimental design – The way in which participants are allocated to levels of the IV (see **repeated measures, independent measures and matched participants designs**).

External reliability – The extent to which a test or measure always produces the same results in the same situation with the same people.

External validity – The extent to which findings from the specific situation in a study, such an experiment in a laboratory, will generalise to other situations, such as to other *settings* (locations or context, e.g. to the 'real world'), to *people* other than the sample of participants and over *time*. **Ecological validity** is an example of external validity.

Extraneous variables – Any factors that can affect the outcome of an investigation other than those being tested. Their influence may be systematic, i.e. have a consistent effect on one level of the IV (confounding variables), or may not be (non-systematic). In either case, they threaten the validity of the findings.

F

Face validity – A simple measure of **validity** indicating whether a measure appears to test what it claims to, i.e. whether it does so at 'face value'.

Falsification – Being able to demonstrate that something is not the case, i.e. that a hypothesis is false.

Fatigue effect – A situation in which participants' performance declines because they have experienced an experimental task more than once, e.g. because of boredom or tiredness.

Field experiment – A study in which the researcher manipulates an IV and measures a DV in the natural setting of the participants for the activity being tested.

Fillers – Questions put into a questionnaire or interview to disguise the aim of the study by hiding the important questions among irrelevant ones

so that participants are less likely to alter their behaviour by working out the aims.

Floor effects – A problematic pattern of results in which the measure of a variable causes scores to cluster at the bottom of the range.

Fraction – A representation of portions of whole numbers such that the number on the top (the numerator) is divided by the number on the bottom (the denominator). For example, 1/4 means '1 divided by 4', which makes 0.25.

Frequency table (tally chart) – A grid used in an observation showing the possible categories of results in which a tick or tally is made each time the item is scored. These can be added together to give a total in each category.

G

Generalisability – The extent to which findings from one situation or sample will apply to other situations or people.

Graph – A visual form of descriptive statistics. See also types of graph: **bar chart, histogram, line graph, pie chart, scatter diagram.**

H

Harm – see **protection of participants**

Histogram – A graph used to illustrate continuous data, e.g. to show the distribution of a set of scores. It consists of bars for each score, or group of scores, along the *x*-axis with the frequency of each category on the *y*-axis.

Hypothesis (plural: hypotheses) – A testable statement predicting a relationship between

variables. The variables should be operationalised. For example, in an experiment, where a change in the IV will produce an increase or a decrease in the DV, or in a correlation, where an increase in one variable will be related to an increase or a decrease in another variable. See also: **alternative hypothesis, null hypothesis, directional hypothesis, non-directional hypothesis.**

Independent measures design – An **experimental design** in which different participants are used for each level of the IV.

Independent variable (IV) – The factor in an experiment that is manipulated, changed or compared by the researcher. It is expected to have an influence on the dependent variable.

Individual differences – Variation between people e.g. in terms of their behaviour, cognitions or emotions (which could lead to differences in their responses in experiments that are not cause by the IV) and which may be genetic or acquired in origin.

Induction – A scientific method that uses observations to generate testable hypotheses, which are developed into theories.

Inferential statistics – Mathematical techniques used to draw meaningful conclusions from numbers, i.e. to make *inferences* about data. As only quantitative data can be used, inferential statistics tend to be used on the results of experimental and correlational studies but also for experimental and correlational analyses of data from observational and self-report studies.

Informed consent – An ethical standard relating to the principle of **respect**, which indicates that participants should have sufficient knowledge about a study to decide whether they want to agree to participate.

Instantaneous scan – A time-sampling technique used in observations in which only the action being performed at the start of each preset interval is recorded. For example, an observer watching a child's play behaviour might record at 5, 10, 15, 20 seconds, etc., whether the child was playing or not, playing alone or with another child, and playing with a toy or not. They would not record any of the child's activity between the time intervals.

Integrity – A principle from the 2014 BPS Code of Human Research Ethics, which states that psychologists should value honesty, accuracy and fairness, and should recognise the importance of the standard relating to deception.

Inter-observer reliability – The extent to which two observers will produce the same records when they watch the same event.

Inter-rater reliability – The extent to which two people coding a variable, such as behaviours in an observation or qualitative responses in an interview, will produce the same records when they are presented with the same raw data.

Internal reliability – The consistency of items within a measure itself, e.g. the extent to which questions in a test or questionnaire all contribute in a similar manner to final outcome. It can be checked using a **split-half** procedure.

Internal validity – This refers to the confidence a researcher has that, within a study, the procedures are achieving the intended manipulations and measures. For example, in an experiment the extent to which they can be sure that the conditions of the IV change the variable in question and no other variables, and that the DV is measuring the effect of those changes rather than any other variables. When internal validity is high, an experimenter can be more sure that changes in the DV are caused by the IV rather than sources of error.

Interval data – A level of measurement that records data as points on a scale that has equal gaps between the points, e.g. standardised measures such as IQ tests, or scientific scales such as centimetres or beats-per-minute.

Interview – A self-report method in which participants reply verbally to questions asked directly, e.g. face-to-face or on the telephone.

Introduction – The main section of a journal article that follows the abstract and discusses the aim in the context of previous research.

IV – see **independent variable**

L

Laboratory experiment – A study conducted in an artificial environment in which the experimenter manipulates an IV and measures the consequent changes in a DV, while carefully controlling extraneous variables to test cause and effect by comparing two or more conditions.

Levels of measurement – The types of quantitative data, i.e. **nominal**, **ordinal** or **interval** data. See also **ratio**.

Levels of significance – The probability (p-value) at which the distribution of results accepted as being significant could, in fact, be due to chance (usually $p \leq 0.05$).

Levels of the IV – The different conditions under which participants are tested in an experiment that are manipulated, changed or compared by the researcher.

Likert scale – A question type that measures attitudes using a statement to which participants respond by choosing an option, typically from choices of 'strongly agree', 'agree', 'don't know', 'disagree' or 'strongly disagree'.

Line graph – A visual way to present frequency data. It is constructed on similar axes to a histogram. The x-axis is a linear scale of a variable, such as the IV in an experiment. The y-axis is the possible frequencies of this variable, eg the number of participants obtaining each score). A point is marked at the height of the frequency of each score. In a frequency polygon these points are joined to form a line. In a frequency distribution curve a smooth line is drawn as a line of best fit between the points. See also **normal distribution curve**.

Longitudinal study – An investigation in which the same participants are followed up at intervals over time to track their development. See also **cross-sectional study**.

M

Magnetic Resonance Imaging (MRI) – A scanning technique using a powerful magnetic field to affect water molecules. The resulting changes are detected by the scanner to produce very detailed images that present different areas – for example of the brain – in shades of black, grey and white.

Manipulation of variables – The way in which variables in an experiment (such as the IV) are changed by the researcher in systematic ways to create different conditions to compare.

Mann Whitney U test – A non-parametric statistical test which is used with ordinal or equal interval data from an experiment with an independent measures design so is therefore looking for a difference in the DV between levels of the IV.

Matched participants design – An experimental design in which participants are arranged into pairs (or threes, etc.). Each pair is similar in ways that are important to the study and one member of each pair performs one of the levels of the IV.

Mean – A **measure of central tendency** worked out by adding up all the scores and dividing by the number of scores.

Measure of central tendency – A mathematical way to describe a typical or average score from a data set (such as using the **mode, median** or **mean**).

Measure of dispersion – A mathematical way to describe the variation or spread in the scores from a data set, such as the **range, variance** and **standard deviation**.

Median – A **measure of central tendency** worked out as the middle score in the list when the data are in rank order (from smallest to largest). If there are two numbers in the middle they are added together and divided by two.

Method – The section of a journal article that give details of the research method, procedure, sample and materials or apparatus. It should give enough detail to allow replication.

Mode – A **measure of central tendency** worked out as the most frequent score(s) in a set of results.

MRI – see Magnetic Resonance Imaging

Mundane realism – The extent to which an experimental task represents a real-world situation.

N

N – The number of scores in the data set.

Naïve participant – A member of the sample who does not know the purpose of the study. This reduces the likelihood that their behaviour will be affected by their beliefs about the aims.

Naturalistic observation – A research method in which behaviours seen in the participants' normal environment are recorded without interference from the researchers in either the social or the physical environment.

Negative correlation – A relationship between two variables such that an increase in one accompanies a decrease in the other.

Negative skew – A non-normal (or 'skewed') frequency distribution, with a long 'tail' of scores to the left (the 'negative' direction). The mode is to the right, the mean to the left (i.e. in the 'tail'), and the median lies in between.

Nominal data – Data in totals of named categories such as the number of kittens who respond to visual stimuli of lines, spots or squares, or the number of participants saying 'yes' or 'no'.

Non-directional (two-tailed) hypothesis – A statement about the aim of a study which predicts that, rather than how, one variable will be related to another. In experiments this will be a difference between the scores on the DV for the different levels of the IV. For a correlation it will be a relationship between the two measured variables. In statistical testing this is referred to as a two-tailed hypothesis.

Non-parametric test – A statistical test for which there are no assumptions about the level of measurement, normal distribution or variance of the data collected, so can be used on data that are nominal or ordinal.

Non-participant observation – A way of collecting data such that the participants' behaviour is recorded by a researcher who is not engaging with them as part of the social setting. The observer may be overt or covert.

Normal distribution – A frequency distribution curve that rises gradually and symmetrically to a single maximum at the point of the mean, median and mode. It is sometimes called 'the bell curve' because of its shape.

Null hypothesis – A testable statement saying that any difference or correlation is due to chance, i.e. that no pattern in the results has arisen because of the variables being studied.

O

Objectivity – Taking an unbiased external perspective that is not affected by an individual or personal viewpoint, so should be consistent between different researchers. See also **subjectivity**.

Observational method – A research method used when watching participants (human or animal) directly in order to obtain data and gather information about their behaviour.

Observed value – The single number calculated by a statistical test from the scores found (i.e. *observed*) in the study. It is compared to a *critical value* to determine whether the pattern in the results is significant.

Observer bias – The tendency of an observer to record behaviours that they believe should or will occur, or to identify behaviours within the context of their subjective perspective, rather than recording those behaviours that are actually occurring.

Observer effects – The influences that the presence of an observer can have on participants in a situation where the observer is overt, or where their role becomes apparent. The participants' awareness that they are being watched prompts changes in their behaviour.

One-tailed (or directional) hypothesis – A statement predicting the nature, i.e. *direction* of a relationship between variables, e.g. in an experiment whether a change in the IV will produce an increase or a decrease in the DV, or in a correlation whether an increase in one variable will be linked to an increase or a decrease in another variable (i.e. positive or negative). This is used in statistical testing.

One-zero sampling – A time-sampling technique used in observations in which the researcher records whether the each behavioural category was exhibited or not within each time period.

Open questions – Questions that allow participants to give full and detailed answers in their own words, i.e. no categories or choices are given. They generate qualitative data.

Operationalisation – The definition of variables so that they can be accurately manipulated, measured or quantified, and replicated.

Opportunity sampling – The selection of participants according to availability. It is non-representative.

Order effects – The consequences of participating more than once in a study, for example in a repeated measures design, which produce changes in performance between conditions that are not the result of the IV, so can obscure the effect on the DV. See also **practice** and **fatigue effects**.

Ordinal data – Data as points along a scale, e.g. from rating or Likert scale, such that the points fall in order but there are not necessarily equal gaps between those points.

Overt observation (disclosed observation) – A procedure in which participants are aware that they are being watched, e.g. if the role of the observer is known to participants.

P

p – The letter *p* is used to represent a probability. In statistical testing it represents the probability that the distribution of results could have arisen by chance. A *p*-value can range from 0 to 1, with 0 representing no influence of chance, and 1 representing a complete influence of chance, so the smaller the *p*-value, the more stringent the statistical test. The *p*-value is written as a proportion e.g. $p \leq 0.05$.

Parametric test – A statistical test that makes assumptions about the data collected. These are that: the data are normally distributed for the population(s) from which the sample was taken; the data from both levels of the IV have equal variance; the level of measurement of the data is equal interval.

Participant observation – A way to collect data such that the participants' behaviour is recorded by a researcher who is engaged with them as part of the social setting.

Participant variables – Individual differences between participants (such as age, skills, personality) that could affect their responses in a study.

Peer review – The process of using other experts, such as fellow professionals, to judge whether a new piece of research (typically a journal article) makes a significant contribution to the body of psychological knowledge, specifically that it is effective in its methodology, data analysis and the drawing of conclusions, as well as adhering to ethical guidelines.

Percentage – A numerical value that is a special fraction in which the denominator is always 100. The resulting number is followed by the sign '%'. So, a half would be written as 50% (because ½ = 50/100). To convert a fraction to a percentage, you multiply 100 by the fraction (e.g. ½ ×100 = 50, so ½ is the same as 50%). To convert a percentage to a fraction, you divide by 100 (e.g. 25% is 25/100 = ¼). To change a decimal to a percentage, multiply by 100 (e.g. 0.75 = 0.75×100 = 75%. To change a percentage to a decimal, divide by 100, e.g. 90% = 90/100 = 9/10.

Physical harm – see **protection of participants**

Pie chart – A circular graph divided into sectors such that each portion represents a numerical proportion of a whole.

Pilot study – A small-scale trial run of a method to identify and resolve any problems with the procedure.

Population – All the people within a given group (e.g. geographical area, religion or school) who could, potentially, be selected for the sample.

Population validity – The extent to which findings from one sample can be generalised to the whole of the **population** from which the sample was taken, and to other populations. It is dependent on factors such as sampling method, sample size and diversity, and the phenomenon being tested.

Positive correlation – A relationship between two variables such that an increase in one accompanies an increase in the other.

Positive skew – A non-normal (or 'skewed') frequency distribution, with a long 'tail' of scores to the right (the 'positive' direction). The mode is to the left, the mean to the right (ie in the 'tail') and the median lies in between.

Practice effect – A situation in which participants' performance improves because they experience an experimental task more than once. They might become more familiar with the task or recall their previous answers. It is a type of **order effect**.

Predominant activity sampling – A time-sampling techniques used in observations in which the observer watches throughout each time interval and records only whichever behaviour the individual performed most during that interval.

Presumptive consent – It can be used when gaining agreement to participate, in principle, from a group of people similar to the intended participants, by asking them if they would object to the procedure. It can be used when to gain informed consent from the participants themselves would lead to their working out the aim of the study.

Primary data – The results of a first-hand investigation; collecting qualitative or quantitative information directly from a sample.

Privacy – The ethical **standards** standard relating to avoiding the invasion of emotions or physical space, e.g. observing participants in locations where they would expect to be unseen.

Probability – see *p*-value.

Protection of participants – An ethical standard relating to the principle of **responsibility**, indicating that participants should not be put at any greater physical or psychological risk than they would expect in their day-to-day lives.

Psychological harm – see **protection of participants**.

Psychometrics – The theory and practice of psychological measurement which attempts to achieve valid assessments that provide numerical measures of human personality traits, attitudes and abilities. Psychometric tools include tests, questionnaires and interviews, e.g. IQ tests.

Q

Qualitative data – Descriptive results indicating the *quality* of a psychological characteristic, i.e. providing in-depth findings. Examples include detailed observational accounts and open question data from questionnaires, interviews or case studies.

Quantitative data – Numerical results indicating the *quantity* of a psychological measure such as time or a score on a personality test.

Quasi-experiment – An experimenter makes use of an existing change or difference in situations to create levels of an IV, and then measures the DV in each condition.

Questionnaire – A self-report method that uses written questions.

R

Random allocation – A way to overcome the effects of confounding variables such as individual differences by ensuring that the participants representing each level of the IV in an experiment have an equal chance of being in any condition.

Random sampling – Selecting participants so that each member of a population has an equal chance of being chosen. It is representative of the population.

Range – A measure of dispersion calculated by taking the smallest from the largest value in the data set and adding 1 to the total.

Rating scale – A numerical scale on which participants indicate the strength of some measure, generating quantitative data. It can be used to give a numerical answer to a question or to indicate the extent to which the participant agrees with a statement.

Ratio – A comparison between values within different categories, e.g. a playgroup has 4 staff and 16 children. The staff:child ratio is 1:4 (as both numbers can be divided by 4). A playgroup with a ratio of 1:8 would have twice as many children per staff member. (NB you may also see 'ratio' used to mean a level of measurement which, like interval data has equal gaps between the points, but this also has an absolute zero.)

Raw data – The original scores obtained from all the participants in a study.

Reference – The citation of details of a piece of research in a conventional way such that others are able to trace it. The *References* section of a journal article lists all the other articles that have been referred to.

Reliability – The consistency of a measure, e.g. whether results that should be the same do indeed stay the same each time. See also **internal**, **external**, **inter-rater** and **inter-observer reliability**.

Repeated measures design – An experimental design in which each participant performs in every level of the IV, i.e. *repeats* their performance.

Replicability – Being able to repeat an original procedure in exactly the same way.

Representativeness – The extent to which a sample is typical of the key features of the population so is likely to produce findings that can be generalised.

Research aim – see **aim**.

Research question – A question that illustrates what a study intends to investigate.

Researcher bias – An unconscious tendency of the researcher to act in ways that alter the results, often in the expected direction.

Researcher effects – The negative influences researchers can have on a study by their presence or beliefs.

Respect – An ethical principle from the BPS Code of Human Research Ethics, which states that researchers should value the dignity and worth of all individuals, including an awareness of people's rights to privacy and self-determination, especially the standards of informed consent, right to withdraw and confidentiality.

Response bias – The tendency of a participant to favour one extreme or the other in the way that they react in a study, such as in their replies on a questionnaire or reaction on a measure of the DV in an experiment. For example, they may tend towards one end of a scale in a questionnaire or to press the right-hand key.

Responsibility – An ethical principle from the BPS Code of Human Research Ethics, which states that psychologists should value their profession and the science of psychology, including avoiding harm and preventing misuse or abuse of contributions to society, and recognising the importance of the standards of protection of participants and the role of the debrief.

Restricted sample – A group of participants having one or more characteristics in common. This may be necessary if the sample needs to contain a particular kind of person, such as people with a particular disorder, or it may be a consequence of the sampling technique and therefore limits the generalisibility of the findings.

Results – The section of a journal article that includes any summary and analysis of the findings from the research.

Right to withdraw – An ethical standard relating to the principle of respect, which indicates that a participant should be aware that they can remove themselves, and their data, from the study at any time.

S

S² – The **variance**.

Sample – The group of people selected from a population to take part in a study whose results represent those of the population.

Sampling bias – A source of **bias** that arises from a systematic tendency to recruit particular types of participants, or for particular types of participants to segregate between levels of the IV. This potentially leads to a difference between conditions that is not due to the IV but is caused by a flaw in the procedure, causing a misrepresentation of the population.

Sampling technique – The way a group of participants (the sample) is selected. See also **snowball, stratified, volunteer, random** and **opportunity sampling**.

Scatter diagram – A graph used to display the data from a correlational study. Each point on the graph represents one participant's score on scales for each of the two measured variables.

Scientific method – The process of developing knowledge through either **induction** or **deduction**.

Secondary data – Information that is obtained about the results of an investigation that has already been conducted by another researcher, possibly for a different purpose. This can then be re-used in a new analysis. See also **primary data**.

Self-report – A research method that obtains data by asking participants to provide information about themselves. See also **interviews, questionnaires**.

Self-selected sampling (volunteer sampling) – A way to recruit people through advertising; the participants respond to a request rather than being approached by the experimenter. It is non-representative.

Semantic differential – A rating scale on which participants choose between two extremes, rating their response towards an opposing pair of descriptive words (bipolar adjectives), such as 'calm' and 'tense'. The participant chooses one of several numerical values (typically 5 or 7).

Semi-structured interview – A type of interview that uses a fixed list of open and closed questions, although the interviewer can introduce additional questions if required.

Sign test – see **binomial sign test**.

Significance level – The probability that a pattern in the results (a difference in an experiment or relationship in a correlation) could have arisen by chance. It is usually set at $p \leq 0.05$.

Significant figure – This is a way to simplify a long number. The first digit is the most important (i.e. 'significant'), but the next number matters too. If it is 5 or more, the first number is rounded up. If it is 4 or less the, first number is not rounded up. So, 6710 becomes 7000 to one significant figure; 0.0438 becomes 0.04 to one significant figure (these would be 6700 and 0.044 to two significant figures).

Single blind – An experimental procedure ensuring that the participants themselves are unaware of the level of the IV in which they are performing, which helps to reduce the effect of demand characteristics.

Single participant experiment – A research method that employs one individual in a repeated measures design. This may be achieved by comparing a variable 'before' and 'after' a significant change, such as surgery, or in different levels of the IV (in an experimental set up), for example, comparing right and left hemisphere responses.

Single-cell recording – A way to measure the activity of individual neurons using a micropipette.

Situational variables – Factors in the environment surrounding participants that could affect their performance on the DV and hence act as confounding variables, obscuring the effect of the IV.

Skewed distribution – A frequency distribution in which (unlike a normal distribution) the measures of central tendency do not lie together in the middle. Instead, there is a greater spread of scores on one side. See also **positive skew** and **negative skew**.

Snowball sampling – A technique for selecting of participants used when they are hard to find or when a particular kind of person is needed. Starting with a very small number of participants, these individuals then recruit further members of the sample (to whom they are in some way connected).

Social desirability – A potential source of bias caused by the tendency of participants to respond in ways that they think reflect what is acceptable in society rather than how they necessarily believe they should or want to respond.

Socially sensitive research – Investigations that have the potential to be offensive or destructive through their methods or findings, for example, by stigmatising certain individuals or groups (e.g. in areas of gender or culture), having political consequences (e.g. have implications for policy change), or having the potential to cause harm (e.g. issues that are highly controversial, private or likely to cause distress)

Spearman's Rho test – A non-parametric statistical test used with ordinal data when the research is correlational to test for a relationship between two measured variables.

Split-half – A measure of reliability that compares two halves of a test, e.g. odd- and even-numbered questions. If the participants' scores on the two halves correlate well, the measure has good reliability.

Standard deviation – A measure of dispersion that calculates the average difference between each score in the data set and the mean, and represents this in the same units as the mean itself. Bigger values indicate greater dispersion It is the square root of the variance.

Standard form – This is a way of representing very small or very large numbers by showing how many 'times tens' the number is multiplied by. For example, 5×10^2 means '5 multiplied by two times ten', i.e. $5 \times (10 \times 10)$ or $5 \times 100 = 500$. When the number to be represented is very small the 'power' that 10 is raised to (2 in the example above) is negative.

Standardisation – The use of set procedures for conducting a study and collecting data across different conditions and participants to limit the effects of uncontrolled variables.

Standardised instructions – A set of spoken, written or recorded instructions presented to participants to tell them what to do. This ensures that all participants receive identical treatment and information, so differences between their performance on the DV are more likely to be the result of the IV.

Statistical test – see **inferential test**.

Stratified sampling – A technique for selecting participants in which individuals are taken to represent each major layer (stratum) within the population (eg socio-economic group, age, locations or ethnic group). In proportionate strata sampling individuals from the different strata are selected according to the incidence of that sub-group within the population. In disproportionate strata sampling the relative incidence of subgroups is not reflected in the sample.

Structured interview – An **interview** method that asks predominantly closed questions in a fixed order. The questions are likely to be scripted so they are standardised, and consistency might even be required for the interviewer's posture, etc.

Structured observation – A research method in which an observer records a specified range of behaviours in predefined categories.

Subjectivity – Taking a biased personal viewpoint that may be influenced by one's own beliefs or experiences, so may differ between individual researchers, i.e. is not independent of the situation. See also **objectivity**.

T

t-test – An example of a parametric statistical test which, like all other statistical tests, produces an observed value. For the t-test this is called 't'

Table – A data record sheet with rows and columns for recording results. In a raw data table, these are the results collected directly from participants in a study, which may be counted using tally marks.

Tally chart – see **frequency table**.

Target population – The group from which a sample is drawn. See also **population**.

Test-retest – A measure of reliability that uses the same test twice. If the participants' two sets of scores correlate well, the measure has good reliability.

Time sampling – A data-collection technique that uses a limited list of possible activities. The occurrence of these activities is recorded in relation to short, specified time intervals.

True experiment – An **experiment** in which the researcher can randomly allocate participants to different levels of the IV. Laboratory and field experiments are examples of true experiments, a quasi experiment is not.

Twin study – A technique used to attempt to separate the effects of genes and family environment. Comparisons may be made between identical twins (MZs) reared together and reared apart, or to assess the relative similarity between identical and non-identical (DZ) twins.

Two-tailed (or non-directional) hypothesis – A statement predicting how one variable will be related to another, e.g. whether there will be a difference in the DV between levels of the IV (in an experiment), or that there will be a relationship between the measured variables (in a correlation).

Type one error – Rejecting the null hypothesis when it is true (and therefore accepting the alternative hypothesis when it is false, an 'optimistic' error: 'o' for 'one' and 'optimistic'). This is more likely when the level of significance is less stringent, e.g. $p \leq 0.1$, than when it is more stringent (e.g. $p \leq 0.05$) as it is easier to reject the null hypothesis at $p \leq 0.1$, than at $p \leq 0.05$.

Type two error – Accepting the null hypothesis when it is false and therefore rejecting the alternative hypothesis when it is true (a 'pessimistic' error). This is more likely when the level of significance is too stringent, e.g. $p \leq 0.01$, than when it is less stringent (e.g. $p \leq 0.05$) as it is harder to reject the null hypothesis at $p \leq 0.01$, than at $p \leq 0.05$.

U

Unstructured interview – An interview method that generally begins with a standard question for all participants but, from there on, questions depend on the respondent's answers. There might be a list of topics for the interviewer to cover.

Unstructured observation – A research method in which an observer records a nonspecified, wide range of behaviours including any that seem relevant.

V

Validity – The extent to which a test or tool measures what it claims to measure. See also **internal**, **external**, **experimental** and **ecological validity**.

Variance – A measure of dispersion that calculates the average difference between each score in the data set and the mean. Bigger values indicate greater dispersion. It is the same calculation as the standard deviation, without the final step of finding the square root.

Volunteer sampling – see **self-selected sampling**.

W

Wilcoxon signed ranks test – A non-parametric statistical test which is used with ordinal or equal interval data from an experiment with a repeated measures (or matched participants) design to look for a difference in the DV between levels of the IV.

Withdrawal – see **right to withdraw**.

X

x – Each score in the data set, i.e. a figure for the variable being measured.

x̄ – The mean of the data set (called the 'sample mean').

α – The Greek letter Alpha, used to refer to an unknown angle. You could encounter it in relation to a pie chart. It is also used to refer to the probability of making a type one error.

Σ – The Greek letter Sigma, meaning 'the sum of', i.e. 'add them all up'.

CHAPTER 7

REVISION

WHEN, WHAT AND HOW

When

Effective revision isn't something that benefits from being done at the last minute. With luck, you will be reading this well in advance and can start early. Your first task is to perfect your exam technique. This takes practice and feedback, and you should work on this *throughout the course*. Your teacher will help, but you can also write essays and mark them yourself using any questions and mark schemes that are available from the OCR examination board. You can download some from their website (www.ocr.org.uk/qualifications/as-a-level-gce-psychology-h167-h567-from-2015/).

Your second task is to learn the course content. Again, learning the material and testing yourself regularly throughout the course will help to consolidate your understanding. However, you will need to dedicate time just to revision in the run-up to the exam period. You are probably studying several subjects and will need to organise your time and stick to a timetable to make sure you get everything done. Plan out in advance how long you will spend on each topic, and be realistic – there is no point in revising a little of the course really well but being unable to remember anything from the rest.

What

Remember that you will be examined on everything that you have done over the full *two years*. Even if you happened to have sat exams at the end of the first year course, this does not count towards your full A level; you will be tested on the same material again, so you need to learn the studies and research methods from Year 1 as well as the applications from Year 2. If you do not have a copy of the specification for your course, it is worth looking at one so that you know exactly what you could be tested on. Look at the examination board website (www.ocr.org.uk/Images/171732-specification-accredited-a-level-gce-psychology-h567.pdf), and use it as a checklist to tick off everything you need to revise. The list on page 328 will help you too.

TABLE 7.1: WHAT YOU WILL NEED TO KNOW FOR EACH PAPER

Paper	% of total A level	Marks and time	What is covered
Research methods (H567/01)	30	90 marks 2 hours	Research methods, both in general and in relation to the core studies. This includes how to plan, conduct, analyse and report psychological research using experimental and non-experimental methods.
Psychological themes through core studies (H567/02)	35	105 marks 2 hours	20 core studies from five areas of psychology. One classic and one contemporary study represent two key themes within each area. The key methodological issues relating to each core study, and how each contributes to perspectives, issues and debates in psychology.
Applied psychology (H567/03)	35	105 marks 2 hours	Three applied areas: Issues in Mental Health (which is compulsory) and then two of the following options: Child Psychology, Criminal Psychology, Environmental Psychology, Sport and Exercise Psychology. Questions can refer to issues and debates.

How

REVISING THE A LEVEL YEAR 2 APPLICATIONS

For 'Issues in Mental Health' you need to learn:

The background, key research and application for each of the three sub-topics: the historical context of mental health, the medical model, and an alternative to the medical model (here you should have learned the behaviourist and cognitive models, plus one of humanistic, psychodynamic or cognitive-neuroscience).

For your two chosen applied topics you need to learn:

The background, key research and application for each of the six sub-topics in each of the two applications. The applications are Child, Criminal, Environmental, and Sport and Exercise. You will be asked questions not only relating to the content you have learned but also about the content in relation to issues and debates. In addition, you need to be able to apply this knowledge to novel situations. For example, to be able to design similar studies to the key research or to suggest ways to use the ideas from the application to new problems.

Use the Question Spotlight features to help you to think about key ideas you need to understand and make sure that you look carefully at the Practice Questions at the end of each chapter. There are exam-style questions that you can use for practice, as well as worked examples from Liam and Rina. To improve your exam technique it is a good idea to attempt the same questions as Liam and Rina before reading the commentary, then compare your responses to theirs. Use this to see how you could have written a better answer and then tackle the remaining questions in the topic. You can use the 'Issues and Debates' features in particular to guide you in your revision of the debates and how they link to the applications.

To help you to learn the details of each of the pieces of key research, these have been summarised for you in the following pages.

SUMMARIES IN BRIEF

CHAPTER 1

Topic 1: The historical context of mental health

Aim: To investigate the reliability of the diagnosis of mental illness

Method: Study 1: Pseudopatients presented themselves to different hospitals across the USA. On admission, they all reported the same symptom (hearing voices). Once diagnosed, they were admitted and showed no further symptoms. Participants kept a written record of their own experiences and those of other patients in the hospital.

Study 2: In a different hospital, staff were made aware of the findings of Study 1. They were led to believe that over three months one or more pseudopatients would attempt to be admitted. They each scored new patients out of 10 as to the probability of their being a sane actor.

Results: In Study 1, all of the pseudopatients were admitted to hospital, none was detected as 'sane' by staff. Participants experienced depersonalisation and powerlessness. In Study 2, approximately 10% of genuine patients were judged to be pseudopatients by at least one psychiatrist and one other staff member.

Conclusion: Psychiatric diagnosis lacks reliability. Labelling people as 'insane' can change subsequent interpretations of their behaviour.

Topic 2: The medical model

Aim: To compare vulnerability to mental illness of offspring with one or both parents having a diagnosis of schizophrenia or bipolar disorder.

Method: Rates of mental illness were compared in Danish people who had both, one or neither parent with a diagnosis of schizophrenia or bipolar disorder.

Results: For both schizophrenia and bipolar disorder having both parents with a diagnosis increased the chances significantly of suffering that disorder (27.3% for schizophrenia and 24.95 for bipolar) and mental illness in general (67.5% and 44.2% respectively). Having one parent with schizophrenia or bipolar disorder carried a more modest risk.

Conclusion: Having both parents with a serious mental illness – and to a lesser extent one parent with a serious mental illness – conveys increased risk of developing mental illness.

Topic 3: Alternatives to the medical model

Aim: To review and update Szasz's own work on beliefs about mental illness, as psychiatry becomes increasingly politicised and medicalised.

Method: Szasz's paper does not include original participant research, but instead outlines his anti-psychiatry arguments.

Results: Szasz rejects the view that those who act in disturbing or disturbed ways should be viewed as mentally ill. The current mental healthcare system treats people as patients with little control over their illnesses. It also frames mental illness as a medical problem, which invokes hierarchies of power and control by professionals over their patients.

Conclusion: Mental illness is little more than a metaphor for the perceived disturbing behaviour of others, and labelling individuals denies them their autonomy and freedom.

CHAPTER 2

Topic 1: Intelligence

Aim: To investigate the relative contributions of genetic and environmental influences in IQ variance and explore reasons for spousal resemblance for intelligence.

Method: A twin-family design was used which included 112 families who were contacted through the Netherlands Twin Registry. Twins were assessed for zygosity. Both adults and children undertook a standardised test of cognitive ability. Statistical modelling was used to compare explanations of spousal resemblance for IQ.

Results: Concordance rates between MZ twins were higher than between any other relatives. Spousal resemblance for intelligence was confirmed, and estimated to be a result of phenotypic assortment. There was evidence of an interaction between genetic and environmental factors.

Conclusion: Genetics are the main influence on intelligence, with environmental factors playing a smaller but still significant role.

Topic 2: Pre-adult brain development

Aim: To test whether adolescents respond differently to rewards than adults, using a task of expect value (EV).

Method: Nineteen adults and 22 adolescents took part in this quasi lab experiment. The participants underwent an fMRI scan whilst completing a gambling simulation task. The task offered them a 50-50 chance of winning or losing differing amounts of money. Participants had to 'accept' or 'reject' gambles in 144 trials.

Results: There was greater activation of the ventral striatum in adolescents than adults as EV increased. Both groups responded similarly to no-risk trials. Adolescents accepted more gambles than adults when the EV was greater.

Conclusion: Adolescents are more sensitive to rewards than adults.

Topic 3: Perceptual development

Aim: To investigate depth perception in infants and young animals.

Method: 36 infants aged 6–14 months were individually placed on the centre of the visual cliff apparatus. The mother of each infant called to them from the cliff and shallow sides in turn. The responses of the infants were observed and recorded. The behaviour of other baby animals was also observed using the visual cliff apparatus.

Results: Infants appeared to rely on visual perception to guide behaviour. The majority of infants moved towards the shallow side of the apparatus, and only three crawled 'off' the visual cliff. Infants often cried or crawled away from their mothers when they stood at the cliff side. All species seemed to perceive and avoid sharp drops.

Conclusion: Most human infants can perceive height distance at the time they begin crawling. Some aspects of visual perception appear to precede the development of physical movement.

Topic 4: Cognitive development and education

Aim: To compare how children of different ages interacted with a tutor on simple construction tasks.

Method: 30 male and female participants of 3, 4 or 5 years of age were sourced from the same area and took part in this quasi-experiment. They were introduced to a tutor and presented with interlocking blocks to play with. A tutor was tasked with individually teaching each child to build a three-dimensional structure which was beyond what they might be expected to create on their own. The data collected were the systematic descriptions of the changing interaction of tutor and child in response to different forms of support during the undertaking of this task.

Results: Age played a key role in the children's success in the tasks, e.g. the older a child was, the more unassisted correct constructions they made. It also affected the tutor's role, which ranged from trying to engaging the 3 year olds with the task, to correcting the 4 year olds' errors and offering confirmation to the 5 year olds who made correct constructions.

Conclusion: Analysis of the observed interactions between children and tutors showed a process of instruction that involved scaffolding.

Topic 5: Development of attachment

Aim: To observe exploratory and attachment behaviours using the Strange Situation test.

Method: A controlled observation was conducted with 56 mother and baby pairs using the Strange Situation test. Two observers tape-recorded covert observations of the interactions. Exploratory behaviours and crying were coded for analysis.

Results: The presence of the mother encouraged exploratory behaviour, and her absence lead to increased attachment behaviours such as crying and searching. In reunion episodes, infants sought contact and proximity to their mothers more frequently. In some infants, contact-resistance increased along with contact-maintaining suggesting ambivalence, and in others proximity-avoidance increased.

Conclusion: When present, the mother offers a secure base for exploration, whilst threatening situations increase attachment behaviours. There are observable individual differences in attachment styles.

Topic 6: Impact of advertising on children

Aim: To examine whether the language used in TV adverts links products to gender stereotypical roles.

Method: Across a range of TV networks, 39 half-hour programmes were recorded and found to include 478 adverts. Toy averts were selected for further analysis due to their frequency, cultural content and likelihood of including gendered material. They were categorised as either boy-oriented, girl-oriented and both boy and girl-oriented. Researchers analysed 188 adverts for evidence of stereotyping, including gender exaggeration and verb elements.

Results: The names of toys and the ways in which they were played with reinforced gender stereotypes. Voice-overs tended to be gender specific to the toy being advertised and there was evidence of gender exaggeration in those voices. Verb element analysis revealed polarised messages, with greater activity, competition and control within boy-oriented adverts and more nurturing and feeling activity within girl-oriented adverts.

Conclusion: Features of discourse included in this analysis have shown that gender stereotyping is prevalent in TV adverts for children's toys.

CHAPTER 3

Topic 1: What makes a criminal?

Aim: To compare the brain activity of murderers and non-murderers.

Method: An experiment comparing two levels of the IV using a group of murderers and a control group in a matched participants design. The DV was the areas of brain activity during a controlled task measured using a PET scan.

Results: The murderers had less brain activity in the prefrontal cortex and corpus callosum than non-murderers and differences in left side and right side activation in the amygdala, temporal lobe, hippocampus and thalamus.

Conclusion: Differences in brain activation areas such as the prefrontal cortex and limbic system may predispose criminals to violence.

Topic 2: The collection and processing of forensic evidence

Aim: To find out whether fingerprint experts are emotionally affected by case details and whether this emotional context biases their judgments.

Method: 70 fingerprint experts volunteered for an experiment in which they were given a latent mark on a £50 and a set of comparison prints to match. They were given either low- or high-emotion case information in an independent measures design. Their reported feelings about the case information and whether this affected their decision about the fingermark match were measured.

Results: 52% of the 30 analysts who had read the high-emotion case information felt affected by it compared to 6% in the low-emotion condition. However, no significant difference was found between the decisions by participants in the two emotional contexts nor in their willingness to present the mark in court, i.e. they were equally confident.

Conclusion: Emotional context affects experts' feelings but not their decision about fingermark matches.

Topic 3: Collection of evidence

Method: A review, structured around the effectiveness of the various components of the Cognitive Interview, the relationship between the Cognitive Interview and other interviewing methods, different measures of memory performance and the effect this has on research findings and interviewer variables and the effect of training quality on interview performance.

Results: The authors make several key points. They argue that context reinstatement is the most effective component of the Cognitive Interview. They claim that comparisons with

the standard police interview are now dated and suggest that future research should compare the Cognitive Interview to the Structured Interview. Finally, they discuss the problems associated with the differing measures of memory and factors such as the quality and length of training given to interviewers.

Conclusion: The authors conclude that there is still a need for good research into the Cognitive Interview. Researchers must ensure that they have appropriate comparison groups and suitable measures of memory.

Topic 4: Psychology and the courtroom

Aim: To test the hypothesis that a Brummie-accented suspect would produce stronger attributions of guilt than a standard-accented suspect. The study also tested whether the race of the suspect and the type of crime would influence this effect.

Method: An experimental design with three independent variables (accent, race and type of crime). 119 undergraduate students listened to one audio recording of a (fake) police transcript and then rated the likely guilt of the accused on a 7-point scale.

Results: The 'Brummie' suspect was rated as the most likely to be guilty. The Brummie accent/black suspect/blue-collar condition had significantly higher guilt ratings than the other conditions.

Conclusion: Accent has a significant effect on judgments of guilt or innocence.

Topic 5: Crime prevention

Aim: To explore the relationship between low-level crime and serious offences within communities.

Method: The authors considered the Newark Foot Patrol Experiment as a case study, and engaged in participant observations of police officers in communities.

Results: Increased foot patrols resulted in better community relations and lowered residents' fear of crime. Fear of crime and poor relations with police can lead to a lack of responsibility and personal involvement in community affairs. Just as a single broken window when ignored can lead to many more being destroyed, serious crime was theorised to emerge from increasing levels of disorder and antisocial behaviour.

Conclusion: The theory of broken windows can help explain the link between public disorder and serious crime.

Topic 6: Effect of imprisonment

Aim: The aim of the study was to investigate the effect of being given the roles of prisoner and guard.

Method: A sample of 24 white, middle-class male college students were randomly assigned the role of prisoner or guard. The study took place in a mock prison at Stanford University.

They were each given uniforms and told the study would last two weeks. The participants were observed and their behaviour was recorded by the experimenters.

Results: Both the prisoners and guards adopted their assigned roles quickly and began to show pathological behaviour. Guards were hostile and aggressive towards the prisoners, some of whom became extremely distressed. The experiment was ended after just six days due to the deterioration of conditions in the prison.

Conclusion: Situational factors offer a better explanation than dispositional factors for the social roles taken on by participants. This has important implications for how prison guards are trained.

CHAPTER 4

Topic 1: Stressors in the environment

Aim: To explore the impact of aircraft noise on the health of a community of people living in areas surrounding Sydney Airport.

Method: In this correlational study, noise measurements were taken from 26 noise stations surrounding Sydney Airport. Questionnaires were sent to 1500 participants in the noise exposure areas and control areas.

Results: Participants in the noise exposure group had significantly higher levels of reported noise stress and aircraft annoyance, as well as lower scores on health measures.

Conclusion: Long-term aircraft noise exposure was significantly associated with chronic noise stress and, in turn, chronic noise stress was significantly associated with prevalence of hypertension.

Topic 2: Biological rhythms

Aim: To examine the experience of individuals working on rotating shift patterns and to test a redesigned shift-work schedule based on knowledge of circadian rhythms.

Method: This study is in two parts. The first part is a natural experiment comparing the experiences of rotating (phase advance) versus non-rotating shift workers. The second part is a field experiment where the researchers manipulated the shift-work patterns so that the workers on phase-advancing schedules were divided into two groups: the first continued to change shifts every week and the second group rotated shifts by phase delay every 21 days.

Results: In the first part of the study, the workers on rotating shifts reported significantly more sleep problems than the non-rotating workers. They also reported that schedules changed too often and that they had problems adjusting their sleep patterns after each change in schedule. In the second part of the study, it was found that workers preferred delay rotating schedules over advance rotating schedules. Those on the 21-day phase-delay shift pattern had increased scores on both the schedule satisfaction index and the health index. In addition, there was an increase in productivity and a decrease in staff turnover.

Conclusion: Workers clearly preferred the phase delay direction of rotation, and the change to this shift schedule also produced improvements in health, an increase in productivity, and a decrease in staff turnover.

Topic 3: Recycling and other conservation behaviours

Aim: This research investigates the effectiveness of a range of different types of messages designed to increase compliance with a recycling programme in the United States. The investigators manipulated several variables including message appeal (positive or negative) and message source (advertising, publicity and personal).

Method: In this field experiment, 140 households were allocated to a condition with a combination of message source (advertisement/newspaper article/personal letter) and message framing (positive/negative). Recycling behaviour was observed through recording of number of items in the recycling bin prior to the message delivery and one week later. Questionnaires were also given to one member of each household, measuring beliefs and attitudes associated with recycling behaviour.

Results: Positive appeals produced the most favourable levels of belief and attitude towards recycling. However the greatest increase in recycling behaviour was seen in the group who were given the negatively framed personal letter.

Conclusion: Factors affecting recycling behaviours are complex and this research highlights this.

Topic 4: Ergonomics

Aim: To evaluate a configural vital signs (CVS) display designed to support rapid detection and identification of physiological change in an intensive care unit (ICU) by graphically presenting patient vital signs data.

Method: 42 ICU nurses interpreted data presented in either a traditional, numerical format or on the CVS display. Response time and accuracy were measured.

Results: Response time and accuracy improved significantly in the CVS display condition.

Conclusion: A display that shows trends and data variability can improve the speed and accuracy of data interpretation by ICU nurses.

Topic 5: Psychological effects of the built environment

Aim: To compare the recovery from surgery in a group of patients undergoing gall bladder surgery who had either a view of trees or a view of a brick wall.

Method: This study was conducted using patient records from a 200-bed hospital. The researcher was able to compare data relating to patients allocated to rooms with a view of trees, with that of patients allocated to rooms with no view. All patients had had the same gall bladder surgery and were matched on a number of other characteristics.

Results: The patients that had the view of the trees spent a shorter amount of time in hospital after their operation and required lower levels of pain relief.

Conclusion: This offers some support for the positive effects of a view of nature.

Topic 6: Territory and personal space

Aim: To determine whether office personalisation is associated with employee well-being and to determine the effect of gender on this relationship.

Method: A survey of 338 office workers at 20 companies. 23 of the participants were also interviewed and their workspaces observed.

Results: Personalisation is associated with satisfaction with the physical work environment and with job satisfaction. These two variables are in turn associated with employee well-being. There were also gender differences in personalisation: women personalised more than men, and men and women personalised with different items and for different reasons.

Conclusion: Personalisation can have positive effects in the work place.

CHAPTER 5

Topic 1: Arousal and anxiety

Aim: To identify limitations with the inverted-U hypothesis and offer an alternative and more sophisticated model of the relationship between sporting anxiety and performance.

Method: The authors reviewed research into three potential limitations of the inverted-U hypothesis; limitations of basic concepts, limitations of supporting evidence and limitations in applications of the model. The authors then proposed an alternative model taking account of these problems.

Results: Serious problems were found with the basic ideas behind the inverted-U hypothesis, its evidence base and practical applications deriving from it. A model taking account of both cognitive and somatic anxiety and inspired by Zeeman's stress machine was proposed. This suggests a three dimensional relationship between performance, cognitive anxiety and somatic anxiety in which excessive cognitive anxiety triggers a performance catastrophe.

Conclusion: The inverted-U hypothesis is an inadequate representation of the relationship between anxiety, arousal and performance. The catastrophe model is a superior model.

Topic 2: Exercise and mental health

Aim: To test the effects of a 10-week programme of dance lessons on the mood of older adults, both sufferers of Parkinson's disease and healthy controls.

Method: 22 older adults with a diagnosis of mild to moderate Parkinson's disease and a control group of 15 were assessed for mood. They undertook a programme of 10 weekly 50-minute dance lessons. Acute mood change was assessed after the first lesson and longer-term change was assessed a few days after the final lesson.

Results: Mood improved after one class and significantly improved after 10 classes. This applied to both the Parkinson's patients and the healthy older people.

Conclusion: Dance lessons are an effective intervention to improve the mood of older people, including those with Parkinson's disease.

Topic 3: Motivation

Aim: To investigate relationships between imagery and self-confidence and self-efficacy in competitive and recreational footballers, in particular to test the hypotheses that Motivational General-Mastery (MG-M) imagery would be strongly associated with confidence and self-efficacy and that these relationships would be stronger in the competitive group.

Method: Tests designed to assess imagery, self-confidence and self-efficacy were administered to 125 Canadian football players, aged 11–14 years.

Results: All types of imagery were positively correlated with self-confidence and self-imagery. As predicted the strongest predictor of self-confidence and self-efficacy was MG-M imagery, however, counter to the second hypothesis the relationship was stronger in the recreational footballers.

Conclusion: Imagery, in particular MG-M imagery, is strongly associated with self-confidence and self-efficacy in child football players. The relationship is stronger in recreational level players than at competitive level.

Topic 4: Personality

Aim: To look for differences in the 16 traits measured by the 16PF between participants in four sports; American football, wresting, karate and gymnastics.

Method: The 16PF was administered to a total of 387 high-level athletes from the four sports. A lie-scale was also administered. Once scores were removed from athletes scoring high in the lie test the personality profiles of the four groups of athletes were compared.

Results: Some significant differences emerged between the four groups. Personality predicted sporting choice around half the time. Gymnasts were particularly shy, intelligent and serious. Karateka were particularly conscientious and independent. Football players and wrestlers were the most group-dependent.

Conclusion: There are significant differences between the personality profiles of high-level athletes competing in different sports.

Topic 5: Performing with others

Aim: To test the effectiveness of a coaching development programme that aimed to improve quality of communication between baseball coaches and child players.

Method: The coaching development programme was administered to an experimental group of coaches, whilst a control group had no intervention. The two groups of coaches were then compared by means of observations and by interviews and questionnaires administered to the children working with the coaches.

Results: Some significant differences emerged between the two groups, in particular in reports given by the children working with the coaches. Coaches who had undertaken the programme were more likely to reinforce and encourage and less likely to punish children. Children reported liking the trained coaches more than others and were more likely to want to play for them again the following season.

Conclusion: Coaching development programmes based on improving quality of communication are effective.

Topic 6: Audience effects

Aim: To test the effects of same-species co-actors and an audience on the time taken for cockroaches to carry out a simple task – running along a straight runway – and a more complex task – running a maze.

Method: In experiment 1 cockroaches ran either a straight runway or a simple maze in order to escape a bright light. They were timed when running alone, with a co-actor or with an audience. In the second experiment they repeated the procedure with either visual stimulus of another cockroach or the smell of other cockroaches.

Results: In experiment 1 cockroaches ran the runway faster in the presence of both an audience and a co-actor. There was an anomalous result in that cockroaches in the presence of an audience ran the maze faster than those working alone. In experiment 2 having either visual or olfactory cues for the presence of other cockroaches resulted in poor performance for the runway.

Conclusion: The results of experiment 1 largely support drive theory in that the presence of others improved performance in the simple task and adversely affected it in the more complex task (the maze). Results of experiment 2 were inconclusive.

REVISING THE CORE STUDIES

Table 7.2 presents a list of the core studies from the first year which you need to learn. For each one, you need to know all of the following details: the background, aims, procedure, findings and conclusions as well as being able to evaluate the study in terms of methodology (including research method, design, sample and sampling methods), in comparison to its paired study, and in terms of its contribution to the psychological area, the key theme and each of the debates. To remind you, the debates are: nature/nurture, freewill/determinism, reductionism/holism, individual/situational explanations, usefulness of research, ethical considerations, conducting of socially sensitive research, psychology as a science, ethnocentrism, validity, reliability and sampling bias. Although not all of the debates are relevant to all of the studies, you could be asked about any of these ideas, so your revision notes should cover as many as possible.

TABLE 7.2: CORE STUDIES

Area	Key theme	Classic study	Contemporary study
Social	Responses to people in authority	Milgram (1963) Obedience	Bocchiaro *et al.* (2012) Disobedience and whistle-blowing
	Responses to people in need	Piliavin *et al.* (1969) Subway samaritan	Levine *et al.* (2001) Cross-cultural autism
Cognitive	Attention	Moray (1959) Auditory attention	Simons and Chabris (1999) Visual inattention
	Memory	Loftus and Palmer (1974) Eyewitness testimony	Grant *et al.* (1998) Context-dependent memory
Developmental	External influences on children's behaviour	Bandura *et al.* (1961) Transmission of aggression	Chaney *et al.* (2004) Funhaler study
	Moral development	Kohlberg (1968) Stages of moral development	Lee *et al.* (1997) Evaluations of lying and truth-telling
Biological	Regions of the brain	Sperry (1968) Split-brain study	Casey *et al.* (2011) Neural correlates of delay of gratification
	Brain plasticity	Blakemore and Cooper (1970) Impact of early visual experience	Maguire *et al.* (2000) Taxi drivers
Individual differences	Understanding disorders	Freud (1909) Little Hans	Baron-Cohen *et al.* (1997) Autism in adults
	Measuring differences	Gould (1982) A nation of morons: Bias in IQ testing	Hancock *et al.* (2011) Language of psychopaths

QUESTION SPOTLIGHT!

Which of the following core studies collected primary data and which collected secondary data?

- Moray (1959) Auditory attention
- Gould (1982) A nation of morons: Bias in IQ testing
- Sperry (1968) Split-brain study

REVISING RESEARCH METHODS

You can work through this section in several ways. It summarises the key ideas from research methods, with – in bold – the terms you need to know. You can challenge yourself to define these and then to check your understanding using the text. You can also revise using the Research Methods A–Z in Chapter 6. Many of the terms are also illustrated using the core studies. These will help to remind you of the meaning of the terms, with practical examples, and of the content of the studies themselves. Finally there are Question Spotlights to encourage you to think about and explain other examples.

You have continued to use the ideas you learned in the first year throughout the course in developing your understanding of the key research in each applied area. However, in the Research Methods paper, you can be asked specific questions about methodological terms and concepts, and about how these apply to the core studies, as well as being required to apply them to novel situations. You therefore need to revise this carefully. To help you with this, the following pages recap the research methods content from year 1.

Psychology in action

Psychologists conduct research using a number of different **research methods**, including experiments, self reports, observations, correlations and case studies. Each of these collects **primary data**, i.e. data gathered directly from the participant themselves. In other cases, psychologists use **secondary data**, i.e. data that is derived from existing sources, such as from news reports or from the results of other studies.

The research that psychologists conduct is reported in scientific journals, which are subject to **peer review**, i.e. they are judged to be worthy and ethical by other experts. Such articles typically follow the same format: an **abstract** (summary at the beginning), and **introduction** (which explains the background), the **method** (including the **design**, **sample**, **materials/apparatus** and **procedure**), the **results**, **discussion**, **references** and **appendices**. The references list all the articles that have been referred to in the article and they follow a system, such as the **Harvard system**, which follows a standard pattern of: author surname, author initial. (date) article title. journal title, volume number (part number), page range. For example: Milgram, S. (1963) Behavioural study of obedience. *Journal of Abnormal and Social Psychology*, 67 (4), 371–378.

Ethics

All psychological research should be ethical, i.e. it should treat its participants and subject matter sensitively. The **British Psychological Society** publishes guidelines based on four principles. '**Respect**' includes ensuring participants give **informed consent** (they know what they are agreeing to), have the **right to withdraw** (i.e. can leave at any time, keeping any payment and taking their data), and are offered **confidentiality** (so that their data is safe and individually unidentifiable). '**Competence**' expects researchers to keep within the limits of their ability, such as not using unfamiliar equipment or procedures or giving advice they are not qualified to offer. '**Responsibility**' requires the **protection of participants** (from physical and psychological harm – they should leave in the same condition as they entered), and that they should have a **debrief**, i.e. they should learn the true aims of the research and be restored to their previous state at the end. **Integrity** refers to honesty, and means that **deception** should not be used (although this may be necessary in some situations).

The key elements of good research

Good research should be **valid** (i.e. it should test what it claims to test) and **reliable** (i.e. it should be consistent).

External reliability is whether a test or measure produces the same results in the same situation with the same people. In a **test-retest** assessment

QUESTION SPOTLIGHT!

From the list of core studies below, identify:
- an experiment
- a self-report
- a study using observations
- a case study

- Maguire *et al.* (2000) Taxi drivers
- Freud (1909) Little Hans
- Bandura (1961) Transmission of aggression
- Grant *et al.* (1998) Context-dependent memory
- Hancock *et al.* (2011) Language of psychopaths

QUESTION SPOTLIGHT!

Think about the experiments by Piliavin *et al.* (1969, Subway samaritan) and Loftus & Palmer (1974, Eyewitness testimony). How does the validity of these two studies differ?

two sets of scores from the same people on the same test will have a high positive correlation if they have high external reliability.

Internal reliability is the consistency of items within the measure itself (such as questions in a test). In a **split-half** assessment, the scores from two halves of a test (e.g. all the even- and all the odd-numbered questions) will have a high positive correlation if the internal reliability is good. **Standardisation** helps to raise reliability, including **inter-rater reliability**, the similarity between the scores produced by two researchers gathering data independently in the same situation (e.g. interpreting the same open-ended response in an interview in the same way).

Internal validity relates to the experimental task, specifically whether changes in the DV are caused by the IV. This can be considered in terms of: **face validity** (whether it measures, at face value, what it claims to), **criterion validity** (whether the phenomenon measured in one way will predict a different but related variable). This predictive relationship can be either at the same time (i.e. concurrent) or in the future, which is called predictive validity. **Concurrent validity** is whether a measure produces a similar score for a particular individual as another test that claims to assess the same phenomenon. **Construct validity** considers whether a measure relates to a real phenomenon, based on a range of sources of theoretical and empirical research.

External validity relates to generalisations to other populations, location or contexts and times. It includes **ecological validity** (whether the situation and task are sufficiently like everyday encounters to generalise), and **population validity** (whether findings from one sample can be generalised to the whole of the population from which the sample was taken, and to other populations). Factors influencing generalisations include the sampling method, the sample size and diversity, the sample and the phenomenon being tested. To be **representative**, samples should include a cross section of the population, so that different categories (of age, gender, ethnic group, job, etc.) are included.

Experiments

Blakemore & Cooper used the **research method** of an **experiment** because the study was looking for a **cause and effect** relationship, i.e. differences between the two levels of the variable that was manipulated, the **IV** (of kittens raised with horizontal or vertical stripes). The effect on the **DV** was **operationalised**, i.e. changes in perceptual development were measured in two ways – through their behaviour in response to objects, and physiologically as the specificity of orientation of neurons in the visual cortex. As this was a **laboratory experiment**, it was possible to implement **controls**, such as raising all the animals in the dark when they were not in the apparatus, and the potential to randomly allocate each kitten to a 'horizontal' or a 'vertical' rearing condition. In contrast, participants cannot be randomly allocated to the different conditions in a **quasi-experiment**, such as that conducted by Baron-Cohen *et al.*, as the participants already belonged to the different conditions of autism, Tourette's and controls. In both of these studies the **experimental design** was **independent measures** as there were different participants in each level of the IV. In contrast, **Moray**'s comparison between attention to affective and non-affective messages was a **repeated measures design**, as each participant was tested in both conditions or levels of the IV, i.e. with and without their own name. Although an independent measures design reduces the risk of participants responding to **demand characteristics** (clues about the aim), because they see only one level of the IV, there is a risk of individual differences between the groups introducing errors. These risks are reversed in a repeated measures design. A **matched participants design**, which allocates participants who are similar in important respects to different conditions, helps to overcome both of these problems.

In a **field experiment**, an IV is manipulated and a DV is measured with participants in the normal environment for the activity being investigated (which can raise ecological validity), although fewer controls are possible than in a laboratory experiment. In **Chaney et al.**'s field experiment, children's and parents' attitudes were measured when the children were using their normal spacer and the Funhaler. **Researcher/observer effect**(s) are likely to be less apparent in field experiments compared to laboratory experiments.

In a **quasi-experiment**, there is an IV, but it cannot be manipulated by the experimenter, although a DV is measured. This makes it possible to test variables that cannot be artificially changed. However, with fewer controls over the participants in each level of the IV, there is a risk of **extraneous variables** affecting the DV. For example, in **Baron-Cohen et al.**'s quasi-experiment, participants could not be allocated to the groups; they already had diagnoses of autism, Tourette's syndrome or had no diagnosis.

A **strength** of experiments is that they have strong controls, so validity is high – the research can be fairly confident that only the IV is causing changes in the DV. Reliability is also high because the procedure is **standardised** so participants are treated in the same way. The quantitative data gained can be easily compared, for example with averages, and statistically analysed. A **weakness** of experiments is that they may be unrealistic in terms of the task (or setting) so the findings may not be **representative**, i.e. they may not be typical of other situations or the wider population. There is also a risk of demand characteristics lowering validity.

Observations

Observations are often used with young children and animals as they cannot respond to questions or follow instructions. Bandura *et al.*'s observation was **controlled** as it was in an environment that was devised for the study, rather than **naturalistic**. The observers were **covert** (the participants were unaware of them) as they were behind a one-way mirror, rather than **overt** (i.e. having their role as observers obvious to the participants). They were also **non-participant** (not part of the social situation), rather than being **participant** observers.

Behavioural categories are pre-decided and defined actions to be observed. In **Bandura et al.**'s study these were the different aggressive actions. This means it was a **structured observation** as there was only a limited range of behavioural categories of interest. A **coding frame** provides a system for recording behavioural categories using codes. The observations of the 'teacher's' behaviour conducted by **Milgram** were **unstructured observations**, because there was no particular set of behaviours to observe.

QUESTION SPOTLIGHT!

1. The cross-cultural study by Lee *et al.* had a cross-sectional design, part of it was repeated measures and part was independent measures. Each child heard both anti-social and pro-social stories but different children were tested at different ages. Which comparison was repeated measures and which was independent measures?
2. Was Chaney *et al.*'s study an independent measures design or a repeated measures design? Why?

QUESTION SPOTLIGHT!

1. Although Bandura *et al.* used observations to measure the DV, the study was an experiment. What kind of experiment was it and which experimental design did they use? Justify your answers.
2. Did Bandura *et al.* collect quantitative data, qualitative data or both? Justify your answer.

QUESTION SPOTLIGHT!

1. Think about Piliavin *et al.*'s observations of helping on the subway. Were they: controlled or naturalistic? Overt or covert? Structured or unstructured? Were the observers participant or non-participant?
2. Although Piliavin *et al.* used observations to measure the DV, the study was an experiment. What kind of experiment was it and which experimental design did they use? Justify your answers.

QUESTION SPOTLIGHT!

1. The test of psychopathy used by Hancock *et al.* asked participants to indicate how much they agreed with statements similar to: 'I am often rude to people'. Is this a Likert scale or a semantic differential?
2. Do Likert scales and semantic differentials produce qualitative or quantitative data?

QUESTION SPOTLIGHT!

1. Which research method was used in the psychometric tests described by Gould?
2. In Bocchiaro *et al.*'s study, participants were scored as obedient or disobedient. Was this nominal or ordinal data?
3. Did Freud collect qualitative or quantitative data? Justify your answer.

In **event sampling**, every occurrence of a behaviour is tallied on a checklist. This provides information about frequency of behaviours but not their duration or the order of behaviours over the whole sampling period. There are several types of **time sampling**, which involves dividing the observation period into short intervals, and recording behaviours per interval. This gives some indication of duration (how long they last) and order (whether they are more common in different intervals during the observational period).

A **strength** of observations, especially if they are covert and naturalistic, is that they are representative of real life as the participant is in their normal environment and unaware of being in a study. Also, it enables the collection of data from participants such as children and animals who cannot be asked questions or given tests. However, a **weakness** is that observers may be biased in their recording or interpretation, especially if they are participant and become involved in the social situation, this could also lead to low **inter-observer reliability**. Furthermore, there are ethical issues when participants are unaware of being observed.

Self reports

A **self report** collects information directly from the participant, using a **questionnaire** (written) or an interview (face-to-face). **Chaney et al.**, used a **structured questionnaire** (the same questions, in the same order for all participants), which consisted of **closed questions** (ones with limited, fixed answer choices). These are examples of numerical or **quantitative data**. The study by **Lee et al.**, used a self report to measure the children's responses to a story. They used a **rating scale** in the form of a seven-point chart to indicate how good or naughty the child in the story was. The **level of measurement** of such data is **ordinal**, as the points lie on a increasing but non-linear scale. Ordinal data are also generated by **Likert rating scales**, rating scales offering choices about statements from 'strongly agree' to 'strongly disagree' and **semantic differential rating scales**, which ask participants to indicate how they feel by choosing a point between two opposite descriptive words (such as calm – tense).

The closed question asked by **Loftus and Palmer** – 'Did you see any broken glass?' – generated **nominal data**, i.e. responses in named categories ('yes' or 'no' in this case). The **interview** used by **Hancock et al.** included **open questions**, which generated descriptive or **qualitative data**.

A **strength** of self reports is that they can be used to generate both qualitative and quantitative data so obtain both numerical data to statistically analyse and qualitative to help to explain findings in terms of the reasons behind people's behaviour. They can also be structured to ensure reliability or, in the case of interviews, **semi-structured** or **unstructured** to offer flexibility by including additional questions as needed. However, a **weakness** is that **social desirability** may prevent people from being honest, lowering validity and sample biases may arise if certain types of people are more or less willing to participate.

Correlations

Maguire et al. used **correlations**, which look for relationships between variables rather than causal effects, to assess the relationship between time spent as a taxi driver and hippocampal volume. They found both a **positive correlation**, where the higher the value on one variable, the higher the score on the other and a **negative correlation**, where the higher the value on one variable, the lower the score on the other. **No correlation** exists when there is no clear relationship between the two variables.

A **strength** of correlations is that they can be used when it would be impractical or unethical to conduct an experiment – if variables could not be manipulated. They therefore offer a way to conduct early studies to find out if a relationships exists that warrants further investigation. However, a **weakness** is that a correlation can only identify a link between two variables, not a cause-and-effect relationship between them. Furthermore, only variables that can be measured on numerical scales can be tested.

Case studies

Freud's study was a **case study**, this method involves the detailed investigation of a single instance (usually just one individual), in this case Little Hans. A **strength** is that they provide in-depth data, which is rich in detail and is likely to be valid because it is collected in context. The qualitative data gained can also explore the reasons behind behaviours, which many other methods cannot do. A **weakness** is that they explore a single case so the findings are unlikely to generalise. Also, the data may be unreliable as a single researcher/observer may be biased in their interpretation of the findings.

Sampling

Milgram and **Bocchario** *et al.* used **self-selected sampling**, that is they advertised for volunteers, whereas **Loftus & Palmer** used university students so this is likely to have been an **opportunity sample**, where participants are readily available to the researchers. Any sample is intended to represent the **target population** (to whom generalisations will be made). Sampling methods such as these are less **representative** than other methods, such as **random sampling** (where any member of the population has an equal chance of being selected), such as used by **Chaney** *et al.* However, they are possibly more representative than **snowball sampling**, in which new participants are gathered from contacts of existing participants. This tends to produce a very homogeneous group which is less likely to produce findings which are **generalisible** to the diversity found in a wider population. For example, if an initial sample for a study on IQ were friends of the researchers, they might tend to be quite intelligent. If these individuals then found more participants, they too might be brighter than average. This would produce a sample biased towards the higher end of the IQ spectrum. Sample biases are problematic as they reduce generalisibility. For example, the main part of **Kohlberg**'s study used only American boys. This may have been important if girls responded to moral dilemmas differently from boys. Although this main sample was from a single culture, comparisons to other cultures suggested that the results were not overly **ethnocentric** (i.e. biased in terms of their generalisibility to other cultures).

Aims and hypotheses

Studies typically begin with a **research aim**, such as to discover the effects of hemispheric deconnection, as **Sperry** did. This is developed into a **research question** which can be tackled through a specific research method. From here, hypotheses can be written. The **alternative hypothesis** predicts the outcome

QUESTION SPOTLIGHT!

1. The Spearman Rho result for the relationship between time spent as a taxi driver and right posterior hippocampal volume (based on VBM) was r=0.6, and between time spent as a taxi driver and anterior hippocampal volume (based on VBM) it was r=–0.6. Which of these was a positive and which a negative correlation?
2. What type of graph would you use to display data from a correlation?

of the research, such as that there will be a difference between conditions of the IV in an experiment, e.g. the verbal ability of the left and right hemispheres, in Sperry's case. This is a **non-directional hypothesis**. A **directional hypothesis** predicts which level of the IV will be 'better'. For example, Sperry might have predicted that the left hemisphere would be more verbally competent than the right.

A non-directional hypothesis in a correlation simply says that there will be a relationship between the two variables. For example, in their cross-cultural study, **Levine *et al.*** might have predicted that 'there will be a relationship between helping and population size'.

When a hypothesis in a correlation predicts a positive (or a negative) correlation rather than a non-specific relationship, this also requires a directional hypothesis. For example, Levine might have predicted that 'People will be less helpful in more individualist cities', which is predicting a negative correlation. When statistical tests are being conducted, directional hypotheses are referred to as **one-tailed hypotheses**. However, it is actually the **null hypothesis**, based on the idea that any difference or relationship could have arisen by chance, which is tested in a statistical test. When a significant difference or correlation is not found the null hypothesis is accepted. In the two examples above, neither of the suggested hypotheses were supported, so the null hypothesis would have been accepted in each case.

Dealing with data

The data collected in a study is put into a **raw data recording table**, such as a **frequency table (tally chart)**. This is typically in whole numbers but can be in **decimal form**, e.g. if it is a small measurement such as centimetres and millimetres. Very large (or very small) numbers may be written in **standard form** (e.g. 10^{-2}).

The raw data is then simplified to give an indication of the typical score, the average, this is the **measure of central tendency**. The **mode**, the most frequent, is the simplest and least informative, the **median** is the middle one of the scores in rank order and the **mean**, calculated by adding all the scores up and dividing by how many there are, is the most informative. **Measures of dispersion** indicate how spread out the scores are and include the **range** (the biggest minus the smallest plus one), and the **variance** and **standard deviation**, which are both calculations based on the average difference of each score from the mean (but the final stage of the standard deviation is a square root). When such calculations are done, the final figure is often quoted to a certain number of **significant figures** (non-zero digits) and **decimal** places. These should not be more than the original accuracy of the measurements. An initial **estimation** can help you to decide if your answer is about right.

Information such as the relative numbers of scores in different categories (or participants in different conditions) can be expressed in different ways, such as **percentages**, **fractions** or **ratios** (the proportion of each type). These summaries, totals, or averages, can all be represented visually, on **line graphs**, **pie charts**, **bar charts** or **histograms**. For correlations, each individual pair of scores is plotted on a **scatter diagram**.

Choosing and using non-parametric statistical tests

When conducting **non-parametric statistical tests**, the correct one must be chosen. For a correlation this is the **Spearman's Rho**. For experiments, the choice depends on the experimental design and the **level of measurement** of the data. For an independent measures design study collecting nominal data, such as the number of adverts for boys, girls or mixed-gender toys in different years, the choice would be **Chi-square**. For an independent measures design study collecting ordinal or interval data, such as comparing IQ between males and females, a **Mann Whitney U test** could be used. For a repeated measures design study collecting nominal data, such as the number of targets a sportsman can hit with or without an audience, the choice would be a **binomial sign test**. For a repeated measures design study collecting ordinal or interval data, such as comparing brain scan data for patients before and after drug treatment, a **Wilcoxon signed-ranks test** could be used. In any of these situations, the test produces an observed value which is compared to a **critical value** from a table. The correct critical value is identified using the following information: the **significance level** (e.g. $p \leq 0.05$, or $p \leq 0.01$, which is more stringent), whether the hypothesis was one or two tailed, and either N (the number of participants) or, for Chi-square, the degrees of freedom.

QUESTION SPOTLIGHT!

1. Loftus & Palmer used the Chi-square test in experiment 2. The observed value was 7.76 and there were 2 degrees or freedom. Use the table on the left to decide whether the difference was significant at $p \leq 0.025$ for a one-tailed test.

df	Level of significance for a two-tailed test			
	0.1	0.05	0.02	0.01
	Level of significance for a one-tailed test			
	0.05	0.025	0.01	0.005
1	3.841	5.024	6.635	7.879
2	5.991	7.378	9.210	10.597
3	7.815	9.348	11.345	12.838
4	9.488	11.143	13.277	14.860

Choosing methods of analysis

The data collected by **Casey et al.** fulfilled the criteria for using **parametric tests**, i.e. they were interval data, with an even **dispersion** and from a population with a **normal distribution**. **Interval data** has points on a linear scale, i.e the gaps between the points are all equivalent. With parametric data, means can be used to measure central tendency and the standard deviation as a measure of dispersion. For parametric tests, the standard deviations should be similar for the levels of the IV. Alternatively, dispersion can be assessed using **normal distribution curves**, which should show similar spread and should be symmetrical around the mean, median and mode, rather than having a **skewed distribution** (where the 'tail' is longer on one side). A normal distribution has all three measures of central tendency in the middle, whereas in a skewed distribution the median and mean are out in the 'tail'.

Type one and type two errors

Whenever a statistical test is conducted, there is a risk that the researcher sets a **probability** at which they accept an error may be made. If the significance level is too optimistic (e.g. $p \leq 0.05$ rather than $p \leq 0.01$), there is a greater risk of a **type one error** – accepting the alternative hypothesis when it is false. However, if the significance level is too stringent (e.g. $p \leq 0.01$ rather than $p \leq 0.05$), there is a greater risk of a **type two error** – rejecting the alternative hypothesis when it is true. Any statistical testing is a compromise between these two problems.

QUESTION SPOTLIGHT!

1. Grant et al. used parametric tests on their data. Which measures of central tendency and spread would have been most appropriate?
2. Simons & Chabris used the Chi-square test. Is this a non-parametric or a parametric test?

PRACTICE QUESTIONS

Here are some of the sorts of questions that you could be asked in your A level exam. The questions below include examples of answers that we believe might be successful and less successful. Additional Research Methods questions are provided on pages 347–8 for you to practise.

SECTION A: MULTIPLE CHOICE

1 The following are times (in seconds) taken to solve an anagram by a group of 10 students.
11, 14, 14, 14, 17, 19, 19, 20, 23, 25.
Which **one** of the following statements is true?
 (a) There are two modal figures
 (b) The mode is 19
 (c) The mode is 14
 (d) The median is 25

2 Which test of difference should be used if data is ordinal and the design was repeated measures?
 (a) Chi-square
 (b) Wilcoxon
 (c) Spearman's Rho
 (d) Mann Whitney

3 Which method was used by Freud in his study of Little Hans?
 (a) An experiment
 (b) An observation
 (c) A correlation
 (d) A case study

4 Identify the independent variable in an investigation to measure whether performance on a card-sorting task is affected by levels of hunger.
 (a) Performance on a card-sorting task
 (b) Time taken to complete a card-sorting task
 (c) Hunger levels
 (d) Whether someone ate lunch or not

5 Which section of a practical report would contain suggestions for further research?
 (a) Method
 (b) Discussion
 (c) Results
 (d) Abstract

6 Which of these is not always a strength of an experiment?
 (a) High levels of control
 (b) The ability to draw cause-and-effect conclusions
 (c) The ability to replicate the study
 (d) High levels of realism

7 What is meant by criterion validity?
 (a) How well findings are matched by other research findings
 (b) How well findings generalise to real-life situations
 (c) How well findings measure what they intend to measure
 (d) How well findings predict what happens beyond the research

8 Which is the correct definition of ethnocentrism?
 (a) Only studying one culture
 (b) Only studying one gender
 (c) Judging everyone by the standards of your own culture
 (d) Judging everyone by the standards of your own gender

SECTION B: RESEARCH DESIGN AND RESPONSE

A psychologist used an observation to investigate what sixth-formers used their sixth-form common room for. The psychologist decided to use a time-sampling approach and to observe every 20 seconds what activities were taking place. They included behaviours such as chatting, eating and working, and four observers were recruited who would each observe one section of the common room for half an hour in the morning and half an hour in the afternoon. Members of the sixth form using the common room made up the sample.

1 Outline **one** strength of using an observation compared to self-report. **[2]**

2 Identify **three** ethical issues that would need to be considered when carrying out this observation. **[3]**

3 The psychologist used a time-sampling approach for their observation.
 (a) Explain **one** strength and **one** weakness of using time sampling for this study. **[6]**
 (b) Name and outline one **other** sampling technique for conducting this study. **[2]**
 (c) Describe **one** strength and **one** weakness of the sampling technique you have chosen in (b). **[4]**

4 You have been asked to carry out a further observational study to investigate the differences in use of the common room in school sixth forms compared to further education colleges. This will be part of a quasi-experiment using one school and one further education college.
Write an alternative hypothesis for your investigation. **[3]**

5* Explain how you would carry out an observation to investigate the differences in use of common rooms in school sixth forms compared to further education colleges. Justify your decisions as part of your explanation. You must refer to:

- structured or unstructured observations
- participant or non-participant observations
- time or event sampling
- collection of data.

You should use your own experience of carrying out an observation to inform your response. **[15]**

SECTION C: DATA ANALYSIS AND INTERPRETATION

A psychoanalyst wanted to test whether males would interpret neutral stimuli more aggressively than females. He decided to use an ink blot as the stimulus.

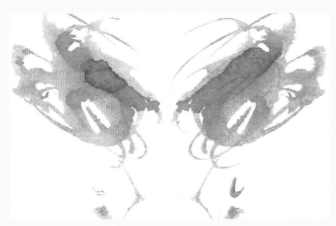

He showed the ink blot to 100 people (50 male and 50 female) attending a creative-writing workshop. He asked them to say what they thought the ink blot looked like and he decided whether their interpretation could be seen as aggressive or non-aggressive. The results are given below.

	Aggressive	Non-aggressive	Total
Male	29	21	50
Female	17	33	50
Total	46	54	100

1 **(a)** Outline **one** finding from the table. **[2]**
  (b) Calculate the percentage of men giving aggressive interpretations of the ink blot. **[2]**
2 Name and briefly describe the sampling method used in this study. **[3]**
3 Explain why this sampling method could be seen as a problem in this study. **[5]**
4 **(a)** Outline the purpose of peer review in psychological research. **[3]**
  (b) As a result of a peer review, the following statement was made about the study above:
    'There is a potential issue with experimenter bias when considering these findings.'
    Explain what this statement means in relation to this study. **[5]**
  (c) Suggest how this experimenter bias could be reduced. **[3]**
5 The psychologist analysed the data using the Chi-square test. Give **one** reason for this choice of test with reference to the study. **[2]**
6 The Chi-square test gave an observed (calculated) value of 5.7
Levels of significance for a one-tailed test

Significance level	0.05	0.025	0.01
Critical value	2.71	3.84	5.41

Using the above critical values, explain whether the psychologist has found a significant difference or not. **[4]**
7 Outline what is meant by each of the following features of science and state how they apply to this study:
  (a) Cause and effect. **[3]**
  (b) Control. **[3]**

Rina's answer:

One strength of observation is that you can see the behaviour happening in real life rather than asking somebody to tell you something. For example if you asked people what they did in the common room they might say that they did their homework but if you watched them you might find that they spent all their time talking.

> **We say:** This is the same point that Liam made but Rina has elaborated on his answer and given a very clear example, which makes it easy to understand.

---

2 Identify **three** ethical issues that would need to be considered when carrying out this observation. **[3]**

Liam's answer:

Physical harm, Consent, Confidentiality, Right to withdraw.

> **We say:** Liam has started with physical harm, which is unlikely to arise in this case. Remember to identify appropriate ethical issues for the study. He has then given three suitable examples, but because the first one was irrelevant, he may not gain the third mark for the final issue of right to withdraw.

Rina's answer:

Privacy – they would have to make sure that they didn't observe students doing things they wouldn't expect to be observed doing, for example if they tried to overhear personal conversations. This invades their right to keep things to themselves.

Deception – if the students asked what they were doing they would have to tell the truth otherwise this would be lying, i.e. deception, e.g. if they said they were helping the college staff.

> **We say:** Rina has provided detail that isn't required; she only needed to state the names of the ethical issues in order to gain marks. This means she has filled the space but has given only two issues, when the question asked for three, so although what she has written is correct, she cannot gain maximum marks.

---

3 The psychologist used a time-sampling approach for their observation.

    (a) Explain **one** strength and **one** weakness of using time sampling for this study. **[6]**

Liam's answer:

Being done in the field is good because it's ecologically valid so is a good thing about observations. Another strength is that recording every 20 seconds is short so there would be unlikely to be any behaviours that they would have missed.

> **We say:** Liam has made a general point about observations first that is not specific to time sampling in this study, which is what the question is asking for so would not earn credit. He then makes a second, better point but it is also a strength. He should have just made the second point and then added a problem for his other point.

Rina's answer:

Time sampling is good because it means you get an idea of when each behaviour occurred as well as how often. So if they chatted often at the beginning of the half hour then ate more at the end you would be able to see this in the pattern of the 20-second intervals. This is better than checklists in event sampling. However, time sampling doesn't tell you about really short behaviours, because they might never be recorded at all. So if they worked but only for less than 20 seconds at a time it might not be in the observation even though it happened, whereas a checklist would give it a tally no matter how short it was.

We say: Rina's answer is good as she has identified a strength of time sampling and related it to the study. She could have gone on to say why it is better than a checklist – because this wouldn't indicate when the different behaviours occurred. The weakness she gives is excellent.

3 (b) Name and outline one **other** sampling technique for conducting this study. **[2]**

Liam's answer:

Random sampling – this is where everybody in the population has an equal chance of being selected.

We say: Although Liam's definition of random sampling is correct, he has mistakenly named and outlined a sampling method for collecting participants in a study, whereas the question is asking for a sampling technique for collecting observational data. This is clear because the question says one other sampling technique. His answer is therefore irrelevant.

Rina's answer:

Event sampling is where ticks are put in a chart each time things happen from a list of behavioural categories.

We say: Event sampling is where ticks are put in a chart each time things happen from a list of behavioural categories.

3 (c) Describe **one** strength and **one** weakness of the sampling technique you have chosen in (b). **[4]**

Liam's answer:

Random sampling is good because you can just go out and collect any random people so it is quick and easy, you just get whoever comes into the common room first. But it's not so good because it's not representative.

We say: Here Liam has continued to misunderstand the meaning of 'sampling technique' and the advantage and disadvantage he describes for random sampling are also incorrect – he is thinking about opportunity sampling here, which is a common mistake!

Rina's answer:

Event sampling is good because it is easy to analyse the results. All you have to do is add up the totals for each behaviour then you can look at the different behaviours to see which is the most frequent (the mode). You could also work out percentages for each behavioural category to compare them. A disadvantage is that even if something is the most frequent you don't know how long was spent on that behaviour, it could be really quick and come up lots in the chart even though in fact less time was spent doing it than some other behaviour that took a really long time but happened only occasionally. For example, the students might chat once for ages then do lots of really short bouts of eating and working and it would look like they had worked more than they really did.

We say: Rina makes a good point about the ease with which event sampling data can be analysed and gives useful examples of the calculations that could be done. She then gives an excellent disadvantage relating to the absence of duration information, which she explains and illustrates well.

You have been asked to carry out a further observational study to investigate the differences in use of the common room in school sixth forms compared to further education colleges. This will be part of a quasi-experiment using one school and one further education college.

4   Write an alternative hypothesis for your investigation. **[3]**

Liam's answer:

There will be differences in behaviour in the common room.

We say: This does not contain all the necessary pieces of information. Liam has identified difference in behaviour but does not include where these differences are being investigated – that is, he has not included the 'school versus further education college', which is the independent variable in this study.

Rina's answer:

Behaviour in a school sixth-form common room will be different from behaviour in a further education common room.

We say: Rina's alternate hypothesis is much clearer. The IV (school versus further education college) is clear and this hypothesis is clearly predicting a difference in behaviour. Note that this is a two-tailed hypothesis in that Rina is not predicting the direction of the difference (such as saying that students are better behaved in one of these environments). It would be acceptable to offer a one-tailed or a two-tailed hypothesis here.

5*   Explain how you would carry out an observation to investigate the differences in use of common rooms in school sixth forms compared to further education colleges. Justify your decisions as part of your explanation. You must refer to:
   •   structured or unstructured observations
   •   participant or non-participant observations
   •   time or event sampling
   •   collection of data.
   You should use your own experience of carrying out an observation to inform your response. **[15]**

Liam's answer:

I would do an observation in one common room in a school sixth form and one common room in a further education college. I would observe what kind of things people were doing with their time such as doing their homework, talking to their friends, using their mobile phones, eating, or working on the computers. I would have to do my observations at different times of the day so that it would not be biased and I would have to make sure that people didn't know that I was observing them because that would be biased as well and I would have to observe for quite a long time. If people knew that I was observing them then their behaviour might change and then my results would not be very good.

Rina's answer:

I think this observation would be best if it was conducted as a participant observation rather than a non-participant observation. I would do the one in the sixth form in a school because this is where I am a pupil, and I would ask a friend at the local further education college if he could carry out the observation there. This would be good because then there won't be a stranger in the room which might significantly change people's behaviour. When I did my observation, nobody took any notice as they were used to seeing me in our form room. A structured observation would be better so that we knew exactly what we were looking for but we would need to plan this carefully. We could both do little pilot studies and make a list of all the activities we see in the common room over a week and then we could use this to create our coding sheets. We would have categories such as: working on computers, chatting with friends, using a mobile phone, watching TV, eating, drinking, reading a book, writing notes by hand, and so on. Once we had this coding scheme we would be ready to carry out our observation. It would be a good idea to have a column headed 'other' for any other behaviours that weren't on the list and then we could add them. Time sampling would be better than event sampling. We would simply observe every 20 seconds, for example, and tick all the behaviours that we could see. I think

We say: Liam has given a little bit of information about how he would conduct this observation although there is quite a lot missing. The first sentence is unnecessary as this information was in the instructions that were given initially. The list of activities is helpful but does not specifically address any of the issues that were asked for. The rest of the answer contains a few brief suggestions that could be seen as discussing collection of data, but there is a great deal more required. Always remember to look at the mark allocations and give yourself enough time to produce the answer.

We say: Rina's answer is far more detailed than Liam's and she has obviously read the instructions much more carefully as she explicitly addresses issues such as participant or non-participant observation, as well as including references to her own observation. There is a lot of good information here and Rina is clearly demonstrating that she has good knowledge of observational methods. Even here, however, there are improvements that could be made. Rina states that 'time sampling would be better than event sampling' but doesn't really explain why, and she could perhaps also consider issues relating to the collection of data, such as where the observers would be and how they would record data without being too obvious. Overall though, this is a very good answer.

we should collect data at three different times of day (morning, lunchtime and afternoon) for about half an hour at a time. If we did this every day for a week then we would get the full range of who was in the common room at any one time because different people have different free lessons depending on what subjects they are doing. This would be better than in my study, as I always saw the same people who were free at the same time as me, so the sample wasn't very representative.

SECTION C

1 (a) Outline **one** finding from the table. **[2]**

Liam's answer:

Men were more aggressive: 29 compared to 17.

We say: This is a very brief answer, and isn't sufficient. Liam could have gone on to say '… than females' and to have described the sense in which they were 'more aggressive', i.e. in their interpretation of the neutral ink blots.

Rina's answer:

The way the females viewed the ink blots was less aggressive than the males. About twice as many non-aggressive ratings compared to aggressive ones were given by females, whereas the men had slightly more aggressive ratings.

We say: Rina's answer is clear and she makes a useful comparison in terms of the ratio of aggressive to non-aggressive interpretations for the females.

1 (b) Calculate the percentage of men giving aggressive interpretations of the inkblot. **[2]**

Liam's answer:

29/46 = 0.63043

0.63043 × 100 = 63%

My answer is 63%

We say: Liam has shown that he can work out a percentage and started with the correct figure of 29, but divided it by the total number of aggressive responses (for men and women) rather than by the total number of responses given by men. This means he has not answered the question.

Rina's answer:

58% of men gave aggressive interpretations.

We say: Here Rina has done the correct calculation, 29/50, but has not shown her working. It is always advisable to do this just in case you make a mathematical error, you may be able to earn some marks for the process you have shown. However, Rina has indicated what the percentage is, and this is also worth remembering, especially if the numbers are specific measurements (such as cm or seconds).

2 Name and briefly describe the sampling method used in this study. **[3]**

Liam's answer:

This was an opportunity sample.

Rina's answer:

This was an opportunity sample of people attending a creative-writing workshop. An opportunity sample is where the experimenter simply uses the people that are available to him or her at the time that he or she wants to conduct the study.

3 Explain why this sampling method could be seen as a problem in this study. **[5]**

Liam's answer:

Opportunity samples are a problem because they are not representative. If the researcher just gets all the participants from one place then it will be really difficult to generalise the results to other people. For example the results from an opportunity sample of people in a pub wouldn't generalise to people who never go to pubs.

Rina's answer:

In this study the experimenter used opportunity sampling of people at a creative-writing workshop. This could create a problem because opportunity sampling does not produce a representative sample anyway and only selecting people from a creative-writing workshop would further limit the generalisability of the sample. People who go to creative-writing workshops are likely to have characteristics that make them different from the general population and as they are obviously more likely to be creative, the types of interpretations that they would make of the ink blots might also be different from those made by another sample.

We say: It is an opportunity sample, although the correct term here would be opportunity sampling as the question is asking about the sampling technique rather than the sample. The main problem with this answer is that the question is worth three marks and Liam has given only one piece of information. It is important to look at the mark allocations for the questions as it does help you to understand how much information you need to give.

We say: Rina has also referred to the sample rather than the sampling method, although the additional detail that she has provided makes it clear that she understands that the question is asking about how the sample was obtained.

We say: Read the question, Liam! The question ends with the words 'in this study'. Whenever you see this you need to make sure that you 'contextualise' your answer. This means relating your answer specifically to the study being asked about. The example Liam has given is a good description of the problem of opportunity sampling but it would have been much better if he had explained what the problem would be in this investigation.

We say: Great answer. Well explained and well contextualised. This shows very good understanding, except that Rina has made a common mistake: she has referred to 'the generalisability of the sample', when she means the generalisability (of the results) *from* the sample.

4 **(a)** Outline the purpose of peer review in psychological research. **[3]**

Liam's answer:

Peer review is a way to find potential issues with experimenter bias when considering the findings of studies.

We say: Liam has simply looked at the question below, which is also about peer review and copied the wording. Although this is one possible thing that peer review might do, it is not an outline of the purpose of peer review, so it does not answer the question. Nice try Liam!

Rina's answer:

When a journal publishes a study written by a psychologist, it will have been read by a panel of experts in the subject. They read it thoroughly, make comments on it and can reject it so it will not get published. The reason this happens is so that things that are published definitely contribute to psychology, they need to have good methodology and data analysis and the conclusions from the data have to be sensible – they can't make wild claims that aren't supported by what they have found. Also, it has to be ethical.

We say: The first part of Rina's answer is irrelevant, she is outlining the process of peer review rather than its purpose. She gets to the point when she says 'The reason…', and from then on it is a good answer. When you are answering questions, make sure you have read them carefully. It was easy here to read 'Outline' then 'peer review' and to make this mistake.

4 **(b)** As a result of a peer review, the following statement was made about the study above: 'There is a potential issue with experimenter bias when considering these findings.' Explain what this statement means in relation to this study. **[5]**

Liam's answer:

It means that the reviewers think that the experimenters were biased when they collected the data.

We say: Liam has done little more here than reword the question again. He needs to explain the statement, not just repeat it.

Rina's answer:

The reviewers think that there may have been a problem because the experimenters weren't entirely neutral and objective in the way they recorded whether the interpretations were aggressive or non-aggressive. Maybe they tended to say that more of the males' interpretations were aggressive because they knew which interpretations had come from men and which from women and because they expected the men to see more violence in the ink blots.

We say: Rina has given a clear and detailed explanation, saying what the problem is and relating it to this particular study. This is a thorough answer.

4 **(c)** Suggest how this experimenter bias could be reduced. **[3]**

Liam's answer:

By giving the male and female participants different ink blots. They should also increase objectivity.

We say: This suggestion isn't going to solve the problem of experimenter bias and could even make the validity of the experiment worse. Although Liam is right, the experimenters need to increase objectivity, he hasn't suggested how this might be done so this point isn't contributing to his answer.

Rina's answer:

By giving the observers a set of guidelines to score the interpretations as aggressive or non-aggressive, this would help to make them less subjective. To make it more valid they could also make sure that the experimenters didn't know whether the interpretation they were judging was from a male or a female, then if they had a bias based on gender differences it couldn't skew the results.

We say: This is a good answer from Rina, she has given two suggestions to reduce bias and has explained both of them clearly, using appropriate terminology. It is important to use methodological terms in a way that connects them to your answer; try not to just 'throw them in'.

5 The psychologist analysed the data using the Chi-square test. Give one reason for this choice of test with reference to the study. **[2]**

Liam's answer:

Because this test is easy to conduct and gives good results.

We say: This is not correct. Researchers have to choose the appropriate test depending on the type of data they have, whether they are looking for a difference or a correlation and what type of design they have used. They don't pick tests because they are easier to conduct!

Rina's answer:

The Chi-square test is used when data is in frequencies.

We say: This is correct. The Chi-square test is the test to use when you have nominal/frequency data that is independent. However, this time Rina has failed to read the question properly and has made no reference to the study. She needed to expand her answer to say that the interpretations were either 'aggressive' or 'non-aggressive' and therefore this is nominal data.

6 The Chi-square test gave an observed (calculated) value of 5.7
Levels of significance for a one-tailed test

Significance level	0.05	0.025	0.01
Critical value	2.71	3.84	5.41

Using the above critical values, explain whether the psychologist has found a significant difference or not. **[4]**

Liam's answer:

Yes there is a significant difference.

We say: Yes, there is a significant difference but this is not an explanation. How do we know that this is significant? Liam needs to explain how he (and the researcher) reached this conclusion.

Rina's answer:

In order to be significant, the calculated value of Chi-square needs to be larger than the number in the table. As 5.7 is larger than 5.41 the results are significant at the 0.01 level and this means that males do give more aggressive interpretations than females.

We say: A good explanation of the process of concluding that there is a significant difference and a very clear link to the study.

Answers to the Section A multiple-choice questions on page 336: 1c, 2b, 3d, 4c, 5b, 6d, 7d, 8c

SECTION A: MULTIPLE CHOICE

Answer all of the questions in Section A.

1 In which one of the following types of observation are participants aware of the role of the observer?

(a) Participant

(b) Non-participant

(c) Overt

(d) Covert **[1]**

2 How was the physiological dependent variable measured in Blackemore & Cooper's (1970) study of early visual experience in cats?

(a) By keeping the kittens in an environment with horizontal or vertical lines

(b) By observing the responses of single brain cells to horizontal or vertical lines

(c) By observing the kittens playing with a horizontal or vertical stick

(d) By keeping the kittens in the dark. **[1]**

3 Look at the following academic reference:
Grant, H.M., Lane, C. Bredahl, J.C., Clay. J., Ferrie, J., Groves, J.E., McDorman, T.A. & Dark, V.J. (1998) Context-dependent memory for meaningful material: Information for students. Applied Cognitive Psychology, 617–623.
What is the error in this Harvard-style reference?

(a) The authors' first names are missing.

(b) The volume number is missing.

(c) The date of the study should be immediately after Grant's name.

(d) The surnames of the researchers should be listed in alphabetical order. **[1]**

4 Which of the following is a suitable null hypothesis for a study looking for improvements in mental health with a new drug?

(a) Patients will have fewer symptoms in the drug condition than when given a placebo.

(b) There will be a difference between the symptoms and the drug condition.

(c) There will be no difference between symptoms in the drug and placebo conditions.

(d) There will be a positive correlation between symptoms and drug use. **[1]**

5 Which inferential test should a researcher use in a study where they have collected nominal data using an independent measures design?

(a) Mann–Whitney U test

(b) Binomial Sign test

(c) Wilcoxon Signed Ranks test

(d) Chi-squared test **[1]**

6 Which is an example of qualitative data?

(a) 10 answers to the question: 'How old were you when you first remember doing something naughty?'

(b) An answer to the question: 'How fast was the car travelling when it hit the bus?'

(c) An answer to the question: 'Why do you believe that you could resist eating that chocolate?'

(d) Five diary entries that tick off a list of things that did or did not happen that day. **[1]**

7 What is the probability of a significant result occurring by chance where the significance level is $p \leq 0.05$?

(a) 5% or less

(b) 50% or less

(c) at least 95%

(d) less than 5% **[1]**

8 Which feature of science refers to the importance of being able to refute a psychologist's claim?

(a) replicability

(b) induction

(c) falsification

(d) verification **[1]**

SECTION B: RESEARCH DESIGN AND RESPONSE

Answer all of the questions in Section B.

A school wanted to know about student preferences for note-taking. The psychology teacher and the computing teacher used a questionnaire to investigate their students' preferences. They wanted to know if they preferred taking notes in class on tablets such as iPads or on paper. A range of question types were used including rating scales and semantic differentials.

1 Outline **one** weakness of using a questionnaire compared to an interview. **[2]**

2 Identify **three** ethical issues that the teachers should consider when planning this research. **[3]**

3 A range of question types were used in the questionnaire, including rating scales and semantic differentials.

(a) Explain **one** strength and **one** weakness of the question type(s) chosen. Your points may refer to the same question type or to different ones. **[6]**

(b) Name and outline **one** other question type that could be used in a questionnaire to find out about opinions. **[2]**

(c) Describe **one** strength and **one** weakness of the question type you have chosen in question 3(b). **[4]**

As part of your psychology class you have been asked to extend the study with a questionnaire for teachers about behaviours such as paying attention, talking in class, and gazing out of the window. The hypothesis for this part of the study is 'These is a difference in concentration level between students who use tablets in class and students who do not'.

4 Explain whether this hypothesis is directional (one-tailed) or non-directional and why this type of hypothesis has been chosen. **[3]**

5* Explain how you would carry out a questionnaire for teachers to investigate whether there is a difference in concentration level between students who use tablets in class and those who do not.

Justify your decisions as part of your explanation. You must include:

- examples of open and closed questions
- the sampling method
- at least two ethical points
- collection of data.

You should use your own experience of carrying out a self report to inform your response. **[15]**

SECTION C: DATA ANALYSIS AND INTERPRETATION

Answer all of the questions in Section C.

A psychologist conducted a pilot study for a correlation to investigate symptoms in patients with schizophrenia. They wanted to know whether there was a relationship between how vivid the hallucinations were and the patients' speech quality. The original sample consisted of 10 patients with schizophrenia. They could not use 2 of them in the study as they did not experience hallucinations.

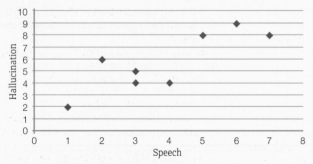

1 **(a)** Describe the pattern in the results on the scatter diagram. **[2]**

(b) Explain why a scatter diagram is appropriate for presenting this data. **[2]**

(c) Express the proportion of patients in the original sample who had and did not have hallucinations as a ratio. **[2]**

The sampling method was random sampling, with patients being taken from hospital records at one hospital.

2 **(a)** Describe how a random sample might have been obtained in this study. **[2]**

(b) Discuss why a random sample might have been better than asking for volunteers for this study. **[5]**

In the full-scale follow-up study, a new sample of 50 participants was obtained, 49 of whom were used.

3 **(a)** Calculate the percentage of the new sample who were used in the follow-up study. Show your workings. **[2]**

(b) In a large population, a normal distribution of scores is typically expected. Sketch a normal distribution graph and explain what it shows. **[4]**

(c) In this study, the results showed a positive skew. Sketch a graph to illustrate a positive skew. **[2]**

(d) Explain the difference in position of measures of central tendency on a normal distribution and a positively skewed distribution. **[2]**

4 The psychologist analysed the data using a Spearman's Rho test. Explain why this was an appropriate test for this study. **[2]**

The Spearman's test gave an observed (calculated) value of Rho of 0.2391.

Critical values for a one-tailed test			
N	0.1	0.05	0.01
48	0.1883	0.2403	0.3348
49	0.1863	0.2377	0.3314
50	0.1843	0.2353	0.3281

Critical values for a two-tailed test			
N	0.1	0.05	0.01
48	0.2403	0.2845	0.3683
49	0.2377	0.2816	0.3646
50	0.2353	0.2787	0.3610

5 Explain whether the table of critical values for a one- or a two-tailed test should be used in this study. **[1]**

6 Using one of the critical value tables above, explain whether the psychologist has found a significant correlation or not. **[3]**

7 Outline what is meant by each of the following features of science and state how they apply to this correlational study:

(a) Cause and effect **[3]**

(b) Standardisation **[3]**

REFERENCES

Abbott, A. and Collins, D. (2004) Eliminating the dichotomy between theory and practice in talent identification and development: considering the role of psychology. *Journal of sports sciences*, 22, 395–408.

Ageton, S.S. and Elliott, D.S. (1974) The effects of legal processing on delinquent orientations. *Social Problems*, 22 (1), 87–100.

Ainsworth, M., Blehar, M., Waters, E. and Wall, S. (1978) *Patterns of Attachment*. Hillsdale, NJ: Erlbaum.

Ainsworth, P. (2000) *Psychology and Crime: Myths and Reality*. United Kingdom: Longman.

Allen, P., Amaro, E., Fu, C.H., Williams, S.C., Brammer, M.J., Johns, L.C. and McGuire, P.K. (2007) Neural correlates of the misattribution of speech in schizophrenia. *The British Journal of Psychiatry*, 190, 162–9.

Altman, I. (1975) *The Environment and Social Behaviour*. Monterey: CA: Brooks/Cole.

American Psychiatric Association (2013) *Diagnostic and statistical manual of mental disorders (DSM-5®)*, American Psychiatric Pub.

Amorose A.J. and Horn T.S. (2001) Pre to post-season changes in the intrinsic motivation of first-year college athletes: relationships with coaching behaviour and scholarship status. *Journal of Applied Sport Psychology*, 13, 355–73.

Anderson, D., Chenery, S. and Pease, K. (1995) *Biting back: Tackling repeat burglary and car crime*. Police Research Group, Home Office Police Department, 1–57.

Arent, S.W., Landers, D.M. and Etner, J.L. (2000) The effects of exercise on mood in older adults: a meta-analytic review. *Journal of Ageing and Physical Activity*, 8, 407–30.

Arnett, J. (1992) Reckless behavior in adolescence: A developmental perspective. *Developmental Review*, 12 (4), 339–73.

Arroll, B., Macgillivray, S., Ogston, S., Reid, I., Sullivan, F., Williams, B. and Crombie, I. (2005) Efficacy and tolerability of tricyclic antidepressants and SSRIs compared with placebo for treatment of depression in primary care: a meta-analysis, Annals of family medicine, 3 (5), 449–56.

Ashford, B., Biddle, S. and Goudas, M. (1993) Participation in community sport centres: motives and predictors of enjoyment. *Journal of sport sciences*, 11, 249–56.

Atkinson, R.C. and Shiffrin, R.M. (1968). Chapter: Human memory: A proposed system and its control processes. In Spence, K.W. and Spence, J.T. *The psychology of learning and motivation* (Volume 2). New York: Academic Press, pp.89–195.

Ayres, A.J. (1961) Development of the body scheme in children. *The American Journal of Occupational Therapy*, 15, 99–102.

Baker, J., Cote, J. and Abernethy, B. (2003) Sport-specific practice and the development of expert decision-making in team ball sports. *Journal of applied sport psychology*, 15 (1), 12–25.

Bandura, A. (1965) Influence of a model's reinforcement contingencies on the acquisition of imitative responses. *Journal of Personality & Social Psychology*, 36, 589–95.

Bandura, A. (1982) Self-efficacy mechanisms in human agency. *American Psychologist*, 37, 122–47.

Bandura, A. (1997) *Self-efficacy. The exercise of control*. New York: W.H. Freeman.

Bandura, A., Ross, D. and Ross, S.A. (1963) Imitation of film-mediated aggressive models. *The Journal of Abnormal and Social Psychology*, 66 (1), 3.

Bankoff (1952) in Police Science Technical Abstracts and Notes 128 (1953–1954), *Journal of Criminal Law, Criminology & Police Science*, 44 (1), article 15.

Bartholomew, J. B., Morrison, D. and Ciccolo, J. T. (2005) Effects of acute exercise on mood and well-being in patients with major depressive disorder. *Medicine and Science in Sports and Exercise*, 37 (12), 2032.

Bass, B.M. and Avolio, B.J. (1994) Transformational leadership and organizational culture. *The International Journal of Public Administration*, 17, 541–54.

Beck, A.T. (1976) *Cognitive therapy and the emotional disorders*. New York: International Universities Press.

Bell, P.A. and Yee, L.A. (1989) Skill level and audience effects on performance of a karate drill. *The Journal of social psychology*, 129 (2), 191–200.

Bem, S.L. (1993) *The lenses of gender: Transforming the debate on sexual inequality*. Yale University Press.

Black, D.A. and Black, J.A. (2007) Aircraft noise exposure and resident's stress and hypertension: A public health perspective for airport environmental management. *Journal of Air Transport Management*, 13 (5), 264–76.

Blakemore, C. and Cooper, G.F. (1970) Development of brain depends on the visual environment. *Nature*, 228, 477–8.

Bohman, M. (1995) *Predisposition to criminality: Swedish adoption studies in retrospect. In Genetics of criminal and antisocial behaviour*, G.D. Bock and J.A. Goode (Eds.), pp.99–114, Ciba Foundation Symposium 194. Chichester: John Wiley & Sons.

Boring, E.G. (1923) Intelligence as the tests test it. *The New Republic*, June, 35–7.

Bowers, K., Johnson, S. and Hirschfield, A. (2004) Closing off opportunities for crime: An evaluation of alley-gating. *European Journal on Criminal Policy and Research*, 10 (4), 285–308.

Bowlby, J. (1944) Forty-four juvenile thieves: Their characters and home life. International *Journal of Psychoanalysis*, 25 (19–52), 107–27.

Bowlby, J. (1951) *Maternal care and mental health*. Bulletin of the World Health Organization.

Bowlby, J. (1957) Symposium on the contribution of current theories to an understanding of child development. *British Journal of Medical Psychology*, 30 (4), 230–40.

Bowlby, J. (1969) *Attachment. Attachment and loss: Vol. 1. Loss*. New York: Basic Books.

Bowling, B. (1999). The rise and fall of New York murder: zero tolerance or crack's decline?. *British Journal of Criminology*, 39 (4), 531–54.

Bramley, G. and Power, S. (2009) Urban form and social sustainability: The role of density and housing type. *Environment and Planning*, 36, 30–48.

Bratton, W. (1997) Crime is Down in New York City: Blame the Police. In N. Dennis. (Ed.), *Zero Tolerance: Policing a Free Society*. London: Institute for Economic Affairs.

Bretherton, I. and Munholland, K.A. (1999) Internal working models revisited. In J. Cassidy and P.R. Shaver (Eds.), *Handbook of attachment: Theory, research, and clinical applications* (pp. 89–111). New York: Guilford Press.

Bretherton, I., Biringen, Z., Ridgeway, D., Maslin, M. and Sherman, M. (1989) *Attachment: The parental perspective*. Infant Mental Health Journal (Special Issue), 10, 203–20.

Breuer J. and Freud S. (1896) *Studies on hysteria. The complete works of Sigmund Freud*, Vol. II. London: Hogarth.

Brewer, K. (2000) *Psychology and Crime*. Oxford: Heinemann.

British Psychological Society (2013) *Prevalence of Depression in the UK*. Retrieved from www.bps.org.uk.

Broeder, D. (1959) The University of Chicago jury project. *Nebraska Law Review*, 38, 744–60.

Bronzaft, A.L. (1981) The effect of a noise abatement program on reading ability. *Journal of Environmental Psychology*, 1, 215–22.

Brook, A. (2011). Ecological footprint feedback: Motivating or discouraging? *Social Influence*, 6 (2), 113–28.

Buchsbaum, M.S., Nuechterlein, K.H. and Haier, R.J. (1990) Glucose metabolic rate in normals and schizophrenics during the continuous performance test assessed by positron emission tomography. *British Journal of Psychiatry*, 156, 216–27.

Buckingham, D., Willett, R., Banaji, S. and Cranmer, S. (2007) Media smart be adwise 2: An evaluation. *Media Smart*.

Bull, R. and McAlpine, S. (1998) Facial appearance and criminality. In Psychology and law: Truthfulness, accuracy and credibility, pp.59–76, In A. Memon, A. Vrij and R. Bull (Eds.). London: McGraw-Hill.

Burns, D. D. (1989) *The feeling good handbook: Using the new mood therapy in everyday life*. New York: William Morrow & Co.

Butler, A.C., Chapman, J.E., Forman, E.M., Beck, A.T. (2006) The empirical status of cognitive-behavioral therapy: A review of meta-analyses. *Clinical Psychology Review.* 26, 17–31.

Callow, N. and Waters, A. (2005) The effect of kinesthetic imagery on the sport confidence of flat-race horse jockeys. *Psychology of Sport and Exercise*, 6, 443–59.

Cannon, W. (1932) *The Wisdom of the Body*. New York: Norton.

Carroll, J.B. (1993) *Human cognitive abilities: A survey of factor-analytic studies*. New York: Cambridge University Press.

Carron, A.V., Bray, S.R. and Eys, M.A. (2002) Team cohesion and team success in sport. *Journal of Sport Sciences*, 20, 119–26.

Carvel, J. (2003, 26 September) TV Ads blamed for rise in childhood obesity. *The Guardian*. Retrieved from http://www.theguardian.com

Casey, B.J., Jones, R.M. and Hare, T.A. (2008) The adolescent brain. *Annals of the New York Academy of Sciences*, 1124 (1), 111–26.

Cattell, H.E. and Mead, A.D. (2008) The sixteen personality factor questionnaire (16PF), *The SAGE handbook of personality theory and assessment*, 2, 135–78.

Cattell, R.B. (1956) Second-order personality factors in the questionnaire realm. *Journal of consulting psychology*, 20, 411.

Charlton, D., Fraser☒Mackenzie, P.A.F. and Dror, I.E. (2010) Emotional experiences and motivating factors associated with fingerprint analysis. *Journal of Forensic Sciences*, 55 (2), 385–93.

Charman, S.D. (2013) The forensic confirmation bias: A problem of evidence integration, not just evidence evaluation. *Journal of Applied Research in Memory and Cognition*, 2, 56–8.

Cheek, J.M. and Buss, A.H. (1981). Shyness and sociability. *Journal of Personality and Social Psychology*, 41, 330–9.

Chelladurai, P. (1993) Leadership. In R. Singer, M. Murphey and L. Tennant (Eds.), *Handbook of research on sport psychology*. New York: Macmillan.

Chenery, S., Holt, J. and Pease, K. (1997) Biting Back II: Reducing Repeat Victimisation in Huddersfield. *Crime Detection and Prevention Series Paper 82*. London, England: Home Office, Police Research Group.

Cialdini, R.B. (2003) Crafting normative messages to protect the environment. *Current Directions in Psychological Science*, 12, 105–9.

Cohen, S., Kamarck, T. and Mermelstein, R. (1983) A global measure of perceived stress. *Journal of Health and Social Behavior*, 24, 385–96.

Collins, N., Clark, C.L. and Shaver, P.R. (1996) Attachment styles and internal working models of self and relationship partners. *Knowledge structures in close relationships: A social psychological approach*, 25.

Conn, S.R. and Rieke, M.L. (1994) *The 16PF Fifth Edition Technical Manual*. Champaign, IL: Institute for Personality and Ability Testing.

Cooper, C. (1972) 'The house as a symbol of self'. In J. Lang (Ed.) *Designing for human behaviour*. Stroudsburg, PA: Dowden, Hutchinson and Ross.

Crowe, T. D. (2000) *Crime prevention through environmental design: Applications of architectural design and space management concepts*. Massachusetts: Butterworth-Heinemann.

Curtiss, S. (1977) *Genie: a psychological study of a modern-day 'wildchild'*. New York: Academic Press.

Czeisler, C.A., Moore-Ede, M.C. and Coleman, R.H. (1982) Rotating shift work schedules that disrupt sleep are improved by applying circadian principles. *Science*, 217 (4558), 460–3.

Dazkir, S. and Read, M. (2011). Furniture Forms and Their Influence on Our Emotional Responses Toward Interior Environments. *Environment and Behavior*.

De Moor, M.H.M., Beem, A.L., Stubbe, J.H., Boomsma, D.I. and De Geus, E.J.C. (2006) Regular exercise, anxiety, depression and personality: a population-based study. *Preventive medicine*, 42 (4), 273–9.

Demetriou, A. (Ed.) (1988) *The neo-Piagetian theories of cognitive development: Toward an integration*. Amsterdam: North-Holland.

Demetriou, A., Efklides, A. and Shayer, M. (Eds.) (2005) *Neo-Piagetian theories of cognitive development: Implications and applications for education*. London: Routledge.

Dennis, N. (Ed.) (1997) *Zero Tolerance: Policing a Free Society*. London: Institute for Economic Affairs.

Dennis, N. and Mallon, R (1997) Confident Policing in Hartlepool. In N. Dennis. (Ed.), *Zero Tolerance: Policing a Free Society*. London: Institute for Economic Affairs.

Department for Transport (2014) *Reported road casualties Great Britain 2013*, Department for Transport, 2014, table RAS30025.

Desrivières, S., Lourdusamy, A., Tao, C., Toro, R., Jia, T., Loth, E. and Schumann, G. (2014) Single nucleotide polymorphism in the neuroplastin locus associates with cortical thickness and intellectual ability in adolescents. *Molecular psychiatry*, 20, 263–74.

DiGiuseppe, R. and Tafrate, R. C. (2003), Anger Treatment for Adults: A Meta-Analytic Review. *Clinical Psychology: Science and Practice*, 10, 70–84.

Donald, I. (1994) Management and change in office environments. *Journal of Environmental Psychology*, 14, 21–30.

Drews, F.A. and Doig, A. (2014) Evaluation of a configural vital sign display for intensive care unit nurses. *The Journal of Human Factors and Ergonomics Society*, 56 (3), 569–80.

Dror, I.E., Champod, C., Langenburg, G., Charlton, D., Hunt, H. and Rosenthal, R. (2011) Cognitive issues in fingerprint analysis: Inter- and intra-expert consistency and the effect of a 'target' comparison. *Forensic Science International*, 208, 10–7.

Dror, I.E., Kassin, S.M. and Kukucka, J. (2013) New application of psychology to law: Improving forensic evidence and expert witness contributions. *Journal of Applied Research in Memory and Cognition*, 2, 78–81.

Dror, I.E., Péron, A.E., Hind, S-L. and Charlton, D. (2005) When Emotions Get the Better of Us: The Effect of Contextual Top-down Processing on Matching Fingerprints. *Applied Cognitive Psychology*, 19, 799–809.

Duda, J. and Pensgaard, A.M. (2002) Enhancing the quantity and quality of motivation: the promotion of task involvement in a junior football team. In I. Cockerill (Ed.), *Solutions in sport psychology*, London: Thomson Learning.

Dwyer, D. (2001) *Angles on Criminal Psychology*. Cheltenham, Glos.: Nelson Thornes.

Ericsson, K.A., Krampe, R.T. and Tesch-Römer, C. (1993) The role of deliberate practice in the acquisition of expert performance. *Psychological review*, 100 (3), 363.

Eron, L.D. and Huesmann, L.R. (1986) The role of television in the development of antisocial and prosocial behavior. In D. Olweus, J. Block and M. Radke-Yarrom (Eds.) *Development of Antisocial and Prosocial Behaviour, Theories and Issues*. New York: Academic Press.

Eron, L.D. Huesmann, L.R., Leftowitz, M.M. and Walder, L.O. (1972) Does television violence cause aggression? *American Psychologist*, 27, 253–63.

Evans, G.W., Bullinger, M. and Hygge, S. (1998) Chronic noise and physiological response: A prospective, longitudinal study. *Psychological Science*, 9, 75–7.

Expert Working Group on Human Factors in Latent Print Analysis (2012) *Latent Print Examination and Human Factors: Improving the Practice through a Systems Approach*. US Department of Commerce, National Institute of Standards and Technology.

Eysenck, H.J., Nias, D.K. and Cox, D.N. (1982) Sport and personality. *Advances in behaviour research and therapy*, 4, 1–56.

Fallis, W.M., McMillan, D.E. and Edwards, M.P. (2011) Napping during night shift: Practices, preferences, and perceptions of critical care and emergency department nurses. *Critical Care Nurse*, 31 (2), e1–11.

Fantz, R.L. (1963) Pattern vision in newborn infants. *Science*, 140, 296–7.

Fazey, J. and Hardy, L. (1988) *The inverted-U hypothesis: A catastrophe for sport psychology*. British Association of Sports Sciences Monograph, No. 1, Leeds: The National Coaching Foundation.

Fazlioğlu, Y. and Baran, G. (2008) A sensory integration therapy program on sensory problems for children with autism 1. *Perceptual and Motor Skills*, 106 (2), 415–22.

Feindler, E. and Guttman, J. (1994) Cognitive-behavioral anger control training for groups of adolescents. In C. W. LeCroy (Ed.), *Handbook of child and adolescent treatment manuals* (pp. 170–99). New York: Lexington Books.

Felipe, N.J. and Somner, R. (1966) Invasions of Personal Space. *Social Problems*, 14, 206–14.

Ferguson, G.S. and Weisman, G.D. (1986) Alternative approaches to the assessment of employee satisfaction within office environments. In J.D. Wineman (Ed.) *Behavioural Issues in Office Design*. New York: Van Nostrum Weinhold.

Fertel-Daly, D., Bedell, G. and Hinojosa, J. (2001) Effects of a weighted vest on attention to task and self-stimulatory behaviors in preschoolers with pervasive developmental disorders. *American Journal of Occupational Therapy*, 55 (6), 629–40.

Festinger, L. (1957). *A Theory of Cognitive Dissonance*. Stanford, CA: Stanford University Press.

Fisher, R.P., Geiselman, R.E. and Amador, M. (1989) Field test of the cognitive interview: Enhancing the recollection of actual victims and witnesses of crime. *Journal of Applied Psychology*, 14 (5), 722–7.

Flynn, J.R. (1987) Massive IQ gains in 14 nations: What IQ tests really measure. *Psychological bulletin*, 101 (2), 171.

Foucault, M. (1961) *Madness and Civilization*. Oxford: Routledge Classics.

Fox, N.J., Joesbury, H. and Hannay, D.R. (1991) Family attachments and medical sociology: a valuable partnership for student learning. *Medical education*, 25 (2), 155–9.

Freedman, A.M., Warren, M.M., Cunningham, L.W. and Blackwell, S.J. (1988) Cosmetic surgery and criminal rehabilitation. *Southern Medical Journal*, 81 (9), 1113–6.

Freud, S. (1896) *The aetiology of hysteria*. Standard Edition, Vol. 3. London, Hogarth Press.

Freud, S. (1905) *Fragment of an Analysis of a Case of Hysteria*, Standard Edition, Vol. 7. London, Hogarth Press.

Freud, S. (1917) *Mourning and melancholia*. Collected works volume 14. London, Hogarth.

Frith, C.D. (1992) *The Cognitive Neuropsychology of Schizophrenia*. Hove: Psychology Press.

Fromm-Reichmann, F. (1948) Notes on the development of treatment of schizophrenics by psychoanalytic psychotherapy. *Psychiatry*, 11, 263–73.

Fuxjager, M.J., Mast, G., Becker, E. A. and Marler, C.A. (2009) The 'home advantage' is necessary for a full winner effect and changes in post-encounter testosterone. *Hormones and behavior*, 56 (2), 214–19.

Gans, J.J., O'Sullivan, P. and Bircheff, V. (2013) Mindfulness based tinnitus stress reduction pilot study. *Mindfulness*, June, 5 (3), 322–33.

Genschow, O., Noll, T., Wänke, M. and Gersbach, R. (2015) Does Baker-Miller pink reduce aggression in prison detention cells? A critical empirical examination. *Psychology, Crime & Law*, 21 (5), 482–9.

Gibson, H.B. (1982) The use of hypnosis in police investigations. *Bulletin of the British Psychological Society*, 35, 138–42.

Goldman-Rakic, P.S., Castner, S.A., Svensson, T.H., Siever, L.J. and Williams, G.V. (2004) Targeting the dopamine D1 receptor in schizophrenia: insights for cognitive dysfunction. *Psychopharmacology*, 174, 3–16.

Goren, C.C., Sarty, M. and Wu, P.Y. (1975) Visual following and pattern discrimination of face-like stimuli by newborn infants. *Pediatrics*, 56 (4), 544–9.

Gottesman, I., Laursen, T.M., Bertelson, A. and Mortenson, P.B. (2010) Severe mental disorders in offspring with two psychiatrically ill parents. *Archives of General Psychiatry*, 67, 252–7.

Gottesman, I.I. (1991) *Schizophrenia genesis: The origins of madness*. WH Freeman/Times Books/ Henry Holt & Co.

Green, S. (1994) *Principles of Biopsychology*. Lawrence Erlbaum Associates.

Greenberg, L.S., Elliott, R.K. and Lietaer, G. (1994) Research on experiential psychotherapies. In

Bergin A.E. and Garfield, S. (Eds.) *Handbook of psychotherapy and behaviour change*. New York: Wiley.

Grossmann, K.E., Grossmann, K., Huber, F. and Wartner, U. (1981) German children's behavior towards their mothers at 12 months and their fathers at 18 months in Ainsworth's Strange Situation. *International Journal of Behavioral Development*, 4 (2), 157–81.

Haier, R.J., Jung, R.E., Yeo, R.A., Head, K. and Alkire, M.T. (2005) The neuroanatomy of general intelligence: sex matters. *NeuroImage*, 25 (1), 320–7.

Hall, C.R., Mack, D., Paivio, A. and Hausenblas, H.A. (1998) Imagery use by athletes: development of the sport imagery questionnaire. *International Journal of Sport Psychology*, 29, 73–89.

Hall, L.J. and Player, E. (2008) Will the introduction of an emotional context affect fingerprint analysis and decision-making? *Forensic Science International*, 181, 36–9.

Hampikian, G., West, E. and Akselrod, O. (2011) The genetics of innocence: analysis of 194 US DNA exonerations. *Annual Review of Genomics & Human Genetics*, 12, 97–120.

Hansen, C.J., Stevens, L.C. and Coast, J.R. (2001) Exercise duration and mood state: how much is enough to feel better? *Health Psychology*, 20 (4), 267.

Harrington, J. (2001). Health effects of shift work and extended hours of work. *Occupational and Environmental Medicine*, 58 (1), 68–72.

Harris, L. and Associates Inc. (1978) *The Steelcase National Study of Office Environments: Do they work?* Grand Rapids, MI: Steelcase.

Health and Safety Executive (2006) *Managing Shift work: health and safety guidance*. Bootle: HSE.

Health and Safety Executive (2012) *Human factors procedures*. Bootle: HSE.

Heseltine, K. (2010) Brief anger interventions with offenders may be ineffective: A replication and extension (report). *Behaviour Research and Therapy*, 48 (3), 246.

Holmes, J. (2002) All you need is cognitive therapy? *British Medical Journal*, 342, 288–94.

Howard, D. (1948) *Territory and Bird Life*. London: Cellan.

Howitt, D. (2009) *Introduction to Forensic and Criminal Psychology*. Harlow: Pearson Education.

Hull, C.L. (1943) *Principles of behavior*. New York: Appleton-Century-Crofts.

Hussar, K. and Horvath, J. (2011). Do children play fair with mother nature? Understanding children's judgments of environmentally harmful actions. *Journal of Environmental Psychology*, 31 (4), 309–13.

Huttenlocher, P.R. (1979) Synaptic density in human frontal cortex-developmental changes and effects of aging. *Brain Research*, 163 (2), 195–205.

Ireland, J. (2000) Do Anger Management Courses Work? *Forensic Updates*, 63, 12–16.

Jacobs, P.A., Brunton, M., Melville, M., Brittain, R.P. and McClemont, W.F. (1965) Aggressive behavior, mental sub-normality and the XYY male. *Nature*, 208 (5017), 1351–2.

Jahoda, G. (1954) A note on Ashanti names and their relationship to personality. *British Journal of Psychology*, 45, 192–5.

Jarvis, M. (2006) *Sport psychology: a student handbook*. London: Routledge.

Jarvis, M., Russell, J., Gauntlett, L. and Lintern, F. (2015) *OCR A-Level Psychology AS and Year 1*, 2nd edn. Oxford: Oxford University Press.

Johnsen, T. and Friborg, O. (2015) The Effects of Cognitive Behavioral Therapy as an Anti-Depressive Treatment is Falling: A Meta-Analysis. *Psychological Bulletin*, 141 (4), 747–68.

Jones, G. (1991) Stress and anxiety. In S.J. Bull (Ed.) *Sport psychology: a self-help guide*, Marlborough: Crowood.

Jones, M.V., Mace, R.D., Bray, S.R., MacRae, A.W. and Stockbridge, C. (2002) The impact of motivational imagery on the emotional state and self-efficacy levels of novice climbers. *Journal of Sport Behaviour*, 25, 57–73.

Jowett, S. and Cockerill, I. M. (2002) Incompatibility in the coach–athlete relationship. *Solutions in sport psychology*, 16–31.

Juckel, G., Schlagenhauf, F., Koslowski, M., Wüstenberg, T., Villringer, A., Knutson, B. and Heinz, A. (2006) Dysfunction of ventral striatal reward prediction in schizophrenia. *Neuroimage*, 29, 409–16.

Junge, A. (2000) The influence of psychological factors on sports injuries review of the literature. *The American Journal of Sports Medicine*, 28 (suppl. 5), S-10.

Kahn, Jr, P., Friedman, B., Gill, B., Hagman, J., Severson, J., Freier, N., Feldman, E., Carrere, S., and Stolyar, A.. (2008). A plasma display window? The shifting baseline problem in a technologically mediated natural world. *Journal of Environmental Psychology*, 28 (2), 192–9.

Kalat, J.W. (1993) *Introduction to Psychology* (3rd Edition). Belmont: CA: Wadsworth

Kassin, S.M., Dror, I.E. and Kukucka, J. (2013) The forensic confirmation bias: Problems, perspectives, and proposed solutions. *Journal of Applied Research in Memory and Cognition*, 2, 42–52.

Katsura, Y., Yoshikawa, T., Ueda, S.Y., Usui, T., Sotobayashi, D., Nakao, H. and Fujimoto, S. (2010) Effects of aquatic exercise training using water-resistance equipment in elderly. *European Journal of Applied Physiology*, 108 (5), 957–64.

Katz, D. (1937) *Animals and Men*. New York: Longmans, Green.

Kennedy, M.M. and Newton, M. (1997) Effect of exercise intensity on mood in step aerobics. *The Journal of Sports Medicine and Physical Fitness*, 37 (3), 200–4.

Kim, J. and de Dear, R. (2013) Workspace satisfaction: The privacy-communication trade-off in open-plan offices. *Journal of Environmental Psychology*, 36 (Dec. 2013), 18–26.

Kim, Y.S., Barak, G. and Shelton, D.E. (2009) Examining the 'CSI-effect' in the cases of circumstantial evidence and eyewitness testimony: multivariate and path analyses. *Journal of Criminal Justice*, 37 (5), 452–82.

Kinnear, N., Lloyd, L., Helman, S., Husband, P., Scoons, J., Jones, S., Stradling, S., McKenna, F. and Broughton, J. (2013) *Novice drivers: Evidence*

Review and Evaluation. Retrieved from https://www.gov.uk/government/uploads/system/uploads/attachment_data/file/249282/novice-driver-research-findings.pdf

Kirkbride, J.B., Errazuriz, A., Croudace, T.J., Morgan, C., Jackson, D., Boydell, J and Jones, P.B. (2012) Incidence of schizophrenia and other psychoses in England, 1950–2009: a systematic review and meta-analyses. *PloS one*, 7 (3), e31660.

Knowles, Z., Tyler, G., Gilbourne, D. and Eubank, M. (2006) Reflecting on reflection: exploring the practice of sports coaching graduates. *Reflective Practice*, 7, 163–79.

Kroll, W. and Crenshaw, W. (1986) Multivariate personality profile analysis of four athletic groups. *Proceedings of the 2nd Congress of Sport Psychology*. Washington DC.

Kuhlthau, K.A., Bloom, S., Van Cleave, J., Knapp, A.A., Romm, D., Klatka, K. and Perrin, J.M. (2011) Evidence for family-centered care for children with special health care needs: a systematic review. *Academic pediatrics*, 11 (2), 136–43.

Kuo, D.Z., Houtrow, A.J., Arango, P., Kuhlthau, K.A., Simmons, J.M. and Neff, J.M. (2012) Family-centered care: current applications and future directions in pediatric health care. *Maternal and child health journal*, 16 (2), 297–305.

Kupersmidt, J.B., Scull, T.M. and Austin, E.W. (2010) Media literacy education for elementary school substance use prevention: study of media detective. *Pediatrics*, 126 (3), 525–31.

Kurtzberg, R.L., Safar, H. and Cavior, N. (1968) Surgical and social rehabilitation in adult offenders. *Proceedings of the 76th Annual Convention of the American Psychological Association*, 3, 649–50.

Labonté-LeMoyne, Santhanam, R., Léger, P., Courtemanche, F., Fredette, M. and Sénécal, S. (2015) The delayed effect of treadmill desk usage on recall and attention. *Computers in Human Behavior*, 46, 1–5.

Lagos, L., Vaschillo, E., Vaschillo, B., Lehrer, P., Bates, M. and Pandina, R. (2008) Heart rate variability biofeedback as a strategy for dealing with competitive anxiety: A case study. *Biofeedback*, 36 (3), 109.

Lakoff, G. (1975) Hedges: A Study in Meaning Criteria and the Logic of Fuzzy Concepts. *Journal of Philosophical Logic*, October 1973, 2 (4), 458–508.

Lang, R., O'Reilly, M., Healy, O., Rispoli, M., Lydon, H., Streusand, W. and Giesbers, S. (2012) Sensory integration therapy for autism spectrum disorders: A systematic review. *Research in Autism Spectrum Disorders*, 6 (3), 1004–18.

Lazarus, R.S. (1966). *Psychological Stress and the Coping Process*. New York: McGrawHill.

Leventhall, G., Benton, S. and Robertson, D. (2008) Coping Strategies for Low Frequency Noise. *Journal of Low Frequency Noise, Vibration and Active Control*, 35–52.

Levine, R., Norenzayan, A. and Philbrick, K. (2001) Cross-cultural differences in helping strangers. *Journal of Cross-cultural Psychology*, 32 (5), 543–60.

Levine, R.V., Lynch, K., Miyake, K. and Lucia, M.(1988) The Type A city: Coronary heart disease and pace of life. Unpublished manuscript, California State University, Fresno, in Bell, P.A., Fisher, J.D., Baum, A. and Greene, T.C. (1996) *Environmental Psychology* (4th Ed). New York: Harcourt Brace.

Lewin, K. (1939/1964) Experiments in social space. In D. Cartwright (Ed.) *Field theory in social science: Selected theoretical papers by Kurt Lewin* (pp.71–83). New York: Harper.

Lewinson, E. (1965) An experiment in facial reconstructive surgery in a prison population. *Canadian Medical Association Journal*, 92 (6), 251–4.

Liebrand, W.B.G. (1984). The effect of social motives, communication and group size on behaviour in an n-person multi stage mixed motive game. *European Journal of Social Psychology*, 14 (3): 239–64.

Lindal, P. and Hartig, T. (2013). Architectural variation, building height, and the restorative quality of urban residential streetscapes. *Journal of Environmental Psychology*, 33, 26–36.

Linn, M.C., de Benedictis, T. and Delucchi, K. (1982) Adolescent reasoning about advertisements: Preliminary investigations. *Child Development*, 1599–1613.

Lombroso, C. (1876) Criminal Man (2006 reprint: Duke University Press). Accessed online.

Lord, K.R. (1994) Motivating recycling behaviour: A quasi-experimental investigation of message and source strategies. *Psychology & Marketing*, 11 (4), 341–358

Lorenz, K. (1935) Der Kumpan in der Umwelt des Vogels. Der Artgenosse als auslösendes Moment sozialer Verhaltensweisen. *Journal für Ornithologie*, 83, 137–215.

Lyons, M.J., True, W.R,. Eisen, S.A., Goldberg, J., Meyer, J.M., Faraone, S.V, Eaves, L.J. and Tsuang, M.T. (1995) Differential heritability of adult and juvenile antisocial traits. *Archives of General Psychiatry*, 52, 906–15.

Mahoney, B., Dixon, J.A. and Cocks, R. (1997) *The Role of Accent and Context on perceptions of Guilt*. BPS Division of Criminological and Legal Psychology Conference, University of Cambridge.

Mann, S., Vrij, A. and Bull, R. (2002) Suspects, Lies and Videotape: An Analysis of Authentic High-Stake Liars. *Law and Human Behavior*, Jun, 26, 3.

McInman, A.D. and Berger, B.G. (1993) Self-concept and mood changes associated with aerobic dance. *Australian Journal of Psychology*, 45 (3), 134–40.

Mearns, D. and Thorne, B. (1988) *Person-centred counselling in action*. London: Sage.

Mednick, S.A., Gabrielli, W.F. and Hutchings, B. (1987) Genetic factors in the etiology of criminal behavior. In S.A. Mednick, T.E. Moffitt and S.A. Stack, *The causes of crime: New biological approaches* (pp.1–6). New York: Cambridge University Press.

Meehl, P.E. (1962) Schizotaxia, schizotypy, schizophrenia. *American psychologist*, 17, 827.

Mehta, R. and Zhu, R. (2009). Blue or Red? Exploring the Effect of Color on Cognitive Task Performances. *Science*. In Press.

Meijers, M. and Rutjens, B. (2014). Affirming belief in scientific progress reduces environmentally friendly behaviour. *European Journal of Social Psychology*, 44 (5), 487–95.

Memon, A. and Stevenage, S.V. (1996). Interviewing witnesses: What works and what doesn't? *Psycoloquy*, 7 (6).

Memon, A., Milne, R., Holley, A., Bull, R. and Koehnken, G. (1994) Towards understanding the effects of interviewer training in evaluating the cognitive interview. *Applied Cognitive Psychology*, 8, 641–59.

Middlemist, R.D., Knowles, E.S. and Matter, C.F. (1972) Personal space invasions in the lavatory: suggestive evidence for arousal. *Journal of Personality and Social Psychology*, 33 (5), 541–6.

Miller, G.A. (1956) The magical number seven, plus or minus two: some limits on our capacity for processing information. *Psychological Review*, 63 (2), 81.

Miller, L.S. (1987) Procedural bias in forensic science examinations of human hair. *Law and Human Behavior*, 11 (2), 157–63.

Milne, R. (1997) *Application and Analysis of the Cognitive Interview*. Doctoral Dissertation. University of Portsmouth.

Milo, T.J., Kaufman, G.E., Barnes, W.E., Konopka, L.M., Crayton, J.W. (2001) Changes in RCBF After Electroconvulsive Therapy for Depression. *Journal of ECT*, 17, 15–21.

Moleski, W.H. and Lang, J.T. (1986). Organizational Goals and Human Needs in Office Planning. In J.D. Wineman (Ed.), *Behavioral issues in office design*. New York, NY: Van Norstrand Reinhold.

Moncrieff, J. (2013) *The bitterest pills: The troubling story of antipsychotic drugs*. Basingstoke, Hampshire: Palgrave Macmillan.

Munroe-Chandler, K., Hall, C. and Fishburne, G. (2008) Playing with confidence: the relationship between imagery use and self-confidence and self-efficacy in youth soccer players. *Journal of Sports Sciences*, 26, 1539–46.

National Institute for Clinical Excellence (2004) Depression: management of depression in primary and secondary care. *Clinical guideline, 23*. London: NICE.

Netz, Y. and Lidor, R. (2003) Mood alterations in mindful versus aerobic exercise modes. The *Journal of psychology*, 137 (5), 405–19.

Newman, O. (1972) *Defensible space*. New York: Macmillan.

Newman, O. and Franck, K.A. (1982) The effects of building size on personal crime and fear of crime. *Population and Environment*, 5 (4), 203-220.

NICE (2009) Depression in adults: The treatment and management of depression in adults. Retrieved from https://www.nice.org.uk/guidance/cg90/ifp/chapter/treatments-for-mild-to-moderate-depression

Nisbet, E. and Zelenski, J. (2011). Underestimating Nearby Nature: Affective Forecasting Errors Obscure the Happy Path to Sustainability. *Psychological Science*, 22 (9), 1101–6.

Nolan, J.M., Schultz, P.W., Cialdini, R.B., Goldstein, N.J. and Griskevicius, V. (2008) Normative social influence is underdetected. *Personality and Social Psychology Bulletin*, 34 (7), 913–23.

Novaco, R. W. (1975) *Anger control: The development and evaluation of an experimental treatment*. Lexington, MA: D.C. Health.

Okken, V., van Rompay, T. and Pruyn, A. (2013). Room to move: On spatial constraints and self-disclosure during intimate conversations. *Environment and Behaviour*, August, 45, 737–60.

Oliver, K. (2002) *Psychology in Practice: Environment*. London: Hodder & Stoughton.

Orne, M.T. (1979) The uses and misuses of hypnosis in court. *International Journal of Clinical and Experimental Hypnosis*, 27, 311–41.

Osborn, S.G. and West, D.J. (1979) Convictions records of fathers and sons compared. *British Journal of Psychology*, 19 (4), 12–33.

Paivio, A. (1985) Cognitive and motivational functions of imagery in human performance. *Canadian Journal of Applied Sport Sciences*, 10, 22–8.

Pavlov, I. (1903) 'The Experimental Psychology and Psychopathology of Animals.' The 14th International Medical Congress. Madrid: Spain.

Peacock, J., Hine, R. and Pretty, J. (2007) *The mental health benefits of green exercise activities and green care*. Report for MIND.

Pedzek, K and Roe, C (1995) The effect of memory trace strength on suggestibility. *Journal of experimental child psychology*, 60, 116–23.

Peluso, M.A.M. and de Andrade, L.H.S. (2005) Physical activity and mood: the association between physical exercise and mood. *Clinics*, 60, 61–70.

Pezdek, K., Sperry, K. and Owens, S. (2007). Interviewing witnesses: The effect of forced confabulation on event memory. *Law and Human Behavior*, 31, 463–78.

Pfeifer, D. and Ogloff, J (1991) Ambiguity and guilt determination: a modern racism perspective. *Journal of Applied Social Psychology*, 23, 767–90.

Piaget, J. (1952) *The origins of intelligence in children*. New York: International Universities Press.

Pine, K.J. and Nash, A. (2002) Dear Santa: The effects of television advertising on young children. International Journal of Behavioral Development, 26 (6), 529–39.

Platt, H. (1959) *Report on the Welfare of Children in Hospital*. London: HMSO.

Plomin, R. and DeFries, J.C. (1998) The genetics of cognitive abilities and disabilities. *Scientific American*, 278 (5), 62–9.

Plowden, B. (1967) *Children and their Primary Schools: A Report of the Central Advisory Council for Education* (England) London: HMSO.

Pollard, C. (1997) Zero Tolerance: Short-term fix, Long-term liability?. In N. Dennis. (Ed.), *Zero Tolerance: Policing a Free Society*. London: Institute for Economic Affairs.

Pollard, R. (1986) Home advantage in soccer: A retrospective analysis. *Journal of sports sciences*, 4 (3), 237–48.

Porter, S., Brinke, L. and Wilson, K. (2009) Crime profiles and conditional release performance of psychopathic and non-psychopathic sexual offenders. *Legal and Criminological Psychology*, 14 (1), 109–118.

Prison Reform Trust (2013) Prison: The Facts. Retrieved from http://www.prisonreformtrust.org.uk/Portals/0/Documents/Prisonthefacts.pdf

Puig, J. and Pummell, B. (2012) 'I can't lose this match!' CBT and the sport psychologist. *Sport & Exercise Psychology Review*, 8 (2), 54–62.

Raine, A., Buchsbaum, M. and LaCasse, L. (1997) Brain abnormalities in murderers indicated by positron emission tomography. *Biological Psychiatry*, 42, 495–508.

Ramzaninezhad, R. and Keshtan, M.H. (2009) The relationship between coach's leadership styles and team cohesion in Iran football clubs professional league. *Brazilian Journal of Biomotricity*, 3, 111–20.

Rice, M. E. (1997) Violent offender research and implications for the criminal justice system. *American Psychologist*, 52, 414–23.

Ripke, S. and the Schizophrenia Working Group of the Psychiatric Genomics Consortium (2014) Biological insights from 108 schiophrenia-associated genetic loci. *Nature*, 511, 421–38.

Robertson (1952) A Two-Year Old Goes to Hospital. [Video]. Robertson Films. Retrieved from: https://www.youtube.com/watch?v=s14Q-_Bxc_U#t=10.

Roediger, H.L. (1980) The effectiveness of four mnemonics in ordering recall. Journal of Experimental Psychology: *Human Learning and Memory*, 6 (5), 558.

Rogers. C.R. (1959) A theory of therapy, personality and interpersonal relationships as developed in the client-centered framework. In S. Koch (Ed.) *Psychology: a study of a science, vol. III. Formulations of the person and the social context* (pp.184–256). New York: McGraw Hill.

Rogers, C.R. (1961) *On becoming a person: a therapist's view of psychotherapy*. Boston, MA: Houghton-Mifflin.

Rutter, M. (1981) Stress, coping and development: Some issues and some questions. *Journal of Child Psychology and Psychiatry*, 22 (4), 323–56.

Sanders, G.S. and Simmons, W.L. (1983) Use of hypnosis to enhance eyewitness accuracy: Does it work? *Journal of Applied Psychology*, 68 (1), 70–7.

Sarkar, M. and Fletcher, D. (2014) Psychological resilience in sport performers: a review of stressors and protective factors. *Journal of sports sciences*, 32 (15), 1419–34.

Scarr, S. (1997) Behavior-genetic and socialization theories of intelligence: Truce and reconciliation. *Intelligence, heredity and environment*, 3–41.

Scarr, S. and Weinberg, R.A. (1978) The influence of 'family background' on intellectual attainment. *American Sociological Review*, 674–92.

Scheiberg, S.L. (1990) Emotions on display. *American Behavioural Scientist*, 33, 330–8.

Schifferm, B. and Champod, C. (2007) The potential (negative) influence of observational biases at the analysis stage of fingermark individualization. *Forensic Science International*, 167, 116–20.

Schunk, D.H. (1991) Self-efficacy and academic motivation. *Educational Psychologist*, 26, 207–31.

Schwartz, S.H. (1992) Universals in the content and structure of values: Theoretical advances and empirical tests in 20 countries. In M. Zanna (Ed), *Advances in experimental social psychology*. Orlando, FL: Academic Press, pp.1–65.

Schweitzer, N.J. and Saks, Michael J. (2007) The CSI Effect: Popular Fiction About Forensic Science Affects Public Expectations About Real Forensic Science. *Jurimetrics*, Spring, Vol. 47, 357.

Scott, M.J. and Stradling, S.G. (2001) *Counselling for Post-Traumatic Stress Disorder*. London: Sage.

Seggie (1983) Accents of Guilt?: Effects of Regional Accent, Race, and Crime Type on Attributions of Guilt. *Journal of Language and Social Psychology*, June 2002, 21, 162–8,

Sheldon, W.H. (1942) *The varieties of temperament: A psychology of constitutional differences*. Harper: Oxford.

Shields, L., Zhou, H., Pratt, J., Taylor, M., Hunter, J. and Pascoe, E. (2012) *Family-centred care for hospitalised children aged 0–12 years*. The Cochrane Library.

Sigall, H. and Ostrove, N. (1975) Beautiful but Dangerous: Effects of Offender Attractiveness and Nature of the Crime on Juridic Judgment. *Journal of Personality and Social Psychology*, 31 (3), 410–14.

Simon, J.J., Billler, A., Walther, A., Roesch-Ely, D., Stippich, C., Weisbrod, M. and Kaiser, S. (2010) Neural correlates of reward processing in schizophrenia. *Schizophrenia Research* 118, 154–61.

Simón, V.M. (1998) Emotional participation in decision-making. *Psychology in Spain*, 2 (1), 100–7.

Simons-Morton, B.G., Bingham, C.R., Falk, E.B., Li, K., Pradhan, A.K., Ouimet, M.C., Almani, F. and Shope, J.T. (2014) Experimental effects of injunctive norms on simulated risky driving among teenage males. *Health Psychology*, 33 (7), 616.

Skinner, B.F. (1938) *The Behavior of organisms: An experimental analysis*. New York: Appleton-Century.

Skinner, B.F. (1974) *About behaviourism*. New York: Random House.

Slater, M.R. and Sewell, D.F. (1994) An examination of the cohesion–performance relationship in university hockey teams. *Journal of sports sciences*, 12, 423–31.

Smith, G.E. (1974) *Ancient Egyptian medicine: the papyrus ebers*. Chicago Ridge, IL: Ares Publishers Inc.

Smith, L.J. (1994) A content analysis of gender differences in children's advertising. *Journal of Broadcasting & Electronic Media*, 323–37.

Smith, P.C., Kendall, L. M. and Hulin, C.L. (1969) *The Measurement of Satisfaction in Work and Retirement*. Rand McNally: Chicago.

Smith. R.E., Smoll, F.L. and Curtis, B. (1979) Coach effectiveness training: a cognitive-behavioural approach to enhancing relationship skills in youth sports coaches. *Journal of Sport Psychology*, 1, 59–75.

Somner, R. (1969) *Personal Space: The behavioural basis of design*. Englewood Cliffs. NJ: Prentice Hall.

Somner, R. (1974) *Tight spaces: hard architecture and how to humanize it.* Englewood Cliffs, NJ: Prentice Hall.

South London and Maudsley NHS Trust (2014) Bethlem Royal Hospital History. Retrieved from www.slam.nhs.uk

Spira, M., Chizen, J.H., Gerow, F.J. and Hardy, S.B. (1966) Plastic surgery in the Texas prison system. *British Journal of Plastic Surgery*, 19 (4), 364–71.

Steg, L., Van den Berg, A.E. and de Groot, J.I.M. (Eds.) (2014) *Environmental Psychology: An Introduction.* BPS Books.

Steinberg, L. (2008) A social neuroscience perspective on adolescent risk-taking. *Developmental Review*, 28 (1), 78–106.

Steptoe, A., Kearsley, N. and Walters, N. (1993) Acute mood responses to maximal and submaximal exercise in active and inactive men. *Psychology & Health*, 8, 89–99.

Stewart, J.E. (1985) Appearance and Punishment: The Attraction-Leniency Effect in the Courtroom. *The Journal of Social Psychology*, 125 (3), 373–8.

Stewart, R.B. (1983) Sibling attachment relationships: Child–infant interaction in the strange situation. *Developmental Psychology*, 19 (2), 192.

Stirling, J., Hellewell, J., Blakey, A. and Deakin, W. (2006) Thought disorder in schizophrenia is associated with both executive dysfunction and circumscribed impairments in semantic function. *Psychological medicine*, 36, 475–84.

Stokols, D., Churchman, A., Scharf, T. and Wright, S. (1990). Workers' experiences of environmental change and transition at the office. In S. Fisher and C.L. Cooper (Eds.) *On the move: the Psychology of change and transition.* New York: Wiley, pp.231–49.

Stroomer, J.W., Vuyk, H.D. and Wielinga, E.W. (1998) The effects of computer simulated facial plastic surgery on social perception by others. *Clinical Otolaryngology & Allied Sciences*, 23 (2), 141–7.

Sturman. T.S. and Thibodeau, R. (2001) Performance-undermining effects of baseball free-agent contracts. *Journal of Sport & Exercise Psychology*, 23, 23–36.

Sugita, Y. (2004) Experience in early infancy is indispensable for color perception. *Current Biology*, 14 (14), 1267–71.

Sundblad, E.-L., Biel, A. and Gärling, T. (2007). Cognitive and affective risk judgements related to climate change. *Journal of Environmental Psychology*, 27, 97–106.

Szasz, T. (1960) The myth of mental illness. *American Psychologist*, 15 (2), 113.

Szasz, T. (1961) *Myth of Mental Illness: Foundations of a Theory of Personal Conduct.* New York: Hoeber-Harper.

Tajadura-Jiménez, A., Pantelidou, G., Rebacz, P., Västfjäll, D. and Tsakiris, M. (2011). I-Space: The Effects of Emotional Valence and Source of Music on Interpersonal Distance. *PLoS ONE*, 6 (10).

Tajfel, H. (1970) Experiments in intergroup discrimination. *Scientific American*, 223, 96–102.

Taylor, G. and Wilson, G.S. (2005) *Applying sport psychology: four perspectives.* Champaign, IL: Human Kinetics.

Taylor, J.C. and Bowers, D.G. (1972) *Survey of Organizations: A machine scored Standardized Questionnaire Instrument.* Ann Arbor, MI: Center for Research on Utilization of Scientific Knowledge, Institute for Social Research, University of Michigan.

Thomas-Peter, B. (2006) The modern context of psychology in corrections: Influences, limitations and values of 'what works'. *Psychological research in prisons*, 24–39.

Thornley, B., Rathbone, J., Adams, C.E. and Awad, G. (2003) *Chlorpromazine versus placebo for schizophrenia.* The Cochrane Library.

Tomei, G., Fioravanti, M., Cerratti, D., Sancini, A., Tomao, E., Rosati, M.V. (2010) Occupational exposure to noise and the cardiovascular system: a meta-analysis. *Science of the Total Environment*, 408 (4), 681–9.

Trzesniewski, K.H., Donnellan, M.B., Moffitt, T.E., Robins, R.W., Poulton, R. and Caspi, A. (2006) Low Self-Esteem During Adolescence Predicts Poor Health, Criminal Behavior, and Limited Economic Prospects During Adulthood. *Developmental Psychology*, 42 (2), 381–90.

Turner, M. and Barker, J.B. (2013) Examining the efficacy of rational-emotive behaviour therapy (REBT) on irrational beliefs and anxiety in elite youth cricketers. *Journal of Applied Sport Psychology*, 25, 131–47.

Tutko, T.A., Lyon, L.P. and Ogilvie, B.C. (1969) *Athletic motivation inventory.* San Jose, CA: Institute for the Study of Athletic Motivation.

Ulrich, R.S. (1984) View through a window may influence recovery from surgery. *Science*, New Series, 224 (4647), 420–1.

US Department of Justice, Office of the Inspector General (2006) *A review of the FBI's handling of the Brandon Mayfield Case. Unclassified executive summary.* Office of the Inspector General: Oversight and Review Division.

Uziel, L. (2007) Individual differences in the social facilitation effect: A review and meta-analysis. *Journal of research in personality*, 41 (3), 579–601.

Vallée, C.N. and Bloom, G.A. (2005) Building a successful university program: Key and common elements of expert coaches. *Journal of Applied Sport Psychology*, 17, 179–96.

Van Goozen, S.H., Cohen-Kettenis, P.T., Gooren, L.J., Frijda, N.H. and Van De Poll, N.E. (1995) Gender differences in behaviour: activating effects of cross-sex hormones. *Psychoneuroendocrinology*, 20 (4), 343–63.

Van Ijzendoorn, M.H. and Kroonenberg, P.M. (1988) Cross-cultural patterns of attachment: A meta-analysis of the strange situation. *Child Development*, 147–56.

Vygotsky, L.S. (1980) *Mind in society: The development of higher psychological processes.* Harvard University Press.

Wallace, H. M., Baumeister, R.F. and Vohs, K.D. (2005) Audience support and choking under pressure: A home disadvantage? *Journal of sports sciences*, 23 (4), 429–38.

Ware, J.E. and Sherbourne, C.D. (1992). The MOS 36-item Short-Form Health Survey (SF-36): I. Conceptual framework and item selection. *Medical Care*, 30, 473–83.

Watson, J. B. and Rayner, R. (1920) Conditioned emotional reactions. *Journal of Experimental Psychology*, 3 (1), 1–14.

Wells, C.M., Collins, D. and Hale, B.D. (1993) The self-efficacy-performance link in maximum strength performance, *Journal of sport sciences*, 11, 167–75.

Wells, G.L., Small, M., Penrod, S., Malpass, R., Fulero, S. and Brimacombe, C.A.E. (1998) Eyewitness identification procedures: Recommendations for lineups and photospreads. *Law & Human Behavior*, 22 (6), 60347.

Wells, M.M. (2000) Office clutter or meaningful personal displays: The role of office personalization in employee and organisational well-being. *Journal of Environmental Psychology*, 20 (3), 239–55.

Wood, D., Bruner, J.S. and Ross, G. (1976) The role of tutoring in problem-solving. *Journal of Child Psychology and Psychiatry*, 17 (2), 89–100.

Worth, P.L. and Roberts, D.F. (2004) Evaluating the Effectiveness of School-Based Media Literacy Curricula. *Communication and Children*, 270.

Yee, N., Bailenson, J.N. and Urbanek, M. (2006) *The unbearable likeness of being digital: The persistence of nonverbal social norms in online virtual environments.* Cyberspace and Behaviour, In Press.

Zahn, C.J. and Hopper, R. (1985) Measuring language attitudes: The Speech Evaluation Instrument. *Journal of Language and Social Psychology*, 4, 113–24.

Zajonc, R.B., Heingartner, A. and Herman, E.M. (1969) Social enhancement and impairment of performance in the cockroach. *Journal of personality & social psychology*, 13, 83–92.

INDEX